Lecture Notes in Computer Science 9295

Commenced Publication in 1973
Founding and Former Series Editors:
Gerhard Goos, Juris Hartmanis, and Jan van Leeuwen

More information about this series at http://www.springer.com/series/7407

Christos Zaroliagis · Grammati Pantziou
Spyros Kontogiannis (Eds.)

Algorithms, Probability, Networks, and Games

Scientific Papers and Essays Dedicated to Paul G. Spirakis
on the Occasion of His 60th Birthday

Springer

Editors
Christos Zaroliagis
University of Patras
Patras
Greece

Spyros Kontogiannis
University of Ioannina
Ioannina
Greece

Grammati Pantziou
Technological Educational Institute
   of Athens
Athens
Greece

Cover illustration: Menger's Theorem for Temporal Graphs
Source: G. Mertzios, O. Michail, I. Chatzigiannakis, P. Spirakis: Temporal Network Optimization Subject to Connectivity Constraints. In: F.V. Fomin, R. Freivalds, M. Kwiatkowska, D. Peleg (Eds.) ICALP 2013, Part II. LNCS, vol. 7966, pp. 657–668. Springer Heidelberg (2013)
Photograph on p. V: The photograph of the honoree was taken by Toms Grinbergs.
© Toms Grinbergs, University of Latvia

ISSN 0302-9743   ISSN 1611-3349   (electronic)
Lecture Notes in Computer Science
ISBN 978-3-319-24023-7   ISBN 978-3-319-24024-4   (eBook)
DOI 10.1007/978-3-319-24024-4

Library of Congress Control Number: 2015948167

LNCS Sublibrary: SL1 – Theoretical Computer Science and General Issues

Springer Cham Heidelberg New York Dordrecht London

Printed on acid-free paper

Springer International Publishing AG Switzerland is part of Springer Science+Business Media
(www.springer.com)

Paul G. Spirakis

Preface

This Festschrift volume is published in honor of Paul G. Spirakis on the occasion of his 60th birthday to celebrate his significant contributions to Computer Science.

The celebration was complemented by a special event that took place in Patras on 16 September 2015 within the frame of ALGO 2015 – the major annual algorithmic event combining the premier algorithmic conference European Symposium on Algorithms (ESA) along with a number of specialized conferences and workshops (ALGO-CLOUD, ALGOSENSORS, ATMOS, IPEC, MASSIVE, WAOA), all related to algorithms and their applications.

Algorithms, Probability, Networks, and Games are the fields of Paul's main research activities and we decided to adopt them as the title of the Festschrift, which is divided into three parts.

Part I contains a modest attempt at a biographical sketch as well as essays from close collaborators and a former PhD student. Part II contains research contributions from the three invited speakers to the special event Shlomi Dolev, Kurt Mehlhorn, and Burkhard Monien, who enthusiastically agreed to participate in the event and to contribute to the Festschrift. Part III contains research contributions mostly from Paul's former PhD students, many of whom now pursue an academic career. The contributions of Part III have undergone the standard peer review process. All research contributions reflect past and current research activities in the fields of *Algorithms, Probability, Networks, and Games*. In each part, the contributions are listed in alphabetic order (w.r.t. author names).

Paul Spirakis is an eminent, talented, and influential researcher that has contributed and keeps contributing significantly to computer science. He is among the most visionary thought leaders of our generation, with a great talent in inspiring and guiding young researchers. We are privileged to have him as mentor, teacher, and friend.

Happy Birthday, Paul!

September 2015

Christos Zaroliagis
Grammati Pantziou
Spyros Kontogiannis

Acknowledgements

We sincerely thank all contributors to this volume as well as the reviewers for their invaluable help. We also thank Andreas Paraskevopoulos for helping with several technical issues during the whole process of this volume production.

List of Contributors

Maria Andreou Professional Training Centre, TC Square Ltd, Nicosia, Cyprus, e-mail: maria@tcsquare.com.cy

Christos Bouras Department of Computer Engineering and Informatics, University of Patras, 26500 Patras, Greece; Computer Technology Institute & Press "Diophantus", N. Kazantzaki Str., Patras University Campus, 26504 Patras, Greece, e-mail: bouras@cti.gr

Ioannis Chatzigiannakis Department of Computer, Control & Informatics Engineering, Sapienza University of Rome, Rome, Italy; Computer Technology Institute & Press "Diophantus", N. Kazantzaki Str., Patras University Campus, 26504 Patras, Greece, e-mail: ichatz@cti.gr

Ka Wong Chong Department of Computer Science, The University of Hong-Kong, Porfulam Road, Hong Kong

Shlomi Dolev Ben-Gurion University of the Negev, Beer Sheva, Israel, e-mail: dolev@cs.bgu.ac.il

Pavlos S. Efraimidis Department of Electrical and Computer Engineering, Democritus University of Thrace, Xanthi, Greece, e-mail: pefraimi@ee.duth.gr

Charilaos Efthymiou College of Computing, Georgia Institute of Technology, 266 Ferst Dr. Atlanta, 30332 Georgia, USA, e-mail: cefthymiou3@mail.gatech.edu

Dimitris Fotakis Division of Computer Science, School of Electrical and Computer Engineering, National Technical University of Athens, 15780 Athens, Greece, e-mail: fotakis@cs.ntua.gr

John D. Garofalakis Department of Computer Engineering and Informatics, University of Patras, 26504 Patras, Greece; Computer Technology Institute & Press "Diophantus", N. Kazantzaki Str., Patras University Campus, 26504 Patras, Greece, e-mail: garofala@ceid.upatras.gr

Anders Gidenstam University of Borås, Sweden, e-mail: anders.gidenstam@hb.se

Vincenzo Gulisano Chalmers University of Technology, Gothenburg, Sweden, e-mail: vincenzo.gulisano@chalmers.se

Vaggelis Kapoulas Department of Computer Engineering and Informatics, University of Patras, 26504 Patras, Greece; Computer Technology Institute & Press "Diophantus", N. Kazantzaki Str., Patras University Campus, 26504 Patras, Greece, e-mail: kapoulas@cti.gr

Spyros Kontogiannis Department of Computer Science and Engineering, University of Ioannina, 45110 Ioannina, Greece; Computer Technology Institute & Press "Diophantus", N. Kazantzaki Str., Patras University Campus, 26504 Patras, Greece, e-mail: kontog@cs.uoi.gr

Dimitrios Koukopoulos Department of Cultural Heritage Management & New Technologies, University of Patras, 30100 Agrinio, Greece, e-mail: dkoukopoulos@upatras.gr

Basilis Mamalis Department of Informatics, Technological Educational Institute of Athens, Greece, e-mail: vmamalis@teiath.gr

Marios Mavronicolas Department of Computer Science, University of Cyprus, 1678 Nicosia, Cyprus, e-mail: mavronic@cs.ucy.ac.cy

Kurt Mehlhorn Max-Planck-Institute for Informatics, 66123 Saarbrücken, Germany, e-mail: mehlhorn@mpi-inf.mpg.de

Othon Michail Computer Technology Institute & Press "Diophantus", N. Kazantzaki Str., Patras University Campus, 26504 Patras, Greece, e-mail: michailo@cti.gr

Burkhard Monien Faculty of Electrical Engineering, Computer Science and Mathematics, University of Paderborn, 33102 Paderborn, Germany, e-mail: bm@upb.de

Athanasios N. Nikolakopoulos Department of Computer Engineering and Informatics, University of Patras, 26504 Patras, Greece; Computer Technology Institute & Press "Diophantus", N. Kazantzaki Str., Patras University Campus, 26504 Patras, Greece, e-mail: nikolako@ceid.upatras.gr

Yiannis Nikolakopoulos Chalmers University of Technology, Gothenburg, Sweden, e-mail: ioaniko@chalmers.se

Sotiris Nikoletseas Department of Computer Engineering and Informatics, University of Patras, 26504 Patras, Greece; Computer Technology Institute & Press "Diophantus", N. Kazantzaki Str., Patras University Campus, 26504 Patras, Greece, e-mail: znikole@cti.gr

Panagiota N. Panagopoulou Computer Technology Institute & Press "Diophantus", N. Kazantzaki Str., Patras University Campus, 26504 Patras, Greece, e-mail: panagopp@cti.gr

Grammati Pantziou Department of Informatics, Technological Educational Institute of Athens, Greece, e-mail: pantziou@teiath.gr

Christos H. Papadimitriou EECS Department, University of California, Berkeley, 94720 California, USA, e-mail: christos@berkeley.edu

Vicky Papadopoulou Lesta Department of Computer Science and Engineering, European University Cyprus, Cyprus, e-mail: v.papadopoulou@euc.ac.cy

Marina Papatriantafilou Chalmers University of Technology, Gothenburg, Sweden, e-mail: ptrianta@chalmers.se

Mikaël Rabie Ben-Gurion University of the Negev, Beer Sheva, Israel, e-mail: rabie@cs.bgu.ac.il

Christoforos L. Raptopoulos Computer Technology Institute & Press "Diophantus", N. Kazantzaki Str., Patras University Campus, 26504 Patras, Greece, e-mail: raptopox@ceid.upatras.gr

Elad M. Schiller Chalmers University of Technology, Gothenburg, Sweden, e-mail: elad@chalmers.se

Paul G. Spirakis Department of Computer Engineering and Informatics, University of Patras, 26504 Patras, Greece; Computer Technology Institute & Press "Diophantus", N. Kazantzaki Str., Patras University Campus, 26504 Patras, Greece; Department of Computer Science, University of Liverpool, Liverpool, UK, e-mail: spirakis@cti.gr

Enea Tsanai Department of Computer Engineering and Informatics, University of Patras, 26504 Patras, Greece, e-mail: tsanai@ceid.upatras.gr

Philippas Tsigas Chalmers University of Technology, Gothenburg, Sweden, e-mail: tsigas@chalmers.se

Klaus W. Wagner Lehrstuhl für Theoretische Informatik, Institut für Informatik, Julius-Maximilians-Universität Würzburg, 97074 Würzburg, Germany, e-mail: wagner@informatik.uni-wuerzburg.de

Christos Zaroliagis Department of Computer Engineering and Informatics, University of Patras, 26504 Patras, Greece; Computer Technology Institute & Press "Diophantus", N. Kazantzaki Str., Patras University Campus, 26504 Patras, Greece, e-mail: zaro@ceid.upatras.gr

Contents

Part I

A Glimpse at Paul G. Spirakis

Ioannis Chatzigiannakis[1,2]([✉]), Dimitris Fotakis[3], Spyros Kontogiannis[1,4],
Othon Michail[1], Sotiris Nikoletseas[1,5], Grammati Pantziou[1,6],
and Christos Zaroliagis[1,5]

[1] Computer Technology Institute and Press "Diophantus", Patras University
Campus, N. Kazantzaki Str., 26504 Patras, Greece
{ichatz,michailo,nikole}@cti.gr
[2] Sapienza University of Rome, Rome, Italy
[3] Division of Computer Science, School of Electrical and Computer Engineering,
National Technical University of Athens, 15780 Athens, Greece
fotakis@cs.ntua.gr
[4] Department of Computer Science and Engineering, University of Ioannina,
45110 Ioannina, Greece
kontog@cs.uoi.gr
[5] Department of Computer Engineering and Informatics, University of Patras,
26504 Patras, Greece
zaro@ceid.upatras.gr
[6] Department of Informatics, Technological Educational Institution of Athens,
Egaleo, Greece
pantziou@teiath.gr

1 Introduction

Paul Spirakis is an eminent, talented, and influential researcher that contributed
significantly to computer science. This article is a modest attempt of a biographical sketch of Paul, which we drafted with extreme love and honor.

2 Childhood, Education and Career

Paul G. Spirakis was born on 29 August 1955 in Didymoteicho, a city in the
northeastern part of Greece, just 2Km from the Greek-Turkish border. His father
George Spirakis originated from that city, while his mother Olga Avgoustinou
originated from the island of Zakynthos (or Zante). She moved to Didymoteicho
as a teacher in an elementary school of the area, where she met Paul's father.
The family is complemented by a daughter (Eleni). Didymoteicho was the home
of the Spirakis family and Paul's parents were among the prominent citizens
of the city. George Spirakis was the City Mayor in the periods 1960–1966 and
1978–1982.

Paul finished the elementary school there as well as the five out of the six
classes of the high-school. He was the top student in all classes with a passionate
love for mathematics. This caused his mathematics teacher in high-school's fifth
class (Mr. Ionas) to convince his parents to let Paul enroll in the advanced 1st

© Springer International Publishing Switzerland 2015
C. Zaroliagis et al. (Eds.): Spirakis Festschrift, LNCS 9295, pp. 3–24, 2015.
DOI: 10.1007/978-3-319-24024-4_1

(public) high-school in Thessaloniki for further training in mathematics. This indeed happened (to the full disappointment of Paul's literature teacher, who was trying to convince him and his parents to study literature) and Paul finished high-school in Thessaloniki in 1973, again as the top student of his class.

During the same academic year (1972–1973) he was also enrolled to a special school preparing students for the National Examinations for University Entrance. His mathematics teacher in that school (Mr. Mpallis), motivated by Paul's passionate love and talent for mathematics, soon developed a close relationship with him and devoted the majority of his time to Paul's further training in mathematics.

As a result, Paul received in 1973 one of the most prestigious prizes in Greece, the First Prize of the Greek Mathematics Society. This prize is awarded after a highly-competitive national examination among students all over Greece. In the same year, he also succeeded in the National Examinations for University Entrance, entering the School of Electrical Engineering at the National Technical University of Athens (NTUA). During his studies, he was constantly among the top 2 % of students, graduating with excellence in 1978 (5-year Diploma in Electrical Engineering from NTUA).

Subsequently, Paul was admitted (with scholarship) at Harvard University for pursuing postgraduate studies. He received his S.M. degree in Applied Mathematics & Computer Science in June 1979, and his Ph.D. in Applied Mathematics & Computer Science in early 1982. His Ph.D. Thesis "Probabilistic Algorithms, Algorithms with Random Inputs and Random Combinatorial Structures", under the supervision of Prof. John Reif, contributed significantly to the field of probabilistic and randomized algorithms.

After his Ph.D, Paul received a post-doctoral research fellowship at Harvard University and in September 1982 was appointed as Assistant Professor in the Courant Institute of Mathematical Sciences at New York University. In the summer of 1985 he was elected Associate Professor in the Department of Computer Engineering and Informatics at the University of Patras, and in October 1990 was promoted to a Full Professor (meanwhile, during the period October 1985–April 1987, he served his obligatory military service in the Greek Army). In 1996, Paul was appointed as the President (Chairman of the Board of Directors) of the Computer Technology Institute & Press "Diophantus". Among others, he is the Head of Research Unit 1 (Foundations of Computer Science, Relevant Technologies and Applications).

Since September 2013 he holds a chair professorship in the Department of Computer Science at the University of Liverpool, UK. He also leads the Networks Sciences and Technologies (NeST) Initiative of the University of Liverpool, and he is the chair of the research committee of the School of Electrical Engineering, Electronics and Computer Science at the same university.

3   Teaching, Mentoring, and Publications

During the 33 years of his academic career, Paul Spirakis taught a variety of classes at both undergraduate and graduate level, covering a broad spectrum of subjects within Computer Science, including *Algorithms and Combinatorial Optimization, Approximation algorithms to Hard Problems, Cryptography, Discrete Mathematics, Distributed Computing and Systems, Game Theory, Economics and Algorithms, Operating Systems, Parallel Algorithms, Probability Theory, Probabilistic Techniques in Algorithms,* and *Theory of Computation.*

Most of these classes were introduced and taught for the first time in a Greek University. All students of those classes surely remember Paul's inspiring lectures, and for most of them those lectures had a predominant influence on their careers.

A key ability of Paul Spirakis is the identification of core problems in technologies that are still in their inception, many years before they become apparent to the scientific community. This requires an almost unique inter-scientific ability to combine a broad set of techniques and methodologies to examine a given problem.

Paul Spirakis is among the most visionary thought leaders of our generation, with a great talent to inspire and guide new researchers. He has invested a huge amount of effort and time in mentoring students and young scientists, and introducing them to the mysteries of computation and its applications. He supervised numerous undergraduate and postgraduate students and he awarded more than 32 doctoral dissertations.

It did not then come as a surprise that, in a study conducted in 2004, he was reported among the *top 50 nurturers* in Computer Science Research [47].

Paul Spirakis has a tremendous publication record. He has published:

- More than 120 research papers in prestigious peer-reviewed journals.
- More than 290 research papers in refereed proceedings of top international computer science conferences.
- 12 books (3 in English and 9 in Greek).
- 17 chapters in books or edited volumes.
- More than 40 research papers in archived repositories (representing work in progress).

His publications have received more than 5300 citations (h-index: 37, g-index: 59).

4 Awards and Distinctions

For his research work and scientific achievements, Paul Spirakis has been honored with numerous awards and distinctions, which include:

- Fellow of the European Association for Theoretical Computer Science (EATCS), since 2014.
- Member of Academia Europaea, since 2010.
- Member of the ACM Europe Council, sice 2009.
- Recipient of a Technology Excellence Award, as a Technology Pioneer, in 2009 in the competition of Technology Excellence Awards 2009 organized by the PC and T3 magazines (Greek Editions).

- Vice President of the European Association for Theoretical Computer Science (elected unanimously), since 2002.
- Member of the Council Board of the European Association for Theoretical Computer Science (elected unanimously), since 1997.
- Acknowledged as among the *top 50 nurturers* in Computer Science Research [47].
- Distinguished Visiting Scientist of the Max-Planck Institute for Informatics, Fall 2001.

5   Research

The research work of Paul Spirakis is so broad that it would be extremely difficult (if at all possible) to describe it in an succinct and unambiguous way. It encompasses two main streams that fruitfully interact with each other throughout his career, *Algorithms and Complexity*, and *Computer Systems and Networks*. The former stream includes his contributions to the foundations of computer science. The latter stream includes mainly applied work that it has heavily benefited from the former stream.

For this reason, we have chosen here to focus on the *Algorithms and Complexity* stream and attempt at providing a short overview of his contributions. In all cases, the vast majority of Paul's work is characterized by a set of recurring themes: probabilistic and randomized approaches, fundamental methods of parallel and distributed computing, graph-theoretic approaches, approximation methods, and (lately) algorithmic game theory and evolution methods & structures.

5.1   Probabilistic and Randomized Algorithms

From the very start of his academic formation, Paul Spirakis developed a fundamental relation to probabilistic methods and their applications in theoretical computer science. In his Ph.D. Thesis, Paul suggested some novel, major uses of discrete probability, in combinatorial structures as well as in the design and analysis of randomized algorithms.

In particular, in [72] he introduced randomness in the fundamental combinatorial structure of matroids, towards its powerful generalization to random matroids. For the independent set problem under this new model, nonconstructive existence proofs as well as efficient randomized algorithms were provided. Also, some nice applications of this structure to classic Erdős-Rényi random graphs were given. The second part of Paul's Ph.D. Thesis anticipated in a characteristic way his major future contributions to randomized methods in distributed computing throughout his career. In [73], he suggested the employment of probabilistic choice for interprocess communication (and symmetry breaking). It is worth noting that this has been one the first few uses of random choice in distributed computing.

Since this early stage, and throughout his career, random methods have been the main connecting thread in the research of Paul Spirakis. Several applications of randomness to diverse topics are also discussed elsewhere in this chapter. We highlight here two fundamental (per se) uses of randomness.

The first one concerns his constant investigation of random combinatorial models. Further to a deep exploration of crucial properties in $G_{n,p}$ random graphs, Paul liked to introduce nice extensions of such models, motivated both by mathematical curiosity and major trends in modern technology. Such extensions characteristically include the introduction of failures to random regular graphs models [65] and the exploration of interesting variations of random intersection graphs [67].

Relevant persistent features of his research include the heavy use of random processes to model and analyze interesting computational phenomena (see e.g., [17,51]) and the use of randomness in algorithms for graph-theoretic problems (see e.g., [19,29]).

In a second line, the exploration of major combinatorial properties of such models has been based on a sophisticated use and even extension of probabilistic techniques collectively referred to as the Probabilistic Method established by Paul Erdős. It is worth noting that Paul Spirakis maintained a deep devotion to such probabilistic techniques, and effectively passed on his dedication to several of his students and colleagues. He not only applied in a brilliant way randomized techniques but several times he also further developed and extended these techniques themselves, such as in [35], where a new series of tail bounds for occupancy problem has been provided.

5.2 Parallel Algorithms and Complexity

A few years after his Ph.D, Paul Spirakis started an intense research activity in the field of parallel algorithms and complexity. He studied various fundamental problems in parallel computing and his results contributed significantly in promoting the field. We mention here a few indicative cases.

One of his first attempts was to devise efficient algorithms that are sensitive to properties of the input which can be determined only at run-time. For instance, in the case of parallel addition in shared memory models, it is interesting to devise algorithms whose bounds depend on the number of non-zero elements. In [77], Paul designed such an algorithm for the fundamental problem of parallel addition. In an input of n numbers, m of which are non-zero entries, he devised a randomized parallel algorithm for a CRCW PRAM, which runs in $O(\log m)$ expected time with m processors using $O(m)$ shared space. He also applied this algorithm to the related problem of processor identification.

A fair part of his work dealt with the development of efficient parallel algorithms and the investigation of the parallel complexity of several problems on graphs within the context of shared memory parallel computing:

- Along the former, he derived (along with Grammati Pantziou and Christos Zaroliagis) efficient deterministic parallel algorithms for shortest paths and other problems (see e.g., [38,71]) as well as parallel algorithms which exhibited a remarkable average case performance. In particular, he studied with John Reif in [76] the parallel average case complexity of several problems on random instances of undirected and directed graphs. In that paper, a bulk of algorithms was developed, based on new results on the diameter of random (directed) graphs, that are able to solve a host of graph problems on an n-node random (directed) graph (connectivity, biconnectivity, transitive closure, minimum spanning trees, and all pairs minimum cost paths) in $O(\log \log n)$ expected parallel time on a CRCW PRAM. These are exponentially faster algorithms than their deterministic counterparts.

– Along the latter, he investigated the parallel complexity of the problem of testing whether a given graph G contains an induced subgraph of vertex (edge) connectivity at least k. Paul Spirakis, with Maria Serna and Lefteris Kirousis, proved in [41] that this problem is P-complete for any fixed $k \geq 3$. This result came as a surprise, since the related problem of computing the triconnected (or Tutte) components of G (maximal subgraphs of G such that for any four vertices in any of them, any two of these vertices can be connected by a path in G that avoids the other two) was known to be in NC. In addition, they provided interesting NC approximability and inapproximability results.

Another thread of his research concerned fault-tolerant parallel computing. Paul Spirakis together with KZvi Kedem and Krishna Palem investigated in [39] the problem of executing efficient robust parallel computations on a PRAM whose processing elements are prone to failure. In particular, they devised a general strategy for simulating an arbitrary step of an ideal CRCW PRAM on a PRAM with faulty processors at a small multiplicative time overhead and at a small (per processor) additive constant space overhead.

An equally important thread of Paul's research focused on more realistic models of parallel computing. In particular, he (along with co-authors) investigated in [4] a quantitative comparison of the BSP and LogP models of parallel computation. Both models are successful paradigms of the so-called bridging models of parallel computation, where one seeks for balancing simplicity (that eases software development), accuracy (to enable realistic performance predictions), and generality (to enable software portability across various architectures). In BSP the fundamental primitives are global barrier synchronization and the routing of arbitrary message sets. LogP lacks explicit synchronization and imposes a more constrained message-passing style which aims at keeping the load of the underlying communication network below a specified capacity limit. Intuitively, BSP offers a more convenient abstraction for algorithm design and programming, while LogP provides better control of machine resources. In [4], very efficient cross simulations between BSP and the stall-free LogP were derived, showing their substantial equivalence for algorithmic design guided by asymptotic analysis. It was also shown that the two models can be implemented with similar performance on most point-to-point networks.

5.3   Networks and Distributed Computing

The contribution of the research work of Paul Spirakis in the field of networks and distributed computing has been very important for the further development of the field. He has coauthored a significant number of research articles while he contributed as a program committee member of related scientific conferences and as editor of journals. In the following, we highlight some of the most important research works of Paul Spirakis and his coauthors in the field.

Paul Spirakis with John Reif addressed in [75] the fundamental problem of synchronizing communication between distributed processes whose speeds vary dynamically, and they showed how to implement a distributed local scheduler to find matching pairs of processes which are willing to communicate. In [73,74] they considered the probabilistic approach to synchronization of communication in a network of distributed asynchronous processes and presented probabilistic synchronization algorithms that have real time response (the establishment of communication is taking place within a specified time interval with high probability). The algorithms are applied to solve a large class of real time resource synchronization problems.

Paul Spirakis with Hermann Jung and Lefteris Kirousis presented in [34] an algorithm for scheduling a DAG of n nodes on a multiprocessor. The algorithm constructs an optimum schedule which uses at most n processors. They also gave lower bound results on the amount of recomputation needed, thus answering an open question posed by Papadimitriou and Yannakakis.

Paul Spirakis with Lefteris Kirousis and Philippas Tsigas addressed in [42] the problem of reading more than one variables in one atomic operation by only one reader while each of the variables is being written by a set of writers. They presented a deterministic protocol with linear in the number of processes space complexity, linear time complexity for a read operation and constant time complexity for a write operation, as well as a simple probabilistic algorithm with sublinear space complexity and time complexity for a read operation, thus improving significantly previous approaches which required at best, quadratic time and space complexity.

Paul Spirakis with Panagiota Fatourou studied in [21] the problem of efficiently scheduling strict multithreaded computations and presented the first fully distributed scheduling algorithm. The algorithm is asynchronous, on-line, and efficient not only in terms of its memory requirements and its execution time, but also in terms of its communication complexity. Their analysis applies to both shared and distributed memory machines.

Paul Spirakis with Josep Diaz, Dimitrios Koukopoulos, Sotiris Nikoletseas, Maria Serna, and Dimitrios Thilikos analyzed in [18] the stability properties of the FIFO protocol in the adversarial queueing model for packet routing. They presented an upper bound result for stability of any network under the FIFO protocol, answering partially an existing open question. In [45] Paul Spirakis with his co-authors Dimitrios Koukopoulos, Marios Mavronicolas, and Sotiris Nikoletseas, studied the problem of how network structure affects the stability properties of greedy contention-resolution protocols in the framework of the adversarial queueing theory. They came up with a comprehensive collection of structural results in the form of stability and instability bounds on injection rate of the adversary.

Another aspect of Paul's research concerned intrusion propagation in networks. In a joint work with Nikoletseas et al. [66], they studied the problem of intrusion propagation under the assumption of a rather limited in power intruder and how (under this assumption) intrusion can propagate in a perhaps highly secure network. To study this problem, they introduced a new general model for such an intrusion and its propagation in networks. As it turned out by analytic and experimental methods, even such an intruder can have a large penetration factor in the network. Moreover, it was also shown that it will not be easy for a detection mechanism to trace the origin of the intrusion, since it will have to trace a number of links proportional to the nodes captured.

Except for pure theoretical work, Paul Spirakis together with Christos Zaroliagis investigated in [78] implementation and experimentation aspects of distributed algorithms. When one engineers distributed algorithms, some special characteristics arise that are different from conventional (sequential or parallel) computing paradigms. These characteristics include: the need for either a scalable real network environment or a platform supporting a simulated distributed environment; the need to incorporate asynchrony, where arbitrary asynchrony is hard (if at all possible) to implement; and the generation of "difficult" input instances which is a particular challenge. In [78], the term *Distributed Algorithm Engineering* was coined to emerge the need for a systematic methodology to address the aforementioned characteristics as well as the considerable effort required to convert theoretically efficient and correct distributed algorithms to efficient, robust, and easily used software implementations on a simulated or real distributed environment. This conversion has to preserve the assumed properties and limitations of the distributed computing model. The study in [78] addresses several methodological issues in Distributed Algorithm Engineering and illustrates certain approaches to tackle them via case studies.

5.4   Internet, Mobile, and Evolution Networks

Paul was always interested in studying the theoretical foundations of networks using different techniques and testing alternative research direction. Yet, one of the most distinguishing aspects of his approach is to steer his theoretical curiosity into real problems emerging from newly introduced technologies. A typical example of this aspect of his research character is the case of the mobile networks.

In the 1990s, mobile telephony networks were attracting a lot of attention and were emerging as a new technological area. As a first attempt to examine this new technology, along with Grammati Pantziou and George Pentaris, he started by looking into the problem of call control using competitive analysis techniques [70]. Almost in parallel, he also looked into the problem of frequency assignment for fixed-infrastructure mobile networks (e.g., mobile telephony networks) along with Dimitris Fotakis, using graph theoretic techniques [30]. This lightning-fast (Blitzkrieg) examination gave him a good first understanding of this new technological area. Paul started to understand the intricacies and was ready to look beyond the first line of research problems and searched for the deep foundational questions.

In 1999 he forsees that apart from the mobile telephony networks, there is another, different kind of mobile networks where no fixed infrastructure exists. In cooperation with Kostas Hatzis, George Pentaris and Vasilis Tampakas they make one of the very first theoretical approaches into studying fundamental network control problems for the so-called "mobile ad-hoc networks" [32,33]. A key concept of this new approach is that nodes are free to move within the network area in any way they deem appropriate. Given this idea of free-mobility, they understand that all existing graph theoretic models where users are represented by the vertices of the graph and edges correspond to wireless communication channels for users that are within each-others communication range, are simply impractical for use in rigorous theoretical analysis. Among the main contribution of their work was the so-called "motion graph", where essentially the graph represents the area where the nodes move. Under this setting, they introduced efficient counting algorithms and proved (using markov chain theory) their correctness even under scenarios of extreme mobility.

The new model of "motion graph" was then used as the basis for studying other fundamental control problems in ad-hoc mobile network along with Ioannis Chatzigiannakis and Sotiris Nikoletseas. Having as a starting point the Markov chain theory, they looked into different network management protocols in large-scale networks, networks with faulty processors and where some nodes volunteer to support the operation of the network (e.g., see [9,11]). The key idea of the communication framework they introduced was to take advantage of the mobile nodes natural movement by exchanging information whenever mobile nodes meet incidentally. In some way, this idea resembled gossip like communication protocols where messages are spread among nodes like rumors.

Almost in parallel to the work of Paul and his team, similar gossip-like concepts were followed in [82] where an *epidemic algorithm* was designed. In their solution, messages are broadcast to all neighbors as long as there is enough storage space to hold the copies. When there is no room in the local storage of a node, oldest messages are evicted. However, in contrast to the work in [82] and other epidemic algorithms introduced later on in the relevant literature, the protocol framework of Paul and his collaborators did not rely on any assumption on the mobility patterns of the nodes. To deal with cases where nodes were spread in remote areas and would not move beyond these areas, they used these volunteer-nodes to reach them and establish connectivity by physically transporting messages between the sender and receiver nodes. Interestingly, these ideas were used to formulate the *Delay Tolerant Networking Architecture* in 2007 [5] and later on, in 2014, test them in the field as part of a project partially supported by NASA: a team of quadcopters was used to establish digital communication networks.

Another typical example of Paul's interest in emerging technologies, was the case of *Smart Dust* networks. These networks share many common points with the ad-hoc networks, however, the main difference is that nodes have extremely limited capabilities (i.e., in terms of computation, memory and energy). Once again his plan was to look into fundamental network management problems—and in particular the problem of event propagation. The first paper [10] in this new area appeared in 2002 in collaboration with Ioannis Chatzigiannakis and Sotiris Nikoletseas, and then another Blitzkrieg followed with a series of collaborators, to name a few: Peter Triantallou and Nikos Ntarmos [81], Tasos Dimitriou and Marios Mavronicolas [6,7], Ioannis Krontiris and Fotios Nikakis [20]. A few years later, the term Smart Dust networks was replaced by that of *Wireless Sensor Networks*, and a bit later with the term *Pervasive Computing*.

Eventually these technologies became broadly known as the *Internet of Things*. Regardless of the name and ephemeral keywords, the technological goal remained the same: to deploy low-cost network nodes and integrate them with the Internet with the ultimate goal to interconnect the digital and physical domains. Paul's innovative ideas of occasionally-connected networks, and the need to provide sets of protocol families are now interwined with the Internet of Things and uniformly considered by all developers and researchers as a basic concepts. Yet at the very beginning of the inception of the *Internet of Things*, this was not the case. Paul Spirakis was among the very few visionary to predict that in order to realize all these new types of applications we would have to address the problem of intermittent connectivity in networks with long delays between sending and receiving messages, or long periods of disconnection.

Moving forward from the *Smart Dust* networks and their evolution into the *Internet of Things*, Paul had in 2007 one more glimpse into the future. His vision on future systems included the orchestration of myriads of units/nodes, web services, business processes, people, companies and institutions that would be continuously integrated and connected, while preserving their individual properties, objectives and action. Paul's idea on the evolution of the *Web* and the *Internet of Things* was about tiny agents that operate using simple local rules and interact by exchanging short messages. Applications are continuous never-ending processes that eventually reach a state where the agents have developed a self-understanding of the global state.

The first attempt to deal with these systems was based on the Population Protocols model of computation that captures the way in which complex behavior of systems can emerge from the underlying local interactions of agents. Agents are usually anonymous and the local interaction rules are scalable (independent of the size n of the population). Such protocols can model the antagonism between members of several "species" and relate to evolutionary games. In the recent past, Paul was involved in joint research studying the discrete dynamics of cases of such protocols for finite populations. Such dynamics are, usually, probabilistic in nature, either due to the protocol itself or due to the stochastic nature of scheduling local interactions. Examples are (a) the generalized Moran process (where the protocol is evolutionary because a fitness parameter is crucially involved) [17] (b) the Discrete Lotka-Volterra Population Protocols (and associated Cyclic Games) [14] and (c) the Majority protocols for random interactions [52].

Such protocols are usually discrete time transient Markov chains. However the detailed states description of such chains is exponential in size and the state equations do not facilitate a rigorous approach. Instead, ideas related to filtering, stochastic domination and Potentials (leading to Martingales) help in understanding the dynamics of the protocols. Paul looked into the question of fast (in time polynomial in the population size) convergence (to an absorbing state). He addressed questions of "most probable" eventual state of the protocols (and the computation of the probability of such states). Several aspects of such discrete dynamics are wide open and it seems that the algorithmic thought can contribute to the understanding of this emerging subfield of science.

5.5   Algorithmic Game Theory

In the last 15 years, Paul has had a significant contribution to Algorithmic Game Theory (AGT) and has played a key role to the development of the field. He has been one of the pioneers in AGT and his ground-breaking work, mostly on algorithmic properties of load balancing and congestion games and on the efficient computation of exact or approximate Nash equilibria. He has significantly advanced our knowledge and has inspired many researchers to work on AGT.

Load-Balancing and Congestion Games. Paul had understood, from the very beginning, that load balancing and congestion games were bound to play a central role in AGT. His work has shaped the research agenda in the topic for many years and touches many important questions, from existence and complexity of Nash equilibria, to the inefficiency of equilibria, and to computationally efficient mechanisms for improving the Price of Anarchy. Notably, the examples below include four of Paul's most cited papers in Scopus.

In one of the first AGT papers, Marios Mavronicolas and Paul Spirakis [49] initiated the study of *fully mixed* Nash equilibria for load balancing games. They determined the fully mixed Nash equilibrium for identical links and weighted players. Building on it, they proved that the Price of Anarchy for n weighted players and m identical links is $O(\ln n / \ln \ln n)$, for $n \geq m$. Shortly afterwards, Koutsoupias et al. [46] improved this bound to an almost tight bound of $\Theta(\ln m / \ln \ln m)$.

Subsequently, Fotakis et al. [27] introduced the notion of *generalized fully mixed* Nash equilibria for uniformly related parallel links and proved that they almost maximize the Price of Anarchy for identical players. They also gave two proofs of the fact that load balancing games admit pure Nash equilibria. The proof techniques, one based on a greedy argument and the other on a lexicographic potential, have found numerous applications since then.

Investigating necessary and sufficient conditions for the existence of pure Nash equilibria in congestion games with weighted players, Fotakis et al. [26] proved that if the delay functions are linear, such games admit a weighted potential function. The construction is versatile and has been extended to several generalizations of congestion games. For instance, Paul and his coauthors extended it for linear congestion games with static coalitions of players [28] and for linear congestion games in a social network [24]. Moreover, Panagopoulou and Spirakis [68] presented a potential function for weighted congestion games with exponential delays. Today we know that there are no other classes of weighted congestion games with a potential function [31].

Investigating the inefficiency of equilibria in congestion games, Christodoulou et al. [13] proved general tight bounds on the Price of Anarchy and the Price of Stability for ε-approximate pure Nash equilibria of congestion games with linear delays.

Trying to eliminate the inefficiency of equilibria, Kaporis and Spirakis [37] introduced the *price of optimum*, namely the smallest fraction of coordinated players required to induce an optimal configuration in Stackelberg routing games, and showed how to efficiently compute it.

A most interesting and counterintuitive fact in selfish routing is the Braess paradox, namely that edge removal may improve the players' delay at equilibrium. Detecting and eliminating the Braess paradox is a notoriously hard computational problem. Fotakis et al. [25] proved that for non-atomic congestion games on single-commodity networks with linear delays, if the delays of almost all edges are strictly increasing, the most severe manifestations of the Braess paradox can be recognized in polynomial time.

Nash Equilibria in Bimatrix Games. One of the most appealing concepts in game theory is the notion of *Nash equilibrium*: A collection of strategies for the players, from which no player has an incentive to unilaterally deviate. The extremely nice thing about Nash equilibria is that they always exist in any finite normal-form game [64]. Nevertheless, the recent advances in the apparent hardness of the problem NASH(k) of computing an arbitrary Nash equilibrium in k-player games [15], even for 2-player (a.k.a. bimatrix) games [12], crucially question its appllicability as a realistic solution concept.

Therefore, a flurry of results have appeared in the literature during the last decade, concerning the polynomial-time construction of either an approximation of a Nash equilibrium for the general case, or an exact Nash equilibrium for certain important classes of bimatrix games. Spirakis has been one of the leading researchers in both these research trends.

With respect to the approximability of Nash equilibria, he essentially initiated the discussion on polynomial-time constructible approximations of NASH(2) [43], in parallel with the group of Papadimitriou [16]. Since then there has been a significant effort in the literature to reduce these upper bounds, for various notions of Nash equilibrium approximations. Spirakis and his colleagues have established novel techniques for constructing approximate equilibria in normalized bimatrix games, which essentially hold the record so far for the two most popular notions of Nash equilibrium approximations:

- For the most common notion of additive ϵ-approximate Nash equilibria (ϵ-NE in short), in which no player may increase its payoff more than an additive term of ϵ given the strategies of the opponents, Spirakis and Tsaknakis [79]

suggested a gradient-based approach on the regret functions of the two players, and proved that it converges in polynomial time to a 0.3393-NE of an
arbitrary normalized bimatrix game. For *symmetric* bimatrix games, Spirakis
and Kontogiannis have provided a polynomial-time algorithm for constructing $(1/3 + \delta)$-NE, for any constant $\delta > 0$ [44], which is also so far the best
polynomial-time approximation guarantee. Although there is to date no theoretical evidence that one cannot go below these thresholds, all experimental
evidence [23,44,80] demonstrate that it is indeed hard to break it with the
existent approaches.

- For the more demanding notion of, again additive, ϵ-well supported approximate Nash equilibria (ϵ-WSNE in short), in which each player may assign
positive probability mass only to actions that are ϵ-approximate best
responses to the opponent's strategy, Spirakis and Kontogiannis suggested
a polynomial-time algorithm that is based on the tractability of linear programming and constructs $(2/3)$-WSNE. This result has only slightly been
improved in [22] to $(2/3 - 0.005913759)$-WSNE. It is also known that going
below the 2/3 threshold, one would need to check profiles of strategies with
at least polylogarithmic support sizes [2], essentially ruling out enumerative
approaches on the support sizes.

Concerning the second research trend, of polynomial-time algorithms for efficiently solving exactly NASH(2) in certain classes of bimatrix games, the most
typical class is that of *constant-sum* games. Spirakis and Kontogiannis have
determined another class of polynomial-time solvable bimatrix games, called
mutually-concave games [44]. The main idea was based on the polynomial-time
tractability of convex quadratic programs, along with a parameterization of the
quadratic-program formulation of Mangasarian and Stone for Nash equilibria in
bimatrix games [48]. It was proved in [44] that this class of games is essentially
equivalent to the class of *strategically-zero-sum* games proposed by Moulin [63],
but the approach in [44] provides a faster algorithm for computing an equillib-
rium than the one suggested by Moulin. The class of mutually-concave games
is strictly larger than that of constant-sum games, and is incomparable to the
other widely studied class of *constant-rank* games, for which it is known that a
FPTAS exists [36]. Spirakis and Panagopoulou have also proved that randomly
constructed bimatrix games are easy to solve [69].

5.6   Population Protocols and Temporal Graphs

In the last 7 years, Paul Spirakis has been studying in a systematic way formal
models and problems inspired from Dynamic Distributed Computing Systems
and Networks. His work on this modern subject can be broken down into two
main strands: *Population Protocols* and *Temporal Graphs*.

Population Protocols (PPs) of Angluin et al. [3] is a distributed computing model of highly restricted computational entities (e.g., tiny sensor nodes or
nanorobots) that move and interact *passively*, following the dynamicity of their
environment. In terms of modeling, the entities are automata that interact in

pairs according to a fair (or random) scheduler. The main result known when Spirakis started working on the subject was that PPs are very limited computationally, being able to compute only *semilinear predicates* on input assignments. The work carried out by Spirakis, together with Othon Michail, Ioannis Chatzigiannakis, and other collaborators, is prominent between those that established PPs as a very active and rapidly growing sub-area of *Distributed Computing*. Working on their *Mediated Population Protocols* (MPPs) [55], an extension that allows the automata to additionally establish (physical or virtual) links with each other, they proved a quite surprising (at that time) result: *the n automata can now be programmed to simulate any nondeterministic Turing machine of space* $O(n^2)$. Recently, building upon the MPP model, Othon Michail and Paul Spirakis initiated the study of protocols that can algorithmically construct stable networks [59], trying at the same time to answer computability questions and questions related to the potential of their model to represent chemical and biological self-assembly processes. Between the several other important contributions of Spirakis and his collaborators on PPs, one can distinguish the parameterized study of PPs according to the size of their local memories [8], papers that have promoted our understanding on the *Termination* problem [61,62], his work with George Mertzios, Sotiris Nikoletseas, and Christoforos Raptopoulos on the *Majority* problem [52], and with Czyzowicz et al. on the dynamics of discrete Lotka-Volterra PPs [14]. His involvement in PPs has led to a remarkable research record since 2008: 1 research monograph [54], 1 book chapter, around 20 publications in prestigious journals and conferences, and numerous invited talks and lectures.

Though very recent, and with its full story remaining to be written, the work of Spirakis on PPs has already been recognized at the highest level, being one of the four research areas for which he received his 2014 EATCS Fellowship (see Sect. 4).

Inspired by the theoretical developments in dynamic distributed computing systems, together with Othon Michail and other collaborators, Paul Spirakis started envisioning a *Temporal* extension of *Graph Theory* and he is currently working intensively to put down its founding stone. Informally, a *temporal graph* is a graph that changes with time. It can be thought of as a special case of labeled graphs, where the (usually discrete) labels represent some measure of time and constrain connectivity to respect the additional time-dimension, captured in the notion of *time-respecting* paths. The work of Spirakis on the subject begins with [50]. That paper has received attention, as it gave the first temporal analogue of Menger's theorem (in contrast to a famous negative result proving that the classical formulation of Menger's theorem fails on temporal graphs [40]) and introduced the intriguing problem of designing a cost-optimal temporal graph under various combinations of connectivity constraints and cost parameters. Together with Othon Michail, he defined and initiated the study of temporal versions of several well-known combinatorial optimization graph-problems, such as the *Temporal Exploration* problem, the *Temporal Traveling Salesman Problem with Costs One and Two*, and the *Temporal Matching* problem, and gave a first set of approximation algorithms and hardness results for them [60]. Moreover, Spirakis may be considered as one of the very few people that have initiated the formal study of *Random Temporal Graphs*, on which he is currently working with Eleni Akrida and other collaborators [1]. For a more detailed introduction to the work of Spirakis and others on the subject of *Temporal Graphs*, the reader is referred to [53], which is included in this volume.

Finally, we should mention that Paul Spirakis, together with Othon Michail and Ioannis Chatzigiannakis, has worked on the modern area of distributed computation in highly-dynamic networks, where protocols must perform their task against a *worst-case adversary* that controls and alters the communication topology. His contribution to the subject can be found in [56–58].

6   Other Professional Activities

Paul Spirakis has been extremely successful in receiving project grants—a condition *sine qua non* for establishing a research group and descent conditions for pursuing research.

He devoted a considerable amount of his time in submitting proposals and getting highly-competitive project grants, most of which came from the European Union (other funding organizations included NSF and the Greek State). Overall, he has been involved in about 50 projects—a fair portion of which he acted as coordinator.

One of Paul's major efforts, since 1996, was to run (as Chairman of the Board of Directors) the Computer Technology Institute & Press "Diophantus" (CTI), one of the largest Research & Development Institutes in Greece. He carried out this challenging job with great success, managing to run CTI without governmental funding. CTI is a self-funded organization employing more than 300 experienced and specialized scientists (including faculty members of the Department of Computer Engineering and Informatics at the University of Patras), engineers, PhD students, and supporting staff. In the last 5 years, CTI has successfully undertaken more than 130 R&D projects, 95 of which were funded by the EC. In the last 20 years, CTI has exhibited substantial basic and applied research activity in areas such as algorithms and complexity, optimization, wired as well as wireless and sensor networks, computer and network security, ubiquitous and distributed computing, e-learning, complex information systems design and development, production systems, embedded systems, integration and sustainable development.

One of the memorable great successes of Paul Spirakis was the development of close ties between CTI and the Greek State, making CTI the official technical consultant of the Ministry of Education on IT issues continuously in the past 20 years. CTI places particular emphasis on education, by developing and deploying conventional and digital media in education and lifelong learning, publishing printed and electronic educational materials, administrating and managing the Greek School Network, and supporting the organization and operation of the electronic infrastructure of the Greek Ministry of Education and all educational units. In addition, CTI undertakes the lifelong training of school teachers in the new education technology and material.

Because of his extensive involvement in the theory and applications of Computer Science (CS) as well as of the Information & Communication Technologies (ICT) in general, Paul Spirakis had a prominent role in promoting the importance and in determining the research agenda of CS and ICT within Europe. He also served as a consultant in numerous bodies of European Union and the Greek State.

Paul writes occasionally articles in Greek newspapers, mostly in special columns devoted to science and technology, as well as articles expressing his liberal opinions about several aspects of our political and socio-economic environment.

7   Contributions to the Scientific Community

Paul Spirakis delivered more than 125 lectures as invited speaker of various scientific conferences, research institutes, and universities around the globe.

He serves in the Editorial Boards of prestigious computer science journals, including *Acta Informatica, Algorithmica, Computer Science Review, International Journal of Computing Theory, Journal of Parallel and Distributed Computing, Parallel Processing Letters, Theoretical Computer Science*, and *Theory of Computing Systems*. He has also been editor of *Computational Geometry Journal—Theory and Applications*, and area editor of the *Encyclopedia of Algorithms*, published by Springer.

Paul Spirakis was the chairman of more than 25 and a member in more than 130 Program Committees of major international conferences in computer science (incuding STOC, ESA, IPDPS, ICALP, PODC, SPAA, and STACS). He has also been editor in several special issues of prestigious journals dedicated to selected papers from some of these major conferences.

8   Personal

Paul Spirakis is married to (the mathematician) Asimina Chrisofaki. They have two daughters, Olga, an actress and choreographer, and Zeta (Georgia), a computer scientist who currently pursues postgraduates studies (MA) in *The London Film School*. Paul has also a grandson from Olga. He greatly believes in the importance of family, having said among others that "investing time on family is a very good investment".

A first acquaintance with Paul makes you immediately realizing that you are confronted with a perspicacious and open-minded man. Paul is warm, generous, and cultured. Despite being an eminent scientist, he remains simple and approachable, and his door is always open to students and young aspiring researchers. Paul greatly believes in the new generation and in the proper education of young people. He is extremely patient with students believing in their potential and helping each one of them self-realize his/her own special talents.

This makes him at the same time a teacher, a good friend, and a father of his students.

Another immediate observation from a first acquaintance with Paul is that he is a heavy smoker and a passionate drinker of Greek Frappe (cold instant) coffee.

He is characterized by an extremely good sense of humor and high optimism, which make him a pleasant company. He laughs out loudly, especially when he listens to or tells a funny joke (something that he enjoys a lot).

Paul tries every day to learn or discover something new in mathematics. If not, he (claims that he) feels guilty. He also studies books and papers from other scientific disciplines (physics, biology, etc.), because he truly believes that multi-disciplinarity is the key to new ideas and approaches. Time seems to have almost no effect on him. He is full of energy and always keen and ready to tackle the next open problem.

In his free time, he likes to read. Among the great variety of subjects that he reads, he is a passionate reader of crime and spy novels, science fiction, and history. Paul is also a very talented chess player.

Paul has a unique talent in accomplishing heavy managerial and administrative duties and at the same time high-level research and teaching. His passion for research was evident at Friday nights, when, after a whole day (and preceding week) of administrative meetings, he remained in the building of CTI (usually until after midnight) in order to have some fruitful research meetings with his students and collaborators.

Paul deeply believes in the ideals of democracy, social justice, and the promotion of individual talents and initiatives.

9 Epilogue

This article offers a glimpse at the life and career of Paul Spirakis. It is an effort (hopefully successful) to present main aspects of his personal and professional life and to emphasize on his visions and achievements. In any case, the goal was to highlight Paul's excessive offering as a teacher, researcher and scientist, and to express our gratitude and appreciation to him.

Acknowledgements. We are indebted to Eleni Spiraki (Paul's sister) for her great help in the preparation of this article.

References

1. Akrida, E., Gasieniec, L., Mertzios, G., Spirakis, P.: Ephemeral networks with random availability of links: diameter and connectivity. In: Proceedings of 26th ACM Symposium on Parallelism in Algorithms and Architectures—SPAA 2014, pp. 267–276 (2014)

2. Anbalagan, Y., Norin, S., Savani, R., Vetta, A.: Polylogarithmic supports are required for approximate well-supported Nash equilibria below 2/3. In: Chen, Y., Immorlica, N. (eds.) WINE 2013. LNCS, vol. 8289, pp. 15–23. Springer, Heidelberg (2013)

3. Angluin, D., Aspnes, J., Diamadi, Z., Fischer, M.J., Peralta, R.: Computation in networks of passively mobile finite-state sensors. Distrib. Comput. 18(4), 235–253 (2006)

4. Bilardi, G., Herley, K., Pietracaprina, A., Pucci, G., Spirakis, P.: BSP versus LogP. Algorithmica 24, 405–422 (1999). Preliminary version in SPAA 1996

5. Cerf, V., Burleigh, S., Hooke, A., Torgerson, L., Durst, B., Scott, K., Fall, K., Weiss, H.: Delay-tolerant networking architecture. Technical report, The IETF Trust (2007)

6. Chatzigiannakis, I., Dimitriou, T.D., Mavronicolas, M., Nikoletseas, S.E., Spirakis, P.G.: A comparative study of protocols for efficient data propagation in smart dust networks. In: Kosch, H., Böszörményi, L., Hellwagner, H. (eds.) Euro-Par 2003. LNCS, vol. 2790, pp. 1003–1016. Springer, Heidelberg (2003)

7. Chatzigiannakis, I., Dimitriou, T., Mavronicolas, M., Nikoletseas, S., Spirakis, P.: A comparative study of protocols for efficient data propagation in smart dust networks. Parallel Process. Lett. 13(4), 615–627 (2003)

8. Chatzigiannakis, I., Michail, O., Nikolaou, S., Pavlogiannis, A., Spirakis, P.: Passively mobile communicating machines that use restricted space. Theor. Comput. Sci. 412(46), 6469–6483 (2011)

9. Chatzigiannakis, I., Nikoletseas, S.E., Paspallis, N., Spirakis, P.G., Zaroliagis, C.D.: An experimental study of basic communication protocols in ad-hoc mobile networks. In: Brodal, G.S., Frigioni, D., Marchetti-Spaccamela, A. (eds.) WAE 2001. LNCS, vol. 2141, pp. 159–171. Springer, Heidelberg (2001)

10. Chatzigiannakis, I., Nikoletseas, S., Spirakis, P.: Smart dust protocols for local detection and propagation. In: Proceedings of 2nd ACM International Workshop on Principles of Mobile Computing—POMC 2002, pp. 9–16 (2002)

11. Chatzigiannakis, I., Nikoletseas, S., Spirakis, P.: Distributed communication algorithms for ad hoc mobile networks. J. Parallel Distrib. Comput. 63(1), 58–74 (2003)

12. Chen, X., Deng, X., Teng, S.-H.: Settling the complexity of computing two-player Nash equilibria. J. ACM 56, 3, Art. No. 14 (2009)

13. Christodoulou, G., Koutsoupias, E., Spirakis, P.: On the performance of approximate equilibria in congestion games. Algorithmica 61(1), 116–140 (2011)

14. Czyzowicz, J., Gąsieniec, L., Kosowski, A., Kranakis, E., Spirakis, P.G., Uznański, P.: On convergence and threshold properties of discrete Lotka-Volterra population protocols. In: Halldórsson, M.M., Iwama, K., Kobayashi, N., Speckmann, B. (eds.) ICALP 2015. LNCS, vol. 9134, pp. 393–405. Springer, Heidelberg (2015)

15. Daskalakis, C., Goldberg, P.W., Papadimitriou, C.H.: The complexity of computing a Nash equilibrium. SIAM J. Comput. 39(1), 195–259 (2009). Preliminary version in ACM STOC 2006

16. Daskalakis, C., Mehta, A., Papadimitriou, C.: A note on approximate Nash equilibria. In: Spirakis, P.G., Mavronicolas, M., Kontogiannis, S.C. (eds.) WINE 2006. LNCS, vol. 4286, pp. 297–306. Springer, Heidelberg (2006)

17. Díaz, J., Goldberg, L.A., Mertzios, G.B., Richerby, D., Serna, M.J., Spirakis, P.: Approximating fixation probabilities in the generalized Moran process. Algorithmica 69(1), 78–91 (2014). Preliminary version in SODA 2012

18. Diaz, J., Koukopoulos, D., Nikoletseas, S., Spirakis, P., Serna, M., Thilikos, D.: Stability and instability of the FIFO protocol. In: Proceedings of 13th ACM Symposium on Parallel Algorithms and Architectures—SPAA 2001, pp. 48–52 (2001)

19. Díaz, J., Serna, M.J., Spirakis, P.: On the random generation and counting of matchings in dense graphs. Theor. Comput. Sci. **201**(1–2), 281–290 (1998)
20. Dimitriou, T.D., Krontiris, I., Nikakis, F., Spirakis, P.G.: SPEED: Scalable Protocols for Efficient Event Delivery in sensor networks. In: Mitrou, N.M., Kontovasilis, K., Rouskas, G.N., Iliadis, I., Merakos, L. (eds.) NETWORKING 2004. LNCS, vol. 3042, pp. 1300–1305. Springer, Heidelberg (2004)
21. Fatourou, P., Spirakis, P.: Efficient scheduling of strict multithreaded computations. Theory Comput. Syst. **33**(3), 173232 (2000)
22. Fearnley, J., Goldberg, P.W., Savani, R., Sørensen, T.B.: Approximate well-supported Nash equilibria below two-thirds. In: Serna, M. (ed.) SAGT 2012. LNCS, vol. 7615, pp. 108–119. Springer, Heidelberg (2012)
23. Fearnley, J., Igwe, T.P., Savani, R.: An empirical study of finding approximate equilibria in bimatrix games. ArXiv/CoRR, abs/1502.04980 (2015)
24. Fotakis, D., Gkatzelis, V., Kaporis, A., Spirakis, P.: The impact of social ignorance on weighted congestion games. Theory Comput, Syst. **50**(3), 559–578 (2012)
25. Fotakis, D., Kaporis, A., Spirakis, P.: Efficient methods for selfish network design. Theor. Comput. Sci. **448**, 9–20 (2012)
26. Fotakis, D., Kontogiannis, S., Spirakis, P.: Selfish unsplittable flows. Theor. Comput. Sci. **348**, 226–239 (2005)
27. Fotakis, D., Kontogiannis, S., Koutsoupias, E., Mavronicolas, M., Spirakis, P.: The structure and complexity of Nash equilibria for a selfish routing game. Theor. Comput. Sci. **410**(36), 3305–3326 (2009)
28. Fotakis, D., Kontogiannis, S., Spirakis, P.: Atomic congestion games among coalitions. ACM Trans. Algorithms **4**, 4 (2008)
29. Fotakis, D., Nikoletseas, S., Papadopoulou, V., Spirakis, P.: Radiocoloring in planar graphs: complexity and approximations. Theor. Comput. Sci. **340**(3), 514–538 (2005)
30. Fotakis, D.A., Spirakis, P.G.: A Hamiltonian approach to the assignment of non-reusable frequencies. In: Arvind, V., Sarukkai, S. (eds.) FST TCS 1998. LNCS, vol. 1530, pp. 18–30. Springer, Heidelberg (1998)
31. Harks, T., Klimm, M., Möhring, R.H.: Characterizing the existence of potential functions in weighted congestion games. Theory Comput. Syst. **49**(1), 46–70 (2011)
32. Hatzis, K., Pentaris, G., Spirakis, P.G., Tampakas, B.: Counting in mobile networks: theory and experimentation. In: Vitter, J.S., Zaroliagis, C.D. (eds.) WAE 1999. LNCS, vol. 1668, pp. 95–109. Springer, Heidelberg (1999)
33. Hatzis, K., Pentaris, G., Spirakis, P., Tampakas, V., Tan, R.B.: Fundamental control algorithms in mobile networks. In: Proceedings of ACM SPAA 1999, pp. 251–260 (1999)
34. Jung, J., Kirousis, L.M., Spirakis, P.: Lower bounds and efficient algorithms for multiprocessor scheduling of directed acyclic graphs with communication delays. Inf. Comput. **105**, 94–104 (1993)
35. Kamath, A., Motwani, R., Palem, K., Spirakis, P.: Tail bounds for occupancy and the satisfiability threshold conjecture. In: Proceedings of 35th IEEE Symposium on Foundations of Computer Science—FOCS 1994, pp. 592–603 (1994)
36. Kannan, R., Theobald, T.: Games of fixed rank: a hierarchy of bimatrix games. Econ. Theory **42**, 157–173 (2010). Preliminary version in ACM-SIAM SODA 2007
37. Kaporis, A., Spirakis, P.: The price of optimum in Stackelberg games on arbitrary single commodity networks and latency functions. Theor. Comput. Sci. **410**(8–10), 745–755 (2009)

38. Kavvadias, D., Pantziou, G., Spirakis, P., Zaroliagis, C.: Hammock-on-Ears decomposition: a technique for the efficient parallel solution of shortest paths and other problems. Theor. Comput. Sci. **168**(1), 121–154 (1996). Preliminary version in MFCS 1994

39. Kedem, Z., Palem, K., Spirakis, P.G.: Efficient robust parallel computations. In: Proceedings of 22nd Annual ACM Symposium on Theory of Computing—STOC 1990, pp. 138–148 (1990)

40. Kempe, D., Kleinberg, J., Kumar, A.: Connectivity and inference problems for temporal networks. In: Proceedings of 32nd ACM Symposium on Theory of Computing—STOC 2000, pp. 504–513 (2000)

41. Kirousis, L., Serna, M., Spirakis, P.: The parallel complexity of the connected subgraph problem. SIAM J. Comput. **22**(3), 573–586 (1993). Preliminary version in FOCS 1989

42. Kirousis, L., Spirakis, P., Tsigas, P.: Reading many variables in one atomic operation solutions with linear or sublinear complexity. IEEE Trans. Parallel Distrib. Comput. **5**(7), 688–696 (1994)

43. Kontogiannis, S.C., Panagopoulou, P.N., Spirakis, P.G.: Polynomial algorithms for approximating nash equilibria of bimatrix games. In: Spirakis, P.G., Mavronicolas, M., Kontogiannis, S.C. (eds.) WINE 2006. LNCS, vol. 4286, pp. 286–296. Springer, Heidelberg (2006)

44. Kontogiannis, S., Spirakis, P.: Approximability of symmetric bimatrix games and related experiments. In: Pardalos, P.M., Rebennack, S. (eds.) SEA 2011. LNCS, vol. 6630, pp. 1–20. Springer, Heidelberg (2011)

45. Koukopoulos, D., Mavronicolas, M., Nikoletseas, S., Spirakis, P.: The impact of network structure on the stability of greedy protocols. Theory Comput. Syst. **38**(4), 425–460 (2005)

46. Koutsoupias, E., Mavronicolas, M., Spirakis, P.: Approximate equilibria and ball fusion. Theory Comput. Syst. **36**, 683–693 (2003)

47. Kumar, B., Srikant, Y.N.: The best nurturers in computer science research. In: Proceedings of 2005 SIAM International Conference on Data Mining, pp. 566–570; also Technical Report IISc-CSA-TR-2004-10, Computer Science and Automation, Indian Institute of Science, India, October 2004

48. Mangasarian, O.L., Stone, H.: Two-person nonzero-sum games and quadratic programming. J. Math. Anal. Appl. **9**(3), 348–355 (1964)

49. Mavronicolas, M., Spirakis, P.: The price of selfish routing. Algorithmica **48**(1), 91–126 (2007)

50. Mertzios, G.B., Michail, O., Chatzigiannakis, I., Spirakis, P.G.: Temporal network optimization subject to connectivity constraints. In: Fomin, F.V., Freivalds, R., Kwiatkowska, M., Peleg, D. (eds.) ICALP 2013, Part II. LNCS, vol. 7966, pp. 657–668. Springer, Heidelberg (2013)

51. Mertzios, G.B., Nikoletseas, S., Raptopoulos, C., Spirakis, P.: Natural models for evolution on networks. Theor. Comput. Sci. **477**, 76–95 (2013)

52. Mertzios, G.B., Nikoletseas, S.E., Raptopoulos, C.L., Spirakis, P.G.: Determining majority in networks with local interactions and very small local memory. In: Esparza, J., Fraigniaud, P., Husfeldt, T., Koutsoupias, E. (eds.) ICALP 2014. LNCS, vol. 8572, pp. 871–882. Springer, Heidelberg (2014)

53. Michail, O.: An introduction to temporal graphs—an algorithmic perspective. In: Algorithms, Probability, Networks, and Games. LNCS, vol. 9295. Springer, New York (2015)

54. Michail, O., Chatzigiannakis, I., Spirakis, P.: New Models for Population Protocols. Synthesis Lectures on Distributed Computing Theory. Morgan & Claypool Publishers, San Rafael (2011)
55. Michail, O., Chatzigiannakis, I., Spirakis, P.: Mediated population protocols. Theor. Comput. Sci. **412**(22), 2434–2450 (2011)
56. Michail, O., Chatzigiannakis, I., Spirakis, P.G.: Naming and counting in anonymous unknown dynamic networks. In: Higashino, T., Katayama, Y., Masuzawa, T., Potop-Butucaru, M., Yamashita, M. (eds.) SSS 2013. LNCS, vol. 8255, pp. 281–295. Springer, Heidelberg (2013)
57. Michail, O., Chatzigiannakis, I., Spirakis, P.: Causality, influence, and computation in possibly disconnected synchronous dynamic networks. J. Parallel Distrib. Comput. **74**(1), 2016–2026 (2014)
58. Michail, O., Chatzigiannakis, I., Spirakis, P.: Computing in dynamic networks. In: Dehmer, M., Emmert-Streib, F., Pickl, S. (eds.) Chapter 6 in Computational Network Theory: Theoretical Foundations and Applications, 1st edn, pp. 173–218, Wiley-VCH Verlag GmbH & Co. KGaA (2015)
59. Michail, O., Spirakis, P.: Simple and efficient local codes for distributed stable network construction. In: Proceedings of 33rd ACM Symposium on Principles of Distributed Computing—PODC 2014, pp. 76–85 (2014)
60. Michail, O., Spirakis, P.G.: Traveling salesman problems in temporal graphs. In: Csuhaj-Varjú, E., Dietzfelbinger, M., Ésik, Z. (eds.) MFCS 2014, Part II. LNCS, vol. 8635, pp. 553–564. Springer, Heidelberg (2014)
61. Michail, O., Spirakis, P.: Terminating population protocols via some minimal global knowledge assumptions. J. Parallel Distrib. Comput. **81**, 1–10 (2015)
62. Michail, O., Spirakis, P.: Distributed computation by connectivity preserving network transformers (2015) (to appear)
63. Moulin, H., Vial, J.P.: Strategically zero-sum games: the class of games whose completely mixed equilibria cannot be improved upon. Int. J. Game Theory **7**(3–4), 201–221 (1978)
64. Nash, J.: Noncooperative games. Ann. Math. **54**, 289–295 (1951)
65. Nikoletseas, S., Palem, K.V., Spirakis, P., Yung, M.: Short vertex disjoint paths and multiconnectivity in random graphs: reliable network computing. In: Proceedings of 21st International Colloquium on Automata, Languages and Programming—ICALP 1994, pp. 508–519 (1994)
66. Nikoletseas, S., Prasinos, G., Spirakis, P., Zaroliagis, C.: Attack propagation in networks. Theory Comput. Syst. **36**, 553–574 (2003). Preliminary version in ACM SPAA 2001
67. Nikoletseas, S.E., Raptopoulos, C., Spirakis, P.G.: The existence and efficient construction of large independent sets in general random intersection graphs. In: Díaz, J., Karhumäki, J., Lepistö, A., Sannella, D. (eds.) ICALP 2004. LNCS, vol. 3142, pp. 1029–1040. Springer, Heidelberg (2004)
68. Panagopoulou, P., Spirakis, P.: Algorithms for pure Nash equilibria in weighted congestion games. ACM J. Exp. Algorithmics **11**, 1–19 (2006)
69. Panagopoulou, P., Spirakis, P.: Random bimatrix games are asymptotically easy to solve (A simple proof). Theor. Comput. Sci. **54**(3), 479–490 (2014)
70. Pantziou, G., Pentaris, G., Spirakis, P.: Competitive call control in mobile networks. In: Algorithms and Computation—ISAAC 1997, pp. 404–413 (1997)
71. Pantziou, G., Spirakis, P., Zaroliagis, C.: Efficient parallel algorithms for shortest paths in planar digraphs. BIT **32**(2), 215–236 (1992). Preliminary vesrion in SWAT 1990

72. Reif, J., Spirakis, P.: Random matroids. In: Proceedings 12th ACM Symposium on Theory of Computing—STOC 1980, pp. 385–397 (1980)
73. Reif, J., Spirakis, P.: Distributed algorithms for synchronizing interprocess communication within real time. In: Proceedings of 13th ACM Symposium on Theory of Computing—STOC 1981, pp. 133–145 (1981)
74. Reif, J., Spirakis, P.: Real time synchronization of interprocess communications. ACM Trans. Programm. Lang. Syst. **6**(2), 215–238 (1984)
75. Reif, J., Spirakis, P.: Unbounded speed variability in distributed systems. SIAM J. Comput. **14**(1), 7592 (1985)
76. Reif, J., Spirakis, P.: Expected parallel time and sequential space complexity of graph and digraph problems. Algorithmica **7**, 597–630 (1992)
77. Spirakis, P.: Optimal parallel randomized algorithms for addition sparse addition and identification. Inf. Comput. **76**, 1–12 (1988)
78. Spirakis, P., Zaroliagis, C.: Distributed algorithm engineering. In: Fleischer, R., Moret, B.M.E., Schmidt, E.M. (eds.) Experimental Algorithmics. LNCS, vol. 2547, pp. 197–228. Springer, Heidelberg (2002)
79. Tsaknakis, H., Spirakis, P.G.: An optimization approach for approximate Nash equilibria. In: Deng, X., Graham, F.C. (eds.) WINE 2007. LNCS, vol. 4858, pp. 42–56. Springer, Heidelberg (2007)
80. Tsaknakis, H., Spirakis, P.G., Kanoulas, D.: Performance evaluation of a descent algorithm for bi-matrix games. In: Papadimitriou, C., Zhang, S. (eds.) WINE 2008. LNCS, vol. 5385, pp. 222–230. Springer, Heidelberg (2008)
81. Triantafillou, P., Ntarmos, N., Nikoletseas, S., Spirakis, P.: Nanopeer networks and P2P worlds. In: Proceedings of 3rd International Conference on Peer-to-Peer Computing—P2P 2003, pp. 40–46 (2003)
82. Vahdat, A., Becker, D.: Epidemic routing for partially connected ad hoc networks. Technical report CS-200006, Duke University (2000)

The Reality Game Theory Imposes
(Short Summary)

Shlomi Dolev[✉]

Department of Computer Science, Ben-Gurion University of the Negev,
Beersheba, Israel
dolev@cs.bgu.ac.il

I was lucky to be exposed to game theory by Paul Spirakis, moreover to have my first PhD student, Elad Schiller staying with Paul as his PostDoc. It was a great opportunity to examine and think about the combination of philosophical and social considerations when examining the rigorous mathematical settings, results and implications of Game Theory. Implications, that should reflect our real life situations. Especially when searching for game theory tools to be used automatically by societies of (users connected to) computers that form a distributed system.

Distributed computing has changed dramatically in recent years where computing devices that participate in the distributed system are not identical anymore, and may have different hardware, software and utilities. In particular, in the scope of the Internet of things technology, heterogeneous, ad-hoc connected entities form the distributed system, implying the need for game theory techniques in managing the distributed system.

Maybe the most popular and simple example in game theory is the prisoner's dilemma. The possible actions are either to betray or be silent, and the outcome is either to be free (when one prisoner chooses to betray while the other prisoner is silent) or be in prison for two years if both betray or three years if one keeps silent while the other betrays. Such a setting is proven to imply a situation in which both betray and both stay two years in prison. Trying to formulate the game in an autonomous computer system requires the restriction of actions to be in the restricted vocabulary of either betray or keep silent, and obviously not including escape as an option. The restriction on using only rules in the game vocabulary is based on our implicit knowledge of society's authority tools and structure, where the role of the police is to prevent out of rule actions. Hence, we should implement *game authority* [2] that will enforce the vocabulary of rules in the game, and the corresponding outcome. A way to implement such an authority by (almost) identical (computer) participants, just as in society, is based on the cooperation of the majority of the individuals in monitoring and enforcing the rules of the games, possibly by using global Byzantine agreement in the distributed system. In turn, there is a need for game adoption decisions prior to the enforcement of game rules, just like the legislative service. One

Partially supported by Rita Altura Trust Chair in Computer Sciences, Lynne and William Frankel Center for Computer Sciences, Israel Science Foundation (grant number 428/11), and Israeli Internet Association.

C. Zaroliagis et al. (Eds.): Spirakis Festschrift, LNCS 9295, pp. 25–26, 2015.
DOI: 10.1007/978-3-319-24024-4_2

should assume that there are moral meta-rules (say, in the style of the ten commandments) agreed upon by the vast majority of the participants. These meta-rules can then imply the majority's choice on moral (rule of) games and enforcement of the agreed upon game rules. Otherwise, when the number of Byzantine participants is more than the threshold, the society may not able to decide on (moral) games and enforce their rules.

Once we have the game authority that enforces the rules and outcomes of the chosen games, there is still free choice for the players to act according to their (possibly unknown) utility function. Sometimes when the rules of the game are known and the utility is clear the argument and computation needed to realize the correct choice is too complicated to comprehend. The situation is even more complicated, as when some of the players deviate from their optimal choice the rest of the players may be dramatically influenced. To overcome this we suggested the *rational authority* which enforces that players choose the best action in the game according to their possible unrevealed utility [3]. The idea behind the rational authority is to provide the player with a procedure to privately compute the best choice, a procedure that also outputs a proof for the optimality of the choice, where the proof itself can be verified by many reputable proof checkers. Thus, the user can find the best action and verify the action optimality without revealing the private utility. Auditing may be used to ensure that indeed a player uses the provided procedure and verification, the user may be asked to keep signed information for future auditing.

Given the game authority and rational authority, game theory results can be applied to real life actions (or scenarios). Is this real life, or the force of democracy to administer games and impose "artificial rational" action? What action is rational, and who's to define a mathematical utility function, when the secret of creation and life is beyond our understanding? Is rationality based on selfishness ([5])? selfishness of genes ([1])? or is it uncertain ([4]) or an outcome of practical reasons ([6])?

In the end, let me reiterate, I am lucky to have the opportunity to work with Paul who introduced me to the fascinating field of Game Theory, given his deep understanding and enthusiasm for research. I wish him great success in the future.

References

1. Dawkins, R.: The Selfish Gene. Oxford University Press, Oxford (1989)
2. Dolev, S., Schiller, E.M., Spirakis, P.G., Tsigas, P.: Game authority for robust and scalable distributed selfish-computer systems. Theor. Comput. Sci. **411**(26–28), 2459–2466 (2010)
3. Dolev, S., Panagopoulou, P.N., Rabie, M., Schiller, E.M., Spirakis, P.G.: Rationality authority for provable rational behavior. In: PODC 2011, pp. 289–290 (2011)
4. Gigerenzer, G.: Rationality for Mortals, How people cope with uncertainty. Oxford University Press, New York (2008)
5. Rand, A.: The Virtue of Selfishness, New American Library (1964)
6. Wallace, J.R.: Practical reason. In: Millgram, E. (ed.) Varieties of Practical Reasoning. MIT Press, Cambridge (2001)

On Neural Networks and Paul Spirakis

Christos H. Papadimitriou

EECS Department, University of California, Berkeley, CA 94720, USA
christos@berkeley.edu

"We are our connectome," this is the tautology du jour. Everything we do, think, remember, say (or *write*), is merely a projection of our current neural configuration. So, here goes.

It was the memorable January of 1978. Boston was recovering from the greatest snowstorm of its recorded history. This was my second year as Assistant Professor at the Aiken Lab, Harvard's fledgling Computer Science department. A senior colleague showed me the file of a PhD applicant. "His is very good," he said, "except that he seems fascinated with neural networks." I stared at the orange-colored wall across the hall. I had no idea what this phrase meant. "Can you talk to him? Find out how serious his interest is? He cannot pursue neural nets here." He winked at me. "He is Greek."

That evening, after reading the application file, and quickly leafing through an article on neural networks in the library, I spoke for the first time to Paul Spirakis.

I cannot recall exactly what was said, but I do remember that, considering the occasion, it was a very comfortable exchange, surprisingly warm and frank. For some reason my recollection is that he addressed me as "brother," as he does now, but this cannot be. In any event, he assured me in no uncertain terms that he has no firm commitment to neural networks as a research subject, and as a result he was welcomed to Harvard's PhD program with open arms.

I am happy to acknowledge that Paul has kept his promise to me. In fact, he kept it in the strongest way possible, because he seems to have worked on every subfield of Computer Science other than neural networks. Starting with a paper in STOC on random matroids, co-authored with his advisor John Reif, he continued into distributed systems and operating systems theory, computational geometry and random graph theory — all themes that would recur often — then parallel algorithms for more than a decade, concurrent with network and database theory and VLSI, then parallel complexity and approximation, queuing theory and later phase transitions, robust and reliable computation as well as network synchronization (plus work combining many of the above themes), routing on meshes and multithreaded computation, security and — finally in 1995 — the web. Next came scheduling, as well as frequency coloring and mobile networks, then, with the new century, game theory — price of anarchy and complexity and approximation of equilibria but also fairness — then networks again, except now it is smart dust and sensor nets and peer-to-peer. It gets more intense: Onward to evolution and electronic voting, deeper into all aspects of game theory, then dynamic and temporal networks, but not without frequent forays back to random graphs and distributed computation and performance evaluation. And of course it is not the

© Springer International Publishing Switzerland 2015
C. Zaroliagis et al. (Eds.): Spirakis Festschrift, LNCS 9295, pp. 27–28, 2015.
DOI: 10.1007/978-3-319-24024-4_3

list that is most impressive, but the timing, the way Paul Spirakis's research path crisscrossed four decades of history of Computer Science, responding to its priorities and aspirations and anxieties. Like a master football player, Paul has always managed to be close to the ball.

It may not be easy for our younger colleagues to understand the force that drives such exquisite breadth. Paul Spirakis belongs in a generation of theoreticians who understood and loved all of Computer Science — we almost felt that we owned Computer Science. Back then, our mission was not only to advance the mathematical elegance and sophistication of our arguments. We considered it our responsibility to outfit with rigorous foundations all the important practical endeavors that were unfolding around us. This is the mindset in the opus of Paul Spirakis.

If there is one thing missing from Paul's formidable research trail so far, it has to be our first joint paper. It is hard to believe that, with all the intersection points of our research and lives, we have yet to prove a theorem together. But I can feel it, it is coming close now.

And maybe it will be on neural networks.

Concurrency, Parallelism, Asynchrony and Life

Marina Papatriantafilou(✉)

Chalmers University of Technology, Gothenburg, Sweden
ptrianta@chalmers.se

Abstract. This is a brief essay in honor of Paul Spirakis on the occasion of his 60th birthday, and a prologue for the articles of this volume titled "Of concurrent data structures and iterations" and "Data-streaming and concurrent data-object co-design: overview and algorithmic challenges".

Patras, Middle of 80's, Some September Late Afternoons

The amphitheater is full, the professor that holds the classes is newly arrived from NYU. With a big smile, full of energy and enthusiasm, he is taking the class by storm, with new knowledge. No slides, just pure, genuine discussion and blackboard. The speed is unbelievable and so is the flow of knowledge. Some of us are wondering "Will he soon start writing backwards on the blackboard? Then we can go even faster, learn even more! (laughter)". Always with a smile and enthusiasm! And of course we loved it!

For the author of this essay, this has been the start of a journey, starting from those lectures on inter-process synchronization and later on, as researcher, moving to concurrency in general, algorithms for multiprocessor and multicore systems, the magic world of distributed computing and the differences between the possible and the impossible.

Three Decades Later

In two of the articles in this volume, it is possible to find an extract of some of the recent work by the author along this journey, coauthored with colleagues. The articles, titled *"Of concurrent data structures and iterations"* and *"Data-streaming and concurrent data-object co-design: overview and algorithmic challenges"*, put together a brief flashback on the needs from implementations of shared objects and their role in concurrency, relatively to efficiency, consistency and determinism. The articles shed light on shared data objects and their role as data exchange and synchronization points in new contexts in demanding applications such as data-streaming, in-memory analysis of large data volumes, with needs for iterations and range queries over the elements of the data structures.

More specifically, the article on concurrent iterations on shared data objects describes recent work on the problem, including a framework of consistency specifications, together with an overview of iteration implementations that have appeared in the research literature, as well as in widely-used programming environments; furthermore, it outlines a range of application targets and challenging

C. Zaroliagis et al. (Eds.): Spirakis Festschrift, LNCS 9295, pp. 29–30, 2015.
DOI: 10.1007/978-3-319-24024-4_4

future directions. The article on concurrent data-stream processing proposes to analyze the related issues through newly proposed data objects and identifies new key challenges to improve data-stream processing through co-design of fine-grain efficient synchronization combined with the data exchange.

To achieve parallelism with consistency, combined with the inherent asynchrony present in systems and applications, has been and continues to be challenging. Asynchronous threads need to do useful work independently, as well as to meet e.g. through synchronization and/or the data that they exchange. The aforementioned articles, contributing to the exploration of these challenges and possibilities in new contexts, also showing new paths, are offspring of a tree planted with enthusiasm and have been written with gratitude to the person who inspired the enthusiasm and who is honored in this volume.

Thank you Paul and Happy Birthday!

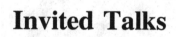

Invited Talks

Rationality Authority for Provable Rational Behavior

Shlomi Dolev[1]([✉]), Panagiota N. Panagopoulou[2], Mikaël Rabie[1],
Elad M. Schiller[3], and Paul G. Spirakis[2,4]

[1] Ben-Gurion University of the Negev, Beer Sheva, Israel
{dolev,rabie}@cs.bgu.ac.il
[2] Computer Technology Institute, and Press "Diophantus", Rio, Greece
{panagopp,spirakis}@cti.gr
[3] Chalmers University of Technology, Gothenburg, Sweden
elad@chalmers.se
[4] University of Liverpool, Liverpool, UK
P.Spirakis@liverpool.ac.uk

Abstract. Players in a game are assumed to be totally rational and absolutely smart. However, in reality all players may act in non-rational ways and may fail to understand and find their best actions. In particular, participants in social interactions, such as lotteries and auctions, cannot be expected to always find by themselves the "best-reply" to any situation. Indeed, *agents* may consult with others about the possible outcome of their actions. It is then up to the counselee to assure the rationality of the consultant's advice. We present a distributed computer system infrastructure, named *rationality authority*, that allows safe consultation among (possibly biased) parties. The parties' advices are adapted only after verifying their feasibility and optimality by standard formal proof checkers. The *rationality authority* design considers computational constraints, as well as privacy and security issues, such as verification methods that do not reveal private preferences. Some of the techniques resembles zero-knowledge proofs. A non-cooperative game is presented by the *game inventor* along with its (possibly intractable) equilibrium. The *game inventor* advises playing by this equilibrium and offers a checkable proof for the equilibrium feasibility and optimality. Standard *verification procedures*, provided by trusted (according to their reputation) *verification procedures*, are used to verify the proof. Thus, the proposed *rationality authority* infrastructure facilitates the applications of game theory in several important real-life scenarios by the use of computing systems.

1 Introduction

Game theory is based on the assumption that (at least, some) players play rationally. This assumption is questionable in the face of the sophistication for obtaining the best strategy in (even simple) games. Thus, the application of game theory in real life is limited by the degree in which the players (who are rarely

© Springer International Publishing Switzerland 2015
C. Zaroliagis et al. (Eds.): Spirakis Festschrift, LNCS 9295, pp. 33–48, 2015.
DOI: 10.1007/978-3-319-24024-4_5

mathematicians, economic experts, or computer scientists) can understand the meaning of the game rules and the way to act. One famous example is auctions where every variant of an auction introduces the need for a new proof that, say, reconfirms that the second price auction is the best to use [5,22]. We have in mind a framework that will let the ordinary and inexperienced Joe and Jane safely figure their best-reply.

Distributed computer systems can implement the *rationality authority* framework that in turn, can enable (and ensure by audit schemes) rational behavior, without sacrificing the players' privacy, e.g., keeping the individual preferences (utilities) private. The framework, as depicted in Fig. 1, includes:

- The *game inventor*, which may possibly gain revenues from the game. We consider *game inventors* that create games for which they could predict the best-reply and prove their feasibility and optimality to the players/*agents*.
- The *agents* are the game participants, for which they receive verifiable advices on the feasible and optimal actions to take.
- The *verifiers* are trustable service providers that profit from selling general purpose *verification procedures*, $v()$, (using formal methods and languages), and therefore would like to have a good long-lasting reputation on being honest in checking (a variety of) proofs. We note the possibility of having several *verifiers*, such that their majority is trusted. The reputation of the *verifiers* can be updated according to the (majority of their) results.

The *verification procedures* supplied by the verifiers may be general purpose procedures, not restricted to the context of the *rationality authority*. They should be able to check proofs [3] in an agreed upon format, a detailed logic proof in 3-SAT or Coq, probabilistically checkable proofs, interactive proofs in the style of zero-knowledge proofs, globally agreed upon, and simple instructions for the *agents* to check the proof (or even an empty proof relying on the verifier procedure to check the suggested actions in the style of nondeterministic Turing machines). The *verifiers* may use a library for the specification of the solution concepts and inform the user concerning the solution concept used and the consequences of the choice.

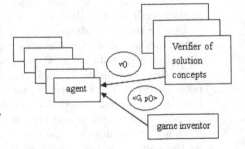

Fig. 1. The inventor sends the game G with a procedure $p()$ to the *agents*, suggesting actions and proofs for the optimality of the suggested actions. A designated verifier $v()$ sends *verification procedures* to the *agents* to allow verification of the proofs.

Verifying a best-reply could be as hard as computing it [24,29]. Computing the best-reply is known to be intractable [6]. However, there are some cases in which the game outcome is known, say, due to human innovation or statistically emerging patterns [14]. For example, taxation authorities or system administrators can sometimes observe the outcome and advise the participants about employing Nash equilibria, as in [32]. Thus, we may study the verification of such advised solutions, rather than only their (possibly unrevealed way of) computation.

Online auctions have gained tremendous popularity in electronic commerce, B2B applications, and Internet ad auction applications [11]. Much of the literature models these auctions as single stage games or as repeated games. In some of our examples for the use of the *rationality authority*, we take a realistic approach in which the *agents* join the game in some random order, rather than participating in all game rounds (see Sects. 5 and 6).

Related Work

All agents are aware of the existence of the *rationality authority* as common knowledge. Since it communicates with agents before they choose their actions, one might view the authority as synchronization mechanisms that are used in correlated equilibria [1] or as moderators that are used in multi-party computation [15]. However, the *rationality authority* is *not* trusted, where as synchronization mechanisms are. Vis., the inventors must demonstrate their trustworthiness and have only the (trusted) verifiers at their disposal. This assumption is directly implied by the separation principles between the inventors and the verifiers.

Guerin and Pitt [19] present a framework for verification and compliance in a multi-*agent* system. They discuss whether the verification depends on the information that may be available (*agent* internals, observable behavior, normative specifications) and the semantic definition of the communication language. Moreover, they consider the types of languages that permit verification and testing in open systems where *agents'* internals are kept private. Their analysis is useful in enforcing compliance in open systems. Guerin [17] explains how to formally specify and verify subgame perfect equilibria. Tadjouddine [29] considers the complexity of verifying an equilibrium. Tadjouddine shows that Nash and Bayesian Nash equilibria can be verified in polynomial time. Moreover, dominant strategy equilibrium is NP-complete. Other related work includes [18,20,28,30,31], to name a few. None of the aforementioned results considers non-revealing verification methods. In [9,10] we proposed the *game authority*, which is a self-stabilizing middleware for assuring that all *agents* honestly follow the rules of the game. In [8,9] we presented a self-stabilizing mechanism for deterring joint deviations.

Our Contribution

We propose the *rationality authority* infrastructure that separates the interest, benefit and goals of the parties (*game inventors, verifiers* and *agents*) that enables *agents* to take rational (feasible and optimal) actions. The separation also includes the disjointment of the *game inventor* from game revenues and the *verifier* from selling reliable *verification procedures*. We propose the following specific case studies for the usefulness of the *rationality authority* framework.

– We explain how to use interactive theorem provers for verifying pure Nash equilibria (Sect. 3).

- We present an equilibrium verification method that does not reveal the *agent* preferences, and by that, preserves the users privacy and secures their actions when acting upon the advised equilibria. As a second case study, we present a general 2-*agents* (bimatrix) game for which a unique Nash equilibrium exists but it is hard to compute. For this game, we present a polynomial-time equilibria verifier with privacy guarantees. Namely, the verifier does not reveal the *agent* preferences in a way that resembles zero-knowledge proofs [16] (Sect. 4).
- We present the *participation* game, which has an equilibrium that is hard to compute without the *game inventor* advice. We show how to use the advice for computing the game equilibrium and verify it (Sect. 5).
- We study competitive on-line games in which each *agent* joins the game at a different time (as in [12]). The *game inventor* keeps statistical information about past *agent* actions. Each *agent*, upon arrival, has to choose a strategy. With probability p, the *agent* follows the inventor's suggested strategy. With probability $(1 - p)$, it chooses a strategy based on its knowledge about the strategic (off-line) version of the game. The inventor chooses a strategy for the *agent* based on its statistics. When the inventor suggests a strategy, it must convince the *agent* that the strategy is beneficial for it. To do so, the inventor provides the *agent* with a formal proof that can be checked by a trusted verifier (Sect. 6).

The *rationality authority* enables *agents* to identify and take rational choices. Not only does the *rationality authority* verify the feasibility and optimality of proposed equilibria, but it can also cooperate with the *game authority* proposed in [9,10] that guarantees that the *agents* employ the strategy equilibrium by following the game rules.

This work appears as a brief announcement in [7].

2   Preliminaries

We use N to denote the set of *agents* that rationally and unilaterally choose an action from the set A_i, where $i \in N$ is an *agent*. A preference relation, $\succsim_i$, expresses the desire of the individual *agent* for one particular outcome over another. For game, G, the relation $\succsim_i$ refers to *agent* i's preferences. We can replace $\succsim_i$ with a *payoff/utility function* $u_i : A \to \mathbb{R}$, for which $u_i(a) \geq u_i(b)$ whenever $a \succsim_i b$. Namely, u_i is a function $A \to \mathbb{Z}$, which associates with the strategies of each *agent* the gain of *agent* i, where $A = A_0 \times \cdots \times A_{n-1}$. We represent single stage games, G, in their strategic form as $\langle N, A = (A_i), \succsim = (\succsim_i) \rangle$ (or $\langle N, A = (A_i)_{i \in N}, U = (u_i)_{i \in N} \rangle$).

Profiles

A strategy *profile* (a strategy combination) $a = (a_i)_{i \in N}$ is a strategy set, one for each *agent*, that completely implies all game actions by specifying a single strategy for each *agent*. We borrow from [27] also the notation of profiles that

---

Types
2 n; *number of agents*

4 TSi; *associate each agent with its number of strategies*

6 Si; *for each agent i, $S_i(i)$ is the strategy played by i*

8 u; $u(i, Si)$ *(utility) is i's gain for the strategy profile Si*

10 **Functions and Properties**
   $change(Si, si, i)$; *a strategy profile that is different from Si by the strategy si for agent i. Note that this function*
12 *can build all the strategies needed for proving that a strategy profile is a Nash Equilibrium*

14 $isStrat(n, TSi, Si)$; *verifies the strategy profile's size*; $\forall i \leq n : Si(i) \leq TSi(i)$

16 $eqStrat(n, Si1, Si2)$; *checks equality of two strategy profiles*; $\forall i \leq n : Si1(i) = Si2(i)$

18 $leStrat(n, u, Si1, Si2)$; *checks incomparability of $Si1$ and $Si2$*; $\exists i, j : u_i(Si1) < u_i(Si2) \wedge u_j(Si2) < u_j(Si1)$

20 $leStrat(n, u, Si1, Si2)$; *checks* $Si1 \leq_u Si2$; $\forall i \leq n : u_i(Si1) \leq u_i(Si2)$

22 **Pure Nash Equilibrium** (**definitions**)
   $isNash(n, u, Si, TSi)$; *verifies that Si is a Nash equilibrium*;
24
   $isStrat(n, TSi, Si) \wedge \forall i \leq n, si \leq Si(i) : u_i(Si) \leq u_i(change(Si, si, i))$
26
   $isMaxNash(n, u, Si, TSi)$; *checks* $isNash \wedge \forall$ *Nash equilibrium* $S'i : Si \leq_s S'i$
28
   Verifying a Nash Equilibrium (**proof scheme**)
30 $allStrat$; $\forall Si : isStrat(n, TSi, Si) \rightarrow eqStrat(n, Si, Si_1) \vee eqStrat(n, Si, Si_2) \vee \ldots eqStrat(n, Si, Si_m)$, where $\{Si_{-j}\}_{j \leq m}$
   are possible strategies
32
   $allNash$; $\forall Si : isNash(n, u, Si, TSi) \rightarrow eqStrat(n, Si, NSi_1) \vee eqStrat(n, Si, NSi_2) \vee \ldots eqStrat(n, Si, NSi_m)$,
34 *where* $\{NSi_j\}_{j \leq m}$ *are Nash equilibrium*

36 $NashMax$; $\forall Si : isNash(n, u, Si, TSi) \rightarrow leStrat(n, u, Si, NSi) \vee noComp(n, u, Si, NSi)$

Fig. 2. Definition of the game model and its equilibria. These definitions are used for verifying Pure Nash equilibria.

do not include the strategy of a single agent, i.e., (a_{-i}, a_i), as well as the profile of action sets, A_{-i}. We say that the strategy profile $s \in A$ is greater than $s' \in A$ if $\forall i \in N : u_i(s) \geq u_i(s')$. We denote $s \geq_u s'$.

Nash Equilibria

A strategy profile $s \in A$ is a pure Nash equilibrium of game $G = \langle N, A = (A_i), \succsim = (\succsim_i) \rangle$, if $\forall i \in N$, $\forall s'_i \in A_i$, $u_i(s) \geq u_i((s_{-i}, s'_i))$. We say that a pure Nash equilibrium (PNE) s is maximal if for any pure Nash equilibrium s', we do not have $s' \geq_u s$.[1] A game may not possess a PNE at all. However, if we extend the game to include *mixed strategy* by allowing each *agent* to choose its strategy with certain probabilities (and if we extend the payoff functions u_i to capture expectation), then an equilibrium is guaranteed to exist [23].

---

[1] Similarly, we can define the minimal Nash equilibria; s is minimal if for any pure Nash equilibrium s', we do not have $s' \leq_u s$.

3   Verifying a Nash Equilibrium Using Coq

Agents are expected to act rationally. We consider *agents* that are offered a strategy for which optimality is claimed. In order to familiarize the reader with equilibria verification, we briefly explain how to verify that a strategy profile, NSi, is a maximal Nash equilibrium. The proof presented in this section enumerates all strategy profiles, i.e., intractable with respect to both time and space for an unbounded number of *agents* or strategies (Sect. 4 addresses these important complexity issues). We sketch the proof of a pure Nash equilibrium using the theorem prover, Coq [2]. We use Coq because it is a standard and well-tested theorem prover.

The proof sketch considers the definitions that appears in Fig. 2. We note that Proposition *all_strat* (line 30) enumerates all strategy profiles. The proof of Proposition *all_strat* (line 30) is demonstrated by destructing all $Si(i)$ as long as $Si(i) \leq TSi(i)$, and then concluding that the equality exists with one of the strategies enumerated. The next step is to show that NSi is an equilibrium. Then, we enumerate all Nash equilibria (constructing a proposition for each of them). For each enumerated strategy in the Proposition *all_strat* (line 30), if it is an equilibrium, we use the corresponding proposition, if it is not, we show a counter-example (i and si such as $u(i, Si) < u(i, change(Si, si, i))$). NSi's optimality is showed by verifying that there is no equilibrium Si greater than the equilibrium NSi (Proposition *Nash_max*, line 36). Proposition *Nash_max* assume that we are looking for a maximal equilibrium and in the opposite case we just have to change $le\_strat(n, u, Si, NSi)$ with $le\_strat(n, u, NSi, Si)$.

4   Provable Rationality Using Interactive Proofs

We study a 2-*agent* game, defined by the $n \times m$ matrices A, B of the payoffs of the two *agents*. Broadly speaking, the equilibrium is hard to compute. We present two interactive proofs that lead to an easy polynomial-time verification. The second proof also has privacy guarantees.

Case Study: A General 2-*agent* Game with Privacy Guarantees

We now turn to consider a 2-*agent* game, defined by the $n \times m$ matrices A, B of the payoffs of the two *agents* (the *row* agent , whose pure strategies are the n rows, and the column *agent*, whose strategies are the m columns). Here an equilibrium is, in general, hard to compute, i.e., complete in the complexity class PPAD, see [6]. However, the interactive proofs P_1 and P_2 (Figs. 3 and 4, respectively) lead to an easy polynomial-time verification with privacy guarantees in the case of P_2.

Lemma 1 shows that P_1's verifier algorithm has polynomial time complexity. The proof follows from the second Nash theorem [23], i.e., that for each strategy of the row *agent* in the support S_1 the expected gain should be the same and no less than the expected gain for strategies not in the support. It is easy to state the Verifier for the column *agent*.

Prover *(inventor)*: Provide each *agent* the *agents'* supports, i.e., strategy profiled played with non-zero probabilities.

Verifier of the row agent i: Let the support S_2 of the other *agent* (the column *agent*) be $\{j_1,\ldots,j_k\}$. Let $y_{j_1},\ldots,y_{j_k}$ be the Nash probabilities of the column *agent*. Let S_1 be the support of the row *agent* and $S_1 = \{i_1,\ldots,i_\ell\}$. The verifier solves the linear system (1) and verifies that $0 \le y_t \le 1$ for all $t \in \{j_1,\ldots,j_k\}$ and also that, for each row $i \notin S_1$, the expected gain $y_{j_1}A(i,j_1)+\cdots+y_{j_k}A(i,j_k) < \lambda_1$.

$$\lambda_1 = y_{j_1}A(i_1,j_1) + y_{j_2}A(i_1,j_2) + \cdots + y_{j_k}A(i_1,j_k) \qquad (1)$$
$$\vdots$$
$$\lambda_1 = y_{j_\ell}A(i_\ell,j_1) + y_{j_2}A(i_\ell,j_2) + \cdots + y_{j_k}A(i_\ell,j_k)$$
$$y_{i_1} + \cdots + y_{j_k} = 1$$

Fig. 3. Interactive prover P_1.

Prover *(inventor)*: Send to each *agent* just *its* support, *its* probabilities, and the values λ_1, λ_2.

Verifier of the row agent i: Agent $i \in \{1,2\}$ asks the prover for two random indices j_1, j_2. If the prover is honest, it will return whether j_1 is in S_2 (or not) and whether j_2 is in S_2 (or not). Then the verifier computes the *expected gains of the other* agent for the two indices, $\lambda_2(j_1)$ and $\lambda_2(j_2)$. The verifier can then check whether
- "both j's in S_2", i.e., $\lambda_2(j_1) = \lambda_2(j_2) = \lambda_2$, and
- "1-in/1-out", say j_1 is in, i.e., $\lambda_2(j_1) = \lambda_2 \ge \lambda_2(j_2)$.

The test is inconclusive for both $j_1, j_2 \notin S_2$ but at least one will be in with probability at least $1/n$. Thus, on average, $O(n)$ random queries of the verifier will verify the equilibrium play.

Fig. 4. A private proof P_2.

Lemma 1. *The interactive proof P_1 has verifier complexity of time $LP(n,m)$ (where LP is the time of a linear program solver of at most n equations and m unknowns) and the number of bits communicated is $O(n+m)$.*

Proof Sketch. The verifier must solve a linear system of $k+1$ equations and $k+1$ unknown variables, where $k \ge \max(n,m)$ as implied by Fig. 3. Also, the prover just sends the two support sets (indices); each is less than $\max(n,m)$ in cardinality. Thus, it can actually send a vector of zeroes and ones, where the ones indicate the support indices. □

Note that our proof P_1 reveals both equilibrium supports to each *agent*. However, P_1 does not need to explicitly send any probability values. Moreover, the verifier algorithm P_2 extends P_1, still has a polynomial time, and yet does not reveal to any *agent* the Support (or probability values) of the other *agents*!

Remark 1. We can generalize the scheme of P_1 and P_2 to n agents. The prover provides the support sets $S_1, \ldots, S_n$ to all. The verifier of each *agent* then solves the corresponding *polynomial system* to find the Nash equilibrium probabilities.

Remark 2. The interactive proof P_2 does not reveal the actual equilibrium to either *agent*. Namely, the row *agent*, for example, cannot in general compute the Support (and hence the probability values) of the column *agent* if the row *agent* knows λ_1, λ_2 and its own Support and probabilities. To see this, consider the example in Fig. 5. Assume that the prover sends to the row *agent* its Support $S_1 = \{A\}$, its probabilities $p_A = 1, p_B = 0$, its payoff $\lambda_1 = 1$, and the payoff of the column player $\lambda_2 = 1$. Then, the row *agent* cannot conclude which is the actual equilibrium, since it is easy to see that any probabilities q_C, q_D of the column *agent* such that $q_C + q_D = 1, q \leq 1/2, q_C \geq 0, q_D \geq 0$ correspond to Nash equilibrium probabilities with $\lambda_2 = 1$.

Remark 3. In the case of large supports, e.g., $\theta(n)$, our verifier can test the equilibrium in a constant, k, number of queries, because the probability is constant in each case. Note that one can get the other's support via n queries, i.e., each query asks "is j in the other's support?" for all j to get all the support of the other *agents*. Thus, our verifier has a definite advantage in this case of large supports. The proposed test is always sublinear in n, except for the case of constant size supports.

	C	D
A	1, 1	1, 1
B	0, 1	2, 0

Fig. 5. A bimatrix game example.

5   Equilibrium Consultant with Provable Advices

We present the *Participation* game in which c is the auction participation fee and no gain is offered to the solo participant. The game's equilibrium is hard to compute without the *rationality authority*'s advice. We explain how the *agent* can use the advice for computing the game equilibrium and verify the *rationality authority*'s advice.

Consider n firms that are eligible to participate in an auction. The auction rules are:

- A firm f gets a value $v > 0$ if at least $k = 2$ firms choose to participate and f chooses *not* to.
- A firm f gets a value $v - c > 0$ when at least $k = 2$ firms participate and f is one of them.
- If nobody participates, then each firm gains zero.
- If firm f participates but the total number of participants is less than k, then f *pays* $c > 0$.

The Participation game is a symmetric game and thus, by Nash's theorem [23], it has a symmetric Nash equilibrium in which each firm decides to participate or not with probability p independent of the others.[2] The equilibrium stability implies equality between the expected payoffs of a firm f for participating and for not participating:

$$(v - c) \cdot \Pr\{\text{at least 1 other participates} \,|\, f \text{ participates}\} - \qquad (2)$$
$$c \Pr\{\text{no other firm participates} \,|\, f \text{ participates}\} =$$
$$v \Pr\{\text{at least 2 other firms participate} \,|\, f \text{ does not}\} +$$
$$0 \cdot \Pr\{\text{at most 1 other firm participates} \,|\, f \text{ does not}\}$$

Equation (2) defines the *equilibrium*'s probability p. Thus, the verifier can verify Eq. (2) by computing Eq. (3).

$$(v - c) \cdot A + (-c) \cdot B = v \cdot C + 0 \cdot D, \qquad (3)$$

where

$A = \Pr\{\text{at least 1 other firm participates} \,|\, f \text{ participates}\} = 1 - (1 - p)^{n-1}$

$B = \Pr\{\text{no other firm participates} \,|\, f \text{ participates}\} = (1 - p)^{n-1}$

$C = \Pr\{\text{at least 2 other participate} \,|\, f \text{ does not}\} = 1 - (1 - p)^{n-1} - (n - 1)p(1 - p)^{n-2}$

$D = \Pr\{\text{at most 1 other participates} \,|\, f \text{ does not}\} = (1 - p)^{n-1} + (n - 1)p(1 - p)^{n-2}$

In fact, our simple example defines an easier job for the verifier since Eq. (3) gives Eq. (4).

$$(v - c) - (v - c)(1 - p)^{n-1} + (-c)(1 - p)^{n-1} = v - v(1 - p)^{n-1} - v(n - 1)p(1 - p)^{n-2}$$
$$(v - c) + (-v + c - c)(1 - p)^{n-1} = v - v(1 - p)^{n-1} - v(n - 1)p(1 - p)^{n-2}$$
$$(v - c) - v(1 - p)^{n-1} = v - v(1 - p)^{n-1} - v(n - 1)p(1 - p)^{n-2}$$
$$c = v(n - 1)p(1 - p)^{n-2} \qquad (4)$$

For $\frac{c}{v} = \frac{3}{8}$, $n = 3$, and $p = \frac{1}{4}$, the firm's expected gain is $v \left(1 - \left(\frac{3}{4}\right)^2 - 2 \cdot \frac{1}{4} \cdot \frac{3}{4}\right) = \frac{v}{16}$. In the case of any k, the prover still has to provide each firm with the equilibrium value of p and the verifier asserts Eq. (5).

$$(v - c) \cdot A_k + (-c) \cdot B_k = v \cdot C_k + 0 \cdot D_k, \quad \text{where} \qquad (5)$$
$$A_k = \Pr\{\text{at least } k \text{ firms participate} \,|\, f \text{ participates}\}$$
$$B_k = \Pr\{\text{at most } k - 1 \text{ firms participate} \,|\, f \text{ participates}\}$$
$$C_k = \Pr\{\text{at least } k \text{ firms participate} \,|\, f \text{ does not}\}$$
$$D_k = \Pr\{\text{at most } k - 1 \text{ firms participate} \,|\, f \text{ does not}\}$$

Note that, now, p's value is hard to compute but, once it is given, it is easy to compute the conditional probabilities A_k, B_k, and C_k and verify the equilibrium

---

[2] We assume that firms do not differ significantly (or that they are aware of any difference among themselves) and thus a symmetric equilibrium, in which each firm participates with probability $p > 0$, is natural to assume.

play in which a firm *expects to get the same* by using p to decide whether to play. Also note that for the Participation game, and for symmetric games in general, the players can cross-check that the prover has sent the *same* probability p to each of them, since it might be the case that more than one symmetric equilibrium exists. The existence of multiple equilibria would allow a dishonest prover to send different probabilities to the players, with each probability corresponding to a different symmetric equilibrium.

On-line Participation. Let us again assume that $k = 2$ and consider the case in which firms need to decide about their participation *at different times*. If firm f is the last to choose, the prover's "proof" is either $p = 1$, when at least one other firm has entered the game, or $p = 0$ otherwise. If the advice is $p = 1$, firm f will gain $v - c = \frac{5v}{8}$ and if $p = 0$, firm f will gain v. In both cases, f gains more in "on-line" advice in this setting. However, this verification method reveals the number of firms that have already played.

Of course, such advice favors the late arriving *agents*. But *if the order of arrivals is random*, the expected gain of any firm after advice is at least $\frac{1}{3} \cdot \frac{5v}{8} = \frac{5v}{24}$, still better than $\frac{v}{16}$ in the off-line case. On the other hand, false advice to the last *agent*, i.e., a flip of the value of p, will result in a loss! Thus it is crucial here to verify that the advice given by the prover is truthful. Namely, that it can lead to a best-reply given past history.

6   On-line Network Congestion Games

We study competitive games in a setting in which each *agent* joins the game at a different time (on-line games [12]). The *game inventor*, named the inventor, keeps statistical information about past *agents*. Each *agent*, upon arrival, has to choose a strategy. With probability p, the *agent* follows the inventor's suggested strategy. With probability $(1 - p)$, it chooses a strategy based on its knowledge about the strategic (off-line) version of the game. The inventor chooses a strategy for the *agent* based on its statistics. When the inventor suggests a strategy, it must convince the *agent* that the strategy is beneficial. To do so, we assume that the inventor provides the *agent* with a formal proof that can be checked by a trusted verifier (as in Sect. 5).

After defining an online variation of congestion games, such as [13], we present a greedy strategy for choosing a path based on the inventor's statistics. Let us consider a communication network, $N = (V, E, (d_e)_{e \in E})$, where V is the set of nodes, E is the set of arcs, and $d_e : \mathbb{R}_+ \to \mathbb{R}_+$ is a non-decreasing function for each $e \in E$, indicating the delay on arc e as a function of its congestion, i.e., the total load on it. Initially, the set of *agents* (the network users) is unknown to the inventor, which in the case of on-line congestion games is the operator of the network. We assume, however, that the number of *agents*, n, is known. Each *agent* i, at some point τ_i, joins the network and chooses a path π_i from a source node $s_i \in V$ to a sink node $t_i \in V$ to route its load $w_i \in \mathbb{R}_+$. The decision of each *agent* on the path is irrevocable. Let $[i] = \{1, \ldots, i\}$. The *configuration* of the network

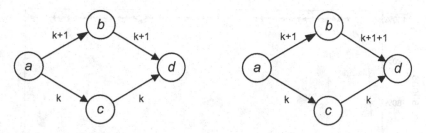

Fig. 6. An example in which the delay of each edge e is $d_e(x) = x$. Consider unit loads, and *agent* $2k+1$ that chooses a path from a to d. Observe that each edge has congestion k. A best-reply for *agent* $2k + 1$ would be $a \to b \to d$ (shortest path). Suppose that the next *agent* to enter the network, *agent* $2k + 2$, has to choose a path from b to d. Its only option is the path $b \to d$. Therefore, at time τ_{2k+2}, the delay experienced by *agent* $2k+1$ is $2k+3$, while its best-reply would be path $a \to c \to d$ with a total delay of $2k + 2$.

at time τ_i (right after *agent* i joins) is $\pi(i) = (\pi_j)_{j \in [i]}$. Given a configuration $\pi(k)$, let $W_e(\pi(k)) = \sum_{j \in [k]: e \in \pi_j} w_j$ denote the total load on arc $e \in E$. At time τ_k, the total delay experienced by *agent* i is then $\lambda_i(\pi(k)) = \sum_{e \in \pi_i} d_e(\pi(k))$.

The goal of each *agent* is to choose a path, π_i, from s_i to t_i so that $\lambda_i(\pi(n))$ is minimized in N. However, an *agent* $i \in [n-1]$ cannot be aware of the final configuration $\pi(n)$. At time τ_i, its best-reply is to choose a shortest path from s_i to t_i, but this path cannot remain a best-reply for *agent* i at time τ_n when the game ends. To see this, consider the network shown in Fig. 6. The goal of the inventor is to minimize total congestion $\Lambda(\pi(n)) = \sum_{e \in E} d_e(\pi(n))$.

Choosing a Path Based on the Inventor's Statistics

The question now is, how should an *agent* choose its path since it is not aware of the final configuration. We let each *agent* i have two options: either to choose a shortest path given $\pi(i-1)$, or to ask the inventor for a suggested path.

What is the statistical information that the inventor maintains? We consider two cases: In the first case, the inventor has *prior* knowledge about the loads of the *agents*, knows for example that they are drawn from some particular probability distribution. In the second case, the inventor dynamically updates its information about the loads. That is, at each time τ_i, assuming that the total number of *agents* n is known, the inventor knows that loads $w_1, \ldots, w_i$ have appeared, and expects for example $(n - i)$ loads of expected value $\frac{\sum_{k=1}^{i} w_k}{i}$.

Greedy Strategies for Parallel Links

Assume that the network consists of a set $[m] = \{1, \ldots m\}$ of m parallel links from a source node s to a sink node t. What is the best-reply of *agent* i of load w_i that arrives at time τ_i? The best-reply is not necessarily the least loaded link at time τ_i, because *agent* i knows that the game has not ended, and expects $n - i$

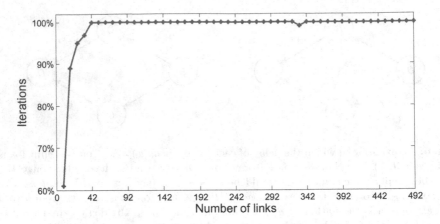

Fig. 7. The number of links (x-axis) and the iteration percentage (y-axis) in which the final assignment is strictly better, w.r.t. makespan, than the greedy strategy, see also Remark 4. We consider 1000 *agents*, uniform load distribution in $[0, 1000]$, the number of (equispeed) links is $m = 2, \ldots 500$.

loads to arrive. Namely, at time τ_i, *agent* i knows: (1) The total congestion on each link by time τ_i, (2) Its own load w_i, and (3) That $n - i$ loads are expected to arrive.

We simulate a simple on-line congestion game where *all agents* ask the inventor, i.e., $p = 1$ (see Fig. 7). We compare the greedy strategy (each *agent* on arrival chooses the least loaded link) to the strategy suggested by the inventor: The inventor takes into consideration the fact that more *agents* are expected. For each *agent* i, the inventor computes the average load $\overline{w_i}$ that has appeared so far.[3] Given the congestion on the links by time τ_i, agent i computes a Nash equilibrium assignment of its own load w_i and of $n - i$ loads $\overline{w_i}$. Namely, each load is assigned to the least loaded link, greatest load first. Then the inventor suggests that *agent* i choose the link that is suggested by that Nash equilibrium assignment. The greedy strategy is natural to assume while it also offers a performance guarantee (see Lemma 2); however, it is clear from the figure that it is outperformed by the strategy suggested by the inventor. The lemma refers to the term *makespan*, which is the maximum load on any link.

Lemma 2 (Greedy Strategy). *Let* $L^1, \ldots L^m$ *be the total loads of links* $1, \ldots m$ *when all* agents *have entered the game.* $L^j \leq \left(2 - \frac{1}{m}\right) \cdot OPT$, *where* OPT *is the optimum makespan (given all* w_i's).

Proof. Let L_{ij} be the total load of link j right after *agent* i enters the game. Clearly, $L_n^j = L^j$. Let i_j be the last *agent* of load w_{i_j} that is assigned to link j.

---

[3] One can consider a way in which the agents can know that the inventor is not cheating about the average loads. For example, the system can require the inventor to publish the average loads with its signature at each round. In everyone record, then the inventor is kept responsible when found cheating, as in [10].

Since each *agent* chooses the least loaded link at the time it enters the game, Expression (6) holds for any link j.

$$L^j_{i_j-1} \leq L^k_{i_j-1} \quad \forall k \in [m] \setminus \{j\} \qquad L^j_n - w_{i_j} \leq L^k_n \quad \forall k \in [m] \setminus \{j\} \qquad (6)$$
$$L^j_{i_j} - w_{i_j} \leq L^k_{i_j} \quad \forall k \in [m] \setminus \{j\} \qquad L^j - w_{i_j} \leq L^k \quad \forall k \in [m] \setminus \{j\}$$

Expression (7) completes the proof by summing for all $k \in [m] \setminus \{j\}$.

$$(m-1)(L^j - w_{i_j}) \leq \sum_{i=1}^n w_i - L^j \qquad (7)$$

$$L^j \leq \frac{\sum_{i=1}^n w_i}{m} + \frac{m-1}{m} w_{i_j} \leq \frac{\sum_{i=1}^n w_i}{m} + \frac{m-1}{m} \max_i w_i \leq \left(2 - \frac{1}{m}\right) \cdot OPT$$

Remark 4. Note that in Fig. 7, we plot the percentage of iterations where the strategy suggested by the inventor outperforms the greedy strategy. Each iteration involves an experiment, which considers random numbers, i.e., the agents' loads. The chart illustrates that, for sufficiently large number of links, obeying to the inventor's suggestion outperforms greediness in the vast majority of iterations. Note that we also observe particular cases in which the greedy strategy outperforms the inventor, e.g., in the experiment with 332 edges, the inventor was better at 99 % of the cases than the greedy strategy.

7   Discussions

This work studies the *rationality authority* infrastructure for encouraging computer *agents* to identify and make rational choices that are feasible and optimal. The *agents* can use this infrastructure for consulting with possibly biased *game inventors*. The *agents* verify these advices by using the *verification procedures*.

Anecdotes

There is a story about two folks, Ron (the rational) and Norton (the irrational), who walk in a far away road in the middle of a rainy night. At some point they both decide to sleep. Ron chooses to sleep on the muddy side of the road, in order to avoid cars that may drive in the paved part of the road. Norton decides to sleep on the more convenient paved part. A car arrives, the driver sees Norton at the last minute, and turns to the side of the road, exactly where Ron decided to sleep... Later, Norton may claim that he could not predict the influence of his irrational action on Ron. The existence of *rationality authority* suggests the way to act and produces a check-able proof for the optimality of the suggestion, eliminates the possible validity of Norton's excuse and may be used (after auditing Norton's actions) to blame Norton for not using the *rationality authority* results to act rationally.

The theory of non-cooperative games considers *agents* that are capable of identifying and making rational choices. However, non-cooperative game analysis is complicated; it is the subject of extensive theoretical study [27]. In certain games the ingenious observations that are needed in order to figure the game outcome are even beyond the computer's capabilities; many solution concepts have no polynomial time decidability [26]. Such difficulties could be circumvented when the *game inventor* has additional capabilities that enables the *game inventor* to compute and propose solutions.

We consider *game inventors* that may have conflicts of interest with the *agents* and attempt to misadvise them. Therefore, we require the *game inventor* to equip the *agents* with a procedure to determine their actions for the game and with a procedure that produces a rationality proof of the chosen actions. The *agent* privately uses the procedures for choosing actions, possibly without revealing their preferences (utilities). The *agents* may suspect that the supplied procedures are biased or incorrect, as the inventor may benefit from the game. Thus, the outcome of the procedure that defines the actions and the outcome of the procedure that supplies the proof for the rationality of the chosen actions are checked using proof *verification procedures* (that are possibly provided by several verifiers).

The *rationality authority* design considers computational constraints as well as computer security considerations. The *game inventor* that suggests the actions and proofs, supplies procedures that are executed by the *agents* on their computers, where users execute the procedures, with their preferences (utilities), that are unknown to the rest of the world. To prevent information leakage, the agents may protect the activity in their computers by isolating them from the communication network. The *rationality authority* is designed to enable rational behavior of *agents*, whether they are humans or processes acting as part of electronic commerce.

Consider lottery with x raffle tickets to be sold. When the lottery is fair, the possibility to win, after buying a raffle ticket, is $1/x$. Suppose that the (*game inventor*, which is the) lottery company, knows that there are fake raffle tickets, which are almost indistinguishable from the valid ones. The lottery company knows that these fake tickets are being sold in a certain geographic area $\mathscr{A}$. The lottery company can advise the lottery participants to avoid buying tickets sold in area $\mathscr{A}$, supplying convincing proofs for identifying these fake raffles. By doing so, the lottery company allows the lottery participants to keep their chances at $1/x$. In this case, the information disclosure is minimal but very useful to the *agents*. The *rationality authority* can support such scenarios.

Conclusions

We focus on verification methods that do not violate the *agents'* privacy by revealing their preferences (utilities). Autonomous *agents* do not voluntarily reveal their preferences, because it could jeopardize the success of their actions. Moreover, even when such preferences are known to a trusted third party, security concerns and privacy restrictions limit the use of such information. This work presents examples in which such parties privately consult the *agents* using knowledge that only they have, as in [32], and yet offer proof for their advices, unlike [32]. Moreover, the local equilibrium verification allows us to consider a more general scenario in which the *agents* have private and public preferences (as in [25]). Future research can further investigate efficient private verification of online games and online best replies [24].

Once the *rationality authority* requirements are satisfied, a *game authority* [9, 10] can guarantee that all *agents* take rational and honest actions; actions that follow the game rules. Moreover, actions of dishonest *game inventors*, *agents*, and *verifiers* can exclude the participant from acting in games and can be reported to a *reputation system* that audits their actions (e.g., see [8,9]).

The ordinary Joe and Jane do not have sufficient experience or the academic background for choosing best-replies and "perfect" maximum expected utility [21]. Interestingly, they are assured of making the right choice when using the *rationality authority*.

References

1. Aumann, R.J.: Subjectivity and correlation in randomized strategies. J. Math. Econ. **1**(1), 67–96 (1974)
2. Bertot, Y., Castéran, P., Huet, G., Paulin-Mohring, C., Pierre, C.: Interactive Theorem Proving and Program Development: Coq'Art: The Calculus of Inductive Constructions. Springer, New York (2004)
3. Brânzei, S., Procaccia, A.D.: Verifiably truthful mechanisms. CoRR abs/1412.0056 (2014)
4. Burkhard, H.-D., Lindemann, G., Verbrugge, R., Varga, L.Z. (eds.): CEEMAS 2007. LNCS (LNAI), vol. 4696, pp. 11–21. Springer, Heidelberg (2007)
5. Coy, P.: The secret to google's success. Business Week/Bloomberg L.P., 6 March 2006. (ts innovative auction system has ad revenues soaring)
6. Daskalakis, C., Goldberg, P.W., Papadimitriou, C.H.: The complexity of computing a nash equilibrium. Commun. ACM **52**(2), 89–97 (2009)
7. Dolev, S., Panagopoulou, P.N., Rabiey, M., Schiller, E.M., Spirakis, P.G.: Brief announcement: Rationality authority for provable rational behavior. In: PODC 2011 TR 2011:03, Department CSE, Chalmers University of Technology (2011)
8. Dolev, S., Schiller, E.M., Spirakis, P.G., Tsigas, P.: Strategies for repeated games with subsystem takeovers implantable by deterministic and self-stabilizing automata. In: Manzalini, A. (ed.) Autonomics. ACM International Conference Proceeding Series, ΛCM (2008)
9. Dolev, S., Schiller, E.M., Spirakis, P.G., Tsigas, P.: Robust and scalable middleware for selfish-computer systems. Comput. Sci. Rev. **5**(1), 69–84 (2011)
10. Dolev, S., Schiller, E.M., Spirakis, P.G., Tsigas, P.: Game authority for robust and scalable distributed selfish-computer systems. Theor. Comput. Sci. **411**(26–28), 2459–2466 (2010)
11. Edelman, B., Ostrovsky, M., Schwarz, M.: Internet advertising and the generalized second-price auction: selling billions of dollars worth of keywords. Am. Econ. Rev. **97**(1), 242–259 (2007)
12. Foster, D.P., Vohra, R.: Regret in the on-line decision problem. Games Econ. Behav. **29**(1–2), 7–35 (1999)
13. Fotakis, D., Kontogiannis, S.C., Spirakis, P.G.: Atomic congestion games among coalitions. ACM Trans. Algorithms **4**(4), 52 (2008)

14. Freund, Y., Schapire, R.E.: Game theory, on-line prediction and boosting. In: COLT, pp. 325–332 (1996)
15. Goldreich, O., Micali, S., Wigderson, A.: How to play any mental game or A completeness theorem for protocols with honest majority. In: Aho, A.V. (ed.) Proceedings of the 19th Annual ACM Symposium on Theory of Computing, 1987, pp. 218–229. ACM, New York (1987)
16. Goldwasser, S., Micali, S., Rackoff, C.: The knowledge complexity of interactive proof-systems (extended abstract). In: Sedgewick, R. (ed.) Proceedings of the 17th Annual ACM Symposium on Theory of Computing, May 6–8, 1985, pp. 291–304. ACM, Providence (1985)
17. Guerin, F.: An algorithmic approach to specifying and verifying subgame perfect equilibria. In: Proceedings of the Eighth Workshop on Game Theoretic and Decision Theoretic Agents (GTDT-2006), Hakodate, Japan (2006)
18. Guerin, F.: Applying game theory mechanisms in open agent systems with complete information. Auton. Agents Multi-Agent Syst. 15(2), 109–146 (2007)
19. Guerin, F., Pitt, J.: Verification and compliance testing. In: Huget, M.-P. (ed.) Communication in Multiagent Systems. LNCS (LNAI), vol. 2650, pp. 98–112. Springer, Heidelberg (2003)
20. Guerin, F., Tadjouddine, E.M.: Realising common knowledge assumptions in agent auctions. In: IAT, pp. 579–586. IEEE Computer Society (2006)
21. Kahneman, D., Tversky, A.: Prospect theory: an analysis of decision under risk. Econometrica 47(2), 263–291 (1979)
22. Mirrokni, V., Muthukrishnan, S., Nadav, U.: Quasi-proportional mechanisms: prior-free revenue maximization. In: López-Ortiz, A. (ed.) LATIN 2010. LNCS, vol. 6034, pp. 565–576. Springer, Heidelberg (2010)
23. Nash, J.F.: Equilibrium point in n-person games. Proc. Nat. Acad. Sci. USA 36, 48–49 (1950)
24. Nikoletseas, S., Panagopoulou, P., Raptopoulos, C., Spirakis, P.G.: On the structure of equilibria in basic network formation. In: Gasieniec, L., Wolter, F. (eds.) FCT 2013. LNCS, vol. 8070, pp. 259–270. Springer, Heidelberg (2013)
25. Nisan, N., Ronen, A.: Algorithmic Mech. Des. 35, 166–196 (2001)
26. Nisan, N., Roughgarden, T., Tardos, E., Vazirani, V.V.: Algorithmic Game Theory. Cambridge University Press, New York (2007)
27. Osborne, M.J., Rubinstein, A.: A Course in Game Theory. MIT Press, Cambridge (1994)
28. Pauly, M.: Programming and verifying subgame-perfect mechanisms. J. Log. Comput. 15(3), 295–316 (2005)
29. Tadjouddine, E.M.: Complexity of verifying game equilibria. CEEMAS 4, 103–112 (2007)
30. Tadjouddine, E.M., Guerin, F.: Verifying dominant strategy equilibria in auctions. In: [4], pp. 288–297(2007)
31. Tadjouddine, E.M., Guerin, F., Vasconcelos, W.W.: Abstractions for model-checking game-theoretic properties of auctions. In: Padgham, L., Parkes, C.D., Müller, J., Parsons, S. (eds.) AAMAS (3), pp. 1613–1616. IFAAMAS, South Carolina (2008)
32. Thaler, R.H., Sunstein, C.R.: Nudge: Improving Decisions About Health, Wealth, and Happiness. Yale University Press, New Haven (2008)

Weighted Boolean Formula Games

Marios Mavronicolas[1]([⊠]), Burkhard Monien[2], and Klaus W. Wagner[3]

[1] Department of Computer Science, University of Cyprus,
1678 Nicosia, Cyprus
mavronic@cs.ucy.ac.cy
[2] Faculty of Electrical Engineering, Computer Science and Mathematics,
University of Paderborn, 33102 Paderborn, Germany
bm@upb.de
[3] Lehrstuhl für Theoretische Informatik, Institut für Informatik,
Julius-Maximilians-Universität Würzburg, 97074 Würzburg, Germany
wagner@informatik.uni-wuerzburg.de

Abstract. We introduce *weighted boolean formula games* (WBFG) as a new class of succinct games. Each *player* has a set of boolean *formulas* she wants to get satisfied; the formulas involve a ground set of boolean *variables* each of which is controlled by some player. The *payoff* of a player is a *weighted* sum of the values of her formulas. We consider both *pure equilibria* and their refinement of *payoff-dominant equilibria* [34], where every player is no worse-off than in any other pure equilibrium. We present both structural and complexity results:

- We consider *mutual weighted boolean formula games* (MWBFG), a subclass of WBFG making a natural mutuality assumption on the formulas of players. We present a very simple *exact potential* for MWBFG. We establish a polynomial monomorphism from certain classes of *weighted congestion games* to subclasses of WBFG and MWBFG, respectively, indicating their rich structure.
- We present a collection of complexity results about decision (and search) problems for both pure and payoff-dominant equilibria in WBFG. The precise complexities depend crucially on five parameters: *(i)* the number of players; *(ii)* the number of variables per player; *(iii)* the number of formulas per player; *(iv)* the *weights* in the payoff functions (whether identical or not), and *(v)* the syntax of the formulas. These results imply that, unless the polynomial hierarchy collapses, decision (and search) problems for payoff-dominant equilibria are harder than for pure equilibria.

A preliminary version of this work appeared in the *Proceedings of the 3rd International Workshop on Internet and Network Economics*, X. Deng and F. Chung Graham eds., pp. 467–481, Vol. 4858, Lecture Notes in Computer Science, Springer-Verlag, December 2007. This work has been partially supported by the German Research Foundation (DFG) within the Collaborative Research Centre "On-the-Fly-Computing" (SFB 901) and by the IST Program of the European Union under contract numbers IST-2004-001907 (DELIS) and 15964 (AEOLUS).

C. Zaroliagis et al. (Eds.): Spirakis Festschrift, LNCS 9295, pp. 49–86, 2015.
DOI: 10.1007/978-3-319-24024-4_6

1   Introduction

1.1   Succinct Games and Equilibria Problems

Nash equilibrium [49] is the dominant solution concept in Game Theory; it represents a stable state of a *game* where no *player* could unilaterally improve her *payoff* by switching her *strategy*. The Nash equilibrium is *pure* when each player chooses a single strategy; when at least one player randomizes over her *strategy set,* the equilibrium is *non-pure* or *mixed.* Deciding the existence of and computing Nash equilibria, whether mixed or pure, for a given game are among the most important problems considered in *Algorithmic Game Theory* – see, for example, [1,5,12,14,16–18,26,31,57]. In the *explicit form* of a game, the players' strategy sets and payoffs are presented explicitly by using a total of $m \cdot k^m$ numbers when there are m players with k strategies per each. The explicit form allows for deciding the existence of and computing a pure equilibrium by a straightforward algorithm, which, however, does *not* scale in m and k.

In a *succinct game,* there is an *implicit* representation, via some model of computation, of strategy sets and payoffs requiring size much smaller than for its explicit form (cf. [51, Sect. 2]). For example, in an *(unweighted) congestion game* [55], the payoffs are represented by explicitly given *payoff functions.* Other interesting examples of succinct games include *graphical games* [41], *sparse games* [14], *symmetric games* [30,49], *anonymous games* [6], *polymatrix games* [36], *local-effect games* [44] and *circuit games* [24,26,57]. The complexity of both pure and mixed equilibria for succinct games has been studied very intensively in the last few years – see, e.g., [1,12,17,19,20,23,25,26,29,41,44,45, 51,57].

Equilibrium selection (cf. [34]) deals with singling out some "best" equilibrium. A criterion for the selection is set by some refinement of equilibrium. *Payoff-dominance* [34] is a well-known refinement; in a *payoff-dominant equilibrium,* every player is no-worse-off than in any other pure equilibrium. Games admitting payoff-dominant equilibria are called *games of common interests* (cf. [2]); simple examples for them include *unanimity games* [40] and *matching games* [3] (cf. [15, Sect. 1]). There are many other, well-studied refinements; we only mention *dominating equilibrium, Pareto-optimality, risk-dominance* [34] and *social welfare maximization.* Due to their strength, refinements of pure equilibria are usually unlikely to exist even when pure equilibria do. For example, the only class of games we know for which Pareto-optimal equilibria always exist are certain, very special *two-person exchange models* [13] of an exchange economy with just two traders. The complexity of deciding the existence and computing such refinements of pure equilibria in succinct games remains largely unexplored.

1.2   Weighted Boolean Formula Games

We introduce *weighted boolean formula games,* abbreviated as WBFG, as an adequate and very general form of succinct games (Definition 1). Here each player controls a set of boolean *variables*; different players control disjoint sets of variables. A *strategy* of a player is a truth assignment to her boolean variables. Each player targets a set of constraints expressed by boolean *formulas*, which she wants to get satisfied; her formulas may also depend on variables owned by other players.[1] Thus, WBFG represent the payoff functions with succinct size: the size of formulas. For each formula, there is an (integer) *weight* expressing the relative priority of the constraint for the player. In an *unweighted boolean formula game,* abbreviated as BFG, all weights are 1. The *payoff* of a player is the *weighted* sum of her satisfied constraints. In a *pure equilibrium,* no player can increase her payoff by flipping the values of her variables. We shall study the structure and complexity of pure and payoff-dominant equilibria for WBFG.

Even though the definition of a WBFG is very simple, any setting in which variables and weighted constraints are distributed among autonomous agents can be expressed as a WBFG. Consider, for example, an economic setting in which a *principal* motivates a team of *agents,* or *schedulers,* each coming with a set of *tasks.* Each agent is bound to a set of *contracts* signed with the principal; however, a contract may involve tasks owned by multiple agents. For each contract, the agent is incentivized via a *payment* conditioned on scheduling all involved tasks; each agent seeks to maximize her total payment. This setting already generalizes *(weighted) congestion games* [47,55] since it allows payments to depend on combinations of scheduled tasks in an arbitrary way. It is straightforward to formalize this example using players, boolean variables, boolean formulas and weights for schedulers, tasks, contracts and payments, respectively.

We shall especially consider a subclass of WBFG, called *mutual weighted boolean formula games* and abbreviated as MWBFG; these add a natural *mutuality* assumption on the constraints targeted by different players. More specifically, whenever some formula of a player involves a variable owned by a second player, then the same formula is a constraint for the second player with the *same* weight. Mutuality is motivated by typical multi-agent systems, where a constraint concerns all agents featuring the involved variables in a uniform way.

1.3 Summary of Results and Significance

We present two types of results.

- We identify structural properties for both WBFG and its subclass of MWBFG.
- We present a comprehensive collection of complexity results about pure and payoff-dominant equilibria; those about the latter are the *first* known complexity results about payoff-dominant equilibria. More specifically, we investigate how the complexity of their decision and search problems depends on five natural parameters:
  - The number of players m.
  - The (maximum) number k of variables per player.

---

[1] A boolean formula is the special case of a *(boolean) circuit* where every *boolean gate* has *fan-out* one; so, a boolean formula is a circuit whose underlying graph is a tree.

- The (maximum) number r of boolean formulas weight-summed into a payoff function.
- The *weights* for the payoff functions — whether WBFG are *weighted* or *unweighted*.
- The syntax of the boolean formulas; WBCG denote weighted boolean *clause* games.

Each of the parameters m, k, and r is either *fixed* to some specific natural number or *non-fixed*. We discover that the choice of these parameters has a crucial impact on complexity. In all cases, complexity results for the search problem accompany those for the decision problem.

Structural Results. We show that a MWBFG is an *exact potential* game [48] (Theorem 1); towards this end, we provide a very simple and intuitive exact potential for a MWBFG with size polynomial in the size of a MWBFG. Thus, a MWBFG has the *Finite Improvement* property [48, Lemma 2.3], so that it admits a pure equilibrium; the corresponding search problem is in $\mathcal{PLS}$ [39] (Corollary 1). We remark that the assumption that variables and formulas are boolean is *not* essential for the proof of Theorem 1: mutuality suffices on its own for the existence of an exact potential.

Recall that (exact) potential games (containing MWBFG) and *unweighted* congestion games are equivalent [48,55]; hence, to obtain a classification of WBFG into known classes of games, we aim at embedding some known class of congestion games more general than unweighted congestion games into WBFG. *Weighted, linear congestion games with player-specific coefficients and constants* from [29,45] is the class we end up with. As a tool for the embedding, we use polynomial *monomorphisms* between classes of games, which not only preserve the pure equilibria of the original game but also create no new pure equilibrium for the resulting game.

We show that every weighted, linear congestion game with player-specific coefficients and constants is polynomial monomorphic to a WBFG (Theorem 2). The particular monomorphism we employ has the form of a linear relation between corresponding payoffs of each player (cf. [34, Sect. 3.4]). In the special case where the coefficients are *player-independent,* the same monomorphism reduces a weighted, linear congestion game with player-specific constants to a MWBFG (Corollary 2).

Complexity Results for Pure Equilibria. We first consider the case where m is *not* fixed while $k \geq 1$ is fixed (Theorem 3, Cases (1), (2) and (3)). For WBFG with $r \geq 1$ fixed or not, the decision problem is $\mathcal{NP}$-complete (Case (1)); for WBCG with $r \geq 2$ fixed or not, the decision problem is still $\mathcal{NP}$-complete (Case (2)). These two results reveal an interesting trade-off between the number (per player) and the syntax of boolean formulas sufficing for $\mathcal{NP}$-hardness: either more than one function or arbitrary syntax were needed for the proofs. We establish that this trade-off is inherent by showing that, even if k is *not* constant, the decision problem for WBCG is in $\mathcal{P}$ when $r = 1$ (Case (3)).

We next consider the case where k is *not* fixed while $m \geq 2$ is fixed or not. We show that the decision problem is Σ_2^P-complete for WBFG with $r \geq 1$ fixed or not (Theorem 3, Case (4)).

These complexity results indicate that, unless the polynomial hierarchy collapses, allowing an arbitrary number of variables per player has a stronger impact on the complexity of deciding the existence of pure equilibria in WBFG than allowing an arbitrary number of players.

Complexity Results for Payoff-Dominant Equilibria. We first consider the case where m is *not* fixed while $k \geq 1$ is fixed (Theorem 4, Cases (1) and (2)). For WBFG with r *not* fixed, the decision problem is Δ_2^P-complete (Case (1)); for BFG with r fixed or not, the decision problem is Θ_2^P-complete (Case (2)).

We next consider the dual case where k is *not* fixed while $m \geq 3$ is fixed or not (Theorem 4, Cases (3) and (4)). For this case we consider further that r is *not* fixed. For WBFG, the decision problem is Δ_3^P-complete (Case (3)); for BFG, the decision problem is Θ_3^P-complete (Case (4)).

Similarly to the complexity results for pure equilibria, these complexity results indicate that, unless the polynomial hierarchy collapses, allowing an arbitrary number of variables per player has a stronger impact on the complexity of deciding the existence of payoff-dominant equilibria in WBFG than allowing an arbitrary number of players. Furthermore, the results indicate that in both cases (m *not* fixed and k *not* fixed, respectively), the impact of weights on this complexity is conditioned on whether the inclusion $\Theta_2^P \subseteq \Delta_2^P$ (resp., $\Theta_3^P \subseteq \Delta_3^P$ is proper or not; it is conjectured in [62, Sect. 2] that on each level $i \geq 1$ of the polynomial hierarchy, the inclusion $\Theta_i^P \subseteq \Delta_i^P$, where $\Theta_i^P = \mathcal{L}^{\Sigma_{i-1}^P}$, is proper.

The Θ_2^P-completeness of deciding the existence of payoff-dominant equilibria in BFG with a *non-fixed* number of players (Theorem 4, Case (2)) provides one of the very rare, truly natural complete problems for Θ_2^P— see [62] for references to other Θ_2^P-complete problems. We feel that this result seconds in importance the Θ_2^P-completeness [35] of deciding who the winner is in the election system, known as *Dodgson Election,* developed back in 1876 by Lewis Carroll. To the best of our knowledge, the Θ_3^P-completeness of deciding the existence of payoff-dominant equilibria in BFG with a *non-fixed* number of variables per player (Theorem 4, Case (4)) provides the *first* truly natural complete problem for Θ_3^P.

1.4 Related Work and Comparison

Succinct games with formalisms similar to WBFG have been considered in *Algorithmic Game Theory*. Several works including [1,4,9,57] have *independently* obtained results related to ours for such succinct games. Since WBFG have a restricted structure, the proofs of the completeness of deciding the existence of pure equilibria for WBFG have required much more delicate arguments than the ones in [1,9,57]. There were no complexity results before for deciding the existence of payoff-dominant equilibria for succinct games.

Circuit Games [57]. In a *circuit game* [57], players still control disjoint sets of variables, but each player's payoff is given by a *single boolean circuit* and there are *no* weights. Note that a WBFG can be encoded as a circuit game since their payoff functions, defined as the weighted sum of boolean formulas, can be evaluated by a *single* boolean circuit. Thus, WBFG make a very restricted subclass of circuit games. So, any hardness result such as the ones in Sects. 5 and 6 about WBFG automatically holds for circuit games. *Boolean circuit games* are the special case of circuit games where each player controls a *single* boolean variable. Circuit games had been earlier studied in [24,26].

The best-known upper bound for the *formula size* $\mathsf{L}(f)$ of a boolean function f in terms of its *(boolean) circuit size* $\mathsf{C}(f)$ is $\mathsf{L}(f) = \mathcal{O}(2^{\mathsf{C}(f)})$ [42,53].[2] So, there is no known polynomial time transformation of a circuit game into a boolean formula game where each player has a *single* equivalent formula. But it is possible to transform a boolean circuit into a polynomial number of boolean *clauses* by introducing new, polynomially many boolean variables to express the correctness of the computations by its individual gates. Hence, there is a polynomial time transformation of a circuit game into a boolean formula game where each player has a polynomial number of clauses. Nevertheless, we aim, in this work, at WBFG where the number of boolean formulas (in particular, clauses) per player is a small constant.

We note that all upper bounds established in this work for WBFG (Propositions 1 and 2) are also valid for circuit games. It is shown [57, Theorem 6.1] that deciding the existence of pure equilibria in *two-player* circuit games is Σ_2^P-complete; this result is *incomparable* to Theorem 3 (Case (4)), which concerns *three-player* boolean formula games. Furthermore, it is shown in [57, Theorem 6.2] that deciding the existence of pure equilibria in boolean circuit games is $\mathcal{NP}$-complete; this result follows trivially from Theorem 3 (Case (1)).

Turing Machine Games [1]. Two different levels (*forms*) of succinct representations of such games are considered in [1]: In the *implicit form,* both the payoff functions and the strategy sets are given implicitly. Thus, the payoff functions are represented by a deterministic Turing Machine (DTM) computing the payoffs, while strategy sets are described succinctly. In the *general form,* payoff functions are represented by a DTM as in the explicit form, but strategy sets are now listed explicitly.

For each form, there are two cases. In the *non-uniform* case, the payoff functions are represented by a tuple $\langle M, 1^t \rangle$, where M is a DTM and t is a natural number bounding its computation time. In the *uniform* case, the payoff functions

---

[2] The straightforward *depth-preserving* conversion of a boolean circuit into an equivalent formula may potentially blow up the size exponentially since pieces of the circuit must be repeated. Nevertheless, the largest *shown* difference between formula size and boolean circuit size is only $\mathsf{L}(f) = \Omega(n^2 \lg^{-1} n)$ and $\mathsf{C}(f) = 2n + o(n)$, where f is the *storage access function* for indirect addressing [54].

are represented by a DTM M computing the payoffs in polynomial time when given the number of players and their strategy sets; so, this case corresponds to games with *polynomial time computable payoffs*.

Recall the folklore facts that Turing machine computations with t steps can be encoded as a boolean circuit of size $\mathcal{O}(t^2)$, and that boolean circuits can be evaluated by Turing machines in polynomial time (cf. [63, Chapter 9]). So, Turing machine games in implicit form and circuit games are computationally equivalent. It follows from the previous discussion on the relation of WBFG to circuit games that WBFG are computationally equivalent to Turing machine games in implicit form.

Considered in [1] is also the *explicit form*, where payoffs are listed explicitly. However, it is *not* possible to obtain from a succinct WBFG such an explicit form in polynomial time.

Completeness results on deciding the existence of pure equilibria are given in [1, Sects. 6 and 7]. The proofs use a simple *gadget game* [1, Sect. 6]. It is straightforward to see that the payoff functions of the gadget game may be expressed as an instance of a WBFG with $r = 5$.

Deciding the existence of pure equilibria is $\mathcal{NP}$-complete for games in general form for both the non-uniform [1, Theorem 6.3] and the uniform [1, Theorem 7.1] cases. It follows from either [1, Theorem 6.3] or [1, Theorem 7.1] that if m is not fixed, then the decision problem for WBFG is $\mathcal{NP}$-complete when $k \geq 2$ is fixed and $r \geq 5$ is fixed or not.

Deciding the existence of pure equilibria is Σ_2^P-complete for games in implicit form for both the non-uniform [1, Theorem 6.3] and the uniform [1, Theorem 7.1] cases. It follows from [1, Theorem 6.3] that if k is *not* fixed, then the decision problem for WBFG is Σ_2^P-complete when $m \geq 3$ is fixed or not and $r \geq 5$ is fixed or not. This implied result is *incomparable* to Theorem 3 (Case (4)).

Deciding the existence of pure equilibria in Turing machine games in explicit form is $\mathcal{P}$-complete [1, Theorem 6.4].

Boolean Games [9, 21, 32, 33]. They were originally introduced in [32, 33] and further studied in [21] as two-player, zero-sum games where the two players control disjoint sets of boolean variables; there is a single propositional formula on the variables, which represents the payoff of player 1. Boolean games were further extended in [9] to games with an arbitrary number of players that are not necessarily zero-sum.[3] In this extended formulation [9], each player attempts to satisfy her own boolean formula, but, unlike WBFG, neither multiple formulas nor weights are allowed. Thus, in those extended boolean games [9], each player has a *dichotomous preference*: either she is satisfied or not. In contrast, WBFG allow for modeling players with *graded* preferences by assigning weights to the boolean formulas. Boolean games are further studied in [10, 11, 22, 37, 38].

A stronger version with $m \geq 2$ (fixed or not) of Case (4) in Theorem 3, holding for $m \geq 3$ (fixed or not), had been *independently* obtained in [9, Proposition 5];

---

[3] We note that the work in [9] appeared for the first time in two conference papers published in 2006 [7, 8]; the formulation of, and results about, WBFG in this paper represents *independent* work.

moreover, their result applies to *zero-sum* (two-player) games. It is proved in [9, Proposition 6] that when k is *not* fixed, the decision problem for boolean games with $m \geq 2$ (fixed or not) is $\mathcal{NP}$-complete when the formula of each player is in disjunctive normal form. That result complements Case (2) in Theorem 3, establishing $\mathcal{NP}$-completeness for clause formulas. Further complexity results about boolean games appeared recently in [22, 37, 38].

Satisfiability Games [4]. *Satisfiability games* were introduced and studied independently and concurrently to our work in [4]. As in WBFG, each player i owns a set of ℓ_i boolean variables; but her strategy set is allowed to be any subset of $\{0, 1\}^{\ell_i}$. (In WBFG, her strategy set is exactly $\{0, 1\}^{\ell_i}$, but this difference is not essential.) There is a ground set $\mathcal{C}$ of boolean formulas, coined as *clauses,* defined over all boolean variables; each clause $C \in \mathcal{C}$ has an associated *weight c.* Associated with player i is the set of clauses $\mathcal{C}^i$ containing at least one literal for a boolean variable owned by the player. For an assignment to the boolean variables, the payoff of player i is the sum of the weights of clauses from $\mathcal{C}^i$ that get satisfied. The difference between WBFG and satisfiability games is that it is not necessary in WBFG for a formula in a player's set to depend on at least one variable owned by her; since this is required in MWBFG, satisfiability games are equivalent to MWBFG. More precisely, equivalent to MWBFG are the *unrestricted satisfiability games* which, unlike the *restricted* ones, put no restriction on how many of her variables a player sets to 1.

Satisfiability games with player-specific payoffs [4] use *player-specific* weights for the clauses; they encompass *all* games even if restricted to conjunctive formulas [4, Theorem 3].

It is shown in [4, Theorem 1] that every satisfiability game is an exact potential game. Since satisfiability games are equivalent to MWBFG, this result is equivalent to Theorem 1.

Other Work. In contrast to the polynomial sized exact potential for MWBFG in Theorem 1, the isomorphic potential game constructed from an unweighted congestion game in [48, 60] has exponential size since its resource set is the strategy set of the unweighted congestion game. The exact potential in [27, Theorem 1] for weighted, linear network congestion games is a special case of the exact potential for their superclass of MWBFG in Theorem 1.

Complexity results for deciding the existence of pure equilibria in other classes of succinct games have been shown for *graphical games* in [19, 25, 31, 41], for symmetric games in [12], and for *weighted (network) congestion games* [47] and *local-effect games* [44] in [20]. The impact of the precise form of succinctness on the complexity of pure equilibria for succinct games has been investigated in [17, 25, 51, 56]. The first complexity result for deciding the existence of pure equilibria in a particular succinct game dates back to 1974 [56, Theorem 2.4.1]. WBFG were recently considered in a study of the complexity of game isomorphism in [28].

1.5   Road Map

The rest of this paper is organized as follows. Section 2 presents the framework and some helpful background. Weighted boolean formula games are introduced in Sect. 3. Mutual weighted boolean formula games are treated in Sect 4. Sections 5 and 6 present the complexity results about pure equilibria and payoff-dominant equilibria, respectively. We conclude, in Sect. 7, with some open problems.

2   Framework and Background

2.1   Notation

For an integer $n \geq 1$, denote as $[n] = \{1, \ldots, n\}$. For a set S, denote as $|S|$ and $\mathbb{P}(S)$ the cardinality and the power set of S, respectively. For a boolean vector $\mathbf{x}$, $|\mathbf{x}|$ denotes the natural number with binary representation $\mathbf{x}$. Denote as $\geq_{cw}$ the *component-wise ordering* relation on vectors. Denote as $\geq_{le}$ the *lexicographic ordering* relation on boolean vectors; for lexicographically ordering two boolean vectors, the comparison goes from left to right till the first bit where the vectors differ is met. We shall sometimes abbreviate *lexicographically maximum* as *lmax*.

2.2   Games and Equilibria

A *game* is a triple $\Gamma = \langle m, (S_i)_{i \in [m]}, (U_i)_{i \in [m]} \rangle$, where m is the number of players, S_i is the *strategy set* of player $i \in [m]$, and $U_i : S_1 \times \ldots \times S_m \to \mathbb{R}$ is the *payoff function* of player $i \in [m]$. The game Γ is *finite* if all strategy sets are finite; all games considered in this paper will be assumed to be finite. For the game Γ, denote $S := S(\Gamma) = S_1 \times \ldots \times S_m$.

A *profile* is a tuple of strategies $\mathbf{s} = \langle s_1, \ldots, s_m \rangle$, one for each player; denote as $\mathbf{s}_{-i}$ the partial profile resulting from eliminating the strategy of player i from $\mathbf{s}$. Given a profile $\mathbf{s}$, a player $i \in [m]$ and a strategy $t \in S_i$, denote as $(\mathbf{s}_{-i}, t) = \langle s_1, \ldots, s_{i-1}, t, s_{i+1}, \ldots, s_m \rangle$; so, $(\mathbf{s}_{-i}, t)$ results by substituting in the profile $\mathbf{s}$ the strategy s_i of player i with t. Associated in the natural way with a profile $\mathbf{s}$ is the *payoff vector* $U(\mathbf{s})$.

A profile $\mathbf{s} \in S$ is a *pure equilibrium* if for each player $i \in [m]$ and for each strategy $t \in S_i$, $U_i(\mathbf{s}) \geq U_i(\mathbf{s}_{-i}, t)$. Denote as $\mathcal{PE}(\Gamma)$ the set of pure equilibria of Γ. A pure equilibrium $\mathbf{s}$ is a *payoff-dominant equilibrium* if for each pure equilibrium $\mathbf{s}'$, for each player $i \in [m]$, $U_i(\mathbf{s}) \geq U_i(\mathbf{s}')$; so, each player has a dominant payoff in a payoff-dominant equilibrium. Denote as $\mathcal{PDE}(\Gamma)$ the set of payoff-dominant equilibria for Γ; so, $\mathcal{PDE}(\Gamma) \subseteq \mathcal{PE}(\Gamma)$. To compare, a pure equilibrium $\mathbf{s}$ is *Pareto-optimal* if for each pure equilibrium $\mathbf{s}'$, there is a player $i \in [m]$ such that $U_i(\mathbf{s}) \geq U_i(\mathbf{s}')$. Clearly, a payoff-dominant equilibrium is Pareto-optimal (but not vice versa).

2.3   Isomorphisms and Monomorphisms

Consider games $\Gamma = \langle m, (S_i)_{i \in [m]}, (U_i)_{i \in [m]} \rangle$ and $\Gamma' = \langle m, (S'_i)_{i \in [m]}, (U'_i)_{i \in [m]} \rangle$ with the same number of players. A *strategy bijection* (resp., *strategy injection*) from Γ to Γ' is an m-tuple $\phi = (\phi_i)_{i \in [m]}$, where each ϕ_i is a bijective (resp., injective) mapping $\phi_i : S_i \to S'_i$. Thus, ϕ maps profiles from S to profiles from S' in the natural way; that is, for a profile $\mathbf{s} \in S$, $\phi(\mathbf{s}) = \mathbf{s}'$ where for each $i \in [m]$, $s'_i = \phi_i(s_i)$.

The games Γ and Γ' are **isomorphic** if there is a strategy bijection ϕ from Γ to Γ' such that for each pair of profiles $\mathbf{s}, \mathbf{t} \in S$, for each player $i \in [n]$, $U_i(\mathbf{s}) < U_i(\mathbf{t})$ if and only if $U_i(\phi(\mathbf{s})) < U_i(\phi(\mathbf{t}))$; then, ϕ is an **isomorphism** from Γ to Γ'. So, an isomorphism from Γ to Γ' preserves the preference relations induced by the payoff functions of the players; hence, ϕ induces a bijection from $\mathcal{PE}(\Gamma)$ to $\mathcal{PE}(\Gamma')$.

The games Γ and Γ' are **monomorphic** if there is a strategy injection ϕ from Γ to Γ' such that (C.1) for each pair of profiles $\mathbf{s}, \mathbf{t} \in S$, for each player $i \in [n]$, $U_i(\mathbf{s}) < U_i(\mathbf{t})$ if and only if $U_i(\phi(\mathbf{s})) < U_i(\phi(\mathbf{t}))$, and (C.2) every pure equilibrium for Γ' is the image under ϕ of a profile of Γ; then, ϕ is a **monomorphism** from Γ to Γ', which still induces a bijection from $\mathcal{PE}(\Gamma)$ to $\mathcal{PE}(\Gamma')$. When both ϕ and ϕ are computable in polynomial time, Γ and Γ' are **polynomial monomorphic** and ϕ is a **polynomial monomorphism**.

A **linear monomorphism** (cf. [34, Sect. 3.4]) from Γ to Γ' is the special case of a monomorphism ϕ where for each player $i \in [m]$, there are constants $\gamma_i > 0$ and ζ_i such that for each profile $\mathbf{s} \in S$,

$$U'_i(\phi(\mathbf{s})) = \gamma_i U_i(\mathbf{s}) + \zeta_i;$$

so, there is a linear relation between payoffs of each player in Γ and Γ', respectively. (A **strong monomorphism** (cf. [49]) is the special case where for each player $i \in [m]$, $\gamma_i = 1$ and $\zeta_i = 0$.) Say then that Γ is **linear monomorphic** to Γ'.

We shall consider extensions of monomorphism from games to classes of games, which takes computation into account. Fix two classes $\mathcal{C}$ and $\mathcal{C}'$ of games. The class $\mathcal{C}$ is **monomorphic** to a subclass of $\mathcal{C}'$ if every game $\Gamma \in \mathcal{C}$ is monomorphic to some game Γ' in the subclass of $\mathcal{C}'$, which can be computed from Γ via a map $\lambda : \mathcal{C} \to \mathcal{C}'$. The class $\mathcal{C}$ is **polynomial monomorphic** to a subclass of $\mathcal{C}'$ if $\mathcal{C}$ is monomorphic to a subclass of $\mathcal{C}'$ via a polynomial time map $\lambda : \mathcal{C} \to \mathcal{C}'$ such that each game $\Gamma \in \mathcal{C}$ is polynomial monomorphic to its image $\lambda(\Gamma) \in \mathcal{C}'$

2.4   Potential Games and Classes of Congestion Games

An **exact potential** or **potential** for short for the game Γ is a function $\Phi : S \to \mathbb{R}$ such that for each profile $\mathbf{s} \in S$, for each player $i \in [m]$ and strategy $t \in S_i$,

$$U_i(\mathbf{s}_{-i}, t) - U_i(\mathbf{s}) = \Phi(\mathbf{s}_{-i}, t) - \Phi(\mathbf{s}).$$

A **potential game** [48, Sect. 2] is one that admits a potential. A potential game has a pure equilibrium [48, Corollary 2.2].

A **weighted, linear congestion game with player-specific coefficients and constants** [29] is a game $\Gamma = \langle m, (S_i)_{i \in [m]}, (U_i)_{i \in [m]} \rangle$ such that:

(1) There is integer $k \geq 2$ such that for each player $i \in [m]$, $S_i \subseteq \mathbb{P}(\{1, 2, \ldots, k\})$. So, $S_i \subseteq \{0, 1\}^k$ and each $e \in \{1, 2, \ldots, k\}$ is called a *resource*.

(2) There are families of integers $(\beta_{ie})_{i \in [m], e \in [k]}$ with $\beta_{ie} \geq 0$ (the *coefficients*), $(\delta_{ie})_{i \in [m], e \in [k]}$ with $\delta_{ie} \geq 0$ (the *constants*), and $(w_i)_{i \in [m]}$ with $w_i \geq 1$ (the *weights*) such that for each profile $\mathbf{s} = \langle s_1, \ldots, s_m \rangle$, for each player $i \in [m]$,

$$U_i(\mathbf{s}) = -\sum_{e \in s_i} \left(\beta_{ie} \cdot \sum_{j \in [m] | e \in s_j} w_j + \delta_{ie} \right).$$

Denote as PSC^2 both a weighted, linear congestion game with player-specific coefficients and constants and the corresponding class of games. Note that PSC^2 is contained in the general class of *weighted congestion games with player-specific payoff functions* [47].

A **weighted, linear congestion game with player-specific constants** [45], denoted as PSC, is the special case of a weighted, linear congestion game with player-specific coefficients and constants where for each resource $e \in [k]$, for each player $i \in [m]$, $\beta_{ie} = \beta_e$ for some constant $\beta_e \geq 0$; so, the coefficients are *player-independent*.

A **weighted, linear congestion game** [27] is the special case of a weighted, linear congestion game with player-specific constants where for each resource $e \in [k]$, for each player $i \in [m]$, $\delta_{ie} = \delta_e$ for some constant $\delta_e \geq 0$; so, both the coefficients and the constants are player-independent.

A game PSC admits a vector potential and a pure equilibrium [45, Theorem 6 and Corollary 7]; but a game PSC^2 does *not* necessarily admit a pure equilibrium [29, Theorem 2].

2.5 Complexity Theory

Classes. We assume familiarity of the reader with some classical complexity classes (cf. [50]):

- $\mathcal{L}$, $\mathcal{P}$, *polynomial local search* $\mathcal{PLS}$ [39], $\mathcal{NP}$ and $\mathcal{PSPACE}$.
- The *polynomial hierarchy* $\mathcal{PH}$ [46,58]; in particular, $\Delta_2^P = \mathcal{P}^{\mathcal{NP}}$, $\Sigma_2^P = \mathcal{NP}^{\mathcal{NP}}$ and $\Delta_3^P = \mathcal{P}^{\mathcal{NP}^{\mathcal{NP}}}$, with $\Delta_2^P \subseteq \Sigma_2^P \subseteq \Delta_3^P$.
- The *bounded query classes* at levels 2 and 3 of $\mathcal{PH}$:
  - $\Theta_2^P = \mathcal{L}^{\mathcal{NP}} = \mathcal{P}^{\mathcal{NP}[\log n]}$ [52]: all languages decidable via parallel access to $\mathcal{NP}$.
  - $\Theta_3^P = \mathcal{L}^{\Sigma_2^P} = \mathcal{P}^{\Sigma_2^P[\log n]} = \mathcal{P}^{\mathcal{NP}^{\mathcal{NP}}[\log n]}$ [62]: all languages decidable via parallel access to Σ_2^P.
  It holds that $\mathcal{NP} \subseteq \Theta_2^P \subseteq \Delta_2^P \subseteq \Sigma_2^P \subseteq \Theta_3^P \subseteq \Delta_3^P$.
- The *function classes* F$\mathcal{P}$, F$\mathcal{NP}$ and FΣ_2^P of function problems associated with languages in $\mathcal{P}$, $\mathcal{NP}$ and Σ_2^P, respectively.

Complete Problems. We recall (in language form) some prominent decision problems which will be used in later reductions. In what follows, H is a propositional formula and C is the special case of a *clause*; each of $\mathbf{x}$ and $\mathbf{y}$ is a vector of n boolean variables.

$$\text{SAT} = \{H(\mathbf{x}) \mid \exists \mathbf{a} \in \{0,1\}^n (H(\mathbf{a}) = 1)\}$$

$$\text{CNF-SAT} = \{H(\mathbf{x}) \mid H(\mathbf{x}) \text{ is in conjunctive normal form and } \exists \mathbf{a} \in \{0,1\}^n (H(\mathbf{a}) = 1)\}$$

$$\Sigma_2 - \text{QBF} = \{H(\mathbf{x}, \mathbf{y}) \mid \exists \mathbf{a} \in \{0,1\}^n \forall \mathbf{b} \in \{0,1\}^n (H(\mathbf{a}, \mathbf{b}) = 1)\}$$

$$\Delta_2\text{-QBF} = \{H(\mathbf{x}) \mid \text{ the lexmax } \mathbf{a} \text{ with}(H(\mathbf{a}) = 1) \text{ has } a_n = 1\}$$

$$\Theta_2\text{-QBF} = \{\langle H(\mathbf{x}), 1^m \rangle \mid \text{ the lmax } \mathbf{a} \text{ with } (H(\mathbf{a}) = 1)\&|\mathbf{a}| \leq m \text{ has } a_n = 1\}$$

$$\Delta_3\text{-QBF} = \{H(\mathbf{x}, \mathbf{y}) \mid \text{ the lmax } \mathbf{a} \text{ with} \forall \mathbf{b} \in \{0,1\}^n (H(\mathbf{a}, \mathbf{b}) = 1) \text{ has } a_n = 1\}$$

$$\Theta_3\text{-QBF} = \left\{ \begin{array}{l} \langle H(\mathbf{x}, \mathbf{y}), 1^m \rangle \mid \\ \text{the lmax } \mathbf{a} \text{ with } \forall \mathbf{b} \in \{0,1\}^n (H(\mathbf{a}, \mathbf{b}) = 1) \text{ and } |\mathbf{a}| \leq m \text{ has } a_n = 1 \end{array} \right\}$$

SAT and CNF-SAT are the prototypical $\mathcal{NP}$-complete problems. Σ_2-QBF is Σ_2^P-complete [58,64]. Δ_2-QBF is Δ_2^P-complete [43,61]. Θ_2-QBF is Θ_2^P-complete [61]; similarly, Θ_3-QBF is Θ_3^P-complete. It is an easy consequence of results from [59] that Δ_3-QBF is Δ_3^P-complete. Consider a subclass Σ_2-RQBF of Σ_2-QBF restricted to the domain

$$R = \{H(\mathbf{x}, \mathbf{y}) \mid \forall \mathbf{a} \in \{0,1\}^n \exists \mathbf{b} \in \{0,1\}^n (H(\mathbf{a}, \mathbf{b}) = 1)\};$$

thus,

$$\Sigma_2\text{-RQBF} = \{H(\mathbf{x}, \mathbf{y}) \in R \mid \exists \mathbf{a} \in \{0,1\}^n \forall \mathbf{b} \in \{0,1\}^n (H(\mathbf{a}, \mathbf{b}) = 1)\}.$$

We observe:

Observation 21. *Σ_2-RQBF is Σ_2^P-complete.*

Proof. By reduction from Σ_2-QBF. Given a propositional formula $H(\mathbf{x}, \mathbf{y})$, construct the propositional formula $H'(\mathbf{x}, u, \mathbf{y}, v) = (H(\mathbf{x}, \mathbf{y}) \bigwedge v) \bigvee \bar{v}$. We prove that $H(\mathbf{x}, \mathbf{y}) \in \Sigma_2$-QBF if and only if $H'(\mathbf{x}, u, \mathbf{y}, v) \in \Sigma_2$-RQBF.

– Assume first that $H(\mathbf{x}, \mathbf{y}) \in \Sigma_2$-QBF. So there is $\mathbf{a}_0$ such that for all $\mathbf{b}$, $H(\mathbf{a}_0, \mathbf{b}) = 1$.
   • Fix arbitrary $\mathbf{a}$ and c. Set $\mathbf{b} := \mathbf{b}_0$ (for an arbitrary $\mathbf{b}_0$) and $d := 0$. Then,

$$H'(\mathbf{a}, c, \mathbf{b}_0, d) = \left(H(\mathbf{a}, \mathbf{b}_0) \bigwedge 0 \right) \bigvee \bar{0} = 1.$$

   So, $H'(\mathbf{x}, u, \mathbf{y}, v) \in R$.
   • Recall $\mathbf{a}_0$ and fix an arbitrary c_0. Consider arbitrary $\mathbf{b}$ and d. Then,

$$H'(\mathbf{a}_0, c_0, \mathbf{b}, d) = \left(H(\mathbf{a}_0, \mathbf{b}) \bigwedge d \right) \bigvee \bar{d} = \left(1 \bigwedge d \right) \bigvee \bar{d} = 1.$$

Hence, $H'(\mathbf{x}, u, \mathbf{y}, v) \in \Sigma_2$-RQBF.

– Assume now that $H'(\mathbf{x}, u, \mathbf{y}, v) \in \Sigma_2\text{-RQBF}$. Then, there are $\mathbf{a}_0$ and c_0 such that for all $\mathbf{b}$ and d, $H'(\mathbf{a}_0, c_0, \mathbf{b}, d) = 1$. Set $d := 1$. It follows that for all $\mathbf{b}$,

$$H'(\mathbf{a}_0, c_0, \mathbf{b}, 1) = \Big(H(\mathbf{a}_0, \mathbf{b}) \bigwedge 1 \Big) \bigvee 0 = 1.$$

It follows that $H(\mathbf{a}_0, \mathbf{b}) = 1$. Hence, $H(\mathbf{x}, \mathbf{y}) \in \Sigma_2\text{-QBF}$.

The proof is now complete.

Similarly, we consider restricted subclasses

$$\Delta_3\text{-RQBF} = \{H(\mathbf{x}, \mathbf{y}) \in R \mid \text{the lmax } \mathbf{a} \text{ with } \forall \mathbf{b} \in \{0,1\}^k (H(\mathbf{a}, \mathbf{b}) = 1) \text{ has } a_n = 1\}$$

$$\Theta_3\text{-RQBF} = \left\{ \langle H(\mathbf{x}, \mathbf{y}), 1^m \rangle \in R \times 1^* \mid \begin{array}{l} \text{the lmax } \mathbf{a} \text{ with } \forall \mathbf{b} \in \{0,1\}^k (H(\mathbf{a}, \mathbf{b}) = 1) \& |\mathbf{a}| \le m \text{ has } a_n = 1 \end{array} \right\}$$

of $\Delta_3\text{-QBF}$ and $\Theta_3\text{-QBF}$, respectively. Similarly to Observation 21, $\Delta_3\text{-RQBF}$ is Δ_3^P-complete and $\Theta_3\text{-RQBF}$ is Θ_3^P-complete.

3   Weighted Boolean Formula Games

3.1   Definition

We introduce:

Definition 1 (Weighted Boolean Formula Game). *Fix a triple of integers* $m \ge 2$, $k \ge 1$ *and* $r \ge 1$. *A game* $\Gamma = \langle m, (S_i)_{i \in [m]}, (U_i)_{i \in [m]} \rangle$, *is a* **weighted** (m, k, r)**-boolean formula game**, *or* **weighted boolean formula game** *for short, if the following conditions hold for each player* $i \in [m]$:

(1) $S_i = \{0, 1\}^k$.
(2) *There is a set*

$$F_i = \{(\mathsf{f}, \alpha) \mid \mathsf{f} \text{ is a } (km)\text{-ary propositional boolean formula and } \alpha \in \mathbb{N}\},$$

with $|F_i| \le r$, *such that for each profile* $\langle s_1, \ldots, s_m \rangle \in S$,

$$U_i(s_1, \ldots, s_m) = \sum_{(\mathsf{f}, \alpha) \in F_i} \alpha \cdot \mathsf{f}(s_1, \ldots, s_m).$$

We also write $\Gamma = \langle m, k, r, (F_i)_{i \in [m]} \rangle$. Set $F := \bigcup_{i \in [m]} F_i$. We use WBFG as an abbreviation for both a weighted boolean formula game, and the corresponding class of games.

An (m, k, r)-**boolean formula game**, denoted as BFG, is the special case of a weighted (m, k, r)-boolean formula game $\Gamma = \langle m, k, r, (F_i)_{i \in [m]} \rangle$ such that for each pair $(\mathsf{f}, \alpha) \in F$, $\alpha = 1$. A **(weighted)** (m, k, r)-**boolean clause game**, denoted as (WBCG) BCG, is the special case of a (weighted) (m, k, r)-boolean formula game $\Gamma = \langle m, k, r, (F_i)_{i \in [m]} \rangle$ such that for each pair $(\mathsf{f}, \alpha) \in F$, f is a *clause*. We now formulate a restricted case of a WBFG.

Definition 2. *A weighted boolean formula game* $\Gamma = \langle m, k, r, (\mathsf{F}_i)_{i \in [m]} \rangle$ *is* **mutual** *if the following condition holds:*

> *For each pair* $(\mathsf{f}, \alpha) \in \mathsf{F}$, *if* f *depends on a variable of player* $i \in [m]$, *then* $(\mathsf{f}, \alpha) \in \mathsf{F}_i$.

So, in a mutual weighted boolean formula game, for each pair $(\mathsf{f}, \alpha) \in \mathsf{F}_i$, if (f, α) depends on a variable of player l with $l \neq i$, then $(\mathsf{f}, \alpha) \in \mathsf{F}_l$ as well. A mutual weighted boolean formula game will be abbreviated as MWBFG; so will be the corresponding class of games.

3.2 Decision and Search Problems

Let $m \in \{2, 3, \dots\}$, $k \in \{1, 2, \dots\}$ and $r \in \{1, 2, \dots\}$. We formulate and study the following decision problems regarding pure and payoff-dominant equilibria:

PROBLEM:	PROBLEM:	GIVEN: A game Γ, which is:
WBF-PURE$_d(m, k, r)$	WBF-PDE$_d(m, k, r)$	Weighted (m, k, r)-boolean formula game
BF-PURE$_d(m, k, r)$	BF-PDE$_d(m, k, r)$	(m, k, r)-boolean formula game
WBC-PURE$_d(m, k, r)$	WBC-PDE$_d(m, k, r)$	Weighted (m, k, r)-boolean clause game
BC-PURE$_d(m, k, r)$	BC-PDE$_d(m, k, r)$	(m, k, r)-boolean clause game
QUESTION: Is $\mathcal{PE}(\Gamma) \neq \emptyset$?	QUESTION: Is $\mathcal{PDE}(\Gamma) \neq \emptyset$?	

Also, we shall treat search problems WBF-PURE$_s(m, k, r)$, BF-PURE$_s(m, k, r)$, WBC-PURE$_s(m, k, r)$, BC-PURE$_s(m, k, r)$ for pure equilibria and corresponding search problems WBF-PDE$_s(m, k, r)$, BF-PDE$_s(m, k, r)$, WBC-PDE$_s(m, k, r)$, BC-PDE$_s(m, k, r)$ for payoff-dominant equilibria, respectively. We shall often consider the case where some of the parameters m, k, and r are not restricted to a fixed value. In this case, such a parameter gets the value $*$. For example, for $k \in \{1, 2, \dots\}$ and $r \in \{1, 2, \dots\}$,

$$\text{BF-PURE}_d(*, k, r) = \bigcup_{m \geq 2} \text{BF-PURE}_d(m, k, r).$$

4 Mutual Weighted Boolean Formula Games

We show:

Theorem 1 (MWBFG is Potential). *Fix a MWBFG* $\Gamma = \langle m, k, r, (\mathsf{F}_i)_{i \in [m]} \rangle$. *Then, the function* $\Phi : (\{0, 1\}^k)^m \to \mathbb{R}$ *with*

$$\Phi(\mathbf{s}) = \sum_{\langle \mathsf{f}, \alpha \rangle \in \mathsf{F}} \alpha \cdot \mathsf{f}(\mathbf{s})$$

is a potential for Γ.

Proof. Consider an arbitrary profile $\mathbf{s} \in S$ and a strategy $t_i \in \{0,1\}^k$ of player $i \in [m]$. Then,

$$
\Phi(\mathbf{s}_{-i}, t_i) - \Phi(\mathbf{s})
$$
$$
= \sum_{\langle f, \alpha \rangle \in F} \alpha \cdot f(\mathbf{s}_{-i}, t_i) - \sum_{\langle f, \alpha \rangle \in F} \alpha \cdot f(\mathbf{s})
$$
$$
= \sum_{\langle f, \alpha \rangle \in F_i} \alpha \cdot f(\mathbf{s}_{-i}, t_i) + \sum_{\langle f, \alpha \rangle \notin F_i} \alpha \cdot f(\mathbf{s}_{-i}, t_i) - \sum_{\langle f, \alpha \rangle \in F_i} \alpha \cdot f(\mathbf{s}) - \sum_{\langle f, \alpha \rangle \notin F_i} \alpha \cdot f(\mathbf{s})
$$
$$
= \sum_{\langle f, \alpha \rangle \in F_i} \alpha \cdot f(\mathbf{s}_{-i}, t_i) - \sum_{\langle f, \alpha \rangle \in F_i} \alpha \cdot f(\mathbf{s}) + \sum_{\langle f, \alpha \rangle \in F \setminus F_i} \alpha \cdot (f(\mathbf{s}_{-i}, t_i) - f(\mathbf{s})).
$$

Since Γ is a MWBFG, it follows that for each pair $\langle f, \alpha \rangle \notin F_i$, $f(s_1, \ldots, s_m)$ does *not* depend on a variable of player i; thus, it does not depend on t_i. Hence, for each pair $\langle f, \alpha \rangle \notin F_i$, $f(\mathbf{s}_{-i}, t_i) = f(\mathbf{s})$, so that

$$
\Phi(\mathbf{s}_{-i}, t_i) - \Phi(\mathbf{s}) = \sum_{\langle f, \alpha \rangle \in F_i} \alpha \cdot f(\mathbf{s}_{-i}, t_i) - \sum_{\langle f, \alpha \rangle \in F_i} \alpha \cdot f(\mathbf{s})
$$
$$
= U_i(\mathbf{s}_{-i}, t_i) - U_i(\mathbf{s}).
$$

It follows that Φ is an exact potential for Γ.

Theorem 1 immediately implies:

Corollary 1. $\text{MWBF-PURE}_d(*, *, *) \in \mathcal{PLS}$.

We now show:

Theorem 2. PSC^2 *is polynomial monomorphic to WBFG.*

In the proof, we identify a set $t \subseteq \{1, \ldots, k\}$ with the *characteristic vector* $\langle \chi_t(1), \ldots, \chi_t(k) \rangle$, where χ_t is the *characteristic function* for t: for each $e \in [k]$, $\chi_t(e) = 1$ if $e \in t$ and 0 otherwise. For a boolean variable x, set $x^{\chi_t(e)} := x$ if $\chi_t(e) = 1$ and $\overline{x}$ otherwise.

Proof. We shall give a polynomial linear monomorphism λ from PSC^2 to WBFG. We define the action of λ on a game PSC^2 $\Gamma = \langle m, (S_i)_{i \in [m]}, (U_i)_{i \in [m]} \rangle$, with $S_i \subseteq \{0,1\}^k$ for each player $i \in [m]$. In the game WBFG, each player $i \in [m]$ has a k-tuple of boolean variables $x_i = \langle x_{i1}, \ldots, x_{ik} \rangle$; so, $S'_i = \{0,1\}^k$. The set F_i consists of:

For each:	The boolean formula:	With weight:
$e \in [k]$:	$f_{ie}(x_1, \ldots, x_m) = \overline{x_{ie}}$	$\alpha_{ie} = \delta_{ie} \cdot w_i$
$j \in [m]$ $e \in [k]$:	$f_{ije}(x_1, \ldots, x_m) = \overline{x_{ie}} \vee \overline{x_{je}}$	$\alpha_{ije} = \beta_{ie} \cdot w_i \cdot w_j$
$t \in S_i$:	$f_{it}(x_1, \ldots, x_m) = \bigwedge_{e \in [k]} x_{ie}^{\chi_t(e)}$	$\alpha_{it} = w_i \cdot \sum_{e \in [k]} \left(\beta_{ie} \cdot \sum_{j \in [m]} w_j + \delta_{ie} \right) + 1$

Clearly, λ is computable in polynomial time. It remains to establish that λ is a monomorphism from Γ to Γ'. For each player $i \in [m]$, set ϕ_i to the identity map on S_i; thus, $\phi\,(\phi_i)_{i\in[m]}$ induces the identity map on $S = \times_{i\in[m]}S_i$. Fix any profile $\mathbf{s}' = \langle s_1', \ldots, s_m' \rangle$ for Γ', where for each player $i \in [m]$, $s_i = \langle s_{i1}', \ldots, s_{ik}' \rangle$. By the definition of WBFG, for each player $i \in [m]$,

$$\mathsf{U}_i'(\mathbf{s}') = \underbrace{\sum_{e\in[k]} \alpha_{ie} \cdot \mathsf{f}_{ie}(\mathbf{s}')}_{\Sigma_1(\mathbf{s}')} + \underbrace{\sum_{j\in[m]} \sum_{e\in[k]} \alpha_{ije} \cdot \mathsf{f}_{ije}(\mathbf{s}')}_{\Sigma_2(\mathbf{s}')} + \underbrace{\sum_{t\in S_i} \alpha_{it} \cdot \mathsf{f}_{it}(\mathbf{s}')}_{\Sigma_3(\mathbf{s}')}.$$

We treat separately each of the three sums $\Sigma_1(\mathbf{s}')$, $\Sigma_2(\mathbf{s}')$ and $\Sigma_3(\mathbf{s}')$.

– For $\Sigma_1(\mathbf{s}')$, note that

$$\Sigma_1(\mathbf{s}') = \sum_{e\in[k]} \delta_{ie} \cdot w_i \cdot (1 - s_{ie}') \;=\; w_i \sum_{e\in[k]} \delta_{ie} - w_i \sum_{e\in s_i'} \delta_{ie}.$$

– For $\Sigma_2(\mathbf{s}')$, note that

$$\Sigma_2(\mathbf{s}') = \sum_{j\in[m]} \sum_{e\in[k]} \beta_{ie} \cdot w_i \cdot w_j - \sum_{j\in[m]} \sum_{e\in[k]} \beta_{ie} \cdot w_i \cdot w_j \left((s_{ie}' \wedge s_{je}') \right).$$

Note that $s_{ie}' \wedge s_{je}' = 1$ if and only if $e \in s_i'$ and $e \in s_j'$. Hence,

$$\Sigma_2(\mathbf{s}') = w_i \sum_{j\in[m]} \sum_{e\in[k]} \beta_{ie} \cdot w_j - w_i \cdot \sum_{e\in s_i'} \sum_{j\mid e\in s_j'} \beta_{ie} \cdot w_j.$$

It follows that

$$\Sigma_1(\mathbf{s}') + \Sigma_2(\mathbf{s}')$$
$$= w_i \sum_{e\in[k]} \delta_{ie} - w_i \sum_{e\in s_i'} \delta_{ie} + w_i \sum_{j\in[m]} \sum_{e\in[k]} \beta_{ie} \cdot w_j - w_i \cdot \sum_{e\in s_i'} \sum_{j\mid e\in s_j'} \beta_{ie} \cdot w_j$$
$$= w_i \sum_{e\in[k]} \left(\beta_{ie} \cdot \sum_{j\in[m]} w_j + \delta_{ie} \right) - w_i \sum_{e\in s_i'} \left(\beta_{ie} \cdot \sum_{j\mid e\in s_j'} w_j + \delta_{ie} \right).$$

– For $\Sigma_3(\mathbf{s}')$, note that

$$\Sigma_3(\mathbf{s}') = \sum_{t\in S_i} \left(w_i \cdot \sum_{e\in[k]} \left(\beta_{ie} \cdot \sum_{j\in[m]} w_j + \delta_{ie} \right) + 1 \right) \cdot \bigwedge_{e\in[k]} (s_{ie}')^{\chi_t(e)}$$
$$= \left(w_i \cdot \sum_{e\in[k]} \left(\beta_{ie} \cdot \sum_{j\in[m]} w_j + \delta_{ie} \right) + 1 \right) \cdot \sum_{t\in S_i} \bigwedge_{e\in[k]} (s_{ie}')^{\chi_t(e)}.$$

We observe that for each $t \in S_i$, $\bigwedge_{e\in[k]}(s'_{ie})^{\chi_t(e)} = 1$ if and only if ($e \in s_i$ if and only if $e \in t$) if and only if $s'_i = t$. Thus,

$$\sum_{t\in S_i} \bigwedge_{e\in[k]} (s'_{ie})^{\chi_t(e)} = \sum_{t\in S_i} (s'_i = t),$$

where $(s'_i = t) = 1$ if and only if $s'_i = t$. Since $\sum_{t\in S_i}(s'_i = t) = \chi_{S_i}(s'_i)$, it follows that

$$\Sigma_3(\mathbf{s}') = \left(w_i \cdot \sum_{e\in[k]} \left(\beta_{ie} \cdot \sum_{j\in[m]} w_j + \delta_{ie} \right) + 1 \right) \cdot \chi_{S_i}(s'_i).$$

We now establish Conditions (C.1) and (C.2) in the definition of monomorphism. For (C.1), consider a profile $\mathbf{s}' \in S'(\Gamma')$ such that $\mathbf{s}' = \phi(\mathbf{s})$ for some profile $\mathbf{s} \in S(\Gamma)$. Hence, for each player $i \in [m]$, $\chi_{S_i}(s_i) = 1$. Since ϕ is the identity map, $\mathbf{s}' = \mathbf{s}$. It follows that for each player $i \in [m]$, $\chi_{S_i}(s'_i) = 1$ as well. So,

$$\mathsf{U}'_i(\phi(\mathbf{s}))$$

$$= w_i \sum_{e\in[k]} \left(\beta_{ie} \sum_{j\in[m]} w_j + \delta_{ie} \right) - w_i \sum_{e\in s'_i} \left(\beta_{ie} \sum_{j|e\in s'_j} w_j + \delta_{ie} \right)$$

$$+ w_i \sum_{e\in[k]} \left(\beta_{ie} \sum_{j\in[m]} w_j + \delta_{ie} \right) + 1$$

$$= -w_i \sum_{e\in s'_i} \left(\beta_{ie} \sum_{j|e\in s'_j} w_j + \delta_{ie} \right) \cdot + 2\, w_i \sum_{e\in[k]} \left(\beta_{ie} \sum_{j\in[m]} w_j + \delta_{ie} \right) + 1$$

$$= -w_i \sum_{e\in s'_i} \left(\beta_{ie} \sum_{j|e\in s_j} w_j + \delta_{ie} \right) + 2\, w_i \sum_{e\in[k]} \left(\beta_{ie} \sum_{j\in[m]} w_j + \delta_{ie} \right) + 1$$

$$= w_i \cdot \mathsf{U}_i(\mathbf{s}) + 2\, w_i \sum_{e\in[k]} \left(\beta_{ie} \sum_{j\in[m]} w_j + \delta_{ie} \right) + 1.$$

Since $w_i > 0$, Condition (C.1) follows. For Condition (C.2), consider a profile $\mathbf{s}' \in S(\Gamma')$ such that there is no profile $\mathbf{s} \in S(\Gamma)$ such that $\mathbf{s}' = \phi(\mathbf{s})$. Since the map induced by ϕ on $S = \times_{i\in[n]} S_i$ is the identity, $\mathbf{s}' \notin S(\Gamma)$. Hence, there is a player $i \in [m]$ such that $s'_i \notin S_i$; so, $\chi_{S_i}(s'_i) = 0$ and $\Sigma_3(\mathbf{s}') = 0$. So,

$$\mathsf{U}'_i(\mathbf{s}') = \Sigma_1(\mathbf{s}') + \Sigma_2(\mathbf{s}') \leq w_i \cdot \sum_{e\in[k]} \left(\beta_{ie} \cdot \sum_{j\in[m]} w_j + \delta_{ie} \right).$$

Assume now that player i switches from strategy $s_i' \notin S_i$ to strategy $s_i'' \in S_i$; thus, $\chi_{S_i}(s_i'') = 1$. Hence,

$$\mathsf{U}_i'(\mathbf{s}_{-i}', s_i'')$$

$$= 2w_i \cdot \sum_{e \in [k]} \left(\beta_{ie} \cdot \sum_{j \in [m]} w_j + \delta_{ie} \right) + 1 - w_i \cdot \sum_{e \in s_i''} \left(\beta_{ie} \cdot \sum_{j \in [m] | e \in s_j''} w_j + \delta_{ie} \right)$$

$$\geq 2w_i \cdot \sum_{e \in [k]} \left(\beta_{ie} \cdot \sum_{j \in [m]} w_j + \delta_{ie} \right) + 1 - w_i \cdot \sum_{e \in [k]} \left(\beta_{ie} \cdot \sum_{j \in [m]} w_j + \delta_{ie} \right)$$

$$= w_i \cdot \sum_{e \in [k]} \left(\beta_{ie} \cdot \sum_{j \in [m]} w_j + \delta_{ie} \right) + 1.$$

Hence, $\mathsf{U}_i'(\mathbf{s}_{-i}', s_i'') > \mathsf{U}_i'(\mathbf{s}')$ and $\mathbf{s}'$ is not a pure equilibrium for Γ'. Condition (C.2) follows.

Consider the restriction of PSC^2 to PSC, where the coefficients $(\beta_{ie})_{i \in [m], e \in [k]}$ become player-independent as $(\beta_e)_{e \in [k]}$. Then, an inspection to the proof of Theorem 2 reveals that the weights for the boolean formula f_{ije}, where $i, j \in [m]$ and $e \in [k]$, satisfy $\alpha_{ije} = \alpha_{jie} = \beta_e w_i w_j$; note that f_{ije} is the only boolean formula owned by more than one player. Thus, the constructed WBFG $\lambda(\Gamma)$ is a MWBFG. Hence, Theorem 2 immediately implies:

Corollary 2. PSC *is polynomial monomorphic to* MWBFG.

5   Pure Equilibria

Note that the existence of a pure equilibrium in a WBFG is expressed by the predicate

$$\exists s_1 \in \{0,1\}^k \ldots \exists s_m \in \{0,1\}^k \forall i \in \{1, \ldots, m\} \forall s_i' \in \{0,1\}^k \left(\mathsf{U}_i(\mathbf{s}) \geq \mathsf{U}_i(\mathbf{s}_{-i}, s_i') \right);$$

this is a Σ_2^P-predicate when k is *not* fixed (even if m is fixed), while it becomes an $\mathcal{NP}$-predicate when k is fixed. Hence, upper bounds on the complexity of deciding the existence of pure equilibria, under corresponding assumptions on the range of values of m, k and r, follow directly from the type of the predicate:

Proposition 1 (Upper Bounds for Pure Equilibria). *Let* $m \in \{2, 3, \ldots\}$, $k \in \{1, 2, \ldots\}$ *and* $r \in \{1, 2, \ldots, *\}$. *Then, we have:*

(1) WBF-PURE$_d(m, k, r) \in \mathcal{P}$ *(and* WBF-PURE$_s(m, k, r) \in \mathrm{F}\mathcal{P}$*).*
(2) WBF-PURE$_d(*, k, r) \in \mathcal{NP}$ *(and* WBF-PURE$_s(*, k, r) \in \mathrm{F}\mathcal{NP}$*).*
(3) WBF-PURE$_d(*, *, r) \in \Sigma_2^P$ *(and* WBF-PURE$_s(*, *, r) \in \mathrm{F}\Sigma_2^P$*).*

We show:

Theorem 3 (Completeness Results for Pure Equilibria). *We have:*

(1) *For $k \in \{1, 2, \ldots\}$ and $r \in \{1, 2, \ldots, *\}$, BF-PURE$_d(*, k, r)$ is $\mathcal{NP}$-complete (and BF-PURE$_s(*, k, r)$ is F$\mathcal{NP}$-complete).*

(2) *For $k \in \{1, 2, \ldots\}$ and $r \in \{2, 3, \ldots, *\}$, BC-PURE$_d(*, k, r)$ is $\mathcal{NP}$-complete (and BC-PURE$_s(*, k, r)$ is F$\mathcal{NP}$-complete).*

(3) *For $k \in \{1, 2, \ldots, *\}$, WBC-PURE$_d(*, k, 1) \in \mathcal{P}$ (and WBC-PURE$_s(*, k, 1) \in$ F$\mathcal{P}$). In fact, every weighted $(*, k, 1)$-boolean clause game has a pure equilibrium.*

(4) *For $m \in \{3, 4, \ldots, *\}$, $r \in \{1, 2, \ldots, *\}$, BF-PURE$_d(m, *, r)$ is Σ_2^P-complete (and BC-PURE$_s(m, *, r)$ is FΣ_2^P-complete).*

Proof. For each of the Cases (1), (2) and (4), membership in the corresponding class is established in Case (2), (2) and (3), respectively, of Proposition 1; it remains to establish hardness. We consider each case separately.

Case(1) : It suffices to prove that BF-PURE$_d(*, 1, 1)$ is $\mathcal{NP}$-hard. Towards this end, we use a reduction from SAT to BF-PURE$_d(*, 1, 1)$. Given a propositional formula $H(x_1, \ldots, x_n)$, construct a BFG $\Gamma_H = \langle n + 2, 1, 1, (F_i)_{i \in [n+2]} \rangle$ as follows:

Player	Variable	Boolean formula
$i \in [n]$	x_i	$f_i(\mathbf{x}) = 0$
$n + 1$	x_{n+1}	$f_{n+1}(\mathbf{x}) = H(x_1, \ldots, x_n) \bigvee (x_{n+1} \oplus x_{n+2})$
$n + 2$	x_{n+2}	$f_{n+2}(\mathbf{x}) = H(x_1, \ldots, x_n) \bigvee (x_{n+1} \oplus x_{n+2} \oplus 1)$

Note that all players $i \in [n]$ do not matter for a pure equilibrium since their payoffs are constant. We now prove that $H(x_1, \ldots, x_n)$ is satisfiable if and only if Γ_H has a pure equilibrium:

Lemma 1. *For all $a_{n+1}, a_{n+2} \in \{0, 1\}$, it holds that $H(a_1, \ldots a_n) = 1$ if and only if $\langle a_1, \ldots a_n, a_{n+1}, a_{n+2} \rangle$ is a pure equilibrium for Γ_H.*

Proof. Assume first that $H(a_1, \ldots, a_n) = 1$. Then, for all $a_{n+1}, a_{n+2} \in \{0, 1\}$,

$$f_{n+1}(a_1, \ldots, a_{n+2}) = f_{n+2}(a_1, \ldots, a_{n+2}) = 1,$$

and no player can improve her payoff $U_i(a_1, \ldots, a_n, a_{n+1}, a_{n+2}) = 1$. It follows that $\langle a_1, \ldots, a_n, a_{n+1}, a_{n+2} \rangle$ is a pure equilibrium for Γ_H.

Assume now that $\langle a_1, \ldots, a_n, a_{n+1}, a_{n+2} \rangle$ is a pure equilibrium for Γ_H. Then:

– Player $n + 1$ cannot increase her payoff by flipping a_{n+1} to $\overline{a_{n+1}}$. It follows that

$$H(a_1, \ldots, a_n) \bigvee (a_{n+1} \oplus a_{n+2}) \geq H(a_1, \ldots, a_n) \bigvee (\overline{a_{n+1}} \oplus a_{n+2}).$$

Hence, either $H(a_1, \ldots, a_n) = 1$ or $a_{n+1} \oplus a_{n+2} = 1$.

– Player $n+2$ cannot increase her payoff by flipping a_{n+2} to $\overline{a_{n+2}}$. It follows that

$$\mathsf{H}(a_1,\ldots,a_n) \bigvee (a_{n+1} \oplus a_{n+2} \oplus 1) \geq \mathsf{H}(a_1,\ldots,a_n) \bigvee (a_{n+1} \oplus \overline{a_{n+2}} \oplus 1).$$

Hence, either $\mathsf{H}(a_1,\ldots,a_n) = 1$ or $a_{n+1} \oplus a_{n+2} \oplus 1 = 1$.

It follows that $\mathsf{H}(a_1,\ldots,a_n) = 1$, so that H is satisfiable.

Case(2) : It suffices to prove that $\mathsf{BC\text{-}PURE}_d(*, 1, 2)$ is $\mathcal{NP}$-hard. Towards this end, we establish a reduction from $\mathsf{CNF\text{-}SAT}$ to $\mathsf{BC\text{-}PURE}_d(*, 1, 2)$. Given a CNF formula $\mathsf{H}(x_1,\ldots,x_n) = \bigwedge_{j\in[m]} \mathsf{C}_j(x_1,\ldots,x_n)$, construct a BCG $\Gamma_{\mathsf{H}} = \langle n + 2m, 1, 2, (\mathsf{C}_{jk})_{j\in[n+2m],k\in[2]}\rangle$ as follows:

Player	Variable	Clause $\mathsf{C}_{j1}(\mathbf{x},\mathbf{y},\mathbf{z})$	Clause $\mathsf{C}_{j2}(\mathbf{x},\mathbf{y},\mathbf{z})$
$j \in [n]$	x_j	0	0
$n + j$ with $j \in [m]$	y_j	$\mathsf{C}_j(\mathbf{x}) \bigvee y_j \bigvee z_j$	$\mathsf{C}_j(\mathbf{x}) \bigvee \overline{y_j} \bigvee \overline{z_j}$
$n + m + j$ with $j \in [m]$	z_j	$\mathsf{C}_j(\mathbf{x}) \bigvee y_j \bigvee \overline{z_j}$	$\mathsf{C}_j(\mathbf{x}) \bigvee \overline{y_j} \bigvee z_j$

Note that all players $j \in [n]$ do not matter for a pure equilibrium since their payoffs are *constant*. In the sequel, we shall use vectors $\mathbf{a}$, $\mathbf{b}$ and $\mathbf{c}$ to denote vectors of values for the boolean variables in the vectors $\mathbf{x}$, $\mathbf{y}$ and $\mathbf{z}$, respectively. We prove:

Lemma 2. *For all boolean vectors $\mathbf{b}, \mathbf{c}$, it holds that $\mathsf{H}(\mathbf{a}) = 1$ if and only if $\langle \mathbf{a}, \mathbf{b}, \mathbf{c}\rangle$ is a pure equilibrium for Γ_{H}.*

Proof. Assume first that $\mathsf{H}(\mathbf{a}) = 1$. It follows that for each index $j \in [m]$, $\mathsf{C}_j(\mathbf{a}) = 1$. Hence, $\mathsf{C}_{j1}(\mathbf{a},\mathbf{b},\mathbf{c}) = \mathsf{C}_{j2}(\mathbf{a},\mathbf{b},\mathbf{c}) = 1$ for all players $n + j$ with $j \in [2m]$. So, each player $n + j$ with $j \in [2m]$ cannot increase her payoff by flipping her variable (y_j or z_j). It follows that for any pair of boolean vectors $\mathbf{b}$ and $\mathbf{c}$, $\langle \mathbf{a}, \mathbf{b}, \mathbf{c}\rangle$ is a pure equilibrium for Γ_{H}.

Assume now that $\langle \mathbf{a}, \mathbf{b}, \mathbf{c}\rangle$ is a pure equilibrium for Γ_{H}. Fix any index $j \in [m]$. Then:

Player $n + j$ cannot increase her payoff by flipping her variable y_j from b_j to $\overline{b_j}$. So,

$$\left(\mathsf{C}_j(\mathbf{a}) \bigvee b_j \bigvee c_j\right) + \left(\mathsf{C}_j(\mathbf{a}) \bigvee \overline{b_j} \bigvee \overline{c_j}\right) \geq \left(\mathsf{C}_j(\mathbf{a}) \bigvee \overline{b_j} \bigvee c_j\right) + \left(\mathsf{C}_j(\mathbf{a}) \bigvee b_j \bigvee \overline{c_j}\right).$$

Player $n + m + j$ cannot increase her payoff by flipping her variable z_j (from c_j to $\overline{c_j}$). So,

$$\left(\mathsf{C}_j(\mathbf{a}) \bigvee b_j \bigvee \overline{c_j}\right) + \left(\mathsf{C}_j(\mathbf{a}) \bigvee \overline{b_j} \bigvee c_j\right) \geq \left(\mathsf{C}_j(\mathbf{a}) \bigvee b_j \bigvee c_j\right) + \left(\mathsf{C}_j(\mathbf{a}) \bigvee \overline{b_j} \bigvee \overline{c_j}\right).$$

The two inequalities imply that

$$\left(C_j(\mathbf{a}) \bigvee b_j \bigvee c_j\right) + \left(C_j(\mathbf{a}) \bigvee \overline{b_j} \bigvee \overline{c_j}\right) = \left(C_j(\mathbf{a}) \bigvee \overline{b_j} \bigvee c_j\right) + \left(C_j(\mathbf{a}) \bigvee b_j \bigvee \overline{c_j}\right).$$

Denote as $g(\mathbf{a}, \mathbf{b}, \mathbf{c}) \in \{0, 1, 2\}$ the common value. We prove that $g(\mathbf{a}, \mathbf{b}, \mathbf{c}) = 2$. Assume, by way of contradiction, that $g(\mathbf{a}, \mathbf{b}, \mathbf{c}) \in \{0, 1\}$. We proceed by case analysis.

- Assume first that $g(\mathbf{a}, \mathbf{b}, \mathbf{c}) = 0$. This implies that $C_j(\mathbf{a}) \bigvee b_j \bigvee c_j = 0$. It follows that $b_j = 0$. Hence, $C_j(\mathbf{a}) \bigvee \overline{b_j} \bigvee \overline{c_j} = 1$, so that $g(\mathbf{a}, \mathbf{b}, \mathbf{c}) = 1$, a contradiction.
- Assume now that $g(\mathbf{a}, \mathbf{b}, \mathbf{c}) = 1$. We proceed by case analysis on the value $C_j(\mathbf{a}) \bigvee b_j \bigvee c_j$.
  - Assume first that $C_j(\mathbf{a}) \bigvee b_j \bigvee c_j = 0$. This implies that $b_j = c_j = 0$. Hence, it follows that $C_j(\mathbf{a}) \bigvee \overline{b_j} \bigvee c_j = C_j(\mathbf{a}) \bigvee b_j \bigvee \overline{c_j} = 1$. So,

$$g(\mathbf{a}, \mathbf{b}, \mathbf{c}) = C_j(\mathbf{a}) \bigvee \overline{b_j} \bigvee c_j + C_j(\mathbf{a}) \bigvee b_j \bigvee \overline{c_j}$$
$$= 2.$$

  A contradiction.
  - Assume now that $C_j(\mathbf{a}) \bigvee b_j \bigvee c_j = 1$. Since

$$g(\mathbf{a}, \mathbf{b}, \mathbf{c}) = \left(C_j(\mathbf{a}) \bigvee b_j \bigvee c_j\right) + \left(C_j(\mathbf{a}) \bigvee \overline{b_j} \bigvee \overline{c_j}\right)$$

and $g(\mathbf{a}, \mathbf{b}, \mathbf{c}) = 1$ (by assumption), it follows that $C_j(\mathbf{a}) \bigvee \overline{b_j} \bigvee \overline{c_j} = 0$. This implies that $b_j = c_j = 1$. Hence, it follows that $C_j(\mathbf{a}) \bigvee \overline{b_j} \bigvee c_j = C_j(\mathbf{a}) \bigvee b_j \bigvee \overline{c_j} = 1$. So,

$$g(\mathbf{a}, \mathbf{b}, \mathbf{c}) = \left(C_j(\mathbf{a}) \bigvee \overline{b_j} \bigvee c_j\right) + \left(C_j(\mathbf{a}) \bigvee b_j \bigvee \overline{c_j}\right)$$
$$= 2.$$

  A contradiction.

Since $g(\mathbf{a}, \mathbf{b}, \mathbf{c}) = 2$,

$$C_j(\mathbf{a}) \bigvee b_j \bigvee c_j = C_j(\mathbf{a}) \bigvee \overline{b_j} \bigvee \overline{c_j} = C_j(\mathbf{a}) \bigvee \overline{b_j} \bigvee c_j = C_j(\mathbf{a}) \bigvee b_j \bigvee \overline{c_j} = 1.$$

It follows that $C_j(\mathbf{a}) = 1$. Since $j \in [m]$ was chosen arbitrarily, this implies that $H(\mathbf{a}) = \bigwedge_{j \in [m]} C_j(\mathbf{a}) = 1$.

Case(3) : Consider any game Γ as input to WBC-PURE$_d(*, k, 1)$. Then, Γ has a pure equilibrium where player i chooses her variables $\mathbf{x}^i = \langle x_{i1}, \ldots, x_{ik} \rangle \in \{0, 1\}^k$ as follows: if x_{ij} appears unnegated in her clause function f_i, then $x_{ij} := 1$, else $x_{ij} := 0$. So, WBC-PURE$_d(*, k, 1) \in \mathcal{P}$.

Player	Variables	Boolean formula
1	$\mathbf{x} \in \{0,1\}^n$	$f_1(\mathbf{x}, \mathbf{y}, \mathbf{z}) = 0$
2	$\mathbf{y} \in \{0,1\}^n$	$f_2(\mathbf{x}, \mathbf{y}, \mathbf{z}) = H(\mathbf{x}, \mathbf{y}) \oplus H(\mathbf{x}, \mathbf{z})$
3	$\mathbf{z} \in \{0,1\}^n$	$f_3(\mathbf{x}, \mathbf{y}, \mathbf{z}) = H(\mathbf{x}, \mathbf{y}) \oplus H(\mathbf{x}, \mathbf{z}) \oplus 1$

Case(4) : It suffices to prove that $\mathsf{BF\text{-}PURE}_d(3, *, 1)$ is Σ_2^P-hard. Towards this end, we use a reduction from $\Sigma_2\text{-RQBF}$ to $\mathsf{BF\text{-}PURE}_d(3, *, 1)$. Given a propositional formula $H(\mathbf{x}, \mathbf{y}) \in R$ with $\mathbf{x} = \langle x_1, \ldots, x_n \rangle$ and $\mathbf{y} = \langle y_1, \ldots, y_n \rangle$, construct a BFG $\Gamma_H = \langle 3, n, 1, (F_i)_{i \in [3]} \rangle$ as follows:

We now prove that $H(\mathbf{x}, \mathbf{y}) \in \Sigma_2\text{-RQBF}$ if and only if Γ_H has a pure equilibrium:[4]

Lemma 3. *There is a boolean vector* $\mathbf{a}$ *for which it holds that* $\forall \mathbf{b}(H(\mathbf{a}, \mathbf{b}) = 1)$ *if and only if* $\langle \mathbf{a}, \mathbf{b}, \mathbf{c} \rangle$ *is a pure equilibrium for* Γ_H *for all pairs of boolean vectors* $\mathbf{b}$ *and* $\mathbf{c}$.

Proof. Assume first that there is a vector $\mathbf{a} \in \{0,1\}^n$ such that for all vectors $\mathbf{d} \in \{0,1\}^n$, $H(\mathbf{a}, \mathbf{d}) = 1$. Fix any such vector $\mathbf{a} \in \{0,1\}^n$. Fix arbitrary vectors $\mathbf{b}, \mathbf{c} \in \{0,1\}^n$ as strategies of players 2 and 3, respectively.

– The choice of $\mathbf{a}$ implies that $f_2(\mathbf{a}, \mathbf{b}.\mathbf{c}) = H(\mathbf{a}, \mathbf{b}) \oplus H(\mathbf{a}, \mathbf{c}) = 0$. Hence, player 2 cannot increase her payoff by switching her strategy $\mathbf{b}$.
– The choice of $\mathbf{a}$ implies that $f_3(\mathbf{a}, \mathbf{b}, \mathbf{c}) = H(\mathbf{a}, \mathbf{b}) \oplus H(\mathbf{a}, \mathbf{c}) \oplus 1 = 1$. Hence, player 3 cannot increase her payoff by switching her strategy $\mathbf{c}$.

Thus, $\langle \mathbf{a}, \mathbf{b}, \mathbf{c} \rangle$ is a pure equilibrium for the game Γ_H.

Assume now that $\langle \mathbf{a}, \mathbf{b}, \mathbf{c} \rangle$ is a pure equilibrium for the game Γ_H. Then:

– Player 2 cannot increase her payoff by switching her strategy $\mathbf{b}$ to a strategy $\mathbf{b}'$. Thus, for all vectors $\mathbf{b}' \in \{0,1\}^n$,

$$H(\mathbf{a}, \mathbf{b}) \oplus H(\mathbf{a}, \mathbf{c}) \geq H(\mathbf{a}, \mathbf{b}') \oplus H(\mathbf{a}, \mathbf{c}).$$

Two cases are now possible:
- $H(\mathbf{a}, \mathbf{b}) \oplus H(\mathbf{a}, \mathbf{c}) = 1$.
- $H(\mathbf{a}, \mathbf{b}) \oplus H(\mathbf{a}, \mathbf{c}) = 0$. This implies that for all vectors $\mathbf{b}' \in \{0,1\}^n$, $H(\mathbf{a}, \mathbf{b}) = H(\mathbf{a}, \mathbf{b}')$.
– Player 3 cannot increase her payoff by switching his strategy $\mathbf{c}$ to a strategy $\mathbf{c}'$. Thus, for all vectors $\mathbf{c}' \in \{0,1\}^n$,

$$H(\mathbf{a}, \mathbf{b}) \oplus H(\mathbf{a}, \mathbf{c}) \oplus 1 \geq H(\mathbf{a}, \mathbf{b}) \oplus H(\mathbf{a}, \mathbf{c}') \oplus 1.$$

---

[4] We **warn** the reader against the formula $G(\mathbf{x}, \mathbf{y}) \equiv 0$ for all $\mathbf{x}$ and $\mathbf{y}$. Note that in the constructed game Γ_G, $f_1 \equiv 0$, $f_2 \equiv 0$ and $f_3 \equiv 1$; so, every profile is a pure equilibrium for Γ_G. But this is *not* a contradiction, since $G \notin R$, which implies that G may *not* be an input for $\Sigma_2\text{-RQBF}$ (even though $G \notin \Sigma_2\text{-RQBF}$). In fact, we used reduction from $\Sigma_2\text{-RQBF}$ (as opposed to $\Sigma_2\text{-QBF}$) in order to eliminate such degenerate formulas from consideration.

Two cases are now possible:
- $H(a, b) \oplus H(a, c) \oplus 1 = 1$.
- $H(a, b) \oplus H(a, c) \oplus 1 = 0$. This implies that for all vectors $c' \in \{0, 1\}^n$, $H(a, c) = H(a, c')$.

Since it is impossible that both $H(a, b) \oplus H(a, c) = 1$ and $H(a, b) \oplus H(a, c) \oplus 1 = 1$, it follows that for all vectors $b' \in \{0, 1\}^n$, $H(a, b) = H(a, b')$. Since $H \in R$, there is a vector $b' \in \{0, 1\}^n$ such that $H(a, b') = 1$. It follows that for all $b' \in \{0, 1\}^n$, $H(a, b') = 1$.

We conclude with two groups of open problems for *(i)* the *two-players* case, and *(ii)* the case where the boolean formulas are clauses and k is *not* fixed, respectively.

Open Problem 51. *Find the complexities of the following problems, where $r \in \{1, 2, \ldots, *\}$:*

(1) BF-PURE$_d(2, *, r)$ *(and* BF-PURE$_s(2, *, r)$*);*
(2) WBF-PURE$_d(2, *, r)$ *(and* WBF-PURE$_s(2, *, r)$*).*

Open Problem 52. *Find the complexities of the following problems, where $m \in \{2, 3, \ldots, *\}$ and $r \in \{1, 2, \ldots, *\}$:*

(1) BC-PURE$_d(m, *, r)$ *(and* BC-PURE$_s(m, *, r)$*);*
(2) WBC-PURE$_d(m, *, r)$ *(and* WBC-PURE$_s(m, *, r)$*).*

6   Payoff-Dominant Equilibria

Upper bounds and completeness results are presented in Subsects. 6.1 and 6.2, respectively.

6.1   Upper Bounds

We show:

Proposition 2 (Upper Bounds for Payoff-Dominant Equilibria). *Let $m \in \{2, 3, \ldots\}$, $k \in \{1, 2, \ldots\}$ and $r \in \{1, 2, \ldots, *\}$. Then, we have:*

(1) WBF-PDE$_d(m, k, r) \in \mathcal{P}$.
(2) BF-PDE$_d(*, k, r) \in \Theta_2^P$.
(3) WBF-PDE$_d(*, k, r) \in \Delta_2^P$.
(4) BF-PDE$_d(*, *, r) \in \Theta_3^P$.
(5) WBF-PDE$_d(*, *, r) \in \Delta_3^P$.

Proof. Consider a query-based algorithm A, taking as input the WBFG $\Gamma = \langle m, k, r, (F_i)_{i \in [m]} \rangle$:

---

1. For each player $i \in [m]$, compute $\mu_i = \max_{\mathbf{s} \in \mathcal{PE}(\Gamma)} U_i(\mathbf{s})$ by a binary search using queries of the kind:

    (Q_1) "Does Γ have a pure equilibrium $\mathbf{s}$ such that $U_i(\mathbf{s}) \geq \ell$?"

2. Output the answer (YES or NO) returned to the query:

    (Q_2) "Does Γ have a pure equilibrium $\mathbf{s}$ such that for each player $i \in [m]$, $U_i(\mathbf{s}) = \mu_i$?"

Clearly, the algorithm A uses a polynomial number of queries of the kind (Q_1) or (Q_2). We proceed to establish upper bounds on the time complexity of A in each case:

(1) With m and k fixed, Case (1) in Proposition 1 implies that each query (Q_1) and (Q_2) is a $\mathcal{P}$-query. Hence, WBF-PDE$_d(m, k, r) \in \mathcal{P}^{\mathcal{P}} = \mathcal{P}$.

(2) With k fixed, Case (2) in Proposition 1 implies that each query (Q_1) and (Q_2) is an $\mathcal{NP}$-query. Since there are no weights and $r \in \{1, 2, \ldots, *\}$, the maximum payoff is $\mathcal{O}(m)$. So, the total number of queries is $\mathcal{O}(\lg m)$. Hence, BF-PDE$_d(*, k, r) \in \mathcal{P}^{\mathcal{NP}[\lg m]} = \Theta_2^P$.

(3) With k fixed, Case (2) in Proposition 1 implies that each query (Q_1) and (Q_2) is an $\mathcal{NP}$-query. Hence, WBF-PDE$_d(*, k, r) \in \mathcal{P}^{\mathcal{NP}} = \Delta_2^P$.

(4) Case (3) in Proposition 1 implies that each query (Q_1) and (Q_2) is a Σ_2^P-query. Since there are no weights and $r \in \{1, 2, \ldots, *\}$, the maximum payoff is $\mathcal{O}(m)$. So, the total number of queries is $\mathcal{O}(\lg m)$. So, BF-PDE$_d(*, *, r) \in \mathcal{P}^{\Sigma_2^P[\lg m]} = \Theta_3^P$.

(5) Case (3) in Proposition 1 implies that each query (Q_1) and (Q_2) is a Σ_2^P-query. Hence, WBF-PDE$_d(*, *, r) \in \mathcal{P}^{\Sigma_2^P} = \Delta_3^P$.

The proof is now complete.

6.2   Completeness Results

We show:

Theorem 4 (Completeness Results for Payoff-Dominant Equilibria). *We have:*

(1) WBF-PDE$_d(*, k, *)$ *is* Δ_2^P*-complete for* $k \in \{1, 2, \ldots\}$.
(2) BF-PDE$_d(*, k, r)$ *is* Θ_2^P*-complete for* $k \in \{1, 2, \ldots\}$ *and* $r \in \{1, 2, \ldots, *\}$.
(3) WBF-PDE$_d(m, *, *)$ *is* Δ_3^P*-complete for* $m \in \{3, 4, \ldots, *\}$.
(4) BF-PDE$_d(m, *, *)$ *is* Θ_3^P*-complete for* $m \in \{3, 4, \ldots, *\}$.

Proof. We consider each case separately.

<u>Case(1)</u>: Membership in Δ_2^P follows from Case (3) in Proposition 2. For Δ_2^P-hardness, it suffices to prove that WBF-PDE$_d(*, 1, *)$ is Δ_2^P-hard. Towards this end, we provide a polynomial time reduction from Δ_2-QBF to WBF-PDE$_d(*, 1, *)$.

Consider a propositional formula $H(\mathbf{x})$ with $\mathbf{x} = \langle x_1, \ldots, x_n \rangle$. Assume, without loss of generality, that $H(0^{n-1}1) = 1$. Construct a weighted $(n + 4, 1, n)$-boolean formula game Γ_H as follows, where $\mathbf{z} = \langle z_1, z_2, z_3, z_4 \rangle$:

Player	Variable	Boolean formulas	Weights
$i \in [n]$	x_i	$f_i(\mathbf{x}, \mathbf{z}) = 0$	$\alpha_i = 1$
$n+1$	z_1	$f_{n+1}(\mathbf{x}, \mathbf{z}) = \mathsf{H}(\mathbf{x}) \bigvee (z_1 \oplus z_2)$	$\alpha_{n+1} = 1$
$n+2$	z_2	$f_{n+1}(\mathbf{x}, \mathbf{z}) = \mathsf{H}(\mathbf{x}) \bigvee (z_1 \oplus z_2 \oplus 1)$	$\alpha_{n+2} = 1$
$n+3$	z_3	$f_{n+3,i}(\mathbf{x}, \mathbf{z}) = x_i,\ i \in [n]$	$\alpha_{n+3,i} = 2^{n-i},\ i \in [n]$
$n+4$	z_4	$f_{n+4}(\mathbf{x}, \mathbf{z}) = x_n$	$\alpha_{n+4} = 1$

We note that the payoffs of all players $i \in [n]$ are constant; the payoffs of players $n+3$ and $n+4$ are independent of their strategies. Hence, neither players $i \in [n]$ nor players $n+3$ and $n+4$ matter for a pure equilibrium. In the sequel, we use $\mathbf{a}$ and $\mathbf{b}$ to denote vectors of values for the vectors $\mathbf{x}$ and $\mathbf{z}$ of variables, respectively. We prove:

Lemma 4. *The following conditions hold:*

(C.1) *Consider a vector* $\mathbf{a} \in \{0,1\}^n$ *such that* $\mathsf{H}(\mathbf{a}) = 1$. *Then, for all vectors* $\mathbf{b} \in \{0,1\}^4$, $(\mathbf{a}, \mathbf{b})$ *is a pure equilibrium for* Γ_{H} *with payoff vector*

$$\mathsf{U}(\mathbf{a}, \mathbf{b}) = \left\langle \underbrace{0, \ldots, 0}_{n}, 1, 1, \sum_{j \in [n]} a_j \cdot 2^{n-j}, a_n \right\rangle.$$

(C.2) *Consider a vector* $\mathbf{a} \in \{0,1\}^n$ *such that* $\mathsf{H}(\mathbf{a}) = 0$. *Then, for all vectors* $\mathbf{b} \in \{0,1\}^4$, $(\mathbf{a}, \mathbf{b})$ *is not a pure equilibrium for* Γ_{H}.

(C.3) $\mathsf{H}(\mathbf{x}) \in \Delta_2$-QBF *if and only if* Γ_{H} *has a payoff-dominant equilibrium.*

Proof. We start with Condition (C.1). We only need to consider players $n+1$ and $n+2$. Since $\mathsf{H}(\mathbf{a}) = 1$, $\mathsf{U}_{n+1}(\mathbf{a}, \mathbf{b}) = \mathsf{U}_{n+2}(\mathbf{a}, \mathbf{b}) = 1$, which cannot be further increased. Hence, $\langle \mathbf{a}, \mathbf{b} \rangle$ is a pure equilibrium for Γ_{H} with payoff vector

$$\mathsf{U}(\mathbf{a}, \mathbf{b}) = \left\langle \underbrace{0, \ldots, 0}_{n}, 1, 1, \sum_{j \in [n]} a_j \cdot 2^{n-j}, a_n \right\rangle.$$

We continue with Condition (C.2). Since $\mathsf{H}(\mathbf{a}) = 0$, $\mathsf{U}_{n+1}(\mathbf{a}, \mathbf{b}) = b_1 \oplus b_2$ and $\mathsf{U}_{n+2}(\mathbf{a}, \mathbf{b}) = b_1 \oplus b_2 \oplus 1$. We proceed by case analysis on the value of $b_1 \oplus b_2$.

- If $b_1 \oplus b_2 = 0$, then player $n+1$ can increase her payoff $\mathsf{U}_{n+1}(\mathbf{a}, \mathbf{b}) = 0$ by flipping b_1.
- If $b_1 \oplus b_2 = 1$, then player $n+2$ can increase her payoff $\mathsf{U}_{n+2}(\mathbf{a}, \mathbf{b}) = 0$ by flipping b_2.

Hence, $(\mathbf{a}, \mathbf{b})$ is *not* a pure equilibrium.

Finally, for Condition (C.3), assume first that $\mathsf{H}(\mathbf{x}) \in \Delta_2$-QBF. Fix the lmax vector $\mathbf{a} \in \{0,1\}^n$ such that $\mathsf{H}(\mathbf{a}) = 1$. Since $\mathsf{H}(\mathbf{x}) \in \Delta_2$-QBF, it follows that

$a_n = 1$. Condition (C.1) implies that $(\mathbf{a}, \mathbf{b})$ is a pure equilibrium for Γ_H with payoff vector

$$U(\mathbf{a}, \mathbf{b}) = \left\langle \underbrace{0, \ldots, 0}_{n}, 1, 1, \sum_{j \in [n]} a_j \cdot 2^{n-j}, a_n \right\rangle.$$

We now prove that $(\mathbf{a}, \mathbf{b})$ is a payoff-dominant equilibrium for Γ_H. Fix any pure equilibrium $(\mathbf{a}', \mathbf{b}')$ for Γ_H. By Condition (C.2), $H(\mathbf{a}') = 1$. Hence, by Condition (C.1),

$$U(\mathbf{a}', \mathbf{b}') = \left\langle \underbrace{0, \ldots, 0}_{n}, 1, 1, \sum_{j \in [n]} a'_j \cdot 2^{n-j}, a'_n \right\rangle.$$

Clearly, we only need to consider players $n + 3$ and $n + 4$.

- Since $\mathbf{a}$ is lmax among all vectors $\mathbf{a}'' \in \{0, 1\}^n$ such that $H(\mathbf{a}'') = 1$, it follows that $\mathbf{a} \geq_{le} \mathbf{a}'$. Hence, $\sum_{j \in [n]} a_j \cdot 2^{n-j} \geq \sum_{j \in [n]} a'_j \cdot 2^{n-j}$, and player $n + 3$ has a dominant payoff in $(\mathbf{a}, \mathbf{b})$.
- Since $a_n = 1$, $a_n \geq a'_n$, and player $n + 4$ has a dominant payoff in $(\mathbf{a}, \mathbf{b})$.

It follows that $(\mathbf{a}, \mathbf{b})$ is a payoff-dominant equilibrium for Γ_H.

Assume now that $H(\mathbf{x}) \notin \Delta_2\text{-QBF}$. Assume, by way of contradiction, that Γ_H has a payoff-dominant equilibrium $(\mathbf{a}, \mathbf{b})$. By Condition (C.2), $H(\mathbf{a}) = 1$, and by Condition (C.1),

$$U(\mathbf{a}, \mathbf{b}) = \left\langle \underbrace{0, \ldots, 0}_{n}, 1, 1, \sum_{j \in [n]} a_j \cdot 2^{n-j}, a_n \right\rangle.$$

Again, by Condition (C.1), $(\tilde{\mathbf{a}}, \mathbf{b})$ is a pure equilibrium for every vector $\tilde{\mathbf{a}} \in \{0, 1\}^n$ with $H(\tilde{\mathbf{a}}) = 1$. Since player $n + 3$ has a dominant payoff in $(\mathbf{a}, \mathbf{b})$, this implies that $\mathbf{a}$ is the lexmax solution to $H(\mathbf{a}) = 1$.

In this case, due to the assumption that $H(\mathbf{x}) \notin \Delta_2\text{-QBF}$, it follows that $a_n = 0$. Hence, player $n + 4$ has payoff 0 in $(\mathbf{a}, \mathbf{b})$.

Since $H(0^{n-1}1) = 1$, it follows, by Condition (C.1), that $(0^{n-1}1, \mathbf{b})$ is also a pure equilibrium with payoff vector

$$U(0^{n-1}1, \mathbf{b}) = \left\langle \underbrace{0, \ldots, 0}_{n}, 1, 1, 1, 1 \right\rangle;$$

thus, player $n + 4$ does *not* have a dominant payoff in $(\mathbf{a}, \mathbf{b})$. A contradiction.

Case(2): Membership in Θ_2^P follows from Case (2) in Proposition 2. We prepare the reader that the proof of Θ_2^P-hardness follows the same structure as the corresponding proof for Case (1). The main difference in the reduction is that player $n+3$ is replaced by players $(n+3, \ell)$, with $\ell \in [m]$, with formulas $(|\mathbf{x}| \geq \ell)$. We continue with the details of the formal proof.

For Θ_2^P-hardness, it suffices to prove that $\mathsf{BF\text{-}PDE}_d(*, 1, *)$ is Θ_2^P-hard. Towards this end, we provide a polynomial time reduction from $\Theta_2\text{-}\mathsf{QBF}$ to $\mathsf{BF\text{-}PDE}_d(*, 1, *)$.

Consider a propositional formula $\mathsf{H}(\mathbf{x})$ with $\mathbf{x} = \langle x_1, \ldots, x_n \rangle$ and an integer $m \geq 1$. Assume, without loss of generality, that $\mathsf{H}(0^{n-1}1) = 1$. Construct a weighted $(n + m + 3, 1, n)$-boolean formula game $\Gamma_{\langle \mathsf{H}, m \rangle}$ as follows, where $\mathbf{z} = \langle z_1, z_2, z_{3,1}, \ldots, z_{3,m}, z_4 \rangle$:

Player	Variable	Boolean formulas
$i \in [n]$	x_i	$f_i(\mathbf{x}, \mathbf{z}) = 0$
$n + 1$	z_1	$f_{n+1}(\mathbf{x}, \mathbf{z}) = (\mathsf{H}(\mathbf{x}) \wedge (|\mathbf{x}| \leq m)) \vee (z_1 \oplus z_2)$
$n + 2$	z_2	$f_{n+1}(\mathbf{x}, \mathbf{z}) = (\mathsf{H}(\mathbf{x}) \wedge (|\mathbf{x}| \leq m)) \vee (z_1 \oplus z_2 \oplus 1)$
$(n + 3, \ell)$, $\ell \in [m]$	$z_{3,\ell}$, $\ell \in [m]$	$f_{n+3,\ell}(\mathbf{x}, \mathbf{z}) = (|\mathbf{x}| \geq \ell)$, $\ell \in [m]$
$n + 4$	z_4	$f_{n+4}(\mathbf{x}, \mathbf{z}) = x_n$

We note that the payoffs of all players $i \in [n]$ are constant; the payoffs of players $(n + 3, \ell)$ with $\ell \in [m]$ and $n + 4$ are independent of their strategies. Hence, neither players $i \in [n]$ nor players $(n + 3, \ell)$ with $\ell \in [m]$ and $n + 4$ matter for a pure equilibrium. In the sequel, we use $\mathbf{a}$ and $\mathbf{b}$ to denote vectors of values for the vectors $\mathbf{x}$ and $\mathbf{z}$ of variables, respectively. We prove:

Lemma 5. *The following conditions hold:*

(C.1) *Consider a vector* $\mathbf{a} \in \{0, 1\}^n$ *such that* $\mathsf{H}(\mathbf{a}) = 1$ *and* $|\mathbf{a}| \leq m$. *Then, for all vectors* $\mathbf{b} \in \{0, 1\}^{m+3}$, $(\mathbf{a}, \mathbf{b})$ *is a pure equilibrium for* $\Gamma_{\langle \mathsf{H}, m \rangle}$ *with payoff vector*

$$U(\mathbf{a}, \mathbf{b}) = \Big\langle \underbrace{0, \ldots, 0}_{n}, 1, 1, \underbrace{0, \ldots, 0}_{m - |\mathbf{a}|}, \underbrace{1, \ldots, 1}_{|\mathbf{a}|}, a_n \Big\rangle.$$

(C.2) *Consider a vector* $\mathbf{a} \in \{0, 1\}^n$ *such that* $\mathsf{H}(\mathbf{a}) = 0$ *or* $|\mathbf{a}| > m$. *Then, for all vectors* $\mathbf{b} \in \{0, 1\}^{m+3}$, $(\mathbf{a}, \mathbf{b})$ *is not a pure equilibrium for* $\Gamma_{\langle \mathsf{H}, m \rangle}$.

(C.3) $\langle \mathsf{H}(\mathbf{x}), 1^m \rangle \in \Theta_2\text{-}\mathsf{QBF}$ *if and only if* $\Gamma_{\langle \mathsf{H}, m \rangle}$ *has a payoff-dominant equilibrium*.

Proof. We start with Condition (C.1). We only need to consider players $n + 1$ and $n + 2$. Since $\mathsf{H}(\mathbf{a}) = 1$ and $|\mathbf{a}| \leq m$, $U_{n+1}(\mathbf{a}, \mathbf{b}) = U_{n+2}(\mathbf{a}, \mathbf{b}) = 1$, which cannot be further increased. Hence, $\langle \mathbf{a}, \mathbf{b} \rangle$ is a pure equilibrium for $\Gamma_{\langle \mathsf{H}, m \rangle}$ with payoff vector

$$U(\mathbf{a}, \mathbf{b}) = \Big\langle \underbrace{0, \ldots, 0}_{n}, 1, 1, \underbrace{0, \ldots, 0}_{m - |\mathbf{a}|}, \underbrace{1, \ldots, 1}_{|\mathbf{a}|}, a_n \Big\rangle.$$

We continue with Condition (C.2). Since $H(\mathbf{a}) = 0$ or $|\mathbf{a}| > m$, $\mathsf{U}_{n+1}(\mathbf{a}, \mathbf{b}) = b_1 \oplus b_2$ and $\mathsf{U}_{n+2}(\mathbf{a}, \mathbf{b}) = b_1 \oplus b_2 \oplus 1$. We proceed by case analysis on the value of $b_1 \oplus b_2$.

- If $b_1 \oplus b_2 = 0$, then player $n + 1$ can increase her payoff $\mathsf{U}_{n+1}(\mathbf{a}, \mathbf{b}) = 0$ by flipping b_1.
- If $b_1 \oplus b_2 = 1$, then player $n + 2$ can increase her payoff $\mathsf{U}_{n+2}(\mathbf{a}, \mathbf{b}) = 0$ by flipping b_2.

Hence, $(\mathbf{a}, \mathbf{b})$ is *not* a pure equilibrium.

Finally, for Condition (C.3), assume first that $\langle H(\mathbf{x}), 1^m \rangle \in \Theta_2\text{-QBF}$. Fix the lmax vector $\mathbf{a} \in \{0,1\}^n$ such that $H(\mathbf{a}) = 1$ and $|\mathbf{a}| \le m$. Since $\langle H(\mathbf{x}), 1^m \rangle \in \Theta_2\text{-QBF}$, it follows that $a_n = 1$. Condition (C.1) implies that $(\mathbf{a}, \mathbf{b})$ is a pure equilibrium for $\Gamma_{\langle H, m \rangle}$ with payoff vector

$$\mathsf{U}(\mathbf{a}, \mathbf{b}) = \Big\langle \underbrace{0, \ldots, 0}_{n}, 1, 1, \underbrace{0, \ldots, 0}_{m - |\mathbf{a}|}, \underbrace{1, \ldots, 1}_{|\mathbf{a}|}, a_n \Big\rangle.$$

We now prove that $(\mathbf{a}, \mathbf{b})$ is a payoff-dominant equilibrium for $\Gamma_{\langle H, m \rangle}$. Fix any pure equilibrium $(\mathbf{a}', \mathbf{b}')$ for $\Gamma_{\langle H, m \rangle}$. By Condition (C.2), $H(\mathbf{a}') = 1$. Hence, by Condition (C.1),

$$\mathsf{U}(\mathbf{a}', \mathbf{b}') = \Big\langle \underbrace{0, \ldots, 0}_{n}, 1, 1, \underbrace{0, \ldots, 0}_{m - |\mathbf{a}'|}, \underbrace{1, \ldots, 1}_{|\mathbf{a}'|}, a_n' \Big\rangle.$$

Clearly, we only need to consider players $(n + 3, \ell)$ with $\ell \in [m]$ and $n + 4$.

- Since $\mathbf{a}$ is lmax among all vectors $\mathbf{a}'' \in \{0,1\}^n$ such that $H(\mathbf{a}'') = 1$ and $|\mathbf{a}''| \le m$, it follows that $\mathbf{a} \ge_{le} \mathbf{a}'$. Hence, for each player $(n + 3, \ell)$ with $\ell \in [m]$, $\mathsf{U}_{(n+3, \ell)}(\mathbf{a}', \mathbf{b}') = 1$ only if $\mathsf{U}_{(n+3, \ell)}(\mathbf{a}, \mathbf{b}) = 1$, and player $(n + 3, \ell)$ has a dominant payoff in $(\mathbf{a}, \mathbf{b})$.
- Since $a_n = 1$, $a_n \ge a_n'$, and player $n + 4$ has a dominant payoff in $(\mathbf{a}, \mathbf{b})$.

It follows that $(\mathbf{a}, \mathbf{b})$ is a payoff-dominant equilibrium for $\Gamma_{\langle H, m \rangle}$.

Assume now that $\langle H(\mathbf{x}), 1^m \rangle \notin \Theta_2\text{-QBF}$. Assume, by way of contradiction, that $\Gamma_{\langle H, m \rangle}$ has a payoff-dominant equilibrium $(\mathbf{a}, \mathbf{b})$. By Condition (C.2), $H(\mathbf{a}) = 1$ and $|\mathbf{a}| \le m$, and by Condition (C.1),

$$\mathsf{U}(\mathbf{a}, \mathbf{b}) = \Big\langle \underbrace{0, \ldots, 0}_{n}, 1, 1, \underbrace{0, \ldots, 0}_{m - |\mathbf{a}|}, \underbrace{1, \ldots, 1}_{|\mathbf{a}|}, a_n \Big\rangle.$$

Again, by Condition (C.1), $(\tilde{\mathbf{a}}, \mathbf{b})$ is a pure equilibrium for $\Gamma_{\langle H, m \rangle}$, for every vector $\tilde{\mathbf{a}} \in \{0,1\}^n$ with $H(\tilde{\mathbf{a}}) = 1$ and $|\tilde{\mathbf{a}}| \le m$. Since each player $(n + 3, \ell)$ with $\ell \in [m]$ has a dominant payoff in $(\mathbf{a}, \mathbf{b})$, this implies that $\mathbf{a}$ is the lexmax solution to $H(\mathbf{a}) = 1$ and $|\mathbf{a}| \le m$.

In this case, due to the assumption that $\langle H(\mathbf{x}), 1^m \rangle \notin \Theta_2\text{-QBF}$, it follows that $a_n = 0$. Hence, player $n + 4$ has payoff 0 in $(\tilde{\mathbf{a}}, \mathbf{b})$.

Since $H(0^{n-1}1) = 1$, it follows, by Condition (C.1), that $(0^{n-1}1, \mathbf{b})$ is also a pure equilibrium for $\Gamma_{\langle H, m \rangle}$ with payoff vector

$$U(0^{n-1}1, \mathbf{b}) = \Big\langle \underbrace{0, \ldots, 0}_{n}, 1, 1, \underbrace{0, \ldots, 0}_{m-1}, 1, 1 \Big\rangle;$$

thus, player $n + 4$ does *not* have a dominant payoff in $(\mathbf{a}, \mathbf{b})$. A contradiction.

Case(3): Membership in Δ_3^P follows from Case (5) in Proposition 2. For Δ_3^P-hardness, it suffices to prove that $\text{WBF-PDE}_d(3, *, *)$ is Δ_3^P-hard. Towards this end, we give a polynomial time reduction from $\Delta_3\text{-RQBF}$ to $\text{WBF-PDE}_d(3, *, *)$.

Consider a propositional formula $H(\mathbf{x}, \mathbf{y}) \in R$ with $\mathbf{x} = \langle x_1, \ldots, x_n \rangle$ and $\mathbf{y} = \langle y_1, \ldots, y_n \rangle$. Assume, without loss of generality, that for every vector $\mathbf{b} \in \{0, 1\}^n$, $H(0^{n-1}1, \mathbf{b}) = 1$. Construct a weighted $(3, n, n+1)$-boolean formula game Γ_H as follows, where $\mathbf{z} = \langle z_1, \ldots, z_n \rangle$:

Player	Variables	Boolean formulas	Weights
1	$\mathbf{x}$	$f_1(\mathbf{x}, \mathbf{y}, \mathbf{z}) = 0$	$\alpha_1 = 1$
2	$\mathbf{y}$	$f_{2,0}(\mathbf{x}, \mathbf{y}, \mathbf{z}) = H(\mathbf{x}, \mathbf{y}) \oplus H(\mathbf{x}, \mathbf{z})$	$\alpha_{2,0} = 1$
		$f_{2,j}(\mathbf{x}, \mathbf{y}, \mathbf{z}) = x_j$ for $j \in [n]$	$\alpha_{2,j} = 2^{n-j}$ for $j \in [n]$
3	$\mathbf{z}$	$f_{3,1}(\mathbf{x}, \mathbf{y}, \mathbf{z}) = H(\mathbf{x}, \mathbf{y}) \oplus H(\mathbf{x}, \mathbf{z}) \oplus 1$	$\alpha_{3,1} = 1$
		$f_{3,2}(\mathbf{x}, \mathbf{y}, \mathbf{z}) = x_n$	$\alpha_{3,2} = 1$

We note that player 1 does not matter for a pure equilibrium since her payoff is constant. Furthermore, we note that

$$U_2(\mathbf{x}, \mathbf{y}, \mathbf{z}) = \sum_{j \in \{0, 1, \ldots, n\}} \alpha_{2,j} \cdot f_{2,j}(\mathbf{x}, \mathbf{y}, \mathbf{z}),$$

while player 2 can influence only $f_{2,0}$. Likewise,

$$U_3(\mathbf{x}, \mathbf{y}, \mathbf{z}) = f_{3,1}(\mathbf{x}, \mathbf{y}, \mathbf{z}) + f_{3,2}(\mathbf{x}, \mathbf{y}, \mathbf{z}),$$

while player 3 can influence only $f_{3,1}$. In the sequel, we use $\mathbf{a}$, $\mathbf{b}$ and $\mathbf{c}$ to denote vectors of values for the vectors $\mathbf{x}$, $\mathbf{y}$ and $\mathbf{z}$, respectively. We prove:

Lemma 6. *The following conditions hold:*

(C.1) *Consider a vector* $\mathbf{a} \in \{0, 1\}^n$ *such that for all vectors* $\mathbf{b} \in \{0, 1\}^n$, $H(\mathbf{a}, \mathbf{b}) = 1$. *Then, for every pair* $(\mathbf{b}, \mathbf{c})$ *with* $\mathbf{b}, \mathbf{c} \in \{0, 1\}^n$, $(\mathbf{a}, \mathbf{b}, \mathbf{c})$ *is a pure equilibrium for* Γ_H *with payoff vector*

$$U(\mathbf{a}, \mathbf{b}, \mathbf{c}) = \Big\langle 0, \sum_{j \in [n]} a_j \cdot 2^{n-j}, 1 + a_n \Big\rangle.$$

(C.2) *Consider a vector* $\mathbf{a} \in \{0,1\}^n$ *such that there is a vector* $\mathbf{b}_\mathbf{a}^0 \in \{0,1\}^n$ *with* $H(\mathbf{a}, \mathbf{b}_\mathbf{a}^0) = 0$. *Then, for every pair* $(\mathbf{b}, \mathbf{c})$ *with* $\mathbf{b}, \mathbf{c} \in \{0,1\}^n$, $(\mathbf{a}, \mathbf{b}, \mathbf{c})$ *is not a pure equilibrium for* Γ_H.

(C.3) $H(\mathbf{x}, \mathbf{y}) \in \Delta_3$-RQBF *if and only if* Γ_H *has a payoff-dominant equilibrium.*

Proof. For Condition (C.1), fix an arbitrary pair $(\mathbf{b}, \mathbf{c})$. We examine players 2 and 3:

– For player 2, fix any arbitrary strategy $\mathbf{b}' \in \{0,1\}^n$. Recall that player 2 can only influence her formula $f_{2,0}$. The assumption on $\mathbf{a}$ implies that

$$f_2(\mathbf{a}, \mathbf{b}', \mathbf{c}) = H(\mathbf{a}, \mathbf{b}') \oplus H(\mathbf{a}, \mathbf{c}) \;=\; 1 \oplus 1 \;=\; 0.$$

So, player 2 cannot unilaterally increase the value $f_{2,0}(\mathbf{a}, \mathbf{b}, \mathbf{c}) = 0$.

– For player 3, fix any arbitrary strategy $\mathbf{c}' \in \{0,1\}^n$. Recall that player 3 can only influence her formula $f_{3,1}$. The assumption on $\mathbf{a}$ implies that

$$f_3(\mathbf{a}, \mathbf{b}, \mathbf{c}') = H(\mathbf{a}, \mathbf{b}) \oplus H(\mathbf{a}, \mathbf{c}') \oplus 1 \;=\; 1 \oplus 1 \oplus 1 \;=\; 1.$$

So, player 3 cannot unilaterally increase the value $f_{3,1}(\mathbf{a}, \mathbf{b}, \mathbf{c}) = 1$.

It follows that $(\mathbf{a}, \mathbf{b}, \mathbf{c})$ is a pure equilibrium with payoff vector

$$U(\mathbf{a}, \mathbf{b}, \mathbf{c}) = \left\langle 0, \sum_{j \in [n]} a_j \cdot 2^{n-j}, 1 + a_n \right\rangle.$$

For Condition (C.2), fix an arbitrary pair $(\mathbf{b}, \mathbf{c})$. We proceed by case analysis on the pair of values $H(\mathbf{a}, \mathbf{b})$ and $H(\mathbf{a}, \mathbf{c})$.

– Assume first that $H(\mathbf{a}, \mathbf{b}) = H(\mathbf{a}, \mathbf{c}) = 0$. Then,

$$f_{2,0}(\mathbf{a}, \mathbf{b}, \mathbf{c}) = H(\mathbf{a}, \mathbf{b}) \oplus H(\mathbf{a}, \mathbf{c}) \;=\; 0 \oplus 0 \;=\; 0.$$

However, since $H(\mathbf{x}, \mathbf{y}) \in R$, there is a vector $\mathbf{b}_\mathbf{a}^1 \in \{0,1\}^n$ with

$$f_{2,0}(\mathbf{a}, \mathbf{b}_\mathbf{a}^1, \mathbf{c}) = H(\mathbf{a}, \mathbf{b}_\mathbf{a}^1) \oplus H(\mathbf{a}, \mathbf{c}) \;=\; 1 \oplus 0 \;=\; 1.$$

So, player 2 can increase $f_{2,0}(\mathbf{a}, \mathbf{b}, \mathbf{c})$ by changing her strategy $\mathbf{b}$ to $\mathbf{b}_\mathbf{a}^1$.

– Assume now that $H(\mathbf{a}, \mathbf{b}) = 0$ and $H(\mathbf{a}, \mathbf{c}) = 1$. (The case where $H(\mathbf{a}, \mathbf{b}) = 1$ and $H(\mathbf{a}, \mathbf{c}) = 0$ is symmetric.) Then,

$$f_{3,1}(\mathbf{a}, \mathbf{b}, \mathbf{c}) = H(\mathbf{a}, \mathbf{b}) \oplus H(\mathbf{a}, \mathbf{c}) \oplus 1 \;=\; 0 \oplus 1 \oplus 1 \;=\; 0.$$

However, by assumption on $\mathbf{a}$,

$$f_{3,1}(\mathbf{a}, \mathbf{b}, \mathbf{b}_\mathbf{a}^0) = H(\mathbf{a}, \mathbf{b}) \oplus H(\mathbf{a}, \mathbf{b}_\mathbf{a}^0) \oplus 1 \;=\; 0 \oplus 0 \oplus 1 \;=\; 1.$$

So, player 3 can increase $f_{3,1}(\mathbf{a}, \mathbf{b}, \mathbf{c})$ by changing her strategy $\mathbf{c}$ to $\mathbf{b}_\mathbf{a}^0$.

– Assume finally that $H(\mathbf{a}, \mathbf{b}) = H(\mathbf{a}, \mathbf{c}) = 1$. Then,

$$f_{2,0}(\mathbf{a}, \mathbf{b}, \mathbf{c}) = H(\mathbf{a}, \mathbf{b}) \oplus H(\mathbf{a}, \mathbf{c}) \quad = \quad 1 \oplus 1 \quad = \quad 0.$$

However, by assumption on $\mathbf{a}$,

$$f_{2,0}(\mathbf{a}, \mathbf{b}_{\mathbf{a}}^0, \mathbf{c}) = H(\mathbf{a}, \mathbf{b}_{\mathbf{a}}^0) \oplus H(\mathbf{a}, \mathbf{c}) \quad = \quad 0 \oplus 1 \quad = \quad 1.$$

So, player 2 can increase $f_{2,0}(\mathbf{a}, \mathbf{b}, \mathbf{c})$ by changing her strategy $\mathbf{b}$ to $\mathbf{b}_{\mathbf{a}}^0$.

The case analysis implies that $\langle \mathbf{a}, \mathbf{b}, \mathbf{c} \rangle$ is *not* a pure equilibrium for Γ_H.

For Condition (C.3), assume first that $H(\mathbf{x}, \mathbf{y}) \in \Delta_3\text{-RQBF}$. Choose the lmax $\mathbf{a} \in \{0, 1\}^n$ such that for all vectors $\mathbf{b} \in \{0, 1\}^n$, $H(\mathbf{a}, \mathbf{b}) = 1$ By definition of $\Delta_3\text{-RQBF}$, it follows that $a_n = 1$. By Condition (C.1), it follows that for every pair $(\mathbf{b}, \mathbf{c})$, $(\mathbf{a}, \mathbf{b}, \mathbf{c})$ is a pure equilibrium for Γ_H with payoff vector

$$U(\mathbf{a}, \mathbf{b}, \mathbf{c}) = \left\langle 0, \sum_{j \in [n]} a_j \cdot 2^{n-j}, 1 + a_n \right\rangle.$$

We now prove that $(\mathbf{a}, \mathbf{b}, \mathbf{c})$ is a payoff-dominant equilibrium for Γ_H. Consider any pure equilibrium $(\mathbf{a}', \mathbf{b}', \mathbf{c}')$ for Γ_H. Condition (C.2) implies that for all vectors $\mathbf{b}'' \in \{0, 1\}^n$, $H(\mathbf{a}, \mathbf{b}'') = 1$. Condition (C.1) implies that the payoff vector for $(\mathbf{a}', \mathbf{b}', \mathbf{c}')$ is

$$U(\mathbf{a}', \mathbf{b}', \mathbf{c}') = \left\langle 0, \sum_{j \in [n]} a_j' \cdot 2^{n-j}, 1 + a_n' \right\rangle.$$

We only need to consider players 2 and 3.

– Since $\mathbf{a}$ is the lmax vector such that for all vectors $\mathbf{b} \in \{0, 1\}^n$, $H(\mathbf{a}, \mathbf{b}) = 1$, it follows that $\mathbf{a} \geq_{le} \mathbf{a}'$. Hence, $\sum_{j \in [n]} a_j \cdot 2^{n-j} \geq \sum_{j \in [n]} a_j' \cdot 2^{n-j}$, and player 2 has a dominant payoff in $(\mathbf{a}, \mathbf{b}, \mathbf{c})$.
– Since $a_n = 1$, $a_n \geq a_n'$, and player 3 has a dominant payoff in $(\mathbf{a}, \mathbf{b}, \mathbf{c})$.

It follows that

$$\left\langle 0, \sum_{j \in [n]} a_j \cdot 2^{n-j}, 1 + a_n \right\rangle \geq_{cw} \left\langle 0, \sum_{j \in [n]} a_j' \cdot 2^{n-j}, 1 + a_n' \right\rangle.$$

Since $(\mathbf{a}', \mathbf{b}', \mathbf{c}')$ was chosen as an arbitrary pure equilibrium for Γ_H, this implies that $(\mathbf{a}, \mathbf{b}, \mathbf{c})$ is a payoff-dominant equilibrium for Γ_H.

Assume now that $H(\mathbf{x}, \mathbf{y}) \notin \Delta_3\text{-RQBF}$. Assume, by way of contradiction, that Γ_H has a payoff-dominant equilibrium $(\mathbf{a}, \mathbf{b}, \mathbf{c})$.

By Condition (C.2), $H(\mathbf{a}, \mathbf{b}') = 1$ for all vectors $\mathbf{b}' \in \{0, 1\}^n$. By Condition (C.1),

$$U(\mathbf{a}, \mathbf{b}, \mathbf{c}) = \left\langle 0, \sum_{j \in [n]} a_j \cdot 2^{n-j}, 1 + a_n \right\rangle.$$

Again, by Condition (C.1), $(\widetilde{\mathbf{a}}, \mathbf{b}, \mathbf{c})$ is a pure equilibrium for Γ_H, for every vector $\widetilde{\mathbf{a}} \in \{0,1\}^n$ such that $H(\widetilde{\mathbf{a}}, \mathbf{b}') = 1$ for all vectors $\mathbf{b}' \in \{0,1\}^n$. Since player 2 has a dominant payoff in $(\mathbf{a}, \mathbf{b}, \mathbf{c})$, it follows that $\mathbf{a}$ is the lexmax solution to $H(\mathbf{a}, \mathbf{b}') = 1$ for all vectors $\mathbf{b}' \in \{0,1\}^n$.

In this case, due to the assumption that $H(\mathbf{x}, \mathbf{y}) \notin \Delta_3\text{-RQBF}$, it follows that $a_n = 0$. Hence, player 3 has payoff 1 in $(\mathbf{a}, \mathbf{b}, \mathbf{c})$.

Recall the assumption that for all vectors $\mathbf{b}' \in \{0,1\}^n$, $H(0^{n-1}1, \mathbf{b}') = 1$. By Condition (C.1), this implies that $\langle 0^{n-1}1, \mathbf{b}, \mathbf{c} \rangle$ is also a pure equilibrium for Γ_H with payoff vector $\langle 0, 1, 2 \rangle$. Hence, player 3 does *not* have a dominant payoff in $(\mathbf{a}, \mathbf{b}, \mathbf{c})$. A contradiction.

Case(4): Membership in Θ_3^P follows from Case (4) in Proposition 2. We prepare the reader that the corresponding proof of Θ_3^P-hardness follows the same structure as the corresponding proof for Case (3). The main difference in the reduction is that now player 1 has the formula $(|\mathbf{x}| \leq r)$ and player 2 has the formulas $f_{2,\ell} = (|\mathbf{x}| \geq \ell)$ with $\ell \in [r]$. We continue with the details of the formal proof.

For Θ_3^P-hardness, it suffices to prove that $\mathsf{BF\text{-}PDE}_d(3, *, *)$ is Θ_3^P-hard. Towards this end, we provide a polynomial time reduction from $\Theta_3\text{-RQBF}$ to $\mathsf{BF\text{-}PDE}_d(3, *, *)$.

Consider a propositional formula $H(\mathbf{x}, \mathbf{y}) \in R$ with $\mathbf{x} = \langle x_1, \ldots, x_n \rangle$ and $\mathbf{y} = \langle y_1, \ldots, y_n \rangle$, and an integer $r \geq 1$. Assume, without loss of generality, that for every vector $\mathbf{b} \in \{0,1\}^n$, $H(0^{n-1}1, \mathbf{b}) = 1$. Construct a $(3, n, r+1)$-boolean formula game $\Gamma_{\langle H, r \rangle}$ as follows, where $\mathbf{z} = \langle z_1, \ldots, z_n \rangle$:

Player	Variables	Boolean formulas
1	$\mathbf{x}$	$f_1(\mathbf{x}, \mathbf{y}, \mathbf{z}) = (|\mathbf{x}| \leq r)$
2	$\mathbf{y}$	$f_{2,0}(\mathbf{x}, \mathbf{y}, \mathbf{z}) = H(\mathbf{x}, \mathbf{y}) \oplus H(\mathbf{x}, \mathbf{z})$
		$f_{2,\ell}(\mathbf{x}, \mathbf{y}, \mathbf{z}) = (|\mathbf{x}| \geq \ell)$ for $\ell \in [r]$
3	$\mathbf{z}$	$f_{3,1}(\mathbf{x}, \mathbf{y}, \mathbf{z}) = H(\mathbf{x}, \mathbf{y}) \oplus H(\mathbf{x}, \mathbf{z}) \oplus 1$
		$f_{3,2}(\mathbf{x}, \mathbf{y}, \mathbf{z}) = x_n$

We note that

$$U_2(\mathbf{x}, \mathbf{y}, \mathbf{z}) = \sum_{\ell \in \{0,1,\ldots,r\}} f_{2,\ell}(\mathbf{x}, \mathbf{y}, \mathbf{z}),$$

while player 2 can influence only $f_{2,0}$. Likewise,

$$U_3(\mathbf{x}, \mathbf{y}, \mathbf{z}) = f_{3,1}(\mathbf{x}, \mathbf{y}, \mathbf{z}) + f_{3,2}(\mathbf{x}, \mathbf{y}, \mathbf{z}),$$

while player 3 can influence only $f_{3,1}$. We prove:

Lemma 7. *The following conditions hold:*

(C.1) *Consider a vector* $\mathbf{a} \in \{0,1\}^n$ *such that for all vectors* $\mathbf{b} \in \{0,1\}^n$, $H(\mathbf{a}, \mathbf{b}) = 1$ *and* $|\mathbf{a}| \leq r$. *Then, for every pair* $(\mathbf{b}, \mathbf{c})$ *with* $\mathbf{b}, \mathbf{c} \in \{0,1\}^n$, $(\mathbf{a}, \mathbf{b}, \mathbf{c})$ *is a pure equilibrium for* $\Gamma_{\langle H, r \rangle}$ *with payoff vector*

$$U(\mathbf{a}, \mathbf{b}, \mathbf{c}) = \langle 1, |\mathbf{a}|, 1 + a_n \rangle.$$

(C.2) *Consider a vector* $\mathbf{a} \in \{0,1\}^n$ *such that there is a vector* $\mathbf{b}_{\mathbf{a}}^0 \in \{0,1\}^n$ *with* $H(\mathbf{a}, \mathbf{b}_{\mathbf{a}}^0) = 0$ *or* $|\mathbf{a}| > r$. *Then, for every pair* $(\mathbf{b}, \mathbf{c})$ *with* $\mathbf{b}, \mathbf{c} \in \{0,1\}^n$, $(\mathbf{a}, \mathbf{b}, \mathbf{c})$ *is not a pure equilibrium for* $\Gamma_{\langle H, r \rangle}$.

(C.3) $H(\mathbf{x}, \mathbf{y}) \in \Theta_3\text{-RQBF}$ *if and only if* $\Gamma_{\langle H, r \rangle}$ *has a payoff-dominant equilibrium.*

Proof. For Condition (C.1), fix an arbitrary pair $(\mathbf{b}, \mathbf{c})$. We examine all players. For player 1, the assumption that $|\mathbf{a}| \leq r$ implies that $U_1(\mathbf{a}, \mathbf{b}, \mathbf{c}) = 1$, which cannot be further increased. For players 2 and 3, the proof follows exactly the proof for Condition (C.1) in Lemma 6.

It follows that $(\mathbf{a}, \mathbf{b}, \mathbf{c})$ is a pure equilibrium with payoff vector

$$U(\mathbf{a}, \mathbf{b}, \mathbf{c}) = \langle 1, |\mathbf{a}|, 1 + a_n \rangle.$$

For Condition (C.2), fix an arbitrary pair $(\mathbf{b}, \mathbf{c})$. If $|\mathbf{a}| > r$, then $U_1(\mathbf{a}, \mathbf{b}, \mathbf{c}) = 0$, and player 1 can unilaterally increase her payoff to 1 by changing her strategy $\mathbf{a}$ to a strategy $\mathbf{a}'$ with $|\mathbf{a}'| \leq r$; so, $(\mathbf{a}, \mathbf{b}, \mathbf{c})$ is *not* a pure equilibrium. So, assume that there is a vector $\mathbf{b}_{\mathbf{a}}^0 \in \{0,1\}^n$ with $H(\mathbf{a}, \mathbf{b}_{\mathbf{a}}^0) = 0$. From this point, the proof that $(\mathbf{a}, \mathbf{b}, \mathbf{c})$ is *not* a pure equilibrium for $\Gamma_{\langle H, r \rangle}$ follows exactly for Condition (C.1) in Lemma 6.

For Condition (C.3), assume first that $H(\mathbf{x}, \mathbf{y}) \in \Theta_3\text{-RQBF}$. Fix the lmax $\mathbf{a} \in \{0,1\}^n$ such that for all vectors $\mathbf{b} \in \{0,1\}^n$, $H(\mathbf{a}, \mathbf{b}) = 1$ By definition of $\Theta_3\text{-RQBF}$, it follows that $a_n = 1$. By Condition (C.1), it follows that for every pair $(\mathbf{b}, \mathbf{c})$, $(\mathbf{a}, \mathbf{b}, \mathbf{c})$ is a pure equilibrium for $\Gamma_{\langle H, r \rangle}$ with payoff vector

$$U(\mathbf{a}, \mathbf{b}, \mathbf{c}) = \langle 1, |\mathbf{a}|, 1 + a_n \rangle.$$

We now prove that $(\mathbf{a}, \mathbf{b}, \mathbf{c})$ is a payoff-dominant equilibrium for $\Gamma_{\langle H, r \rangle}$. Consider any pure equilibrium $(\mathbf{a}', \mathbf{b}', \mathbf{c}')$ for $\Gamma_{\langle H, r \rangle}$. Condition (C.2) implies that for all vectors $\mathbf{b}'' \in \{0,1\}^n$, $H(\mathbf{a}', \mathbf{b}'') = 1$ and $|\mathbf{a}'| \leq r$. Condition (C.1) implies that the payoff vector for $(\mathbf{a}', \mathbf{b}', \mathbf{c}')$ is

$$U(\mathbf{a}', \mathbf{b}', \mathbf{c}') = \langle 1, |\mathbf{a}'|, 1 + a_n' \rangle.$$

We only need to consider players 2 and 3.

- Since $\mathbf{a}$ is the lmax vector such that for all vectors $\mathbf{b} \in \{0,1\}^n$, $H(\mathbf{a}, \mathbf{b}) = 1$, it follows that $\mathbf{a} \geq_{le} \mathbf{a}'$. Hence, $|\mathbf{a}| \geq |\mathbf{a}'|$ and player 2 has a dominant payoff in $(\mathbf{a}, \mathbf{b}, \mathbf{c})$.
- Since $a_n = 1$, $a_n \geq a_n'$, and player 3 has a dominant payoff in $(\mathbf{a}, \mathbf{b}, \mathbf{c})$.

It follows that

$$\langle 1, |\mathbf{a}|, 1 + a_n \rangle \geq_{cw} \langle 1, |\mathbf{a}'|, 1 + a_n' \rangle.$$

Since $(\mathbf{a}', \mathbf{b}', \mathbf{c}')$ was chosen as an arbitrary pure equilibrium for $\Gamma_{\langle H,r \rangle}$, this implies that $(\mathbf{a}, \mathbf{b}, \mathbf{c})$ is a payoff-dominant equilibrium for $\Gamma_{\langle H,r \rangle}$.

Assume now that $H(\mathbf{x}, \mathbf{y}) \notin \Theta_3$-RQBF. Assume, by way of contradiction, that $\Gamma_{\langle H,r \rangle}$ has a payoff-dominant equilibrium $(\mathbf{a}, \mathbf{b}, \mathbf{c})$.

By Condition (C.2), $H(\mathbf{a}, \mathbf{b}') = 1$ for all vectors $\mathbf{b}' \in \{0,1\}^n$. By Condition (C.1),

$$U(\mathbf{a}, \mathbf{b}, \mathbf{c}) = \langle 1, |\mathbf{a}|, 1 + a_n \rangle.$$

Again, by Condition (C.1), $(\widetilde{\mathbf{a}}, \mathbf{b}, \mathbf{c})$ is a pure equilibrium for $\Gamma_{\langle H,r \rangle}$, for every vector $\widetilde{\mathbf{a}} \in \{0,1\}^n$ such that $H(\widetilde{\mathbf{a}}, \mathbf{b}') = 1$ for all vectors $\mathbf{b}' \in \{0,1\}^n$. Since player 2 has a dominant payoff in $(\mathbf{a}, \mathbf{b}, \mathbf{c})$, it follows that $\mathbf{a}$ is the lexmax solution to $H(\mathbf{a}, \mathbf{b}') = 1$ for all vectors $\mathbf{b}' \in \{0,1\}^n$.

In this case, due to the assumption that $H(\mathbf{x}, \mathbf{y}) \notin \Theta_3$-RQBF, it follows that $a_n = 0$. Hence, player 3 has payoff 1 in $(\mathbf{a}, \mathbf{b}, \mathbf{c})$.

Recall the assumption that for all vectors $\mathbf{b}' \in \{0,1\}^n$, $H(0^{n-1}1, \mathbf{b}') = 1$. Note also that $|0^{n-1}1| = 1 \leq r$. By Condition (C.1), these imply that $\langle 0^{n-1}1, \mathbf{b}, \mathbf{c} \rangle$ is also a pure equilibrium for $\Gamma_{\langle H,r \rangle}$ with payoff vector $\langle 1, 1, 2 \rangle$. Hence, player 3 does *not* have a dominant payoff in $(\mathbf{a}, \mathbf{b}, \mathbf{c})$. A contradiction.

We conclude with a group of open problems.

Open Problem 61. *Find the complexities of the following problems:*

(1) WBF-PDE$_d$($*, k, r$) *(and* WBF-PDE$_s$($*, k, r$)*) for* $k \in \{1, 2, \ldots\}$ *and* $r \in \{1, 2, \ldots\}$.
(2) BF-PDE$_d$($m, *, r$) *(and* BF-PDE$_s$($m, *, r$)*) for* $m \in \{2, 3, \ldots\}$, $r \in \{1, 2, \ldots\}$.
(3) WBF-PDE$_d$($2, *, *$) *(and* WBF-PDE$_s$($2, *, *$)*)*.
(4) BF-PDE$_d$($2, *, *$) *(and* BF-PDE$_s$($2, *, *$)*)*.

7   Open Problems

Our work raises far more interesting open problems than it answers; beyond the concrete ones in Open Problems 51, 52 and 61, we mention a few additional here.

1. On the most concrete level, what is the complexity of other refinements of pure equilibrium (e.g., dominating equilibrium, Pareto-optimal equilibrium, risk-dominant equilibrium, etc.) in WBFG? What is the complexity of payoff-dominant equilibria in MWBFG?
2. What is the complexity of *mixed* payoff-dominant equilibria in WBFG, or in other classes of succinct games?

3. We identified natural refinements of pure equilibrium (including itself) that are complete for some of the lowest levels of $\mathcal{PH}$ (not exceeding the third level). Is there for *any* level k of $\mathcal{PH}$, some natural refinement of pure equilibrium that is complete for Θ_k^P, Δ_k^P, Σ_k^P or Π_k^P? Is there some natural refinement of pure equilibrium that is complete for $\mathcal{PSPACE}$?
3. Theorem 1 identifies mutuality as a sufficient condition for a WBFG to admit an exact potential; a corresponding necessary condition is missing.
4. Theorem 2 and Corollary 2 identify classes of congestion games that are polynomially embeddable in WBFG and MWBFG, respectively. Which other classes of congestion games and, in general, succinct games are so embeddable?

Acknowledgements. We would like to thank Paul Spirakis and Karsten Tiemann for many helpful discussions and comments on earlier versions of this work.

References

1. Álvarez, C., Gabarró, J., Serna, M.: Equilibria problems on games: complexity versus succinctness. J. Comput. Syst. Sci. **77**(6), 1172–1197 (2011)
2. Aumann, R.J., Sorin, S.: Cooperation and bounded recall. Game. Econ. Behav. **1**(1), 5–39 (1989)
3. Bacharach, M., Bernasconi, M.: An experimental study of the variable frame theory of focal points. Game. Econ. Behav. **19**(1), 1–45 (1997)
4. Bilò, V.: On satisfiability games and the power of congestion games. In: Kao, M.-Y., Li, X.-Y. (eds.) AAIM 2007. LNCS, vol. 4508, pp. 231–240. Springer, Heidelberg (2007)
5. Bilò, V., Mavronicolas, M.: The complexity of decision problems about nash equilibria in win-lose games. In: Serna, M. (ed.) SAGT 2012. LNCS, vol. 7615, pp. 37–48. Springer, Heidelberg (2012)
6. Blonski, M.: Characterization of pure-strategy equilibria in finite anonymous games. J. Math. Econ. **34**(2), 225–233 (2000)
7. Bonzon, E., Lagasquie-Schiex, M.-C., Lang, J., Zanuttini, B.: Boolean games revisited. In: Proceedings of the 17th European Conference on Artificial Intelligence, Series Frontiers in Artificial Intelligence and Applications, vol. 141, pp. 265–269, August/September 2006
8. Bonzon, E., Lagasquie-Schiex, M.-C., Lang, J.: Compact preference representation for boolean games. In: Yang, Q., Webb, G. (eds.) PRICAI 2006. LNCS (LNAI), vol. 4099, pp. 41–50. Springer, Heidelberg (2006)
9. Bonzon, E., Lagasquie-Schiex, M.-C., Lang, J., Zanuttini, B.: Compact preference representation and boolean games. Auton. Agents Multi-Agent Syst. **18**(1), 1–35 (2009)
10. Bonzon, E., Lagasquie-Schiex, M.-C., Lang, J.: Dependencies between players in boolean games. Int. J. Approximate Reasoning **50**(6), 899–914 (2009)
11. Bonzon, E., Lagasquie-Schiex, M.-C., Lang, J.: Effectivity functions and efficient coalitions in boolean games. Synthese **187**(1 Supplement), 73–103 (2012)
12. Brandt, F., Fischer, F., Holzer, M.: Symmetries and the complexity of pure nash equilibrium. J. Comput. Syst. Sci. **75**(3), 163–177 (2009)

13. Case, J.: A class of games having pareto optimal nash equilibria. J. Optim. Theory Appl. **13**, 379–385 (1974)
14. Chen, X., Deng, X., Teng, S.-H.: Settling the complexity of two-player nash equilibria. J. ACM **56**(3), 14 (2009)
15. Colman, A.M., Bacharach, M.: Payoff dominance and the stackelberg heuristic. Theory Decis. **43**(1), 1–19 (1997)
16. Conitzer, V., Sandholm, T.: Complexity results about nash equilibria. Game. Econ. Behav. **63**(2), 621–641 (2008)
17. Daskalakis, C., Fabrikant, A., Papadimitriou, C.: The game world is flat: the complexity of nash equilibria in succinct games. In: Bugliesi, M., Preneel, B., Sassone, V., Wegener, I. (eds.) ICALP 2006. LNCS, vol. 4051, pp. 513–524. Springer, Heidelberg (2006)
18. Daskalakis, C., Goldberg, P.W., Papadimitriou, C.H.: The complexity of computing a nash equilibrium. SIAM J. Comput. **39**(1), 195–259 (2009)
19. Daskalakis, K., Papadimitriou, C.: The complexity of games on highly regular graphs. In: Brodal, G.S., Leonardi, S. (eds.) ESA 2005. LNCS, vol. 3669, pp. 71–82. Springer, Heidelberg (2005)
20. Dunkel, J., Schulz, A.S.: On the complexity of pure-strategy nash equilibria in congestion and local-effect games. MatH. Oper. Res. **33**(4), 851–868 (2008)
21. Dunne, P.E., van der Hoek, W.: Representation and complexity in boolean games. In: Alferes, J.J., Leite, J. (eds.) JELIA 2004. LNCS (LNAI), vol. 3229, pp. 347–359. Springer, Heidelberg (2004)
22. Dunne, P.E., Wooldridge, M.: Towards tractable boolean games. In: Proceedings of the 11th International Conference on Autonomous Agents and Multiagent Systems, vol. 2, pp. 939–946, June 2012
23. Fabrikant, A., Papadimitriou, C.H., Talwar, K.: The complexity of pure nash equilibria. In: Proceedings of the 36th Annual ACM Symposium on Theory of Computing, pp. 604–612, June 2004
24. Feigenbaum, J., Koller, D., Shor, P.: A game-theoretic classification of interactive complexity classes. In: Proceedings of the 10th Annual IEEE Conference on Structure in Complexity Theory, pp. 227–237, June 1995
25. Fischer, F., Holzer, M., Katzenbeisser, S.: The influence of neighbourhood and choice on the complexity of finding pure nash equilibria. Inf. Process. Lett. **99**(6), 239–245 (2006)
26. Fortnow, L., Impagliazzo, R., Kabanets, V., Umans, C.: On the complexity of succinct zero-sum games. Comput. Complex. **17**(3), 353–376 (2008)
27. Fotakis, D., Kontogiannis, S., Spirakis, P.: Selfish unsplittable flows. Theoret. Comput. Sci. **348**(2–3), 226–239 (2005)
28. Gabarró, J., García, A., Serna, M.: The complexity of game isomorphism. Theoret. Comput. Sci. **412**(48), 6675–6695 (2011)
29. Gairing, M., Monien, B., Tiemann, K.: Routing (un-)splittable flow in games with player-specific linear latency functions. ACM Trans. Algorithms **7**(3), 31 (2011)
30. Gale, D., Kuhn, H.W., Tucker, A.W.: On symmetric games. Contributions to the Theory of Games. Annals of Mathematics Studies, vol. 24. Princeton University Press, Princeton (1950)
31. Gottlob, G., Greco, G., Scarcello, F.: Pure nash equilibria: hard and easy games. J. Artif. Intell. Res. **24**, 357–406 (2005)
32. Harrenstein, P., van der Hoek, W., Meyer, J.-J., Witteveen, C.: Boolean games. In: Proceedings of the 8th Conference on Theoretical Aspects of Rationality and Knowledge, pp. 287–298, July 2001

33. Harrenstein, P.: Logic in conflict, Ph.D. thesis, Utrecht University (2004)
34. Harsanyi, J.C., Selten, R.: A General Theory of Equilibrium Selection in Games. The MIT Press, Cambridge (1988)
35. Hemaspaandra, E., Hemaspaandra, L.A., Rothe, J.: Exact analysis of dodgson elections: lewis carroll's 1876 voting system is complete for parallel access to $\mathcal{NP}$. J. ACM **44**(6), 806–825 (1997)
36. Howson, J.T.: Equilibria of polymatrix games(Part I). Manag. Sci. **18**(5), 312–318 (1972)
37. Ianovski, E.: DValue for boolean games is $\mathcal{EXP}$-Hard. In: CoRR, abs/1403.7428 (2014)
38. Ianovski, E., Ong, L.: ∃GuaranteeNash is $\mathcal{NEXP}$-Hard. In: Proceedings of the 14th International Conference on Knowledge Representation and Reasoning, July 2014
39. Johnson, D.S., Papadimitriou, C.H., Yannakakis, M.: How easy is local search? J. Comput. Syst. Sci. **37**(1), 79–100 (1988)
40. Kalai, E., Samet, D.: Unanimity games and pareto optimality. Int. J. Game Theory **14**(1), 41–50 (1985)
41. Kearns, M.J., Littman, M.L., Singh, S.P.: Graphical models for game theory. In: Proceedings of the 17th Conference on Uncertainty in Artificial Intelligence, pp. 253–260, August 2001
42. Krapchenko, V.M.: Complexity of the realization of a linear function in the class of Π-circuits. Math. Notes Acad. Sci. USSR **9**(1), 21–23 (1971)
43. Krentel, M.W.: The complexity of optimization problems. J. Comput. Syst. Sci. **36**(3), 490–509 (1988)
44. Leyton-Brown, K., Tennenholtz, M.: Local-effect games. In: Proceedings of the 18th International Joint Conference on Artificial Intelligence, pp. 772–780, August 2003
45. Mavronicolas, M., Milchtaich, I., Monien, B., Tiemann, K.: Congestion games with player-specific constants. In: Kučera, L., Kučera, A. (eds.) MFCS 2007. LNCS, vol. 4708, pp. 633–644. Springer, Heidelberg (2007)
46. Meyer, A.R., Stockmeyer, L.J.: The equivalence problem for regular expressions with squaring requires exponential time. In: Proceedings of the 13th Annual IEEE Symposium on Switching and Automata Theory, pp. 125–129, October 1972
47. Milchtaich, I.: Congestion games with player-specific payoff functions. Game. Econ. Behav. **13**(1), 111–124 (1996)
48. Monderer, D., Shapley, L.S.: Potential games. Game. Econ. Behav. **14**(1), 124–143 (1996)
49. Nash, J.F.: Non-cooperative games. Ann. Math. **54**, 286–295 (1951)
50. Papadimitriou, C.H.: Computational Complexity. Addison-Wesley, Boston (1994)
51. Papadimitriou, C.H., Roughgarden, T.: Computing correlated equilibria in multi-player games. J. ACM **55**(3), 14 (2008)
52. Papadimitriou, C.H., Zachos, S.: Two remarks on the power of counting. In: Cremers, A.B., Kriegel, H.-P. (eds.) Theoretical Computer Science. LNCS, vol. 145, pp. 269–275. Springer, Heidelberg (1983)
53. Paterson, M., Valiant, L.G.: Circuit size is nonlinear in depth. Theoret. Comput. Sci. **2**(3), 397–400 (1976)
54. Paul, W.: A 2.5 lower bound on the combinatorial complexity of boolean functions. SIAM J. Comput. **6**(3), 427–443 (1977)
55. Rosenthal, R.W.: A class of games possessing pure strategy nash equilibria. Int. J. Game Theory **2**(1), 65–67 (1973)
56. Sahni, S.: Computationally related problems. SIAM J. Comput. **3**(4), 262–279 (1974)

57. Schoenebeck, G., Vadhan, S.: The computational complexity of nash equilibria in concisely represented games. ACM Trans. Comput. Theory **4**(2), 4 (2012)
58. Stockmeyer, L.J.: The polynomial time hierarchy. Theoret. Comput. Sci. **3**(1), 1–22 (1976)
59. Vollmer, H., Wagner, K.W.: Complexity classes of optimization functions. Inf. Comput. **120**(2), 198–218 (1995)
60. Voorneveld, M., Borm, P., van Megan, F., Tijs, S., Facchini, G.: Congestion games and potentials reconsidered. Int. Game Theory Rev. **1**(3–4), 283–299 (1999)
61. Wagner, K.W.: More complicated questions about maxima and minima, and some closures of $\mathcal{NP}$. Theoret. Comput. Sci. **51**(1–2), 53–80 (1987)
62. Wagner, K.W.: Bounded query classes. SIAM J. Comput. **19**(5), 833–846 (1990)
63. Wegener, I.: The Complexity of Boolean Functions. Wiley, New York (1991)
64. Wrathall, C.: Complete sets and the polynomial time hierarchy. Theoret. Comput. Sci. **3**(1), 23–33 (1976)

On the Implementation of Combinatorial Algorithms for the Linear Exchange Market

Kurt Mehlhorn[✉]

Max-Planck-Institute for Informatics, Saarbrücken, Germany
mehlhorn@mpi-inf.mpg.de

Abstract. Duan and Mehlhorn and Duan, Garg, and Mehlhorn presented polynomial time combinatorial algorithms [DM13, DGM15] for the computation of equilibrium prices in linear exchange markets. I am currently implementing these algorithms. I discuss the questions that I hope to answer through the implementation.

1 Introduction

In the linear exchange market model [Wal74] there are n agents and n goods; agent i owns good i. Agents have preferences over goods. Let $u_{ij} \in \mathbb{N}_{\geq 0}$ be the utility of agent i if all of good j is allocated to him. Goods are divisible. At a certain vector $p = (p_1, \ldots, p_n)$ of prices, agents are only willing to spend money on goods that give them maximum utility per unit of money. Agents are sellers and buyers, i.e., if agent i sells his good completely, he has a budget of p_i units of money. The task is to compute prices at which the market clears, i.e., all goods are completely sold and all money is completely spent. Formally, we want to find a positive price vector p and a nonnegative flow of money $f = (f_{ij})$ such that

$$
\begin{aligned}
p_i &= \textstyle\sum_j f_{ij} \quad \text{for all } i && \text{money is completely spent} \\
p_j &= \textstyle\sum_i f_{ij} \quad \text{for all } j && \text{goods are completely sold} \\
f_{ij} > 0 &\implies \tfrac{u_{ij}}{p_j} = \max_\ell \tfrac{u_{i\ell}}{p_\ell} && \text{agents are selfish}
\end{aligned}
$$

Fig. 1 shows an example.

The problem is solvable in polynomial time. Jain and Ye [Jai07, Ye07] gave algorithms based on the Ellipsoid and interior point method, respectively. Duan and Mehlhorn [DM13] provided a combinatorial algorithm which was recently improved by Duan, Garg, and Mehlhorn [DGM15]. We review the former algorithm in Sects. 2 and 3. We have recently started to implement the algorithm. In Sect. 4 we discuss the questions that we want to address through the implementation. A detailed description of the implementation is under preparation.

2 The Algorithm

This section and the next are based on [DM13]. Each agent only buys its favorite goods. Define the *bang per buck* of buyer b_i to be $\alpha_i = \max_j u_{ij}/p_j$. For a price

© Springer International Publishing Switzerland 2015
C. Zaroliagis et al. (Eds.): Spirakis Festschrift, LNCS 9295, pp. 87–94, 2015.
DOI: 10.1007/978-3-319-24024-4_7

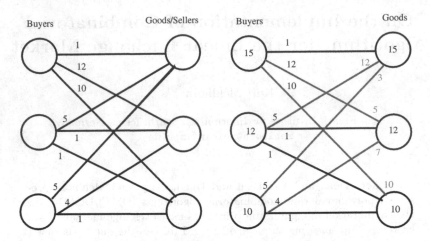

Fig. 1. The input is shown on the left. Each agent is shown twice, once in its role as seller or owner of a good and once in his role as buyer. The utility u_{ij} is indicated on the edge from the i-th buyer to the j-th good. A solution is shown on the right. The prices of the goods (= budgets of the buyers) are shown inside the nodes. The bang-for-buck edges and the money flow are shown in blue.

vector p, the *equality network* N_p is a flow network with vertex set $\{s, t\} \cup B \cup C$, where s is a source node, t is a sink node, $B = \{b_1, \ldots, b_n\}$ is the set of buyers, and $C = \{c_1, \ldots, c_n\}$ is the set of goods, and the following edge set:

- An edge (s, b_i) with capacity p_i for each $b_i \in B$.
- An edge (c_i, t) with capacity p_i for each $c_i \in C$.
- An edge (b_i, c_j) with infinite capacity whenever $u_{ij}/p_j = \alpha_i$. We use E_p to denote these edges.

Our task is to find a positive price vector p such that there is a flow in which all edges from s and to t are saturated. When this is satisfied, all goods are sold and all of the money earned by each agent is spent on goods of maximum utility per unit of money. With respect to a flow f, define the surplus $r(b_i)$ of a buyer i as $r(b_i) = p_i - \sum_j f_{ij}$, where f_{ij} is the amount of flow on the edge (b_i, c_j), and define the surplus $r(c_j)$ of a good j as $r(c_j) = p_j - \sum_i f_{ij}$. Define the surplus vector of buyers to be $r = (r(b_1), r(b_2), ..., r(b_n))$. Also, define the total surplus to be $|r| = \sum_i r(b_i)$, which is also $\sum_j r(c_j)$ since the total capacity from s and to t are both equal to $\sum_i p_i$. For convenience, we denote the surplus vector of flow f' by r'. In the network corresponding to market clearing prices, the total surplus of a maximum flow is zero.

A maximum flow f in N_p is *balanced* if it minimizes the 2-norm $\|r\|_2$ of the surplus vector of the buyers among all maximum flows. Balanced flows were introduced in [DPSV08] and shown to be computable by n maxflow computations in N_p. The equality graph may have as many as $\Theta(n^2)$ edges and hence, assuming the use of an $O(nm + n^2 \log n)$ maxflow algorithm, a balanced flow can

---

Set $\epsilon = 1/(8n^{4n}U^{3n})$, where $U = \max_{ij} u_{ij}$;

Set $p_i = 1$ for all i and set f to a balanced flow in N_p;

Repeat

 Sort the buyers by their surpluses in decreasing order: $b_1, b_2, ..., b_n$;

 Find the smallest ℓ for which $r(b_\ell)/r(b_{\ell+1}) > 1 + 1/n$, and
         let $\ell = n$ when there is no such ℓ;

 Let $S = \{b_1, \ldots, b_\ell\}$;

 Compute $x = \min(x_{eq}, x_{23}, x_{24}, x_2)$.

 Multiply prices of goods in $\Gamma(S)$ and flows into these goods by x.

 Extend f to a balanced flow (goods of surplus zero must keep surplus zero);

Until $|r(B)| < \epsilon$;

Extract a linear system from N_p and compute equilibrium prices from it.

Fig. 2. The algorithm

be computed with $O(n^4)$ arithmetic operations. The algorithm for computing a balanced flow is based on the following characterization of balanced flows.

Lemma 1 [DPSV08]. *A maximum flow f is balanced if for any two edges (b_i, c_k) and (b_j, c_k) on the equality graph with $f_{ik} > 0$, either $r(b_i) = r(b_j)$ or $(r(b_i) > r(b_j)$ and $f_{jk} = 0)$.*

The algorithm is shown in Fig. 2. It starts with all prices p_i equal to one and a balanced flow f in N_p. It works in phases. In each phase, we first number the buyers in order of decreasing surpluses: $b_1, \ldots, b_n$. Let ℓ be minimal such that $r(b_\ell)$ is by a factor of $1 + 1/n$ larger than $r(b_{\ell+1})$; $\ell = n$ if there is no such ℓ. By this choice of ℓ, $r(b_\ell) \geq |r(B)|/(e \cdot n)$ and $r(b_i) \leq e \cdot r(b_\ell)$ for all i is guaranteed.[1] Let $S = \{b_1, \ldots, b_\ell\}$ and let $\Gamma(S) = \{c \in C \mid (b, c) \in E_p \text{ for some } b \in S\}$ be the goods that are adjacent to a buyer in S in the equality graph. Since every buyer has at least one incident edge in the equality graph, $\Gamma(S)$ is non-empty. All flow from buyers in S goes to goods in $\Gamma(S)$ and all buyers in S have surplus. Thus the goods in $\Gamma(S)$ have no surplus, since the current flow is maximum, and the demand for them at the current prices exceeds their supply.

Let $\bar{S} = B \setminus S$. Since the flow is balanced and the buyers in S have larger surplus than the buyers in $\bar{S}$, there is no flow from $\bar{S}$ to $\Gamma(S)$. We raise the prices of the goods in $\Gamma(S)$ and the flow on the edges incident to them by a common factor $x > 1$. We also increase the flow from s to buyers in S such that flow conservation holds. This give us a new price vector p' and a new flow f'. Observe that the surpluses of the goods in $\Gamma(S)$ stay zero. Formally,

---

[1] Clearly $b_1 \geq |r(B)|/n$. Also, $r(b_j)/r(b_{j+1}) \leq 1 + 1/n$ for $j < \ell$, and hence $r(b_\ell) \geq r(b_1)/(1 + 1/n)^{-n} \geq r(b_1)/e \geq |r(B)|/(e \cdot n)$.

$$p'_j = \begin{cases} x \cdot p_j & \text{if } c_j \in \Gamma(S); \\ p_j & \text{if } c_j \notin \Gamma(S). \end{cases} \quad (1) \qquad f'_{ij} = \begin{cases} x \cdot f_{ij} & \text{if } c_j \in \Gamma(S); \\ f_{ij} & \text{if } c_j \notin \Gamma(S). \end{cases} \quad (2)$$

The changes on the edges incident to s and t are implied by flow conservation.

The change of prices and flows affects the surpluses of the buyers, some go up and some go down.

Lemma 2 [DM13]. *Given a balanced flow f in N_p, a set S of buyers such that all goods in $\Gamma(S)$ are completely sold and there is no flow from $\bar{S}$ to $\Gamma(S)$, and a sufficiently small parameter $x > 1$, the flow f' defined in (2) is a feasible flow in the equality network with respect to the prices in (1). The surplus of each good remains unchanged, and the surpluses of the buyers become:*

$$r'(b_i) = \begin{cases} x \cdot r(b_i) & \text{if } b_i \in S, c_i \in \Gamma(S) \text{ (type 1 buyer)}; \\ (1-x)p_i + x \cdot r(b_i) & \text{if } b_i \in S, c_i \notin \Gamma(S) \text{ (type 2 buyer)}; \\ (x-1)p_i + r(b_i) & \text{if } b_i \notin S, c_i \in \Gamma(S) \text{ (type 3 buyer)}; \\ r(b_i) & \text{if } b_i \notin S, c_i \notin \Gamma(S) \text{ (type 4 buyer)}. \end{cases}$$

Proof. See [DM13]. For the definition of the factor x, we perform the following thought experiment. We increase the prices of the goods in $\Gamma(S)$ and the flow on the edges incident to them continuously by a common factor x until one of three events happens: (1) a new edge enters the equality graph or (2) the surplus of a type 2 buyer and a type 3 or 4 buyer become equal or (3) the surplus of a type 2 buyer becomes zero. The third event can only happen if $S = B$ and hence there are no type 3 and type 4 buyers.

The increase of prices of goods in $\Gamma(S)$ makes the goods in $C \setminus \Gamma(S)$ more attractive to the buyers in S and hence an equality edge connecting a buyer in S with a good in $C \setminus \Gamma(S)$ may arise. This will happen at $x = x_{eq}(S)$, where

$$x_{eq}(S) = \min \left\{ \frac{u_{ij}}{p_j} \cdot \frac{p_k}{u_{ik}} \mid b_i \in S, (b_i, c_j) \in E_p, c_k \notin \Gamma(S) \right\}.$$

When we increase the prices of the goods in $\Gamma(S)$ by a common factor $x \leq x_{eq}(S)$, the equality edges in $(S \times \Gamma(S)) \cup (\bar{S} \times (C \setminus \Gamma(S)))$ will remain in the network. Equality edges in $\bar{S} \times \Gamma(S)$ will disappear, but they carry no flow and hence may disappear.

The surplus of type 1 and 3 buyers increases, the surplus of type 2 buyers decreases, and the surplus of type 4 buyers does not change. Since the total surplus does not change (recall that the surpluses of the goods are not affected by the price update), the decrease in surplus of the type 2 buyers is equal to the increase in surplus of the type 1 and 3 buyers. In particular, there are type 2 buyers. We define quantities $x_{23}(S)$ and $x_{24}(S)$ at which the surplus of a type 2 and type 3 buyer, respectively type 4 buyer, becomes equal, and a quantity x_2 at which the surplus of a type 2 buyer becomes zero.

$$x_{23}(S) = \min \left\{ \frac{p_i + p_j - r(b_j)}{p_i + p_j - r(b_i)} b_i \text{ is type 2 and } b_j \text{ is type 3 buyer} \right\},$$

$$x_{24}(S) = \min \left\{ \frac{p_i - r(b_j)}{p_i - r(b_i)} b_i \text{ is type 2 and } b_j \text{ is type 4 buyer} \right\},$$

$$x_2(S) = \min \left\{ \frac{p_i}{p_i - r(b_i)} b_i \text{ is type 2 buyer} \right\}.$$

The quantity $x_2(S)$ is only relevant, if $S = B$. It guarantees that surpluses of buyers stay nonnegative.

Lemma 3 [DM13]. *With* $x = \min(x_{eq}(S), x_{23}(S), x_{24}(S), x_2(S))$ *and* S *as defined in the algorithm,* f' *is a feasible flow in* $N_{p'}$.

Proof Obvious. We complete the phase by extending f' to a balanced flow. In this step, we make sure that goods with surplus zero keep surplus zero. This ends the description of the algorithm. Correctness follows from the following lemma.

Lemma 4 [DM13]. *Once the surplus of a good becomes zero, it stays zero. As long as a good has non-zero surplus, its price stays at one.*

3   A Glimpse of the Analysis

The analysis uses two potential functions, namely the product $P = \prod_i p_i$ of all prices and the 2-norm $\|r(B)\|_2$ of the surplus vector of the buyers.

Lemma 5 [DM13]. *In the course of the algorithm, all prices stay bounded by* $(nU)^n$.

Lemma 6 [DM13]. *For a phase* h*, let* $x_h > 1$ *be the factor by which the prices in* $\Gamma(S)$ *are increased. Then*

$$\prod_h x_h \le (nU)^{n^2}.$$

Let $x_{\max} := 1 + \frac{1}{48e^2n^3}$. Call a phase h an $x_{\max}$-phase if $x_h \ge x_{\max}$ and call it a balancing phase otherwise.

Lemma 7 [DM13]. *The number of* $x_{\max}$*-phases is* $O(n^5 \log(nU))$.

Proof. Let T be the number of $x_{\max}$-phases. In an $x_{\max}$-phase, the product P of the prices grows by at least a factor $x_{\max}$. Therefore $x_{\max}^T \le (nU)^{n^2}$.

The 2-norm of the surplus vector is used to bound the number of balancing phases. The next lemma justifies the name.

Lemma 8 [DM13]. *In a phase* h *with* $x_h < x_{\max}$*, the 2-norm of the surplus vector of the buyers is reduced by a factor* $1 - O(1/n^3)$.

Lemma 9 [DM13]. *Over all $x_{\max}$-phases, the 2-norm of the surplus vector of the buyers increases by at most a multiplicative factor $(nU)^{n^2}$.*

Lemma 10 [DM13]. *The number of balancing phases is $O(n^5 \log(nU))$.*

Proof. Let T be the number of balancing phases. The initial 2-norm of the surplus vector is at most $\sqrt{n}$. The total multiplicative increase is at most $(nU)^{n^2}$ and the total multiplicative decrease in balancing phases is at least $(1 - O(1/n^3))^T$. The algorithm terminates once the 1-norm of the surplus vector is less than ϵ. This is guaranteed if the 2-norm is less than $\epsilon/\sqrt{n}$. The bound follows.

Theorem 1 [DM13]. *The total number of arithmetic operations required by the algorithm is $O(n^9 \log(nU))$.*

Polynomial Time: Since we assume utilities to be integers and the algorithm uses only the basic arithmetic operations, the computation stays within the rationals. However, it is not clear whether the size of the rationals stays polynomially bounded. It is conceivable that the size of the rationals doubles in each phase.

Duan and Mehlhorn guarantee polynomial time as follows. Firstly, they approximate utilities u_{ij} by powers of $1 + 1/L$, where $L = 16n^5(nU)^n/\epsilon = 126n^{5n+5}U^{4n}$. Secondly, they observe that it suffices to approximate x_{23}, x_{24} and x_2 by a nearby power of $1 + 1/L$ and that only x_{eq} needs to be computed exactly. As a consequence, all prices are powers of $1 + 1/L$. Since prices are bounded by $(nU)^n$, the exponents in the representations are between 0 and $\log_{1+1/L}(nU)^n = O(nL \log(nU))$. The bitlength of the exponents is $O(n \log(nU))$.

Theorem 2 [DM13]. *The total number of arithmetic operations required by the algorithm is $O(n^9 \log(nU))$. Arithmetic on integers with $O(n \log(nU))$ bits suffices.*

4   Questions

Through the implementation, we address the following questions:

1. Do the rationals really explode? Or does it suffice to keep them normalized, i.e., to keep numerators and denominators relatively prime? For Gaussian elimination over the rationals it is known [Edm67] that keeping the rationals normalized suffices to control their size.
2. The known algorithm for computing a balanced flow requires up to n maxflow computations in a graph with $2n$ nodes and $O(n^2)$ edges.
   (a) Cycles in the equality graph can only arise if there are dependencies between the utilities. Let $b_{i_0}, c_{j_0}, b_{i_1}, c_{j_1}, \ldots, b_{i_{k-1}}, c_{j_{k-1}}, b_{i_0}$ be a cycle in the equality graph with respect to a price vector p. Then

$$\frac{u_{i_\ell, j_{\ell-1}}}{p_{j_{\ell-1}}} = \frac{u_{i_\ell, j_\ell}}{p_{j_\ell}}$$

for all ℓ, since b_{i_ℓ} is connected to $c_{j_{\ell-1}}$ and c_{j_ℓ} in the equality graph (interpret -1 as $k-1$) and hence

$$\prod_{0\le\ell\le k-1} u_{i_\ell,j_{\ell-1}} = \prod_{0\le\ell\le k-1} u_{i_\ell,j_\ell}.$$

If no such dependency exists, the equality graph E_p is a tree and contains at most $2n-1$ edges. Thus the maxflow computations would be in graphs with only a linear number of edges and special structure. Perturbation of the utilities can guarantee that there are no dependencies. What is the arithmetic cost of perturbation in this context? Does the rounding of the utilities required to make the algorithm polynomial time counteract perturbation and introduce dependencies?

(b) The algorithm for computing a balanced flow works recursively. The divide step answers the question whether all surpluses can be made equal. Note that the average surplus of a buyer is $r_{ave} := (\sum_{i\in B}(p_i - \sum_j f_{ij}))/n$. We set the capacity of the edge from s to b_i to $p_i - r_{ave}$ and recompute the maximum flow. If the entire flow can still be routed, all surpluses are equal to r_{ave} in a balanced flow and we are done. Otherwise, let S be the set of buyers and goods reachable from s in the residual graph and let T be their complement. The nodes in $S \cap B$ have surplus at least r_{ave} in a balanced flow and the nodes in $B \cap T$ have surplus at most r_{ave}. One deletes all edges from buyers in T to goods in S from the equality graph and recurses on the graphs $s \cup S \cup t$ and $s \cup T \cup t$. Actually, the two recursive calls can be combined into one as there are no edges connecting nodes in S and nodes in T. In this way, the number of recursive calls is equal to the recursion depth. Can one control the recursion depth, by using a value different from r_{ave} in the divide step?

Note that the networks for the recursive calls are obtained by deleting some edges and changing the capacities of the edges incident to s. Does one have to start the maxflow computations from scratch or can one reuse the results of earlier computations.

(c) Can one use parametric maxflow [GGT89] to speed up the computation?

(d) It seems that one can do with a weaker version of balanced flows, namely $1+1/(cn)$-balanced flows where c is a small constant. A maximum flow is $1+1/(cn)$-balanced if for any two edges (b_i, c_k) and (b_j, c_k) in the equality graph with $f_{ik} > 0$, we have either $r(b_j) \ge r(b_i)/(1+1/cn)$ or $f_{jk} = 0$.

3. What is the behavior of the algorithm on random inputs? Are their inputs that force the algorithm into its worst-case running time or close to the worst-case running time.

4. Are balanced flows really needed? Garg, Duan, and Mehlhorn [DGM15] have recently shown that the use of balanced flows can be avoided. This reduces the complexity of a phase to $O(n^2)$. Does this theoretical improvement show in the implementation?

5. The main loop terminates when the 1-norm of the surplus vector of the buyers is less than ϵ. At this point, one can extract a linear system from the equality graph E_p. The equilibrium prices are the solution to this linear system.

Of course, one can extract a linear system from E_p at any time during the execution and compute prices from it. Since it is easily checked whether a set of prices is a set of equilibrium prices (one maxflow computation), it makes sense to extract earlier. If the cost of extracting and solving the system is C, one should extract after spending cost $O(C)$ in the main loop. In this way the extraction attempts can be amortized over the cost of the main loop.

6. What problem size can be solved with an $O(n^{10})$ algorithm? In the worst case? On average? Are economists interested in exact solutions to problems of this size?

References

[DGM15] Duan, R., Garg, J., Mehlhorn, K.: A improved combinatorial algorithm for the linear arrow-debreu marketTODO (2015). Forthcoming

[DM13] Duan, R., Mehlhorn, K.: A combinatorial polynomial algorithm for the linear arrow-debreu market. In: Fomin, F.V., Freivalds, R., Kwiatkowska, M., Peleg, D. (eds.) ICALP 2013, Part I. LNCS, vol. 7965, pp. 425–436. Springer, Heidelberg (2013)

[DPSV08] Devanur, N.R., Papadimitriou, C.H., Saberi, A., Vazirani, V.V.: Market equilibrium via a primal-dual algorithm for a convex program. J. ACM 55(5), 22:1–22:18 (2008)

[Edm67] Edmonds, J.: Systems of distinct representatives and linear algebra. J. Res. Nat. Bur. Stan.(B) 71, 241–245 (1967)

[GGT89] Gallo, G., Grigoriadis, M.D., Tarjan, R.E.: A fast parametric maximum flow algorithm and applications. SIAM J. Comput. 18, 30–55 (1989)

[Jai07] Jain, K.: A polynomial time algorithm for computing an Arrow-Debreu market equilibrium for linear utilities. SIAM J. Comput. 37(1), 303–318 (2007)

[Wal74] Walras, L.: Elements of Pure Economics, or the Theory of Social Wealth (1874)

[Ye07] Ye, Y.: A path to the Arrow-Debreu competitive market equilibrium. Math. Program. 111(1), 315–348 (2007)

Regular Contributions

On Radiocoloring Hierarchically Specified Planar Graphs: $\mathcal{PSPACE}$-completeness and Approximations

Maria Andreou[1], Dimitris Fotakis[2], Vicky Papadopoulou Lesta[3]([✉]),
Sotiris Nikoletseas[4], and Paul Spirakis[5,6,7]

[1] Professional Training Centre, TC Square Ltd, Nicosia, Cyprus
maria@tcsquare.com.cy
[2] Division of Computer Science, School of Electrical and Computer Engineering,
National Technical University of Athens, Athens, Greece
fotakis@cs.ntua.gr
[3] Department of Computer Science and Engineering, European University Cyprus,
Egkomi, Cyprus
v.papadopoulou@euc.ac.cy
[4] Computer Technology Institute and Press Diophantus (CTI) and University
of Patras, Patras, Greece
nikole@cti.gr
[5] Department of Computer Science, University of Liverpool, Liverpool, UK
P.Spirakis@liverpool.ac.uk
[6] Department of Computer Engineering and Informatics,
University of Patras, Patras, Greece
[7] Computer Technology Institute and Press Diophantus, Patras, Greece

Abstract. Hierarchical specifications of graphs have been widely used in many important applications, such as VLSI design, parallel programming and software engineering. A well known hierarchical specification model, considered in this work, is that of Lengauer [21,22], referred to as *L-specifications*. In this paper we discuss a restriction on the L-specifications resulting to graphs which we call Well-Separated (WS). This class is recognized in polynomial time.

In this work we study the Radiocoloring Problem (RCP) on WS L-specified hierarchical planar graphs. The optimization version of RCP studied here, consists in assigning colors to the vertices of a graph, such that any two vertices of distance at most two get different colors. The objective here is to minimize the number of colors used.

We first show that RCP is $\mathcal{PSPACE}$-complete for WS L-specified hierarchical planar graphs. Second, we present a polynomial time 3-approximation algorithm as well as a more efficient asymptotic 10/3-approximation algorithm for RCP on graphs of this class. We note that,

A preliminary version of this work appeared in preliminary form in the *Proceedings of the 27th International Symposium on Mathematical Foundations of Computer Science*, pp. 81–92, Vol. 2420, LNCS, Springer-Verlag, August 2002, [2].
S. Nikoletseas—This work was partially supported by FET IP Project MULTIPLEX 317532.

© Springer International Publishing Switzerland 2015
C. Zaroliagis et al. (Eds.): Spirakis Festschrift, LNCS 9295, pp. 97–132, 2015.
DOI: 10.1007/978-3-319-24024-4_8

the best currently known approximation ratio for the RCP on ordinary (non-hierarchical) planar graphs of general degree is 5/3 asymptotically ([27,28]).

1   Introduction, Our Results and Related Work

1.1   Motivation

Many practical applications of graph theory and combinatorial optimization in CAD systems, VLSI design, parallel programming and software engineering involve the processing of large (but regular) objects constructed in a systematic manner from smaller and more manageable components. As a result, the graphs that abstract such circuits (designs) also have a regular structure and are defined in a systematic manner using smaller graphs. The methods for specifying such large but regular objects by small specifications are referred to as *succinct specifications*. One way to succinctly represent objects is to specify the graph hierarchically. Hierarchical specifications are more concise in describing objects than ordinary graph representations. A well known hierarchical specification model, considered in this work, is that of Lengauer, introduced in [21,22], referred to as *L-specifications*. According to this specification, a graph is defined by a polynomial set of graphs, each of which may contain (call) some of the other graphs as a subgraph, in a hierarchical manner. Due to the 'calls' of one subgraph to other graphss, the resulting graph obtaned by this structure might be of *exponential* size compare to the set of graphs used in the specification. For example, a binary tree with $2^{\Omega(N)}$ nodes can be specified using an L-specification of size $O(N)$.

In modern networks, Frequency Assignment Problems (FAP) have important applications in efficient bandwidth utilization, by trying to minimize the number (or the range) of frequencies used, in a way that however keeps the interference of nearby transmitters at an acceptable level. Problems of assigning frequencies in networks are usually abstracted by variations of coloring graphs. An important version of Frequency Assignment Problems is the Radiocoloring Problem (RCP). The radiocoloring problem (RCP), first introduced by Griggs and Yeh [15], is the problem of assigning radio frequencies (integers) to transmitters such that transmitters that are close (distance 2 apart) to each other receive different frequencies and transmitters that are very close together (distance 1 apart) receive frequencies that are at least two apart. The objective there is to minimize the maximum integer used by the assignment (*min span RCP*). The term *radiocoloring* is attributed to Harary [17]. The optimization version of RCP studied here, consists in assigning colors (frequencies) to the vertices (transmitters) of a graph (network), so that any two vertices of distance at most two get different colors. The objective here is to minimize the number of distinct colors used (also called *min order RCP*). In the sequel, since the paper concerns only min order RCP, for simplicity we refer to it as RCP.

In this work we study RCP on L-specified hierarchical graphs. Note that RCP is equivalent to the problem of vertex coloring the square of a graph G,

G^2, where G^2 has the same vertex set as G and there is an edge between any two vertices of G^2 if their distance in G is at most 2. We study here planar hierarchical graphs.

Also, our interest in coloring the square of a hierarchical planar graph is inspired by real communication networks, especially wireless and large ones, that may be structured in a hierarchical way and are usually planar.

1.2 Summary of Our Results

We investigate the computational complexity and provide efficient approximation algorithms for the RCP on a class of L-specified hierarchical planar graphs which we call Well-Separated (WS) graphs. In such graphs, levels in the hierarchy are allowed to directly connect *only* to their immediate descendants. In particular:

1. We prove that the decision version of the RCP for Well-Separated L-specified hierarchical planar graphs is $\mathcal{PSPACE}$-complete.
2. We present two approximation algorithms for RCP for this class of graphs. These algorithms offer alternative trade-offs between the quality and the efficiency of the solution achieved. The first one is a simple and very efficient 10/3-approximation algorithm asymptotically, while the second one achieves a better solution; it is a 3-approximation algorithm, but is less efficient, although polynomial.

A critical observation about the constructions exploited in the $\mathcal{PSPACE}$-completeness proofs of this work, is that such constructions have to exhibit some *locality characteristics* in order to be of polynomial time in the size of the L-specification of the hierarchical graph. Another important issue for the $\mathcal{PSPACE}$-completeness reductions is whether an already known $\mathcal{NP}$-completeness proof for the same problem, that fulfills the desired locality characteristics, can be modified so that to apply for a hierarchical graph G. Unfortunately, in our case, there was no such a 'local' $\mathcal{NP}$-completeness reduction available. Therefore, we provide a new $\mathcal{NP}$-completeness reduction for the RCP of ordinary planar graphs which exhibits locality properties and then, based on this construction, we design the $\mathcal{PSPACE}$-completeness reduction of the RCP of L-specified hierarchical planar graphs.

As far as the algorithmic part of the paper is concerned, remark that an approximation algorithm for hierarchically specified graphs has to compute a feasible solution to the problem for the hierarchical graph, of size exponential in its specification, using only time and space polynomial in its specification. Our approximation algorithms get as input the L-specification of a hierarchical graph and, in time and space polynomial in the size of this specification, compute a feasible solution for the RCP on the hierarchical graph. Moreover, the solution output is produced using the hierarchical specification, thus, requiring only polynomial space to be described.

We note that the class of WS L-specified hierarchical graphs considered here can lead to graphs that are exponentially large in the size of their specification. The WS class is a subclass of the class of L-specified hierarchical graphs considered in [23], called k-level-restricted graphs.

1.3   Related Work and Comparison

In a fundamental work, Lengauer and Wagner [22] proved that the following problems are $\mathcal{PSPACE}$-complete for L-specified hierarchical graphs: 3-coloring, hamiltonian circuit and path, monotone circuit value, network flow and independent set. For L-specified graphs, Lengauer ([21]) have given efficient algorithms to solve several important graph theoretic problems including 2-coloring, min spanning forest and planarity testing.

We remark that the $\mathcal{PSPACE}$-completeness proof of planar 3-coloring of WS L-specified hierarchical graphs provided in this work, is not implied by known $\mathcal{PSPACE}$-completeness results of the same problem for similar (but different) classes of planar graphs. This is so because our $\mathcal{PSPACE}$-completeness proof for planar 3-coloring concerns a subclass studied in [24] of the L-specified hierarchical planar graphs for the same problem. Moreover, the $\mathcal{PSPACE}$-completeness proof of planar 3-coloring of [25] for L-specified hierarchical graphs which are simultaneously planar and unit disks concerns a different class of hierarchical planar graphs than the class of WS L-specified hierarchical planar graphs considered here.

Marathe et al. in [23,24] studied the complexity and provided approximation schemes for several graph theoretic problems for L-specified hierarchical planar graphs including maximum independent set, minimum vertex cover, minimum edge dominating set, max 3SAT and max cut.

Note, however, that most of the work done so far on approximations of $\mathcal{PSPACE}$-complete problems, has basically addressed such "finding a subset" problems and not coloring problems. The methodologies applied for such problems, such as maximum independent set in [23], do not directly apply to coloring problems, since they exclude from a solution some vertices of each graph of the L-specification of the hierarchical graph, something not allowed in graph coloring problems. To our knowledge, the only work studying approximations to coloring problems on hierarchical graphs is the work of [25], studing a special kind of hierarchical graphs (k-level restricted unit disk graphs) achieving a 6-approximation solution. We do not see an easy way of using their algorithm for the radiocoloring problem studied here.

The RCP was studied in [29], called *distance-2-coloring*. There, it was proved there the problem is $\mathcal{NP}$-complete even for planar graphs and a 9-approximation algorithm was presented. Note that a lower bound on the number of colors needed in a radiocoloring assignment is the maximum degree of the graph G, $\Delta(G)$ (or Δ for simplicity). This is so because in vertex of maximum degree, all of its neighbors need to take distinct colors, since they are located at distance two apart. A sequence of papers concentrated in the case of planar graphs and showed upper bounds and approximation algorithms for RCP. van den Heuvel and McGuiness in [18] proved an upper of $2\Delta + 25$. Agnarsson and Halldórsson in [1] showed a bound of $\lceil 9\Delta/5 \rceil + 2$ for $\Delta \geq 749$ and $\lceil 9\Delta/5 \rceil + 1$ for $\Delta \geq 47$ by Borodin, Broersma, Glebow and van den Heuvel [7]. The best currently known upper bound for RCP which result also to a polynomial time approximation algorithm is due to Molloy and Salavatipour [27,28]: $\lceil 5\Delta/3 \rceil + 78$, for all Δ.

As it concerns the min span RCP (where the objective is to minimize the maximum color used), the problem was proved to be $\mathcal{NP}$-complete even for graphs of diameter two [11,14]. It has been proved to be $\mathcal{NP}$-complete even for planar graphs in [6,9,10]. However, exact results have been obtained for certain special class of graphs such as trees [15], cacti, unicycles, bicycles [16]. Approximate upper bounds of the problem have been presented for other graph families such as the bipartite graphs, outerplanar graphs, split graphs [6], chordal graphs [30] and unigraphs [8]. A generalized version of min span RCP, called $L(p,q)$-*labeling*, asks for an assignment of integers to the nodes of the graph so that any two vertices of distance one get colors that differ by at least p and any two nodes of distance two get integers that differ by at least q, that minimizes the maximum integer used, denoted as $\lambda_{p,q}(G)$. Note that $L(p,q)$-labeling coincides with min order RCP when $p = q = 1$. For the $L(p,q)$-labeling problem restricted on planar graphs, Van den Heuvel and McGuinness [18], showed a first upper bound: $\lambda_{p,q}(G) \leq 2(2q-1)\Delta + 10p + 38q - 24$. This bound was improved by [27] showing that $\lambda_{p,q}(G) \leq q\lceil \frac{5}{3}\Delta \rceil + 18p + 77q - 18$.

2 Preliminaries

Consider a simple, undirected graph $G(V, E)$, where V denotes its vertex set and E denotes its edge set. For any two vertices $u, v \in V$, denote as $d(u, v)$ the distance between u and v in G. The Radiocoloring problem is defined as follows:

Definition 1. Radiocoloring Problem: *Given a graph $G(V, E)$, find a radio-coloring assignment of G, i.e. a coloring function $\Lambda_{RCP} : V \to \mathbb{N}$ assigning integers (colors) to the vertices of the graph G such that $\Lambda_{RCP}(u) \neq \Lambda_{RCP}$ if $d(u, v) = 2$ and $|\Lambda_{RCP}(u) - \Lambda_{RCP}(v)| \geq 2$ if $d(u, v) = 1$.*

In this work we study an optimization version of the Radiocoloring problem ([9]), where the objective is to minimize *the number* of colors used. In this case, the problem can be quivalently defined as follows (see [9] for details):

Definition 2. Min order RCP: *Given a graph $G(V, E)$, find an assignment of G, i.e. a coloring function $\Lambda : V \to \mathbb{N}$ assigning integers (colors) to the vertices of G such that $\Lambda(u) \neq \Lambda(v)$ if $d(u, v) \leq 2$, that uses a minimum number of distinct colors. The number of different integers in such an assignment, is called* the *order of RCP on G and is denoted here by $\lambda(G)$.*

We remark that although the two functions Λ_{RCP} and Λ refer to the same problem, the RCP, they are different: In function Λ_{RCP} for any two neighbour vertices u, v, we require the colors (integers) assigned to them, $\Lambda_{RCP}(u)$, $\Lambda_{RCP}(v)$, to differ by at least two, i.e., $|\Lambda_{RCP}(u) - \Lambda_{RCP}(u)| \geq 2$. In contrast, in min order RCP, this restriction is relaxed; we require just $\Lambda_{RCP}(u) \neq \Lambda_{RCP}(u)$. For simplicity reasons, in the sequel we refer to it as the RCP. Remark that:

Proposition 1. *The min order RCP of a given graph G is equivalent to the problem of coloring the square of the graph G, G^2. G^2 has the same vertex set as G and there is an edge between any two vertices of G^2 if their distance in G is at most 2.*

We study the RCP on hierarchical graphs as specified by Lengauer [21].

Definition 3 (L-specifications, [21]). *An L-specification $\Gamma = (G_1, \cdots, G_i, \cdots, G_n)$, where n is the number of levels in the specification, of a graph G is a sequence of labeled undirected simple graphs G_i called* cells. *The graph G_i has m_i edges and n_i vertices. The p_i of the vertices are called pins. The other $(n_i - p_i)$ vertices are called inner vertices. The r_i of the inner vertices are called nonterminals. The $(n_i - r_i)$ vertices are called terminals. The remaining $n_i - p_i - r_i$ vertices of G_i that are neither pins nor nonterminals are called* explicit vertices.

Each pin of G_i has a unique label, its name. The pins are assumed to be numbered from 1 to p_i. Each nonterminal in G_i has two labels (v,t), a name and a type. The type t of a nonterminal in G_i is a symbol from $G_1, \cdots, G_{i-1}$. The neighbours of a nonterminal vertex must be terminals. If a nonterminal vertex v is of type G_j in G_i, $1 \leq j \leq i-1$, then v has degree p_j and each terminal vertex that is a neighbor of v has a distinct label (v,l) such that $1 \leq l \leq p_j$. We say that the neighbor of v labeled (v,l) matches the l-th pin of G_j.

See Fig. 1(a) for an example of an L-specification. Note that a terminal vertex may be a neighbor of several nonterminal vertices. Given an L-specification Γ, $N = \sum_{1 \leq i \leq n} n_i$ denotes the *vertex number* and $M = \sum_{1 \leq i \leq n} m_i$ denotes the

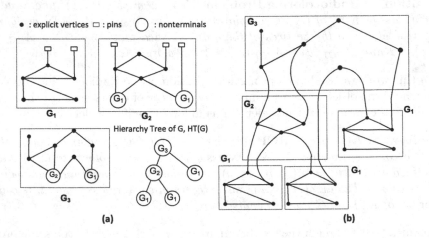

Fig. 1. (a) An L-specification $\Gamma = (G_1, G_2, G_3)$ of a graph G and its hierarchy tree $HT(G)$. (b) The expansion of the graph G.

edge number of Γ. The size of Γ, denoted by $size(\Gamma)$, is $N + M$. For simplicity reasons, we assume that $n_{max} = \max\{\max_i\{n_i\}, n\}$.

This work considers L-specified hierarchical graphs. In the sequel, for simplicity reasons we also refer to them as *hierarchical graphs*.

Definition 4 (Expansion of an L-specificied hierarchical graph, [21]).
Let any L-specified hierarchical graph, given by $\Gamma = (G_1, \cdots, G_n)$. The expanded graph $E(\Gamma)$ (i.e. the graph associated with Γ) is iteratively obtained as follows:
  $k = 1$: $E(\Gamma) = G_1$.
  $k > 1$: *Repeat the following step for each nonterminal v of G_k say of the type G_j: delete v and the edges incident on v. Insert a copy of $E(\Gamma_j)$ by identifying the l-th pin of $E(\Gamma_j)$ with the node in G_k that is labeled (v, l). The inserted copy of $E(\Gamma_j)$ is called a subcell of G_k.*

The expansion $E(\Gamma)$ is the graph associated with the L-specification Γ with vertex number N. Note that the total number of nodes in $E(\Gamma)$ can be $2^{\Omega(N)}$. For example, a complete binary tree with $2^{\Omega(N)}$ nodes can be specified using an L-specification of size $O(N)$.

For example, the expansion of the hierarchical graph G of Fig. 1(a) is shown in Fig. 1(b). To each L-specification $\Gamma = (G_1, \cdots, G_n)$, we associate a labeled rooted unoriented tree $HT(\Gamma)$ depicting the insertions of the copies of the graphs $E(\Gamma_j)$ $(1 \le j \le n - 1)$, made during the construction of $E(\Gamma)$ as follows:

Definition 5 (Hierarchy Tree of an L-specification, [21]). *Let $\Gamma = (G_1, \cdots, G_n)$, be an L-specification of the graph $E(\Gamma)$. The hierarchy tree of Γ, denoted by $HT(\Gamma)$, is a labeled rooted unordered tree defined as follows:*

1. *Let r be the root of $HT(\Gamma)$. The label of r is G_n. The children of r in $HT(\Gamma)$ are in one-to-one correspondence with the nonterminal vertices of G_n as follows: The label of the child s of r in $HT(\Gamma)$ corresponding to the nonterminal vertex (v, G_j) of G_n is (v, G_j).*
2. *For all other vertices s of $HT(\Gamma)$ and letting the label of $s = (v, G_j)$, the children of s in $HT(\Gamma)$ are in one-to-one correspondence with the nonterminal vertices of G_j as follows: The label of the child t of s in $HT(\Gamma)$ corresponding to the nonterminal vertex (w, G_l) of G_j is (w, G_l).*

See Fig. 1(a) for an example of a hierarchical graph G and its associated hierarchical tree $HT(G)$.

We consider hierarchical planar graphs as studied in [21]:

Definition 6 (Strongly planar hierarchical graph, [21]). *An L-specified hierarchical graph G given by $\Gamma = (G_1, \ldots, G_n)$ is strongly planar if $E(\Gamma)$ has a planar embedding such that for each $E(\Gamma_i)$ all pins of it occur around a common face and the rest of $E(\Gamma_i)$ is completely inside this face.*

In fact, we here study a subclass of strongly planar hierarchical graphs:

Definition 7 (Fully planar hierarchical graph). *An L-specified strongly planar hierarchical graph G given by $\Gamma = (G_1, \ldots, G_n)$ is fully planar if all of its graphs G_i, $1 \le i \le n$, are planar.*

In the sequel, and when there is no ambiguity, we refer to fully planar hierarchical graphs simply as *hierarchical planar graphs*.

Moreover, we concentrate on a class of L-specified hierarchical graphs which
we call Well-Separated (WS) graphs, defined in the sequel using the followings:

Consider an L-specified hierarchical graph G, given by $\Gamma = (G_1, \ldots, G_n)$.
For each graph G_i ($1 \leq i \leq n$), we define the following subgraphs:

Definition 8. Inner subgraph of graph G_i, **$G_{\text{in } i}$**: *is induced by the explicit vertices of G_i not connected to any pin or nonterminal of G_i.*

Definition 9. Outer-up subgraph of graph G_i, **$G_{\text{outUp } i}$**: *is induced by the
explicit vertices of G_i connected to at least one pin of G_i.*

Definition 10. Outer-down subgraph of graph G_i, **$G_{\text{outDown } i}$**: *is induced by
the explicit vertices of G_i connected to at least one nonterminal of G_i.*

For each G_i, $1 \leq i \leq n$, let also **$G_{\text{first inner } i}$** be the subgraph of G_i obtained
by the neighbours of vertices of $G_{outUp\,i}$ in G_i and let **$G_{\text{last inner } i}$** be the subgraph of G_i obtained by the neighbours of vertices of $G_{outDown\,i}$ in G_i. For an
example of the subgraphs defined above for a hierarchical graph, see Fig. 2.

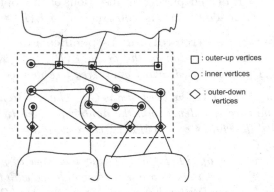

Fig. 2. An example of a graph G_i of a hierarchical graph G, considering inner, outer
up and outer down subgraphs of G_i

Remark 1. Generally, an explicit vertex of G_i might belong to both outer-up,
outer-down subgraphs of G_i. However, note that in the class of graphs considered
in this work (see the following Definition), an explicit vertex, which is not inner,
is either outer up or outer down:

Definition 11 (Well-Separated, WS). *We call Well-Separated graphs the
class of L-specified hierarchical graphs of which any explicit vertex of G_i, $1 \leq i \leq
n$, belongs either to $G_{outDown\,i}$ or $G_{outUp\,i}$ or none of them, but not to both of
them. Moreover, any vertex of $G_{outDown\,i}$ is located at distance at least 3 from
any vertex of $G_{outUp\,i}$.*

Observe that the WS class of hierarchical graphs is testable in time polynomial in the size of the L-specification of a hierarchical graph.

Note that another class of L-specified hierarchical graphs, studied by Marathe et al. [19], is defined as follows:

Definition 12 ([19]). *An L-specified graph G, with $\Gamma = (G_1, \ldots, G_n)$, is k-level-restricted if for all edges $(u; v)$ of E_i (E_i is the edge set of G_i), either (1) nu and nv are the same vertex of $HT(G_i)$, or (2) one of nu or nv is an ancestor of the other in $HT(G_i)$ and the length of the path between nu and nv in $HT(G_i)$ is no more than k.*

Proposition 2. *The class of WS hierarchically specified graphs is a subclass of the k-level-restricted graphs.*

Proof. A WS graph is an 1-level-restricted graph, which additionally has the property that for each G_i, $1 \le i \le n$, any outer up vertex of it is at distance at least 3 from any outer down vertex of it. $\qquad\square$

The following definitions and results are needed by our approximation algorithms.

Proposition 3. *The **maximum degree of an L-specified hierarchical graph** G, $\Delta(G)$, is the maximum degree of a vertex in the expansion of the graph, $E(\Gamma)$.*

Definition 13 (k-outerplanar graph G, [3]). *A k-outerplanar graph G is defined recursively by taking an embedding of the planar graph G, finding the vertices in the exterior face of the graph and removing those vertices and the edges incident to them. Then, the remaining graph should be a $(k-1)$-outerplanar graph. A 1-outerplanar graph is an outerplanar graph.*

Note that every planar graph is k-outerplanar for some k. Moreover, given a planar graph G, a k-outerplanar graph G, for which k is minimal can be found in time polynomial to the number of vertices ([4]).

Definition 14 ([5]). *The class of **k-trees** is recursively defined as follows:*

(a) *A clique of size $k+1$ is a k-tree.*

(b) *If $G(V, E)$ is a k-tree and k vertices $v_1, v_2, \cdots, v_k$ induce a complete subgraph of G, then $G' = (V \bigcup \{w\}, E \bigcup \{(v_i, w) : 1 \le i \le k\})$ is a k-tree, where w is a new vertex not contained in G.*

(c) *All k-trees can be formed with rules (a) and (b).*

Any subgraph of a k-tree is called *partial k-tree*. The minimum value of k for which a graph is a subgraph of a k-tree is called the *treewidth* of the graph.

An alternative approach of defining treewidth is via the means of *tree decomposition* [5]. This leads to an equivalent Definition.

Definition 15 ([5]). *A tree-decomposition of a graph $G(V, E)$ is a tree $T = (V_T, E_T$ with V_T a family of subsets of V satisfying the following properties.*

(i) $\bigcup_{X_i \in V_T} X_i = T$

(ii) For every edge $e(v,w) \in E$, there is a node $X_i \in V_T$ with $v, w \in X_i$ and

(iii) If node X_j lies on the path in T from node X_i to node X_l, then $X_i \cap X_l \subseteq X_j$.

Our work utilize the following theorems on bounded treewidth graphs:

Theorem 1 ([5]). *Any k-outerplanar graph is a $3k-1$ bounded treewidth graph.*

Theorem 2 ([31]). *Let $G(V,E)$ be a k-tree of n vertices given by its tree-decomposition, let C be a set of colors, and let $\alpha = |C|$. Then, it can be determined in polynomial time $T(n,k)$, whether G has a radiocoloring that uses the colors of set C, and if such a radiocoloring exists, it can found in the same time, where $T(n,k) = O(n(2\alpha + 1)^{2^{2(k+1)(l+2)+1}} + n^3)$, $l = 2$ and $n = |V|$.*

3   The Complexity of the Radiocoloring Problem

In this section, we study the complexity of RCP on L-specified hierarchical planar graphs. A critical observation about the constructions utilized in the $\mathcal{PSPACE}$-completeness proofs, is that such constructions have to exhibit some *locality characteristics*. That is, the new graph G' obtained by the initial graph G in the reduction should be computed based on local transformations applied on the vertices or edges of each graph G_i of the L-specification of the graph G without involving the transformation of the whole graph G. Moreover, the transformation should be such that the graph G'_i, resulting by applying the transformation on G_i, is the same for all appearances of G_i in the expansion of G. These properties enable to compute graphs G'_i, $1 \leq i \leq n$ only once, and from those graphs to be able to construct the new hierarchical graph G' with the desired properties, in time polynomial in the size of the L-specification of the initial graph G.

Another important issue for the $\mathcal{PSPACE}$-completeness reductions is whether an already known $\mathcal{NP}$-completeness proof for the same problem, that fulfills such locality characteristics, can be modified so that to apply for a hierarchical graph G. This technique has been used in previous papers to get $\mathcal{PSPACE}$-completeness results for a number of problems considered (e.g. [25]).

In our case, there was no such 'local' $\mathcal{NP}$-completeness reduction available. The corresponding $\mathcal{NP}$-completeness reductions that *both* could be adapted for the hierarchical case are the reductions of [26,29]. However, although the reduction of [29] is local that of [26] is not. Henceforth, they can not be used to get the $\mathcal{PSPACE}$-completeness of L-specified hierarchical planar graphs.

For these reasons, we have developed a new $\mathcal{NP}$-completeness proof for the RCP of ordinary planar graphs which reduces it from the problem of 3-coloring planar graphs. The construction satisfies the desired locality characteristics and thus, we can utilize it to get the $\mathcal{PSPACE}$-completeness proof of the RCP for L-specified hierarchical planar graphs.

3.1   The $\mathcal{NP}$-Completeness of RCP for Planar Graphs

In this section we provide a new $\mathcal{NP}$-completeness proof for the problem of radiocoloring for ordinary (non-hierarchical) planar graphs, which is 'local'.

We remark that this reduction is the only one that works for the cases where $\Delta(G) < 7$ ($\Delta(G) \geq 3$), in contrast to the only known $\mathcal{NP}$-completeness proof of [29]. In fact, we prove that even for graphs of maximum degree $\Delta(G) = 3$, it is $\mathcal{NP}$-complete to decide whether G is 4-radiocolorable or not. Note that, interestingly, the only graphs not included in this $\mathcal{NP}$-completeness result, are graphs that contain only lines and cycles.

Theorem 3. *The following decision problem is $\mathcal{NP}$-complete:*
  Input: A planar graph $G(V, E)$.
  Question: Is $\lambda(G) \leq 4$?

Proof. It can be easily seen that the problem belongs to $\mathcal{NP}$. Let any planar graph G. We reduce RCP from the 3-coloring problem of planar graphs, which is known to be $\mathcal{NP}$-complete ([13]). I.e. we will construct in polynomial time a new graph G', which is 4-radiocolorable if and only if G is 3-colorable. The reduction employs the component design technique.

The construction replaces every vertex u of degree d_u of the initial graph G with a component, called 'cycle node'. The cycle node obtained by a vertex of degree d_u is said to be 'a cycle node of degree d_u'. An instance of it is shown in Fig. 3(a). A cycle node of degree d_u is constructed as follows:

1. Add a cycle of $3d_u$ vertices, called 'outer cycle node'. Group the first three vertices into a group named a and call them a_1, a_2, a_3, the second triad of vertices into a group named b and call them b_1, b_2, b_3, end so on until the d_u-th triad of it, which is named using the d_u-th latin letter. Call the first vertex of each group, $a_1, b_1, c_1, \ldots$, as 'first' vertex, the second $a_2, b_2, c_2, \ldots$, as 'second' and the third $a_3, b_3, c_3, \ldots$ as 'third'.
2. For each group $a, b, c, \ldots$ of vertices of the outer cycle node, add one more vertex, called the 'fourth' and label it as $a_4, b_4, c_4, \ldots$ accordingly.
3. Now connect the fourth vertex of each group with the second (e.g. a_2), and third (e.g. a_3) vertex of the group, as shown in Fig. 3.
4. For each such sequence of four vertices, add one more vertex, call it 'fifth' and name it as $a_5, b_5, c_5, \ldots$ accordingly.
5. Connect the 'fifth' vertex of each group to the 'first' vertex of the group.
6. Add another cycle of vertices, call it 'inner cycle node'. The cycle consists of d_u triads of vertices as the outer cycle. The j-th group is named as the $d_u + j$-th letter of the latin alphabet. In the example of Fig. 3 these are groups e, f, g, h. The vertices of each group, assume one called x, are called as follows: The middle vertex of the group is called 'first' and is labeled x_1, the right one (clockwise) is called 'second' and is labeled x_2 and the left one (clockwise) is called 'third' and is labeled x_3.
7. Similarly to the outer cycle node, add one more vertex for each triad of the inner cycle, call it 'fourth' and label it based on from which group of vertices it is obtained by; for the example of Fig. 3 they are labeled as e_4, f_4, g_4, h_4. Then, connect the fourth vertex (e.g. e_4) of each group with the second (e.g. e_2) and the third (e.g. e_3) vertex of the group. (See Fig. 3.)

8. For each group of four vertices of the outer cycle, assume the i-th, add an edge connecting the fourth vertex (e.g. a_4) of the group to the first vertex (e.g. e_1) of the i-th group of the inner cycle.

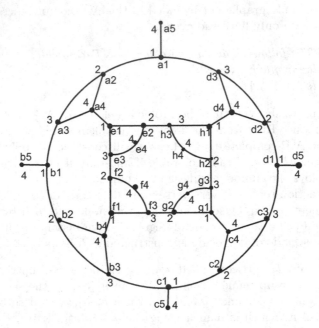

Fig. 3. (a) The 'cycle node' for a vertex of degree 4 and a 4-radiocoloring of it. (b) A graph G with a 3-coloring and the graph G' obtained with the resp. 4-radiocoloring.

In the sequel, we explain how the cycle node is used to construct in polynomial time from any planar graph G a new planar graph G', with the desired properties. We consider a planar embedding of graph G. The new graph G' is constructed as follows (See Fig. 4 for an example):

1. Replace each vertex of degree d_u of the initial graph G, with a cycle node of degree d_u.
2. For each vertex u of graph G, number the edges incident to u, in increasing, clockwise, order.
3. For every edge of the initial graph $e = (u, v)$ connecting u and v, let u_i be the number of edge e given by vertex u and let v_j be the number of the edge e given by vertex v. Then, take the fifth vertex of the u_i-th group of the cycle node of vertex u and the fifth vertex of the v_j-th group of the cycle node of vertex v and collapse them to a single vertex uv.

An example of a graph G and the new graph G' obtained is shown in Fig. 4 (depicted in a compact way). It can easily be seen that the new graph G' is a planar graph. We next prove two Lemmas showing that G' is 4-radiocolorable if and only if the initial graph G is 3-colorable.

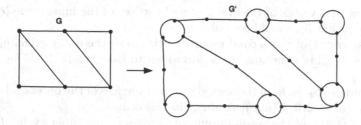

Fig. 4. An instance of the graph G with a 3-coloring and the new graph G' obtained with the respective 4-radiocoloring.

Lemma 1. *If $\chi(G) \leq 3$ then $\lambda(G') \leq 4$.*

Proof. Consider a 3-coloring of the initial graph G, using colors $\{1, 2, 3\}$. Let the following radiocoloring assignment on the graph G' using 4 colors:

For any vertex u of the initial graph colored i, $i \in \{1, 2, 3\}$: (i) Color the 1-st vertices of the cycle node of vertex u in G', (vertices $a_1, b_1, c_1, \dots$) with color i. Let $j, j' \in \{1, 2, 3\}$ with $j \neq j'$, $j, j' \neq i$. (ii) Color all 2-nd vertices of the cycle node of u with color j. (iii) Color all 3-rd vertices of the cycle node of u with color j'. (iv) Color all 4-th vertices of the cycle node of u with color 4. (v) Color all 5-th vertices with the same color as the 4-th vertices, color 4.

We now prove that the suggested radiocoloring assignment is valid. An example for such a radiocoloring for a cycle node of degree 4 is shown in Fig. 3. It can be easily seen that there is no conflict between any two vertices of the cycle node.

Consider now any neighbour cycle nodes, i.e. nodes that are obtained by neighbour vertices in G. We argue that there is no conflict between the colors of any two vertices of the two cycle nodes. To see why, recall that the 'fifth' vertex, call it f, connecting the two cycle nodes is colored 4. Also, the corresponding 'first' vertices of the two cycle nodes, connected to the 'fifth' vertex f, are colored using colors of set $\{1, 2, 3\}$. Each of them is forbidden to take, besides the colors of the vertices of its cycle node, also the color of the other first vertex in the other cycle node. This color is different from its color since the two vertices took the color that their corresponding vertices take in the 3-coloring of G. Thus, there is no conflict between any two vertices of neighbour cycle nodes. Consequently, the suggested radiocoloring of G' is valid.   □

The next four claims are needed to prove that if $\lambda(G') \leq 4$, then $\chi(G) \leq 3$.

Claim 4. *If $\lambda(G') \leq 4$ then for any cycle node u, all of its first vertices (of its outer and inner cycle) take the same color.*

Proof. Consider any radiocoloring assignment of G'. Assume that the a_1-vertex of a cycle node u is colored by j, and w.l.o.g. let $j = 1$. Then, we get:

– The vertices a_2, a_3, a_4 of the first group of vertices of the outer cycle, should take colors $2, 3, 4$ (not necessarily in this order).

- Then, the first vertex of the first group of vertices of the inner cycle (e_1 in the example of Fig. 3), should get color 1.
- The first vertex of the second group of vertices of the outer cycle, b_1 should get color 1. This is because b_1 is forbidden to take colors $2, 3, 4$ by vertices a_2, a_3, a_4.
- Thus, vertices b_2, b_3, b_4 of the second group of vertices of the outer cycle, should take the colors $2, 3, 4$ (not necessarily in this order).
- The first vertex of the second group of vertices of the inner cycle (f_1 in the example of Fig. 3), should get color 1.
  Continuing in the same way for the remaining groups of vertices of the cycle node, for a group of vertices of the outer cycle, assume one named x, we get that:
- The 2nd, 3th and 4th vertex of group x of vertices of the outer cycle, should take colors $2, 3, 4$ (not necessarily in this order).
- Then, the first vertex of group x of vertices of the inner cycle, should get color 1.
- Also, the first vertex of the group $x + 1$ of vertices of the outer cycle, should get color 1 (we use $x + 1$ here to denote the letter following x in the latin alphabet). This is because this vertex is forbidden to take colors $2, 3, 4$ by the 2nd, 3th and 4th vertex of the group x of vertices of the outer cycle.

We conclude that for any cycle node of the graph G', if one first vertex is colored j then all first vertices of it (of the outer and inner cycle of it) get the color j. □

Claim 5. *If $\lambda(G') \leq 4$ then for any cycle node u, all of its fourth vertices (of its outer and inner cycle) take the same color.*

Proof. Consider any radiocoloring assignment of G'. Assume that the a_4-vertex of a cycle node u is colored by j, and w.l.o.g. let $j = 4$. By Claim 4, we know that all of its first vertices are colored with the same color (different than color 4), assume 1. Furthermore, we have:

- The vertices a_2, a_3 of the first group of vertices of the outer cycle, should take colors $2, 3$ (not necessarily in this order).
- Then, the 2nd and 3rd vertices of the first group of vertices of the inner cycle, (e_2, e_3 in the example of Fig. 3), should take colors $2, 3$. This is because they can not take colors $1, 4$ by vertices e_1, a_4.
- The 4th vertex of the first group of vertices of the inner cycle, (e_4 in the example of Fig. 3), should take color 4. This is because it is forbidden to take colors $1, 2, 3$ of vertices e_1, e_2, e_3.
- Then, the 2nd vertex of the second group of vertices of the inner cycle node (f_2 in our example), is forbidden to take colors $1, 2$ (*or* 3), 4 of vertices e_1, e_3, e_4. Thus, it can take color 3 *or* 2.
- The 4th vertex of the second group of vertices of the inner cycle, (f_4 in the example of Fig. 3), should take color 4. This is because it is forbidden to take colors $1, 2, 3$ of vertices f_1, f_2, e_3.

- Then, the 3rd vertex of the second group of vertices of the inner cycle node, (f_3 in our example) is forbidden to take colors $1, 3$ (or 2), 4 by vertices f_1, f_2, f_4. Thus, it can take color 3 or 2.
- Thus, the 4th vertex of the second group of vertices of the outer cycle, b_4, is forbidden to take colors $1, 2, 3$ by vertices f_1, f_2, f_3. Hence, vertex b_4 can only take color 4.
  Continuing in the same way for the rest groups of vertices of the cycle node, for a group of vertices of the outer cycle, assume one named x, we get that:
- The vertices x_2, x_3 of group x of vertices of the outer cycle, should take colors $2, 3$ (not necessarily in this order). This is because vertices x_1, x_4 are colored $1, 4$.
- Take the group of vertices of the inner cycle corresponding to group x. Assume that is named x'. The 2nd and 3rd vertices of group x', vertices x'_2, x'_3, should take colors $2, 3$, not necessarily in this order. This is because they can not take colors $1, 4$ of vertices x'_1, x_4.
- The 4th vertex of group x of vertices of the inner cycle, (x'_4), should take color 4. This is because it is forbidden to take colors $1, 2, 3$ by vertices x'_1, x'_2, x'_3.
- Then, the 2nd vertex of group $x'+1$ of vertices of the inner cycle node ($x'+1$ denotes the letter following x' in the latin alphabet), $(x'+1)_2$ is forbidden to take colors $1, 2$ (or 3), 4 by vertices x'_1, x'_3, x'_4. Thus, it can take color 3 (or 2).
- The 4th vertex of group $x'+1$ of vertices of the inner cycle, $(x'+1)_4$, should take color 4. This is because it is forbidden to take colors $1, 2, 3$ of vertices $(x'+1)_1, (x'+1)_2, x'_3$.
- Then, the 3th vertex of group $x'+1$ of vertices of the inner cycle node, $((x'+1)_3$ in our example) is forbidden to take colors $1, 3$ (or 2), 4 by vertices $(x'+1)_1, (x'+1)_2, (x'+1)_4$. Thus, it can take color 3 (or 2).
- Thus, the 4th vertex of group $x+1$ of vertices of the outer cycle, $(x+1)_4$, is forbidden to take colors $1, 2, 3$ by vertices $(x'+1)_1, (x'+1)_2, (x'+1)_3$. Hence, vertex $(x+1)_4$ can take only color 4.

We conclude that for any cycle node of the graph G', if one fourth vertex is colored j then all fourth vertices of it (of the outer and inner cycle of it) get the color j.   □

Claim 6. *If $\lambda(G') \leq 4$ for any cycle node u, all of its fifth vertices take the same color and this color is the same as the color of the fourth vertices of the cycle node.*

Proof. Consider any radiocoloring assignment of G'. By Claim 4, we know that all of its first vertices are colored with the same color, assume w.l.o.g. color 1. Moreover, by Claim 5, we know that all of its fourth vertices are colored with the same color (different than the color of the first vertices) assume 4. Furthermore, we have:

- The vertices a_2, a_3 of the first group of vertices of the outer cycle, should take colors $2, 3$, assume a_2 takes color 2 and a_3 takes color 3.

- Then, the 2nd vertex of the second group of vertices of the outer cycle, b_2, should take color 2. This is because it is forbidden to take colors $1, 3, 4$ by vertices b_1, a_3, b_4.
- The 5th vertex of the second group of vertices of the outer cycle, b_5, should take color 4. This is because it is forbidden to take colors $1, 2, 3$ by vertices b_1, b_2, a_3.
- The 3rd vertex of the second group of vertices of the outer cycle, b_3, should take color 3. This is because it is forbidden to take colors $1, 2, 4$ by vertices b_1, b_2, b_4.

Continuing in the same way for the rest groups of vertices of the cycle node, for a group of vertices of the outer cycle, assume one named x, we get that:

- The 2nd vertex of group x of vertices of the outer cycle, x_2, should take color 2. This is because it is forbidden to take colors $1, 3, 4$ by vertices $x_1, (x-1)_3, x_4$.
- Then, the 5th vertex of group x of vertices of the outer cycle, x_5, should take color 4. This is because it is forbidden to take colors $1, 2, 3$ by vertices $x_1, x_2, (x-1)_3$.
- The 3rd vertex of the second group of vertices of the outer cycle, x_3, should take color 3. This is because it is forbidden to take colors $1, 2, 4$ by vertices x_1, x_2, x_4.

We conclude that for any cycle node of the graph G', if one fifth vertex is colored j then all fifth vertices of it (of the outer and inner cycle of it) get the color j. □

Claim 7. *If $\lambda(G') \leq 4$ then all fifth vertices of all cycle nodes take the same color.*

Proof. Consider a vertex of the initial graph G and the cycle node in G' corresponding to it, let u. Let a fifth vertex of it; assume w.l.o.g. that it is colored 4. Then, by Claim 6, all fifth vertices of the cycle node get color 4.

Consider any neighbour to u cycle node, v. The cycle nodes of the two nodes are connected through a fifth vertex of their cycle nodes, let it be uv. By Claim 6 all fifth vertices of the cycle node v get the same color as vertex uv, i.e. 4. Recall that vertex uv is connected to a first vertex of node u, call it u'_1 and to a first vertex of the cycle node v, call it v'_1.

Applying the same arguments to the rest of the neighbours of u, we get that all fifth vertices of their cycle nodes get color 4. Continuing, in the same way, for each neighbour, we finally get that all fifth vertices of all cycle nodes of the whole graph get the same color. □

Lemma 2. *If $\lambda(G') \leq 4$ then $\chi(G) \leq 3$.*

Proof. Consider any radiocoloring of G' using 4 colors. Consider a vertex of the initial graph G and the cycle node in G' corresponding to it, u. Let a fifth vertex of it; assume w.l.o.g. that it is colored 4. Then, by Claim 7, all fifth vertices of all cycle nodes of G' get the same color, 4.

Since every first vertex of any cycle node of G' is at distance one from a fifth vertex (colored 4), it is forbidden to take color 4. Thus, any first vertex of any cycle node of G' can take only three of the four colors of the palette, that is the colors $\{1, 2, 3\}$. By Claim 4, all first vertices of any cycle node colored i, get the same color i, $i \in \{1, 2, 3\}$.

Now return to G. Let the following coloring of G, f: Assign to each vertex u of the graph G the color that the first vertices of the corresponding to it cycle node take in the radiocoloring of G' considered. We argue that this is a valid 3-coloring of the graph G. To see why observe that, as we have shown above, all first vertices of G' take only 3 colors. Thus, the assignment f of G uses 3 colors. Moreover, recall also that, by Claim 4, all first vertices of a cycle node colored i get the same color i. Thus, in G', for each cycle node u, all of it first vertices (colored with the same color) 'see' the colors of the corresponding first vertices of all neighbour cycle nodes of u. This is equivalent to the colors that the corresponding to u vertex in G 'see' by all of its neighbours. Hence, since the first vertices of G' have no conflicts with their neighbour first vertices, there is no conflict with the colors of any vertex in G and its neighbours. Thus, if G' can be radiocolored with 4 colors, then there is a 3-coloring of G.   □

This completes the $\mathcal{NP}$-completeness proof.   □

3.2   The $\mathcal{PSPACE}$-Completeness of RCP for Hierarchical Planar Graphs

The $\mathcal{PSPACE}$-completeness reduction for the RCP of L-specified hierarchical planar graphs, utilizes the construction of the $\mathcal{NP}$-completeness proof of the radiocoloring problem for ordinary planar graphs, given in Sect. 3.1, Theorem 3, exploiting its locality properties in order to achieve a construction of time polynomial in the size of the L-specification of the hierarchical graph.

The $\mathcal{PSPACE}$-completeness proofs use the following *categorization of the edges of G_i into 3 kinds*: (a) edges connecting an explicit vertex of G_i to another explicit vertex, called *explicit edges*, (b) edges connecting an explicit vertex with a pin of G_i, called *pin edges*, (c) edges connecting an explicit vertex of G_i with a nonterminal called by G_i, which we call *nonterminal edges*.

The $\mathcal{PSPACE}$-completeness of 3-coloring for hierarchical planar graphs. In order to be able to utilize the $\mathcal{NP}$-completeness reduction of Theorem 3 to prove the $\mathcal{PSPACE}$-completeness of RCP for hierarchical planar graphs we need to know that the 3-coloring problem of L-specified hierarchical planar graphs is $\mathcal{PSPACE}$-complete.

Theorem 8. *The following decision problem is $\mathcal{PSPACE}$-complete:*
   Input: A fully planar hierarchical graph G, given by the L-specification $\Gamma = (G_1, \ldots, G_n)$.
   Question: Is $\chi(G) \leq 3$?

Proof. We adapt the $\mathcal{NP}$-completeness construction of [12].
   Membership in $\mathcal{PSPACE}$: For a given hierarchical planar graph G one chooses nondeterministically a color from $\{1, 2, 3\}$ for every vertex of $E(\Gamma)$ and

checks whether this is really a coloring of $E(\Gamma)$. If this is done in a depth-first manner in the expansion tree $E(\Gamma)$, then such an algorithm can be accomplished using polynomial space.

$\mathcal{PSPACE}$-**completeness**: We reduce the problem of 3-coloring an L-specified hierarchical planar graph from the 3-coloring of L-specified hierarchical general graphs adapting the $\mathcal{NP}$-completeness construction of [12]. The 3-coloring of L-specified hierarchical general graphs is known to be $\mathcal{PSPACE}$-complete ([22]).

Let any L-specified hierarchical general graph G. From the L-specification of G, $\Gamma = (G_1, G_2, \ldots, G_n)$, we construct in polynomial time to the size of the L-specification of G, a new L-specified hierarchical planar graph G', defined by $\Gamma' = (G'_1, G'_2, \ldots, G'_n)$.

First recall that in the transformation of [12] each edge having a crossing is replaced by a component of Fig. 5, called '*diamond*', where H is the subgraph presented in the same Figure. The component has as many 'diamonds' as the number of crossings of the edge.

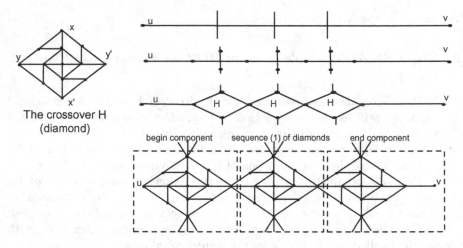

The crossover H
(diamond)

begin component   sequence (1) of diamonds   end component

Fig. 5. The Crossover H (diamond) and the transformation of an edge to a sequence of diamonds.

Observe also that the component that replaces an edge is not a symmetric graph. We call the left part of the component shown in Fig. 5 as *begin component*, the internal part that contains the sequence of diamonds, also shown in Fig. 5, as *sequence of diamonds* and the right part of the component, shown in Fig. 5, as *end component*.

Let $G_i = (V_i, E_i)$ be any graph of the L-specification of G. For each G_i we consider a topology such that all of its pins are located in the boundary face of the graph.

For each graph G_i, we construct a new graph $G'_i = (V'_i, E'_i)$ using the following rules:

1. The graph G'_i has the same explicit and nonterminal vertices as the graph G_i. However, the type of each nonterminal called by G_i, assume G_j, is changed to G'_j.
2. The transformation of each edge of G_i is almost the same as that of [12]. Each kind of edges of G_i (explicit, nonterminal, pin edges) is transformed as follows:
   (a) For each explicit edge uv having i crossings, replace it by a component of Fig. 5 having i diamonds. The begin of the component can be either vertex u or v.
   (b) For each nonterminal edge connecting an explicit vertex u with a nonterminal node, assume one of type G_j:

   – If the edge has no crossing, then replace it by the begin component shown in Fig. 6 (a).

   – If the edge has k crossings ($k \geq 1$), then replace it by a begin component and a sequence of $k - 1$ diamonds as shown in Fig. 6 (b) for the case where $k = 2$.

   Note that in both cases, the edge connecting u to the nonterminal G_j, is replaced by a component that has three edges connected to the nonterminal G_j. As we will show in the next case (c), the pins of the nonterminal will also be triplicated so that each such edge will match the appropriate pin.
   (c) For each pin edge connecting an explicit vertex v with a pin of G_i, p:

   – If the edge has no crossing, then replace it by the end component of Fig. 6 (c).

   – If the edge has k crossings ($k \geq 1$), then replace it by an end component and a sequence of $k-1$ diamonds as shown in Fig. 6 (d) for the case where $k = 2$.

   Note that, again, in both cases, the edge connecting v to the pin p, is replaced by a component that has three pins. In this way, the pins of G'_i are triplicated compared to the pins of G_i.

We now prove that graphs $G'_1, G'_2, \ldots, G'_n$ obtained by the graphs $G_1, G_2, \ldots, G_n$ of the L-specification of G, define a new L-specified hierarchical graph G'.

Consider any graph G'_i. From it, applying the constructive Definition 4, we can get the graph $E(\Gamma'_i)$. To see why take any nonterminal G'_j called by G'_i. Recall that by the transformation, each pin p of G_j is replaced in G'_j by three pins p_1, p_2, p_2. Moreover, note that each edge e of G_i connected to G_j is replaced in G'_i by three edges e_1, e_2, e_3 connected to G'_j. Hence, in $E(\Gamma'_i)$ every edge connected to a nonterminal called by it, matches the appropriate pin of the nonterminal. Finally, from G'_n applying Definition 4, we get $E(\Gamma'_n)$. Thus, in this way, graphs $G'_1, \ldots, G'_n$ define a new hierarchical graph G' specified by $\Gamma' = (G'_1, \ldots, G'_n)$ using the L-specification. Moreover, observe that since the transformation eliminates all crossings the new hierarchical graph obtained is a planar graph. Finally, note that since the transformation is applied only once to each G_i, the construction of G' is performed in polynomial time to the size of the L-specification of G.

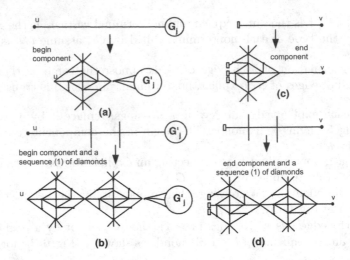

Fig. 6. The edge transformation of a nonterminal edge and pin edge.

Next, we prove that the new planar graph G' obtained by G is 3-colorable if and only if G is 3-colorable. In particular, we will show that the expansion of the hierarchical planar graph G', $E(\Gamma')$ obtained by G exhibits the same properties as the graph obtained by the expansion of G, $E(\Gamma)$, when the transformation of [12] is applied on it.

To see why, consider the expansion $E(\Gamma'_i)$ of the graph G'_i obtained by graph G_i. This graph is the same as the corresponding graph obtained using the construction of [12], except that: (1) In [12] only the edges that have a crossing are replaced by the component of Fig. 5, while in our construction, all edges corresponding to pin or nonterminal edges are replaced by the component of Fig. 5. (2) An edge in the construction of [12] having k ($k \geq 1$) crossings is replaced by a sequence of k diamonds. In our construction it is replaced by a sequence of at most $k + 1$ diamonds.

We argue that these two differences do not have any influence on the desired properties of the new graph $E(\Gamma'_i)$ obtained. As it far as it concerns the first difference, note that after the transformation of each such edge uv, the two neighbour vertices u and v 'see' the color of the other vertex as in [12]. As far as it concerns the second difference, note that although the diamonds of the component might be more than those of the corresponding component in [12], the property of the transformation still holds; that is the two neighbour vertices u and v 'see' the color of the other neighbour vertex as in [12].

Since the two constructions are equivalent, we can use the same arguments used in [12] to prove that the new hierarchical planar graph G' is 3-colorable if and only if the initial hierarchical graph G is 3-colorable.

Finally, we prove that the resulting L-specified graph is a fully planar hierarchical graph. This is true because (i) For each G_i we consider a topology such that all of its pins are located in the boundary face of the graph. Thus, in the resulting graph the corresponding pins are also located in the boundary face of the graph. (ii) For each G_i, the transformation eliminates all crossings; henceforth, we get that each G_i' is a planar graph. The above two conditions prove that the resulting L-specified hierarchical graph G' is a fully planar graph.   □

Comment. A similar result has been proved in [25] for a restricted class of L-specified hierarchical graphs which are simultaneously planar and unit disks. However their reduction does not clearly address the case of strongly planar graphs. Notice that our class is slightly different and neither a subset nor a superset of their class.

The $PSPACE$-completeness of RCP for hierarchical planar graphs. Before introducing the $PSPACE$-completeness Theorem, the following observation is needed. We denote by $d(u)_H$ the degree of vertex u in graph H.

Observation 1. *Let any graph G_i of the L-specification of a hierarchical graph G. Then, for any explicit vertex u in G_i, it holds that $d(u)_{G_i} = d(u)_{E(\Gamma)}$*

Proof. Recall Definition 4. For any explicit vertex v of G_i, any explicit edge incident to u remains the same in $E(\Gamma)$. Any pin edge incident to u in G_i, in $E(\Gamma)$ is replaced by a single edge connecting u to the corresponding vertex of a graph that calls G_i, in every appearance of G_i in $E(\Gamma)$. Thus, in this case, too, the degree of vertex u does not change in $E(\Gamma)$.   □

Theorem 9. *The following decision problem is $PSPACE$-complete:*
   Input: A WS fully planar hierarchical graph G, given by the L-specification $\Gamma = (G_1, \ldots, G_n)$.
   Question: Is $\lambda(G) \leq 4$?

Proof. **Membership in $PSPACE$:** Similar to the $PSPACE$-membership of 3-coloring a hierarchical planar graph of Theorem 8.

   $PSPACE$-**completeness**: We reduce the RCP for hierarchical planar graphs from the 3-coloring of fully planar hierarchical graphs proved to be $PSPACE$-complete in Theorem 8. Our reduction uses that construction of Theorem 3 used to prove the NP-completeness of RCP for ordinary planar graphs.

   Let any L-specified hierarchical planar graph G, given by $\Gamma = (G_1, \ldots, G_n)$. For each graph $G_i = (V_i, E_i)$ of its L-specification we construct a new graph $G_i' = (V_i', E_i')$ using the rules of Theorem 3:

1. Each explicit vertex u of degree d_u of G_i is replaced by a 'cycle node' of degree d_u defined in Theorem 3.
2. Take each edge $e = (u, v)$ of G_i connecting two explicit vertices u and v, and take the corresponding fifth vertices of the cycle nodes of vertices u and v. Collapse it to a single vertex uv connecting the corresponding 'first' vertices of the two cycle nodes. See Fig. 7(a).
3. All nonterminal vertices of G_i are present in G_i'. However, the type of a nonterminal, assume one of type G_j is changed to G_j'.
4. Take each $e = (u, t)$ of G_i connecting an explicit vertex u to a nonterminal vertex t called by G_i, assume of type G_j. Assume moreover, that the edge has label (t, l), i.e. u matches the l-th pin of the graph G_j. Then, connect the

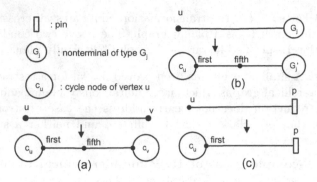

Fig. 7. The transformation of graph G_i to graph G'_i.

corresponding fifth vertex f of the cycle node of u to the nonterminal t and associate it with the label (t, l) (i.e. vertex f matches the l-th pin of G_j). See Fig. 7(b).

5. All pins vertices of G_i are present in G'_i.
6. Take each edge $e = (u, p)$ of G_i connecting an explicit vertex u to a pin p of G_i, numbered as the l-th. Then, remove the corresponding fifth vertex of the cycle node of vertex u and connect the corresponding first vertex of the cycle node to the pin p. See Fig. 7(c).

Observe that the above procedure applied on all graphs $G_1, G_2, \ldots, G_n$ of G, only once for each G_i, results to a set of graphs $G'_1, G'_2, \ldots, G'_n$ that define a new L-specified hierarchical graph G', given by $\Gamma' = (G'_1, G'_2, \ldots, G'_n)$. To see why note that the same graph G'_i results applying the above procedure in any appearance of the graph G_i in the hierarchical tree $HT(\Gamma)$ of G. Note also that the graph G'_i calls the same set of terminals as G_i. Finally, observe that the graph G'_i obtained by G_i by the above procedure has the same pins as G_i. The next lemmas prove that the new graph is 4-radiocolorable if and only if the initial graph is 3-colorable.

Lemma 3. *If $\chi(G) \leq 3$ then $\lambda(G') \leq 4$.*   □

Lemma 4. *If $\lambda(G') \leq 4$, then $\chi(G) \leq 3$.*   □

The two lemmas are proved using the same arguments as those in the proofs of Lemmas 1, 2, respectively, and the observation that the expansion of the graph G' obtained, $E(\Gamma')$, is the same graph as the graph obtained by the construction of Theorem 3 when applied on the expansion of the initial hierarchical graph G.

Next, we prove that the resulting graph is a fully planar hierarchical graph: Observe that, (i) the initial graph G is a hierarchical graph and the transformation introduces no crossings, satisfying the second condition of fully planar hierarchical graphs, (ii) the transformation keeps the pins of the resulting graph in the outside face of the graph, satisfying the first condition of such graphs.

Finally, we prove that the resulting graph is a WS hierarchical graph: Take any outer up vertex u of any G'_i of G', connected to a pin p. In the worst case, the vertex is also an outer down vertex. Let v the nonterminal connected to v. Thus, the degree of the vertex is at least 2. By the transformation, it is replaced by a cycle node of degree at least 2. Recall that a first vertex of the cycle node, call it f, is connected to pin p of G'_i and a fifth vertex, call it t, of the cycle node is connected to nonterminal v of G'_i. Observe now, that the first vertex f is located at distance at least 4 from the fifth vertex t of the cycle node. Since, we get the same result for each graph G_i, $1 \leq i \leq n$, we conclude that the resulting graph G' is a WS fully planar hierarchical graph. $\square$

4   Approximations to RCP for WS Fully Planar Graphs

In this section, we present two approximation algorithms for the min order RCP on WS fully planar hierarchical graphs: a simple and fast algorithm, that achieves an approximation ratio of $10/3$ (asymptotically), and a more sophisticated one which, being still polynomial, achieves a 3-approximation ratio. These algorithms offer alternative options that trade-off the efficiency of the algorithm and the quality of the solution achieved. Both algorithms utilize a bottom up methodology of radiocoloring an L-specified hierarchical planar graph G, given by $\Gamma = (G_1, \ldots, G_n)$. By this method the algorithms radiocolor graphs G_1, G_2, and so on up to G_n in G's specification. Actually, they compute at most $n - i$ radiocolorings for a subgraph of each graph G_i, $1 \leq i \leq n$, and use these radiocolorings for all copies of G_i in the expansion $E(\Gamma)$ of G. This enables them to run in time only polynomial to the size of the L-specification of G.

More analytically, we wish to compute only one radiocoloring assignment for each G_i, and use this in all appearances of G_i in the expansion $E(\Gamma)$ of G. However, due to the structure of L-specified hierarchical graphs, the distance two neighborhood of the outer vertices of each G_i, may differentiate for every call of G_i by other graphs G_j. Henceforth, a radiocoloring for such a vertex (the outer ones) may become invalid due to a change of the distance two neighborhood of the vertex. Since each graph G_i may be called by at most $n - i$ other graphs, we need to compute at most $n - i$ radiocolorings of those (outer) vertices.

Moreover, we need to guarantee that the different radiocolorings of the outer part of G_i do not introduce any implication in the radiocoloring of its inner part. By having only one radiocoloring for the inner part of G_i, we manage to have also no implications to the radiocoloring of the subtree of G_i, $HT(G_i)$.

Based on this design approach, both algorithms partition appropriately, each G_i into three parts: (1) *the inner part*, (2) *the outer up* and (2) *the outer down part*. Remark, that these subgraphs might be different from the inner, outer up, outer down subgraphs of G_i defined in the Definitions 8, 9 and 10.

Then, the algorithms radiocolor the inner part of G_i only once, using, each of them, a different method. However, both of them, group and radiocolor the outer down part of it together with the outer up parts of the graphs called by it, using the best known approximation algorithm.

4.1   A 10/3-Approximation Algorithm RC_Approx

We first provide a simple and efficient algorithm (RC_Approx) that achieves an asymtotic 10/3-approximation for RCP on WS fully planar hierarchical graphs. Let A_1, B_1 two disjoint sets of colors of size $\lceil 5\Delta(G)/3 \rceil + 78$ each, where $\Delta(G)$ is the maximum degree of G.

Overview of the RC_Approx Algorithm: First, the algorithm defines for each G_i its inner, outer up and outer down parts to be the inner, outer up and outer down subgraphs $G_{in\ i}$, $G_{outUp\ i}$ and $G_{outDown\ i}$, respectively.

Then, the algorithm radiocolors the inner part of the graph G_i using the best known approximation algorithm i.e. the algorithm of [27,28] using the color set A_1. Finally, the algorithm radiocolors the outer down part of the graph G_i together with the outer up parts of its children using again the best known approximation algorithm (i.e. algorithm of [27,28]) with the color set B_1. Recall that the radiocoloring algorithm of [27,28] uses at most $\lceil 5\Delta(G)/3 \rceil + 78$ colors.

The description of algorithm RC_Approx appears in Fig. 8.

RC_Approx Algorithm

For each G_i, $1 \leq i \leq n$ do:

1. Let $G'_{in\ i} = G_{outUp\ i} \bigcup G_{in\ i} \bigcup G_{outDown\ i}$.
2. Apply the best known radiocoloring algorithm, i.e. the algorithm of [28, 27], for ordinary planar graphs on Gin'_i using colors of set A_1. Ignore the coloring of vertices of $G'_{in\ i}$ that are not in $Gin_{in\ i}$ (outer up, down vertices of G_i).
3. Let $G_{out\ i} = G_{outDown\ i} \bigcup_{\forall\ j\ called\ by\ G_i} \{\cup G_{outUp\ j}\}$. Also, let
   $$G'_{out\ i} \quad = \quad G_{last\ inner\ i} \bigcup G_{outDown\ i} \bigcup_{\forall\ j\ called\ by\ G_i} \{\cup G_{outUp\ j} \quad \cup$$
   $G_{first\ inner\ j}\}$
4. Apply the best known radiocoloring algorithm, i.e. the algorithm of [28, 27], for ordinary planar graphs on $G'_{out\ i}$ using colors of set B_1. Ignore the coloring of vertices of $G'_{out\ i}$ not in $G_{out\ i}$ (last inner vertices of G_i and first inner vertices of its children).

Fig. 8. Algorithm RC_Approx

Analysis of the RC_Approx algorithm

Theorem 10. *Algorithm $RC\_Approx(G)$ produces a radiocoloring of a WS fully planar hierarchical graph G in time $O(n_{max}^5)$ and achieves a 10/3-approximation ratio, asymptotically.*

Proof. Correctness

Observe first that the algorithm, during the radiocoloring of the subgraphs of each graph G_i, it considers 'extensions' of those subgraphs. E.g. in order to get a radiocoloring of $G_{in\ i}$, it considers $G'_{in\ i}$, which contains $G_{in\ i}$ but also subgraphs $G_{outUp\ i}$ and $G_{outDown\ i}$. This is required in order to get a valid radiocoloring of $G_{in\ i}$, because, a vertex of those graphs ($G_{outUp\ i}$ and $G_{outDown\ i}$) may be connected to more than one vertex of $G_{in\ i}$ making those vertices of $G_{in\ i}$ distance two neighbours. Similar arguments prove that graphs $G'_{out\ i}$, $G'_{out\ j}$ (G_j calls G_i) are required in order to produce valid radiocolorings for graphs $G_{out\ i}$, $G_{out\ j}$, respectively.

The radiocoloring assignment for each subgraph of G is computed using the best known radiocoloring algorithm (i..e the algorithm of [27,28]) for ordinary planar graphs. Since these algorithms require for the radiocoloring of a graph G with maximum degree $\Delta(G)$, at most $\lceil 5\Delta/3 \rceil + 78$ colors, the sets A_1, B_1 of the same size can be used to produce a valid radiocoloring on any subgraph of G.

We next prove that there is no conflict between any two vertices of a graph G_i or a vertex of G_i and a nearby vertex of a graph that calls G_i or a graph that is called by G_i. Recall that:

Each G_i is partitioned into 3 parts:

- $G_{up\ i}$: is radiocolored together with each graph G_j that calls G_i, and the other outer up vertices of the graphs that are also called by G_j, graph $G_{out\ j}$, using color set A_1.
- $G_{in\ i}$: is radiocolored using color set B_1.
- $G_{down\ i}$: is radiocolored together with the outer up vertices of the graphs that are called by G_i, graph $G_{out\ i}$, using color set A_1.

Since $G_{up\ i}$ and $G_{in\ i}$ are radiocolored using different colors, there is no conflict between them. $G_{up\ i}$ and $G_{down\ i}$ are radiocolored using the same set of colors, A_1. However, there is no conflict because there are located at distance at least 3 apart by the definition of class WS of hierarchical graphs considered here. Also, there is no conflict between $G_{up\ i}$ (colored in $G_{out\ j}$) and $G_{in\ j}$ because they are radiocolored using different color sets. Finally, there is no conflict between $G_{down;i}$ (colored in $G_{out\ i}$) and $G_{in\ j}$ (G_j is a child of G_i) because they are radiocolored using a different set of colors.

The above arguments prove that the *RC_Approx* algorithm produces a valid radiocoloring of the hierarchical planar graph G.

Performance and Approximation ratio

The algorithm for each G_i computes a radiocoloring assignment using the best known radiocoloring algorithm ([27,28]). That algorithm require $O(n^2)$ time for the radiocoloring of a graph of size n. Remark that when considering the outer down vertices of G_i and their possible children, we get a subgraph of size (number of vertices) n_i^2. Thus, the radiocoloring algorithm used needs time $O(n_i^4)$. Since this procedure is called for each G_i, $1 \leq i \leq n$, the algorithm needs $O(n_{max}^5)$ time in total.

To compute the approximation ratio of *RC_Approx* algorithm, recall that it uses two sets of colors of size $\lceil 5\Delta(G)/3 \rceil + 78$ each. Observe also that the maximum degree of the graph G, $\Delta(G)$ is a lower bound on the number of colors needed for the radiocoloring of the graph G. Since *RC_Approx* algorithm uses color sets A_1, B_1 for the radiocoloring computed, it uses $2(\lceil 5\Delta(G)/3 \rceil) + 156$ colors in total. Thus, for large values of Δ the algorithm achieves a 10/3-approximation ratio. $\square$

4.2   A 3-Approximation Algorithm RC_Levels

Overview of the Algorithm: We provide a more sophisticated radiocoloring algorithm, that achieves a 3-approximation ratio rather than 10/3, for fully planar hierarchical graphs of class WS. The basic idea of the algorithm, called RC_Levels, is to partition the vertices of each graph G_i into outerplanar *levels* using a BFS (similar to [3,20]) and define the three parts of each G_i based on this search.

The *outer up part of* G_i consists of the first level of the BFS tree obtained. Thus, it is the outer up subgraph of G_i, $G_{outUp\,i}$. The *outer down part of* G_i consists of the graph induced by the vertices of the BFS tree of levels D up to the end of the tree, where D is the first level of the tree having an outer down vertex of G_i. The *inner part of* G_i *is the rest of the graph* G_i.

More analytically, the *inner part of* G_i *is radiocolored* as follows: Radiocolor every two successive levels of the inner part of G_i optimally interchanging color sets A, B, where $|A| = |B| = OPT(G)$ and $OPT(G)$ is the optimal number of colors needed to radiocolor G. We prove that this can be achieved in polynomial time and without any conflicts. We first show that any two successive levels, call them a double level, is a 4-outerplanar graph. Thus, by Theorem 1, it is a bounded treewidth graph. Consequently, applying Theorem 2, each double level can be radiocolored optimally in polynomial time. Moreover, by the BFS partitioning procedure, there is no conflict between double levels colored using the same color set.

The *outer down part of* G_i *is radiocolored* together with the outer up parts of its children using the best known approximation radiocoloring algorithm, i.e. the asymptically 5/3-approximation algorithm of [27,28] for ordinary planar graphs, using the color sets A and C, where $|C| = |A| = OPT(G)$. Since the algorithm uses only color sets A, B, C, it is a 3-approximation algorithm.

Description of the RC_Levels algorithm

Partitioning and Grouping procedures The algorithm applies a number of procedures in each G_i, partitioning the graph into smaller subgraphs and then radiocolor the produced subgraphs:

1. Partitioning Procedure of G_i: We partition the graph G_i into *outerplanar* subgraphs, called *single levels* according to the following procedure: Add a new vertex in G_i, called *virtual vertex* and connect it to all vertices of $G_{outUp\,i}$. Note that this can be done without creating any crossings because each vertex of $G_{outUp\,i}$ is connected to a pin and each pin is replaced by a vertex that calls G_i in the expansion of the hierarchical graph. Then, construct a BFS tree T rooted on the virtual vertex. That is, starting from this vertex, find all of its neighbours. Next, find the neighbours of those vertices, and so on. Number the levels of the BFS tree using successive integers starting with 0 for the root. Now, partition the vertices of G_i into levels according to their distance from the root of the tree T. That is, a vertex which is at distance k from the root belongs to level k. Let M_i be the number of the levels of the partition. Also, let $l_{i\,m}$ the subgraph of G_i induced on vertices of level m. Finally, remove the virtual vertex.

Observation 2. *The subgraph induced by vertices of level 1 resulting by the partitioning procedure on G_i is in fact the subgraph $G_{outUp\ i}$.*

Let D_i the first level of the partition that contains a vertex of the outer down subgraph of G_i, $G_{outDown\ i}$ that is, $D_i = \min\{l_u : u \in G_{outDown\ i}\}$, where l_u is the level of vertex u. For simplicity reasons, and where there is no confusion, in the sequel we use the term D to refer to the level D_i of G_i.

Observation 3. *By the definition of class WS, at least the 2nd and the 3rd level of the partition of G_i consist only of inner vertices.*

2. Grouping Procedure: Next, we group together the levels of the partition of G_i as follows:

1. *First Level Subgraph:* The subgraph induced by the vertices of the first level of the partition (outer up vertices). It is denoted by $G_{first\ level\ i}$.
2. *Inner Levels Subgraph:* The subgraph induced by the vertices of levels 2 to level $D - 1$. Note that the subgraph for graphs of class WS, consists only of inner vertices. Denote it by $G_{inner\ levels\ i}$.
3. *Down Levels Subgraph:* The subgraph induced by the vertices of levels D up to the last level M_i. Note that this subgraph, for graphs of class WS, consists only of inner and outer down vertices. Denote it by $G_{down\ levels\ i}$.

3. Partitioning into double levels Procedure: Group together every two successive levels of the partition of $G_{inner\ levels\ i}$ as follows:
For $m = 1, \ldots, \frac{D-2}{2}$, group together levels $2m$ and $2m + 1$ and call the subgraph obtained as m-*th double level* of G_i, denoted by $L_{i\ m}$. If the number of double levels is even, we extend the last odd level with the rest of the levels of $G_{inner\ levels\ i}$, so that the number of double levels of $G_{inner\ levels\ i}$ to be an odd number.

4. Constructing extended double levels Procedure: Take the single levels preceding and following level $L_{i\ m}$, $l_{i\ 2(m-1)+1}$ and $l_{i\ 2(m+1)}$.

We define the extended level of $L_{i\ m}$, denoted by $Le_{i\ m}$, to be the subgraph induced by the vertices of $L_{i\ m}$ and their neighbours: $Le_{i\ m} = l_{i\ 2(m-1)+1} \bigcup L_{i\ m} \bigcup l_{i\ 2(m+1)}$.

Note that for the first double level $m = 1$, we have $Le_{i\ 1} = G_{outUp\ i} \bigcup L_{i\ 1} \bigcup l_{i\ 3}$. For the last double level, we have $Le_{i\ m} = L_{i\ 2(m-1)+1} \bigcup L_{i\ m} \bigcup l_{i\ 2(m+1)}$, where $m = \frac{D-2}{2}$.

5. Constructing the extended down-levels subgraph Procedure: Consider the subgraph $G_{Down\ Levels\ i}$ of G_i. Let H the multiset of nonterminals called by G_i. For each $G_j \in H$ take the subgraphs $G_{first\ level\ j}$ and $G_{first\ inner\ j}$ of G_j. Let $GD_i = G_{Down\ Levels\ i} \bigcup_{G_j \in H} \{\cup G_{first\ level\ j}\}$.

Also, let $GDe_i = l_D \bigcup G_{Down\ Levels\ i} \bigcup_{G_j \in H} \{G_{first\ level\ j} \cup G_{first\ inner\ level\ j}\}$.

We can now proceed with the description of the the algorithm *RC_Levels* appearing in Fig. 9.

RC_Levels algorithm (high level description)
For each G_i, $1 \leq i \leq n$, do:

1. Apply the *partitioning Procedure* on G_i. Next, apply the *Grouping Procedure* of G_i.
2. Apply the *partitioning into double levels Procedure* on $G_{inner\ levels\ i}$.
3. Radiocolor optimally each *odd* (even) extended double level subgraphs, $Le_{i\ m}$, $1 \leq m \leq \frac{D-2}{2}$, m odd (even), together using color set B (A). Then, ignore the coloring of the vertices of $Le_{i\ m}$ not in $L_{i\ m}$.
4. Apply the best known radiocoloring algorithm for ordinary planar graphs, i.e. the algorithm of [28, 27], on GDe_i using color sets A and C. Ignore the colors of the vertices of GDe_i not in GD_i.

Fig. 9. Algorithm *RC_Levels*

Analysis of the *RC_Levels* algorithm

Lemma 5. *The colors assigned to any double level of G_i, $L_{i\ m}$, $1 \leq m \leq \frac{D-2}{2}$, do not conflict with the colors of other levels of G_i or the colors of vertices of any graph that calls G_i or which is called by G_i.*

Proof. The lemma is proved by the following three claims.

Claim 11. *Any vertex of a level k is at distance greater than two from any vertex in a level $> k + 2$ and $< k - 2$ of G_i.*

Proof. Assume that this is not true. That is there is a vertex u at level k which at distance at most two from a vertex v at level $k + j$, $j > 2$ (or $k - j$). However, note that vertex v should be contained in level $k + 1$ or $k + 2$ (or $k - 1$ or $k - 2$, respectevely) according to the way the partition is constructed, a contradiction. $\square$

Claim 12. *For any $1 < m < \frac{D-2}{2}$, the colors assigned to any double level of G_i, $L_{i\ m}$, do not conflict with the colors of other levels of G_i.*

Proof. Consider any such level $L_{i\ m}$. We study the colors of the vertices outside $L_{i\ m}$.

Consider a vertex of the first level of it, $l_{i\ 2m}$. Such a vertex might be at distance one from a vertex in level $l_{i\ 2(m-1)+1}$, at distance two from a vertex at level $l_{i\ 2(m-1)}$ and at distance two from a vertex of level $l_{i\ 2m+2}$. The vertices of levels $l_{i\ 2(m-1)}$ and $l_{i\ 2(m-1)+1}$ belong to the double level $L_{i\ (m-1)}$. The vertices of level $l_{i\ 2m+2}$ belong to the double level $L_{i\ (m+1)}$. Recall that the algorithm radiocolors levels $L_{i\ m-1}$, $L_{i\ m}$ and $L_{i\ m+1}$ interchanging the set of colors A and B. Thus, there is no conflict between the vertices of level $l_{i\ 2m}$ and the vertices of levels $L_{i\ m-1}$ or $L_{i\ m+1}$.

Moreover, any vertex of $l_{i\ 2m}$ is at distance greater than two from any vertex of levels $l_{i\ 2(m-2)}$ or less, that is vertices of double levels $L_{i\ m-2}$ or less. Although the algorithm radiocolors levels $L_{i\ m}$ and $L_{i\ m-2}$ with the same set of colors, the above observation implies that there is no conflict between a vertex in $l_{i\,2m}$ and a vertex of levels $L_{i\,m-2}$ or less.

Consider now a vertex of the second level of $L_{i\,m}$, $l_{i\,2m+1}$. Such a vertex might be at distance one or two from the following vertices outside $L_{i\,m}$: It might be at distance one from a vertex of level $l_{i\,2m+1}$, at distance two from a vertex of level $l_{i\,2(m+1)+1}$ and at distance two from a vertex of level $l_{i\,2m-1}$. The vertices of levels $l_{i\,2(m+1)}$ and $l_{i\,2(m+1)+1}$ belong to the double level $L_{i\,(m+1)}$. The vertices of level $l_{i\,2m-1}$ belong to the double level $L_{i\,m-1}$. Recall that the algorithm radiocolors levels $L_{i\,m-1}$, $L_{i\,m}$ and $L_{i\,m+1}$ interchanging the set of colors A and B. Thus, there is no conflict between the vertices of level $l_{i\,2m}$ and the vertices of levels $L_{i\,m-1}$ and $L_{i\,m+1}$.

Moreover, any vertex of $l_{i\,2m+1}$ is at distance greater than two from any vertex of levels $l_{i\,2(m+2)}$ or greater, that is vertices of double levels $L_{i\,m+2}$ or greater. Although the algorithm radiocolors levels $L_{i\,m}$ and $L_{i\,m+2}$ with the same set of colors, the above observation implies that there is no conflict between a vertex in $l_{i\,2m}$ and a vertex of levels $L_{i\,m+2}$ or greater.   □

Claim 13. *The colors assigned to the first and the last double level of $G_{inner\ levels\ i}$, i.e. levels $L_{i\,1}$ and $L_{i\,\frac{D-2}{2}}$, do not conflict with the colors of other levels of G_i or the colors of vertices of any graph that calls G_i or it is called by G_i.*

Proof. Consider the first double level $L_{i\,1}$. We study the colors of the vertices outside $L_{i\,1}$. Recall that the algorithm radiocolors the vertices of this double level using color set B.

Consider the levels preceding level $L_{i\,1}$:

– Consider a vertex of the first level of $L_{i\,1}$, $l_{i\,2}$. As far as it concerns the levels preceding level $L_{i\,1}$, a vertex of $l_{i\,2}$ might be at distance one from a vertex in level $l_{i\,1}$ and at distance two from a vertex of a graph G_j that calls G_i. Recall that the algorithm radiocolors the vertices of level $l_{i\,1}$ together with the vertices of the graph G_j connected to them, using the sets of colors A and C. Thus, there is no conflict between the vertices of level $l_{i\,2}$ and the vertices of level $l_{i\,1}$ or the vertices of any graph G_j that calls G_i.

– Consider now a vertex of the second level of $L_{i\,1}$, $l_{i\,3}$. The vertices of previous double levels, near the vertices of level $l_{i\,3}$ are only a subset of the vertices at distance one or two from the vertices of level $l_{i\,2}$. Thus, there is no conflict between the vertices of level $l_{i\,3}$ and the vertices of any previous level outside it.

Consider the levels following level $L_{i\,1}$:

– Consider a vertex of the second level of $L_{i\,1}$, $l_{i\,3}$. As far as it concerns the next double levels, a vertex of $l_{i\,3}$ might be at distance one from a vertex of level $l_{i\,4}$ and at distance two from a vertex of level $l_{i\,5}$. The vertices of levels $l_{i\,4}$ and $l_{i\,5}$ belong to the double level $L_{i\,2}$. Recall, that the algorithm radiocolors level $L_{i\,1}$ using the set of colors B. Also, it radiocolors level $L_{i\,2}$ with a different set of colors, A. Thus, again there is no conflict between the vertices of the two levels.

– Consider now a vertex of the first level of $L_{i\,1}$, $l_{i\,2}$. The vertices of next double levels, outside level $L_{i\,1}$, near the vertices of level $l_{i\,2}$ are only a subset of the vertices at distance one or two from the vertices of $l_{i\,3}$. Thus, there is no conflict between the vertices of level $l_{i\,2}$ and the vertices of any next level outside it.

Consider the last double level $L_{i\,\frac{D-2}{2}}$. We study the colors of the vertices outside the level.

Consider the levels following level $L_{i\,\frac{D-2}{2}}$:

– Consider a vertex of the second level of $L_{i\,\frac{D-2}{2}}$, $l_{i\,D-1}$. As far as it concerns the next double levels, such a vertex might be at distance one from a vertex of level $l_{i\,D}$ and at distance two from a vertex of level $l_{i\,D+1}$. The vertices of levels $l_{i\,D}$ and $l_{i\,D+1}$ belong to the subgraph $G_{down\ levels\ i}$. Recall that the algorithm radiocolors level $L_{i\,\frac{D-2}{2}}$ using the set B. This is because the algorithm, if the number of double levels is odd, then obviously uses color set B at the last double level and otherwise (if this number is even) we are done by extending the last odd double level with the rest of the levels of G_i. It also radiocolors the vertices of $G_{down\ levels\ i}$ together with the first level subgraph of all graphs called by G_i using the sets of colors A and C. Thus, there is no conflict between the vertices of level $l_{i\,D-1}$ and the vertices of levels $l_{i\,D}$, $l_{i\,D+1}$ or greater.

– Consider now a vertex of the first level of $L_{i\,\frac{D-2}{2}}$, $l_{i\,D-2}$. The vertices of next levels, near the vertices of level $l_{i\,D-2}$ are only a subset of the vertices at distance one or two from the vertices of $l_{i\,D-1}$. Thus, there is no conflict between the vertices of level $l_{i\,D-2}$ and the vertices of any next level outside it.

Consider the levels preceding level $L_{i\,\frac{D-2}{2}}$:

– Consider a vertex of the first level of $L_{i\,\frac{D-2}{2}}$, $l_{i\,D-2}$. As far as it concerns the previous double levels, such a vertex might be at distance one from a vertex of level $l_{i\,D-3}$ and at distance two from a vertex of level $l_{i\,D-4}$. The vertices of levels $l_{i\,D-3}$ and $l_{i\,D-4}$ belong to the double level $L_{i\,(\frac{D-2}{2}-1)}$. Recall that the algorithm radiocolors level $L_{i\,\frac{D-2}{2}}$ using the set B. It also radiocolors the vertices of $L_{i\,(\frac{D-2}{2}-1)}$ using the set A. Thus, there is no conflict between the vertices of level $l_{i\,D-2}$ and the vertices of double levels $L_{i\,(\frac{D-2}{2}-1)}$ or less.

– Consider now a vertex of the second level of $L_{i\,\frac{D-2}{2}}$, $l_{i\,D-1}$. The vertices of previous levels, near the vertices of level $l_{i\,D-1}$ are only a subset of the vertices at distance one or two from the vertices of $l_{i\,D-2}$. Thus, there is no conflict between the vertices of level $l_{i\,D-1}$ and the vertices of any previous level outside it. □

The previous 3 claims prove Lemma 5. □

The following lemma is needed in order to manage to radiocolor optimally each double level in polynomial time.

Lemma 6. *For any double level $L_{i\,m}$ of $G_{inner\ levels\ i}$, $1 \leq m \leq \frac{D-2}{2}$ the subgraph $Le_{i\,m}$ is a 4-outerplanar graph.*

Proof. The lemma is proved by the following 3 claims.

Claim 14. *The subgraph l_{im}, $1 \leq m \leq D-1$ is an outerplanar graph.*

Proof. By the way the partition is constructed, using a BFS tree. □

Claim 15. *The subgraph $L_{i\,m} = l_{i\,2m} \bigcup l_{i\,2m+1}$, for any m, $1 \le m \le \frac{D-2}{2}$ is a 2-outerplanar graph.*

Proof. The claim is proved by the way the partition is constructed, using a BFS tree and the previous claim.

Consider the last extended level $m = \frac{D-2}{2}$. For this case we have $L_{i\,m} = l_{i\,D-2} \bigcup l_{i\,D-1}$. Note that $L_{i\,m}$ does not to belong to $G_{inner\,levels\,i}$ but to the subgraph $G_{down\,levels\,i}$. However, $L_{i\,m}$ was constructed by the partition into levels procedure applied on G_i. Thus, by the way the levels are constructed, we get the claim.   □

Claim 16. *The subgraph $Le_{i\,m} = l_{i\,2(m-1)+1} \bigcup L_{i\,m} \bigcup l_{i\,2(m+1)}$, for any m, $1 \le m \le \frac{D-2}{2}$, is a 4-outerplanar graph.*

Proof. Consider any extended level m with $1 < m < \frac{D-2}{2}$. For this case the claim is proved by combining the two previous claims.

Consider the first extended level $m = 1$. For this case we have $Le_{im} = l_{i\,1} \bigcup L_{i\,1} \bigcup l_{i\,3} = G_{outUp\,i} \bigcup L_{i\,1} \bigcup l_{i\,3}$. Note that $G_{outUp\,i}$ does not belong to $G_{inner\,levels\,i}$ but to the subgraph $G_{first\,level\,i}$. However, $G_{outUp\,i}$ was constructed by the partitioning into levels procedure applied on G_i. Thus, by the way the levels are constructed, we get the claim.

Consider the last extended level $m = \frac{D-2}{2}$. For this case we have $Le_{i\,m} = l_{i\,2(m-1)+1} \bigcup L_{i\,m} \bigcup l_{i\,2(m+1)} = l_{i\,D-3} \bigcup L_{i\,\frac{D-2}{2}} \bigcup l_{i\,D-1}$. Note that $L_{i\,m}$ does not to belong to $G_{inner\,levels\,i}$ but to the subgraph $G_{down\,levels\,i}$. However, $L_{i\,m}$ was constructed by the partition into levels procedure applied on G_i. Thus, by the way the levels are constructed, we get the claim.   □

The previous 3 claims prove Lemma 6.   □

Lemma 7. *The RC_Levels algorithm radiocolors any extended double level $Le_{i\,m}$ optimally in polynomial to the size of G_i time. This procedure produces a valid radiocoloring of double level L_{im}.*

Proof. Recall that *RC_Levels* gets a radiocoloring of the vertices of $L_{i\,m}$ by radiocoloring the extended level $Le_{i\,m}$. In order to prove the Lemma we have to prove that (i) the algorithm radiocolors optimally level $Le_{i\,m}$ in polynomial time (ii) By radiocoloring $Le_{i\,m}$, we get an optimal radiocoloring of $L_{i\,m}$.

(i) By Claim 16 (used in the proof of Lemma 6), $Le_{i\,m}$ is a 4-outerplanar graph. Thus, by Theorem 1, it is a bounded treewidth graph (11-bounded treewidth graph). Hence, by Theorem 2, it can be radiocolored optimally in polynomial time.

(ii) In order to prove that the radiocoloring of $L_{i\,m}$ resulting by the radiocoloring of $Le_{i\,m}$ is valid, we have to prove that the radiocoloring of the vertices of $L_{i\,m}$ is valid in G_i as far as it concerns those vertices. The subgraph $Le_{i\,m}$ consists of the vertices of the double level $L_{i\,m}$ and their neighbours. Observe that, the subgraph of G_i^2 induced by vertices of $L_{i\,m}$ is a subgraph of $Le_{i\,m}^2$. Thus, the radiocoloring of the vertices of $Le_{i\,m}$ constitutes a valid radiocoloring of the vertices of $L_{i\,m}$ on G_i.   □

Theorem 17. *RC_Levels Algorithm produces a valid radiocoloring of a WS fully planar hierarchical graph G using at most $3 \cdot (\max\{OPT(G), \lceil 5\Delta/3 \rceil + 78\})$ colors, where $OPT(G)$ is the optimal number of colors needed for the radiocoloring of G. It runs in $O(n_{max}^2 \cdot T(n_{max}, k) + n_{max}^5)$ time, where $T(n, k)$ is a polynomial time function for the optimal radiocoloring of a k-tree of size n ([31]).*

Proof. (Approximation ratio):

Consider any graph G_i in the hierarchy tree of G. The algorithm radio-colors the down levels subgraph of G_i together with the first level subgraphs of the graphs called by G_i (graph GD_i) using color sets A and C applying any known polynomial time radiocoloring algorithm. Employing the algorithm of [27,28] we can compute such a radiocoloring in polynomial time using at most $\lceil 5\Delta/3 \rceil + 78$ colors. Hence, the sets of colors A and C of colors, with $|A| = |C| = \max\{\lceil 5\Delta/3 \rceil + 78, OPT(G)\}$, used by the algorithm, are enough to produce a valid radiocoloring algorithm for GD_i.

The inner levels subgraph of G_i is radiocolored using, at the first double level $(L_{i\,1})$, colors of set B, in the next double level colors of set A, etc., until the last double level $(\frac{D-2}{2})$ which is radiocolored again using colors of set B. The first and the last double level are colored using color set B because the algorithm, if the number of double levels is odd, then obviously uses color set B at the last double level and otherwise (if this number is even) we are done by extending the last odd double level with the rest of the levels of G_i. As we showed in Lemmas 7 and 5, the radiocoloring computed of any double level is optimal and with no conflicts with the other levels of G_i or the vertices of the graphs that are called by it or call G_i.

But, what about the case where the inner levels subgraph consists of less than two levels? In this case a vertex of first level subgraph of G_i may be at distance 2 from a vertex of down levels subgraph of G_i. In this case since the two subgraphs are radiocolored using the same sets of colors (sets A, C) there might be conflicts between them. However, such a case does not appear in the class WS of hierarchical graphs considered here (definition 11), since any vertex of first level subgraph is at distance greater than two from any vertex of down levels subgraph.

We conclude that for any graph G_i of the hierarchical graph G there is no conflict either between any two vertices in G_i or between a vertex of G_i and a vertex that is called by G_i or calls G_i.

Finally, since for the radiocoloring of all graphs G_i of G we use colors of sets A, B, C, the RC_Levels algorithm obtains a 3-approximation ratio for the radiocoloring of the hierarchical planar graph G.

See Fig. 10 for a graphical illustration of the radiocoloring produced by the algorithm $RC\_Levels(G)$.

(Time complexity):

For each graph G_i we have the following computations:

The inner levels subgraph of G_i is radiocolored only once. The algorithm radiocolors the levels of the subgraph independently using the theorem of [31] (Theorem 2 here). Since each level is of size $O(n)$, we require time $O(n \cdot T(n, k))$ for all levels to be optimally radiocolored. Since this procedure is called for

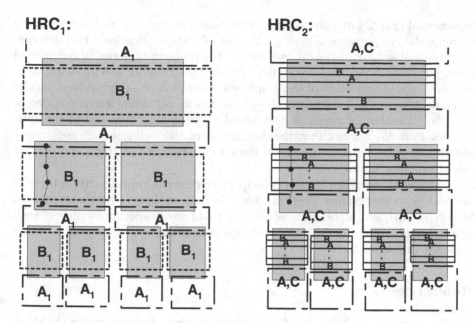

Fig. 10. The radiocoloring of a subtree of the hierarchical tree of G as specified by algorithms RC_Approx, and RC_Levels. Note that for RC_Approx, $|A_1| = |B_1| = \lceil 5\Delta/3 \rceil + 78$ and for RC_Levels, $|A| = |B| = |C| = \max\{\lceil 5\Delta/3 \rceil + 78, OPT(G)\}$, where $OPT(G)$ is the optimal number of colors needed to radioclor the graph G.

each G_i, $1 \leq i \leq n$, the optimal radiocoloring of the levels of all graphs needs $O(n^2 \cdot T(n,k))$ time in total.

The down levels subgraph of G_i is also radiocolored only once together with the first level subgraphs of the graphs that are called by G_i using the algorithm of [27,28]. That algorithm requires $O(n^2)$ time for the radiocoloring of a graph of size n. Remark that when considering the down levels subgraph of G_i and the outer up vertices of the graphs called by G_i, we get a subgraph of size (number of vertices) n^2. Thus, the radiocoloring algorithm used needs time $O(n^4)$. Since this procedure is called for each G_i, $1 \leq i \leq n$, the algorithm needs $O(n^5)$ time in total.

Summing up, we get that the algorithm takes $O(n^2 \cdot T(n,k) + n^5)$ time in total, where $T(n,k) = O(n(2\alpha+1)^{2^{2(k+1)(l+2)+1}} + n^3)$, $l = 2$ and $\Delta(G) \leq \alpha \leq \lceil 5\Delta/3 \rceil + 78$.   □

5   Discussion and Open Problems

In this work we investigated a variation of the fundamental coloring problem, i.e. the Radiocoloring problem, on a class of hierarchically specified planar graphs, i.e. the WS L-specified hierarchical planar graphs. In those graphs the actual graph can be exponential to the size of its specification. We showed $\mathcal{PSPACE}$-completeness of the problem through *local* reductions that apply not to the whole exponential graph, but only to its (polynomial) specification and hence can be accomplished in polynomial time (to the size of the specification). Furthermore, we presented approximation algorithms for the problem that run in polynomial time. For those algorithms, we applied suitable partitioning and grouping techniques on the specification of the graph, solve the radiocoloring problem locally on those instances and then reuse those colorings for obtaining a radiocoloring of the whole hierarchical graph of guaranteed performance compared to the optimal solution. We remark that the description of the radiocoloring assignment obtained is polynomial to the size of the specification of the graph and not the actual exponential graph.

The work is one of the few works ([25]) presenting coloring algorithms on hierarchically specified graphs. There are many fundamental problems that remain to be solved on those graphs, such as coloring problems in specific families of such graphs but also other fundamental problems such as the max clique, the traveling salesman problem, etc.

References

1. Agnarsson, G., Halldórsson, M.M.: Coloring powers of planar graphs. SIAM J. Discrete Math. **16**(4), 651–662 (2003)
2. Andreou, M.I., Fotakis, D.A., Nikoletseas, S.E., Papadopoulou, V.G., Spirakis, P.G.: On radiocoloring hierarchically specified planar graphs: $\mathcal{PSPACE}$-Completeness and approximations. In: Diks, K., Rytter, W. (eds.) MFCS 2002. LNCS, vol. 2420, pp. 81–92. Springer, Heidelberg (2002)
3. Baker, B.S.: Approximation algorithms for NP-complete problems on planar graphs. J. ACM **41**, 153–180 (1994)
4. Bienstoc, D., Monma, C.L.: On the complexity of embedding planar graphs to minimize certain distance measures. Algorithmica **5**, 93–109 (1990)
5. Bodlaender, H.L.: Planar graphs with bounded treewidth. TR RUU-CS-88-14, Department of Computer Science, University of Utrecht, The Netherlands, March 1988
6. Bodlaender, H.L., Kloks, T., Tan, R.B., van Leeuwen, J.: λ-Coloring of Graphs. In: Reichel, H., Tison, S. (eds.) STACS 2000. LNCS, vol. 1770, pp. 395–406. Springer, Heidelberg (2000)
7. Borodin, O.V., Broersma, H.J., Glebov, A., van den Heuvel, J.: Stars and bunches in planar graphs. Part II: General planar graphs and colourings. CDAM Research Report **2002-2005** (2002)
8. Calamoneri, T., Petreschi, R.: $L(2,1)$-Coloring Matrogenic Graphs. In: Rajsbaum, S. (ed.) LATIN 2002. LNCS, vol. 2286, pp. 236–247. Springer, Heidelberg (2002)
9. Fotakis, D.A., Nikoletseas, S.E., Papadopoulou, V.G., Spirakis, P.G.: NP-completeness results and efficient approximations for radiocoloring in planar graphs. In: Nielsen, M., Rovan, B. (eds.) MFCS 2000. LNCS, vol. 1893, pp. 363–372. Springer, Heidelberg (2000)
10. Fotakis, D., Nikoletseas, S., Papadopoulou, V.G., Spirakis, P.G.: Radiocoloring in planar graphs: complexity and approximations. Theoret. Comput. Sci. **340**, 514–538 (2005). Elsevier

11. Fotakis, D., Pantziou, G., Pentaris, G., Spirakis, P.: Frequency assignment in mobile and radio networks. In: Networks in Distributed Computing, DIMACS Series in Discrete Mathematics and Theoretical Computer Science, vol. 45, pp. 73–90. American Mathematical Society, Providence (1999)
12. Garey, M.R., Johnson, D.S., Stockmeyer, L.: Some simplified NP-complete graph problems. Theor. Comput. Sci. 1, 237–267 (1976)
13. Garey, M.R., Johnson, D.S.: Computers and Intractability: A guide to the Theory of NP-completeness. W.H./Freeman and Company (1979)
14. Griggs, J., Liu, D.: Minimum span channel assignments. Recent Advances in Radio Channel Assignments, Invited Minisymposium, Discrete Mathematics (1998)
15. Griggs, J.R., Yeh, R.K.: Labeling graphs with a condition at distance 2. SIAM J. Disc. Math. 5, 586–595 (1992)
16. Jonas, T.K.: Graph Coloring Analogues With a Condition at Distance Two: L(2, 1)- Labelings and List λ-Labelings. Ph.D. thesis, Department of Mathematics, University of South Carolina, Columbia, SC (1993)
17. Harary, F.: Private communication to Paul Spirakis
18. Van den Heuvel, J., McGuinness, S.: Coloring the square of a planar graph. J. Graph Theory 42(2), 110–124 (2003)
19. Hunt III, H.B., Marathe, M.V., Radhakrishnan, V., Ravi, S.S., Rosenkrantz, D.J., Stearns, R.E.: NC-approximation schemes for NP- and PSPACE-hard problems for geometric graphs. In: van Leeuwen, J. (ed.) ESA 1994. LNCS, vol. 855, pp. 468–477. Springer, Heidelberg (1994)
20. Krumke, Marathe, M.V., Ravi, S.S.: Approximation algorithms for channel assignment in radio networks. In: DIALM for Mobility, 2nd International Workshop on Discrete Algorithms and methods for Mobile Computing and Communications, Dallas, Texas (1998)
21. Lengauer, T.: Hierarchical planarity testing. J. ACM 36(3), 474–509 (1989)
22. Lengauer, T., Wagner, K.W.: Correlation between the complexities of the of hierarchical and hierarchical versions of graph problems. J. Comput. Syst. Sci. 44, 63–93 (1992)
23. Marathe, M.V., Hunt III, H.B., Stearns, R.E., Radhakrishnan, V.: Approximation algorithms for PSPACE-hard hierarchically and periodically specified problems. In: Proceedings of the 26th Annual ACM Symposium on the Theory of Computing (STOC), pp. 468–478, May 1994. A complete version appears in SIAM Journal on Computing 27(5), 1237–1261 (1998)
24. Marathe, H., Hunt III, H., Stearns, R., Radhakrishnan, V.: Complexity of hierarchically and 1-dimensioned periodically specified problems. In: Theory and Applications, DIMACS Workshop on Satisfiability Problem (1996)
25. Marathe, M.V., Radhakrishnan, V., Hunt III, H.B., Ravi, S.S.: Hierarchically specified unit disk graphs. In: van Leeuwen, J. (ed.) WG 1993. LNCS, vol. 790, pp. 21–32. Springer, Heidelberg (1994). Journal version appears in Theoretical Computer Science, 174(1-2), pp. 23-65, March 1997
26. McCormick, S.T.: Optimal approximation of sparse hessians and its equivalence to a graph coloring problem. Technical Report SOL 81–22, Department of Operations Research, Standford University (1981)
27. Molloy, M., Salavatipour, M.R.: A bound on the chromatic number of the square of a planar graph. J. Combin. Theory Ser. B 94, 189–213 (2005)
28. Molloy, M., Salavatipour, M.R.: Frequency channel assignment on planar networks. In: Möhring, R.H., Raman, R. (eds.) ESA 2002. LNCS, vol. 2461, pp. 736–747. Springer, Heidelberg (2002)

29. Ramanathan,S., Loyd, E.R.: The complexity of distance2-coloring. In: 4th International Conference of Computing and information, pp. 71–74 (1992)
30. Sakai, D.: Labeling chordal graphs: distance two condition. SIAM J. Discrete Math. **7**, 133–140 (1994)
31. Zhou, X., Kanari, Y., Nishizeki, T.: Generalized vertex-coloring of partial k-trees. IEICE Trans. Foundamentals EXX-A(1) (2000)

Performance Evaluation of Routing Mechanisms for VANETs in Urban Areas

Christos Bouras[1,2](✉), Vaggelis Kapoulas[1,2], and Enea Tsanai[2]

[1] Computer Technology Institute and Press "Diophantus",
Patras, Greece
{bouras,kapoulas}@cti.gr

[2] Computer Engineering and Informatics Department, University of Patras,
Patras, Greece
{bouras,kapoulas,tsanai}@ceid.upatras.gr

Abstract. Mobile Ad hoc Networks (MANETs) and especially Vehicular Ad hoc Networks (VANETs) have recently gained large interest and their performance is heavily studied. A great challenge in VANETs, especially in an urban setting, is the routing scheme used and the subsequent performance obtained. This work presents an experimental performance evaluation of routing mechanisms in VANETs, using simulation, within an urban Manhattan grid like environment. It also describes and evaluates an enhancement of the Greedy Perimeter Stateless Routing (GPSR) protocol that takes into account the motion of the vehicles and the nature of the urban environment. The simulation results demonstrate that the proposed enhancement to the GPSR protocol manages to significantly increase the delivery ratio without increasing the power consumption; nevertheless, in some cases the improvement on delivery ratio is achieved at the expense of slightly increased end-to-end delay.

Keywords: Ad-hoc networks · MANETs · VANETs · Routing protocols

1 Introduction

Vehicular Ad hoc Networks (VANETs) represent a special class of Mobile Ad hoc Networks (MANETs) with unique characteristics. Similar to MANETs, VANETs are an autonomous and self-configured wireless network that allows communications without any dependency on infrastructures or a central coordinator. The moving rates in a VANET are generally higher than that in a typical MANET but more predictable for nodes traveling on the same direction. This means that nodes in a VANET moving towards the same direction in a roadway, maintain similar speeds and thus longer radio connectivity periods than those moving in opposite directions. Another unique characteristic of VANETs is their challenging surrounding environment that contains blocks of buildings, roadways that limit the possible node movements and roadside infrastructures that may provide access points to the internet along with a rich variety of services and applications.

© Springer International Publishing Switzerland 2015
C. Zaroliagis et al. (Eds.): Spirakis Festschrift, LNCS 9295, pp. 133–153, 2015.
DOI: 10.1007/978-3-319-24024-4_9

A great challenge in VANETs is the routing performance [16]. Importing existing MANET routing protocols directly into VANETs may lead to unsatisfactory network performance. Compared to MANETs, the node movement in VANETs is more predictable allowing more effective position allocation algorithms and routing protocols that benefit from the availability of the Global Positioning System (GPS) and electronic maps. However, node density may vary a lot due to traffic conditions. An important issue in the environment of VANETs is the presence of buildings in rural areas which adds signal weakening and noise. Implementing a routing protocol able to select the best possible path which avoids passing through buildings and other obstacles in the topology is not an easy task.

Routing in VANETs has been an important field of research the last years. Numerous works exist which study and analyze routing in VANETs. In [9,13,15] several routing protocols in MANETs and VANETs are being studied and categorized according to their routing strategy. A comparative performance analysis of the Ad Hoc On-Demand Distance Vector (AODV), Destination Sequenced Distance Vector (DSDV) and Dynamic Source Routing (DSR) protocols is conducted in [1] for rural and urban scenarios. In [12], general design ideas and components are being presented for reliable routing design and implementation and in [8], a quantitative model for evaluating routing protocols on highway scenarios is proposed. In [17], three realistic radio propagation models are presented that increase the simulation results accuracy.

A novel routing protocol for reliable vehicle to roadside Access Point (AP) connection is proposed in [21] that uses an algorithm for predicting the wireless links' lifetime. In [18], a road based VANET routing protocol is proposed that uses real-time vehicular traffic information to form the paths and is compared against existing well-known routing protocols. In [11], a cross-layer position based routing algorithm for VANETs is presented that performs better than the Greedy Perimeter Stateless Routing (GPSR) protocol. The algorithm, named Cross-Layer, Weighted, Position-based Routing (CLWPR), uses information about link layer quality and positioning from navigation.

In this paper we conduct an experimental performance evaluation of efficient routing mechanisms in MANETs, using simulation, for the case of VANETs within an urban environment (modeled by Manhattan grid). We also propose an enhancement of the GPRS protocol that takes into account the motion of the vehicle to estimate their position at future times, as well as the nature of the urban environment (i.e. the grid, in order to favor vehicles at crossroads as the intermediary nodes). The study compares Ad Hoc On-Demand Distance Vector (AODV), Destination Sequenced Distance Vector (DSDV), Dynamic Source Routing (DSR), Optimized Link State Routing (OLSR), Greedy Perimeter Stateless Routing (GPSR) and the above proposed modification of the GPSR, and measures the packet delivery ratio, the end to end delay and the power consumption for each routing protocol in various scenarios. The results show that the proposed enhancement to the GPSR protocol outperforms all the other protocols in all cases.

The remainder of the paper is organized as follows: Sect. 2 provides an overview of the routing protocols used in MANETs and VANETs that are the subject of study, and describes the challenges associated with VANETs in an urban setting; Sect. 3 describes the proposed enhancement to the GPRS protocol (named GPRS-Modified of GPRS-M for short); Sect. 4 presents the simulation setting and the reference scenario; Sect. 5 presents and discusses simulation results; and finally Sect. 6 presents our conclusions and ideas for future work.

2   Overview of Routing in MANETs and VANETs

2.1   Routing Protocols

The routing protocols compared in this paper are briefly introduced below. The GPSR protocol is presented in more detail to ease the understanding of the proposed enchancement in Sect. 3.

AODV. The Ad Hoc On-Demand Distance Vector [19] routing is intended for use by mobile nodes in an Ad Hoc network. It offers swift adaptation to dynamic link conditions, low processing and memory overhead, low network utilization, and determines unicast routes to destinations within the Ad Hoc network. It uses destination sequence numbers to ensure loop freedom at all times avoiding common problems associated with classical distance from vector protocols.

DSDV. Destination Sequenced Distance Vector routing [5] is adapted from the conventional Routing Information Protocol (RIP) to an Ad Hoc network routing. It adds a new attribute and sequence number to each route table entry of the conventional RIP. Using the newly added sequence number, the mobile nodes can distinguish stale route information from the new one, thus preventing the formation of routing loops.

DSR. Dynamic Source Routing [7] uses source routing, that is, the source indicates in a data packets sequence of intermediate nodes on the routing path. In DSR, the query packet stores within its header the IDs of the so far traversed intermediate nodes. The destination then retrieves the entire path from the query packet and uses it to respond to the source. As a result, the source can establish a path to the destination. If the destination is allowed to send multiple route replies, the source node may receive and store multiple routes from the destination. An alternative route can be used when some link in the current route breaks. In a network with low mobility, this is advantageous over AODV since the alternative route can be tried before DSR initiates another flood for route discovery.

OLSR. Optimized Link State Routing [6] operates as a table driven, proactive protocol, i.e., exchanges topology information with other nodes of the network regularly. Each node periodically constructs and maintains the set of neighbors that can be reached in 1 hop and 2 hops. Based on this, the dedicated MPR algorithm minimizes the number of active relays needed to cover all 2-hops neighbors. Such relays are called Multi-Point Relays (MPR). A node forwards a packet if and only if it has been elected as MPR by the sender node. In order to construct and maintain its routing tables, OLSR periodically transmit link state information over the MPR backbone. Upon convergence, an active route is created at each node to reach any destination node in the network. The protocol is particularly suited for large and dense networks, as the optimization done using MPRs works well in this context. The larger and more dense a network, the more optimization can be achieved compared to the classic link state algorithm.

GPSR. The Greedy Perimeter Stateless Routing [10] is based on positioning of the routers and assumes that every node has access to a location service and knows its position coordinates. It also assumes that the source node is aware of the final destination nodes location. The GPSR allows routers to be nearly stateless, and requires propagation of topology information for only 1 hop. This means that each node need only to store information about its neighbors positions. The aim of GPSR is to take advantage of geographys properties in routing and allow high performance in forwarding without using other information. The GPSR operates in two modes based on the position of the index node, the neighbors and the final destination.

The first mode, the "greedy mode", is the main strategy of forwarding packets through intermediate nodes that are considered as best next hops. As best next hop is considered the neighbor node with the least distance from the destination. Packets are directly forwarded to this neighbors and form a short path to the destination based on positioning. The operation of this mode is illustrated in the left part of Fig. 1. Although this is the main state of the GPSR, there are cases where the density and the positioning of the nodes is such that does not allow forwarding using this approach.

When the greedy forwarding is impossible, the algorithm recovers by routing around the perimeter of the region. This is the second forwarding mode or else the "recovery/perimeter mode". When entering this mode, packets are marked for their new state and are forwarded according to the counterclockwise rule in relation to the source–destination line; i.e., neighboring nodes are tried as next hops, in the order they are encountered when starting from the source–destination line and turning around counterclockwise. The operation of this mode is illustrated in the right part of Fig. 1 and goes on until a node closer to the final destination than the recovery entry node is found. In the right part of Fig. 1 the orange node is the recovery entry node that informs the source node S about not having a neighbor with less distance to the destination D than itself.

2.2   Challenges

In an urban setting the presence of buildings in the area of the network topology plays a crucial role on the packet delivery success rate and adds a great complexity and challenge on the routing level. Buildings affect radio transmission

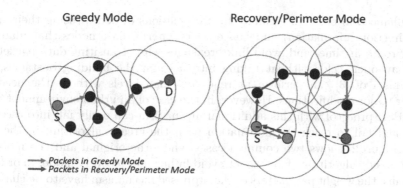

Fig. 1. The Greedy and the Recovery/Perimeter modes of the Greedy Perimeter State-less Routing.

and restrict the communication between the nodes of the VANET. The fact that communication in VANETs takes place in the high frequency of 5GHz (which is more-or-less the standard frequency used in VANETs) makes the communication in areas with buildings even harder. These difficulties arise from penetration through buildings, reflections, refractions, diffractions, etc. At the same time the relatively high speed of the nodes, the resulted increased mobility and the frequent topology changes add additional challenge to the problem of establishing routes between the nodes of the VANET. Multi-hop communication and route maintenance in these scenarios are very challenging as links can be established only when the nodes are within line of sight (LOS) or slightly out of LOS (e.g., just behind corners and close to road intersections) and possibly for a relatively small time period as the involved vehicles may move in different directions.

   As a result, the existing routing protocols are not expected to perform satisfactorily; indeed, as shown in Sect. 5, their performance is rather poor. This highlights the need to come up with solutions that take into account the urban setting and design routing protocols that a are more suitable for it. In this direction the proposed enhancement (described in the following section) takes into account the nodes motion information to better estimate their position at each time, and also identifies that the crossroads are the places where nodes can be better intermediates. Thus, it tries to select as next hop a node that, at the time of the transmission, is estimated to be at a crossroad (i.e., the best intermediate).

3 Proposed Enhancement to GPSR

3.1 Overview of the Proposed Enhancement

The challenge for GPSR is to avoid as much as possible any route dead ends and recovery mode entries. Our proposed implementation for propagation in an area with buildings is based on a previous approach for optimization on highways and areas without obstacles. In the previous approach [3], the GPSR routing protocol was enhanced in order to estimate future positions of nodes (using their speed and direction information) and hence select intermediate nodes that maintain higher route lifetimes and avoid link breakages while transiting data packets.

In an open field, without taking into account the building obstacles, the mechanism of [3] can perform at relatively high levels without the need for further major modifications. However, in the case of an urban environment case, the GPSR protocol with this additional mechanism can easily fall into recovery mode and fail to reach the destination with the greedy algorithm in the first place. Figure 2, shows two common cases where the original and the modified GPSR greedy algorithm of [3] cannot avoid falling into recovery mode. In order to solve this, the weight parameters of the proposed mechanism have to be changed.

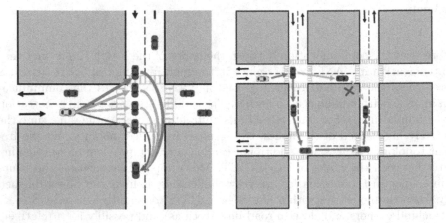

Fig. 2. Two common cases where the GPSR greedy algorithm falls in recovery mode. Left: The routes are chosen in an order from red to green as the vehicles, in the vertical road, move and successively fall out of reach. Right: The yellow route is chosen as first optimal path but fails to reach the destination. The green route is formed in recovery mode (Color figure online).

A key factor for multi-hop communications in a Manhattan-like grid with buildings seems to be any node located inside or very close to road intersections. Road intersections can function as joints for multi hop routes that do not follow a straight line. Figure 3, illustrates such a case.

In the new extension of the GPSR routing protocol, the neighbor nodes that are predicted to be located for the longest time period on a road intersection (and thus in the LOS with the index node), will be assigned less weight among the other neighbors. The new proposed weighting algorithm assigns higher priority to neighbor nodes moving towards the destination and those that are going to be longer inside the next road intersection in the same time. With this approach, the probability of keeping a route up is higher as intersections provide direct visibility with nodes on more directions.

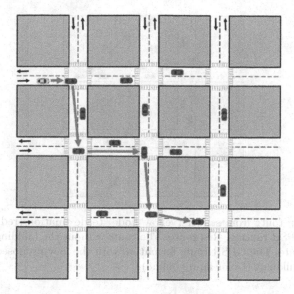

Fig. 3. Multi-hop route from source (yellow node) to destination (red node). Nodes moving in road intersections function as route connectors (Color figure online).

Figure 4, shows the formation of 3 routes while utilizing the GPSR routing. The red route depicts the case of not including buildings on the propagation. As expected, the signal cannot reach the next desired hop by penetrating the building. The yellow one is the case of forming a route while utilizing the default (and first proposed mechanism) GPSR routing. As the algorithm is greedy and based only on current and predicted future positions, it eventually reaches a dead end. The green route, which is formed when using the new proposed mechanism and giving priority on nodes located in intersections, manages to reach the destination (red node) without falling on recovery mode.

3.2   Algorithm and Architecture

Figure 5 presents a simplified overview of the architecture of the GPSR routing protocol with the enhanced methods and sub procedures. The top procedures (grey color) run periodically according to the hello interval initialization. The remainder procedures run on demand, when a packet transmission is required.

The proposed extensions and modifications include:

- GPSR hello packet header: Addition of a vector velocity field that is going to be used for position prediction and direction determination for every neighbor node.
- SNR Tag. Addition of a piggy back field to hello messages for the SNR value from the MAC layer during packet receipt. This field may be used while storing neighbors to the index neighbor table.
- Modifications and additions on the presented procedures in Fig. 4:

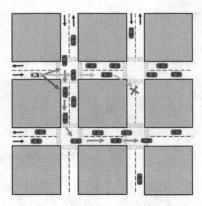

Fig. 4. Multi-hop route from sender (yellow node) to destination (red node). Yellow route: Default GPSR routing. Red route: The route without the buildings propagation model. Green route: The GPSR route formation with the new proposed extension for scenarios with buildings (Color figure online).

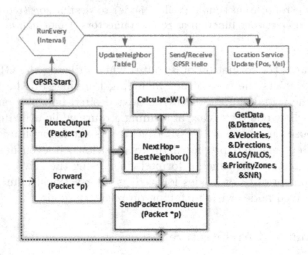

Fig. 5. Enhanced GPSR architecture.

1. RouteOutput(): Calls the modified BestNeighbor()
2. Forward(): Calls the modified BestNeighbor()
3. SendPacketFromQueue(): Calls the modified BestNeighbor()
4. BestNeighbor(): Uses the modified CalculateW()
5. CalculateW(): The weight calculation process for the next hop
6. GetData(): This sub process is in fact a simplified set of implemented methods that calculate specific parameters

The main procedures of the proposed mechanism are the BestNeighbor and CalculateW and are executed every time a node executes the RouteOutput, Forward or SendPacketFromQueue.

The BestNeighbor procedure iterates through all the stored nodes in the neighbour table of the index node and executes the CalculateW for each of them. After the weight of each neighbour node has been calculated, the procedure compares the weight of the index node with the smallest weight found in the neighbour table. If a node in the neighbour table has a smaller weight than the index node, then it is defined as the best neighbour and eventually as the next hop. In the opposite case, the procedure returns a null IP address to the caller function and eventually the GPSR enters the recovery mode. This procedure is presented in Algorithm 1.

Algorithm 1. Procedure BestNeighbor

> **procedure** BESTNEIGHBOR(myPos, myVel, dstPos, dstVel)
>   initialW = calculateW (myPos, myVel, -, -, dstPos, dstVel);
>   W = calculateW (myPos, myVel, neighborTable.begin()→Pos,
>   neighborTable.begin()→Vel, dstPos, dstVel);
>   **for** (i = neighborTable.begin(); i != neighborTable.end(); i++) **do**
>   **if** (W > calculateW (myPos, myVel, i→pos, i→vel, dstPos, dstVel)) **then**
>   W = calculateW(myPos, myVel, i→pos, i→vel, dstPos, dstVel);
>   nextHop.addr = i→addr;
>   **end if**
>   **if** (initialW > W) **then**
>   return nextHop;
>   **else**
>   return IpV4Address::GetZero();
>   **end if**
>   **end for**
> **end procedure**

The CalculateW procedure is invoked for every neighbor node of the index node through the BestNeighbor procedure and returns the calculated weight of the examined node based on the input routing data. The CalculateW contains 2 modes based on the LOS and NLOS situation between the source and the final destination. The first mode is triggered when the source and destination node are within Line Of Sight and the second when they are not. For each case, a different calculation method of W is followed. In the first mode, the algorithm prioritizes neighbour nodes moving in similar way (same road and direction) with the source and destination and maintaining short future distances with the destination. The second mode, recognises 3 priority zones where zone 1 has the least weight and zone 3 the most. Zone1 covers areas in road intersections while zone 2 covers the areas that are in LOS with the destination. Finally, Zone 3 covers the remaining areas that have the least priority. See Fig. 6 for an explanation of the two modes of the CalculateW procedure.

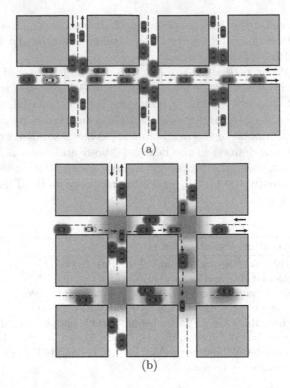

(a)

(b)

Fig. 6. Modes in CalculateW. (a): LOS – greatest priority (Green), medium priority (Yellow), least priority (Red). (b): NLOS – Priority zone 1 with gradual weight (Green), zone 2 (Blue), zone 3 (Red) (Color figure online).

CalculateW uses specific routing data in order to proceed with the weight calculations. This data is received from the procedure GetData and is mostly related to current and future node positions, velocities and directions. In addition, several auxiliary procedures define whether a node is located in an intersection and whether it is within LOS with another node. Some of these auxiliary methods are the inIntersectionTime, inLos, inLosTime, getDirections and dt. All these auxiliary procedures are called directly or indirectly form CalculateW. The pseudocode of CalculateW procedure is presented in Algorithm 2.

The required location data for the calculation of W is provided by the auxiliary GetData sub procedure which is in Algorithm 3.

The previously described procedures are called when a need for packet transmission occurs. Algorithm 4 presents the forward procedure of the GPSR that calls the previously described BestNeighbor and its modified sub procedures.

The described mechanism and the integration with the GPSR routing protocol have been implemented in the NS-3 simulator. The full source code with the implementation of the proposed routing mechanism, the propagation model used in this work and its Pyviz extensions for NS-3 can be found in http://ru6. cti.gr/ru6/research-areas/network-simulations.

Algorithm 2. Procedure CalculateW

```
procedure CALCULATEW(IndxPos, IndxVel, DstPos, DstVel, SrcPos, SrcVel)
    GetData ();
    W = +∞;
    if (inLoS (SrcPos, DstPos)) then  ▷ /* Mode 1: Source &destination in LOS */
        double w1 = 0.25, w2 = 0.1;
        if (inLoS (IndxFutPos, DstFutPos)) then
            if (getDirection (IndxVel) == getDirection (DstVel)) then
                w1 = 0.0;
            else
                w1 = 0.75;
            end if
        end if
        if (inLoS (IndxFutPos, SrcFutPos)) then
            if (getDirection (IndxVel) == getDirection (SrcVel)) then
                w2 = 0.0;
            else
                w2 = 0.01;
            end if
        end if
        W = Node_DestFutDist*(1+ w1 + w2);
    else                              ▷ /* Mode 2: Source & destination in NLOS */
        w1 = 0.5, w2 = 2; InterSectionT = 0.0;
        if    (inIntersection(IndxPos,   IndxVel)   &&   ((Indx_DestFutDist   -
0.25*Src_DstFutDist) < Src_DstFutDist)) then                    ▷ /* Zone 1 */
            InterSectionT = inIntersectionTime (IndxPos, IndxVel);
            W = Indx_DestFutDist*(1-w1-InterSectionT/100 );
        else
            if ((((Indx_DestFutDist - 0.25*Src_DstFutDist) < Src_DstFutDist) &&
(inLoS (IndxFutPos, DstFut-Pos))) || (((Indx_DestCurDist - 0.25*Src_DstCurDist)
< Src_DstCurDist) && (inLoS (IndxPos, DstPos)))) then          ▷ /* Zone 2 */
                W = Indx_DestFutDist + w2*Indx_SrcFutDist;
            else                                                ▷ /* Zone 3 */
                W = 2*Indx_DestFutDist + w2*Indx_SrcFutDist;
            end if
        end if
    end if
    return W;
end procedure
```

4   Simulation Settings

4.1   Reference Scenario

In this work, the studied topology is a Manhattan grid area with blocks of buildings and all simulations are conducted in the network simulator NS-3. Compared
to scenarios in open space (i.e., without buildings), this scenario's propagation

---

Algorithm 3. Procedure GetData

```
procedure GETDATA
    SrcSpeed = sqrt(pow(SrcVel.x, 2.0) + pow(SrcVel.y, 2.0));
    IndxSpeed = sqrt(pow(IndxVel.x, 2.0) + pow(IndxVel.y, 2.0));
    DstSpeed = sqrt(pow(DstVel.x, 2.0) + pow(DstVel.y, 2.0));
    SrcFutPos.x = SrcPos.x + SrcVel.x * dt(SrcSpeed);
    SrcFutPos.y = SrcPos.y + SrcVel.y * dt(SrcSpeed);
    IndxFutPos.x = IndxPos.x + IndxVel.x * dt(IndxSpeed);
    IndxFutPos.y = IndxPos.y + IndxVel.y * dt(IndxSpeed);
    DstFutPos.x = DstPos.x + DstVel.x * dt(DstSpeed);
    DstFutPos.y = DstPos.y + DstVel.y * dt(DstSpeed);
    Src_DstCurDist = GetDistance (SrcPos, DstPos);
    Src_DstFutDist = GetDistance (SrcFutPos, DstFutPos);
    Indx_SrcFutDist = GetDistance (IndxFutPos, SrcFutPos);
    Indx_DestCurDist = GetDistance (IndxPos, DstPos);
    Indx_DestFutDist = GetDistance (IndxFutPos, DstFutPos);
end procedure
```

Algorithm 4. Procedure forward

```
procedure FORWARD(packet)
    myPos = locationService→GetPos(indx);
    myVel = locationService→GetVel(indx);
    dst = packet→GetDst();
    dstPos = packet→GetDstPos();
    dstVel = packet→GetDstVel();
    /* Get the best next hop */
    if (neighborTable.isNeighbor(dst)) then
        nextHop = dst;
    else
        nextHop= neighborTable.BestNeighbor(myPos, myVel, dstPos, dstVel);
    end if
    if (nextHop.addr→isValid()) then
        route→SetGateway(nextHop);
        return;
    else
        RecoveryMode(route);
        return;
    end if
end procedure
```

---

model computes the effects of the buildings presence to the signal path loss in street canyons.

In particular, the B1 – Urban micro-cell scenario of the WINNER II Channel Models [14] is used in our tests. As described in [14], all antennas are below the height of surrounding buildings and both Line Of Sight (LOS) and Not Line Of Sight (NLOS) cases are modeled. The signal reaches the receiver nodes as a result of the propagation around corners, through buildings, and between them.

The path loss calculations of the B1 Winner Model in LOS and in NLOS can be found in the summary table of the path-loss models, in [14].

Figure 7, shows the simulated network graph for 200 wireless ad hoc nodes in NS-3 for the cases where buildings are absent or present in the scenario. As seen, in the case without buildings, the resulting graph has a very large number of links (the relevant part of the figure is difficult to see because of the number of links) and it is very strongly connected. In the case with the buildings, the resulting graph has a greatly reduced number of links and this already indicates that the expected performance of the routing protocols will be much different.

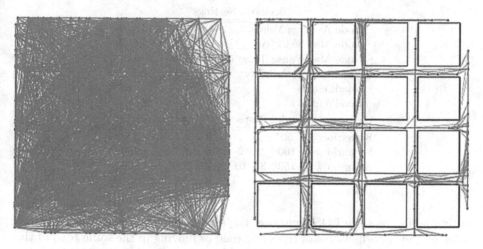

Fig. 7. Network graph for 200 nodes. Left: No buildings are modeled in propagation. Right: buildings are modeled with the 1 Winner Model.

4.2 Experiments and Parameters

For the evaluation of the studied routing protocols of this work as well as the proposed GPSR routing protocol with the integration of the previously presented mechanism, 2 set of simulations are conducted in the reference scenario. Each set is conducted for 3 scenario settings. For each scenario setting, each set of simulation is conducted for 5 different random node placements and mobility. For the node mobility generation the BonnMotion [2] software is used. All the network parameters and the scenario setting are presented in Table 1. Please note, that the density of the nodes is kept almost invariant, as the number of nodes increases with the size of the grid.

The first set of simulations is conducted to evaluate the performance of the studied and proposed routing protocols in the case of LOS between sender and final receiver. In this set, during the whole transmission, the sender and receiver maintain positions within LOS. This case depicts the common case of vehicles moving on the same road along the same direction. In order to evaluate the

Table 1. Simulation Parametes.

Network Parameters

Node Transmission Range	250m
Mac Layer	IEEE 802.11p Wave
PhyMode	Ofdm3mbs10MHz
Propagation Model	Winner B1 Model
Packet Size	256 Bytes
Packet Interval	0.01s
Flow duration	20 sec
Application	Udp UDP Server-Client

Scenario Settings

Node Average Velocity	40 km/h
Node Max Velocity	65 km/h
Node Max Pause Time (traffic light)	5 sec
Node turn probability	0.5
RoadLength	150 m
RoadWidth	20 m

	Nodes	Hops	Grid (roads)	Area (m^2)
Scenario #1	50	2 - 4	3 x 3	500
Scenario #2	100	2 - 7	4 x 4	700
Scenario #3	150	3 - 10	5 x 5	800

routing performance in LOS scenarios, the sender and receiver nodes are either stable on the opposite edges of the same road or moving in the same road of the Manhattan grid area. The intermediate nodes are randomly placed and moving to random directions in the grid. This set of experiments triggers the mode1 of the proposed mechanism.

The second set of experiments evaluates the performance of the studied and proposed routing protocols in the case of NLOS between the sender and final receiver. In this set, during the whole transmission, the sender and receiver maintain positions that are in NLOS. This case depicts a challenging scenario as the sender and final receiver are located and moving on different roads for the whole packet transmission. In this set of simulations, the sender and receiver nodes are either stable in different roads or moving in different roads of the Manhattan grid area. The intermediate nodes are again randomly placed and moving to random directions in the grid. This set of experiments triggers the mode2 and mode1 (for less common cases where the previous hop is in LOS with the destination) of the proposed mechanism.

5   Results and Discussion

The first set of experiments has been conducted for the case where the sender and the receiver are in a line-of-sight (i.e. they are both in the same street in the Manhattan grid). This mostly presents the best case scenario for all algorithms and is used to set a base of what performance each algorithm can achieve without complicating the examined scenario.

Figure 8 shows the average (over the different simulation runs) packet delivery ratio achieved by each routing protocol, for the case there is line-of-sight between the sender and the receiver. In accordance with the results from [3], the worst performer or this case is AODV, for all the different Manhattan grid sizes. The delivery ratio of GPSR is better that the delivery ratio of the other existing routing protocols, and this is due to the knowledge of the positions of the neighboring nodes that the protocol takes advantage of to select as the next hop the node closer to destination. As the existence of the buildings should not play a major role in this case, GPSR makes good choices and maintain a high delivery ratio. However the proposed modification to the GPSR protocol boosts the delivery ratio quite higher than the unmodified GPSR and is the best performer in terms of the packet delivery ratio achieved.

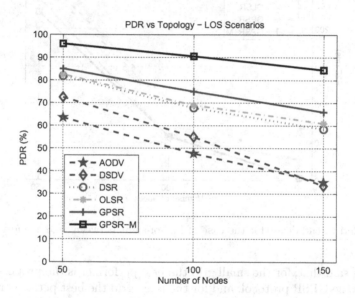

Fig. 8. Packet delivery ratio, for the case of line-of-sight between sender and receiver.

It should be noted that the delivery ratio drops as the size of the grid and the number of the nodes increase (maintaining almost the same node density). This is due to the fact that with larger grids more hops are required and the chances that there is a "gap" without intermediates, in the line-of-sight, becomes bigger and bigger and in that case the route has to make a "detour", which is no longer a simple case. The effect will be more evident with the end-to-end delay. However it is worth noting that the rate that the delivery ratio drops, as the grid increases in size, is less for the proposed modification to the GPSR protocol.

Figure 9 shows the average (over the different simulation runs) end-to-end delay achieved by each routing protocol, for the case there is line-of-sight between the sender and the receiver (please note that the ordering of the routing protocols and the grid sizes is different from the previous figure, so that larger bars do not obscure smaller ones). It should be noted that end-to-end delay increases rapidly with the size of the grid and the number of nodes (while node density remains almost the same). As already mentioned this is due to the "gaps", without nodes, that appear in the line-of-sight and require that another route is formed that detours the "gap". As already hinted this is not easily done in the urban setting, and for larger grid this case starts to look more like the case where there is no line-of-sight between the sender and the receiver.

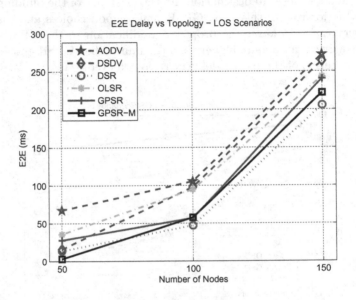

Fig. 9. End-to-end delay, for the case of line-of-sight between sender and receiver.

Having said that, for the small grid the best performer is the proposed modification to the GPSR protocol, and for the large grid the best performer is DSR. This can be explained by the fact that the GPSR-M protocol, maintains routes that deliver more packets even if for some of them the delay is large; i.e., there is a tradeoff between delivery ratio and delay. Still the proposed modification to the GPSR protocol manages to have better end-to-end delay than the rest of the routing protocols concerned.

Figure 10 shows the average (over the different simulation runs) power consumption for each routing protocol, for the case there is line-of-sight between the sender and the receiver (again, note the ordering of the routing protocols and the grid). The less power is consumed by the use of the DSR protocol. AODV, OLSR, GPSR and the proposed modification to the GPSR demonstrate a similar power usage. For the proposed modification to the GPSR protocol this means that the modifications can provide their benefits without increasing the power consumption.

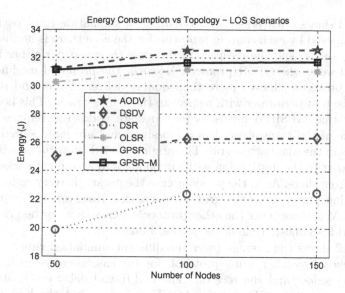

Fig. 10. Power consumption, for the case of line-of-sight between sender and receiver.

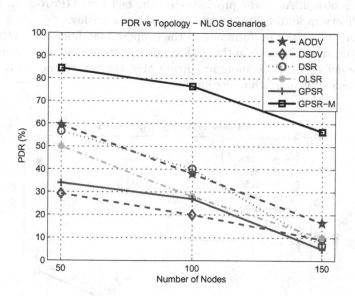

Fig. 11. Packet delivery ratio, for the case there is no line-of-sight between sender and receiver.

The second set of experiments where done for the generic (and more interesting) case where there is no line-of-sight between the sender and the receiver (i.e. they are in different streets in the Manhattan grid). This presents the most usual case for all algorithms.

Figure 11 shows the average (over the different simulation runs) packet delivery ratio achieved by each routing protocol, for the case there is no line-of-sight between the sender and the receiver. In this case the worst performer is DSDV, with second-worst the GPSR protocol. However the proposed modification to the GPSR protocol achieves more than double delivery ratio, and makes the GPSR-M the best performer with respect to the delivery ratio. This is explained by the fact that GPSR-M favors as intermediate nodes the vehicles that are (at the time of the transmission) in a crossroad and are more suited to route packets within the Manhattan grid. The original GPSR protocol greedily selects the node closer to the destination without taking into account if packets can be forwarded from there. As in the previous case the packet delivery ratio decreases for all routing protocols as the grid size increases. However, the improvement that GPSR-M achieves over the other protocols increases with the grid size (for the large grid is almost triple of the second best).

Figure 12 shows the average (over the different simulation runs) end-to-end delay achieved by each routing protocol, for the case there is no line-of-sight between the sender and the receiver. The end-to-end delay of GPSR-M is on the same level as the DSR and the AODV protocols, but the best performer is the OLSR protocol. Still GPSR-M greatly enhances the end-to-end delay of the GPSR protocol. As in the previous case the fact that GPSR-M has a much greater delivery ratio impacts the average end-to-end delay.

However, the overall performance of the proposed modification to the GPSR protocol is deemed higher than the performance of the remainder routing protocols, as the delivery ratio is more important that the end-to-end delay, and the resulting tradeoff is more than acceptable.

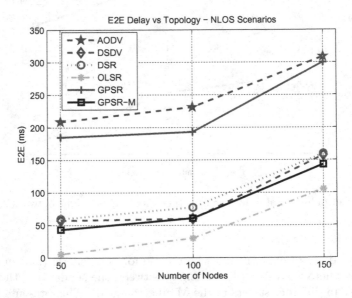

Fig. 12. End-to-end delay, for the case there is no line-of-sight between sender and receiver.

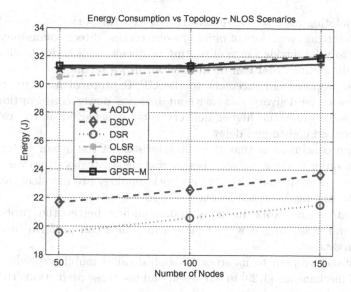

Fig. 13. Power consumption, for the case of no line-of-sight between sender and receiver.

Figure 13 shows the average (over the different simulation runs) power consumption of each routing protocol, for the case there is no line-of-sight between the sender and the receiver. Again, the less power is consumed by the use of the DSR protocol. AODV, OLSR, GPSR and the proposed modification to the GPSR demonstrate similar power usage. For the proposed modification to the GPSR protocol this means that the modifications can provide their benefits without increasing the power consumption.

The overall results demonstrate that the proposed mechanism greatly improves the GPSR performance for both LOS and NLOS scenarios and outperforms the other examined routing protocols. In all cases, the modified GPSR achieved higher packet delivery ratio and maintained quite satisfactory results even in very challenging scenarios of NLOS cases. Therefore, the proposed enhancement is a strong contender to be implemented together with GPSR.

6   Conclusions and Future Work

In this work we presented an experimental performance evaluation of routing mechanisms in MANETs, using simulation, for the case of VANETs within an urban environment (modeled by Manhattan grid). We also described and evaluated an enhancement of the GPRS protocol that takes into account the motion of the vehicles to estimate their position at future times, as well as the nature of the urban environment (i.e. the grid, in order to favor vehicles at crossroads as the intermediary nodes).

The simulation results have demonstrated that the performance of VANETs in an urban setting (with lots of buildings obstructing direct communications) is not satisfactory for a wide range of routing protocols. This is due to the reduced number of direct links that can be utilized in such a setting.

Still the proposed enhancement to the GPSR protocol manages to significantly increase the delivery ratio without increase power consumption; nevertheless, in some cases the higher delivery ratio is achieved at the expense of slightly increased end-to-end delay.

The main conclusion is that the characteristics of the urban setting can be exploited in order to come up with better routing strategies. However, the limitations imposed by the nature of the network topology are not clear, as it is not clear how far the performance increase can go.

Thus, our future work includes understanding better the problem, and proposing and evaluating new routing schemes that can perform much better in an urban setting.

In addition, we plan to incorporate sophisticated mobility prediction algorithms and mechanisms [4,20] in our work, and use these predictions to influence and improve the routing logic.

Acknowledgment. We would like to thank Prof. Paul G. Spirakis for his valuable guidance to our academic and professional careers.

References

1. Abbas, S.F., Chaudhry, S.R., Yasin, G.: VANET route selection in urban/rural areas using metric base traffic analysis. In: UBICOMM 2013, The Seventh International Conference on Mobile Ubiquitous Computing, Systems, Services and Technologies, pp. 85–91 (2013)
2. Aschenbruck, N., Ernst, R., Gerhards-Padilla, E., Schwamborn, M.: BonnMotion: a mobility scenario generation and analysis tool. In: Proceedings of the 3rd International ICST Conference on Simulation Tools and Techniques (ICST), p. 51, March 2010. http://dl.acm.org/citation.cfm?id=1808143.1808207
3. Bouras, C., Kapoulas, V., Tsanai, E.: A GPSR enhancement mechanism for routing in VANETs. In: Proceedings of the 13th International Conference on Wired & Wireless Internet Communications (WWIC 2015), Málaga, Spain, 25–27 May 2015
4. Gavalas, D., Konstantopoulos, C., Mamalis, B., Pantziou, G.: Mobility prediction in mobile ad-hoc networks. In: Pierre, S. (ed.) Next Generation Mobile Networks and Ubiquitous Computing, pp. 226–240. IGI Global, Hershey (2010)
5. He, G.: Destination-sequenced distance vector (DSDV) protocol. Helsinki University of Technology, Networking Laboratory (2002)
6. Jacquet, P., Mühlethaler, P., Clausen, T.H., Laouiti, A., Qayyum, A., Viennot, L.: Optimized link state routing protocol for ad hoc networks. In: IEEE International Multi Topic Conference. pp. 62–68 (2001)
7. Johnson, D.B., Maltz, D.A.: Dynamic source routing in ad hoc wireless networks. In: Imielinski, T., Korth, H.F. (eds.) Mobile Computing. The Kluwer International Series in Engineering and Computer Science, vol. 353, pp. 153–181. Springer, Heidelberg (1996). http://www.springerlink.com/index/10.1007/b102605

8. Kaisser, F., Johnen, C., Vèque, V.: Quantitative model for evaluate routing protocols in a vehicular ad hoc networks on highway. In: Vehicular Networking Conference (VNC 2010), pp. 330–337. IEEE (2010)

9. Kakarla, J., Sathya, S.S., Laxmi, B.G., Babu, B.R.: A survey on routing protocols and its issues in VANET. Int. J. Comput. Appl. **28**(4), 38–44 (2011). http://www.ijcaonline.org/volume28/number4/pxc3874663.pdf

10. Karp, B., Kung, H.T.: GPSR: greedy perimeter stateless routing for wireless networks. In: Proceedings of the 6th annual international conference on Mobile computing and networking, pp. 243–254. ACM (2000)

11. Katsaros, K., Dianati, M., Tafazolli, R., Kernchen, R.: CLWPR - a novel cross-layer optimized position based routing protocol for VANETs. In: IEEE Vehicular Networking Conference (VNC), pp. 139–146 (2011)

12. Kim, J.H., Lee, S.: Reliable routing protocol for vehicular ad hoc networks. AEU-Int. J. Electron. Commun. **65**(3), 268–271 (2011)

13. Kumar, R., Dave, M.: A comparative study of various routing protocols in VANET. arXiv preprint. arXiv:1108.2094 (2011)

14. Kyösti, P., Meinilä, J., Hentilä, L., Zhao, X., Jämsä, T., Schneider, C., Narandzić, M., Milojević, M., Hong, A., Ylitalo, J., Holappa, V.M., Alatossava, M., Bultitude, R., de Jong, Y., Rautiainen, T.: WINNER II Channel Models. Technical report, EC FP6 (2007). http://www.ist-winner.org/deliverables.html

15. Lee, K.C., Lee, U., Gerla, M.: Survey of routing protocols in vehicular ad hoc networks. In: Advances in vehicular ad-hoc networks: Developments and challenges, pp. 149–170 (2010)

16. Maan, F., Mazhar, N.: MANET routing protocols vs mobility models: a performance evaluation. In: 2011 Third International Conference on Ubiquitous and Future Networks (ICUFN), pp. 179–184 (2011)

17. Martinez, F.J., Toh, C.K., Cano, J.C., Calafate, C.T., Manzoni, P.: Realistic radio propagation models (RPMs) for VANET simulations. In: Wireless Communications and Networking Conference (WCNC 2009), pp. 1–6. IEEE (2009)

18. Nzouonta, J., Rajgure, N., Wang, G., Borcea, C.: VANET routing on city roads using real-time vehicular traffic information. IEEE Trans. Veh. Technol. **58**(7), 3609–3626 (2009)

19. Perkins, C., Belding-Royer, E., Das, S.: Ad hoc On-Demand Distance Vector (AODV) Routing (2003). http://www.ietf.org/rfc/rfc3561.txt

20. Su, W., Lee, S.J., Gerla, M.: Mobility prediction and routing in ad hoc wireless networks. Int. J. Netw. Manag. **11**(1), 3–30 (2001). http://dx.doi.org/10.1002/nem.386

21. Wan, S., Tang, J., Wolff, R.S.: Reliable routing for roadside to vehicle communications in rural areas. In: IEEE International Conference on Communications (ICC 2008), pp. 3017–3021. IEEE (2008)

Pioneering the Establishment of the Foundations of the Internet of Things

Ioannis Chatzigiannakis[1,2](✉)

[1] Sapienza University of Rome, Rome, Italy
ichatz@dis.uniroma1.it
[2] Computer Technology Institute & Press "Diophantus",
Patras, Greece

Abstract. In the Internet of Things era, every one of over a trillion everyday items will include at least some ability to store and process information. And, more important, to share that information over the global Internet with the other trillion items. In order to support this technological evolution, among the first problems that were addressed by the research community was that of basic network communication as existing, conventional (Internet-like) networking approaches were either unworkable or impractical. One of the solutions proposed is the so-called "Support Approach" that was proposed in 2000 and rigorously studied using a combination of theoretical and practical research. In this paper we present the main findings and we comment on the research methodology that led to these results.

1 The Internet of Things and Intermittent Connectivity

Many new technologies seem to arrive out of nowhere—and then, suddenly, everyone is talking about them. That is the case with the Internet of Things (IoT). The term was first coined by Kevin Ashton back in 1999, yet it became a standard term in scientific conferences and research forums after about 10 years. After 15 years, in 2014 it became a hot-topic in the business world, with numerous reports presenting the business opportunities of bringing forward from the research labs this now-stable paradigm to realize applications and services that were impossible to develop with already existing technologies.

During this period of 15 years, various other terms were used before the term Internet of Things became dominant. In early 2000, the Mobile Ad-hoc Networks was the most commonly used term. A few years later, the term Wireless Sensor Networks was introduced, and a bit later the term Pervasive Computing appeared in the scene.

Regardless of the name and ephimeral keywords, the technological goal remained the same: to integrate Internet and the Web with everyday objects (such as doors, chairs, electric appliances, cars, etc.) and ultimately interconnect the digital and physical domains. Clearly, the types of objects to be connected with the Internet, e.g., in terms of usage, size, and numbers, is extremely diverse thus having different computation and communication requirements. For this

© Springer International Publishing Switzerland 2015
C. Zaroliagis et al. (Eds.): Spirakis Festschrift, LNCS 9295, pp. 154–168, 2015.
DOI: 10.1007/978-3-319-24024-4_10

reason, a large number of computing architectures and networking paradigms have been proposed and different networking standards have been developed.

In most cases, the operational and performance characteristics of the newly introduced technologies made conventional (Internet-like) networking approaches either unworkable or impractical. Concepts of occasionally-connected networks became common in the real-world applications developed; real-world cases that suffer from frequent partitions and that rely on more than one divergent set of protocols or protocol families.

Today these characteristics are interwined with the Internet of Things and uniformly considered by all developers and researchers as a basic challenge. Yet at the very beginning of the inception of the Internet of Things, this was not the case. Paul Spirakis was among the very few visionary to predict that in order to realize all these new types of applications we would have to address the problem of intermittent connectivity in networks with long delays between sending and receiving messages, or long periods of disconnection.

In 1999, Paul Spirakis commenced the study of such networks by guiding one of his graduate students to work on this area [10]. During that time, the most common way to establish communication was to form paths of intermediate nodes that lie within one another's transmission range and could directly communicate with each other, see e.g., [29]. The mobile nodes would have to act as nodes and routers at the same time in order to propagate packets along these paths. The approach of maintaining a global structure with respect to the temporary network was a difficult problem. Since nodes constantly move, the underlying communication graph is changing, and the nodes have to adapt quickly to such changes and reestablish their routes. It was in 2005 when Busch and Tirthapura [8] provided the first analysis of the performance of some characteristic protocols [20, 29] and shown that in some cases they require $\Omega(l^2)$ time to stabilize (where l is the number of nodes), i.e., be able to provide communication.

In 2000, the first results of Spirakis' team was published under the title *"Analysis and Experimental Evaluation of an Innovative and Efficient Routing Protocol for Ad-hoc Mobile Networks"* [14]. Their work introduced a new communication mechanism for highly dynamic networks where the nodes are partitioned for arbitrary periods of time. In contrast to all techniques available at that time, the new approach proposed to utilize a (mobile) small-sized *support* subnetwork, i.e., a subset of nodes that are controlled by the network and move in a coordinated way acting as an intermediate storage of messages. In [15] (2001) the innovative mechanism was shown to establish communication between *any pair* of nodes in *small, a-priori guaranteed expected time bounds* even when the nodes of the network are disconnected for *arbitrary* period of times.

In [18] different methods to organize the *support subnetwork* were studied and their effect on the correctness and efficiency of the communication mechanism. Using rigorous mathematical tools it was shown that the studied organization schemes are correct, efficient, and totally avoid message flooding. Interestingly they are inherently scalable to the number of nodes that comprise the network. This was fundamentally different to other techniques introduced later on, that relied on epidemic processes that required the message to reach out all nodes of the network to guarantee the correct propagation of the information, see e.g., [26].

Their research work concluded in 2003, after a series of research results that established the theoretical foundations for routing in networks that experience partitions for arbitrary durations of time. In 2008 their innovative communication technique was included in the Encyclopedia of Algorithms, published by Springer [27], under the title *"Communication in Ad Hoc Mobile Networks Using Random Walks"* [11].

Interestingly, after four years, due to the study of the Interplanetary Internet, which focused primarily on the issue of deep space communication in high-delay environments, these ideas were used to form the concept of Delay Tolerant Networking [7]. Shortly after, the paradigm introduced and studied by Spirakis et al. was used to develop routing protocols for delay tolerant networks. In [26] the term *support subnetwork* was replaced by the term *Oracle-based routing* to better describe the routing mechanism in networks with frequent disconnections. Eventually the term DTN (Delay Tolerant Networks) became dominant and created a sub-area of research that led in 2007 in the formation of the *Delay-Tolerant Networking Architecture* under the RFC4838 [9].

2   Modeling Mobile and Dynamic Networks

Like almost all scientific fields, theoretical models are of central importance as they influence the ability to answer fundamental questions. The choice of a particular model usually depends on what problem is studied and what type of algorithm is presented. In the attempt to theoretically evaluate the performance of mobile and dynamic networks, several different models of mobile information processing have been studied. Yet, until 1999, the vast majority of the body of research followed the approach of slowly-changing communication graphs: modelling nodes motions only implicitly, i.e., via a pre-assumed upper bound on the rate of virtual link changes.

In 1998, Paul Spirakis et al. realized that the motions of the nodes are the cause of the fragility of the virtual links and followed a completely different approach by proposing an *explicit model of motions*. In a seminal work [23], they presented the *motion graph model* that distinguishes explicitly between (a) the fixed (for any algorithm) space of possible motions of the mobile nodes and (b) the kind of motions that the nodes perform inside this space. The space of motions is only combinatorially modelled, i.e., as a graph. Based on this new model, in [23] they studied the problem of leader election in mobile networks.

The newly introduced model stated that the space of possible motions of the mobile nodes is combinatorially abstracted by a *motion-graph*, i.e., the detailed geometric characteristics of the motion are neglected. Each node is assumed to have a transmission range represented by a sphere tr centered by itself. Any other node inside tr can receive any message broadcast by this node. This sphere is approximated by a cube tc with volume $\mathcal{V}(tc)$, where $\mathcal{V}(tc) < \mathcal{V}(tr)$. The size of tc can be chosen in such a way that its volume $\mathcal{V}(tc)$ is the maximum that preserves $\mathcal{V}(tc) < \mathcal{V}(tr)$, and if a mobile node inside tc broadcasts a message, this message is received by any other node in tc. Given that the mobile nodes are moving in the space $\mathcal{S}$, $\mathcal{S}$ is divided into consecutive cubes of volume $\mathcal{V}(tc)$.

Definition 1. *The motion graph $G(V, E)$, ($|V| = n$, $|E| = m$), which corresponds to a quantization of some space $\mathcal{S}$ is constructed in the following way: a vertex $u \in G$ represents a cube of volume $\mathcal{V}(tc)$ and an edge $(u, v) \in G$ exists if the corresponding cubes are adjacent.*

For an example of the quantization process see Fig. 1. The number of vertices n, actually approximates the ratio between the volume $\mathcal{V}(\mathcal{S})$ of space $\mathcal{S}$, and the space occupied by the transmission range of a mobile node $\mathcal{V}(tr)$. In the extreme case where $\mathcal{V}(\mathcal{S}) \approx \mathcal{V}(tr)$, the transmission range of the nodes approximates the space where they are moving and $n = 1$. Given the transmission range tr, n depends linearly on the volume of space $\mathcal{S}$ regardless of the choice of tc, and $n = O\left(\frac{V(\mathcal{S})}{V(tr)}\right)$. The ratio $\frac{V(\mathcal{S})}{V(tr)}$ is the *relative motion space size* and is denoted by ρ. Since the edges of G represent neighboring polyhedra each vertex is connected with a constant number of neighbors, which yields that $m = \Theta(n)$. In this example where tc is a cube, G has maximum degree of six and $m \leq 6n$. Thus *motion graph G* is (usually) a *bounded degree graph* as it is derived from a regular graph of small degree by deleting parts of it corresponding to motion or communication obstacles. Let Δ be the maximum vertex degree of G.

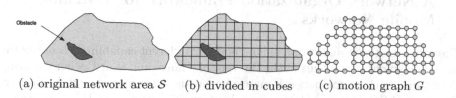

(a) original network area $\mathcal{S}$ (b) divided in cubes   (c) motion graph G

Fig. 1. The original network area $\mathcal{S}$, how it is divided in consecutive cubes of volume $\mathcal{V}(tc)$ and the resulting motion graph G

The *motion graph model* was extended in [17] to incorpotate the motion the nodes perform during the execution of a particular application. The core idea of the extension was that nodes' motion is controlled by an *adversary*—a higher level entity that determines the way that the nodes move. Then the application may be aware of these motions (using some particular technology, or by simply having the users to input their motion patterns) or can be totally unknown.

In the general case, the extension states an *oblivious adversary* or *restricted motion adversary*, that is the adversary determines motion patterns in any possible way but independently of the distributed application executed by the nodes. The central idea here is to exclude cases where some of nodes are deliberately trying to *maliciously affect* the application (e.g., to avoid specific nodes with central node in the application and network management).

For purposes of studying the efficiency of distributed applications for dynamically changing networks *on the average*, the model extensions abstracted the motion of the nodes by *concurrent and independent random walks*. Having the mobile users move randomly, either according to uniformly distributed changes in their directions and velocities or according to the random waypoint mobility model by picking random destinations, was quite common at that point of time and was used by other researchers (see e.g. [21,24]).

The key observation that led to the use of random walks was a fundumental result of graph theory, according to which, dense graphs look like random graphs in many of their properties. This was already noticed for expander graphs at least by [1,3] and captured by the famous Szemeredi's Regularity Lemma [31] (in some sense most graphs can be approximated by random-looking graphs).

In analogy, Spirakis and his student conjectured that any set of *dense (in number)* but arbitrary otherwise motions of many nodes in the motion space can be approximated (at least with respect to their meeting and hitting times statistics) by a set of concurrent dense *random walks*. But the meeting times statistics of the nodes essentially determine the virtual fragile links of any ad-hoc network. They believed that the suggestion for adoption of concurrent random walks as a model for input motions, was not only a tool for average case performance analysis but it might in fact approximate well any mobile network of dense motions.

3   A Network Organization Framework for Dynamic Mobile Networks

The problem of communication among nodes of different capabilities is one of the most fundamental problems in the Internet of Things and is at the core of many algorithms, such as for network management, data processing and fusion, etc. The work of Spirakis and Chatzigiannakis focused on networks that are subject to highly dynamic structural changes created by mobility, channel fluctuations and device failures [17,19]. These changes affect topological connectivity, occur with high frequency and may not be predictable in advance. The problem of establishing communication is such networks is now widely known as the problem of *Routing in Low Power and Lossy Networks* and standardization efforts are coordinated by the Internet Engineering Task Force (IETF) charter ROLL[1].

The key idea of the communication framework is to take advantage of the mobile nodes natural movement by exchanging information whenever mobile nodes meet incidentally. This idea resembles gossip like communication protocols where messages are spread among nodes like rumors. If we assume that the nodes will meet often enough, and moreover, if we assume that they will not try to avoid specific areas of the area covered by the network, then it is reasonable to accept that eventually one of the many copies of the original message will reach the intended receiver. During the same time of the work of Spirakis and

---

[1] https://datatracker.ietf.org/wg/roll/charter/.

his team, this approach was followed by [32] where an *epidemic algorithm* was designed. In their solution, messages are broadcast to all neighbors as long as there is enough storage space to hold the copies. When there is no room in the local storage of a node, oldest messages are evicted.

In contrast to the work of [32] and other epidemic algorithms introduced later on in the relevant literature, the protocol framework of Spirakis et al. removes these assumptions on the mobility patterns of the nodes. It was evident to them that if the nodes would be spread in remote areas and they would not move beyond these areas, then there would no way for information to reach them, unless the application took special care of such situations. To solve this problem, they introduced the idea to force only a small subset of the nodes to move as per the needs of the application; they called this subset of nodes the *support* of the network. The idea of a support team was eventually tested in the field after 14 years, in 2014 as part of a project partially supported by the US National Aeronautics and Space Administration (NASA); a team of quadcopters was used to establish digital communication networks.

Assuming the availability of such nodes, the support nodes can be used to provide a simple, correct and efficient strategy for communication between any pair of nodes of the network that avoids message flooding. Actually the support can assist by providing efficient, secure and robust network management and organization. Interestingly, this idea creates a new class of protocols (distributed algorithms) for ad-hoc mobile networks, which is defined as follows:

Definition 2. Non-Compulsory *protocols are the ones whose execution does not affect the movement of the mobile hosts. On the other hand,* compulsory *protocols are the those that require all hosts to perform certain moves in order to ensure the correct protocol execution. Finally, the class of ad-hoc mobile network protocols which enforce a (small) subset of the mobile hosts to move in a certain way is called the class of* semi-compulsory *protocols.*

Essentially, non-compulsory protocols are gossip based protocols that try to take advantage of the mobile hosts natural movement by exchanging information whenever mobile hosts meet incidentally. On the other hand, Compulsory protocols force the mobile hosts to move according to a specific scheme in order to meet the protocol demands (i.e. meet more often, spread in a geographical area, etc.) and speed up the spreading of messages.

Definition 3. *The subset of the mobile hosts of an ad-hoc mobile network whose motion is determined by a network protocol P is called the support Σ of $\mathcal{P}$. The part of P which indicates the way that members of Σ move and communicate is called the support management subprotocol M_Σ of $\mathcal{P}$.*

This definition captures network management ideas for ad-hoc mobile networks. The scheme of Spirakis et al. defines a support (and its management subprotocol) suitable not only for pairwise communication but also for a whole set of basic problems including many-to-one communication, information spreading and multicasting.

Definition 4. *Consider a family of protocols, $\mathcal{F}$, for a mobile ad-hoc network, and let each protocol $\mathcal{P}$ in $\mathcal{F}$ have the same support (and the same support management subprotocol). Then Σ is called the support of the family $\mathcal{F}$.*

The scheme follows the general design principle of mobile networks (with a fixed subnetwork however) called the "two-tier" principle [25] which says that any protocol should try to move communication and computation to the fixed part of the network. The idea of the support Σ is a simulation of such a (skeleton) network by moving hosts, however.

In addition, the network designer may wish that the way hosts in Σ move (maybe coordinated) and communicate is robust (i.e. that it can tolerate failures of hosts). In the original work of Spirakis et al., they considered permanent host failures (i.e. stop failures). That is, once such a fault happens then the host of the fault does not participate in the ad-hoc mobile network anymore.

Definition 5. *A support management subprotocol, M_Σ, is k-faults tolerant, if it still allows the members of $\mathcal{F}$ (or $\mathcal{P}$) to execute correctly, under the presence of at most k permanent faults of hosts in Σ ($k \geq 1$).*

4   Basic Communication Algorithms for Dynamic Mobile Networks

A *basic communication problem*, in dynamic mobile networks, is to send information from some *sender* user, MH_S, to another designated *receiver* user, MH_R.

Let k nodes be a predefined set of nodes that become the nodes of the support. These nodes move randomly and fast enough so that they visit in sufficiently short time the entire motion graph. When some node of the support is within transmission range of a sender, it notifies the sender that it may send its message(s). The messages are then stored "somewhere within the support structure". When a receiver comes within transmission range of a node of the support, the receiver is notified that a message is "waiting" for him and the message is then forwarded to the receiver.

Protocol 1. The "Snake" Support Motion Coordination Protocol. *Let $S_0, S_1, \ldots, S_{k-1}$ be the members of the support and let S_0 denote the leader node (possibly elected). The protocol forces S_0 to perform a random walk on the motion graph and each of the other nodes S_i execute the simple protocol "move where S_{i-1} was before". When S_0 is about to move, it sends a message to S_1 that states the new direction of movement. S_1 will change its direction as per instructions of S_0 and will propagate the message to S_2. In analogy, S_i will follow the orders of S_{i-1} after transmitting the new directions to S_{i+1}. Movement orders received by S_i are positioned in a queue Q_i for sequential processing. The very first move of S_i, $\forall i \in \{1, 2, \ldots, k-1\}$ is delayed by a δ period of time.*

The purpose of the random walk of the head S_0 is to ensure a *cover*, within some finite time, of the whole graph G without knowledge and memory, other than local, of topology details. This memoryless motion also ensures fairness, low-overhead and inherent robustness to structural changes.

Consider the case where any sender or receiver is allowed a general, unknown motion strategy, but its strategy is provided by a restricted motion adversary. This means that each node not in the support either (a) executes a deterministic motion which either stops at a vertex or cycles forever after some initial part or (b) it executes a stochastic strategy which however is *independent* of the motion of the support. The authors in [19] prove the following correctness and efficiency results. The reader can refer to the excellent book by Aldous and Fill [2] for a nice introduction on Makrov Chains and Random Walks.

Theorem 1. *The support and the "snake" motion coordination protocol guarantee reliable communication between any sender-receiver (A, B) pair in finite time, whose expected value is bounded only by a function of the relative motion space size ρ and does not depend on the number of nodes, and is also independent of how MH_S, MH_R move, provided that the mobile nodes not in the support do not deliberately try to avoid the support.*

Theorem 2. *The expected communication time of the support and the "snake" motion coordination protocol is bounded above by $\Theta(\sqrt{mc})$ when the (optimal) support size $k = \sqrt{2mc}$ and $c = \frac{e}{e-1}u$, with u being the "separation threshold time" of the random walk on G.*

Theorem 3. *By having the support's head move on a regular spanning subgraph of G, there is an absolute constant $\gamma > 0$ such that the expected meeting time of A (or B) and the support is bounded above by $\gamma \frac{n^2}{k}$. Thus the protocol guarantees a total expected communication time of $\Theta(\rho)$, independent of the total number of mobile nodes, and their movement.*

The analysis assumes that the head S_0 moves according to a continuous time random walk of total rate 1 (rate of exit out of a node of G). If S_0 moves ψ times *faster* than the rest of the nodes, all the estimated times, except the inter-support time, will be divided by ψ. Thus the expected total communication time can be made to be as small as $\Theta\left(\gamma \frac{\rho}{\sqrt{\psi}}\right)$ where γ is an absolute constant. In cases where S_0 can take advantage of the network topology, all the estimated times, except the inter-support time are improved:

Theorem 4. *When the support's head moves on a regular spanning subgraph of G the expected meeting time of A (or B) and the support cannot be less than $\frac{(n-1)^2}{2m}$. Since $m = \Theta(n)$, the lower bound for the expected communication time is $\Theta(n)$. In this sense, the "snake" protocol's expected communication time is optimal, for a support size which is $\Theta(n)$.*

The "on-the-average" analysis of the time-efficiency of the protocol assumes that the motion of the mobile nodes not in the support *is a random walk on the motion graph G*. The random walk of each mobile node is performed independently of the other nodes.

Theorem 5. *The expected communication time of the support and the "snake" motion coordination protocol is bounded above by the formula*

$$E(T) \leq \frac{2}{\lambda_2(G)} \Theta\left(\frac{n}{k}\right) + \Theta(k)$$

The upper bound is minimized when $k = \sqrt{\frac{2n}{\lambda_2(G)}}$, where λ_2 is the second eigenvalue of the motion graph's adjacency matrix.

The way the support nodes move and communicate is robust, in the sense that it can tolerate failures of the support nodes. The types of failures of nodes considered are permanent, i.e. stop failures. Once such a fault happens, the support node of the fault does not participate in the ad hoc mobile network anymore. A communication protocol is β-*faults tolerant*, if it still allows the members of the network to communicate correctly, under the presence of at most β permanent faults of the nodes in the support ($\beta \geq 1$). In [19] it is shown that:

Theorem 6. *The support and the "snake" motion coordination protocol is 1-fault tolerant.*

4.1 Alternative Implementations of the Support

A different approach to implement Σ is to allow each member of Σ not to move in a snake-like fashion, but to perform an *independent* random walk on the motion graph G, i.e., the members of Σ can be viewed as "runners" running on G. In other words, instead of maintaining at all times pairwise adjacency between members of Σ, all hosts sweep the area by moving independently from each other. When two runners meet, they exchange any information given to them by senders encountered using a synchronization subprotocol. Similar to the snake protocol case, the same approach is used to notify the sender that it may send its message(s) when within communication range of a node of the support.

As presented in [13], the runners protocol does not use the idea of a (moving) backbone subnetwork. However, all communication is still routed through the support Σ and we expect that the size k of the support (i.e., the number of runners) will affect performance in a more efficient way than that of the snake approach. This expectation stems from the fact that each host will meet each other in parallel, accelerating the spread of information (i.e., messages to be delivered).

The design of network organization and management protocol for networks that dynamically change in terms of network area size, structure and also in terms of number users and needs is a challenging task. Especially when these changes are unpredictable and *not known* in advance and happen in an area of deployment which is not fixed.

Examples of such changes in the network's area topology can result by introducing possible obstacles or by creating new paths for hosts' movement. These changes may have significant effect on the size and the shape of the network's area. As an example showing the dramatic impact on the size of the area of deployment of such changes, note that even a single connectivity change may cut off entire parts of the network area in a permanent way.

In such *highly changing* networks, a "static" implementation of the runners approach is not satisfactory, i.e. having a fixed k will not suffice. Indeed, note that even an initially optimal runners implementation (by choosing an optimal, as possibly implied by the analysis, number of runners) may soon become *inefficient*, leading to big communication times (in the case where the network area grows significantly and/or obstacles appear) or employing an unnecessarily high number of runners (in the case where the network's area size shrinks).

It is therefore necessary that the network protocols anticipate such changes and modify accordingly their internal operation in order to maintain adequate levels of service quality.

Towards this end, the *adaptive-compulsory version* of the support approach is introduced. The adaptive support management protocol builds upon the "runners" protocol by incorporating an adaptation protocol. Clearly such an adaptive approach can also use the "snake" protocol (see previous section) and possibly other support management protocols since the basic building blocks of the support are also used by the adaptive support management protocol.

The basic idea of the adaptive support protocol is that the execution of the protocol evolves in phases of possible adaptation. In the beginning of each such phase the protocol tries to sense the need or not for an adaptation. This is done without assuming knowledge of the network size at any stage, since the need for an adaptation is sensed implicitly, by taking related measurements, such as communication times. When such measurements indicate a certain behavior (i.e. communication times that progressively become significantly bigger or smaller, respectively), the protocol adapts by respectively changing the support size (increasing or reducing it). The adaptation is done progressively, by adding (or removing) support members in each step of the adaptation procedure in a geometrically growing fashion. This progressive adaptation allows to sense reaching a new optimal support size, when the changes in the measured communication times exhibit a certain limiting behavior, in the sense that further change does not incur a significant effect on communication times anymore.

5   Exploiting the Theoretical and Practical Dimensions of Research in Parallel

A standard scientific method for *understanding* complicated situations is to analyze them in a top-down, hierarchical manner. This approach also works well for *organizing* a large variety of structures; that is why a similar hierarchical, centralized approach has worked extremely well for employing computers in so many aspects of our life.

On the other hand, our world has become increasingly complex. The resulting challenges have become so demanding that it is impossible to ignore that a large variety of systems have a very different structure: the stability and effectiveness of our modern political, social and economic structures relies on the fact that they are based on decentralized, distributed and self-organizing mechanisms.

The Internet of Things is a characteristic example of such an approach in technology. We are just beginning to see the effects of turning a vast number of heterogeneous objects into one large and decentralized network; in particular, the large-scale effects of the interaction between hardware, software, algorithms and data are just starting to show, and many of the resulting emerging phenomena come as surprises, rather than by design.

Turning from centralized algorithms for individual processors (albeit locally interacting ones) to large-scale mechanisms for decentralized and self-organizing networks has been one of the crucial paradigm shifts of computer science and its applications in recent years; it is analogous to shifting from studying individual neural cells to the analysis and even the design (!) of a complex brain.

To make the Internet of Things a reality, innovative technology is being developed at both theoretical and technological level. Advancements have been made in the physical hardware level, embedded software in the sensor devices, systems for future sensing applications and fundamental research in new communication and networking paradigms. Although these research attempts have been conducted in parallel, in most cases they were also done in isolation, making it difficult to converge towards a unified global framework. Most currently deployed solutions lack the necessary sophistication, innovation, and efficiency, while state-of-the-art foundational approaches are often too abstract, missing a satisfactory accuracy of important technological details and specifications.

Paul Spirakis was among the first to observe that to be effective and to produce applicable results, it is important to encourage interaction and bridge the gap between fundamental approaches and technological/practical solutions. As a trully visionary researcher, he realized from the very beginning that future research on the Internet of Things will exploit its theoretical and practical dimensions in parallel via simple and efficient communication channels. It should depend on tools and processes that follow good practices, independent of the current available technologies, and that offer effective abstractions for future systems. It should be based on methodologies for which the complementarity of experimentation and analysis is always visible. In [30], for the first time, he formulated the notion of *distributed algorithm engineering* that essentially involves the considerable effort required to convert theoretically efficient and correct distributed algorithms to effective, robust and easily used software implementations on a simulated or real distributed environment, usually accompanied by thorough experimentation, fine-tuning and testing.

From the very beginning of this line of research, a dual approach was followed to study the new communication paradigm for highly dynamic networks with intermittent connectivity. The publication of theoretical results was always accompanied by experimental research. The first set of research results, [14], appeared in a scientific conference on Algorithmic Engineering. The alternative mechanisms proposed in [18] were also studied using an experimental methodology and the results where presented in [13]. In [16] the communication framework is further developed to support large scale deployments using a *hierarchy of support subnetworks*. The experimental investigation significantly helped to study the operation of the newly introduced communication mechanism and understand how to fine-tune the operation of the network, e.g., in relation to the memory available to the *support subnetwork* and how it affects the communiation times.

The complete set of results of the experimental study was published in [19]. This publication included experiments modeling the different possible situations regarding the geographical area covered by a dynamically changing mobile network. It considered different kinds of motion graphs, unstructure (random) and more structured ones. The experiments examined the correctness of the communication framework under different operational conditions and also under the presence of failures. It studied the message delivery delays under different communication patterns and the inherent ability of the framework to scale in networks of large number of nodes. It also included results from experiments that evaluated the utilization of the *support subnetwork* in terms of total number of multiple message copies stored in the support subnetwork at any given time, as well as the message delivery rate.

The examination of the performance of the communication framework in such detail led to the key observation that the *mobility (or motion) rate* of the nodes is the parameter that dominates mostly the performance and the correctness of the protocols regardless of the approach followed. A first attempt to exploit this observation was presented in [12] where the communication framework was combined with pre-existing routing protocols such as the DSR protocol [6] and the ZRP protocol [22,28]. A protocol synthesis approach was followed towards designing new routing protocols that achieve good results (in terms of message delivery rates and delays) in dynamic mobile networks consisting of mobile hosts with mixed mobility patterns. The experimental studies shown that this method provided good results and in fact in some cases the resulting synthesized protocol outperformed the original ones by achieving lower message delivery delays while keeping high success rates.

This line of research was further expanded and in 2006 [4,5] it produced an adaptive protocol framework for exploiting the usually different mobility rates of the nodes by adopting the routing strategy during execution. The adaptation between different strategies was based on a newly defined metric that captured the relative mobility of the nodes. This metric was used to determine, for any pair of origin and destination, the routing technique that best corresponded to their mobility properties. Special care was taken for nodes remaining almost stationary or moving with high (relative) speeds. The performance of the proposed framework was studied using experimental evaluation methodology. The results demonstrate that the proposed adaptive framework improved, in certain cases, the performance of the existing routing protocols.

6   Closing Remarks

We have presented an overview of one of the lines of research conducted by Paul Spirakis and his team, during 1999...2003 at the Computer Technology Institute (CTI) and the University of Patras. We believe that the particular case depicts the ability of Paul Spirakis to identify core problems of technologies that are still in their inception, many years before they become apparent to the scientific community. Moreover, this case is a clear indication of an almost unique multiscientific ability to combine a broad set of techniques and methodologies to examine a given problem. Paul Spirakis is among the most visionary thought leader of our generation, with a great talent to inspire and guide new researchers.

References

1. Ajtai, M., Komlos, J., Szemeredi, E.: Deterministic simulation in logspace. In: 19th Annual Symposium on Theory of Computing, ACM, 1987, pp. 132–140
2. Aldous, D., Fill, J.: Reversible markov chains and random walks on graphs (1999). http://stat-www.berkeley.edu/users/aldous/book.html
3. Alon, N., Chung, F.R.K.: Explicit construction of linear sized tolerant networks. Discrete Math. **72**, 15–19 (1998)
4. Bamis, A., Boukerche, A., Chatzigiannakis, I., Nikoletseas, S.E.: A mobility sensitive approach for efficient routing in ad hoc mobile networks. In: Alba, E., Chiasserini, C-F., Abu-Ghazaleh, N.B., Lo Cigno, R. (eds.) Proceedings of the 9th International Symposium on Modeling Analysis and Simulation of Wireless and Mobile Systems, MSWiM 2006, Terromolinos, Spain, October 2–6, pp. 357–364. ACM (2006)
5. Bamis, A., Boukerche, A., Chatzigiannakis, I., Nikoletseas, S.E.: A mobility aware protocol synthesis for efficient routing in ad hoc mobile networks. Comput. Netw. **52**(1), 130–154 (2008)
6. Broch, J., Johnson, D.B., Maltz, D.A.: The dynamic source routing protocol for mobile ad-hoc networks. In: Technica report, IETF, Internet Draft, December 1998. draft-ietf-manet-dsr-01. txt
7. Burleigh, S., Hooke, A., Torgerson, L., Fall, K., Cerf, V., Durst, B., Scott, K., Weiss, H.: Delay-tolerant networking: an approach to interplanetary internet. IEEE Commun. Mag. **41**(6), 128–136 (2003)
8. Busch, C., Tirthapura, S.: Analysis of link reversal routing algorithms. SIAM J. Comput. **35**(2), 305–326 (2005)
9. Cerf, V., Burleigh, S., Hooke, A., Torgerson, L., Durst, B., Scott, K., Fall, K., Weiss, H.: Delay-tolerant networking architecture. In: Technical report, The IETF Trust (2007)
10. Chatzigiannakis, I.: Design and analysis of distributed algorithms for basic communication in ad-hoc mobile networks. Ph.D. dissertation, Department of Computer Engineering and Informatics, University of Patras, Greece, May 2003
11. Chatzigiannakis, I.: Communication in ad hoc mobile networks using random walks. Encyclopedia of Algorithms, Springer, Heidelberg (2008)
12. Chatzigiannakis, I., Kokkinos, P., Zaroliagis, C.: Synthesizing routing protocols for ad-hoc mobile networks. In: 12th Annual International Symposium on Modeling, Analysis and Simulation of Computer and Telecommunication Systems (MASCOTS 2004), Poster Paper, pp. 24–27 (2004)

13. Chatzigiannakis, I., Nikoletseas, S.E., Paspallis, N., Spirakis, P.G., Zaroliagis, C.D.: An experimental study of basic communication protocols in ad-hoc mobile networks. In: Brodal, G.S., Frigioni, D., Marchetti-Spaccamela, A. (eds.) WAE 2001. LNCS, vol. 2141, p. 159. Springer, Heidelberg (2001)
14. Chatzigiannakis, I., Nikoletseas, S.E., Spirakis, P.G.: Analysis and experimental evaluation of an innovative and efficient routing protocol for ad-hoc mobile networks. In: Näher, S., Wagner, D. (eds.) WAE 2000. LNCS, vol. 1982, pp. 99–110. Springer, Heidelberg (2001)
15. Chatzigiannakis, I., Nikoletseas, S.E., Spirakis, P.G.: An efficient communication strategy for Ad-hoc mobile networks. In: Welch, J.L. (ed.) DISC 2001. LNCS, vol. 2180, pp. 285–299. Springer, Heidelberg (2001)
16. Chatzigiannakis, I., Nikoletseas, S., Spirakis, P.: An efficient routing protocol for hierarchical ad-hoc mobile networks. In: 1st International Workshop on Parallel and Distributed Computing Issues in Wireless Networks and Mobile Computing, 2001, IPDPS Workshops (2001)
17. Chatzigiannakis, I., Nikoletseas, S., Spirakis, P.: On the average and worst-case efficiency of some new distributed communication and control algorithms for ad-hoc mobile networks. In: 1st ACM International Annual Workshop on Principles of Mobile Computing (POMC 2001), pp. 1–19 (2001)
18. Chatzigiannakis, I., Nikoletseas, S., Spirakis, P.: Self-organizing ad-hoc mobile networks: the problem of end-to-end communication. In: 20th ACM Annual Symposium on Principles of Distributed Computing (PODC 2001), pp. 320–322 (2001)
19. Chatzigiannakis, I., Nikoletseas, S., Spirakis, P.: Distributed communication algorithms for ad hoc mobile networks. J. Parallel Distrib. Comput. (JPDC) **63**(1), 58–74 (2003). (Special Issue on Wireless and Mobile Ad-hoc Networking and Computing, edited by Boukerche, A.)
20. Gafni, E., Bertsekas, D.P.: Distributed algorithms for generating loop-free routes in networks with frequently changing topology. IEEE Trans. Commun. **29**(1), 11–18 (1981)
21. Haas, Z.J., Pearlman, M.R.: The performance of a new routing protocol for the reconfigurable wireless networks. In: International Conference on Communications, IEEE (1998)
22. Haas, Z.J., Pearlman, M.R: The zone routing protocol (ZRP) for ad-hoc networks. In: Technical report, IETF, Internet Draft, June 1999. draft-zone-routing-protocol-02. txt
23. Hatzis, K.P., Pentaris, G.P., Spirakis, P.G., Tampakas, V.T., Tan, R.B.: Fundamental control algorithms in mobile networks. In: 11th Annual Symposium on Parallel Algorithms and Architectures (SPAA 1999), pp. 251–260. ACM (1999)
24. Holland, G., Vaidya, N.: Analysis of TCP performance over mobile ad hoc networks. In: 5th ACM/IEEE Annual International Conference on Mobile Computing (MOBICOM 1999), pp. 219–230 (1999)
25. Imielinski, T., Korth, H.F.: Mobile Computing. Kluwer Academic Publishers, Dordrecht (1996)
26. Sushant, J., Kevin, F., Rabin, P., Routing in a delay tolerant network. In: Proceedings of the 2004 Conference on Applications, Technologies, Architectures, and Protocols for Computer Communications (New York, NY, USA), SIGCOMM 2004, pp. 145–158. ACM (2004)
27. Kao, M.-Y. (ed.): Encyclopedia of Algorithms. Springer, Heidelberg (2008)
28. Pearlman, M., Haas, Z.: Determining the optimal configuration for the zone routing protocol. IEEE J. Sel. Areas Commun. **17**(8), 1395–1414 (2003)

29. Perkins, C.E., Royer, E.M.: Ad-hoc on demand distance vector (AODV) routing. In: 2nd IEEE Annual Workshop on Mobile Computing Systems and Applications, 1999, pp. 90–100 (1999)
30. Spirakis, P., Zaroliagis, C.: Distributed algorithm engineering. Experimental Algorithmics, pp. 197–228 (2002)
31. Szemeredi, E.: Regular partitions of graphs, Colloques Internationaux C. N. R. S 260, pp. 399–401 (1976). Problemes Combinatoires et Theorie des Graphes
32. Vahdat, A., Becker, D.: Epidemic routing for partially connected ad hoc networks. In: Technical report, Duke University, 2000, Technical Report CS-200006 (2000)

An Optimal Parallel Algorithm for Minimum Spanning Trees in Planar Graphs

Ka Wong Chong[1] and Christos Zaroliagis[2,3]($\boxtimes$)

[1] Department of Computer Science, The University of Hong-Kong,
Porfulam Road, Porfulam, Hong Kong
[2] Department of Computer Engineering and Informatics,
University of Patras, 26504 Patras, Greece
zaro@ceid.upatras.gr
[3] Computer Technology Institute and Press "Diophantus", N. Kazantzaki Str.,
Patras University Campus, 26504 Patras, Greece

Abstract. We present an optimal deterministic $O(n)$-work parallel algorithm for finding a minimum spanning tree on an n-vertex planar graph. The algorithm runs in $O(\log n)$ time on a CRCW PRAM and in $O(\log n \log^* n)$ time on an EREW PRAM. Our results hold for any sparse graph that is closed under taking of minors, as well as for a class of graphs with non-bounded genus.

1 Introduction

The minimum spanning tree problem is one of the most fundamental problems in network optimization with a wealth of theoretical and practical applications (see e.g., [1]). Given a connected n-vertex, m-edge undirected graph G with real edge weights, the *minimum spanning tree* (MST) problem is to find a spanning tree of minimum total weight among all spanning trees of G. The problem has been extensively studied both in sequential and in parallel computation.

In sequential computation, the MST problem has started being investigated as early as 1926 [4]. The currently best deterministic sequential algorithms [5, 15, 27] run in almost linear time. The first two [5, 15] run on the (classical) unit-cost random access machine (RAM) model of computation, where the only operations allowed on the edge weights are binary comparisons, while the third one [27] is optimal and runs on the pointer machine. Better, linear-time algorithms are known if randomization is allowed [25], or if the input graph is planar [6], or if more powerful models of computation are used [14].

In parallel computation, the MST problem has been studied in the parallel random access machine (PRAM) model of computation, the parallel version of the unit-cost RAM (for more on PRAMs see e.g., [21,26]). In the parallel context, there is a close relationship between the connected components and the MST problem in the sense that almost all parallel algorithms for either of the problems use the *hook-and-contract* approach (also known as Sollin's or Boruvka's approach): initially each vertex represents a component by itself. Then, every

© Springer International Publishing Switzerland 2015
C. Zaroliagis et al. (Eds.): Spirakis Festschrift, LNCS 9295, pp. 169–182, 2015.
DOI: 10.1007/978-3-319-24024-4_11

component C_i hooks to another component C_j by selecting an edge whose one endpoint is in C_i and the other in C_j. After hooking, every (new) component is contracted into a single vertex. The hooking and contraction steps are repeated until there are no more edges connecting different components. While in computing connected components the selection of the hooking edge can be arbitrary, in the MST problem this selection is critical: it has to be the edge with minimum weight. This particular difficulty usually increases the running time and/or the work of the MST algorithms. Further, it has been shown in [24] that the MST problem can be reduced to a connected components problem without an increase in the time; however, the number of processors used (and hence the work) is increased to $m^{1+\varepsilon}$, for some $\varepsilon > 0$.

The results of [8,23] for the MST problem on the EREW PRAM came therefore as a surprise since they matched the corresponding connected components bounds in [9,22]. Namely, in [23] an algorithm for the MST problem is presented running in $O(\log^{3/2} n)$ time and performing $O(m \log^{3/2} n)$ work. In [8] this result is improved to $O(\log n \log \log n)$ time and $O(m \log n \log \log n)$ work. Note that both MST results used much different techniques from those used in the corresponding connected components algorithms. The time for MST (and connected components) on the EREW PRAM was ultimately reduced to $O(\log n)$ in a breakthrough result [10] that used a new technique based on concurrent threads. The algorithm in [10] performs $O((n + m) \log n)$ work.

On the CRCW PRAM, there is still a certain gap in the work performed between the best deterministic connectivity algorithm [13] and the best MST algorithm [29]. The connected components algorithm in [13] runs in $O(\log n)$ time and performs $O(m\alpha(m, n))$ work on an ARBITRARY CRCW PRAM. The MST algorithm in [29] runs in $O(\log n)$ time and performs $O(m \log n)$ work on a COMMON CRCW PRAM. Previous approaches for the MST problem [2,13] achieve similar bounds but on the much stronger PRIORITY CRCW PRAM model.

Optimal-work parallel MST algorithms are known only for the case where randomization is allowed, or for the case of special classes of graphs. Regarding the former, a randomized algorithm is presented in [11] that runs in $O(\log n)$ time and performs $O(m)$ work on an ARBITRARY CRCW PRAM, while an EREW PRAM algorithm with the same bounds was presented in [28]. Regarding the latter, for very dense graphs (i.e., $m = \Omega(n^2)$) a CREW PRAM algorithm was given in [7] that runs in $O(\log^2 n)$ time and performs $O(n^2)$ work. For the case of planar graphs, $O(n)$-work deterministic parallel algorithms running in $O(\log n \log^* n)$ time on an EREW PRAM and in $O(\log n)$ time on a CRCW PRAM were given in [18].

In this paper, we present another optimal deterministic parallel algorithm that solves the MST problem in the important case of planar graphs. Our algorithm runs in $O(\log n \log^* n)$ time on an EREW PRAM, or in $O(\log n)$ time on an ARBITRARY CRCW PRAM, and performs $O(n)$ work. Our algorithm matches the bounds in [18] as well as those of the best parallel algorithm for computing connected components on the same models of computation and for the same classes of graphs [17]. Our algorithm uses different techniques compared to those in [17, 18] and might constitute a simpler alternative to those algorithms. In addition, our results hold for any sparse graph that is closed under taking of minors, as well as for a class of graphs with non-bounded genus.

The main idea of our algorithm is the following. We perform a number of iterations (as in the hook-and-contract approach), but we maintain the property that the graph we are dealing with has constant degree. However, after a contraction the maximum degree of a graph may increase and hence after a few iterations is no longer bounded by a constant. To overcome this problem, we *expand* the graph into a new one with maximum degree 3 (Sect. 2). The expansion is done such that an MST of the original graph can be easily found from an MST of the expanded graph. Moreover, we can guarantee that for the graphs considered the "contraction rate" is larger than the "expansion rate" so that the algorithm terminates after a logarithmic number of iterations. For simplicity, we present first our algorithm for the case of planar graphs (Sects. 3 and 4). Later (Sect. 5) we discuss how it extends to any class of sparse graphs that is closed under taking of minors, as well as for a class of non-bounded genus graphs.

2 Preliminaries

All graphs throughout the paper are undirected and are assumed to be given in its adjacency list representation. Let $G = (V, E)$ be a connected graph, where $|V| = n$ and $|E| = m$. Let also $w(\cdot)$ be a weight function on the edges of G and let $deg_G(v)$ denote the degree of v in G. If $\forall v \in V$, $deg_G(v) \leq \delta$, then we shall call G a *degree-δ* graph. For any spanning tree T of G, we define its weight, $w(T)$, as the sum of the weights of all the edges in T. Then, a minimum spanning tree of G, denoted by T_G^*, is the one with the minimum weight. Throughout the paper we shall not distinguish between a spanning tree T and its set of edges (unless stated otherwise). To simplify our discussion, we make the following assumptions concerning the minimum spanning tree problem.

A1. No two edges in G have the same weight and consequently T_G^* is unique. We can easily fulfill this assumption by considering the triple $\langle w(e), u, v \rangle$ as the weight of the edge $e = (u, v)$ in the adjacency list of u and compare edge weights using the lexicographic order.

A2. The weight function takes values on the positive reals, i.e., $w : E \to I\!R^+$. This is not a restriction, since we can always add to all edge weights in G a sufficiently large number $L > 0$ to make them positive. Moreover, it is easy to verify that the MST, say T^+, found in this case is isomorphic to T_G^* and that $w(T_G^*) = w(T^+) - (n - 1)L$.

Let $G' = (V', E')$ be a connected subgraph of G, where $V' \subseteq V$ and $E' \subseteq E$. We call the edges in E' *internal* edges of G', and the edges of G with only one endpoint in V' *external* edges of G'. Throughout the paper, the *contraction of G' into a single vertex* is an operation defined as follows: first, remove all internal edges in G' and all but one vertices in V' (the remaining vertex is the vertex representing G' in the contracted graph). Then, replace all multiple edges that may have been created with the one of minimum weight. (The latter step guarantees that the contracted graph is a simple graph.)

Let $F \subset E$ be a subset of edges of G. Consider the subgraphs of G induced by the edges in F. If every such induced subgraph is a tree, then we say the F *induces a forest* in G. If a vertex $v \in V$ has no edge from F incident on it, then v induces a tree by itself.

We shall need the following well-known property of MSTs (for a proof see e.g., [1]).

Lemma 1. *Let F be a set of edges of G such that F induces a forest in G and $F \subseteq T_G^*$. Let (u, v) be the external edge of minimum weight of a tree in F. Then, a minimum spanning tree of G contains the edge (u, v) and all edges in F.*

The following properties of a planar graph will be useful later.

Lemma 2. *Let G be a weighted planar graph and let F be a set of edges of G that induce a forest in G. Then:*
(i) The number of edges m in G is no more than $3n - 6$.
(ii) If we contract each tree (connected component) in F into a single vertex, the contracted graph G' is still planar.
(iii) If $F \subseteq T_G^*$, then $T_G^* = T_{G'}^* \cup F$.

Properties (i) and (ii), in the above lemma, are well-known properties of planar graphs (see e.g., [20]). Property (iii) follows by Lemma 1.

The following concept plays a key role in our algorithm.

Definition 1. *Let H be a weighted graph and let S be a subset of edges of H that induce a forest. Then, S is said to be a $(c, f(c))$-**connector** of H if every edge of S belongs to T_H^* and for each tree T induced by S in H, $c \le |T| \le f(c)$, where $|T|$ denotes the number of vertices in T and $f(c)$ is a function of c. By convention, if H has less than c vertices, then $S = T_H^*$.*

In all applications of the above definition, throughout the paper, c will always be a constant. As we shall see in Sect. 4, a $(c, f(c))$-connector S, for constant c, can be computed very efficiently. After contracting the trees induced by S, the graph H is contracted by a factor of at least c. Since further each tree of S contains at most $f(c)$ vertices, the contraction can be done in $O(1)$ time, resulting in a (new) contracted graph H'. The remaining of the edges of T_H^* can now be found in H' (according to Lemma 2 (iii)).

During the execution of our algorithm, we want to maintain the invariant that the graph in processing satisfies the property that every vertex has degree bounded by a fixed constant. However, it can be easily verified that after contracting a graph the maximum degree may increase (i.e., the maximum degree of H' may be larger than that of H). We deal with this problem by expanding the graph. In the following, we describe a simple transformation that implements the expansion. More precisely, the transformation takes as input a graph G and outputs a graph H in which every vertex has degree bounded by 3. Moreover, the minimum spanning tree of H naturally defines the minimum spanning tree of G (see Lemma 5 below).

The expansion transformation is defined as follows. For every vertex v of G, if $deg_G(v) \leq 3$, then include v and all its edges into H directly. Otherwise, if $deg_G(v) > 3$, we create $t = deg_G(v) - 2$ new vertices, $v_1, v_2, \ldots, v_t$, in H. (We alternatively say that v is *split* into t vertices.) Let $e_1, e_2, \ldots, e_{t+1}, e_{t+2}$ be the edges incident on v in G. Then in H, make e_1 and e_2 incident on v_1, make e_i incident on v_{i-1}, for $3 \leq i \leq t$, and make e_{t+1} and e_{t+2} incident on v_t. Finally, add edges between v_i and v_{i+1}, for $1 \leq i \leq t-1$. Each of these new edges is associated with zero weight. The expansion transformation is illustrated in Fig. 1.

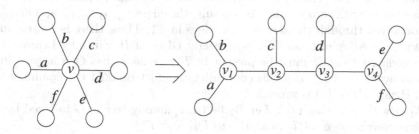

Fig. 1. A vertex v with degree 6, incident on edges a, b, c, d, e, and f, is transformed into four vertices, v_1, v_2, v_3, and v_4. The three new edges $(v_1, v_2), (v_2, v_3)$, and (v_3, v_4) are associated with zero weight.

Lemma 3. *(i) The transformation of a graph G into a degree-3 graph H can be done in $O(\log d)$ time and $O(m)$ work on an EREW PRAM, where d is the maximum degree of a vertex in G.*
(ii) If G is planar, then H is also planar and $n_h \leq 5n - 12$, where n_h is the number of vertices in H.

Proof. (i) It can be easily done using list ranking and segmented parallel prefix computations [21].

(ii) The planarity of H is obvious. For the number of vertices in H, we have that $n_h \leq \sum_{v \in G} \max\{deg_G(v) - 2, 1\} \leq 2m - 2n + n = 2m - n$. As $m \leq 3n - 6$ (Lemma 2 (i)), we have $n_h \leq 5n - 12$.   □

The degree-3 graph H, resulting from this transformation, has some useful properties which we discuss next and which allow us to find easily the MST of G, if the MST of H is given.

Lemma 4. *Every edge in H with zero weight belongs to T_H^*.*

Proof. Consider a greedy (e.g., Kruskal's) algorithm that finds T_H^* by selecting edges in non-decreasing order of weight, and discards an edge if it creates a cycle with already selected edges. (The correctness of this approach can be easily verified using Lemma 1.) Now, all zero weight edges must be present in T_H^*, since their weight is smaller than those of the remaining edges in H and they do not form any cycle.   □

Lemma 5. *The edges with non-zero weight in T_H^* are the edges of T_G^*.*

Proof. It suffices to prove that: (a) all the non-zero weight edges of T_H^* induce a spanning tree in G; and (b) this spanning tree is the MST of G.

To prove claim (a), first observe that in H there are $n_h - n$ edges which have zero weight. Let X be the non-zero weight edges of T_H^*. By Lemma 4, all the zero weight edges of H must be in T_H^*. Therefore, $|X| = n_h - 1 - (n_h - n) = n - 1$.

Suppose on the contrary that X does not induce a spanning tree in G. Then, there must be a simple cycle $C \subseteq X$ induced by X. Let $u_0, u_1, \ldots, u_{k-1}$ be the vertices of C and $e_0, e_1, \ldots, e_{k-1}$ be its edges, where u_i, $0 \le i \le k - 1$, is incident on edges $e_{(i-1) \bmod k}$ and $e_i \bmod k$. By the transformation, each u_i will be split into several vertices which are connected through (a path consisting of) the new edges with zero weight. As a result, the edges $e_{(i-1) \bmod k}$ and $e_i \bmod k$ are connected through the zero weight edges in T_H^*. Thus, there is a cycle in H involving the edges of C and the zero weight edges of H. Since by Lemma 4 all zero weight edges of H must be present in T_H^*, we have that C is a cycle in H induced by edges of T_H^*. But this contradicts the fact that T_H^* is a spanning tree of H. Hence, claim (a) is proved.

We now turn to claim (b). Let T_G be the spanning tree in G induced by the non-zero weight edges of T_H^*. Clearly, $w(T_G) = w(T_H^*)$.

Suppose on the contrary that T_G is not the minimum spanning tree and let T_G' be the MST in G. Then, $w(T_G') < w(T_G)$. By the transformation, T_G' defines a spanning tree T_H in H consisting of all the edges of T_G' and all the zero weight edges of H. But then $w(T_H) = w(T_G') < w(T_G) = w(T_H^*)$, a contradiction to the assumption that T_H^* is the MST of H. This ends the proof of claim (b) and the proof of the lemma.   □

3   The Algorithm

Our algorithm works in phases, where in each phase we find some edges of T_G^*. The input to Phase i is a planar degree-3 graph G_i. Initially, G is transformed into a degree-3 graph which is the graph G_0. Let T_i^* be the minimum spanning tree of G_i. Phase i proceeds in three steps. First, we find a $(c, 2c^4)$-connector S_i of G_i, where c is a constant (whose value will be determined later). Each tree induced by S_i has size at most $2c^4$ and the non-zero weight edges of S_i belong to T_G^*. Second, we contract each tree induced by S_i in G_i into a single vertex. Let G_i' be the contracted graph. Third, we transform G_i' into a degree-3 graph to meet the input requirements of the next phase. A less informal description of the algorithm follows.

Algorithm: MST-Planar
Input: A planar graph G.
Output: The minimum spanning tree, T_G^*, of G.
   1. Transform G into a degree-3 graph G_0;
   2. $i = 0$;
   3. **While** G_i contains more than one vertex **do**

   (a) Find a $(c, 2c^4)$-connector S_i in G_i, where c is a constant;
   (b) Contract each tree induced by S_i in G_i and let G'_i be the resulting graph;
   (c) Transform G'_i into a degree-3 graph G_{i+1};
   (d) $i = i + 1$;
od
4. Return the non-zero weight edges in $\bigcup_{j=0}^{i-1} S_j$, which are the edges of T_G^*;

   We first discuss the correctness of the algorithm. Let Z_i denote the set of zero weight edges in G_i.

Lemma 6. $T_i^* = (T_{i+1}^* - Z_{i+1}) \cup S_i = (T_{i+1}^* \cup S_i) - Z_{i+1}$.

Proof. Consider the graph G'_i which is formed by contracting the trees induced by S_i in G_i. By Lemma 2 (iii), we have that $T_i^* = T_{G'_i}^* \cup S_i$. On the other hand, by Lemma 5 we have that $T_{G'_i}^* = T_{i+1}^* - Z_{i+1}$. Therefore, $T_i^* = (T_{i+1}^* - Z_{i+1}) \cup S_i = (T_{i+1}^* \cup S_i) - Z_{i+1}$, where the last equality is true because $S_i \cap Z_j = \emptyset$ for $i \neq j$. □

Lemma 7. *Let t be the total number of iterations of Algorithm MST-Planar. Then, $T_G^* = \bigcup_{i=0}^t S_i - \bigcup_{i=0}^t Z_i$.*

Proof. By Lemma 5 we have that $T_G^* = T_0^* - Z_0$. Now, by repeated applications of Lemma 6, we get:

$$
\begin{aligned}
T_G^* = T_0^* - Z_0 &= ((T_1^* \cup S_0) - Z_1) - Z_0 \\
&= ((((T_2^* \cup S_1) - Z_2) \cup S_0) - Z_1) - Z_0 \\
&= ((((T_2^* \cup S_1) \cup S_0) - Z_2) - Z_1) - Z_0 \\
&= \cdots \\
&= ((\cdots ((T_{t+1}^* \cup S_t) \cup S_{t-1}) \cdots \cup S_0) - Z_{t+1}) - Z_t) - \cdots) - Z_0 \\
&= \bigcup_{i=0}^t S_i - \bigcup_{i=0}^t Z_i
\end{aligned}
$$

where the last equality follows from the fact that $T_{t+1}^* = Z_{t+1} = \emptyset$ and $\bigcap_{i=0}^t Z_i = \emptyset$. □

   Hence, the correctness of Algorithm MST-Planar has been established. We now turn to the resource bounds. We shall need the following lemma, whose proof is given in Sect. 4.

Lemma 8. *For all constant c, a $(c, 2c^4)$-connector of a degree-3 graph G with n vertices can be computed: (i) in $O(1)$ time using $O(n)$ work on a CRCW PRAM; (ii) in $O(\log^* n)$ time using $O(n \log^* n)$ work on an EREW PRAM; (iii) in $O(\log n)$ time using $O(n)$ work on an EREW PRAM.*

   The transformation of the input graph G into a degree-3 graph G_0, in Step 1 of the algorithm, can be done in $O(\log n)$ time and $O(n)$ work on an EREW PRAM (Lemma 3 (i)). Step 4 can be implemented within the same resource bounds.

Let us now consider the resource bounds of Step 3. Let n_i and n_i' denote the number of vertices in G_i and G_i', respectively. The bounds of Step 3(a) are given by Lemma 8. In Step 3(b), we have first to contract each tree in G_i induced by S_i. This means that we have to remove internal edges in such a tree and replace multiple edges between two vertices by the one with minimum weight. Since each tree in S_i has size at most $2c^4$, and c is a constant, Step 3(b) takes $O(1)$ time using $O(n_i)$ work on an EREW PRAM. Moreover, since each tree in S_i has size at least c, we have that $n_i' \leq n_i/c$. Note that G_i' is also a (simple) planar graph (Lemma 3 (ii)). Finally, Step 3(c) needs $O(1)$ time using $O(n_i)$ work on an EREW PRAM, by Lemma 3 (i). Consequently, each iteration of the while-loop in Step 3 is dominated by the resource bounds of Step 3(a).

To bound the number of iterations, note that by Lemma 3 (ii), $n_{i+1} \leq 5n_i' - 12 \leq 5n_i/c - 12$. Hence, by choosing $c = 10$, we have that $n_{i+1} \leq n_i/2$. Thus, the number of iterations of the while-loop in Step 3 is $\lceil \log n \rceil$.

Now, on a CRCW PRAM, each iteration takes $O(1)$ time and $O(n_i)$ work, by Lemma 8 (i). Therefore, in total Step 3 can be implemented in $O(\log n)$ time and $O(\sum_{i=0}^{\lceil \log n \rceil} n_i) = O(n)$ work.

Similarly, Step 3 can be implemented in $O(\log n \log^* n)$ time and $O(n \log^* n)$ work on an EREW PRAM, since each iteration takes $O(n_i \log^* n)$ work and $O(\log^* n)$ time by Lemma 8 (ii). To achieve optimal work on an EREW PRAM, we additionally use the implementation of the $(c, 2c^4)$-connector which runs in $O(\log n)$ time and $O(n_i)$ work (Lemma 8 (iii)). Having these two EREW PRAM implementations of a $(c, 2c^4)$-connector, we apply the method given in [19, Sect. 4] or in the proof of Theorem 5.1 in [12]: we run in the first $O(\log^* n)$ iterations the optimal implementation (Lemma 8 (iii)), and in the remaining iterations the non-optimal one (Lemma 8 (ii)). This results (again) in a running time of $O(\log n \log^* n)$, but now a simple simulation argument (see [19, Sect. 4] or [12, Theorem 5.1]) shows that the algorithm can be performed using only $O(n)$ work.

We have therefore established the following.

Theorem 1. *A minimum spanning tree of an n-vertex weighted planar graph G can be found: (i) in $O(\log n)$ time and $O(n)$ work on a CRCW PRAM; (ii) in $O(\log n \log^* n)$ time using $O(n)$ work on an EREW PRAM.*

4   Finding a $(c, f(c))$-Connector in a Degree-3 Graph

In this section, we shall prove Lemma 8. Let H be a degree-3 graph with n vertices. Recall that a $(c, f(c))$-connector of H is a set of edges $S \subseteq T_H^*$ such that for each tree T induced by S in H $c \leq |T| \leq f(c)$, where $|T|$ denotes the number of vertices in T and $f(c)$ is a function of c.

Note that one should be careful in finding a $(c, f(c))$-connector, in the sense that there are many simple ways to do it, but they result in a value for $f(c)$ which may be exponential in c. Hence, a different idea is required in order to avoid such a huge value for $f(c)$. In this section, we shall show how to achieve $f(c) = 2c^4$.

We find the $(c, f(c))$-connector in two stages. In the first stage we find a set of edges $K \subseteq T_H^*$ such that each tree induced by K in H contains at least c vertices. However, there may be some trees having as many as $\Theta(n)$ vertices. Then in the second stage, we remove some edges from K in order to break down these "big" trees into trees of bounded size. The remaining edges in K form a $(c, f(c))$-connector of G.

The first stage consists of a number of iterations, where iteration i finds a set of edges $K_i \subseteq K$. Let F_i be the set of trees induced by K_i in H (where each tree in F_0 is a single vertex). The first stage of the $(c, f(c))$-connector algorithm is implemented as follows.

Stage 1 of the $(c, f(c))$-connector algorithm:
1. $i = 0$; $K_i = \emptyset$; $M = \emptyset$;
2. Let F_i be the set of trees induced by K_i in H;
3. **while** $\exists$ tree T in F_i such that $|T| < c$ **do**
    Find the minimum-weight external edge of T and add it to M;
    $K_{i+1} = K_i \cup M$; Let F_{i+1} be the set of trees induced by K_{i+1} in H;
    $M = \emptyset$; $i = i + 1$;
od

Observe that each tree in F_i contains at least 2^i vertices. Thus, after $\lceil \log c \rceil$ iterations, every tree contains at least c vertices. Let $K = K_{\lceil \log c \rceil}$. Since only trees with less than c vertices participate in every iteration, it follows that each iteration can be done in $O(\log c)$ time using $O(n)$ work. (*Remark*: within the same resouce bounds we can also check whether $|T| < c$.) Hence, the first stage runs in $O(\log^2 c)$ time using $O(n \log c)$ work.

In the second stage, we have to remove some edges in K to obtain a $(c, f(c))$-connector of H. Let T be a tree induced by K. Recall that every internal vertex in T has degree bounded by 3 and $|T| \geq c$. To find a $(c, f(c))$-connector of H, it suffices to find a $(c, f(c))$-connector in every such tree T; then, the union of the $(c, f(c))$-connectors of every tree T is a $(c, f(c))$-connector of H.

The second stage consists also of a number of iterations. In each iteration we contract a subtree of T (in a manner to be discussed). Let T_i denote T at the beginning of the ith iteration. Initially, $T_0 = T$ and $i = 0$.

Every vertex $v \in T_i$ represents a (contracted) connected subtree of T_{i-1} and hence of T. Let $size(v)$ denote the number of vertices of T that v represents (i.e., they have been contracted into v). Since every vertex of T has degree at most 3, the degree of v in T_i is at most $3size(v) - 2(size(v) - 1) = size(v) + 2$.

Let v be a vertex of T_i. Then: (i) v is called *inactive* if $size(v) \geq c$; (ii) v is called *neutral* if $size(v) < c$ and all adjacent vertices of v are inactive; and (c) v is called *active*, in all other cases. Note that the degree of an active vertex in T_i is at most $c + 1$. Stage 2 is implemented as follows:

Stage 2 of the $(c, f(c))$-connector algorithm:
for every tree T induced by K **pardo**
1. $i = 0$; $T_i = T$; $A_i = \{v | v \in T_i\}$; **forall** $v \in T_i$ **pardo** $size(v) = 1$ **odpar**;

2. **while** $|A_i| > 1$ **do**
   (a) Find a maximal independent set I in A_i, where A_i is the set of active vertices in T_i;
   /* Perform a selective contraction */
   (b) Every $u \in A_i - I$ selects one of its neighbors in I;
   (c) **if** $\exists v \in I$ that has not been selected **then**
       v selects (arbitrarily) one of its neighbors in $A_i - I$;
   (d) The selection process defines connected subtrees of T_i consisting of active vertices. Then, contract each such subtree into a single vertex z and compute $size(z)$;
   (e) Call the resulting tree T_{i+1} and set $i = i + 1$;
   od
3. Every neutral vertex in T_i selects arbitrarily one of its adjacent inactive vertices to hook (i.e., to merge together in a single component). Contract each such component into a single vertex and call the resulting tree T_f;
odpar

At the end of the ith iteration, every active vertex in T_i has $size$ at least 2^i. Hence, after at most $\lceil \log c \rceil$ iterations there are no more active vertices. Furthermore, the total number of active vertices that define a connected subtree of T_i (to be contracted) is at most $(c + 2) + c(c + 1)$ (where the first term comes from Step 2(b) and the second term from Step 2(c)), which is $c^2 + 2c + 2$. Since every active vertex has $size$ at most $c - 1$, we have that the $size$ of a vertex $u \in T_{i+1}$, at the beginning of the $(i + 1)$th iteration, is $size(u) \leq (c^2 + 2c + 2)(c - 1) = c^3 + c^2 - 2$.

Let $T_{\lceil \log c \rceil}$ be the tree at the end of Step 2. Note that every vertex in $T_{\lceil \log c \rceil}$ is either inactive or neutral, and that T_f (the tree at the end of Step 3) contains only inactive vertices. Let v be an inactive vertex in $T_{\lceil \log c \rceil}$. Since $size(v) \leq c^3 + c^2 - 2$, there are at most $size(v) + 2$ neutral vertices adjacent to it (each of $size$ at most $c - 1$). Consequently, an inactive vertex $u \in T_f$ has $size(u) \leq c^3 + c^2 - 2 + (c^3 + c^2)(c - 1) = c^4 + c^3 - 2 \leq 2c^4$. Hence, every vertex $u \in T_f$ satisfies $c \leq size(u) \leq 2c^4$ and represents a connected subtree U of T, where $|U| = size(u)$. Moreover, every edge of U belongs to T_H^*, as a consequence of Stage 1. Therefore, the union of all these subtrees U, or alternatively the set of edges in $T - T_f$, constitutes the required $(c, f(c))$-connector of T, where $f(c) = 2c^4$.

Let us now consider the complexity of Stage 2. Observe that since T is a tree, no multiple edges are created in every contraction of a subtree of T, and consequently there is no need to invoke a sorting procedure to eliminate all but one multiple edges. Hence, every contraction of a subtree of T of size p can be done in $O(\log p)$ time and $O(p)$ work on an EREW PRAM.

We first discuss the EREW PRAM complexity. Step 3 takes $O(\log c)$ time and $O(n \log c)$ work over all trees T. The resource bounds of each iteration of Step 2 are dominated by those of Step 2(a) to find a maximal independent set in a tree. This requires (over all trees T) $O(\log^* n)$ time and $O(n \log^* n)$ work [16, Theorem 4], or alternatively $O(\log n)$ time and $O(n)$ work [17, Lemma 7]. Hence, Stage 2 runs in $O(\log^2 c \log^* n)$ time and $O(n \log c \log^* n)$ work, or in $O(\log^2 c \log n)$ time and $O(n \log c)$ work.

We now turn to the CRCW PRAM complexity. Unfortunately, the maximal independent set algorithm of [16] cannot take advantage of this model to solve the problem faster. Instead, we use an algorithm from [3] that computes a so-called *fractional* independent set. More precisely, the following result is proved in [3, Sect. 6]: Let G be an n-vertex graph of constant degree. Then, an independent set I such that $|I| \geq \varepsilon n$, where $0 < \varepsilon < 1$ is a constant, can be found in $O(1)$ time and $O(n)$ work on a CRCW PRAM.

Now, in Step 2(a) we do not find a maximal independent set, but a fractional one using the algorithm of [3]. Note that in this case we cannot guarantee that at the end of the ith iteration every active vertex has *size* at least 2^i. However, we can guarantee that in every iteration a constant fraction of the (remaining) active vertices $\varepsilon|A_i|$ perform a selective contraction. Consequently, at the beginning of the next iteration, there are at most $(1-\varepsilon)|A_i| \leq (1-\varepsilon)|T_i| \leq (1-\varepsilon)^i |T_0|$ active vertices. Hence, we need $\lceil \log_{(\frac{1}{1-\varepsilon})} c \rceil = O(\log c)$ iterations to eliminate all active vertices. This implies that Stage 2 can be implemented to run in $O(\log^2 c)$ time and $O(n \log c)$ work on a CRCW PRAM.

The bounds of Lemma 8 follow now from the fact that c is always a constant in all applications of the $(c, f(c))$-connector algorithm with $f(c) = 2c^4$.

5   Extensions of Our Results

Following [17], a class $\mathcal{G}$ of undirected graphs is called *linearly contractible* if: (1) for all G in $\mathcal{G}$ $m \leq kn$, where k is a constant; and (2) $\mathcal{G}$ is closed under taking of minors, i.e., every subgraph and every *elementary contraction* of a graph in $\mathcal{G}$ is in $\mathcal{G}$. An *elementary contraction* of a graph G is a new graph obtained from G by contracting two adjacent vertices u and v into a single vertex z. Examples of the class of linearly contractible graphs are planar graphs, graphs of bounded treewidth and graphs of bounded genus.

Observe that the only properties that our algorithm requires from a planar graph are those stated in Lemma 2 (i) and (ii), and which are included in the above definition of the linearly contractible graphs. Hence, Lemma 2 is satisfied (in a sense) by any graph belonging to a linearly contractible class, with the difference that part (i) now becomes $m \leq kn$. This implies that the number n_h of vertices of the transformed graph (Lemma 3) is now bounded by $n_h \leq 2m - n = (2k-1)n$. To achieve again a number of $\lceil \log n \rceil$ iterations of our MST algorithm in Sect. 3, it suffices to choose $c = 4k - 2$ in the construction of the $(c, 2c^4)$-connector. We have therefore established the following.

Theorem 2. *A minimum spanning tree of an n-vertex weighted graph G, drawn from a linearly contractible class, can be found: (i) in $O(\log n)$ time and $O(n)$ work on a CRCW PRAM; (ii) in $O(\log n \log^* n)$ time using $O(n)$ work on an EREW PRAM.*

We can further achieve optimal results in the case of graphs with non-bounded genus. The idea is as follows.

Let G be a graph with genus γ. Then, $m \leq 3n + 6\gamma - 6$ [20]. Note that when G is contracted, the genus of the resulting graph may remain unchanged and the total number of edges may not decrease accordingly. However, if γ is very small compared to the number of vertices in the graph, the total number of edges contributed by the "6γ" term is also very small. In particular, we can assume that $m \leq 4n$, when $\gamma = o(n)$. Therefore, our algorithm can still work properly for a number of iterations, as long as the condition $\gamma = o(n_i)$ in every iteration is satisfied (n_i being the number of vertices at iteration i), for some suitable value of γ and choice of c. As soon as, after a particular iteration, $\gamma \geq n_i$, we switch to another algorithm. Next we show that if $\gamma \leq 2^{\frac{\log n}{\log \log n}}$, the above approach gives an optimal algorithm to compute T_G^*. Note that $2^{\frac{\log n}{\log \log n}} = \Omega(\text{poly}\log n)$.

We find T_G^* in two phases. In Phase I, we run Algorithm MST-Planar up to the ith iteration, where $i = \log n - \log n / \log \log n$ and we choose the constant c to be 14. At the end of Phase I, we obtain a graph G_{i+1} in which the total number of vertices is no more than $2^{\frac{\log n}{\log \log n}}$. In Phase II, we use the algorithm of [8] to find T_{i+1}^* in G_{i+1}. The edges found in the two phases form the MST of G.

Phase I takes $O(\log n \log^* n)$ time using $O(n)$ work on an EREW PRAM, or $O(\log n)$ time using $O(n)$ work on a CRCW PRAM.

Phase II takes $O(\log n' \log \log n')$ time using $O(m' \log n' \log \log n')$ work. As $n' = 2^{\frac{\log n}{\log \log n}}$, Phase II runs in $O(\log n)$ time using no more than $O(n)$ work on an EREW PRAM. Thus we have established the following.

Theorem 3. *A minimum spanning tree of an n-vertex weighted graph G with genus $\gamma \leq 2^{\frac{\log n}{\log \log n}}$ can be found: (i) in $O(\log n)$ time and $O(n)$ work on a CRCW PRAM; (ii) in $O(\log n \log^* n)$ time using $O(n)$ work on an EREW PRAM.*

6   Conclusions

We presented an $O(n)$ work parallel algorithm for solving the MST problem on planar, minor closed, and a class of non-bounded genus graphs. The algorithms runs in $O(\log n \log^* n)$ time on an EREW PRAM and in $O(\log n)$ time on a CRCW PRAM.

An interesting open problem is to develop a $O(n)$-work deterministic EREW PRAM algorithm for these graph classes that runs in $O(\log n)$ time.

Acknowledgements. The last author is indebted to his mentor Paul Spirakis, who taught him by example to be a scientist and who uniquely affected the shaping of his career.

References

1. Ahuja, R., Magnanti, T., Orlin, J.: Network Flows. Prentice-Hall, Englewood (1993)
2. Awerbuch, B., Shiloach, Y.: New connectivity and MSF algorithms for shuffle-exchange network and PRAM. IEEE Trans. Comput. **36**(10), 1258–1263 (1987)

3. Bodlaender, H., Hagerup, T.: Parallel algorithms with optimal speedup for bounded treewidth. SIAM J. Comput. **27**(6), 1725–1746 (1998)
4. Boruvka, O.: O jistém problému minimálním. Práca Moravské Přírodovědecké Společnosti **3**, 37–58 (1926)
5. Chazelle, B.: A minimum spanning tree algorithm with inverse-Ackermann type complexity. J. ACM **47**(6), 1028–1047 (2000)
6. Cheriton, D., Tarjan, R.E.: Finding minimum spanning trees. SIAM J. Comput. **5**, 724–742 (1976)
7. Chin, F.Y., Lam, J., Chen, I.N.: Efficient parallel algorithms for some graph problems. Commun. ACM **25**(9), 659–665 (1982)
8. Chong, K.W.: Finding minimum spanning trees on the EREW PRAM. In: Proceedings of the International Computer Symposium—ICS'96, pp. 7–14. Taiwan (1996)
9. Chong, K.W., Lam, T.W.: Finding connected components in $O(\log n \log \log n)$ time on the EREW PRAM. J. Algorithms **18**, 378–402 (1995)
10. Chong, K.W., He, Y., Lam, T.W.: Concurrent threads and optimal parallel minimum spanning trees algorithm. J. ACM **48**(2), 297–323 (2001)
11. Cole, R., Klein, P.N., Tarjan, R.E.: Finding minimum spanning forests in logarithmic time and linear work using random sampling. In: Proceedings of the 8th ACM symposium on Parallel Algorithms and Architectures (ACM), pp. 243–250 (1996)
12. Cole, R., Vishkin, U.: Deterministic coin tossing with applications to optimal parallel list ranking. Inf. Control **70**, 32–53 (1986)
13. Cole, R., Vishkin, U.: Approximate and exact parallel scheduling with applications to list, tree and graph problems. In: Proceedings of the 27th IEEE Symposium on Foundations of Computer Science, pp. 478–491. IEEE (1986)
14. Fredman, M., Willard, D.E.: Trans-dichotomous algorithms for minimum spanning trees and shortest paths. J. Comput. Syst. Sci. **48**, 533–551 (1994)
15. Gabow, H., Galil, Z., Spencer, T., Tarjan, R.E.: Efficient algorithms for finding minimum spanning trees in undirected and directed graphs. Combinatorica **6**(2), 109–122 (1986)
16. Goldberg, A., Plotkin, S., Shannon, G.: Parallel symmetry-breaking in sparse graphs. SIAM J. Discrete Math. **1**, 434–446 (1988)
17. Hagerup, T.: Optimal parallel algorithms on planar graphs. Inf. Comput. **84**, 71–96 (1990)
18. Hagerup, T.: Optimal Parallel Computation of Minimum Spanning Forests in Planar Graphs, Technical Report 11/1990. Universität des Saarlandes, May 1990
19. Hagerup, T., Chrobak, M., Diks, K.: Optimal parallel 5-colouring of planar graphs. SIAM J. Comput. **18**(2), 288–300 (1989)
20. Harary, F.: Graph Theory. Addison-Wesley, Reading (1969)
21. JáJá, J.: An Introduction to Parallel Algorithms. Addison-Wesley, Reding (1992)
22. Johnson, D.B., Metaxas, P.: Connected components in $O(\log^{3/2} |V|)$ parallel time for the CREW PRAM. In: Proceeings of 32nd IEEE Symposium on Foundations of Computer Science, pp. 688–695, IEEE (1991)
23. Johnson, D.B., Metaxas, P.: A parallel algorithm for computing minimum spanning trees. J. Algorithms **19**, 383–401 (1995)
24. Karger, D.R.: Approximating, verifying, and constructing minimum spanning trees. Unpublished manuscript (1992)
25. Karger, D.R., Klein, P.N., Tarjan, R.E.: A randomized linear-time algorithm to find minimum spanning trees. J. ACM **42**(2), 321–328 (1995)

26. Karp, R., Ramachandran, V.: Parallel Algorithms for Shared-Memory Machines. In: van Leeuwen, J. (ed.) Handbook of Theoretical Computer Science, vol. A, pp. 869–941. Elsevier, Amsterdam (1990)
27. Pettie, S., Ramachandran, V.: An optimal minimum spanning tree algorithm. J. ACM **49**(1), 16–34 (2002)
28. Pettie, S., Ramachandran, V.: A randomized time-work optimal parallel algorithm for finding a minimum spanning forest. SIAM J. Comput. **31**(6), 1879–1895 (2002)
29. Zaroliagis, C.D.: Simple and work-efficient parallel algorithms for the minimum spanning tree problem. Parallel Process. Lett. **7**(1), 25–37 (1997)

Weighted Random Sampling over Data Streams

Pavlos S. Efraimidis[✉]

Department of Electrical and Computer Engineering,
Democritus University of Thrace, Xanthi, Greece
pefraimi@ee.duth.gr

1 Introduction

The problem of random sampling calls for the selection of m random items out of a population of size n. If all items have the same probability to be selected, the problem is known as uniform random sampling. If each item has an associated weight and the probability of each item to be selected is determined by these item weights, then the problem is called weighted random sampling (WRS).

Weighted random sampling, and random sampling in general, is a fundamental problem with applications in several fields of computer science including databases, data streams, data mining and randomized algorithms. Moreover, random sampling is important in many practical problems, like market surveys, quality control in manufacturing, statistics and on-line advertising.

There are several factors that have to be taken into account, when facing a WRS problem. It has to be defined if the sampling procedure is with or without replacement, whether the sampling procedure has to be executed over data streams, and what the semantics of the item weights are. In this work, we present a comprehensive treatment of WRS over data streams. In particular, we examine the above problem parameters and describe efficient solutions for different WRS problems that arise in each case.

- **Weights.** In WRS the probability of each item to be selected is determined by its weight with respect to the weights of the other items. However, for random sampling schemes without replacement there are at least two natural ways to interpret the item weights. In the first case, the relative weight of each item determines the probability that the item is in the final sample. In the second, the weight of each item determines the probability that the item is selected in each of the explicit or implicit item selections of the sampling procedure. Both cases will become clear in the sequel.
- **Replacement.** Like other sampling procedures, the WRS procedures can be with replacement or without replacement. In WRS with replacement, each selected item is replaced in the main lot with an identical item, whereas in WRS without replacement each selected item is simply removed from the population.
- **Data Streams.** Random sampling is often applied to very large datasets and in particular to data streams. In this case, the random sample has to be generated in one pass over an initially unknown population. An elegant and

© Springer International Publishing Switzerland 2015
C. Zaroliagis et al. (Eds.): Spirakis Festschrift, LNCS 9295, pp. 183–195, 2015.
DOI: 10.1007/978-3-319-24024-4_12

efficient approach to generate random samples from data streams is the use of a reservoir of size m, where m is the sample size. The reservoir-based sampling algorithms maintain the invariant that, at each step of the sampling process, the contents of the reservoir are a valid random sample for the set of items that have been processed up to that point. There are many random sampling algorithms that make use of a reservoir to generate uniform random samples over data streams [17].

- **Feasibility of WRS.** When considering the problem of generating a weighted random sample in one pass over an unknown population one may doubt that this is possible. In [1], the question whether reservoir maintenance can be achieved in one pass with arbitrary bias functions, is stated as an open problem. In this work, we bring to the fore two algorithms [3, 8] for the two, probably most important, flavors of the problem. In our view, the above results, and especially the older one, should become more known to the databases and algorithms communities.

- **A Standard Class Implementation.** Finally, we believe that the algorithms for WRS over data streams can and should be part of standard class libraries at the disposal of the contemporary algorithm or software engineer. To this end, we design an abstract class for WRS and provide prototype implementations of the presented algorithms in Java.

Contribution and Related Work. Random sampling is a classic, well studied field, and the volume of the corresponding literature is enormous. See for example [11, 12, 14, 16, 17] and the references therein. These results concern uniform random sampling, random sampling with a reservoir (which can be used on data streams), and weighted random sampling but not over data streams. An efficient algorithm for weighted random sampling with a reservoir which can support data streams is presented in [8]. Another weighted random sampling algorithm, which is less known to the computer science community and which uses a different interpretation for the item weights, is presented in [3]. This algorithm, too, is efficient and can be applied to data streams.

Random sampling is still an active research field and new sampling schemes are studied in various contexts; some indicative examples are sampling from sliding windows [13], from distributed data streams [4,5,15], from streams with time decay [6], independent range sampling [10], sampling on very large file systems [9], and stratified reservoir sampling [2]. In light of the above results (which are mainly from the data streams field), we consider the algorithms of [3] and [8] as fundamental sampling schemes for general purpose weighted random sampling over data streams.

In this work, we present a comprehensive treatment of general purpose weighted random sampling (WRS) over data streams. More precisely, we identify and examine two natural interpretations of the item weights, describe an existing algorithm for each case [3,8], discuss sampling with and without replacement and show adaptations of the algorithms for several WRS problems and evolving data streams. Moreover, we bring to the fore the sampling algorithm of Chao and show how to apply the jumps technique on it. Finally, we propose an abstract class definition for weighted random sampling over data streams and present a prototype implementation for this class.

Outline. The rest of this work is organized as follows: Notation and definitions for WRS problems are presented in Sect. 2. Core algorithms for WRS are described in Sect. 3. The treatment of representative WRS problems is described in Sect. 4. In Sect. 5, a prototype implementation and experimental results are presented. Finally, the role of item weights is examined in Sect. 6 and an overall conclusion of this work is given in Sect. 7.

2   Weighted Random Sampling (WRS)

Given an instance of a WRS problem, let V denote the population of all items and $n = |V|$ the size of the population. In general, the size n will not be known to the WRS algorithms. Each item $v_i \in V$, for $i = 1, 2, \ldots, n$, of the population has an associated weight w_i. The weight w_i is a strictly positive real number $w_i > 0$ and the weights of all items are initially considered unknown. The WRS algorithms will generate a weighted random sample of size m. If the sampling procedure is without replacement then it must hold that $m \leq n$. All items of the population are assumed to be discrete, in the sense that they are distinguishable but not necessarily different. The distinguishability can be trivially achieved by assigning an increasing ID number to each item in the population, including the replaced items (for WRS with replacement). We define the following notation to represent the various WRS problems:

$$\mathrm{WRS} - < \mathrm{rep} > - < \mathrm{role} >, \tag{1}$$

where the first parameter specifies the replacement policy and the second parameter the role of the item weights.

- Parameter **rep**: This parameter determines if and how many times a selected item can be replaced in the population. A value of "N" means that each selected item is not replaced and thus it can appear in the final sample at most once, i.e., sampling without replacement. A value of "R" means that the sampling procedure is with replacement and, finally, an arithmetic value k, where $1 \leq k \leq m$, defines that each item is replaced at most $k - 1$ times, i.e., it can appear in the final sample at most k times.
- Parameter **role**: This parameter defines the role of the item weights in the sampling scheme. As already noted, we consider two natural ways to interpret item weights. In the first case, when the role has value P, the probability of an item to be in the random sample is proportional to its relative weight. In the second case, the role is equal to W and the relative weight determines the probability of each item selection, if the items would be selected sequentially.

Moreover, WRS-P will denote the whole class of WRS problems where the item weights directly determine the selection probabilities of each item, and

WRS-W the class of WRS problems where the items weights determine the selection probability of each item in a supposed[1] sequential sampling procedure. A summary of the notation for different WRS problems is given in Table 1.

Table 1. Notation for WRS problems.

WRS problem		Notation
With replacement		WRS-R
Without replacement	Probabilities	WRS-N-P
	Weights	WRS-N-W
With $k-1$ replacements	Weights	WRS-k-W

Definition 1. *Problem WRS-R (Weighted Random Sampling with Replacement).*

Input: A population of n weighted items and a size m for the random sample.
Output: A weighted random sample of size m. The probability of each item to occupy each slot in the random sample is proportional to the relative weight of the item, i.e., the weight of the item with respect to the total weight of all items.

Definition 2. *Problem WRS-N-P (Weighted Random Sampling without Replacement, with defined Probabilities).*

Input: A population of n weighted items and a size m for the random sample.
Output: A weighted random sample of size m. The probability of each item to be included in the random sample is proportional to its relative weight.

Intuitively, the basic principle of WRS-N-P can be shown with the following example. Assume any two items v_i and v_j of the population with weights w_i and w_j, respectively. Let $c = w_i/w_j$. Then the probability p_i that v_i is in the random sample is equal to $c p_j$, where p_j is the probability that v_j is in the random sample. For heavy items with relative weight larger than $1/m$ we say that the respective items are "infeasible". If the inclusion probability of an infeasible item would be proportional to its weight, then this probability would become larger than 1, which of course is not possible. As shown in Sect. 3.1, the infeasible items are handled in a special way that guarantees that they are selected with probability exactly 1.

Definition 3. *Problem WRS-N-W (Weighted Random Sampling without Replacement, with defined Weights).*

---

[1] We say "supposed" because even though WRS is best described with a sequential sampling procedure, it is not inherently sequential. Algorithm A-ES [8] which we will use to solve WRS-W problems can be executed on sequential, parallel and distributed settings.

Input: A population of n weighted items and a size m for the random sample. Output: A weighted random sample of size m. In each round, the probability of every unselected item to be selected in that round is proportional to the relative item weight with respect to the weights of all unselected items.

The definition of problem WRS-N-W is essentially the following sampling procedure. Let S be the current random sample. Initially, S is empty. The m items of the random sample are selected in m rounds. In each round, the probability for each item in $V - S$ to be selected is $p_i(k) = \frac{w_i}{\sum_{s_j \in V - S} w_j}$. Using the probabilities $p_i(k)$, an item v_k is randomly selected from $V - S$ and inserted into S. We use two simple examples to illustrate the above defined WRS problems.

Example 1. Assume that we want to select a weighted random sample of size $m = 2$ from a population of $n = 4$ items with weights $1, 1, 1$ and 2, respectively. For problem WRS-N-P the probability of items 1, 2 and 3 to be in the random sample is 0.4, whereas the probability of item 4 is 0.8. For WRS-N-W the probability of items 1, 2 and 3 to be in the random sample is 0.433, while the probability of item 4 is 0.7.

Example 2. Assume now that we want to select $m = 2$ items from a population of 4 items with weights $1, 1, 1$, and 4, respectively. For WRS-N-W the probability of items 1, 2 and 3 to be in the random sample is 0.381, while the probability of item 4 is 0.857. For WRS-N-P, however, the weights are infeasible because the weight of item 4 is infeasible. In particular, the product m times the relative weight of item 4 is $2 \cdot (4/7)$ which is larger than 1 and cannot be used as a probability. This case is handled by assigning with probability 1 a position of the reservoir to item 4 and filling the other position of the reservoir randomly with one of the remaining (feasible) items. Note that if the sampling procedure is applied on a data stream and a fifth item, for example with weight 3, arrives, then the instance becomes feasible with probabilities 0.2 for items 1, 2 and 3, 0.8 for item 4 and 0.6 for item 5. The possibility for infeasible problem instances or temporary infeasible evolving problem instances over data streams is an inherent complication of the WRS-N-P problem that has to be handled in the respective sampling algorithms.

3   The Two Core Algorithms

The two core algorithms that we use for the WRS problems of this work are the *General Purpose Unequal Probability Sampling Plan* of Chao [3] and the *Weighted Random Sampling with a Reservoir* algorithm of Efraimidis and Spirakis [8]. We provide a short description of each algorithm while more details can be found in the respective papers.

3.1   A-Chao

The sampling plan of Chao [3], which we will call A-Chao, is a reservoir-based sampling algorithm that processes sequentially an initially unknown population V of weighted items.

A typical step of algorithm A-Chao is presented in Fig. 1. When a new item is examined, its relative weight is calculated and used to randomly decide if the item will be inserted into the reservoir. If the item is selected, then one of the existing items of the reservoir is uniformly selected and replaced with the new item. The trick here is that, if the probabilities of all items in the reservoir are already proportional to their weights, then by selecting uniformly which item to replace, the probabilities of all items remain proportional to their weight after the replacement.

Algorithm A-Chao (sketch)

Input : Item v_k for $m < k \leq n$
Output : A WRS-N-P sample of size m
1 : Calculate the probability $p_k = w_k/(\sum_{i=1}^{k} w_i)$ for item v_k
2 : Decide randomly if v_k will be inserted into the reservoir
3 :   if No, do nothing. Simply increase the total weight
4 :   if Yes, choose uniformly a random item from the
            reservoir and replace it with v_k

Fig. 1. A sketch of algorithm A-Chao. We assume that all the positions of the reservoir are already occupied and that all item weights are feasible.

The main approach of A-Chao is simple, flexible and effective. There are however some complications inherent to problem WRS-N-P that have to be addressed. As shown in Example 2, an instance of WRS-N-P may temporarily not be feasible, in case of data streams, or may not be feasible at all. This happens when the (current) population contains one or more infeasible items, i.e., items each of which has a relative weight greater than $1/m$. The main idea to handle this case, is to sample each infeasible item with probability 1. Thus, each infeasible item automatically occupies a position in the reservoir. The remaining positions are assigned with the normal procedure to the feasible items. In case of sampling over a data stream, an initially infeasible item may later become feasible as more items arrive. Thus, with each new item arrival the relative weights of the infeasible items are updated and if an infeasible item becomes feasible it is treated as such. Appropriate procedures to initialize the reservoir and to handle the infeasible items are described in [3].

3.2 A-ES

The algorithm of Efraimidis and Spirakis [8], which we call A-ES, is a sampling scheme for problem WRS-N-W. In A-ES, each item v_i of the population V independently generates a uniform random number $u_i \in (0,1)$ and calculates a key $k_i = u_i^{1/w_i}$. The items that possess the m largest keys form a weighted random sample. We will use the reservoir-based version of A-ES, where the algorithm maintains a reservoir of size m with the items with m largest keys.

The basic principle underlying algorithm A-ES is the remark that a uniform random variable can be "amplified" as desired by raising it to an appropriate power (Remark 1). A high level description of algorithm A-ES is shown in Fig. 2.

Remark 1 [8]. Let U_1 and U_2 be independent random variables with uniform distributions in $[0, 1]$. If $X_1 = (U_1)^{1/w_1}$ and $X_2 = (U_2)^{1/w_2}$, for $w_1, w_2 > 0$, then
$$P[X_1 \le X_2] = \frac{w_2}{w_1 + w_2}.$$

Algorithm A-ES (High Level Description)

Input :   A population V of n weighted items
Output :   A WRS-N-W sample of size m

1:   For each $v_i \in V$, $u_i = random(0,1)$ and $k_i = u_i^{\frac{1}{w_i}}$
2:   Select the m items with the largest keys k_i

Fig. 2. A high level description of algorithm A-ES.

3.3   Algorithm A-Chao with Jumps

A common technique to improve certain reservoir-based sampling algorithms is to change the random experiment used in the sampling procedure. In normal reservoir-based sampling algorithms, a random experiment is performed for each new item to decide if it is inserted into the reservoir. In random sampling with jumps instead, a single random experiment is used to directly decide which will be the next item that will enter the reservoir. Since each item that is processed will be inserted with some probability into the reservoir, the number of items that will be skipped until the next item is selected for the reservoir, is a random variable. In uniform random sampling it is possible to generate an exponential jump that identifies the next item of the population that will enter the reservoir [7], while in [8] it is shown that exponential jumps can be used for WRS with algorithm A-ES.

In this work, we show that a jumps approach can be used for algorithm A-Chao too, albeit in a slightly more complicated way than for algorithm A-ES. The reason is that in WRS-N-W the probability that an item will be the next item that will enter the reservoir can be directly obtained from its weight and the total weight of the items preceding it, while in WRS-N-P the respective probabilities have to be computed.

Assume for example a typical step of algorithm A-Chao. A new item v_i has just arrived and with probability p_i it will be inserted into the reservoir. The probability that v_i will not be selected, but the next item, v_{i+1}, is selected, is $(1 - p_i)\,p_{i+1}$. In the same way the probability that items v_i and v_{i+1} are not selected and that item v_{i+2} is selected is $(1 - p_i)\,(1 - p_{i+1})\,p_{i+2}$. Clearly, if the stream continues with an infinite number of items then with probability 1 some item will be the next item that will enter the reservoir. Thus, we can generate a uniform random number u_j in $[0, 1]$ and add up the probability mass of each new item until the accumulated probability exceeds the random number u_j. The selected item is then inserted into the reservoir with the normal procedure of algorithm A-Chao.

The main advantage of using jumps in reservoir-based sampling algorithms is that, in general, the number of random number generations can be dramatically reduced. For example, if the item weights are independent random variables with a common distribution, then the number of random numbers is reduced from $O(n)$ to $O(m \log(n/m))$, where n is the size of the population [8]. In contexts where the computational cost for qualitative random number generation is high, the jumps versions offer an efficient alternative for the sampling procedure. From a semantic point of view, the sampling procedures with and without jumps are identical.

4   Algorithms for WRS Problems

Both core algorithms, A-Chao and A-ES, are efficient and flexible and can be used to solve fundamental but also more involved random sampling problems. We start with basic WRS problems that are directly solved by A-Chao and A-ES. Then, we present sampling schemes for two WRS problems with a bound on the number of replacements and discuss the sampling problem in the presence of stream evolution.

4.1   Basic Problems

- **Problem WRS-N-P:** The problem can be solved with algorithm P-Chao. In case no infeasible items appear in the data stream, the cost to process each item is $O(1)$ and the total cost for the whole population is $O(n)$. The complexity of handling infeasible items is higher. For example, if a heap data structure is used to manage the current infeasible items, then each infeasible item costs $O(\log m)$. An adversary could generate a data stream where each item would be initially (at the time it is feeded to the sampling algorithm) infeasible and this would cause a total complexity of $\Theta(n \log m)$ to process the complete population. However, this is a rather extreme example and in reasonable cases the total complexity is expected to be linear on n.
- **Problem WRS-N-W:** The problem can be solved with algorithm A-ES. The reservoir-based implementation of the algorithm requires $O(1)$ computational steps for each item that is not selected and $O(\log m)$ for each item that enters the reservoir (if, for example, the reservoir is organized as a heap). In this case too, an adversary can prepare a sequence that will require $O(n \log m)$ computational steps. In common cases, the cost for the complete population will be $O(n) + O(m \log(n/m))O(\log m)$, which becomes $O(n)$ if n is large enough with respect to m.
- **Problem WRS-R:** In WRS with replacement the population remains unaltered after each item selection. Because of this, WRS-R-P and WRS-R-W coincide and we call the problem simply WRS-R. In the data stream version, the problem can be solved by running concurrently m independent instances of WRS-N-P or WRS-N-W, each with sample size $m' = 1$. Both algorithms A-Chao and A-ES in both their versions, with and without jumps, can efficiently solve the problem. In most cases, the version with jumps of A-Chao or A-ES should be the most efficient approach.

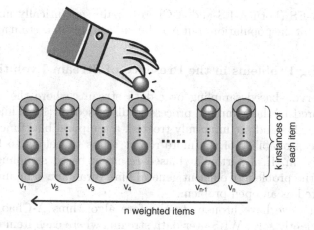

Fig. 3. WRS-k-W, n weighted items with k instances of each item.

Note that sampling with replacement is not equivalent to running the experiment on a population V' with m instances of each original item of V. The sample space of the later experiment would be much larger than in the case with replacement.

4.2   Sampling with a Bounded Number of Replacements

We consider weighted random sampling from populations where each item can be replaced at most a bounded number of times (Fig. 3). An analogy would be to randomly select m products from an automatic selling machine with n different products and k instances of each product. The challenge is of course that the weighted random sample has to be generated in one-pass over an initially unknown population.

- **Problem WRS-k-W:** Sampling from a population of n weighted items where each item can be selected up to $k \leq m$ times. The weights of the items are used to determine the probability that each item is selected at each step.
  A general solution, in the sense that each item may have its own multiplicity $k_i \leq k$, is to use a pipeline of m instances of a A-ES, where each instance will generate a weighted random sample of size 1. Note that either algorithm A-Chao or A-ES can be used, because for samples of size 1 the outcomes of the two algorithms are equivalent. If the first instance is at item ℓ, then each other instance is one item behind the previous instance. Thus, an item of the population is first processed by instance 1, then by instance 2, etc. If at some point the item has been selected k_i times, then the item is not processed by the remaining instances and the information up to which instance the item has been processed is stored. If the item is replaced in a reservoir at a later step, then it is submitted to the next instance of A-ES. Note that in this approach, some items might be processed out of their original order. This is fine with

algorithm A-ES (both A-ES and A-Chao remain semantically unaffected by any ordering of the population) but may be undesirable in certain applications.

4.3 Sampling Problems in the Presence of Stream Evolution

A case of reservoir-based sampling over data streams where the more recent items are favored in the sampling process is discussed in [1]. While the items do not have weights and are uniformly treated, a temporal bias function is used to increase the probability of the more recent items to belong to the random sample. Finally, in [1], a particular biased reservoir-based sampling scheme is proposed and the problem of efficient general biased random sampling over data streams is stated as an open problem.

In this work, we have brought to the fore algorithms A-Chao and A-ES, which can efficiently solve WRS over data streams where each item can have an arbitrary weight. This should provide an affirmative answer to the open problem posed in [1]. Moreover, the particular sampling procedure presented in [1] is a special case of algorithm A-Chao.

Since algorithms A-Chao and A-ES can support arbitrary item weights, a bias favoring more recent items can be encoded into the weight of the newly arrived item or in the weights of the items already in the reservoir. Furthermore, by using algorithms A-Chao and A-ES the sampling process in the presence of stream evolution can also support weighted items. This way the bias of each item may depend on the item weight and how old the item is, or on any other factor that could be taken into account. Thus, the sampling procedure and/or the corresponding applications in [1] can be generalized to items with arbitrary weights and other, temporal or not, bias criteria.

The way to increase the selection probability of a newly arrived item is very simple for both algorithms, A-Chao and A-ES.

- **A-Chao:** By increasing the weight of the new item.
- **A-ES:** By increasing the weight of the new item or decreasing the weights of the items already in the reservoir.

5 An Abstract Data Structure for WRS

We designed an abstract class StreamSampler with the methods feedItem() and getSample(), and a set of auxiliary classes for the weighted items to capture the basic functionality for weighted random sampling over data streams (Fig. 4). Then, we developed descendant classes that implement the functionality of the StreamSampler class for algorithms A-Chao and A-ES, both with and without jumps. The descendant classes are StreamSamplerChao, StreamSamplerES, StreamSamplerESWithJumps and StreamSamplerChaoWithJumps [18].
Preliminary experiments with random populations (with uniform random item weights) showed that all algorithms scale linear on the population size and at most linear on the sample size. Indicative measurements are shown in Fig. 5.

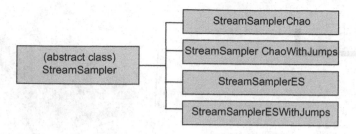

Fig. 4. The class hierarchy for sampling over data streams.

While there is still room for optimization of the implementations of the algorithms, the general behavior of the complexities is evident in the graphs. The experiments have been performed on the Sun Java 1.6 platform running on an Intel Core 2 Quad CPU-based PC and all measurements have been averaged over 100 (at least) executions.

6   The Role of Weights

The problem classes WRS-P and WRS-W differ in the way the item weights are used in the sampling procedure. In WRS-P the weights are used to directly determine the final selection probability of each item and this probability is easy to calculate. On the other hand, in WRS-W the item weights are used to determine the selection probability of each item in each step of a supposed sequential sampling procedure. In this case it is easy to study each step of the sampling procedure, but the final selection probabilities of the items seem to be hard to calculate. In the general case, a complex expression has to be evaluated in order to calculate the exact inclusion probability of each item and we are not aware of an efficient procedure to calculate this expression. An interesting feature of random samples generated with WRS-W is that they support the concept of order for the sampled items. The item that is selected first or simply has the largest key (algorithm A-ES) can be assumed to take the first position, the second largest the second position etc. The concept of order can be useful in certain applications. We illustrate the two sampling approaches in the following example.

Example 3. On-line advertisements. A search engine shows with the results of each query a set of k sponsored links that are related to the search query. If there are n sponsored links that are relevant to a query then how should the set of k links be selected? If all sponsors have paid the same amount of money then any uniform sampling algorithm without replacement can solve the problem. If however, every sponsor has a different weight then how should the k items be selected? Assuming that the k positions are equivalent in "impact", a sponsor who has the double weight with respect to another sponsor may expect its advertisement to appear twice as often in the results. Thus, a reasonable approach

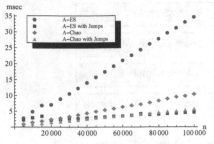 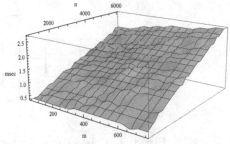

(a) Measurements for m=200 and n rang-   (b) The complexity of A-ES for m ranging
ing from 5000 to 100000.   from 50 to 750 and n from 1000 to 6000.

Fig. 5. Time measurements of the WRS sampling algorithms.

would be to use algorithm A-Chao to generate a WRS-N-P of k items. If however, the advertisement slots are ordered based on their impact, for example the first slot may have the largest impact, the second the second largest etc., then algorithm A-ES may provide the appropriate solution by generating a WRS-N-W of k items.

When the size of the population becomes large with respect to the size of the random sample, then the differences in the selection probabilities of the items in WRS-P and WRS-W become less important. The reason is that if the population is large then the change in the population because of the removed items has a small impact and the sampling procedure converges to random sampling without replacement. As noted earlier, in random sampling with replacement the two sampling approaches coincide.

7 Discussion

We presented a comprehensive treatment of WRS over data streams and showed that efficient sampling schemes exist for fundamental but also more specialized WRS problems. The two core algorithms, A-Chao and A-ES have been proved efficient and flexible and can be used to build more complex sampling schemes.

Acknowledgments. The present work was supported in part by the project ATLAS (Advanced Tourism Planning), GSRT/CO-OPERATION/11SYN-10-1730, and by national ETAA funds.

References

1. Aggarwal, C.C.: On biased reservoir sampling in the presence of stream evolution. In: VLDB 2006: Proceedings of the 32nd International Conference on Very Large Data Bases, pp. 607–618. VLDB Endowment (2006)

2. Al-Kateb, M., Lee, B.S.: Adaptive stratified reservoir sampling over heterogeneous data streams. Inf. Syst. **39**, 199–216 (2014)
3. Chao, M.T.: A general purpose unequal probability sampling plan. Biometrika **69**(3), 653–656 (1982)
4. Cormode, G., Muthukrishnan, S., Yi, K., Zhang, Q.: Optimal sampling from distributed streams. In: Proceedings of the Twenty-ninth ACM SIGMOD-SIGACT-SIGART Symposium on Principles of Database Systems, PODS 2010, pp. 77–86. ACM, New York (2010)
5. Cormode, G., Muthukrishnan, S., Yi, K., Zhang, Q.: Continuous sampling from distributed streams. J. ACM **59**(2), 10:1–10:25 (2012)
6. Cormode, G., Shkapenyuk, V., Srivastava, D., Xu, B.: Forward decay: a practical time decay model for streaming systems. In: Proceedings of the 2009 IEEE International Conference on Data Engineering, ICDE 2009, pp. 138–149. IEEE Computer Society, Washington, DC (2009)
7. Devroye, L.: Non-Uniform Random Variate Generation. Springer, New York (1986)
8. Efraimidis, P.S., Spirakis, P.G.: Weighted random sampling with a reservoir. Inf. Process. Lett. **97**(5), 181–185 (2006)
9. Goldberg, G., Harnik, D., Sotnikov, D.: The case for sampling on very large file systems. In: 30th Symposium on Mass Storage Systems and Technologies (MSST), pp. 1–11, June 2014
10. Hu, X., Qiao, M., Tao, Y.: Independent range sampling. In: Proceedings of the 33rd ACM SIGMOD-SIGACT-SIGART Symposium on Principles of Database Systems, PODS 2014, pp. 246–255. ACM, New York (2014)
11. Knuth, D.E.: The Art of Computer Programming: Seminumerical Algorithms, vol. 2, 2nd edn. Addison-Wesley Publishing Company, Reading (1981)
12. Li, K.-H.: Reservoir-sampling algorithms of time complexity o(n(1 + log(n/n))). ACM Trans. Math. Softw. **20**(4), 481–493 (1994)
13. Longbo, Z., Zhanhuai, L., Yiqiang, Z., Min, Y., Yang, Z.: A priority random sampling algorithm for time-based sliding windows over weighted streaming data. In: Proceedings of the 2007 ACM Symposium on Applied Computing, SAC 2007, pp. 453–456. ACM, New York (2007)
14. Olken, F.: Random sampling from databases. Ph.D. thesis, Department of Computer Science, University of California at Berkeley (1993)
15. Tirthapura, S., Woodruff, D.P.: Optimal random sampling from distributed streams revisited. In: Peleg, D. (ed.) Distributed Computing. LNCS, vol. 6950, pp. 283–297. Springer, Heidelberg (2011)
16. Vitter, J.S.: Faster methods for random sampling. Commun. ACM **27**(7), 703–718 (1984)
17. Vitter, J.S.: Random sampling with a reservoir. ACM Trans. Math. Softw. **11**(1), 37–57 (1985)
18. WRS.: A stream sampler for weighted random sampling. https://euclid.ee.duth.gr/demo/wrs/

Random Instances of Problems in NP – Algorithms and Statistical Physics

Charilaos Efthymiou[✉]

Georgia Institute of Technology, College of Computing,
266 Ferst Dr. Atlanta, 30332 Atlanta, GA, USA
cefthymiou3@mail.gatech.edu

Abstract. One of the most intriguing discoveries made by Erdös and Rényi in the course of their investigating random graphs is the so-called *phase transition phenomenona*, like the sudden emergence of the giant component. Since then, this kind of phenomena have been observed in many, diverse, areas of combinatorics and discrete mathematics in general. Typically, the notion of phase transition in combinatorics is related to a sudden change in the structural properties of a combinatorial construction, e.g. a (hyper)graph, arithmetic progressions e.t.c. However, it seems that the study of phase transitions goes much further. There is an empirical evidence that certain phase transition phenomena play a prominent role in the performance of algorithms for a lot of natural computational problems. That is, phase transitions are related to the, somehow elusive, notion of computational intractability. The last fifteen-twenty years, there has been serious attempts to put this relation on a mathematically rigorous basis. Our aim is to highlight some of the most central problems that arise in this endeavor.

1 Introduction

In one or another way, our main focus is algorithms for problems in NP. NP is a class of tremendous wealth of important natural computational problems. Many computational problems in several application areas call for the design of mathematical objects of various sorts (paths in graphs, solutions of equations, traveling salesman routes and so on). Sometimes we seek the optimum among all possible alternatives and other times we are satisfied with any object that fits some specifications. These mathematical objects are abstractions of actual physical objects of real-life. Hence, it is natural that in most applications the *certificates of solutions* are not astronomically large in terms of the input data while specifications are usually simple and checkable quickly. The class NP consists exactly of this kind of computational problems, i.e. those whose solution can be certified *efficiently*.

Many problems in NP can be cast naturally as *Constraint Satisfaction Problems* (CSP), e.g. graph k-colourability, k-satisfiability and many others. An instance of CSP is defined by a set of n *variables*, $x_1, \ldots, x_n$ each of them ranging over a small domain $\mathbf{D}$ and a set of m *constraints*. A constraint is a k-tuple

© Springer International Publishing Switzerland 2015
C. Zaroliagis et al. (Eds.): Spirakis Festschrift, LNCS 9295, pp. 196–222, 2015.
DOI: 10.1007/978-3-319-24024-4_13

of variables, e.g. $(x_1, \ldots x_k)$, for some small k. Each constraint *forbids certain combinations of values* among its variables. That is, assigning the variables of a constraint a "forbidden" combination makes the constraint *unsatisfied*. Otherwise, the constraint is *satisfied*. A CSP is *satisfiable* if there is at least one assignment which satisfies all the constraints simultaneously.

One example of CSP is the "k-colourability problem". Given a graph $G = (V, E)$ and a set of k-colours, the problem is to decide whether there is an assignment of colours to the vertices such that no two adjacent vertices take on the same colour. Following the above definition of CSP we can formulate the k-colouring problem as follows: The set of variables corresponds to the set of vertices V. Each variable has domain $\mathbf{D} = \{1, \ldots, k\}$, i.e. the set of colors. The set of constraints corresponds to the set of edges E, i.e. two variables in the constrain are not allowed to take the same value.

The task of finding a satisfiable assignment of a CSP can be accomplished by just enumerating all the $|\mathbf{D}|^n$ possible assignments of the variables. However, even for moderate values of n this exponential running is impractical. Yet, for many CSPs, no better algorithm is known.

The theory of NP-completeness established by the seminal works of Cook and Karp in the early 1970 s enabled us to distinguish the most difficult among the NP problems, the NP-*complete* problems. However, there has been only a little evidence to illuminate the conceptual origin of their computational intractability. That is, it is not clear why the attempts to find efficient algorithms for the NP-complete problems have failed. On the other hand, there are many cases in practice where instances of NP-complete problems can be solved "quickly". Hence computational intractability is a rather elusive phenomenon.

A major research effort over the past 40 years has been the study of random instances of NP-complete problems, particularly *random Constrains Satisfaction Problems* (rCSP). At first the main objective of this endeavor was to show that NP-complete problems are easy "*on the average*", i.e. hard instances are rare and exceptional.

Yet in various setting rCSPs do not comply with the above picture. Random graph colouring is a case in the point. Let $G(n, m)$ by a graph created by choosing at random a graph on n vertices and $m = dn/2$ edges, where d is constant. It has been shown that in typical instances of $G(n, m)$ χ the minimum number of colours needed for k-colouring the vertices of $G(n, m)$ is $d/(2 \ln d)$, see [5, 21]. However, the best algorithm there exists for colouring typical instances of $G(n, m)$ is a very simple greedy one and requires as many as 2χ colours and it was proposed around 40 years ago [40]. Since then there has been no other efficient algorithm, howsoever sophisticated, that can outperform this simple (almost naive) algorithm, in term of number of colours.

The state of affairs leads to the question whether rCSP such as random graph colouring are computationally "hard", at least under certain conditions. If so, then for some very natural problems computational intractability would be the typical behaviour, rather than a rare exception. In fact it would be easy to generate hard problem instances. While this scenario might seem frustrating from an algorithmic perspective, it is no exaggeration to say that a proof of some natural type of a rCSP is hard would revolutionize computational complexity and cryptography.

From a different starting point, rCSP have been studied in *statistical mechanics* as models of *disordered systems*. Starting with the work of Marc Mézard and Giorgio Parisi in the 1980s physicists have developed ingenious, however mathematically highly non-rigorous ideas for the study of these objects. Over the past decade, the ideas pioneered by Mézard and Parisi have grown into a generic toolkit called *Cavity method* [57]. Cavity method makes impressively strong predictions about fundamental properties of rCSP which seem to affect the performance of algorithms.

Cavity method does not include any computational complexity theoretic predictions. However, the empirical performance of all known algorithms and heuristics for finding satisfying assignments of rCSP instances appear to go along with certain *phase transition* phenomena predicted by this method. A case in the point is the problem of colouring we describe above. Acquiring a $(2+\epsilon)\chi$ colouring of $G(n,m)$ efficiently is a trivial task. On the other hand, there is not any efficient algorithm that can $(2-\epsilon)\chi$ colour $G(n,m)$. Technically speaking, the difficulty in the later case seems to rely on the fact that the choices that are made by some *local algorithm* have *global impact*. A folklore term that describes this phenomenon is *"freezing"*, [1]. In a typical $(2-\epsilon)\chi$ colourings of $G(n,m)$ it is impossible to alter the colour assignment of a vertex and keep the colouring proper. To do so, one has to change the colour assignments of a significant number of vertices. The phenomenon of freezing is rather exceptional among the $(2+\epsilon)\chi$-colourings of $G(n,m)$.

Of course, freezing on its own is not sufficient to provide any hardness results, in a rigorous sense. However, it is a remarkable coincidence that all the algorithms or heuristics we have for colouring a $G(n,m)$ seem to be suffer from this phenomenon.

1.1   Algorithms for rCSP

There is a wide variety of algorithms-heuristics applied to rCSP. A lot of them are motivated from the study of the problem from statistical physics e.g. *Glauber Dynamics, Metropolis process* [52], *Belief Propagation*, [62] *Survey Propagation* [11] *Simulated Annealing* [48]. Other have more CS-Mathematical flavor, e.g. *Walksat* [65], *DPLL* and many others.

Remark 1. We wish to distinguish the notion of heuristics from algorithm in that, a heuristic is a method whose performance guarantees are not (mathematically) rigorously established, as opposed to the algorithms which are.

The rage of the aforementioned algorithm is by no means restricted to rCSP. The spectrum of their applications varies from combinatorial algorithms for approximate counting of combinatorial objects [44], computing the permanent of a matrix [45], to optimization [48], information theory e.g. for the LDPC codes [64], Artificial Intelligence [62] and Computer Vision [34].

In this survey we focus mainly on algorithms which are motivated by to ideas coming from statistical physics, e.g. *algorithm dynamicses* like Glauber Dynamics, Metropolis process or *message passing algorithms* like Belief Propagation, Survey Propagation. Especially, the algorithm dynamicses are a natural family of algorithms since they simulate certain kinds of *random walks* on the solution space of the rCSP. These algorithms are very *simple, local* and *easy to implement*. They are studied in the context of Markov Chain Monte Carlo sampling as well as for optimization[1]. On the other hand, the message passing algorithms is an attempt to turn the cavity method to an algorithm.

The behavior of all the above algorithms as well as many other algorithms for rCSP depends heavily on phenomena predicted by the (non rigorous) the cavity method. In particular, it seems that a prominent role in studying most of the algorithms above plays the so called *Gibbs distribution* over the solutions of a given rCSP instance. The cavity method predicts a series of phase transitions regarding the structure of the Gibbs distribution which in turn affect the empirical performance of the algorithms.

2 Predictions from Statistical Physics - "Cavity Method"

The study of phase transitions in rCSP is done with respect to a parameter called *density*. Density is defined as the ratio of the *number of constraints m* over *the number of variables, n*. The notion of *phase transition* implies a sudden, usually dramatic, change in some property (or properties) of a rCSP as a result of a relatively small change in the value of the density.

For the shake of concreteness we use the graph colouring problem to describe the predictions from the cavity method. Very similar predictions hold for other rCSP like independent set problem, k-SAT and many others. We should remark that the cavity method is a generic tool whose applications go *beyond* the study of rCSP. The presentations of the results are from [50].

The setting which we use to present the results is more or less standard in the study of phase transitions. We consider the following *graph-process*: Start with an empty graph on n vertices, i.e. G_0. This is *step* 0. Given G_{t-1}, at *step t* we "throw a random edge" into G_{t-1}. That is, we choose a pair of non-adjacent vertices of G_{t-1} at random and we connect them by introducing a new edge. Then, it is standard to show that G_m is an instance of random graph $G(n, m)$. We denote with d the expected degree of $G(n, m)$, which is equal to twice the density as $d = 2m/n$.

In the above graph-process we study how does the set of k-colourings of G_t evolve with t. Assume that the number of colours k is fixed. The evolution of the set of k-colourings is w.r.t. the following phenomenon: each time t we throw a new edge into the graph a large number of k-colourings of G_{t-1} has to be disregarded. E.g. if the new edge connects the vertices v and u, then the new set of k-colourings should disregard all the previous k-colourings which assign v and u the same colour.

---

[1] As local greedy algorithms.

The cavity method predicts a very exciting scenario for the evolution of the set of k-colourings both in terms of its *geometry* as well as the *structure* of the corresponding Gibbs distribution. Gibbs (or Boltzmann) distribution of a rCSP is a natural distribution defined on the set of satisfying assignments. E.g. for the k-colourings it is just the uniform distribution over all possible k-colourings of the underlying graph (Fig. 1).

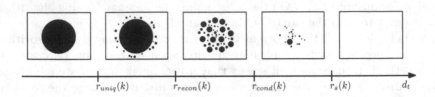

Fig. 1. Geometry evolution

We start by considering the geometry first. The evolution of the geometry of the k-colourings during the graph process is illustrated in Fig. 2. Given k there is a set of four critical values, $r_{uniq}(k), r_{recon}(k), r_{cond}(k), r_s(k)$ for the expected degree (equiv. density) which signify 5 different phases.

The first phase is for expected degree $d < r_{uniq}$, this is the so-called "*uniqueness*" region. There, the set of k-colourings looks like a giant "connected" ball. By connected we mean that there is a path connecting any two k-colourings. Two k-colourings are adjacent in the path if their hamming distance is very small, e.g. fixed. For two colourings σ and τ their *hamming distance* is equal to the number of assignments that the two colorings disagree.

As the graph process continuous to add edges into the graph, the expected degree increases. As soon as d becomes larger than r_{uniq} we get to a new phase the so-called "*non-reconstruction*". Geometrically, this phase is not so much different than the previous one. It is just an exponentially small fraction of solutions that gets disconnected from the giant ball. Disconnection means that the solutions that do not belong to the giant ball are separated from it with linear hamming distance.

When d passes beyond a critical value r_{recon} we have a sudden, very dramatic, change in the geometry of the solution space. The space "shatters" into exponentially many small balls. Each of the small balls contains an exponentially small fraction of the k-colourings. Any two k-colourings in each ball are connected with each other. However, any two k-colouring from different balls are separated with linear hamming distance. This is called the "*reconstruction*" region. The k-colourings within each ball are highly correlated, i.e. most of the colour assignments are the same for all k-colourings in the ball.

Remark 2. From an algorithmic perspective, in the reconstruction region, we have the phenomenon of frozen variables [1]. For the majority of vertices the following is true: so as to change the assignment of a variable we need to change the assignments of a substantial number of vertices in the graph so as to keep the colouring proper.

Remark 3. All the known efficient algorithms which find solutions stop to work in the reconstruction region. In other words, given some k, there is not any efficient algorithm which can find a k-colouring of $G(n, m)$ if its expected degree $d > r_{recon}(k)$.

Next, there is the *condensation phase*. As soon as d gets $d > r_{cond}$ the k-colourings start to disappear rapidly as d increases. This means that the balls -clusters of solutions- from the previous phase start shrinking rapidly and a lot of them disappear. From those which survive in the condensation phase, there is only a small, constant, fraction of balls which dominates. These, constant many, dominating balls gather a constant fraction of the k-colourings. A basic feature of this phase is that the k-colourings are *extremely correlated* with each other.

Finally, as soon as d gets $d > r_s$ the k-colourings disappear, i.e. the graph is not k-colourable any more. This is the *unsatisfiability phase*.

Alternatively, the cavity method considers the *Gibbs distribution* which is defined as follows: We have an "energy" function $\mathcal{H}(\cdot)$ from the set of assignments to the positive real numbers. This function is called *Hamiltonian*. It is necessary to remark that the Hamiltonian is defined for every possible assignment of the variables, satisfying or not. Given $\mathcal{H}$, the Gibbs distribution assigns the configuration σ probability measure

$$\mu(\sigma) = \frac{1}{Z_\beta} \exp\left(-\beta \cdot \mathcal{H}(\sigma)\right), \tag{1}$$

where β is a parameter of the system and it is called *inverse temperature*. The inverse temperature takes on either some real value or it is infinity. Z_β is a normalizing quantity which is called *"partition function"*.

Remark 4. In a physics' perspective, $\mathcal{H}(\sigma)$ corresponds to the "energy" that configuration σ has. In that terms, Gibbs distribution gives greater probability measure to the configurations with smaller energy.

For the k-colourings of a graph G, the corresponding Gibbs distribution is defined as follows: For every assignment of colours $\sigma \in [k]^{V(G)}$ it holds that

$$\mathcal{H}(\sigma) = \sum_{\{v,u\} \in E(G)} \delta(\sigma_v, \sigma_u),$$

where $\delta(\sigma_v, \sigma_u)$ is Kronecker's delta function, i.e.

$$\delta(\sigma_v, \sigma_u) = \begin{cases} 1 & \text{if } \sigma_v = \sigma_u \\ 0 & \text{otherwise.} \end{cases}$$

Essentially, $\mathcal{H}(\sigma)$ counts the number of monochromatic edges of G under σ.

In order to guarantee that the Gibbs distribution has support the proper k-colourings of G only, we set $\beta = \infty$. E.g. every non proper takes probability measure 0 while each proper k-colouring takes the same probability measure as the other proper k-colourings.

Remark 5. Studying the problem of graph colouring for general β has gathered a lot of attention in statistical physics literature. The corresponding distribution is also known as *Potts model*. In computer science the focus is mainly on the most challenging case where $\beta = \infty$.

The study of Gibbs distribution μ mainly focuses on its *spatial correlation decay* properties. Consider a small subset of vertices $\Lambda \subseteq V(G)$. Roughly speaking, the spatial correlation studies the difference between the projection (marginal) of Gibbs distribution on Λ and the projection of the Gibbs distribution on Λ when we condition on the configuration of some other set Λ' which is at graph distance r from Λ.

So as to compare two distributions ν, ξ on some discrete space S, we use the notion of *total variation distance*, denoted as $||\nu - \xi||$. Total variation distance is defined as follows:

$$||\nu - \xi|| = \max_{A \subseteq S} |\nu(A) - \xi(A)|.$$

For a pair of distribution ν, ξ on the set of k-colourings of a graph G and $\Lambda \subseteq V(G)$, we let $||\nu - \xi||_\Lambda$ denote the total variation distance of the projections of the two distributions on the vertex set Λ.

In what follows, given some vertex v and some integer r we let $B_{v,r}$ denote the set of vertices which are within graph distance r from v. We denote $\bar{B}_{v,r}$ the complement of the set $B_{v,r}$.

The different phases regarding the geometry of the configuration space correspond to different spatial correlation decay properties for the corresponding Gibbs measure μ on $G(n, m)$. More specifically, as long as $d < r_{uniq}$, i.e. in the uniqueness region, it holds that

$$\mathbb{E}\left[\sup_{\sigma_{\bar{B}_{v,r}}} ||\mu(\cdot | \sigma_{\bar{B}_{v,r}}) - \mu(\cdot)||_{\{v\}}\right] = o_r(1), \tag{2}$$

where $o_r(1)$ is a vanishing function of r. The expectation is taken w.r.t. the graph instances.

In words, the above relation implies the following: Consider some "typical" instance of $G(n, m)$ with $d < r_{uniq}$ and some "typical" vertex in that graph. Take a random k-colouring of this graph. In this random colouring, the assignment of the vertex v is asymptotically independent, w.r.t. r, from the colour assignments in $\bar{B}_{v,r}$. The specific notion of independence assumes a *worst case* boundary condition for $\bar{B}_{v,r}$, e.g. we take the supremum over $\sigma_{\bar{B}_{v,r}}$. For this reason it is rather strong. The condition in (2) is called *Gibbs uniqueness condition*.

Remark 6. Gibbs uniqueness is one of the most basic and most fundamental properties in the study of Gibbs distribution for such models (also called "*spin systems*" in statistical physics literature) see [38].

When d is in the non-reconstruction region, then (2) does not hold. There are boundary conditions on $\bar{B}_{v,r}$ which have substantial influence on the distribution of the colour assignment of v, regardless of r. However, there is a weaker condition that holds,

$$\mathbb{E}\left[\sum_{\sigma_{\bar{B}_r}} \mu(\sigma_{\bar{B}_r}) \cdot \|\mu(\cdot|\sigma_{\bar{B}_r}) - \mu(\cdot)\|_{\{v\}}\right] = o_r(1). \tag{3}$$

In words, the above condition implies that the colour assignment of v is asymptotically independent of "typical" boundary conditions on $\bar{B}_{v,r}$. That is the boundaries conditions on $\bar{B}_{v,r}$ that have great influence on the distribution of the colouring on v are somehow *exceptional* under the Gibbs distribution.

When d is in the reconstruction regime the l.h.s. of (3) is bounded away from zero. Then we have the following situation. Let $\mathbf{S} = \{v_1, \ldots, v_l\}$ be a set of l randomly chosen vertices, for some fixed number $l > 0$. Let $\mu_{\mathbf{S}}$ and μ_{v_i} denote the Gibbs marginals of $\mathbf{S}$ and the vertex $v_i \in \mathbf{S}$, respectively. Then it holds that

$$\mathbb{E}\left[\sum_{\sigma_{\mathbf{S}}} \left|\mu_{\mathbf{S}}(\sigma_{\mathbf{S}}) - \prod_{i=1}^{l} \mu_{v_i}(\sigma_{v_i})\right|\right] = o_n(1). \tag{4}$$

The above expectation is w.r.t. both graph instances and set of vertices.

In word, what the above relation implies is that the joint distribution of the vertices in $\mathbf{S}$ factorizes as a product of marginals of the individual vertices in the set. The condition implies that each of the possible combinations of colorings of the vertices $v_1, \ldots, v_l$ appear in, roughly, the same number of balls of solutions.

Finally, in condensation phase, (4) does not hold. The expectation now is bounded away from zero. This is mainly because the colouring of the vertices $v_1, \ldots, v_l$ is hugely influenced by the assignments induced by the dominating balls of solutions.

Remark 7. The spatial mixing conditions in (4) gives rise to the study of spatial mixing properties of new probability measures, e.g. measures over the clusters. This motivates the well known algorithm *Survey Propagation* [11].

2.1 Rigorous Results

The cavity method describes in a very precise way the location of all the aforementioned thresholds. The most fundamental question in this context is specifying the satisfiability threshold. In a separate paragraph we focus on this very interesting subject, i.e. Sect. 3. In the rest of this short section we focus on presenting some, rigorous, results which are related to predictions of the cavity method we refer above.

In [1, 16] the authors give rigorous result about geometric predictions of the cavity method, as far as k-colouring, k-SAT, hypergraph 2 colouring and independent set problem are regarded. These results are for predictions up to condensation threshold. Also in [18, 33] we show that for the k-colouring problem, the non-reconstruction threshold is true for the case of k-colourings. In particular in

[18] we show that up to condensation threshold, the Gibbs distribution over the k-colourings of $G(n, m)$ converges, in a specific way, to the Gibbs distribution of the k-colouring of a Galton-Watson tree with offspring distribution $2m/n$.

Also in [8] the authors prove rigorously the existence of the condensation phase and give the precise location of the threshold for the case of k-colourings.

There is a number of papers which consider the problems not on random graphs or random hypergraphs but on random regular graphs. It is expected that there are a lot of similarities between regular rCSP and their random counterparts. We mention some results on regular rCSP [10,17,24,25].

3   Satisfiability Thresholds

Possibly the most fundamental endeavor in the study of rCSP is to find precisely the satisfiability threshold for the corresponding model. The existence of satisfiability threshold for rCSP has been conjectured to exists few decades ago. In this section, we provide a high level description of the approaches used for estimating this threshold. Due to the fact that random k-SAT has focused the greatest attention, the corresponding satisfiability threshold has the best estimates so far. Our presentation focuses on this problem.

Consider a set of n boolean variables, $x_1, \ldots, x_n$. A literal is either a variable x_i or its negation. A random k-CNF formula $F_{n,m,k}$ is the conjunction of m clauses such that each clause is a disjunction of a random subset of k out the $2n$ literals.

Given some random k-CNF formula $F_{n,m,k}$ we let $\mathrm{SAT}(F_{n,m,k}) = $ "$F_{n,m,k}$ is satisfiable". The satisfiability threshold conjecture stipulates that given some fixed k, there is a critical value r_s such that

$$Pr[\mathrm{SAT}(F_{n,m,k})] = \begin{cases} 1 & \text{if } m/n < r_s \\ 0 & \text{if } m/n > r_s \end{cases}$$

The work [35], by Freidgut, as well as further results like [3], established that indeed there is such critical value for the satisfiability of various rCSP like k-SAT or k-colouring.

Remark 8. The aforementioned results about the existence of satisfiability threshold do not exclude the possibility that the threshold depends on n, i.e. $r_s = r_s(n)$.

Usually the attempt is to determine upper and lower bounds for the satisfiability threshold, i.e. r_s^-, r_s^+ such that $r_s^- \leq r_s \leq r_s^+$. Ideally we would like to have $r_s^- = r_s = r_s^+$. The attempts to estimate r_s^-, r_s^+ follow more or less a standard approach. Given some formula $F_{n,m,k}$ we define an appropriate variable $\mathcal{Z} = \mathcal{Z}(F)$ such that $\mathcal{Z} > 0$ if the formula is satisfiable and $\mathcal{Z} = 0$, otherwise. Then the aim is to show that

$$\lim_{n \to \infty} Pr[\mathcal{Z} > 0] = \begin{cases} 1 & \text{if } m/n < r_s^- \\ 0 & \text{if } m/n > r_s^+ \end{cases}$$

The most natural candidate for $\mathcal{Z}$ is the number of satisfying assignments of $F_{n,m,k}$. This was the case in the early attempts to get bounds for r_s. For upper bounding r_s the attempt was to find the minimum possible r_s^+ such that $\mathbb{E}[\mathcal{Z}] = o(1)$ whenever $m/n > r_s^+$. Then, non-satisfiability follows by using the *first moment method*, i.e. Markov's inequality,

$$Pr[\mathcal{Z} > 0] \leq \mathbb{E}[\mathcal{Z}].$$

This approach implies that $r_s^+ = 2^k \ln 2$. The authors in [49] improve further on the upper bound from the first moment and get $r_s^+ = 2^k \ln 2 - (1 + \ln 2)/2 + o_k(1)$ which is correct in the second order asymptotic term.

Someone could expect that the lower bound r_s^- would follow by using the *second moment method*. That is, for r_s^- as big as possible to show that $\mathbb{E}[\mathcal{Z}] \to \infty$, while $\mathbb{E}[\mathcal{Z}^2] \sim \mathbb{E}^2[\mathcal{Z}]$, for any $m/n < r_s^-$. Then, using Payley-Sigmund inequality we could get that

$$Pr[\mathcal{Z} > 0] \geq \frac{\mathbb{E}^2[\mathcal{Z}]}{\mathbb{E}[\mathcal{Z}^2]} = 1 - o(1). \tag{5}$$

It turns out that the use of the second moment method as we describe above is not possible. The reason why the above does not hold is because $\mathbb{E}[\mathcal{Z}^2] = \omega(1)\mathbb{E}^2[\mathcal{Z}]$. That is, the second moment of the number of solutions of a random k-SAT formula is *asymptotically greater* than the square of the first moment. To this end, the attempt was to construct an algorithm which finds satisfying solutions on typical instances of $F_{n,m,k}$ when $m/n < r_s^-$, i.e. show that solutions exist by finding one.

Remark 9. In a retrospect we know that any algorithmic approach has to deal with the reconstruction phase transition. The reconstruction threshold is much lower, density-wise, than the satisfiability threshold.

It is elementary to see that finding a solution requires more "effort" than just showing that one exists. Returning to the second moment approach, it turns out that it is possible to circumvent to above problems by noting the following. The fact that $\mathbb{E}[\mathcal{Z}^2] = \omega(1)\mathbb{E}^2[\mathcal{Z}]$ is mainly because the solutions of a random formula $F_{n,m,k}$ are "too correlated" with each other. In particular, the performance of the the the second moment method relies on the pairwise independence between the solutions.

In these terms, there was a breakthrough in [4]. There the authors, developed a new setting where they can use the second moment method to show existence of solutions. This method turned out to be much stronger that any algorithmic attempt. They circumvent the correlation problems by taking $\mathcal{Z}$ so that it counts the size of a special subset of solutions, rather than the whole set. In particular, in [4] the authors improve on the lower bound on satisfiability be setting $\mathcal{Z}$ to count the so-called "Not-All-Equal" (NAE) satisfying assignments of $F_{n,m,k}$. A NAE satisfying assignment stipulates that each clause should have one literal which is satisfied and one that is not. The choice of counting the number of this kind of solutions was not a coincidence. Somehow, random pairs of NAE solutions are pairwise independent. This new approach showed that $r_s^- \geq 2^{k-1} \ln 2 - O(1)$. This result was a great improvement compared to the previous, algorithmic, lower bound which was $\Omega(2^k/k)$ [22].

In particular, the author in [4] showed that for densities up to $2^{k-1} \ln 2 - O(1)$ it holds that $\mathbb{E}[\mathcal{Z}^2] \leq C \cdot \mathbb{E}^2[\mathcal{Z}]$ for sufficiently large fixed number $C > 0$. This result combined with (5) implies that a random formula $F_{n,m,k}$ is satisfiable with *strictly positive probability*. Then, it follows that the satisfiability holds with probability $1 - o(1)$ by using standard arguments about sharp thresholds [35].

Subsequent to [4], the result in [6] estimates the satisfiability threshold up to some quantity $O(k)$. In particular they show that $r_s^- = 2^k \ln 2 - O(k)$. The technique in this result apart from choosing appropriately solutions it also imposes weights to each solution.

Further results [15, 19] consider densities inside the condensation phase. This is highly challenging as in this phase the solutions become *extremely correlated*. An ingredient of the works in [15, 19] is that a lot of their techniques are motivated by the prediction from statistical physicist we presented in Sect. 2. This gives even better bounds for r_s, i.e. $r_s^+ - r_s^- = \epsilon_k$ where $\lim_{k \to \infty} \epsilon_k = 0$. In particular it holds

$$r_s = 2^k \ln 2 - \frac{1}{2}(1 + \ln 2) + \epsilon_k. \tag{6}$$

However, the above bound is not sufficient to show the satisfiability conjecture for random k-SAT. Quite recently, the work [26] resolves the satisfiability threshold conjecture. That is, improving on ideas from [15], the authors in [26] find precisely the satisfiability threshold r_s, which is of similar form as in (6). The authors in [26] show that if the density deviates by $o(n)$ around the critical value r_s, then we get from almost certain satisfiability to almost certain unsatisfiability.

Remark 10. Currently, the best algorithm find that solutions of typical instances of k-SAT for densities up to $2^k \ln k/k$, [14].

Estimations of the satisfiability thresholds for other rCSP problems can be found in [20, 21, 23].

4   Algorithm Dynamics

One could claim that algorithm dynamics are, at least, as old as the use of programmable computers by physicists. These kind of algorithms are studied from computer scientists usually in the context of *Markov Chain Monte Carlo* sampling and *optimization*. Most popular examples are *Glauber Dynamics* [44], *Metropolis Process* [56] and *Simulated Annealing* [48]. These algorithms, the dynamicses, are simple randomized processes. Mostly they simulate a certain kind of *random walk* on the solution space of a given rCSP instance. To that extent, this makes them a quite natural class of algorithms.

Even though they are very *simple, local* and *easy to implement,* understanding the behaviour of these dynamicses, largely, has been elusive. Analyzing their performance is far from a trivial task. In most cases of interest, the gap between their conjectured and their rigorously proved performance is big.

Remark 11. The physicists' insight on this comes mainly from the analogy between the dynamics of algorithms and the physical dynamics of systems in nature.

Each dynamics gives rise to a well defined equilibrium distribution, which usually is the Gibbs distribution. Given such a process, one objective is to study the *rate of convergence,* i.e. how fast does the process converge to its equilibrium distribution. Another aspect of these process involves studying them in the context of *optimization.* That is, we view the rCSP as an optimization problem and use the dynamics to get a solution as close to the optimal as possible.

4.1 Convergence of Glauber Dynamics

Mathematically, we model the dynamics by using finite state, (discrete time) *Markov chains.* Typically, the state space Ω is the solutions of a given rCSP instance. The transition rule of the Markov chain specifies the kind of dynamics we use, e.g. here we consider Glauber dynamics. Typically, we focus on the cases where the chain satisfies a set of conditions which come with the name *ergodicity.* In our setting, ergodicity is equivalent to having a connected state space, i.e. the chain can get from one state to any other state by using a sequence of transitions such that each one of the transitions has strictly positive probability. It is well known that an ergodic Markov chain converges to a well defined *equilibrium distribution.* For the Glauber dynamics the equilibrium distribution is the Gibbs distribution.

Remark 12. In what follows the Markov chains we consider are *discrete time* ones.

For the sake of concreteness our focus is on the Glauber dynamic on the k-colourings of $G(n, m)$. This corresponds to a Markov chain with state space Ω the set of proper k-colouring of $G(n, m)$. The equilibrium distribution is the uniform distribution over the k-colourings of the underlying graph (Gibbs distribution).

In what follows we describe, in its simples form, the Markov chain which corresponds to Glauber dynamics. We let $\{X_t\}_{t \geq 0}$ denote the state of the chain at time t. The initial configuration X_0 is, usually, an arbitrary configuration. For every $t \geq 0$, given X_t, we get to the state X_{t+1} as follows:

1. Choose uniformly at random on vertex v from the set of vertices
2. Set $X_{t+1}(w) = X_t(w)$, for every vertex $w \neq v$
3. Set $X_{t+1}(v)$ according to Gibbs distribution conditional the colouring of the rest of the graph.

The last step implies that for $X_{t+1}(v)$ we choose uniformly at random a colour among those which do not appear in the neighborhood of the vertex v under X_t.

The above method of updates is called *single site* update since each transition changes the colour of a single vertex. Alternatively, some can choose to update small blocks of vertices than single vertices. This alternative for updates is known as *block dynamics*. Here we consider block dynamics.

The idea is to use an algorithm to simulate the aforementioned Markov chain. The measure of performance is the rate of convergence to the equilibrium distribution. For this we use the notion of *mixing time*. The mixing time is defined as the number of transitions required from the chain to reach within total variation distance $1/e$ from the equilibrium distribution, regardless of its initial state. What is desirable is to have *rapid mixing*. We say that a chain is rapidly mixing when its mixing time is upper bounded by some polynomial of the size of underlying graph instance.

Remark 13. For an efficient random colouring algorithm, additionally to rapid mixing, it is necessary that we get a proper k-colouring of the underlying graph efficiently. For the range of k we consider here, k-colouring the underlying graph can be done efficiently by using standard methods.

The problem of establishing rapid mixing when the underlying graph is $G(n, m)$ is a rather interesting one. There are many ingredients into the problem which make it challenging. The first one, and possibly the most obvious, is that someone has to deal with the so called *high degree effect*. That is, there is a relative large fluctuation on the degrees of the vertices in the random graph. E.g. it is elementary to show that typical instances of $G(n, m)$ with fixed expected degree d have maximum degree which is equal to $\Theta\left(\frac{\log n}{\log\log n}\right)$, while more than, say, 99.999 % of the vertices have degree in the interval $(1 \pm 10^{-3})d$. Usually the bounds for rapid mixing in terms of k are expressed as functions of the maximum degree, e.g. see [29,37,39,41,54,55,63,66,67]. However, from the above discussion it seems natural that for the case of $G(n, m)$ the bound for mixing time should depend on the *expected degree* rather than the *maximum degree*. This picture is also supported not only by non rigorous predictions but from a series of rigorous results too, i.e. [31,61].

In what follows, we give a brief overview of the work in [31] which provides the best bound for rapid mixing of Glauber dynamics for k-colouring[2] of $G(n, m)$ with expected degree $d = 2m/n^3$.

It seems natural to consider block updates rather than single vertex updates. That is, there is a collection of appropriately defined blocks $\mathcal{B}$ and at each step t the Markov chain updates the colouring of a randomly chosen block from $\mathcal{B}$. This approach relies on the observation from [27] that the effect of high degrees

---

[2] The interested reader can find rapid mixing bound fro the *hard-core model* (weighted independent sets), too.

[3] The paper in [31] is for $G(n, p)$ model for $p = d/n$, the result for $G(n, m)$ follow by using standard arguments.

somehow diminishes when high degree vertices are away from the boundary of their block. Devising such a block construction is a complex task. Examples of strategies for creating blocks can also be found in [27,31,61].

The rapid mixing property of the algorithm follows from using the well-known *Path Coupling* technique [13]. The technique summarizes as follows: For the sake of brevity, assume initially that we have single site updates instead of block dynamics. Consider any two copies of the Markov chain, i.e. at state X_0, Y_0, respectively. We take arbitrary X_0, Y_0 on the condition that they have exactly one disagreement, i.e. their Hamming distance $H(X_0, Y_0) = 1$. The coupling carries out one transition of each copy of the chain. Let X_1, Y_1 be the colouring after each transition, respectively. A sufficient condition for rapid mixing is to exist a coupling such that

$$\mathbb{E}[H(X_1, Y_1) | X_0, Y_0] \leq 1 - \Theta\left(n^{-1}\right), \tag{7}$$

where the expectation is w.r.t. the coupling.

To study the path coupling technique further, assume now that for $w \in V$ we have $X_0(w) \neq Y(w)$. It is natural to use a coupling that updates the same vertex in both copies. The cases that matter are only those where the coupling chooses to update either the disagreeing vertex w or one of its neighbours. If the update involves the vertex w, then, trivially, we get that $X_1 = Y_1$. This happens with probability $1/n$, where $|V| = n$. On the other hand, if the update involves a neighbour of w, then X_1, Y_1 may have an extra disagreement. In particular, the update of a neighbour of w generates an extra disagreement with probability at most $\frac{1}{k-\Delta}$. Since the disagreeing vertex w has at most as many neighbours as the maximum degree Δ, the probability of having an extra disagreement is at most $\frac{\Delta}{n}\frac{1}{k-\Delta}$. Taking $k \geq 2\Delta + 1$, it is direct that (7) is satisfied.

In our setting, we consider two copies of the chain at states X_0, Y_0. The states differ only on the assignment of the vertex w. The coupling chooses uniformly at random a block B from the set of blocks $\mathcal{B}$ and updates the colouring of B in both chains. It turns out that the crucial case for proving (7) is when the outer boundary of B is not the same for both chains, i.e. the disagreeing vertex w is outside the block B but it is adjacent to some vertices in B. There, we need to upper bound the expected number of *disagreements*, the vertices which take different colour assignments after the update of the colouring. Note that the new disagreements are only among the vertices of B. The construction of the blocks in $\mathcal{B}$ should be such that the expected number of disagreements is minimized.

We use the well-known "*disagreement percolation*" coupling construction, [9] to bound the expected number of disagreements during the update of block B. The disagreement at the boundary of B prohibits identical coupling of $X_1(B)$ and $Y_1(B)$. The disagreement percolation assembles the coupling in a stepwise fashion moving away from w. Disagreements propagates into B along paths from w. A disagreement at vertex $u' \in B$ at distance r from w propagates to a neighbour u at distance $r + 1$ if $X_1(u) \neq Y_1(u)$. The disagreement percolation is dominated by an *independent* process such that each vertex $v \in B$ is disagreeing with probability

$$\varrho_v = \begin{cases} \frac{2}{k-(1+\alpha)d} & \text{if } \mathbf{degree}(v) \leq (1+\alpha)d \\ 1 & \text{otherwise,} \end{cases}$$

where $\alpha > 0$ is some small constant and $k \geq 5.5d$. The disagreement propagates over the path L that start from w with probability at most $\prod_{u \in L \setminus \{w\}} \varrho_u$. The expected number of disagreements is at most the expected number of paths of disagreements that start from w and propagate inside B.

Intuitively, high degree vertices are expected to have an increased contribution to the number of disagreements. Mainly this is due to the following reason: If a high degree vertex is disagreeing, it has an increased number of neighbours to propagate the disagreement. However, for typical $G(n, m)$ and $k \geq \frac{11}{2}d$, it turns out that the larger the distance between a high degree vertex from w the less probable is for the disagreement to reach it. This balances "on average" the increased contribution that high degree vertices have. We exploit this observation in the block construction.

To be more concrete, we introduce a weighting schema as follows: Each vertex u, of degree $\mathbf{degree}(u)$ in $G(n, m)$, is assigned weight $W(u)$ such that

$$W(u) = \begin{cases} (1+\gamma)^{-1} & \text{if } \mathbf{degree}(u) \leq (1+\alpha)d \\ d^c \cdot \mathbf{degree}(u) & \text{otherwise,} \end{cases} \tag{8}$$

for appropriate real numbers $\alpha, \gamma, c > 0$. Given the weights of the vertices, each block $B \in \mathcal{B}$ should satisfy the following two properties:

1. B is either a tree or a unicyclic graph
2. For every path L between a vertex at the outer boundary of B and a high degree vertex inside B it should hold that $\prod_{u \in L} W(u) \leq 1$.

Roughly speaking, 1. guarantees that the updates can be implemented efficiently, while 2. guarantees that the disagreement percolation coupling construction we describe above satisfies (7). For further details on how does 2. with Path coupling implies rapid mixing for the block updates, see in [31].

Efficient Colour Updates. For the algorithm to be efficient it is necessary that it can implement the update of each block in $\mathcal{B}$ in polynomial time. In our case, the updates can be implemented efficiently due to the fact that each block is a tree with at most one extra edge.

It is well known that someone can take a random k-colouring of a tree of maximum degree $O(\ln n)$ in polynomial time, as long as k is fixed. This can be done by just using *Dynamic Programming* (DP) to enumerate all the k-colourings of the tree and then choose one at random. This implies that the Glauber dynamics, above, can update the colouring of a block when this block is a tree.

For the case where the block is a unicyclic graph, i.e. tree with an extra edge, it is still possible to take a random k-colouring. In this case, we consider all the possible $k(k-1)$ possible colorings of the ends of the extra edge. For every such colouring we employ DP and count, in polynomial time, the k-colourings of the remaining structure which now is a tree. Clearly, this implies that we can count efficiently all the k-colouring of the unicyclic block in polynomial time. In turn, this means that we can generate one at random.

Efficient Block Creation. Another important issue for the efficiency of the algorithm is to be able to create a set of block which has the aforementioned properties. For creating such a set of blocks, we need to distinguish the vertices u in $G(n, m)$ such that all the paths that emanate from u are of low weight, i.e. weight less than 1. These vertices are important for the creation of blocks and we call them *break points*.

Definition 1 (Influence). *For a vertex v, let $\mathcal{P}(v)$ denote the set of all paths of length at most $\frac{\ln n}{d^{2/5}}$ that start from v. We call "influence" on the vertex v, denoted as $E(v)$, the following quantity:*

$$E(v) = \max_{L \in \mathcal{P}(v)} \left\{ \prod_{u \in L} W(u) \right\}.$$

A vertex v is considered to be under no influence if $E(v) \leq 1$. The vertices under no influence are the break points. It is necessary to make the following observation: For typical instances of $G(n, m)$, if for some vertex v the influence $E(v) < 1$, then there is no path L that emanates from v such that $|L| > \log n / d^{2/5}$ while $\prod_{u \in L} W(u) > 1$.

The break points are used to specify the boundaries of the blocks. In what follows, a path L that does not contain break-points is called *"influence path"*.

Block Creation: We have two different kinds of blocks. Let $\mathcal{C}$ denote the set of all cycles of length at most $4 \frac{\ln n}{\ln^5 d}$ in $G(n, m)$.

1. For each $C \in \mathcal{C}$ we have a block which contains every vertex $v \in C$ as well as all the vertices that are reachable from v through an influence path that does not use vertices of $C \backslash \{v\}$.
2. The remaining blocks are created as follows:
   (a) Pick a vertex v which is not a break point and does not belong to any block, so far. Consider as a new block the vertex v and all the vertices that are reachable from v through an influence path.
   (b) Each vertex which does not belong to a block after steps 1 and 2.a can only be a break point. Each break point becomes a single vertex block.

For typical instances of $G(n, m)$, the above construction gives rise to a set of blocks $\mathcal{B}$ such that each block in the set is a tree with at most one extra edge. This follows mainly because the influence paths considered during the construction are rather short, while the graph $G(n, m)$ is locally either tree-like or unicyclic.

The challenging part for creating the blocks is to distinguish which vertices are the break points. This can be done in polynomial time due to the following reasons: (A) We need to check the weight of relatively short paths around each vertex i.e. length $l_0 = \ln n / d^{2/5}$. (B) The structure within distance $\ln n / d^{2/5}$ around each vertex, in typical instances of $G(n, m)$, is a tree with at most one extra edge. This means that we need to check only polynomially many paths around each vertex so as to decide if it is a break point or not. For further details see in [31].

Main Result. With probability $1-o(1)$ over the instances of $G(n,m)$ the following is true: The graph admits a block partition $\mathcal{B}$ as we describe above. The Glauber block dynamics, with set of blocks $\mathcal{B}$, over the k-colourings of $G(n,m)$ has rapid mixing for any fixed $k \geq 5.5d$.

Concluding Remarks - Cavity Method's Perspective. It is an empirical fact that the rate of convergence of the Glauber dynamics is hugely affected by the phase transitions predicted by the cavity method. As far as the k-colourings problem is regarded, the picture seems to be as follows: In the uniqueness region, the dynamics has rapid mixing regardless of its initial state. In the non-reconstruction region the state space is not connected, which implies that the chain is non-ergodic. However, restricting the dynamics on the colourings of the giant ball (which includes all but an exponentially small fraction of colourings) we expect to have rapid mixing. On the other hand, in subsequent phases, i.e. from the reconstruction phase and on, there is no ergodicity at all[4].

It wouldn't be far fetched to conjecture that the spatial mixing conditions in (2) and (3) imply rapid mixing for the Glauber dynamics in the way we describe above. How this can be established for $G(n,m)$ remains a challenging open problem.

4.2   Dynamics and Optimization

For certain cases (e.g. [1,16]) it has been proven that from the reconstruction phase and on, the dynamicses do not converge fast, or they do not converge at all. It could seem that this behaviour limits the applicability of the dynamics. It turns out that this is not the case. There is a wealth of different kind of problems that the dynamics may find applications. The new setting now is the *optimization problems.*

The general framework is the following one: we consider a set of configurations and some cost function. The dynamics starts from some "easily accessible" configuration. Then, iteratively it tries to get to a better configuration, i.e. better w.r.t to the cost function. A set of different rearrangement operations can be applied until some configuration that improves the cost function is discovered. The rearranged configuration then becomes the new configuration of the dynamics. The process is continued until no further improvements can be found[5].

For the shake of exposition we shift problem by considering the independent set problem, instead of k-colouring. That is, we consider the problem of finding

---

[4] There are cases where the dynamics remains ergodic beyond non-reconstruction, e.g. hard-core model. In these cases the non-ergodicity is substituted by "low conductance", which implies slow mixing.

[5] Since this search usually gets stuck in a local but not a global optimum, it is customary to carry out the process several times, starting from different configurations, and save the best result.

an independent set[6] of a graph G of a specific size k. For the cases where the underlying graph is $G(n, m)$, the Metropolis process [56] has been proposed for solution [43]. This problem is closely related to the problem of finding (hidden) cliques in random graphs [7].

Let us give a brief description of the Metropolis process. There is a parameter $\lambda \geq 1$, called *fugacity*. Given a graph G the state space of the process is the set of all independent sets of G. The process is a discrete time one. Let I_t be the state at step t. Given I_t we get I_{t+1} as follows:

1. Choose a vertex $v \in G$ uniformly at random.
2. If $v \notin I_t$ but also v's neighbour do not belong in I_t, then $I_{t+1} = I_t \cup \{v\}$
3. If $v \in I_t$, then
   (a) with probability $1/\lambda$ set $I_{t+1} = I_t \setminus \{v\}$, i.e. remove v from I_t
   (b) with probability $1 - 1/\lambda$ set $I_{t+1} = I_t$

The process above always converges to an equilibrium distribution μ which assigns to each independent set σ probability measure $\mu(\sigma)$ such that

$$\mu(\sigma) = Z^{-1}\lambda^{|\sigma|},$$

where $|\sigma|$ is the cardinality of σ and Z is a normalizing quantity. The above Gibbs distribution is also known as the *Hard-Core model* with underlying graph G. We have seen the normalizing quantity Z in Sect. 2 under the name partition function.

In particular, for the case of $G(n, m)$, someone can control to a great precision the size of the independent set that the process is going to be in its equilibrium. That is, the independent sets of a specific size dominate the equilibrium measure. Clearly, one could get a large independent set by setting λ appropriately and run the Metropolis process and wait until the process gets close to equilibrium.

Unfortunately the above approach for finding large independent sets is far from efficient. It is well known that the size of maximum independent set of $G(n, m)$ is $2n \ln d/d$, e.g. see [23]. The independent sets which correspond to the "reconstruction" region are those of size bigger than half the maximum, i.e. of size $(1 + \epsilon)n \ln d/d$. It does not come as a surprise that when we set λ so as to the equilibrium measure is dominated by independent sets of size $(1 + \epsilon)n \ln d/d$, the mixing time is exponential in n. This follows by just using geometric arguments like *conductance* as in [16, 43].

It seems that waiting for the process to converge rapidly is asking too much! From optimization's perspective, Metropolis process can be seen as a *greedy, randomized* algorithm which *backtracks*. I.e. it is a reminiscent of the famous *Karp-Sipser algorithm* [46], with backtracking (step 3(a)). Backtracking helps the process to get unstuck from a local maxima. It is natural to ask what is the probability for the process to hit a large independent set, within a not so long period of time, e.g. within polynomially many number of transitions. It seems

---

[6] Independent set of a graph is any subset of its vertices which do not span any edge with each other.

that the choice of the initial configuration is important for the performance of the process. To analyze the process in this setting we need to study its behaviour when it is in away from equilibrium.

It is not hard to draw a parallel between the abstract description of the optimization process we presented and the example of Metropolis process. Of course one does not need to restrict only on the Metropolis process, there are many alternatives e.g. *Simulated Annealing* [48]. Even though the idea of using such dynamics for combinatorial optimization goes back many decades, the performance of these algorithms is not so well understood.

The recent developments in the cavity method, provide explanations (to a certain extent) and hints about the behaviour of the algorithms above. However, it seems that their analysis calls for an approach somehow complementary to what the cavity method provides. Essentially we need to analyzing the drift of these processes as the evolve in their configuration space. Interestingly, the new questions call for a more elaborate description of the geometry than what we get from cavity method.

5   Algorithms Beyond Dynamics

Spatial mixing expresses in a very specific way a notion of locality about the Gibbs distribution. The promise of locality we get from conditions such as (2), (3) makes it natural to ask whether we can use them for novel algorithms which achieve the same objectives as the Monte Carlo ones. In this section we discuss exactly this prospect.

The spatial mixing conditions in (2), (3) suggest that there is a weak dependence between the colour assignment of some vertex v and colouring of relatively distant vertices. E.g. the Gibbs marginal of the colour assignment of a vertex v is a "*local quantity*". The algorithmic question now is, how can we use this "local quantities" to create an approximate sample of the Gibbs distribution. Or, even if this is not possible, how can we compute *arithmetically* good approximations of marginals of the Gibbs distribution[7].

The above question motivated, recently, many new algorithms, mostly non Monte Carlo ones. In a sense, these new algorithms seem to be "more deterministic" than their Monte Carlo counterparts. Usually the approximation guarantees they achieve are weaker. On the other hand, they tend to be more robust, e.g. they do not require conditions like ergodicity e.t.c. Furthermore, they tend to be more susceptible to analysis. Our focus is on two different categories of algorithms of these kinds. The first involves a combinatorial one while the second involves numerical.

5.1   Combinatorial Algorithms

In what follows we provide a high level description of an algorithm, introduced in [30], for approximate random colourings of $G(n,m)$[8]. The best bound in terms of

---

[7] Somehow the problem of computing marginals turns out to be easier than sampling.

[8] The algorithm in [30] is for the related $G(n,p)$ where $p = d/n$. result for $G(n,m)$ follows by just using standard arguments.

k for this algorithm is $k = (1 + \epsilon)d$ and appears in [32]. This is the best efficient algorithm for approximate sampling colourings of $G(n, m)$ in terms of minimum number of colours required.

It is well known that the typically the structure of $G(n, m)$ is highly complex. This is the reason why random colouring typical instances of $G(n, m)$ is a highly non trivial computational task. The idea now is the following: First, remove edges of the input instance of $G(n, m)$ until it becomes so simple that we can take a random colouring the resulting graph in polynomial time. Then, we *rebuild* the graph by adding *iteratively* the edges we deleted in the first place. Additionally, every time we add a new edge we *update the colouring*. I.e. whenever a new edge is inserted some vertices' colour assignments is updated so that the resulting colouring remains random[9]. The algorithm is efficient because the updates are implemented efficiently.

So as to give a high level description of the algorithm, first we need to introduce the notion of *switching* colouring. For this we define the *disagreement graph*. Consider a fixed graph G and let v be a distinguished vertex in G. Let σ be a k-colouring of G and let some colour $q \neq \sigma(v)$. Under the colouring σ, we denote by $V_{\sigma(v)}, V_q$ the colour classes of $\sigma(v)$, and q, respectively. We call *disagreement graph* $Q_{\sigma(v),q}$ the maximal, connected, induced subgraph of G which includes v and vertices only from the set $V_{\sigma_v} \cup V_q$. E.g. in Fig. 2, the disagreement graph $Q_{B,G}$ is the one with the fat lines.

Definition 2 (switching). *Consider G, v, σ and q as specified above. The "q-switching of σ" corresponds to the proper colouring of G which is derived by exchanging the assignments in the two colour classes in $Q_{\sigma_v,q}$.*

Figure 3 illustrates a switching of the colouring in Fig. 2. Observe that the colouring in Fig. 3 differs from the colouring in Fig. 2 to that we have exchanged the two colour classes of the subgraph with the fat lines. We would like to emphasize that the q-switching of any proper colouring of G is always a proper colouring too.

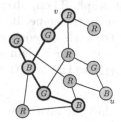

Fig. 2. "Disagreement graph".

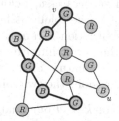

Fig. 3. "g-switching".

Now, we proceed with a high level description of the algorithm. The input is an instance of $G(n, m)$ with expected degree d and k, the numbers of colours.

---

[9] To be more precise the colour remains asymptotically random.

The algorithm is as follows:

Set Up: We construct a sequence $G_0, \ldots, G_r$ such that every G_i is a subgraph of $G(n, m)$. The graph G_r is identical to $G(n, m)$. Each G_i is derived by deleting from G_{i+1} the edge $\{v_i, u_i\}$. This edge is chosen at random among those which do not belong to a *short cycle* of G_{i+1}. We call short, any cycle of length less than $(\log n)/(9 \log d)$. G_0 is the graph we get when there are no other edges to delete.

With probability $1 - n^{-\Omega(1)}$, over the instances of $G(n, m)$, G_0 is very simple, in terms of its component structure. In particular, each component of G_0 is either an isolated vertex, or an isolated simple cycle. It is standard to show how to colour randomly G_0 in polynomial number of step, i.e. use Dynamic Programing see [32]. Assuming that we deal with such an instance, the algorithm works as follows:

The Updates: Take a random colouring of G_0. Let Y_0 be that colouring. Colour the rest graphs according to the following inductive rule: Given that G_i is coloured Y_i, so as to get Y_{i+1}, the colouring for the graph G_{i+1} we distinguish two cases

Case (a): Under Y_i (the colouring of G_i) the vertices v_i and u_i are assigned
    different colours, i.e. $Y_i(v_i) \neq Y(u_i)$.
Case (b): Under Y_i the vertices v_i and u_i are assigned the same colour, i.e.
    $Y_i(v_i) = Y(u_i)$.

In the first case, we just set $Y_{i+1} = Y_i$, i.e. G_{i+1} gets the same colouring as G_i. In the second case, we choose q uniformly at random among all the colours but $Y_i(v_i)$. Then we set Y_{i+1} equal to the q-switching of Y_i. The q-switching is w.r.t. the vertex v_i.

With the above, we finish the high level description of the algorithm.

The reader may have observed that the switching does not necessarily provide a k-colouring where the assignments of v_i and u_i are different. That is, it may be that both vertices v_i, u_i belong to the disagreement graph. Then, after the q-switching of Y_i the colour assignments of v_i and u_i remain the same. It turns out that this situation is rare as long as $k \geq (1 + \epsilon)d$. For such k, most of the times, after the q-switching the vertices v_i, u_i get different colour assignments. The approximate nature of the algorithm amounts exactly to the fact that on some, rare, occasions the switching somehow fails.

Remark 14. For $k \leq d$ our analysis cannot guarantee that the switching fails only on rare occasions.

Main Result. Let $k \geq (1 + \epsilon)d$, for fixed $\epsilon > 0$ and sufficiently large d. With probability $1 - o(1)$ over the input instances $G(n, m)$ with expected degree d, the above algorithm returns, in polynomial time, a k-colouring whose distribution ν has the following property

$$||\nu - \mu||_{TV} \le n^{-\Omega(1)},$$

where μ is the Gibbs distribution of the input graph.

Remark 15. For the MCMC algorithms, the more we allow the algorithm to run the smaller the error at the out gets. The the error of the above algorithm is a vanishing function of n which does not depend on the execution time of the algorithm.

The success of the algorithm relies on the fact that, at each iteration, the recolouring takes place only on a restricted part of the graph. In particular, what we want to have is that the colouring of a single vertex should have a vanishing effect on the distribution of the colouring of distant vertices. This condition is equivalent to non-reconstruction condition. Somehow the algorithm in [30] is the first sampling algorithm whose accuracy is proved to depend on non-reconstruction. Actually this relation is immediate.

The fact that the algorithm, in its current form, requires $(1 + \epsilon)d$ colours while non-reconstruction holds for $(1 + \epsilon)d/\ln d$ implies that there is room for improvement. The current approach does not seem to take full advantage of the of the spatial mixing condition required due to its update rule, i.e. an improved, rule is required.

Another very interesting direction for study is to investigate whether the ideas in [30] can be exploited for different models, like hard core model (weighted independent sets), random k-SAT e.t.c. The main difference between colouring and the other models is that colouring is, somehow, symmetric and this helps the algorithm (the update rule).

5.2   Numerical Algorithms - Message Passing

This category includes the well known *Belief Propagation* (BP) [62] and *Survey Propagation* (SP) [11] algorithms. Both of them belongs to the family of the so-called *message passing algorithms*. BP is closely related to *sum-product* algorithms from *information theory* [51]. We should mention that the applicability of message passing algorithm goes far beyond the algorithmic theory of r-CSP. They are widely used in *information theory* e.g. for the so-called LDPC codes, e.g. [64], in Artificial Intelligence e.g. [62] Computer Vision, e.g. [34], and many other areas.

In our context, BP and SP can be viewed as an attempt to turn the cavity method into an efficient algorithm. Roughly speaking, their basic objective is the following one: There is a target distribution, typically, a Gibbs distribution (or a "Gibbs-like" distribution). W.l.o.g. in what follows, the reader may very well consider the Gibbs distribution over the k-colouring. The algorithm computes numerically approximations of marginals of the target distribution. In order to do so it performs a certain kind of fixed point computations. The accuracy of these computations depends heavily on certain *spatial mixing properties* of the target distribution.

In more standard terms, BP (and SP) computes marginals by using *dynamic programming* (DP). DP is a basic and widely known technique for computations which is based on the *divide and conquer* principle. So as the message passing algorithm to use dynamics programing it exploits the fact that the typical instances of rCSP, locally, look tree-like. Of course the global structure is way more complicated than a tree. The idea is that spatial mixing properties of the target distribution, somehow, prevents the rest of the graph to affect too much the computations of the marginals.

An additional feature of the message passing algorithms is that they compute the dynamic program in parallel for every variable. Somehow, the results of the local computations travel among variables of the same constrains by using the so-called messages[10].

Worst case spatial mixing conditions such as uniqueness somehow suffices to show that the algorithm converges, i.e. computes with reasonable accuracy the marginals. In particular this happens regardless of the initial conditions of the dynamic program. It is believed that this is the case when *weaker spatial mixing conditions* hold, like non-reconstruction. However, for weaker conditions it is not straightforward what is the behaviour of the algorithm. It seems that the initial conditions of the algorithm may be very influential on the convergence. That is, it is not clear whether there is something that prevents things go "wrong" when the algorithm starts from some "bad" initial condition. The hope is that somehow every vertex tries to compute the correct marginal and somehow this help the rest vertices to compute more accurately their marginals and so on. What is the exact behaviour of the algorithm is not well understood yet.

As far as SP is regarded the study of its behaviour seems even more challenging. It is supposed that it computes marginals from reconstruction region and on. The target distribution is considered w.r.t. clusters of solutions (not the actual solutions as the Gibbs distribution does). The hypothesis is that SP is sufficiently accurate due to certain spatial mixing conditions of its target distribution.

Of course, the study of message passing algorithm in the context of rCSP goes much further. E.g. it can consider the so-called *dissemination processes*. This means that we assign each variable iteratively by using marginals that are computed by the algorithm. That is, at each iteration the, say, BP computes Gibbs marginals. Then we pick one vertex and assign it a value according to the marginal the algorithm has computed. In the next iteration the algorithm repeats the computations with the value of this variable fixed. This process is even more complicate to analyze as as we need to establish spatial mixing conditions when some variables have fixed values (not necessarily according to Gibbs distribution).

Acknowledgement. Most of the material in the introduction come from discussions with Amin Coja-Oghlan. For this reason I would like to thank him.

---

[10] This justifies the name message passing algorithm.

References

1. Achlioptas, D., Coja-Oghlan, A.: Algorithmic Barriers from Phase Transitions. In: Proceedings of 49th IEEE Symposium on Foundations of Computer Science, FOCS (2008)
2. Achlioptas, D., Coja-Oghlan, A., Ricci-Tersenghi, F.: On the solution-space geometry of random constraint satisfaction problems. Random Struct. Algorithms **38**(3), 251–268 (2011)
3. Achlioptas, D., Friedgut, E.: A sharp threshold for k-colorability. Random Struct. Algorithms **14**(1), 63–70 (1999)
4. Achlioptas, D., Moore, C.: Random k-SAT: two moments suffice to cross a sharp threshold. SIAM J. Comput. **36**(3), 740–762 (2006)
5. Achlioptas, D., Naor, A.: The two possible values of the chromatic number of a random graph. Ann. Math. **162**(3), 1333–1349 (2005)
6. Achlioptas, D., Peres, Y.: The threshold for random k-SAT is $2^k \log 2 - O(k)$. J. AMS **17**, 947–973 (2004)
7. Alon, N., Krivelevich, M., Sudakov, B.: Finding a large hidden clique in a random graph. In: Proceedings of 9th ACM-SIAM Symposium on Discrete Algorithms, SODA 1998 (1998)
8. Bapst, V., Coja-Oghlan, A., Hetterich, S., Rassmann, F., Vilenchik, D.: The condensation phase transition in random graph coloring. In: proceedings of APPROX-RANDOM 2014, pp. 449–464 (2014)
9. van den Berg, J., Maes, C.: Disagreement percolation in the study of Markov fields. Ann. Probab. **22**, 749–763 (1994)
10. Bhatnagar, N., Sly, A., Tetali, P.: Decay of Correlations for the Hardcore Model on the d-regular Random Graph. http://arxiv.org/abs/1405.6160
11. Braunstein, A., Mézard, A., Zecchina, R.: Survey propagation: an algorithm for satisfiability. Random Struct. Algorithms **27**, 201–226 (2004)
12. Brightwell, G., Winkler, P.: A second threshold for the hard-core model on a Bethe lattice. Random Struct. Algorithms **24**, 303–314 (2004)
13. Bubley, R., Dyer, M.: Path coupling: a technique for proving rapid mixing in markov chains. In: proceedings of 38th FOCS, pp 223–231 (1997)
14. Coja-Oghlan, A.: A Better Algorithm for Random k-SAT. In: proceedings of ICALP (1) 2009: 292–303. SIAM J. Comput. **39**(7) 2823–2864 (2010)
15. Coja-Oghlan, A.: The asymptotic k-SAT threshold. In: proceedings of STOC 2014: 804–813 (2014)
16. Coja-Oghlan, A., Efthymiou, C.: On independent sets in Random Graphs. In: Proceedings of 22nd ACM-SIAM Symposium on Discrete Algorithms, SODA 2011, pp 136–144 (2011)
17. Coja-Oghlan, A., Efthymiou, C., Hetterich, S.: On the chromatic number of random regular graphs. http://arxiv.org/abs/1308.4287
18. Coja-Oghlan, A., Efthymiou, C., Jaafari, N.: Local convergence of random graph colorings. http://arxiv.org/abs/1501.06301
19. Coja-Oghlan, A., Panagiotou, K.: Going after the k-SAT threshold. In: procedings of STOC 2013: 705–714 (2013)
20. Coja-Oghlan, A., Panagiotou, K.: Catching the k-NAESAT threshold. In: proceedings of STOC 2012: 899–908 (2012)
21. Coja-Oghlan, A., Vilenchik, D.: Chasing the k-colorability threshold. In: Proceedings of 54th IEEE Symposium on Foundations of Computer Science, FOCS 2013, pp 380–389 (2013)

22. Chvátal, V., Reed, B.: Mick gets some (the odds are on his side). In: Proceedings of the 33rd Annual IEEE Symposium on Foundations of Computer Science, pp. 620–627 (1992)
23. Dani, V., Moore, C.: Independent sets in random graphs from the weighted second moment method. In: Goldberg, L.A., Jansen, K., Ravi, R., Rolim, J.D.P. (eds.) RANDOM 2011 and APPROX 2011. LNCS, vol. 6845, pp. 472–482. Springer, Heidelberg (2011)
24. Ding, J., Sly, A., Sun, N.: Maximum independent sets on random regular graphs. http://arxiv.org/abs/1310.4787
25. Ding, J., Sly, A., Sun, N.: Satisfiability threshold for random regular NAE-SAT. In: proceedings of STOC 2014: 814–822 (2014)
26. Ding, J., Sly, A., Sun, N.: Proof of the satisfiability conjecture for large k. To appear in STOC 2015 (2015)
27. Dyer, M., Flaxman, A., Frieze, A.M., Vigoda, E.: Random colouring sparse random graphs with fewer colours than the maximum degree. Random Struct. Algorithms **29**, 450–465 (2006)
28. Dyer, M.E., Frieze, A.M.: The solution of some random np-hard problems in polynomial expected time. J. Algorithms **10**(4), 451–489 (1989)
29. Dyer, M., Frieze, A.M., Hayes, A., Vigoda, E.: Randomly colouring constant degree graphs. In proceedings of 45th FOCS, pp 582–589 (2004)
30. Efthymiou, C.: A simple algorithm for random colouring $G(n, d/n)$ using $(2 + \epsilon)d$ colours. In: Proceedings of the 23rd ACM-SIAM Symposium on Discrete Algorithms, SODA 2012 (2012)
31. Efthymiou, C.: MCMC sampling colourings and independent sets of G(n, d/n) near the uniqueness threshold. In: proceedings of Symposium on Discrete Algorithms, SODA (2014)
32. Efthymiou, C.: Switching colouring of $G(n,d/n)$ for sampling up to gibbs uniqueness threshold. In: Schulz, A.S., Wagner, D. (eds.) ESA 2014. LNCS, vol. 8737, pp. 371–381. Springer, Heidelberg (2014)
33. Efthymiou, C.: Reconstruction/Non-reconstruction Thresholds for Colourings of General Galton-Watson Trees. CoRR abs/1406.3617 (2014)
34. Freeman, W.T., Paztor, E.C., Carmichael, O.T.: Learning low-level vision. Int. J. Comput. Vis. **40**, 25–47 (2000)
35. Friedgut, E.: Necessary and sufficient conditions for sharp thresholds of graph properties, and the k-SAT problem. J. Amer. Math. Soc. **12**, 1017–1054 (1999)
36. Frieze, A.M.: On the independence number of random graphs. Discrete Math. **81**(183), 171–175 (1990)
37. Frieze, A.M., Vera, J.: On randomly colouring locally sparse graphs. Discrete Math. & Theor. Comput. Sci. **8**(1), 121–128 (2006)
38. Georgii, H.O.: Gibbs Measures and Phase Transitions, de Gruyter Stud. Math. 9, de Gruyter, Berlin (1988)
39. Goldberg, L.A., Martin, R.A., Paterson, M.: Strong spatial mixing with fewer colors for lattice graphs. SIAM J. Comput. **35**(2), 486–517 (2005)
40. Grimmett, G.R., McDiarmid, C.J.H.: On colouring random graphs. Math. Proc. Camb. Phil. Soc. **77**(02), 313–332 (1975)
41. Hayes, T., Vera, J., Vigoda, E.: Randomly coloring planar graphs with fewer colors than the maximum degree. In: proceedings of 39th STOC, pp 450–458 (2007)
42. Held, M., Karp, R.M.: The traveling-salesman problem and minimum spanning trees. Oper. Res. **18**(6), 1138–1162 (1970)
43. Jerrum, M.R.: Large cliques elude the Metropolis process. Random Struct. Algorithms **3**, 347–359 (1992)

44. Jerrum, M.R., Sinclair, A.: The Markov chain Monte Carlo method: an approach to approximate counting and integration. In: Approximation Algorithms for NP-hard Problems, (Dorit Hochbaum, ed.), PWS (1996)
45. Jerrum, M., Sinclair, A., Vigoda, E.: A polynomial-time approximation algorithm for the permanent of a matrix with non-negative entries. J. ACM **51**(4), 671–697 (2004)
46. Karp, R., Sipser, M.: Maximum matchings in sparse random graphs. In: proceedings of FOCS 1981, pp. 364 375 (1981)
47. Kelly, F.P.: Loss networks. Ann. Appl. Probab. **1**(3), 319–378 (1991)
48. Kirkpatrick, S., Gelatt, C., Vecchi, M.: Optimisation by simulated annealing. Science **220**, 671–680 (1983)
49. Kirousis, L.M., Kranakis, E., Krizanc, D., Stamatiou, Y.C.: Approximating the unsatisfiability threshold of random formulas. Random Struct. Algor. **12**(3), 253–269 (1998)
50. Krzakala, F., Montanari, A., Ricci-Tersenghi, F., Semerjianc, G., Zdeborova, L.: Gibbs states and the set of solutions of random constraint satisfaction problems. Proc. Natl. Acad. Sci. **104**, 10318–10323 (2007)
51. Kschischang, F., Frey, B., Loeliger, H.A.: Factor graphs and the sum-product algorithm. IEEE Trans. Inf. Theory **47**, 498519 (2001)
52. Levin, D., Peres, Y., Wilmer, E.: Markov Chains and Mixing Times. American Mathematical Society (2008)
53. Lovász, L., Vempala, S.: Simulated annealing in convex bodies and an $O * (n^4)$ volume algorithm. In: Proceedings of the 44th IEEE Foundations of Computer Science (FOCS 2003) (2003). Also in JCSS (FOCS 2003 special issue)
54. Lucier, B., Molloy, M., Peres, Y.: The Glauber Dynamics for Colourings of Bounded Degree Trees. In: proceedings of RANDOM 2009, pp 631–645 (2009)
55. Martinelli, F., Sinclair, A., Weitz, D.: Fast mixing for independent sets, colorings and other models on trees. In: proceedings of 15th SODA, pp 456–465 (2004)
56. Metropolis, N., Rosenbluth, A.W., Rosenbluth, M.N., Teller, A.H., Teller, E.: Equation of state calculations by fast computing machines. J. Chem. Phys. **21**, 1087–1092 (1953)
57. Mézard, M., Parisi, G., Zecchina, R.: Analytic and algorithmic solution of random satisfiability problems. Science **297**(5582), 812–815 (2002)
58. Molloy, M.: The Glauber dynamics on the colourings of a graph with large girth and maximum degree. SIAM J. Comput. **33**, 721–737 (2004)
59. Montanari, A., Restrepo, R., Tetali, P.: Reconstruction and clustering in random constraint satisfaction problems. SIAM J. Discrete Math. **25**(2), 771–808 (2011)
60. Montanari, A., Shah, D.: Counting good truth assignments of random k-SAT formulae. In: proceedings of the 18th Annual ACM-SIAM, SODA 2007, pp 1255–1264 (2007)
61. Mossel, E., Sly, A.: Gibbs rapidly samples colorings of $G_{n,d/n}$. J. Probab. Theory Relat. fields **148**, 1–2 (2010)
62. Pearl, J.: Probabilistic reasoning in intelligent systems: Networks of plausible inference. Morgan-Kaufmann, Palo Alto (1988)
63. Restrepo, R., Stefankovic, D., Vera, J.C., Vigoda, E., Yang, L.: Phase transition for glauber dynamics for independent sets on regular trees. In: proceedings SODA 2011, pp 945–956 (2011)
64. Richardson, T., Urbanke, R.: The capacity of low-density parity check codes under message passing deconding. IEEE Trans. Inf. Theory **47**, 599–618 (2001)

65. Schöning, U.: A probabilistic algorithm for k-SAT and constraint satisfaction problems. In: proceedings of Symposium on Foundations of Computer Science, FOCS 1999, pp 410–419 (1999)
66. Tetali, P., Vera, J.C., Vigoda, E., Yang, L.: Phase transition for the mixing time of the glauber dynamics for coloring regular trees. In: proceedings of SODA 2010, pp 1646–1656 (2010)
67. Vigoda, E.: Improved bounds for sampling colorings. J. Math. Phys. **41**(3), 1555–1569 (2000). A preliminary version appears in FOCS 1999

A Selective Tour Through Congestion Games

Dimitris Fotakis[✉]

Division of Computer Science, School of Electrical and Computer Engineering,
National Technical University of Athens, 15780 Athens, Greece
fotakis@cs.ntua.gr

Abstract. We give a sketchy and mostly informal overview of research
on algorithmic properties of congestion games in the last ten years. We
discuss existence of potential functions and pure Nash equilibria in games
with weighted players, simple and fast algorithms that reach a pure Nash
equilibrium, and efficient approaches to improving the Price of Anarchy.

1 Introduction

Congestion games and their different variants and generalizations provide an elegant model for competitive resource allocation in large-scale telecommunication
and transportation networks and have been the subject of intensive research in
Algorithmic Game Theory. In an *atomic congestion game*, a finite set of non-
cooperative players, each controlling an unsplittable amount of traffic demand,
compete over a finite set of resources. All players using a resource experience a
delay given by a non-negative and non-decreasing function of the resource's load.
Among a given set of resource subsets (or strategies), each player selects one self-
ishly trying to minimize her *individual delay*, that is the sum of the delays on
the resources in the chosen strategy. A natural solution concept is that of a *pure
Nash equilibrium*, a configuration where no player can decrease her individual
delay by unilaterally switching to a different strategy. In other applications, we
consider *non-atomic congestion games* (or *selfish routing games*) where the traffic demand is divided among an infinite number of players, each controlling an
infinitesimal amount of traffic. Then, the Nash equilibrium is essentially unique,
under mild assumptions on the delay functions, and all players use strategies of
equal minimum delay at equilibrium.

The prevailing research questions about algorithmic properties of congestion
games have to do either with establishing the existence of pure Nash equilibria
and of potential functions for variants and generalizations of atomic games (see
e.g., [23,29,30,34,47]), or with bounding the convergence time to a pure Nash
equilibrium if the players select their strategies in a selfish and decentralized

This work was supported by the project Algorithmic Game Theory, co-financed
by the European Union (European Social Fund—ESF) and Greek national funds,
through the Operational Program "Education and Lifelong Learning", under the
research funding program Thales.

© Springer International Publishing Switzerland 2015
C. Zaroliagis et al. (Eds.): Spirakis Festschrift, LNCS 9295, pp. 223–241, 2015.
DOI: 10.1007/978-3-319-24024-4_14

fashion (see e.g., [1,22,23,26,27,29,47]), or with quantifying and mitigating the inefficiency due to the players' selfish behavior using the Price of Anarchy (see e.g., [2,6,11,13,14,17,21,22,24,29,33,41,43,44,49]).

As for several other areas of Theoretical Computer Science, Paul Spirakis has contributed interesting and significant results in all the three directions above. On the occasion of Paul's 60th birthday, I took the opportunity to write this (highly biased and selective) survey on algorithmic properties of congestion games that focuses either on our joint work with Paul (and with a few other dear friends) or on research work that has been directly inspired by Paul's contribution in the area.

It was a sort of an obvious choice for me, since Paul was the person who introduced me to the main research questions about algorithmic properties of congestion games. In fall 2001, when I was a postdoc and Paul was a distinguished visiting scientist at Max-Planck Institut für Informatik, in Saarbrücken, Paul insisted that we should start working together on congestion games on parallel links with linear delays and weighted players (a.k.a. load balancing games). As our first problem, he proposed us to investigate the existence and efficient computation of pure Nash equilibria and the conjecture that the mixed Nash equilibrium with full support (a.k.a. the fully-mixed equilibrium) maximizes the Price of Anarchy for the objective of maximum delay of the players (the latter was motivated by Paul's previous work in [40,44]). Fotakis et al. [29] was the result of this effort and the beginning of a fruitful and really enjoyable collaboration with Paul (and also with Spyros, Alexis, Vasilis, Thanasis and others) on algorithmic properties of congestion games. Back in Patras, in fall 2003, Paul, Spyros and I started looking at potential functions for congestion games with weighted players and simple algorithms for efficient computation of pure Nash equilibria (the motivation came from [19,46]). What happened next is described in the following pages. *Paul, thank you for everything and happy birthday!*

1.1 Organization

After a formal definition of atomic and non-atomic congestion games and related notions (Sect. 2), we discuss existence of potential functions for atomic games with weighted players (Sect. 3). Next, we show how a pure Nash equilibrium can be reached, using simple and natural algorithms, after as many steps as the number of players in series-parallel and extension-parallel networks (Sect. 4). In the final part, we bound the Price of Anarchy for atomic congestion games on extension-parallel networks (Sect. 5.1) and discuss how we can use tolls (Sect. 5.2), Stackelberg routing (Sect. 5.3) and the Braess paradox (Sect. 5.4) to improve the Price of Anarchy of congestion games. With the exception of the results about the Braess paradox, which apply to non-atomic congestion games, we mostly focus on algorithmic properties of atomic congestion games.

2 Congestion Games and Nash Equilibria

An *atomic congestion game* consists of a finite set $N = \{1, \ldots, n\}$ of players, a finite set $E = \{e_1, \ldots, e_m\}$ of edges (or resources), a strategy space $\Sigma_i \subseteq 2^E \setminus \{\emptyset\}$

for each player i, and a non-negative and non-decreasing delay function $d_e(x)$ associated with each edge e. A congestion game has *weighted players* if there is a positive weight w_i associated with each player i. Otherwise, the players are unweighted and we have that $w_i = 1$ for each player i. Throughout this survey, we assume that the players are unweighted, unless stated otherwise. A congestion game has *symmetric strategies* if all players share a common strategy space Σ. A congestion game is *symmetric* if it is unweighted and has symmetric strategies. A congestion game is *linear* if every edge e is associated with a linear delay function $d_e(x) = a_e x + b_e$, with $a_e, b_e \geq 0$.

In many parts of this survey, we consider *symmetric network* congestion games. Then, the players' strategies are determined by a directed network $G(V, E)$ with a distinguished origin o and destination t (a.k.a. an $o - t$ network). The common strategy space of the players is the set of (simple) $o - t$ paths in G, denoted $\mathcal{P}$. To be consistent with the definition of strategies as edge subsets, we regard paths as sets of edges. An $o - t$ network is a *parallel-link* network if each path in $\mathcal{P}$ consists of a single edge. Hence, in congestion games on parallel links the players' common strategy space consists of m singleton strategies, one for each edge.

A *configuration* is a tuple $s = (s_1, \ldots, s_n)$ consisting of a strategy $s_i \in \Sigma_i$ for each player i. For every edge e, we let $s_e = |\{i \in N : e \in s_i\}|$ denote the congestion (or load) induced on e by s. If the congestion game has weighted players, e's load in s is $s_e = \sum_{i:e \in s_i} w_i$. Given a congestion game on a directed network G, a configuration s is *acyclic* if there is no directed cycle in G with positive load on all its edges. For a configuration s and a path $p \in \mathcal{P}$, we let $s_p^{\min} = \min_{e \in p}\{s_e\}$ denote the minimum load on some edge of p.

Pure Nash Equilibrium. The individual delay (or cost) of player i in the configuration s is $c_i(s) = \sum_{e \in s_i} d_e(s_e)$. A configuration s is a *pure Nash equilibrium* if no player can improve her individual delay by unilaterally changing her strategy. Formally, s is a pure Nash equilibrium if for every player i and all strategies $s_i' \in \Sigma_i$, $c_i(s) \leq c_i(s_{-i}, s_i')$.

2.1 Price of Anarchy and Price of Stability

We evaluate configurations using the objective of (weighted) *total delay*. The (weighted) total delay $C(s)$ of a configuration s in a congestion game (with weighted players) is the (weighted) sum of players' individual delays in s, namely

$$C(s) = \sum_{i \in N} w_i c_i(s) = \sum_{e \in E} s_e d_e(s_e).$$

The *optimal configuration*, usually denoted o, achieves a minimum (weighted) total delay $C(o)$ among all configurations.

The *Price of Anarchy* (PoA) of a congestion game is the maximum ratio $C(s)/C(o)$ over all pure Nash equilibria s of the game. The *Price of Stability* (PoS) is the minimum ratio $C(s)/C(o)$ over all pure Nash equilibria s of the game. In words, the Price of Anarchy (resp. the Price of Stability) is equal to

$C(s)/C(o)$, where s is the pure Nash equilibrium of maximum (resp. minimum) total delay. The Price of Anarchy (resp. the Price of Stability) for a class of congestion games is the maximum PoA (resp. PoS) of any game in this class.

2.2   Potential Functions and Best Responses

A function Φ that assigns a non-negative number $\Phi(s)$ to each configuration s is an exact (resp. weighted) *potential function* if when a player i moves from her current strategy s_i to a new strategy $s_i' \in \Sigma_i$, the difference in the potential value equals the difference in the individual delay of player i (resp. times some function of i's weight w_i). Namely, Φ is an exact potential function if

$$\Phi(s_{-i}, s_i') - \Phi(s) = c_i(s_{-i}, s_i') - c_i(s).$$

If a game admits an (exact or weighted) potential function, its pure Nash equilibria correspond to the local minima of the potential function.

Rosenthal [48] proved that the pure Nash equilibria of an (unweighted) congestion game correspond to the local optima of the following potential function

$$\Phi(s) = \sum_{e \in E} \sum_{k=1}^{s_e} d_e(k).$$

Hence every congestion game admits at least one pure Nash equilibrium (and possibly many of them). For symmetric network congestion games with general delay functions, Fabrikant, Papadimitriou and Talwar [19] proved that the global minimum of the potential function Φ, and thus a pure Nash equilibrium, can be computed in polynomial time by a min-cost flow computation.

A strategy $s_i \in \Sigma_i$ is a *best response* of player i to a configuration s_{-i} of the remaining players if for all strategies $s_i' \in \Sigma_i$, $c_i(s_{-i}, s_i) \leq c_i(s_{-i}, s_i')$. A strategy $s_i' \in \Sigma_i$ is an *improvement move* of player i in a configuration s if $c_i(s_{-i}, s_i') < c_i(s)$. For a congestion game that admits a potential function, every improvement move decreases the potential value. Therefore, the Nash dynamics, namely, any sequence of improvement moves, converges to a pure Nash equilibrium in a finite number of steps.

2.3   Non-atomic Congestion Games

In non-atomic congestion games (or *selfish routing games*), the number of players is infinite and each player controls an infinitesimal amount of traffic. Unless stated otherwise, we assume that the traffic rate is $r = 1$. For simplicity and convenience, when we consider non-atomic congestion games, we focus on symmetric games on an $o-t$ network G. Everything else is defined as above, with the important difference that since the number of players is infinite, a configuration s should be regarded now as a *flow* $s = (s_p)_{p \in \mathcal{P}}$ that assigns an amount of traffic $s_p \geq 0$ to each path p so that $\sum_{p \in \mathcal{P}} s_p = r$.

The delay on each path $p \in \mathcal{P}$ in a configuration s is $d_p(s) = \sum_{e \in p} d_e(s_e)$. A configuration s is a *Nash equilibrium* if it routes all traffic on minimum delay paths, i.e., if for every path p with $s_p > 0$, and every path p', $d_p(s) \leq d_{p'}(s)$. Hence, in a Nash equilibrium s, all players incur the same delay $D(s) = \min_{p:s_p>0} d_p(f)$ and the total delay is $C(s) = rD(s)$.

Since the equivalent of Rosenthal's potential function is convex for non-atomic games, the Nash equilibrium is essentially unique (under mild assumptions on the delay functions). Therefore, the Price of Anarchy and the Price of Stability coincide and are equal to $C(s)/C(o)$, where s is the Nash equilibrium configuration and o is the configuration of minimum total delay.

3   Potential Functions for Weighted Players

In [46], Monderer and Shapley presented conditions for the acyclicity of Nash dynamics and for the existence of pure Nash equilibria in non-cooperative games. Most of these conditions are naturally associated with potential functions and their generalizations. One of the most interesting results in [46] is that every finite non-cooperative game with an exact potential function is isomorphic to a congestion game. Motivated by [46], we investigated in [30] which classes of congestions games with weighted players admit a potential function and to which extent we can generalize existence of pure Nash equilibria on parallel-link games with weighted players [29]. We proved that linear congestion games with weighted players admit a weighted potential function that naturally generalizes the potential function of Rosenthal. Hence, any sequence of improvement moves converges to a pure Nash equilibrium.

Theorem 1 *([30]). Every linear congestion game with weighted players admits a weighted potential function and thus, a pure Nash equilibrium.*

Proof. The intuition is that Rosenthal's potential can be generalized to weighted players if the order of the players in the sum of their delays does not make any difference (just as in the case of unweighted players). So, any deviating player can be considered as the last player in the sum. This holds for linear delay functions, since their derivative is constant.

Formally, let s be any configuration of a linear congestion game with weighted players. We let

$$U(s) = \sum_{i \in N} w_i \sum_{e \in s_i} (a_e w_i + b_e)$$

be the weighted total delay of the players in s, if each player was alone in the game. We also recall that

$$C(s) = \sum_{i \in N} w_i c_i(s) = \sum_{i \in N} w_i \sum_{e \in s_i} (a_e s_e + b_e) = \sum_{e \in E} s_e (a_e s_e + b_e)$$

is the weighted total delay of the players in configuration s.

We next show that $\Phi(s) = (C(s) + U(s))/2$ is a weighted potential function (note that for unweighted players and linear delays, $\Phi(s)$ becomes Rosenthal's potential). To this end, we let i be some player switching from her strategy s_i in s to a different strategy s_i' and let $s' = (s_{-i}, s_i')$ be the resulting configuration. We observe that

$$U(s') - U(s) = w_i \sum_{e \in s_i' \setminus s_i} (a_e w_i + b_e) - w_i \sum_{e \in s_i \setminus s_i'} (a_e w_i + b_e)$$

and that

$$C(s') - C(s) = w_i \sum_{e \in s_i' \setminus s_i} [a_e(2s_e + w_i) + b_e] - w_i \sum_{e \in s_i \setminus s_i'} [a_e(2s_e - w_i) + b_e].$$

Using that for all $e \in s_i' \setminus s_i$, $s_e' = s_e + w_i$, that for all $e \in s_i \setminus s_i'$, $s_e' = s_e - w_i$, and that for all $e \in s_i' \cap s_i$, $s_e' = s_e$, we conclude that

$$\begin{aligned}
\Phi(s') - \Phi(s) &= (C(s') - C(s) + U(s') - U(s))/2 \\
&= w_i \sum_{e \in s_i' \setminus s_i} [a_e(s_e + w_i) + b_e] - w_i \sum_{e \in s_i \setminus s_i'} (a_e s_e + b_e) \\
&= w_i(c_i(s') - c_i(s)).
\end{aligned}$$

Therefore, $\Phi(s) = (C(s) + U(s))/2$ is a weighted potential function for linear congestion games with weighted players. $\qquad\square$

The potential function of Theorem 1 is versatile and works for several other generalizations of linear congestions games, by appropriately adapting U in each case. It works e.g., for linear congestion games with static coalitions of players [27, Sect. 6], for linear congestion games in a social context of surplus collaboration [5], and for graphical linear games with weighted players [23].

In [30], we proved that Theorem 1 is essentially best possible, in the sense that (i) congestion games with weighted players and linear delays are not exact potential games, and that (ii) there is a simple congestion game with only two weighted players and delay functions that are either linear or 2-wise linear which admits neither a generalized potential function nor a pure Nash equilibrium.

Shortly after [30], Panagopoulou and Spirakis [47] presented a weighted potential function for congestion games with weighted players and delays given by an exponential function. Subsequently, Harks, Klimm and Möhring [34] significantly strengthened the negative result of [30] by proving that for congestion games with weighted players even the slightest deviation from the settings that guarantee weighted potential functions in [30, 47] leads to games that do not admit weighted potentials.

4   Reaching a Pure Nash Equilibrium

The existence of a potential function for congestion games and for linear congestion games with weighted players implies that any sequence of improvement moves converges to a pure Nash equilibrium. Nevertheless, Fabrikant,

Papadimitriou and Talwar [19] proved that it is **PLS**-complete to compute a pure Nash equilibrium in symmetric congestion games and in non-symmetric network congestion games. **PLS**-completeness holds even if the delay functions are linear. Moreover, Ackermann, Röglin and Vöcking [1] proved that in symmetric network congestion games with linear delays, where a pure Nash equilibrium can be computed in polynomial time by min-cost flow techniques, there are instances and initial configurations from which any best response sequence is exponentially long. On the positive side, [1] proved that in asymmetric congestion games with general delays, best response dynamics converges fast to a pure Nash equilibrium if (and essentially only if) the strategy space of each player is a matroid.

4.1   Series-Parallel Networks

For symmetric network congestion games, the matroid property corresponds to very simple networks consisting of bunches of parallel links connected in series. Trying to identify some more general classes of symmetric network congestion games where natural and efficient algorithms reach a pure Nash equilibrium, we considered, in [31], series-parallel networks and the so-called Greedy Best Response approach. We recall that an $o - t$ network is *series-parallel* if it consists of either a single edge (o, t) or two series-parallel networks composed either in series or in parallel.

Greedy Best Response, or GBR in brief, considers the players one-by-one in an arbitrary order. Each player adopts her best response strategy given the strategies of the previous players. The choice is irrevocable, in the sense that no player can switch to a different strategy afterwards. We proved that for series-parallel networks, GBR maintains a pure Nash equilibrium. Namely, after a new player selects her strategy, the other players do not have an incentive to deviate.

Theorem 2 *([31]). Greedy Best Response applied to symmetric congestion games on series-parallel networks with general delays maintains a pure Nash equilibrium in time $O(nm \log m)$.*

In [31], we show that for any non-series-parallel network, we can select linear edge delays so that GBR does not maintain a pure Nash equilibrium even for two players. Moreover, we prove that Theorem 2 can be generalized to congestion games with weighted players that satisfy the *common best response* property, namely that all players agree on their best responses with respect to any given collection of edge loads.

4.2   Extension-Parallel Networks

An interesting generalization of congestion games on parallel links is that of symmetric games on extension-parallel networks. An $o - t$ network is *extension-parallel* if it consists of either (i) a single edge (o, t), or (ii) a single edge and an extension-parallel network composed in series, or (iii) two extension-parallel networks composed in parallel. An interesting property of extension-parallel networks is that they have *linearly independent* $o - t$ *paths*, in the sense that every $o - t$ path contains at least one edge not belonging to any other $o - t$ path (and thus, it is not possible to express a path as the symmetric difference of some other paths, see [35,45]).

In [22], we proved that for symmetric congestion games on extension-parallel networks[1], each player moves at most once in any sequence of best response moves. More formally, we show the following:

Lemma 1 *([22]). For a symmetric congestion game on an extension-parallel network, let s be the current configuration and let i be a player switching from her current strategy s_i to her best response s_i'. Then, for every player j whose current strategy s_j is a best response to s, s_j remains a best response of j to the new configuration $s' = (s_{-i}, s_i')$.*

Lemma 1 directly implies that in extension-parallel networks, the best response dynamics converges to a pure Nash equilibrium in at most n steps. One can also show that the following theorem is essentially best possible, in the sense that it does not hold for any generalization of extension-parallel networks.

Theorem 3 *([22]). For any n-player symmetric congestion game on an extension-parallel network, every sequence of best response moves converges to a pure Nash equilibrium in at most n steps.*

5   The Price of Anarchy and How to Deal with It

Since the seminal paper of Koutsoupias and Papadimitriou [41], the Price of Anarchy of both atomic and non-atomic congestion games has been investigated extensively. Lücking et al. [43] were the first to consider the PoA of atomic congestion games for the objective of total delay. The proved that for parallel-link games with linear delays, the PoA is 4/3. For parallel-link games with polynomial delays of degree d, Gairing et al. [33] proved that the PoA is at most $d + 1$. Awerbuch, Azar and Epstein [6] and Christodoulou and Koutsoupias [13] proved independently that the PoA of congestion games is 5/2 for linear delays and $d^{\Theta(d)}$ for polynomial delays of degree d. Subsequently, Aland et al. [2] obtained exact bounds on the PoA of congestion games with polynomial delays.

For non-atomic congestion games, Roughgarden [49] proved that the PoA is independent of the strategy space and equal to $\rho(\mathcal{D})$, where ρ depends on the class of delay functions $\mathcal{D}$ only. Specifically, for a non-negative and non-decreasing function $d(x)$,

$$\rho(d) = \sup_{x \geq y \geq 0} \frac{x d(x)}{y d(y) + (x - y) d(x)}.$$

---

[1] Note that matroid congestion games and congestion games on extension-parallel networks have a different combinatorial structure and may have quite different properties. E.g., a network consisting of two parallel-link networks composed in series is not extension-parallel, but corresponds to a symmetric matroid congestion game.

For a non-empty class $\mathcal{D}$ of delay functions, $\rho(\mathcal{D}) = \sup_{d \in \mathcal{D}} \rho(d)$. For example, ρ is equal to $4/3$ for linear delays, to $\frac{27+6\sqrt{3}}{23}$ for quadratic delays and to $\Theta(d/\ln d)$ for polynomial delays of degree d. Subsequently, Correa, Schulz, and Stier-Moses [17] introduced the quantities $\beta(d) = 1 - 1/\rho(d)$ and $\beta(\mathcal{D}) = 1 - 1/\rho(\mathcal{D})$, as alternatives to $\rho(d)$ and $\rho(\mathcal{D})$, respectively, and gave a simple and elegant proof of the same bound.

The general picture is that the PoA of atomic congestion games can be quite large and there is a considerable gap between the PoA of atomic and non-atomic congestion games. In fact, for polynomial delays of degree d, this gap is exponential in d. Therefore, it is natural to ask about possible ways of improving the PoA of atomic congestion games either to 1 or at least close to the PoA of non-atomic congestion games. Moreover, it is interesting to investigate possible approaches to further improving the PoA of non-atomic congestion games without expensive changes in the structure of the game.

5.1 The Price of Anarchy for Extension-Parallel Networks

A possible approach to improving the PoA of atomic congestion games is to consider special classes of networks. In contrast to non-atomic games, where the PoA is independent of the strategy space, the PoA of atomic games crucially depends on it (e.g., the PoA of linear congestion games is $4/3$ for parallel-links [43] and $5/2$ in general [6,13]). In this direction, we [21] and Caragiannis et al. [11] proved independently that the PoA of atomic congestion games on parallel links with delay functions in class $\mathcal{D}$ is at most $\rho(\mathcal{D})$, i.e., it is bounded from above by the PoA of non-atomic congestion games.

Theorem 4 ([11, 21]). *The Price of Anarchy of atomic congestion games on parallel links with delay functions in class $\mathcal{D}$ is at most $\rho(\mathcal{D})$.*

Proof. We consider a congestion game on a set E of parallel links with delay functions $\{d_e(x)\}_{e \in E} \subseteq \mathcal{D}$. Let o be the optimal configuration, and let s be the pure Nash equilibrium of maximum total delay. For every link $e \in E$,

$$s_e d_e(s_e) = o_e d_e(s_e) + (s_e - o_e) d_e(s_e)$$
$$\leq o_e d_e(o_e) + \beta(\mathcal{D}) s_e d_e(s_e) + (s_e - o_e) d_e(s_e), \tag{1}$$

where the inequality follows from the definitions of $\beta(d)$ and $\beta(\mathcal{D})$.

For every link e with $o_e > s_e$,

$$s_e d_e(s_e) = o_e d_e(o_e) - o_e d_e(o_e) + s_e d_e(s_e)$$
$$\leq o_e d_e(o_e) - (o_e - s_e) d_e(s_e + 1). \tag{2}$$

The inequality follows from $d_e(s_e) \leq d_e(s_e + 1)$ and $d_e(s_e + 1) \leq d_e(o_e)$, because the delays are non-decreasing and $s_e + 1 \leq o_e$.

Now, let us assume that the following holds:

$$\sum_{e : s_e > o_e} (s_e - o_e) d_e(s_e) \leq \sum_{e : o_e > s_e} (o_e - s_e) d_e(s_e + 1). \tag{3}$$

Then, using (1), for links e with $s_e \geq o_e$, using (2), for links e with $o_e > s_e$, and employing (3), we obtain that:

$$C(s) \leq \sum_{e \in E} o_e d_e(o_e) + \beta(\mathcal{D}) \sum_{e:s_e \geq o_e} s_e d_e(s_e) +$$

$$\sum_{e:s_e > o_e} (s_e - o_e)d_e(s_e) - \sum_{e:o_e > s_e} (o_e - s_e)d_e(s_e + 1)$$

$$\leq C(o) + \beta(\mathcal{D})C(s).$$

Therefore, $C(s) \leq (1 - \beta(\mathcal{D}))^{-1}C(o) = \rho(\mathcal{D})C(o)$, i.e., the PoA is at most $\rho(\mathcal{D})$.

For parallel-link games, (3) is an immediate consequence of the pure Nash equilibrium condition. Formally, since s is a pure Nash equilibrium, for every link e with $s_e > o_e$ (which implies that $s_e \geq 1$) and every link e',

$$d_e(s_e) \leq d_{e'}(s_{e'} + 1).$$

Then, (3) follows from the fact that

$$\sum_{e:s_e > o_e} (s_e - o_e) = \sum_{e:o_e > s_e} (o_e - s_e),$$

because in parallel-link networks, $\sum_{e \in E} s_e = \sum_{e \in E} o_e$.   □

We observe that in the proof of Theorem 4, the assumption of parallel-link networks is used only to establish (3). Everything else holds for general symmetric congestion games. Therefore, the upper bound of $\rho(\mathcal{D})$ on the PoA (or, more generally, on the inefficiency of a pure Nash equilibrium s) holds if the strategy space and the selected configuration s are such that (3) is satisfied. In [22], we observed that if we regard configurations s and o as flows, (3) essentially states that switching from s to o does not increase the value of Rosenthal's potential function. Intuitively, in such cases, one can reduce (3) to the absence of a negative cost cycle in the circulation $o - s$ with Rosenthal's potential as a cost function. Based on this intuition, one can show that for symmetric network congestion games, (3) holds if s is a minimizer of Rosenthal's potential function. Then, we immediately obtain that:

Theorem 5 *([4, 22]).* *For any symmetric network congestion game with delay functions in class $\mathcal{D}$, the Price of Stability is at most $\rho(\mathcal{D})$.*

Moreover, in [22, 35], it is shown that if the network is extension-parallel, any pure Nash equilibrium is a minimizer of Rosenthal's potential function. Therefore, the PoA of symmetric congestion games on extension-parallel networks is bounded from above by the PoA of non-atomic congestion games.

Theorem 6 *([22]).* *For symmetric network congestion games on extension-parallel networks with delay functions in class $\mathcal{D}$, the Price of Anarchy is at most $\rho(\mathcal{D})$.*

In [22], we presented a congestion game with 3 players on a simple series-parallel network with linear delays and PoA equal to $15/11 > 4/3$, i.e., larger than the PoA of non-atomic congestion games with linear delays.

5.2 Optimal Tolls for Atomic Congestion Games

With the PoA of (atomic and non-atomic) congestion games very well understood, a few natural approaches to reducing it have been investigated. A strong approach is to introduce economic incentives, usually modeled as edge-dependent per-unit-of-traffic *tolls*, that influence the players' selfish choices and induce the optimal configuration as a pure Nash equilibrium (and in the ideal case, as the unique pure Nash equilibrium) of the modified game with tolls.

In a modified congestion game with tolls $t = (t_e)_{e \in E}$, the individual cost of a player i in configuration s is equal to $c_i'(s) = \sum_{e \in s_i}(d_e(s_e) + t_e)$, i.e., equal to the total delay through the edges in her strategy s_i plus the tolls for using the edges in s_i. Nash equilibria are now defined with respect to the modified costs $c_i'(s)$ that also account for include tolls. However, most of the literature assumes that the tolls are *refundable* to the players and thus, do not affect the social cost. Therefore, each configuration s is evaluated by (and the PoA is defined with respect to) the total delay $C(s) = \sum_{e \in E} s_e d_e(s_e)$ of the players in s. The goal in this research direction is to find a set of moderate and efficiently computable *optimal tolls*, under which the Nash equilibria of the modified game coincide with the optimal configuration o.

Existence and efficient computation of optimal tolls for non-atomic congestion games have been investigated extensively. A classical result is that the optimal configuration o is realized as the Nash equilibrium of a non-atomic congestion game with *marginal cost tolls* [8]. If the delay functions are differentiable, the marginal cost toll of each edge e is $t_e = o_e d_e'(o_e)$, where $d_e'(x)$ denotes the first derivative of $d_e(x)$. Cole, Dodis, and Roughgarden [16] considered *heterogeneous* players, who may have different valuations of time (delay) in terms of money (toll), and established the existence of optimal tolls for non-atomic symmetric network congestion games through a non-costructive proof based on Brouwer's fixed point theorem. Subsequently, Fleischer, Jain, and Mahdian [20] and Karakostas and Kolliopoulos [37] proved independently that the existence of optimal tolls for non-atomic congestion games with heterogeneous players follows directly from Linear Programming duality. Therefore, optimal tolls can be computed efficiently by solving a Linear Program. These results (and essentially all known results about existence and efficient computation of tolls for non-atomic games) crucially depend on uniqueness of the Nash equilibrium.

For atomic congestion games, that may admit many different pure Nash equilibria, one has to distinguish between the case where a set of tolls *weakly enforces* the optimal configuration o, in the sense that o is realized as some pure Nash equilibrium of the modified game with tolls, and the case where a set of tolls *strongly enforces* o, in the sense that o is realized as the unique pure Nash equilibrium of the modified game with tolls.

Caragiannis, Kaklamanis, and Kanellopoulos [12] considered atomic congestion games with linear delays and homogeneous players and investigated existence of optimal tolls and how much tolls can improve the Price of Anarchy. They presented a simple non-symmetric congestion game for which the PoA remains at least 6/5 under any set of tolls. Therefore, they proved that non-symmetric congestion games do not necessarily admit strongly optimal tolls. On the positive side, [12] presented (i) a set of strongly optimal tolls for linear congestion games on parallel links, and (ii) efficiently computable tolls that reduce to the PoA to 2 for linear games with arbitrary strategies (and even with weighted players).

Motivated by [12], we investigated in [32] the existence of optimal tolls for symmetric atomic network congestion games with homogeneous players and general delay functions. In [32], we presented a natural toll mechanism, called *cost-balancing tolls*, which are motivated by the optimal tolls for non-atomic games in [20, 37]. A set of cost-balancing tolls for a given configuration turns every path with positive load on its edges into a minimum cost path (the optimal tolls for linear games on parallel links in [12] are also based on the same principle). Formally, a set of tolls t is cost-balancing for a configuration s if for every path $p \in \mathcal{P}$ with $s_p^{\min} > 0$ and every path $p' \in \mathcal{P}$,

$$\sum_{e \in p} (d_e(s_e) + t_e) \leq \sum_{e \in p'} (d_e(s_e) + t_e).$$

Essentially by definition, any given configuration s is induced as a pure Nash equilibrium of the modified congestion game with cost-balancing tolls for s. We proved that every acyclic configuration s admits cost-balancing tolls. Moreover, the computation of cost-balancing tolls for s naturally reduces to a longest path computation from the origin in the subnetwork used by s. Using the fact that the optimal configuration o in symmetric network congestion games is acyclic, we proved the following.

Theorem 7 *([32]). For every symmetric network congestion game, the optimal configuration o is weakly enforceable by cost-balancing tolls t for o, which satisfy the following properties:*

(a) *Given the optimal configuration o, t is computed in time linear in the size of the network.*

(b) *The maximum toll on any edge is at most $t^{\max} = \delta + \max_{p \in \mathcal{P}} \sum_{e \in p} d_e(n)$, for any $\delta > 0$. Every edge with toll $t^{\max}$ is not used in any pure Nash equilibrium of the modified game with tolls.*

(c) *The total amount of tolls paid by any player in any pure Nash equilibrium of the modified game with tolls does not exceed $\max_{p:o_p^{\min}>0} \sum_{e \in p} d_e(o_e)$.*

In [32], we gave a simple example where the optimal configuration cannot be weakly enforced by tolls substantially smaller than the cost-balancing tolls of Theorem 7. Therefore, there are symmetric network games where tolls as large as cost-balancing tolls are also necessary for weakly enforcing the optimal configuration. In [28], we generalized Theorem 7 and proved that cost-balancing tolls exist and can be computed efficiently even for heterogeneous players.

The main result of [32] is that for symmetric congestion games on series-parallel networks with increasing delay functions, the optimal configuration is strongly enforceable by the corresponding cost-balancing tolls. Therefore, symmetric congestion games on series-parallel networks with increasing delays admit a set of moderate optimal tolls computable in linear time.

Theorem 8 *([32]). Every symmetric congestion game on a series-parallel network with increasing delay functions admits a set of strongly optimal tolls with the properties (a), (b), and (c) of Theorem 7.*

Interestingly, games on series-parallel networks admit many different pure Nash equilibria in general. However, games on series-parallel networks with cost-balancing tolls admit an essentially unique pure Nash equilibrium that coincides with the optimal configuration!

If the network is not series-parallel, cost-balancing tolls may not strongly enforce the optimal solution even for linear delay functions. Moreover, Theorem 8 cannot be generalized to heterogeneous players. In [28], we presented a simple congestion game on parallel links with linear delay functions and heterogeneous players for which the PoA remains at least $28/27$ under any set of tolls.

Given the existence of efficiently computable strongly optimal tolls for congestion games on series-parallel networks, it is natural to ask for optimal tolls that minimize some objective function (e.g. the sum of tolls, the maximum toll, etc.) on the amount of tolls charged to the players. In [32], we proved that even for 2-player linear congestion games on series-parallel networks, it is **NP**-hard to distinguish between the case where the optimal configuration is the unique pure Nash equilibrium (and thus, tolls only serve to increase the players' disutility) and the case where there is another pure Nash equilibrium of total delay at least $6/5$ times the optimal total delay (and hence some tolls are required to strongly enforce the optimal configuration).

An intriguing problem that remains open in this research direction is whether strongly optimal tolls exist for symmetric network congestion games with homogeneous players.

5.3   Stackelberg Routing

A different simple and appealing approach to reducing the PoA is *Stackelberg routing* [39]. The idea is to exploit a small fraction of centrally routed (a.k.a. coordinated) players to improve the quality of the Nash equilibrium reached by the remaining selfish players. A *Stackelberg policy* is an algorithm that determines the strategies of the coordinated players. Given the strategies of (and the congestion caused by) the coordinated players, the selfish players lead the system to a configuration where they are at a pure Nash equilibrium. Our goal is to find a Stackelberg policy of minimum Price of Anarchy, that is the worst-case ratio of the total delay of all (coordinated and selfish) players at a Nash equilibrium for the selfish players to the optimal total delay. The PoA of a given Stackelberg strategy is a non-increasing function of the fraction of coordinated players, usually denoted by α, and ideally is given by a continuous curve decreasing from the value of PoA if all players are selfish to 1 if all players are coordinated.

There has been a significant volume of work on the PoA of Stackelberg routing in non-atomic congestion games. For non-atomic linear games on parallel links, Roughgarden [50] proved that it is **NP**-hard to compute an optimal Stackelberg configuration for a given fraction of coordinated players. To deal with

NP-hardness, he proposed two "heuristic" Stackelberg policies, called SCALE and LARGEST LATENCY FIRST (LLF), and investigated their worst-case PoA as a function of the fraction α of coordinated players. SCALE simply employs the optimal configuration scaled by α. LLF assigns the coordinated players to the largest cost strategies in the optimal configuration. Roughgarden proved that the PoA of LLF on parallel links is $1/\alpha$ for general delay functions and $4/(3+\alpha)$ for linear delays.

Swamy [52] and independently Correa and Stier-Moses [18] proved that the PoA of LLF is at most $1+1/\alpha$ for series-parallel networks with general delay functions. Moreover, Swamy proved that the PoA of LLF is at most $\alpha + (1-\alpha)\rho(\mathcal{D})$ for parallel links with delay functions in class $\mathcal{D}$. The best known upper and lower bounds on the PoA of LLF and SCALE for non-atomic congestion games on general networks with linear and polynomial delays are due to Karakostas and Kolliopoulos [38]. An upper bound for SCALE with linear delays in [38] is $4(1-\alpha^2/4)/3$. Other upper bounds for SCALE and the upper bounds for LLF are rather too complicated for stating (and explaining) them in this survey.

In [21], we investigated the PoA of SCALE and LLF for atomic congestion games on general networks with linear delays and on parallel-links with general delay functions. We proved that the PoA of LLF is at most $\min\{(20-11\alpha)/8, (3-2\alpha+\sqrt{5-4\alpha})/2\}$ and at least $5(2-\alpha)/(4+\alpha)$. For SCALE, we proved that the PoA is at most $\max\{(5-3\alpha)/2, (5-4\alpha)/(3-2\alpha)\}$. These bounds are continuous functions of α and drop from $5/2$ to 1, as α grows from 0 to 1. For parallel-link games, we prove that the PoA of LLF matches that for non-atomic games on parallel links, i.e., it is at most $1/\alpha$ for general delays and at most $\alpha + (1-\alpha)\rho(\mathcal{D})$ for delay functions in class $\mathcal{D}$.

The general picture is that for parallel-link networks with general delays and for general networks with polynomial delays, the coordinated players can be allocated so that the PoA decreases smoothly as the fraction α of the coordinated players increases. Unfortunately, there are non-atomic games on $o-t$ networks with delay functions chosen so that the PoA cannot be bounded by any function of α under any Stackelberg configuration [9].

In a different and also very interesting research direction, Kaporis and Spirakis [36] introduced the *price of optimum*, namely the smallest fraction of coordinated players required to induce an optimal configuration. They presented efficient algorithms for computing the price of optimum in Stackelberg routing for non-atomic games on parallel links and on general $o-t$ networks. An interesting consequence of their work is that there are instances where enforcing the optimal configuration may require a large fraction of the coordinated traffic to be sacrificed through slower paths, since optimal configurations can be quite unfair with respect to the players' individual delay.

5.4   Approximate Network Design for Non-Atomic Games

A simple, albeit counterintuitive, way of improving the Price of Anarchy is to exploit the essence of the Braess paradox [10], namely the fact that removing some network edges may improve the players' delay at equilibrium (see Fig. 1

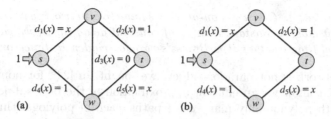

Fig. 1. (a) The optimal total delay is $3/2$, achieved by splitting the traffic among the paths (s, v, t) and (s, w, t). In the Nash equilibrium, all traffic goes through the path (s, v, w, t) and has delay 2. This gives a PoA of $4/3$. (b) If we remove the edge (v, w), the Nash equilibrium coincides with the optimal configuration. Hence the network on the left is *paradox-ridden*, and the network on the right is its *best subnetwork*.

for a non-atomic congestion game suffering from the paradox). Since Braess's paradox have been studied mostly for non-atomic symmetric network congestion games, we restrict our attention to such games throughout this section.

Focusing on understanding to which extent the PoA can be improved by exploiting the Braess paradox, Roughgarden [51], introduced the optimization problem of the *best subnetwork* (a.k.a. *network design*). Namely, given a non-atomic symmetric network congestion game, to compute the subnetwork induced by edge deletions that minimizes the players' delay at Nash equilibrium (we recall that for non-atomic games, the Nash equilibrium is unique and all players incur the same delay in it). Roughgarden proved that it is **NP**-hard not only to find the best subnetwork, but also to compute any meaningful approximation to the equilibrium delay on the best subnetwork. In particular, he proved that even for linear delays, it is **NP**-hard to distinguish between *paradox-free* instances, where edge removal cannot improve the equilibrium delay, and *paradox-ridden* instances, where the total equilibrium delay on the best subnetwork is equal to the optimal total delay on the original network. Furthermore, Roughgarden proved that for any $\varepsilon > 0$, it is **NP**-hard to approximate the equilibrium delay on the best subnetwork within a factor of $4/3 - \varepsilon$ for linear delays, and within a factor of $\lfloor |V|/2 \rfloor - \varepsilon$ for general delays, where $|V|$ is the number of nodes in the network. Hence, the only general algorithm for approximating the equilibrium delay on the best subnetwork is the trivial one, which does not remove any edges from the network. This algorithm achieves an approximation ratio of $4/3$ for linear delays and of $\lfloor |V|/2 \rfloor$ for general delays.

Despite the strong and discouraging results of [51], we proved, in [24], that paradox-ridden instances of the best subnetwork problem can be recognized in polynomial time for networks with strictly increasing linear delay functions. The idea is that if the delay functions are linear and strictly increasing, then the optimal configuration is unique. Therefore, a non-atomic game is paradox-ridden if and only if the unique optimal configuration is a Nash equilibrium for the subnetwork consisting of the edges used by it. In [24], we further generalized this result using properties of Linear Programming and proved the following.

Theorem 9 *([24]). Given a non-atomic symmetric network game with linear delays and at most a constant number of constant delay edges, we can recognize in polynomial time whether it is Braess's-paradox-ridden instance or not.*

If the network is not paradox-ridden, we sought, in [24], for nontrivial special cases that allow for an efficient approximation of the best subnetwork. For networks with polynomially many $o - t$ paths, each of polylogarithmic length, and arbitrary linear delays, we presented a subexponential-time approximation scheme for the equilibrium delay of the best subnetwork. For any $\varepsilon > 0$, the algorithm computes a subnetwork and an ε-Nash equilibrium[2] in it so that the players' delays are within an additive term of $\varepsilon/2$ from the equilibrium delay on the best subnetwork. The running time is exponential in $\mathrm{poly}(\log m)/\varepsilon^2$. The analysis is based on an application of the Probabilistic Method, motivated by Althöfer's Sparsification Lemma [3] and its application to the computation of approximate Nash equilibria for bimatrix games [42]. In particular, we apply the Probabilistic Method and show that any configuration admits an ε-approximate "sparse" configuration that assigns traffic only to $O(\log m/\varepsilon^2)$ paths.

In a subsequent work [25], we presented a subexponential-time approximation for the best subnetwork in sparse random networks. The motivation came from the works of Valiant and Roughgarden [53] and Chung and Young [15], who proved that the Braess paradox occurs with high probability in random $\mathcal{G}_{n,p}$ networks with $p = \Omega(\ln n/n)$, i.e., just greater than the connectivity threshold, and linear delays drawn independently from a natural probability distribution. Our result in [25] is essentially an approximation scheme for a class of so-called *good* instances, which includes the random instances of [15,53] as a special case. Namely, given a good instance and any constant $\varepsilon > 0$, we compute a configuration that (i) is an ε-Nash equilibrium for the subnetwork consisting of the edges used by it, and (ii) has maximum delay no greater than $(1+\varepsilon)D^* + \varepsilon$, where D^* is the equilibrium delay on the best subnetwork.

Our main contribution in [25] is a polynomial-time approximation-preserving reduction of the best subnetwork problem for a good $o - t$ network G to a best subnetwork problem for a 0-*delay simplified network* G_0. The latter is a layered network obtained from G if we keep only o, t and their immediate neighbors, and connect all neighbors of o and t by direct edges of 0 delay. In [25], we proved that the equilibrium delay of the best subnetwork does not increase when we consider the 0-delay simplified network G_0. Although this may sound reasonable, one should be very careful because decreasing edge delays to 0 may trigger the Braess paradox (e.g., starting from the network in Fig. 1.a with $\hat{d}_3(x) = 1$ and decreasing it to $d_3(x) = 0$ is just another way of triggering the paradox). Given the 0-latency simplified network G_0, we can employ the approximation scheme of [24] and approximate the best subnetwork problem on G_0.

The final (and crucial) step of the approximation preserving reduction of [25] is to start with the solution to the best subnetwork problem for the 0-delay

---

[2] For some $\varepsilon > 0$, a configuration s is an ε-Nash equilibrium if for every path p with $s_p > 0$ and every path p', $d_p(s) \leq d_{p'}(s) + \varepsilon$.

simplified network and extend it to a solution to the best subnetwork problem for the original good network G. In [25], we show how to "simulate" 0-delay edges by low delay paths in the original good network G. Intuitively, this is possible because due to the expansion properties and the random delay functions of G, the intermediate subnetwork of G, connecting the neighbors of o to the neighbors of t, essentially behaves as a complete bipartite network with 0-delay edges. Interestingly, this is also the key step in the approach of [15,53], showing that the Braess paradox occurs in good networks with high probability. Hence, one could say that the reason that the Braess paradox exists in good networks is the very same reason that the paradox can be efficiently approximated.

Since the approximation preserving reduction above runs in polynomial time, we could replace the subexponential-time approximation scheme of [24], for approximating the best subnetwork on the 0-delay simplified network G_0, with an improved approximation scheme based on the generalization of Althöfer's Sparsification Lemma presented in [7]. We believe that this approach could lead to a polynomial-time approximation scheme for many interesting classes of good instances.

References

1. Ackermann, H., Röglin, H., Vöcking, B.: On the impact of combinatorial structre on congestion games. J. Assoc. Comput. Mach. **55**(6), 1–22 (2008)
2. Aland, S., Dumrauf, D., Gairing, M., Monien, B., Schoppmann, F.: Exact price of anarchy for polynomial congestion games. SIAM J. Comput. **40**(5), 1211–1233 (2011)
3. Althöfer, I.: On sparse approximations to randomized strategies and convex combinations. Linear Algebra Appl. **99**, 339–355 (1994)
4. Anshelevich, E., Dasgupta, A., Kleinberg, J.M., Tardos, É., Wexler, T., Roughgarden, T.: The price of stability for network design with fair cost allocation. SIAM J. Comput. **38**(4), 1602–1623 (2008)
5. Ashlagi, I., Krysta, P., Tennenholtz, M.: Social context games. In: Papadimitriou, C., Zhang, S. (eds.) WINE 2008. LNCS, vol. 5385, pp. 675–683. Springer, Heidelberg (2008)
6. Awerbuch, B., Azar, Y., Epstein, A.: The price of routing unsplittable flow. In: Proceedings of the 37th ACM Symposium on Theory of Computing (STOC 2005), pp. 57–66 (2005)
7. Barman, S.: Approximating Carathéodory's theorem and nash equilibria. In: Proceedings of the 47th ACM Symposium on Theory of Computing (STOC 2015) (2015)
8. Beckmann, M., McGuire, C.B., Winsten, C.B.: Studies in the Economics of Transportation. Yale University Press, New Haven (1956)
9. Bonifaci, V., Harks, T., Schäfer, G.: Stackelberg routing in arbitrary networks. Math. Oper. Res. **35**(2), 330–346 (2010)
10. Braess, D.: Über ein paradox aus der Verkehrsplanung. Unternehmensforschung **12**, 258–268 (1968)
11. Caragiannis, I., Flammini, M., Kaklamanis, C., Kanellopoulos, P., Moscardelli, L.: Tight bounds for selfish and greedy load balancing. Algorithmica **61**(3), 606–637 (2011)

12. Caragiannis, I., Kaklamanis, C., Kanellopoulos, P.: Taxes for linear atomic congestion games. ACM Trans. Algorithms **7**(1), 13 (2010)
13. Christodoulou, G., Koutsoupias, E.: The Price of anarchy of finite congestion games. In: Proceedings of the 37th ACM Symposium on Theory of Computing (STOC 2005), pp. 67–73 (2005)
14. Christodoulou, G., Koutsoupias, E., Spirakis, P.G.: On the performance of approximate equilibria in congestion games. Algorithmica **61**(1), 116–140 (2011)
15. Chung, F., Young, S.J.: Braess's paradox in large sparse graphs. In: Saberi, A. (ed.) WINE 2010. LNCS, vol. 6484, pp. 194–208. Springer, Heidelberg (2010)
16. Cole, R., Dodis, Y., Roughgarden, T.: How much can taxes help selfish routing? J. Comput. Syst. Sci. **72**(3), 444–467 (2006)
17. Correa, J.R., Schulz, A.S., Stier, N.E.: Moses. selfish routing in capacitated networks. Math. Oper. Res. **29**(4), 961–976 (2004)
18. Correa, J.R., Stier-Moses, N.E.: Stackelberg Routing in Atomic Network Games. In: Technical report DRO-2007-03, Columbia Business School (2007)
19. Fabrikant, A., Papadimitriou, C., Talwar, K.: The complexity of pure nash equilibria. In: Proceedings of the 36th ACM Symposium on Theory of Computing (STOC 2004), pp. 604–612 (2004)
20. Fleischer, L., Jain, K., Mahdian, M.: Tolls for heterogeneous selfish users in multicommodity networks and generalized congestion games. In: Proceedings of the 45th IEEE Symposium on Foundations of Computer Science (FOCS 2004), pp. 277–285 (2004)
21. Fotakis, D.: Stackelberg strategies for atomic congestion games. Theory Comput. Syst. **47**(1), 218–249 (2010)
22. Fotakis, D.: Congestion games with linearly independent paths: convergence time and price of anarchy. Theory Comput. Syst. **47**(1), 113–136 (2010)
23. Fotakis, D., Gkatzelis, V., Kaporis, A.C., Spirakis, P.G.: The impact of social ignorance on weighted congestion games. Theory Comput. Syst. **50**(3), 559–578 (2012)
24. Fotakis, D., Kaporis, A.C., Spirakis, P.G.: Efficient methods for selfish network design. Theor. Comput. Sci. **448**, 9–20 (2012)
25. Fotakis, D., Kaporis, A.C., Lianeas, T., Spirakis, P.G.: Resolving braess's paradox in random networks. In: Chen, Y., Immorlica, N. (eds.) WINE 2013. LNCS, vol. 8289, pp. 188–201. Springer, Heidelberg (2013)
26. Fotakis, D., Kaporis, A.C., Spirakis, P.G.: Atomic congestion games: fast, myopic and concurrent. Theory Comput. Syst. **47**(1), 38–59 (2010)
27. Fotakis, D., Kaporis, A.C., Spirakis, P.G.: Efficient methods for selfish network design. Theor. Comput. Sci. **448**, 9–20 (2012)
28. Fotakis, D., Karakostas, G., Kolliopoulos, S.G.: On the existence of optimal taxes for network congestion games with heterogeneous users. In: Kontogiannis, S., Koutsoupias, E., Spirakis, P.G. (eds.) SAGT 2010. LNCS, vol. 6386, pp. 162–173. Springer, Heidelberg (2010)
29. Fotakis, D., Kontogiannis, S.C., Koutsoupias, E., Mavronicolas, M., Spirakis, P.G.: The structure and complexity of Nash equilibria for a selfish routing game. Theor. Comput. Sci. **410**(36), 3305–3326 (2009)
30. Fotakis, D., Kontogiannis, S.C., Spirakis, P.G.: Selfish unsplittable flows. Theor. Comput. Sci. **348**, 226–239 (2005)
31. Fotakis, D.A., Kontogiannis, S.C., Spirakis, P.G.: Symmetry in network congestion games: pure equilibria and anarchy cost. In: Erlebach, T., Persinao, G. (eds.) WAOA 2005. LNCS, vol. 3879, pp. 161–175. Springer, Heidelberg (2006)

32. Fotakis, D., Spirakis, P.G.: Cost-balancing tolls for atomic network congestion games. Internet Math. **5**(4), 343–363 (2008)
33. Gairing, M., Lücking, T., Mavronicolas, M., Monien, B., Rode, M.: Nash equilibria in discrete routing games with convex latency functions. J. Comput. Syst. Sci. **74**(7), 1199–1225 (2008)
34. Harks, T., Klimm, M., Möhring, R.H.: Characterizing the existence of potential functions in weighted congestion games. Theory Comput. Syst. **49**(1), 46–70 (2011)
35. Holzman, R., Law-Yone, N.: (Lev-tov). Network structure and strong equilibrium in route selection games. Math. Soc. Sci. **46**, 193–205 (2003)
36. Kaporis, A.C., Spirakis, P.G.: The price of optimum in Stackelberg games on arbitrary single commodity networks and latency functions. Theor. Comput. Sci. **410**(8–10), 745–755 (2009)
37. Karakostas, G., Kolliopoulos, S.: Edge pricing of multicommodity networks for heterogeneous selfish users. In: Proceedings of the 45th IEEE Symposium on Foundations of Computer Science (FOCS 2004), pp. 268–276 (2004)
38. Karakostas, G., Kolliopoulos, S.: Stackelberg strategies for selfish routing in general multicommodity networks. Algorithmica **53**(1), 132–153 (2009)
39. Korilis, Y.A., Lazar, A.A., Orda, A.: Achieving network optima using Stackelberg routing strategies. IEEE/ACM Trans. Networking **5**(1), 161–173 (1997)
40. Koutsoupias, E., Mavronicolas, M., Spirakis, P.: Approximate equilibria and ball fusion. Theory Comput. Syst. **36**, 683–693 (2003)
41. Koutsoupias, E., Papadimitriou, C.H.: Worst-case equilibria. Comput. Sci. Rev. **3**(2), 65–69 (2009)
42. Lipton, R.J., Markakis, E., Mehta, A.: Playing large games using simple strategies. In: Proceedings of the 4th ACM Conference on Electronic Commerce (EC 2003), pp. 36–41 (2003)
43. Lücking, T., Mavronicolas, M., Monien, B., Rode, M.: A new model for selfish routing. Theor. Comput. Sci. **406**(3), 187–206 (2008)
44. Mavronicolas, M., Spirakis, P.G.: The price of selfish routing. Algorithmica **48**(1), 91–126 (2007)
45. Milchtaich, I.: Network topology and the efficiency of equilibrium. Games Econ. Behav. **57**, 321–346 (2006)
46. Monderer, D., Shapley, L.: Potential games. Games Econ. Behav. **14**, 124–143 (1996)
47. Panagopoulou, P.N., Spirakis, P.G.: Algorithms for pure Nash equilibria in weighted congestion games. ACM J. Exp. Algorithmics **11**, 1–19 (2006)
48. Rosenthal, R.W.: A class of games possessing pure-strategy nash equilibria. Int. J. Game Theory **2**, 65–67 (1973)
49. Roughgarden, T.: The price of anarchy is independent of the network topology. In: Proceedings of the 34th ACM Symposium on Theory of Computing (STOC 2002), pp. 428–437 (2002)
50. Roughgarden, T.: Stackelberg scheduling strategies. SIAM J. Comput. **33**(2), 332–350 (2004)
51. Roughgarden, T.: On the severity of Braess's paradox: designing networks for selfish users is hard. J. Comput. Syst. Sci. **72**(5), 922–953 (2006)
52. Swamy, C.: The effectiveness of stackelberg strategies and tolls for network congestion games. In: Proceedings of the 18th ACM-SIAM Symposium on Discrete Algorithms (SODA 2007), pp. 1133–1142 (2007)
53. Valiant, G., Roughgarden, T.: Braess's paradox in large random graphs. Random Struct. Algorithms **37**(4), 495–515 (2010)

Data-Streaming and Concurrent Data-Object Co-design: Overview and Algorithmic Challenges

Vincenzo Gulisano, Yiannis Nikolakopoulos, Marina Papatriantafilou[✉],
and Philippas Tsigas

Chalmers University of Technology, Gothenburg, Sweden
ptrianta@chalmers.se

Abstract. Processing big volumes of data generated on-line, implies needs to carry out computations on-the-fly, in the streams of data. In parallel data-stream computing, the underlying data objects can provide the means for exchanging the data so that the communication and the work imbalance between the concurrent threads performing the computation are reduced, while the pipeline parallelism is enhanced. By shedding light on the concurrent data objects and their role as articulation points in data-stream processing, we place some cornerstones to analyze the problems, propose appropriate new data structures suitable for a set of functions and identify new key challenges to improve data-stream processing through co-design with fine-grain efficient synchronization combined with the data exchange.

It is interesting to point out that research in distributed computing on multiprocessor efficient and consistent data sharing through fine-grain synchronization emerged from questions in concurrent database-related research; approximately three decades since then, it is interesting to see several returns of the fruits of this expedition, helping with the new problems in the massive-data research domain, with applications in e.g. cyberphysical systems.

Keywords: Concurrent data structures · Data-streaming · Stream processing engines · In-memory data analysis

1 Introduction

Concurrent data objects are commonly described as implementations of Abstract Data Types (ADTs) shared by concurrent execution threads or processes. ADTs form abstractions of high re-usability across different applications and provide structured access to the data through their interface. The goals of the algorithmic implementation are about correctness and minimal complexity overhead of data-access, modification and retrieval.

One of the challenges in parallel and concurrent programs and applications, that also applies to their data objects, stems from the communication overhead, which needs to be minimized, too — besides the computational complexity—, so as to ensure that the underlying system's parallelism is properly utilized. Consequently, concurrent data structures need to integrate communication patterns,

© Springer International Publishing Switzerland 2015
C. Zaroliagis et al. (Eds.): Spirakis Festschrift, LNCS 9295, pp. 242–260, 2015.
DOI: 10.1007/978-3-319-24024-4_15

besides access patterns, that will serve the needs of the application domain that they will be used in.

In the journey from traditional methods for implementing shared objects through mutual exclusion to *lock-free* or *wait-free* algorithmic implementations, motivation and boost came from research communities focusing on the analysis and exploration of data. Nearly concurrently with the very important foundational steps in formalization of concurrency requirements in database-transactions [44,45,52], there came ideas of allowing concurrency in shared data object algorithmic implementations; e.g. first through proposing to safely allow read-only operations to execute concurrently with each-other in [14], later on with the seminal step by Lamport in [33], providing algorithms that allow concurrent reading and writing without assuming process synchrony or mutual exclusion, while also guaranteeing safety properties of the values obtained.

The above are all the more important in the new era of cyberphysical systems, with needs for computationally- and energy-efficient systems to analyse the big streams of data and extract useful information [18–20]. While the leveraging of concurrent algorithmic implementation of shared data objects might have been limited by the earlier times nature of analysis needs by applications —based on stored-data, rather than in-memory data— we now are in an era where data is generated in massive rates —e.g. by cyberphysical systems— and where in-memory analysis is needed to cope with such rates. Leveraging the concurrent data objects that best fit the needs of an application in a concurrent environment is a key issue, as highlighted by Michael in the "Balancing act of choosing non-blocking features" [40]. Moreover, quoting from [3], *"Not having to read from the disk and write computation results back saves hours to days of scientific work, giving scientists more time to investigate the data"*. To process data in such a fashion, *data-streaming* is one of the new computation methodologies that have been proposed [2,5,8,9,21,25]. In data streaming, continuous queries, defined as Directed Acyclic Graphs (DAGs) of interconnected operators, are executed by Stream Processing Engines (SPEs) that process incoming data and produce results in a continuous fashion, without the necessity of storing the data. As highlighted in [16], parallelism is a necessity due to the low-latency and high-throughput requirements of such continuous real-time complex processing of increasingly large data volumes.

What are the shared objects that meet the needs of concurrent data streaming applications is an important issue that has only recently been brought for addressing in the literature [13]. By shedding light on the data structures, these recent findings place essential cornerstones in this study avenue and identify new key challenges to improve data streaming. In other words, what we observe is that in the journey where big data and concurrent data transactions meet concurrent data objects, there is a new crossing: data and computation meet in new forms and with new needs. In-memory, close-to-source analysis of data can provide useful information and services in cyberphysical systems. Data-streaming is significant in this context [20]. Concurrent data objects are a means to enhance the data streaming parallelism as needed, while new data objects and interfaces are required to be defined to meet the needs of data streaming.

Outline of the Paper. In the rest of this paper we outline the key points in the aforementioned findings, emphasizing the role of concurrent data objects serving as articulation points in data streaming and stream processing engines in particular. We highlight new challenges and the benefits that can be brought by the co-design of data stream processing and concurrent object co-design.

Section 2 provides a short overview of the evolution of concurrency in shared objects algorithmic implementations. Section 3 provides an introduction to data streaming and the requirements in synchronization and determinism in data processing. Subsequently, Sects. 4 and 5 elaborate on architectural aspects of Stream Processing Engines and the challenges in parallelization, in connection to the way that concurrent threads process and exchange data, in order to meet the above requirements. Section 6 introduces a new abstract data type, whose concurrent lock-free and linearizable implementation can allow threads to work efficiently in an asynchronous fashion and meet the requirements for synchronization and determinism in data stream processing. Section 7 provides an example evaluation of possible throughput and latency improvements in data streaming, by the use of the new shared object and its concurrent algorithmic implementation. Section 8 concludes with a discussion, pointing out also directions for further research.

2   Concurrent object Algorithmic Implementations - Preliminaries

As discussed in Sect. 1, shared objects have been traditionally implemented through mutual exclusion. The first steps in introducing true concurrency in shared object implementations [14,33] can be characterized as ideas and results that opened a big avenue in research. Setting the foundations for arguing about concurrency in shared object implementations that allowed concurrent access became an important next goal. In this context, we can find Lamport's definitions [34] of shared object implementations with progress guarantees (*wait-freeness*) and safety properties (*safeness, regularity, atomicity*) of such, describing the data consistency. The latter were proposed to formulate requirements for the object constructions and assumptions of the underlying system description. It was argued that they can e.g. describe consistency guarantees of asynchronous hardware. Related here is also the work by Misra [42], formulating axioms for memory access in asynchronous hardware systems, and by Lynch and Tuttle [38] setting foundations for hierarchical correctness proofs for distributed algorithms through automata and executions on them. Another significant step has been the formulation of *linearizabilty* as correctness condition for concurrent objects, by Herlihy and Wing [31].

For ease of reference, we paraphrase here the definitions of some of the key terms, that are also used later in the paper. A *wait-free* object implementation ensures that any operation on the object can complete in bounded number of steps, independently of other contending processes. A relaxed condition is lock-freedom: a *lock-free* object implementation ensures that at least one of the contending operations makes progress in a finite number of its own steps. These properties are often referred to in the literature as *non-blocking*. An implementation of an object is *linearizable* if each operation execution appears to take effect at some point (linearization point) between its invocation and response; thus, given an execution of concurrent operations and by using the linearization points, it should be able to define a total order of the operations, which is consistent with their real-time ordering and their effects are consistent with the sequential semantics of the data structure.

Following the foundations, there was a "movement" in the scientific community, providing challenging algorithmic implementations of shared data objects allowing concurrency and guaranteeing a variety of safety properties (linearizability or weaker forms) and progress properties (e.g. wait-freeness, lock-freeness, obstruction-freeness); we refer the reader to [6,11,29,37] and references therein, for overview and more detailed presentations of key results.

In parallel, the hardware point of view is also worthwhile to comment on. At the first stages, the concept of asynchronous parallel hardware was mainly studied from a theoretical point of view, with the exception of some elegant efforts such as the work by the group of Ebergen [15,46]. Similar has been the perspective of massive parallelism, until the relatively recent era of multicore and manycore systems in hardware. The latter triggered a new "movement", that brought changes including the consideration of new abstractions, most notably the one of transactional memory [28,47] as well as the deeper consideration of asynchronous hardware [26]. This evolution makes the need for asynchronous concurrent implementations of shared objects even more significant.

3   Data Streaming - Preliminaries

In this section, we introduce basic concepts of the data streaming processing paradigm. We also illustrate them through a sample data streaming continuous query that analyzes traffic gathered from the *SoundCloud* [48] social network. Besides, we overview the evolution of Stream Processing Engines (SPEs) from centralized to parallel-distributed ones, also introducing the definition of *deterministic processing* (also referred to as *semantic transparency* [22]).

Data Streaming Model. A data stream S is an unbounded sequence of tuples sharing a given schema composed by attributes $\langle ts, A_1, A_2, \ldots, A_n \rangle$. We refer to attribute A_i of tuple t as $t.A_i$. Attribute $t.ts$ represents the time when the tuple is created. As common in the literature [12], we assume that tuples generated by a given data source and delivered through the same data stream have non-decreasing ts values. We also suppose data sources have clocks that are well-synchronized using a clock synchronization protocol like NTP [41].

Table 1 presents a sample schema, composed of four attributes, for tuples carrying comments (exchanged by users in relation to songs) from the SoundCloud platform.

It should be noted that tuples belonging to the same *logical* data stream, sharing the same schema and carrying similar information (e.g., comments about

Table 1. Sample tuple schema.

Attribute	Content
ts	The creation timestamp of the tuple
user	The user commenting a song
song	The song to which the comment refers to
comment	The comment itself

songs, as in Table 1), might be delivered by multiple distinct *physical* streams (e.g., generated by crawlers running at different physical nodes). As we explain in the following, such distinction plays an important role if tuples must be processed deterministically. In the remainder, we refer to logical streams simply as streams, specifying explicitly when physical streams are in focus.

In the data streaming model, input tuples coming from one or multiple input streams are consumed by *Continuous Queries* (or simply queries in the following), which subsequently produce one or more output streams. A query, defined as a directed acyclic graph (DAG) with additional input and output edges, produces results "continuously" while consuming input tuples. Vertexes represent operators that consume tuples (from at least one input stream) and produce output tuples (for at least one output stream). Edges define how input and output tuples flow among the operators of a query.

Data Streaming Operators. Data streaming operators, the base unit used to process and produce tuples, are classified depending on whether they maintain a state that evolves accordingly with the input tuples being processed. *Stateless operators* such as *Map*, *Filter* and *Union* do not maintain such a state and perform a one-by-one processing of input tuples. On the other hand, *stateful operators* such as *Aggregate* and *Join* maintain a state and process multiple input tuples in order to produce one output tuple. Due to the unbounded nature of data streams, stateful computations are usually performed over *sliding windows* covering portions of the input tuples. Time based windows are defined over period of times (e.g., tuples received in the last 10 min) while tuple based windows are defined over the number of stored tuples (e.g., last 50 received tuples).

Continuous Query Example. Let us take a look at a sample continuous query that consumes the tuples sharing the schema presented in Table 1 to count the number of positive comments (i.e., comments containing certain predefined keywords) exchanged by users in relation to each song. As presented in Fig. 1[1], the query is composed by three operators.

An initial *Map* operator transforms each comment (attribute *comment* into a stream of words typed by users in relation to songs. Its resulting output stream schema is composed by attributes $\langle ts, song, word \rangle$. Subsequently, a *Filter* operator is used to forward only the words that belong to a given subset of positive

---

[1] Tuples shown in this example are not extracted from SoundCloud, but handcrafted for the specific example.

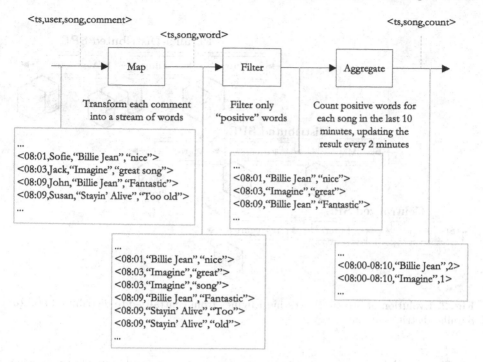

Fig. 1. Sample query that consumes tuples sharing the schema in Table 1 and counts the number of positive comments exchanged by users in relation to each song.

words (e.g., nice, great or fantastic). The output tuples produced by this operator share the same schema of its input tuples. Finally, an *Aggregate* operator is used to count, for each song, how many positive words are received over a sliding window of 10 min and to produce a new result every 2 min.

3.1 Parallel Data Streaming and Deterministic Processing

As emphasized in [16], real-time continuous processing of large volumes of data demand for low-latency and high throughput processing. During the last decade, such increasing demand drove the evolution of SPEs from centralized [2,5,9] to distributed [1] and to parallel-distributed ones [17,22,23]. As shown in Fig. 2 (in relation to the sample query of Fig. 1), queries are entirely deployed and run by exactly one SPE instance when the latter is centralized. By providing *inter-operator* parallelism, distributed SPEs allow for the execution of different operators belonging to the same query at different SPE instances. Finally, by providing *intra-operator* parallelism, parallel-distributed SPEs also allow for a single operator to be executed at multiple SPE instances. For simplicity, the figure shows distinct SPE instances running at distinct physical machines. Nevertheless, multiple SPE instances can be deployed within the same physical node (e.g., to leverage multi-core architectures).

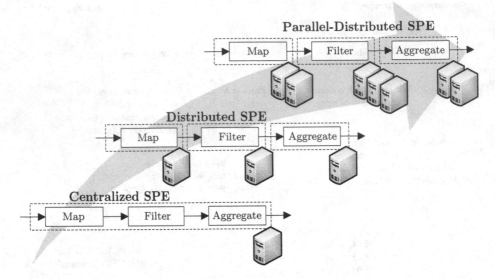

Fig. 2. Evolution of Stream Processing Engines from centralized to distributed and to parallel-distributed ones.

The parallel execution of data streaming operators (and thus of the queries they compose) is the only means for a single operator to avoid to get overloaded because of its volume of input data; the latter would of course be unwanted as it would degrade the performance of the entire data streaming query. Challenging aspects in the design and implementation of parallel data streaming operators do not only aim at improving their performance, but also aim at preserving their semantic.

Definition 1. *[22, 23] The property of semantic transparency or deterministim in parallel stream processing guarantees that, by consuming the tuples delivered by a given set of physical input streams, a parallel operator produces exactly the same output that would be produced by its centralized counterpart.*

As explained in [13], a condition to enforce deterministic processing for the operators of a query is to process tuples delivered by distinct physical streams in timestamp-order (that is, to process them deterministically independently of their inter-arrival times). In the context of parallel-distributed SPEs, the distinct physical input streams of an operator do not only refer to the physical streams generated by distinct sources, but also to the distinct physical streams generated by the multiple instances of a parallel operator. In the example in Fig. 1, distinct physical streams could be delivered to the Map operator by distinct sources, while distinct physical streams could be delivered to the aggregate from the multiple SPE instances running the Filter operator in parallel. In [12], the authors introduce the concept of *ready* tuple as follows:

Definition 2. *Let t_i^j be the i-th tuple in timestamp-sorted physical stream j. Tuple t_i^j is ready to be processed if $t_i^j.ts \leq merge_{ts}$, where $merge_{ts}$ is the minimum among the latest timestamps from each timestamp-sorted physical stream j, i.e. $merge_{ts} = min_j\{max_i(t_i^j.ts)\}$*

Based on this definition, deterministic processing is enforced if operators consume timestamp-sorted *ready* tuples from their physical input streams.

It should be noticed that the way in which input tuples are distinguished between the ones that are *ready* and the ones that are not is not orthogonal to the data structures used to maintain such tuples. Naïve solutions that rely on data structures oblivious to the concept of *ready* tuples bound the parallelism and concurrency degree of the analysis, usually incur in high processing costs and introduce processing bottlenecks. On the other hand, streaming-aware data structures enable for finer-grained and scalable cooperation among the different threads operating on them, as we will explain in Sect. 5.

4   Inter-thread Communication in SPEs Architecture

In this section, we present the common architecture of a SPE, focusing especially on the data structures defined for each SPE instance to maintain the tuples being consumed and produced in a deterministic fashion and the threads operating on them. For the clarity of the discussion, we illustrate the architecture of a SPE considering a single query consuming one input stream and producing one output stream, and do not overview the data structures internal to the query's operators (maintaining partial computations and windows). While overviewing the architecture, we also discuss its limitations motivating the discussion that follows, in Sect. 5.

Common SPE Architecture. The common architecture of a SPE (presented in Fig. 3) usually defines three main modules, which we refer to as M_{in}, M_{proc} and M_{out}[1,2,22,36][2]. Module M_{in} maintains the queues in which tuples from a given set of physical input streams $I_1, \ldots, I_n$ are collected from the network. The collection of such tuples is usually performed by a dedicated thread, which we refer to as T_{in}, running the *add* method. Tuples from each physical input stream can be maintained at individual queues [22,23] or concurrent data structures such as the LMAX Disruptor [50] (as for the Storm [36] SPE).

Tuples stored at M_{in} are subsequently copied to M_{proc} and consumed by the different data streaming operators composing the query run by the SPE. More concretely, a dedicated thread (T_{proc}):

1. copies the tuples from each physical input stream (method *copy*),

---

[2] Complementary modules, not in the scope of this discussion, might be defined for features such as fault tolerance, scheduling, balancing or self-provisioning and self-decommissioning.

2. merges the timestamp-sorted physical streams into a single timestamp-sorted logical stream of tuples in order for the query to process tuples deterministically (method *merge*),
3. processes them (method *process*) and, finally,
4. stores the resulting output tuples in a dedicated queue (method *store*).

Each time an output tuple is produced, a dedicated thread T_{out} copies it to the queue maintained at the M_{out} module (method *copy*) and, finally, forwards it to other SPE instances or to the external user applications (method *forward*)[3].

Basic Architecture

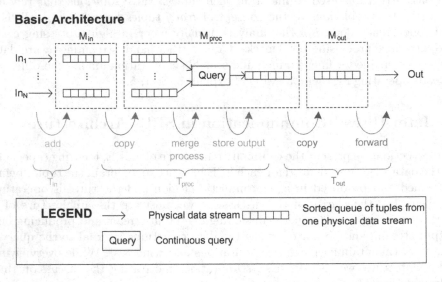

Fig. 3. Basic architecture of a SPE, presenting the different modules and threads operating on them.

Enforcing Deterministic Processing. As presented in Fig. 3, the execution of the method *process* is preceded by the execution of the method *merge* for thread T_{proc}. The merging of the physical streams referring to the same logical stream of tuples fed to the query is performed in order to enforce deterministic process (as discussed in Sect. 3.1). The merging of the physical input streams can happen in different ways. On one hand, each new tuple from a physical stream I_i can be compared with the ones previously received from any physical stream $I_j | j \neq i$ in order to identify the *ready* tuples and process them. Such aggressive merging, performed by operators such as the Transparent Input Merger [22] or the SUnion operator [7], results in low processing latency, as each tuple is processed as soon as it becomes ready. On the other hand, the tuples from the different physical streams can also be sorted periodically, by using punctuation tuples [49] or by performing the sorting each time a given time period expires.

---

[3] Depending on how the data structures in modules M_{in}, M_{proc} and M_{out} are defined, locking mechanism can be in place, as in [23].

With respect to the output tuples produced by the query running at the SPE, the method *forward* is executed by exactly one thread in order for the output tuples to be delivered in timestamp order to the following SPE instance or to the end user application.

Shortcomings. The architecture outlined above results in several shortcomings, as we explain in the following.

First, by keeping dedicated threads for the different stages, it is prone to unbalanced work (and thus does not leverage at their full potential the available threads). As it can be observed, threads T_{in} and T_{out} perform a reduced set of methods (*add*, *copy* and *forward*) with respect to thread T_{out}. Moreover, such operations are light when compared with computational intensive operations such as *merge* and *process* (the latter depending on the number of operators composing the query run by the SPE).

Secondly, *copy* operations are performed by both the T_{in} and T_{out} threads in order to retrieve the tuples from their preceding modules. As discussed in [4], the copies required to maintain tuples at different queues incur in a significant cost, which in turns affects the performance of the SPE.

Finally, independently of whether tuples are sorted periodically or upon reception of each new incoming tuple, the merging techniques proposed in the literature [7,22] usually have a processing cost that grows linearly in the number of physical streams being merged. Moreover, the merging itself constitutes a *potential bottleneck* for the entire system (whose throughput is bounded by the speed with which input tuples can be merged) and it limits the pipelining of the operations performed by the different threads. That is, independently of the rate at which input tuples are retrieved by thread T_{in}, as long as available tuples are not merged, no tuple can be processed by thread T_{proc} and, consequently, no new result can be forwarded by the thread T_{out}.

5   Leveraging Concurrent Data Structures in SPEs

As we discuss in this section, three main actions can be undertaken to balance the work of the different threads running within a SPE instance and thus enhance its inner concurrency and maximize its performance. As we complement in our evaluation, such actions result in a significant performance improvement for the throughput of a SPE.

Switch from Inter-module to Intra-module Data Access. The first action towards an improved architecture is for modules to share the data structures where tuples retrieved from the network are maintained before being fed to the query. While the thread(s) operating on such modules can be in charge of different tasks (either retrieving tuples from the network or consume input tuples), the joint access prevents unnecessary copies of tuples across modules M_{in} and M_{proc}. In this context, fine-grained synchronization mechanisms should be defined for threads M_{in} and M_{proc} intercommunication.

A) Shared and Concurrent access to input tuples

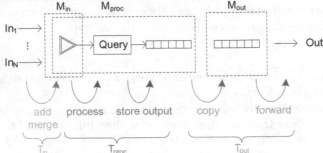

B) Shared and concurrent access to input and output tuples

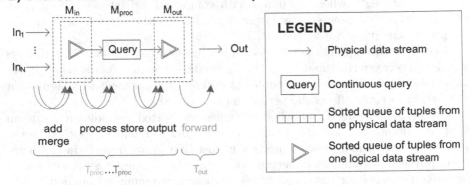

Fig. 4. SPE architectures leveraging concurrent data structures.

Merge Physical Streams Concurrently. As discussed in Sect. 3.1, the tuples delivered by timestamp-sorted physical input stream streams of a query must be merged and fed in timestamp order in order to enforce deterministic processing. Hence, the second action is to enable for the merging of tuples delivered by physical streams to happen concurrently with their processing (as presented in Fig. 4A). This approach provides a better balancing of the threads work by shifting the *merge* operation to thread T_{in}.

Consume Logical Streams Concurrently. The third action aims at overcoming the potential bottleneck caused by merging the tuples delivered by the distinct physical input streams. This can be achieved by relying on a concurrent data structure that not only enables for concurrent addition of tuples (being merged) and retrieval of tuples (being processed), but also allows for such operations to be performed by arbitrarily number of processing threads. Such an architecture allows the parallelism degree of a SPE instance to grow beyond the number of threads usually defined by the latter. In such a case, though, the synchronization is no only required for the merging of input tuples, but also for the merging of output ones (as presented in Fig. 4B). That is, since multiple physical output streams are produced by the processing threads running at the

SPE, the former must be merged deterministically into a single logical stream. As we explain in [12, 24], the way in which input tuples are processed by the different threads depends on the semantics of the operators running at the SPE instance.

6 ScaleGate: A Novel, Concurrency- and Streaming-Aware Data Object

As discussed in Sect. 5, a shared data structure that enables for concurrent addition and merging of tuples delivered by multiple physical streams, while also allowing for an arbitrary number of threads to retrieve *ready* tuples in timestamp order, is the key to balance the workload of an arbitrary number of processing threads running in a SPE instance. In the following, we overview such a data structure, *ScaleGate*, focusing on its functionality and core ideas and also presenting its interface. We refer the reader to [24] for its implementation details.

Overview and Interface. The common architecture of SPEs outlined in Sect. 4, can be seen as a pipeline where data is continuously produced, processed and consumed across the different stages, in this case the three main modules. In a parallel implementation, each computational thread associated with one or more modules will communicate with the rest by accessing and/or modifying the shared data structures, which are the focal point of this section. The ideal concurrent data structures should organize the data so that the communication cost and computational complexity of each access is minimized while the parallelism within the modules and the overall system efficiency is maximized. Moreover, this should be done under an interface that provides semantics that enhance the parallelism across modules.

ScaleGate is a recently proposed abstract data type that becomes a cornerstone in achieving the parallelization challenges presented in the previous section. *ScaleGate* guarantees properties essential for concurrently merging physical streams at the articulation points where data and threads meet, while it integrates the necessary synchronization for allowing multiple threads to consume *ready* tuples concurrently. It allows for an arbitrary number of timestamp-sorted streams, each delivered by a *source* thread, to be merged into a timestamp-sorted stream of *ready* tuples (Definition 2). At the same time, it allows for an arbitrary number of *reader* threads to consume in timestamp order all the *ready* tuples of the resulting timestamp-sorted stream. *ScaleGate* integrates, in a decentralized manner, the necessary communication between the source and reader threads in order to decide whether a tuple is *ready* or not. The interface of *ScaleGate* provides the following methods:

- addTuple(timestamp,tuple,sourceID): which allows a tuple from the source thread sourceID to be merged by *ScaleGate* in the resulting timestamp-sorted stream of *ready* tuples.

- getNextReadyTuple(readerID): which provides to the calling reader thread readerID the next earliest *ready* tuple that has not been yet consumed by the former.

Algorithmic Design for Concurrent Implementation of *ScaleGate*. As explained earlier in the paper, synchronization is one of the fundamental design considerations for a concurrent data structure implementation. Lock-free (a.k.a. non-blocking) implementations ensure system-wide progress, by guaranteeing at least one of the threads operating on the data structure to make progress independently of the behavior of other threads. Following the expectations based on their basic properties, such implementations demonstrate higher scalability and better fairness when compared with coarse- or fine-grain locking mechanisms [10,35,39]. This behavior remains across several multiprocessor hardware architectures, with varying characteristics such as uniform/non-uniform memory access, or memory hierarchies. All the above contribute to the choice in [24], for lock-free algorithmic implementation of the *ScaleGate*.

A basic requirement for an algorithmic implementation of the *ScaleGate* is to maintain items in a sorted manner. Tree-like implementations, especially balanced ones, have not been proven efficient in concurrent environments due to the strong dependencies that appear in balancing operations [30]. On the contrary, shared concurrent skip lists [27,51] have been used extensively for such requirements. In a nutshell, skip lists maintain a sorted linked list of elements (e.g., tuples), while allowing for probabilistically logarithmic concurrent insertions of new elements and the concurrent deletion of existing ones. This is made possible by multiple levels (pointers), for each element, that act as shortcuts for quickly locating the appropriate insertion position of a new element. The number of additional levels for each element is chosen randomly during its allocation.

Inspired by skip lists, the *ScaleGate* algoritmic implementation incorporates a multi-level pointer mechanism adapted to its requirements. Such adaption aims at enabling fine-grained synchronization that boosts parallelism and is carried out (1) by making *ScaleGate* inherently aware of the concept of *ready* tuples and (2) by exploiting the specific access patterns of *ready* tuples (e.g. consumed in timestamp order by the threads executing the queries) and thus allowing for a more lightweight implementation than the general purpose delete operations of skip lists (such operations carry a considerable overhead in the respective implementations).

Claim. The concurrent implementation of *ScaleGate* in [12,24] follows the above elements and satisfies strong safety and liveness requirements, namely linearizability and lock-freedom. Also, as shown in [12,24], *ScaleGate* enables deterministic execution of data streaming operators.

7   Evaluation Study

In this section we describe an experimental study of how concurrent data structures can enhance the performance of SPE by finer-grained synchronization among the threads operating on the tuples. This is not meant to be a thorough evaluation of the proposed data structure and stream processing engine designs. Some detailed experimental studies for a range of operators and input streams that vary in character and volumes can be found in [12,13,24].

In particular, here we show an evaluation of the performance for the query introduced in Sect. 3, in different SPE architectures presented in Figs. 3 and 4. More concretely, we measure both their per-tuple processing time (in μs) and overall throughput (in tuples/second, t/s). We begin by discussing the evaluation setup.

Experiment Setup

This evaluation study has been run with a workstation equipped with a 2.0 GHz Intel Xeon E5-2650 (16 cores over 2 sockets) and 64 GB of memory. The different data structures and modules of SPEs' architectures have been implemented in Java. We use a dataset, which we refer to as SC, collected from the online audio distribution platform SoundCloud from a subset of approximately $40,000$ users exchanging comments about $250,000$ songs between 2007 and 2013. Tuples contain comments sent by users in relation to songs and are composed by the attributes $\langle ts, user, song, comment \rangle$.

We fed tuples from the SC dataset into the query presented in Sect. 3, which counts the number of positive comments (a comment is considered as positive if it contains keywords such as nice, great, fantastic and so on) in relation to each song given a window of size 10 min and advance 2 min. In all the experiments, we assume input tuples are delivered to the query by 20 distinct physical input streams.

We refer to the basic architecture (Fig. 3), the architecture defining shared and concurrent access to the input tuples (Fig. 4A) and the one defining shared and concurrent access for both input and output tuples (Fig. 4B) as architectures A_1, A_2 and A_3, respectively. In all the experiments, we measure the average per-tuple processing time based on the operation performed by threads T_{in} and T_{proc} in the different architectures. Subsequently, we compute the maximum expected throughput based on such per-tuple processing time. Since both threads T_{in} and T_{proc} perform the same operations for architecture A_3, we refer to the threads as T_1 and T_2 in all the experiments. All the presented results are averaged over 100 runs. In all the experiments, we do not take into account the per-tuple processing time incurred by the thread T_{out} in order to forward each output tuple to the following SPE instance or the external end-user application.

Illustrative Outcome and Discussion. In the following, we present the results for the three different setups we considered, namely A_1, A_2 and A_3. Results about the per-tuple processing time are summarized in Fig. 5 while throughput results are summarized in Fig. 6.

Architecture A_1 (Fig. 3). In the first experiment, we consider the SPE architecture presented in Fig. 3, in which thread T_{in} is in charge of the *add* operation while thread T_{proc} is in charge of the *copy, merge, process* and *store* operations.

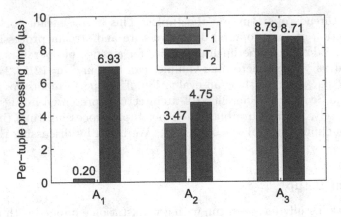

Fig. 5. Per-tuple average processing time for threads T_1 and T_2 and the different architectures A_1, A_2 and A_3.

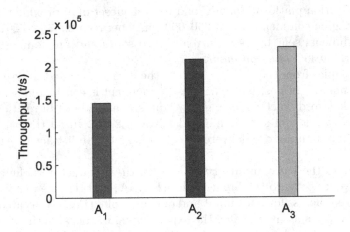

Fig. 6. Throughput achieved by the different architectures A_1, A_2 and A_3.

As presented in Fig. 5 and explained in Sect. 4, the two threads are heavily unbalanced. Thread T_{in} is responsible for a single, lightweight operation which on average takes 0.2 ms to be run. At the same time, thread T_{proc} is responsible for merge sorting all the input tuples and process them, which on average takes 6.9 ms (that is, the per-tuple processing time for thread T_{proc} is 35 times higher than the one for thread tone). For such a setup, the operations run by thread T_{proc} result in a bottleneck of the system, allowing for a maximum throughput of 150, 000 t/s.

Architecture A_2 (Fig. 4A). For this architecture, the *merge* operation is now performed by thread T_{in} rather than T_{proc}. While the work between the two threads is still unbalanced, it can be observed that thread T_{in} per-tuple processing now grows to approx 3.5 ms while thread T_{proc} per-tuple processing time decreases to 4.8 ms. As a result, while still containing a bottleneck, this setup allows for an increased throughput, up to 200,000 t/s (thus increasing the baseline A_1 throughput by 33 %).

Architecture A_3 (Fig. 4B). For this architecture, the operations *add*, *copy*, *merge*, *process* and *store* are not partitioned among the two threads T_{in} and T_{proc} but rather executed (all of them) by both threads in a parallel and concurrent fashion. As we explained in Sect. 5, while such an architecture requires extra synchronization in order for the output tuples produced by each thread to be merged into a single logical stream (in order to enforce deterministic processing), it allows for the parallel and concurrent execution of an arbitrary number of processing threads (as long as the merging of their output tuples does not constitute a bottleneck).

As presented in Fig. 5, the per-tuple processing time incurred by both threads grows to approximately 8.7 ms. As only one of them is needed in order to process a tuple and each of them is able to process 115000 t/s, independently from the other, the overall throughput of the system grows to 230000 t/s (thus increasing the baseline A_1 throughput by more than 50 %).

Overview Comment. The significant improvements are achieved through more balanced work among the threads and the possibility for each thread to make progress asynchronously and nearly independent of the progress of the other threads. These are enabled through the*ScaleGate* concurrent object, as expected.

8   Conclusions

In this paper we give an overview of the motivation and the idea of co-design of data stream processing and concurrent data structures. We point out that abstract data types and their concurrent implementations play a key role in data streaming efficiency and we give examples of newly proposed ones that can offer significant benefits. Symmetrically, we show that stream processing designs can benefit significantly by awareness of the concurrency in the "articulation" points, where data and computation "meet". This is all the more important given the needs for processing in the continuously increasing data volumes in e.g. cyber-physical systems [20], where data streaming becomes a must in order to extract efficiently useful information from the data and justify the existence of these systems.

Continued research in this new space is expected to have significant impact, both from the point of view of concurrent algorithmic challenges that are brought in, as well as from the point of view of usefulness in actual applications' needs. Possible topics include efficiency and consistency (and their trade-offs) in the context of intra-node and inter-node concurrency for data streaming operators, as well as in the context of operations such as range queries, possibly through snapshots or iterations on these objects [32,43]; the analysis of data transformation pipelines (with a query) given the progress properties of the concurrent object implementations; new abstract data types and efficient concurrent implementations that can improve such pipelines.

References

1. Abadi, D.J., Ahmad, Y., Balazinska, M., Çetintemel, U., Cherniack, M., Hwang, J.-H., Lindner, W., Maskey, A., Rasin, A., Ryvkina, E., Tatbul, N., Xing, Y., Zdonik, S.B.: The design of the borealis stream processing engine. In: CIDR, pp. 277–289 (2005)
2. Abadi, D.J., Carney, D., Cetintemel, U., Cherniack, M., Convey, C., Lee, S., Stonebraker, M., Tatbul, N., Zdonik, S.: Aurora: a new model and architecture for data stream management. VLDB J. **12**, 12–139 (2003)
3. Ailamaki, A., Kantere, V., Dash, D.: Managing scientific data. Commun. ACM **53**(6), 68–78 (2010)
4. Akram, S., Marazakis, M., Bilas, A.: Understanding and improving the cost of scaling distributed event processing. In: Proceedings of the 6th ACM International Conference on Distributed Event-Based Systems, DEBS 2012, pp. 290–301. ACM, New York (2012)
5. Arasu, A., Babcock, B., Babu, S., Cieslewicz, J., Datar, M., Ito, K., Motwani, R., Srivastava, U., Widom, J.: Stream: the stanford data stream management system. Book chapter (2004)
6. Attiya, H., Welch, J.: Distributed Computing: Fundamentals. Simulations and Advanced Topics, Wiley Online Library (2004)
7. Balazinska, M., Balakrishnan, H., Madden, S.R., Stonebraker, M.: Fault-tolerance in the Borealis distributed stream processing system. ACM Trans. Database Syst. **33**(1), 3 (2008)
8. Callau-Zori, M., Jiménez-Peris, R., Gulisano, V., Papatriantafilou, M., Fu, Z., Patiño Martínez, M.: Stone: a stream-based ddos defense framework. In: Proceedings of the 28th Annual ACM Symposium on Applied Computing, SAC 2013, pp. 807–812. ACM (2013)
9. Carney, D., Cetintemel, U., Cherniack, M., Convey, C., Lee, S., Seidman, G., Stonebraker, M., Tatbul, N., Zdonik, S.: Monitoring streams: a new class of data management applications. In: Proceedings of the 28th International Conference on Very Large Data Bases, VLDB 2002. VLDB Endowment (2002)
10. Cederman, D., Chatterjee, B., Nguyen, N., Nikolakopoulos, Y., Papatriantafilou, M., Tsigas, P.: A study of the behavior of synchronization methods in commonly used languages and systems. In: IEEE 27th International Symposium on Parallel and Distributed Processing (IPDPS) (2013)
11. Cederman, D., Gidenstam, A., Ha, P., Sundell, H., Papatriantafilou, M., Tsigas, P.: Lock-free concurrent data structures (2013). arXiv:1302.2757
12. Cederman, D., Gulisano, V., Nikolakopoulos, Y., Papatriantafilou, M., Tsigas, P.: Concurrent data structures for efficient streaming aggregation. Technical report, Chalmers University of Technology (2013)
13. Cederman, D., Gulisano, V., Nikolakopoulos, Y., Papatriantafilou, M., Tsigas, P.: Brief announcement: concurrent data structures for efficient streaming aggregation. In: Proceedings of the 26th ACM Symposium on Parallelism in Algorithms and Architectures, SPAA 2014, pp. 76–78 (2014)
14. Courtois, P.-J., Heymans, F., Parnas, D.L.: Concurrent control with readers and writers. Commun. ACM **14**(10), 667–668 (1971)

15. Ebergen, J.: Circuits without clocks: what makes them tick? In: Papatriantafilou, M., Hunel, P. (eds.) OPODIS 2003. LNCS, vol. 3144, pp. 2–2. Springer, Heidelberg (2004)
16. Gedik, B., Bordawekar, R.R., Philip, S.Y.: Cell Join: a parallel stream join operator for the cell processor. VLDB J. **18**, 501–519 (2009)
17. Gulisano, V.: StreamCloud: An Elastic Parallel-Distributed Stream Processing Engine. Ph.D. thesis, Universidad Politécnica de Madrid (2012)
18. Gulisano, V., Almgren, M., Papatriantafilou, M.: Metis: a two-tier intrusion detection system for advanced metering infrastructures. In: Proceedings of the 5th International Conference on Future Energy Systems, e-Energy 2014, pp. 211–212. ACM (2014)
19. Gulisano, V., Almgren, M., Papatriantafilou, M.: Online and scalable data validation in advanced metering infrastructures. In: Innovative Smart Grid Technologies Conference Europe (ISGT-Europe), 2014 IEEE PES, pp. 1–6 (2014)
20. Gulisano, V., Almgren, M., Papatriantafilou, M.: When smart cities meet big data. ERCIM News. Smart Cities, p. 40 (2014)
21. Gulisano, V., Jimenez-Peris, R., Patiño-Martinez, M., Soriente, C., Valduriez, P.: A big data platform for large scale event processing. ERCIM News **2012**(89), 2 (2012)
22. Gulisano, V., Jimenez-Peris, R., Patino-Martinez, M., Soriente, C., Valduriez, P.: Streamcloud: an elastic and scalable data streaming system. IEEE Trans. Parallel Distrib. Syst. **99** (2012)
23. Gulisano, V., Jiménez-Peris, R., Patiño-Martínez, M., Valduriez, P.: Streamcloud: a large scale data streaming system. In: ICDCS 2010: International Conference on Distributed Computing Systems (2010)
24. Gulisano, V., Nikolakopoulos, Y., Papatriantafilou, M., Tsigas, P.: ScaleJoin: a deterministic, disjoint-parallel and skew-resilient stream join enabled by concurrent data structures. Technical report, Chalmers University of Technology (2014)
25. Gulisano, V., Nikolakopoulos, Y., Walulya, I., Papatriantafilou, M., Tsigas, P.: DEBS grand challenge: deterministic real-time analytics of geospatial data streams through scalegate objects. In: DEBS 2015: the 9th ACM International Conference on Distributed Event-Based Systems (2015)
26. Hardavellas, N., Ferdman, M., Falsafi, B., Ailamaki, A.: Toward dark silicon in servers. IEEE Micro. **31**(EPFL-ARTICLE-168285), 6–15 (2011)
27. Herlihy, M.P., Lev, Y., Luchangco, V., Shavit, N.N.: A simple optimistic skiplist algorithm. In: Prencipe, G., Zaks, S. (eds.) SIROCCO 2007. LNCS, vol. 4474, pp. 124–138. Springer, Heidelberg (2007)
28. Herlihy, M., Moss, J.E.B.: Transactional memory: architectural support for lock-free data structures. In: Proceedings of the 20th Annual International Symposium on Computer Architecture, ISCA 1993, pp. 289–300. ACM, New York (1993)
29. Herlihy, M., Shavit, N.: The Art of Multiprocessor Programming. Morgan Kaufmann, Boston (2008)
30. Herlihy, M., Shavit, N.: The Art of Multiprocessor Programming. Elsevier, Revised Reprint (2012)
31. Herlihy, M.P., Wing, J.M.: Linearizability: a correctness condition for concurrent objects. ACM Trans. Program. Lang. Syst. **12**(3), 463–492 (1990)
32. Kirousis, L.M., Spirakis, P.G., Tsigas, P.: Reading many variables in one atomic operation: solutions with linear or sublinear complexity. IEEE Trans. Parallel Distrib. Syst. **5**(7), 688–696 (1994)
33. Lamport, L.: Concurrent reading and writing. Commun. ACM **20**(11), 806–811 (1977)

34. Lamport, L.: On interprocess communication. Part I: basic formalism. Distrib. Comput. **1**(2), 77–85 (1986)
35. Liu, Y., Zhang, K., Spear, M.: Dynamic-sized nonblocking hash tables. In: Proceedings of the 2014 ACM Symposium on Principles of Distributed Computing, PODC 2014. ACM (2014)
36. LMax Disruptor. https://lmax-exchange.github.io/disruptor/
37. Lynch, N.A.: Distributed Algorithms. Morgan Kaufmann, San Francisco (1996)
38. Lynch, N.A., Tuttle, M.R.: Hierarchical correctness proofs for distributed algorithms. In: Proceedings of the Sixth Annual ACM Symposium on Principles of Distributed Computing, Vancouver, British Columbia, Canada, August 10–12, 1987, pp. 137–151 (1987)
39. Michael, M.M.: High performance dynamic lock-free hash tables and list-based sets. In: Proceedings of the Fourteenth Annual ACM Symposium on Parallel Algorithms and Architectures, SPAA 2002. ACM (2002)
40. Michael, M.M.: The balancing act of choosing nonblocking features. Commun. ACM **56**(9), 46–53 (2013)
41. Mills, D.L.: A brief history of ntp time: memoirs of an internet timekeeper. Comput. Commun. Rev. **33**, 9–21 (2003)
42. Misra, J.: Axioms for memory access in asynchronous hardware systems. ACM Trans. Program. Lang. Syst. **8**(1), 142–153 (1986)
43. Nikolakopoulos, Y., Gidenstam, A., Papatriantafilou, M., Tsigas, P.: A consistency framework for iteration operations in concurrent data structures. In: IEEE 29th International Symposium on Parallel and Distributed Processing (IPDPS) (2015)
44. Papadimitriou, C.H.: The serializability of concurrent database updates. J. ACM **26**(4), 631–653 (1979)
45. Papadimitriou, C.H.: The Theory of Database Concurrency Control. Computer Science Press, Rockville (1986)
46. Papatriantafilou, M., Hunel, P. (eds.): OPODIS 2003. LNCS, vol. 3144. Springer, Heidelberg (2004)
47. Shavit, N., Touitou, D.: Software transactional memory. In: Proceedings of the Fourteenth Annual ACM Symposium on Principles of Distributed Computing, PODC 1995, pp. 204–213. ACM, New York (1995)
48. SoundCloud. https://soundcloud.com/
49. Srivastava, U., Widom, J.: Flexible time management in data stream systems. In: Proceedings of the Twenty-Third ACM SIGMOD-SIGACT-SIGART Symposium on Principles of Database Systems, pp. 263–274. ACM, New York (2004)
50. Storm project. http://storm.incubator.apache.org/
51. Sundell, H., Tsigas, P.: Fast and lock-free concurrent priority queues for multi-thread systems. J. Parallel Distrib. Comput. **65**, 609–627 (2005)
52. Tuzhilin, A., Spirakis, P.G.: A semantic approach to correctness of concurrent transaction executions. In: Proceedings of the Fourth ACM SIGACT-SIGMOD Symposium on Principles of Database Systems, PODS 1985, pp. 85–95. ACM, New York (1985)

Stability in Heterogeneous Dynamic Multimedia Networks

Dimitrios Koukopoulos[✉]

Department of Cultural Heritage Management and New Technologies,
University of Patras, 30100 Agrinio, Greece
dkoukopoulos@upatras.gr

Abstract. Internet and other multimedia packet-switched networks are *heterogeneous* due to the simultaneous running (composition) of different contention-resolution protocols over different network hosts and the existence of various types of network links. Also, real networks are dynamic in their nature due to intentional or unintentional changes on network link service rates or tra nsient link failures. Our interest is focused on FIFO compositions with other contention-resolution protocols due to the FIFO popularity for offering best-effort services in packet-switched networks. A packet-switched network is stable, if the number of packets in the network remains bounded at all times against any adversary. We use an enhanced adversarial framework that is based on an adversary that controls packet injection rates, along with packet paths, and manipulates link slowdowns or capacities. Within this framework, we study the impact of specific compositions of FIFO with other protocols on the network stability using as a test-bed specific network topologies which have been proved forbidden for stability for a single protocol, fixed link slowdowns/capacities and packet paths without repeated links/edges. Our results suggest that the instability behavior of a network using FIFO compositions under adversarial attacks, that dynamically change link slowdowns/capacities, is not only maintained, but, also, may become worse than in the case of attacks that do not change slowdowns/capacities or when a single protocol, like FIFO, is employed on all network queues for contention-resolution. We believe that this study can advance the research for the provision of trustworthy heterogeneous networks.

1 Introduction

Motivation-Objectives. The provision of efficient multimedia content distribution services to the consumers/end-users is a necessity in today's large-scale multimedia networks like Internet. The goal for efficient multimedia services should be two-fold. High-speed network infrastructure should be combined with reliability and robustness against adversarial attacks, even worst-case ones. Modern multimedia networks should handle efficiently changing loading conditions due

This research is dedicated to my teacher Prof. Spirakis, who contributed decisively to the formation of my academic personality, in honor of his 60th birthday.

© Springer International Publishing Switzerland 2015
C. Zaroliagis et al. (Eds.): Spirakis Festschrift, LNCS 9295, pp. 261–280, 2015.
DOI: 10.1007/978-3-319-24024-4_16

to versatile data loads or passing changes in network topology due to network link failures. A reliable multimedia network must be capable to support communication services, even if network links face service rate fluctuations or failures. The most common adversarial attacks that may lead a network to performance degradation due to service rate fluctuations or transient link failures are denial of service attacks. Such attacks flood the network (or a subnetwork) with dummy packets preventing end-users from having access to the network services [29,31]. Multimedia network administrators should be given suitable tools in order to handle such dangers. The degree of robustness of multimedia networks to such dangers could be considered as a measure of trustworthiness for those networks. Successively, highly-trustworthy multimedia networks will improve user confidence that the network will be able to provide the required service to satisfy user needs.

A network condition that is closely related to the robustness of a network infrastructure against worst-case adversarial attacks is stability. Stability requires that the number of packets in the network remains bounded at all times by a constant against any adversary [10]. There is a number of factors that affect this constant: packet injection rate into the network, initial number of network packets at the beginning of network operation, network topology, link slowdown (which is the time delay an outgoing packet suffers on a link), link capacity (which is the rate at which a link forwards outgoing packets) and protocol or composition of protocols used for contention resolution in the network queues [10,11,23]. However, it is not sure that those factors are the only ones that affect stability. Therefore, it is not easy to study the stability behavior of multimedia networks, even if they are small ones.

Here, we aim at studying the stability of large-scale heterogeneous dynamic multimedia networks, such as the Internet. Internet is heterogeneous and dynamic in its nature due to its ability to support multiple contention-resolution protocols running on different network hosts and multiple network links with varying service rates (wired, satellite, mobile, etc.) that can suffer from link failures [16]. We are further interested in the investigation of networks that use compositions of FIFO with other contention-resolution protocols on their queues because FIFO is very popular in packet-switched networks due to its simplicity. A very natural question that arises in such common settings of multimedia networks concerns the degradation of network stability under adversarial attacks that change dynamically network link slowdowns/capacities. The study of stability in multimedia networks which use compositions of FIFO with other protocols for contention resolution on their queues and suffer from adversarial attacks that change dynamically link slowdowns/capacities can help to establish design criteria for the implementation of trustworthy networks.

Framework. We adopt a model of worst-case continuous packet arrivals, originally proposed in [10] and termed Adversarial Queuing Model (AQM) [10]. Roughly speaking, AQM views the operation of a packet-switched communication network as a game between an adversary and a contention-resolution protocol or a composition of protocols. At each time step, the adversary may inject a set of packets into some nodes with predetermined paths. When more than one packets wish to cross a link during a time step and only one should be forwarded, we have a conflict and a greedy contention-resolution protocol is employed to resolve it. The power of the adversary is the manipulation of packet injection rate r ($0 < r \leq 1$). However there is a restriction to injection rate manipulation. The adversary should inject into the network at most $r|I|$ packets with paths that contain any particular edge in any time interval I.

It is well motivated to consider that one packet can cross a network link in a single time step assuming that all network links are identical and there are not link failures. However, this is not common in large-scale packet-switched multimedia networks, like Internet, due to the variety of their network links. Also, real networks, like Internet, often suffer from link failures due to natural disasters, human or malicious software action (like hacker attacks or denial of service attacks) or by unintentional software failures. In order to model this reality, it is well motivated to allow the dynamic change of network link slowdowns or capacities. In particular, for the efficient handling of network link failures, we assume an adversarial model where a slowdown is assigned to each network link. A model that satisfies this condition has been proposed by Borodin et al. in [11]. Here we adopt the weakest possible model of dynamically changing slowdowns of the models implied in [11] as in [17]. According to [17], each link slowdown takes on values in the two-valued set of integers $\{1, D\}$ for $D > 1$. The assigning of slowdown D to a link can be considered approximately as a link failure, while the assigning of unit slowdown to a link can be considered as the proper service rate.

Furthermore, the realization of the variety of links in a large network motivates the assignment of a capacity to each link [11]. Here, we adopt the weakest possible model of dynamically changing capacities of the models implied in [11] as proposed by Prof. Spirakis team in [25]. According to [25] each link capacity takes on values in the two-valued set of integers $\{1, C\}$ for $C > 1$. This assumption realizes the condition where a link guarantees a minimum service rate in the worst case and a maximum service rate in the most optimistic case.

Prof. Spirakis team initiated the subfield of study concerning the stability behavior of contention-resolution protocol compositions in [23]. In this work, we focus on how FIFO compositions with other protocols affect the stability behavior of heterogeneous multimedia networks where packets are injected with predetermined fixed paths (that do not contain repeated links, but they can contain repeated nodes) against adversarial attacks that dynamic change link slowdowns/capacities. The study of the stability behavior of networks where packets are injected into paths without repeated links/edges was an interesting subfield initiated in [4]. In particular, it has been shown that the family of undirected-path universally stable graphs is minor-closed and that there exists a finite set of basic undirected graphs such that a graph is stable, if and only if it does not contain any of the graphs of that set as a minor [4]. We believe that establishing specific criteria from such a study promotes the trustworthiness of a heterogeneous multimedia network.

We say that a contention-resolution protocol (or a composition of protocols) P is stable on a network G against an adversary A of rate r, if there is a constant B for which the number of packets in the network is bounded at all times by B [10]. On the other hand, we say that a protocol (or a composition of protocols) P is universally stable, if it is stable against any adversary of rate less than 1 and on any network [10]. We also say that a network G is universally stable, if any greedy protocol is stable against any adversary of rate less than 1 on G [10]. According to [1], a directed network graph where packets are injected in paths that do not contain repeated links/edges, but they can contain repeated nodes/vertices, is universally stable, if and only if it does not contain as subgraph any graph that is obtained by replacing any edge of the graphs U_1 or U_2 by disjoint directed paths (Fig. 1). The graphs U_1 and U_2 are called forbidden subgraphs for universal stability [1]. Network graphs U_1 and U_2 have been proved unstable when a single contention-resolution protocol resolves packet conflicts on network queues under AQM attacks (where link slowdowns/or capacities are unit) [1].

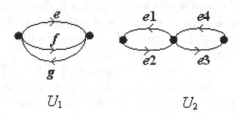

$$U_1 \qquad\qquad U_2$$

Fig. 1. Forbidden subgraphs for universal stability [1].

Here, we consider greedy contention-resolution protocols on network queues. In particular, we consider FIFO (First-In-First-Out), NTG (Nearest-To-Go) and LIS (Longest-in-System) protocols. FIFO protocol gives priority to the earliest arrived packet at the queue when a queue faces packet conflict. NTG protocol gives priority to the nearest packet to its destination when a queue faces a packet conflict. LIS protocol gives priority to the least recently injected packet into the network when a queue faces a packet conflict. As far as the stability behavior of those protocols is concerned, FIFO and NTG protocols have been proved unstable in AQM model, while LIS protocol has been proved universally stable in AQM model [4]. Here, we assume FIFO as tie breaking rule for the protocols in order to be unambiguously defined.

Contribution and Comparison. The contribution of this work is two-fold. First, it focuses on the study of the stability behavior of multimedia networks that use compositions of FIFO with other contention-resolution protocols (LIS, NTG) and face adversarial attacks that change dynamically network link slowdowns between two values, unit and a high slowdown D > 1. Second, it studies the stability behavior of multimedia networks which face adversarial attacks that change dynamically network link capacities between two values, unit and a high capacity $C > 1$ under the protocol composition (FIFO, NTG, LIS). This study permits the comparison of the network stability results obtained under the two dynamic network models and the traditional AQM model [10]. We adopt as a test-bed the set of forbidden subgraphs $\mathcal{U}_1$ and $\mathcal{U}_2$ for universal stability (Fig. 1) [1]. We apply on these network structures specific adversarial constructions that lead them to instability when these adversarial constructions are combined with the use of specific protocol compositions on different network queues. Especially, we consider specific compositions of FIFO with any of NTG and LIS protocols or both of them on the queues of network subgraphs $\mathcal{U}_1$ and $\mathcal{U}_2$ when link slowdowns change dynamically. Furthermore, we study the behavior of protocol composition (FIFO, NTG, LIS) on $\mathcal{U}_1$ and $\mathcal{U}_2$ when link capacities change dynamically.

From our results we can conjecture that when protocol compositions of FIFO with NTG and LIS protocols are employed on different network queues of $\mathcal{U}_1$ and $\mathcal{U}_2$ under adversarial attacks that change link slowdowns, the instability behavior of $\mathcal{U}_1$ and $\mathcal{U}_2$ becomes very bad. Actually, our results suggest that the instability behavior of $\mathcal{U}_1$ and $\mathcal{U}_2$ in such conditions can be even worse comparing to the case those network structures face AQM attacks either a single protocol [1] or a protocol composition is used for contention-resolution on network queues [20]. The same conjecture holds on the case of protocol composition (FIFO, NTG, LIS) on $\mathcal{U}_1$ and $\mathcal{U}_2$ when link capacities change dynamically. However, there is an exception concerning network $\mathcal{U}_2$ for protocol composition (FIFO, NTG) and dynamically changing link slowdowns where the instability injection rate bound is greater than the case of unit slowdowns [1,20]. On the other hand, comparing the theoretical instability results for the protocol composition (FIFO, NTG, LIS) on $\mathcal{U}_1$ and $\mathcal{U}_2$ for both dynamic models we can conclude that the $\mathcal{U}_1$ and $\mathcal{U}_2$ networks face similar instability behavior in both cases. However, the experimental evaluation of the two dynamic models in Sect. 6 shows that the instability behavior of $\mathcal{U}_1$ and $\mathcal{U}_2$ for the same protocol composition (FIFO, NTG, LIS) on the same network queues and for the same injection rate into the networks is worse in the case of dynamically changing link capacities than in the case of dynamically changing link slowdowns. That is the total number of packets on network queues increases faster in the case of changing link capacities than in the case of changing slowdowns.

More specifically, we proved lower instability bounds on the injection rate for networks $\mathcal{U}_1$ and $\mathcal{U}_2$ when protocol compositions (FIFO, NTG), (FIFO, LIS) and (FIFO, NTG, LIS) are employed on network queues and link slowdowns change dynamically than the corresponding instability bounds for AQM model specified in [1] ($r \geq 0.841$) where only a single protocol is applied on $\mathcal{U}_1$ and $\mathcal{U}_2$ (Theorems 1, and 3–6). Furthermore, in [20] it has been proved that the protocol composition (FIFO, NTG) leads $\mathcal{U}_1$ and $\mathcal{U}_2$ to instability for $r \geq 0.841$ ($\mathcal{U}_1$) and $r \geq 0.867$ ($\mathcal{U}_2$) under AQM attacks. Here the instability behavior of the protocol composition (FIFO, NTG) is even worse on $\mathcal{U}_1$ when it faces attacks that change dynamically link slowdowns leading to instability for $r \geq 0.794$ (Theorem 1). On the other hand, we show the instability behavior of $\mathcal{U}_2$ under the composition (FIFO, NTG) when link slowdowns change dynamically for $r \geq 0.893$ (Theorem 2). In [18], the stability behavior of $\mathcal{U}_1$ and $\mathcal{U}_2$ is examined when link capacities change dynamically and protocol compositions (FIFO, NTG) and (FIFO, LIS) are employed on network queues. Here, we extend this study investigating the instability behavior of $\mathcal{U}_1$ and $\mathcal{U}_2$ for the composition of three protocols (FIFO, NTG, LIS) when link capacities change dynamically.

It is interesting to stress that $\mathcal{U}_2$ has been proved stable when only FIFO is used for contention resolution on all network queues under AQM attacks [32]. However $\mathcal{U}_2$ has been proved unstable when a specific composition of FIFO and NTG protocols are used for resolving packet conflicts on different network queues under AQM attacks [20]. Here we show that the instability behavior of $\mathcal{U}_2$ holds for the protocol composition (FIFO, NTG) under attacks that change link slowdowns (Theorem 2). Also, although LIS is a universally stable protocol [4] when it is composed with FIFO for content-resolution on different network queues on $\mathcal{U}_2$ it leads the network to worst instability behavior (Theorem 4) comparing to the case FIFO is composed with a protocol which is not universally stable like NTG under attacks that change link slowdowns (Theorem 2). This implies that the composition of a universally stable protocol with a non-universally stable protocol on different queues of the same network may lead the network to worse instability behavior comparing to the case we apply a composition of two contention-resolution protocols (which are not universally stable) on different network queues under attacks that change dynamically link slowdowns. Also, as far as the instability behavior of $\mathcal{U}_1$ and $\mathcal{U}_2$ is concerned when protocol composition (FIFO, NTG, LIS) is employed on network queues under attacks that change link capacities, we proved lower instability bounds on the injection rate (Theorems 7 and 8) than the corresponding instability bounds for AQM model specified in [1] where only a single contention-resolution protocol is applied on network queues. Those instability bounds (Theorems 7 and 8) are the same as in the case of dynamically changing link slowdowns. Finally, we present an experimental evaluation of the stability behavior of the set of forbidden subgraphs for universal stability for any composition of FIFO with LIS and NTG protocols under attacks that change dynamically link slowdowns and the specific composition of (FIFO, LIS, NTG) under attacks that change link capacities.

Roadmap. The paper is organized as follows: In Sect. 2, some related works regarding intrusion attacks, adversarial environments and stability results are discussed. Section 3 presents theoretical framework definitions. Section 4 demonstrates the instability behavior of FIFO protocol compositions under adversarial attacks that change dynamically network link slowdowns. Section 5 shows the instability behavior of a specific FIFO composition with other protocols when it is applied on the set of forbidden network subgraphs for universal stability under attacks that change dynamically link capacities. Section 6 makes an experimental evaluation of the stability behavior of FIFO protocol compositions under dynamic attacks. Finally, Sect. 7 makes some concluding remarks along with proposals for future research directions.

2 Related Work

Intrusion Attacks. Adversarial environments can be used to model intrusion attacks as an intruder can behave like an adversary that tries to change network environment parameters concerning network link slowdowns or capacities, packet injection rate or the used contention-resolution protocols. In particular, adversarial attacks act as denial of service attacks flooding the network with dummy packets in order to overload the network. The study of intrusion detection and the proposal of methods for guaranteed quality service against various attacks received a lot of interest [31, 33].

Adversarial Environments. A lot of adversarial environments related to network stability behavior have been proposed in the literature [3, 9–14]. However, in the community of stability, Adversarial Queueing Model [10] received a lot of interest in the study of network performance issues as a more realistic model that replaces traditional stochastic assumptions made in Queuing Theory by more robust, worst-case ones [1, 4, 10, 17, 20, 23, 27].

Stability Results. Due to the popularity of FIFO, the investigation of its stability behavior when it is used alone or in compositions with other protocols against various adversarial models occupied many research works [3, 7, 8, 14, 15, 18, 28, 32]. The universal stability of various natural greedy protocols (LIS) and the instability of other protocols (NTG, FIFO) under AQM model were proved in [4]. The first result concerning the stability of FIFO protocol was presented in [15]. The issue of composing distributed protocols to obtain other protocols, and the properties of the resulting (composed) protocols, has a rich record in Distributed Computing Theory [30]. In [17] the stability of networks that use compositions of NTG with LIS protocols for contention-resolution is studied because these protocols are commonly-used on simple networks and their stability has been investigated in many adversarial environments [4, 11, 21, 27].

The impact of network structure on the stability behavior of greedy protocols was studied in detail by Prof. Spirakis team [22]. The stability behavior of forbidden subgraphs for universal stability was studied in [1] presenting instability lower bounds of 0.841 for U_1 and U_2 under a single protocol and in [20] presenting instability lower bounds of 0.841 for U_1 and 0.794 for U_2 when NTG protocol is composed with LIS protocol on different network queues under AQM attacks. Also, the stability behavior of forbidden subgraphs for universal stability was studied in [20] presenting instability lower bounds of 0.841 for U_1 and 0.867 for U_2 when NTG protocol is composed with FIFO protocol on different network queues under AQM attacks. In [24] performance and stability bounds for dynamic networks have been presented. Instability behavior of networks with quasi-static link capacities has been investigated in [25, 26]. Also, dynamic adversarial attacks were investigated in [11, 17, 19, 21, 26]. In [21, 26] the stability behavior of forbidden subgraphs U_1 and U_2 is examined when protocol NTG-U-LIS is employed on network queues and link slowdowns or capacities change dynamically. Especially, the stability of heterogeneous multimedia networks under adversarial attacks dynamically changing network link slowdowns/capacities was studied in [17, 19].

In particular, [17,19] study the stability behavior of networks when different compositions of contention-resolution protocols NTG, LIS and FFS (Furthest-From-Source) are composed on top of them under adversarial attacks that change dynamically network link slowdowns/capacities. In [19] the study of the stability behavior of the protocol compositions of NTG with any of LIS and FFS or both of them uses as a test-bed a specific set of network structures called forbidden subgraphs for simple-path universal stability (packets are injected in paths that cannot contain repeated edges or vertices) [1]. Furthermore, stability in adversarial environments where networks face node and link failures was studied in [2]. Systematic simulation studies of network stability behavior have been presented recently in [5,6].

3   Theoretical Framework

Our study of the stability of heterogeneous multimedia dynamic networks follows the definitions of the adversarial model in [10]. According to [10] a routing network is modelled by a directed graph $\mathcal{G}$ on n vertices and m edges. Each vertex of $\mathcal{G}$ represents a communication switch (node), and each edge of $\mathcal{G}$ represents a link between two switches. In each node, there is a queue associated with each outgoing link. Time proceeds in discrete time steps. Queues store packets. Packets are injected into the network with a route. A packet route is a simple directed path in $\mathcal{G}$. When a packet wants to travel along an edge e at a particular time step, but it is not forwarded, it waits in the queue for the edge e. We say that a packet p requires an edge e at time t, if the edge e lies on the path from its position to its destination at t. We call system a triple of the form $\langle \mathcal{G}, \mathcal{A}, \mathsf{P} \rangle$ where $\mathcal{G}$ is a network, $\mathcal{A}$ is an adversary and P is the used composition of protocols on the network queues.

However, the adversarial model in [10] assumes unit link capacities and slowdowns. Here, we study dynamic networks with varying link slowdowns as in [11], but we address the weakest possible model of changing slowdowns (AQMDS model) as in [17]. Edges can have different integer slowdowns, which may or may not vary over time. $\mathsf{D}_e(t)$ denotes the *slowdown* of the edge e at time step t. When we use $\mathsf{D}_e(t)$ for an edge e, we mean that if a packet p is scheduled to traverse the edge e at time t, then packet p completes the traversal of e at time $t + \mathsf{D}_e(t)$ and during this time interval, no other packet can be scheduled on e. We assume that $\mathsf{D} > 1$ is an integer parameter. The slowdown of any edge e at any time step t can get only two values 1 and D. Denote $w \geq 1$ an arbitrary positive integer. For any network edge e and any sequence of w consecutive time steps, $N(w, e)$ is the number of paths injected by the adversary during w time steps requiring to traverse e. For any constant injection rate r, $0 < r \leq 1$, an adversary injects packets such that for every edge e and every sequence τ of w consecutive time steps, $N(\tau, e) \leq r \sum_{t \in \tau} \frac{1}{\mathsf{D}_e(t)}$.

Also, we study dynamic networks with varying link capacities as in [11], but we adopt the weakest possible adversarial model of changing capacities (AQMDC model) as in [25]. $\mathsf{C}_e(t)$ denotes the capacity of the edge e at time step t.

When we use $C_e(t)$ for an edge e, we mean that the edge e can simultaneously forwards up to $C_e(t)$ packets at time t. We assume that $C > 1$ is an integer parameter. The capacity of any edge e at any time step t can get only two values 1 and C. Denote $w \geq 1$ an arbitrary positive integer. For any network edge e and any sequence of w time steps, $N(w, e)$ is the number of paths injected by the adversary during w time steps requiring to traverse e. For any constant injection rate r $(0 < r \leq 1)$, an adversary injects packets such that for every edge e and every sequence τ of w consecutive steps, $N(\tau, e) \leq r \sum_{t \in \tau} C_e(t)$.

In the adversarial constructions we study here for proving instability, we split time into phases. In each phase, we consider consecutive non-overlapping time rounds. Each phase is split into the same number of time rounds. During the same round of any phase the adversarial strategy is the same. We use inductive arguments to show that the number of packets into the network queues increases forever. This network condition is sufficient to guarantee instability. Our inductive hypothesis is based on the assumption of an initial network configuration of specific number of packets in specific network queues with predetermined paths at the beginning of a phase. The induction step we prove is that at the end of the phase there will be more packets in the same network queues than at the phase beginning. Determining the adversarial strategy in every round of the phase we prove the induction step. Therefore, network instability is shown applying this inductive argument repeatedly.

4   Instability of FIFO Protocol Compositions Under AQMDS Model

First we examine whether the composition (FIFO, NTG) is stable on the network $\mathcal{U}_1$ (Fig. 1) under the AQMDS model. We show:

Theorem 1. *Let* $r = 0.8$. *For the network* $\mathcal{U}_1$ *there is an adversary* $\mathcal{A}$ *of rate* r *that can change the link slowdowns of* $\mathcal{U}_1$ *between* $\{1, D > 1000\}$ *such that the system* $\langle \mathcal{U}_l, \mathcal{A}, (\mathsf{FIFO}, \mathsf{NTG}) \rangle$ *is unstable. When* $D \to \infty$ *the system* $\langle \mathcal{U}_l, \mathcal{A}, (\mathsf{FIFO}, \mathsf{NTG}) \rangle$ *is unstable for* $r \geq 0.794$.

Proof. The queue of the edge e uses FIFO protocol, while the queues of the edges f and g use NTG protocol.

Inductive Hypothesis: At the beginning of phase j, there are s_j packets (called S packet set) that are queued in the queues of the edges f, e requiring to traverse the edge g.

Induction Step: At the beginning of phase $j + 1$, there will be $s_{j+1} > s_j$ packets that will be queued in the queues of the edges f, e requiring to traverse the edge g.

We will construct an adversary $\mathcal{A}$ such that the induction step will hold. Then, we will prove that the induction step holds in order to ensure that the inductive hypothesis will hold at the beginning of the next phase $j + 1$ with an increased value of s_j, $s_{j+1} > s_j$. During phase j the adversary plays four rounds of packet injections as follows:

Round 1: It lasts $|T1| = s_j$ time steps. During this round all the network edges have unit slowdown. The adversary injects in the queue of the edge g a set X of $|X| = r|T1|$ packets with path g, f. The packets of the set S delay the packets of the set X in the queue g. Therefore, X packets remain at queue g at the end of this round.

Round 2: It lasts $|T2| = rs_j$ time steps. During this round all the network edges have unit slowdown. The adversary injects a set Y of $|Y| = r|T2|$ packets in the queue of the edge g requiring to traverse the edges g, e and a set Z of $|Z| = r|T2|$ packets in the queue of the edge f requiring to traverse the edge f. The X packets delay the Y packets in the queue of the edge g and the Z packets in the queue of the edge f. All the Y packets remain in g. In the queue of the edge f a set $Z1$ of $|Z1| = r|T2|$ packets remain wanting to traverse the edge f.

Round 3: It lasts $|T3| = r^2 s_j$ time steps. During this round the edge e has high slowdown D, while all the other network edges have unit slowdown. The adversary injects a set $Z2$ of $|Z2| = r|T3|$ packets in the queue of the edge f requiring to traverse the edges f, g. The packets of the set $Z1$ delay the packets of $Z2$ in the queue of the edge f. Furthermore, the packets of Y are delayed in e due to the high slowdown of the edge e during this round. Thus, the remaining Y packets in the queue of the edge e at the end of this round is a set $Y1$ of $|Y1| = |Y| - |T3|/D$ packets.

Round 4: It lasts $|T4| = |Y1|$ time steps. During this round the edge f has high slowdown D, while all the other edges have unit slowdown. The adversary injects a set $Z3$ of $|Z3| = r|T4|$ packets in the queue of the edge e requiring to traverse the edges e, g. The $Y1$ packets delay the $Z3$ packets in the queue e. Moreover, the packets of $Z2$ are delayed in f because edge f has high slowdown during this round. Therefore, the packets of $Z2$ in the queue of the edge f at the end of this round can be considered as a set $Z4$ of $|Z4| = |Z2| - |T4|/D$ packets. Thus, the number of packets in the queues of the edges f, e requiring to traverse the edge g at the end of this round is $s_{j+1} = |Z3| + |Z4|$.

In order to have instability, we must have $s_{j+1} > s_j$. Replacing s_{j+1} and s_j in the previous inequality we take $r^3 - r^4/D + r^3 - (r^2 - (r^3/D))/D > 1$. The inequality holds for $D = 1000$ and $r = 0.8$. When $D \to \infty$, it holds that $1/D^k \to 0$ for all $k \geq 1$. Then, the inequality gives $2r^3 - 1 > 0$ which is true for $r \geq 0.794$. This argument can be repeated for an infinite and unbounded number of phases ensuring that the number of packets in the queues of the edges f, e requiring to traverse the edge g at the end of a phase is larger than at the phase beginning. □

Now, we consider the network $\mathcal{U}_2$ (Fig. 1). Theorem 2 is proved similarly to Theorem 1. To prove the instability of the system $\langle \mathcal{U}_2, \mathcal{A}', (\text{FIFO}, \text{NTG}) \rangle$, we assume that the queue of the edge $e2$ uses FIFO protocol and the rest of the queues use NTG protocol. We split time into phases where each phase consists of four distinguished and consecutive time rounds.

Inductive Hypothesis: At the beginning of phase j, there are s_j packets (called S packet set) that are queued in the queues of the edges $e2$, $e4$ requiring to traverse the edge $e1$.

Induction Step: At the beginning of phase $j+1$, there will be $s_{j+1} > s_j$ packets that will be queued in the queues of the edges $e2$, $e4$ requiring to traverse the edge $e1$.

The adversarial strategy during a phase j follows:

Round 1: It lasts $|T1| = s_j$ time steps. During this round all the network edges have unit slowdown. The adversary injects in the queue of the edge $e1$ a set X of $|X| = r|T1|$ packets wanting to traverse the edges $e1, e2, e3$. The packets of the set S delay the packets of the set X in the queue of the edge $e1$. Therefore, X packets remain at the queue of the edge $e1$ at the end of this round.

Round 2: It lasts $|T2| = rs_j$ time steps. During this round all the network edges have unit slowdown. The adversary injects a set Y of $|Y| = r|T2|$ packets in the queue of the edge $e2$ requiring to traverse the edge $e2$ and a set Z of $|Z| = r|T2|$ packets in the queue of the edge $e3$ requiring to traverse the edges $e3, e4$. X and Y arrive simultaneously at the edge $e2$. Thus, $|X'| = \frac{|X|}{|X|+|Y|}|T2|$ packets of X will manage to traverse edge $e2$ towards $e3$. X' packets will delay Z packets at $e3$. Thus, a number of $|Z'| = |Z| - (|T2| - |X'|)$ will remain at $e3$ wanting to traverse the edges $e3, e4$ at the end of this round. Moreover, at the end of this round $r^2 s_j$ packets will remain at the queue of the edge $e2$.

Round 3: It lasts $|T3| = r^2 s_j$ time steps. During this round the edge $e2$ has high slowdown D, while all the other edges have unit slowdown. The adversary injects a set $Z1$ of $|Z1| = r|T3|$ packets in the queue of the edge $e4$ requiring to traverse the edges $e4, e1$. Z' packets delay $Z1$ packets at edge $e4$. At the end of this round $|Z1'| = |Z1| - (|T3| - |Z'|)$ packets will remain at $e4$ wanting to traverse the edges $e4, e1$. Moreover, a set K of $|K| = |Y| - \frac{|T3|}{D}$ packets will remain at $e2$ at the end of this round.

Round 4: It lasts $|T4| = |Y| - \frac{|T3|}{D}$ time steps. During this round the edge $e4$ has high slowdown D, while all the other edges have unit slowdown and the adversary injects a set $Z2$ of $|Z2| = r|T4|$ packets in the queue of the edge $e2$ requiring to traverse the edges $e2, e1$. At the end of this round K packets delay $Z2$ packets at queue $e2$ and $|Z1'| - \frac{|T4|}{D}$ packets will remain at queue $e4$ wanting to traverse the edges $e4, e1$.

Theorem 2. *Let* $r = 0.9$. *For the network* $\mathcal{U}_2$ *there is an adversary* $\mathcal{A}'$ *of rate* r *that can change the link slowdowns of* $\mathcal{U}_2$ *between* $\{1, D > 1000\}$ *such that the system* $\langle \mathcal{U}_2, \mathcal{A}', (\text{FIFO}, \text{NTG}) \rangle$ *is unstable. When* $D \to \infty$ *the system* $\langle \mathcal{U}_2, \mathcal{A}', (\text{FIFO}, \text{NTG}) \rangle$ *is unstable for* $r \geq 0.893$.

Now, we consider the network $\mathcal{U}_1$ (Fig. 1) under protocol composition (FIFO, LIS). Then, similarly to Theorem 1, we can prove Theorem 3.

Adversary's Strategy in Network $\mathcal{U}_1$. For the system $\langle \mathcal{U}_1, \mathcal{A}_1, (\text{FIFO}, \text{LIS}) \rangle$ the queue of the edge e uses FIFO protocol and the queues of the rest edges use LIS protocol. The strategy of the adversary is the same as the adversary's strategy in the system $\langle \mathcal{U}_1, \mathcal{A}_1, (\text{FIFO}, \text{NTG}) \rangle$ (Theorem 1).

Theorem 3. *Let* $r = 0.8$. *For the network* $\mathcal{U}_1$ *there is an adversary* $\mathcal{A}_1$ *of rate* r *that can change the link slowdowns of* $\mathcal{U}_1$ *between* $\{1,\ \mathsf{D} > 1000\}$ *such that the system* $\langle \mathcal{U}_1, \mathcal{A}_1, (\text{FIFO}, \text{LIS}) \rangle$ *is unstable. When* $\mathsf{D} \to \infty$ *the system* $\langle \mathcal{U}_1, \mathcal{A}_1, (\text{FIFO}, \text{LIS}) \rangle$ *is unstable for* $r \geq 0.794$.

Now, we consider the network $\mathcal{U}_2$ (Fig. 1) under composition (FIFO, LIS).

Adversary's Strategy in Network $\mathcal{U}_2$. For the system $\langle \mathcal{U}_2, \mathcal{A}_2, (\text{FIFO}, \text{LIS}) \rangle$ the queue of the edge $e4$ uses FIFO protocol and the queues of the rest edges use LIS protocol. We consider that each phase consists of three distinguished time rounds.

Inductive Hypothesis: At the beginning of phase j, there are s_j packets (called S packet set) that are queued in the queues of the edges $e2, e3$ requiring to traverse the edge $e1$ and the edges $e4, e1$ correspondingly.

Induction Step: At the beginning of phase $j + 1$, there will be $s_{j+1} > s_j$ packets that will be queued in the queues of the edges $e2, e3$ requiring to traverse the edge $e1$ and the edges $e4, e1$ correspondingly.

The adversary's strategy during a phase j follows:

Round 1: It lasts $|T1| = s_j$ time steps. During this round all the network edges have unit slowdown and the adversary injects in the queue of the edge $e1$ a set X of $|X| = r|T1|$ packets wanting to traverse the edges $e1, e2, e3$. The packets of the set S delay the packets of the set X in the queue of the edge $e1$. Therefore, X packets remain at the queue of the edge $e1$ at the end of this round.

Round 2: It lasts $|T2| = r|T1|$ time steps. During this round all the network edges have unit slowdown and the adversary injects a set Y of $|Y| = r|T2|$ packets in the queue of the edge $e2$ requiring to traverse the edges $e2, e1$ and a set Z of $|Z| = r|T2|$ packets in the queue of the edge $e3$ requiring to traverse the edges $e3, e4$. The X packets delay the Y packets in the queue of the edge $e2$ and the Z packets in the queue of the edge $e3$. All the Y packets remain in $e2$, and all the Z packets remain in $e3$.

Round 3: It lasts $|T3| = r|T2|$ time steps. During this round the edge $e2$ has high slowdown D, while all the other edges have unit slowdown and the adversary injects a set $Z1$ of $|Z1| = r|T3|$ packets in the queue of the edge $e3$ requiring to traverse the edges $e3, e4, e1$. $Z1$ packets are delayed in the queue of the $e3$. Also, at the end of this round a set Y' of $|Y'| = |Y| - \frac{|T3|}{\mathsf{D}}$ packets will remain at queue $e2$ wanting to traverse the edges $e2, e1$.

Theorem 4. *Let* $r = 0.76$. *For the network* $\mathcal{U}_2$ *there is an adversary* $\mathcal{A}_2$ *of rate* r *that can change the link slowdowns of* $\mathcal{U}_2$ *between* $\{1,\ \mathsf{D} > 1000\}$ *such that the system* $\langle \mathcal{U}_2, \mathcal{A}_2, (\text{FIFO}, \text{LIS}) \rangle$ *is unstable. When* $\mathsf{D} \to \infty$ *the system* $\langle \mathcal{U}_2, \mathcal{A}_2, (\text{FIFO}, \text{LIS}) \rangle$ *is unstable for* $r \geq 0.755$.

Now, we consider the network $\mathcal{U}_1$ (Fig. 1) under protocol composition (FIFO, NTG, LIS). Then, similarly to Theorems 1 and 3 we can prove Theorem 5.

Adversary's Strategy in Network $\mathcal{U}_1$. For the system $\langle \mathcal{U}_1, \mathcal{A}_1, (\text{FIFO}, \text{NTG}, \text{LIS}) \rangle$ the queue of the edge g uses LIS protocol, f uses NTG protocol and the queue of the edge e uses FIFO protocol. The strategy of the adversary is the same in this system as the adversary's strategy in the systems $\langle \mathcal{U}_1, \mathcal{A}_1, (\text{FIFO}, \text{NTG}) \rangle$ (Theorem 1) and $\langle \mathcal{U}_1, \mathcal{A}_1, (\text{FIFO}, \text{LIS}) \rangle$ (Theorem 3).

Theorem 5. *Let $r = 0.8$. For the network $\mathcal{U}_1$ there is an adversary $\mathcal{A}_1$ of rate r that can change the link slowdowns of $\mathcal{U}_1$ between $\{1, \text{D} > 1000\}$ such that the system $\langle \mathcal{U}_1, \mathcal{A}_1, (\text{FIFO}, \text{NTG}, \text{LIS}) \rangle$ is unstable. When $\text{D} \to \infty$ the system $\langle \mathcal{U}_1, \mathcal{A}_1, (\text{FIFO}, \text{NTG}, \text{LIS}) \rangle$ is unstable for $r \geq 0.794$.*

Now, we consider the network $\mathcal{U}_2$ (Fig. 1) under protocol composition (FIFO, NTG, LIS). Then, similarly to Theorem 4 we can prove Theorem 6.

Adversary's Strategy in Network $\mathcal{U}_2$. For the system $\langle \mathcal{U}_2, \mathcal{A}_2, (\text{FIFO}, \text{NTG}, \text{LIS}) \rangle$ the queue of the edge $e4$ uses FIFO protocol, the queue of the edge $e1$ uses NTG protocol and the queues of the rest edges use LIS protocol. The strategy of the adversary is the same in this system as the adversary's strategy in the system $\langle \mathcal{U}_1, \mathcal{A}_1, (\text{FIFO}, \text{LIS}) \rangle$ (Theorem 4).

Theorem 6. *Let $r = 0.76$. For the network $\mathcal{U}_2$ there is an adversary $\mathcal{A}_2$ of rate r that can change the link slowdowns of $\mathcal{U}_2$ between $\{1, \text{D} > 1000\}$ such that the system $\langle \mathcal{U}_2, \mathcal{A}_2, (\text{FIFO}, \text{NTG}, \text{LIS}) \rangle$ is unstable. When $\text{D} \to \infty$ the system $\langle \mathcal{U}_2, \mathcal{A}_2, (\text{FIFO}, \text{NTG}, \text{LIS}) \rangle$ is unstable for $r \geq 0.755$.*

We should mention that the higher link slowdown in all the above theorems is $\text{D} > 1000$. For values of D less than 1000 the instability injection rates are higher than the obtained ones.

5   Instability of a FIFO Composition with Other Protocols Under AQMDC Model

In order to compare the instability behaviour of networks using compositions of FIFO with other greedy protocols in other dynamic environment concepts, we consider the stability behaviour of the composition of FIFO with NTG and LIS protocols when network link capacities can vary dynamically (AQMDC model). As a test-bed we use the set of forbidden subgraphs for universal stability $\mathcal{U}_1$ and $\mathcal{U}_2$ [1]. First we examine whether the composition (FIFO, NTG, LIS) is stable on the network $\mathcal{U}_1$ (Fig. 1). We show:

Theorem 7. *Let $r = 0.8$. For the network $\mathcal{U}_1$ there is an adversary $\mathcal{A}_1$ of rate r that can change the link capacities of $\mathcal{U}_1$ between $\{1, \text{C} > 1000\}$ such that the system $\langle \mathcal{U}_1, \mathcal{A}_1, (\text{FIFO}, \text{NTG}, \text{LIS}) \rangle$ is unstable. When $\text{C} \to \infty$ the system $\langle \mathcal{U}_1, \mathcal{A}_1, (\text{FIFO}, \text{NTG}, \text{LIS}) \rangle$ is unstable for $r \geq 0.794$.*

Proof. The queue of the edge e uses FIFO protocol, the queue of the edge g uses LIS protocol and the queue of the edge f uses NTG protocol.

Inductive Hypothesis: At the beginning of phase j, there are s_j packets (called S packet set) that are queued in the queues of the edges f, e requiring to traverse the edge g.

Induction Step: At the beginning of phase $j + 1$, there will be $s_{j+1} > s_j$ packets that will be queued in the queues of the edges f, e requiring to traverse the edge g.

We will construct an adversary $\mathcal{A}_1$ such that the induction step will hold. Then, we will prove that the induction step holds in order to ensure that the inductive hypothesis will hold at the beginning of the next phase $j + 1$ with an increased value of s_j, $s_{j+1} > s_j$. During phase j the adversary plays four rounds of packet injections as follows:

Round 1: It lasts $|T1| = s_j/C$ time steps. During this round all the network edges have high capacity C. The adversary injects in the queue of the edge g a set X of $|X| = rC|T1|$ packets with path g, f. The packets of the set S delay the packets of the set X in the queue g. Therefore, X packets remain at queue g at the end of this round.

Round 2: It lasts $|T2| = rs_j/C$ time steps. During this round all the network edges have high capacity C. The adversary injects a set Y of $|Y| = rC|T2|$ packets in the queue of the edge g requiring to traverse the edges g, e and a set Z of $|Z| = rC|T2|$ packets in the queue of the edge f requiring to traverse the edge f. The X packets delay the Y packets in the queue of the edge g and the Z packets in the queue of the edge f. All the Y packets remain in g. In the queue of the edge f a set $Z1$ of $|Z1| = rC|T2|$ packets remain wanting to traverse the edge f.

Round 3: It lasts $|T3| = r^2 s_j/C$ time steps. During this round the edge e has unit capacity, while all the other network edges have high capacity C. The adversary injects a set $Z2$ of $|Z2| = rC|T3|$ packets in the queue of the edge f requiring to traverse the edges f, g. The packets of the set $Z1$ delay the packets of $Z2$ in the queue of the edge f. Furthermore, the packets of Y are delayed in e due to the unit capacity of the edge e during this round. Thus, the remaining Y packets in the queue of the edge e at the end of this round is a set $Y1$ of $|Y1| = |Y| - |T3|$ packets.

Round 4: It lasts $|T4| = |Y1|/C$ time steps. During this round the edge f has unit capacity, while all the other edges have high capacity C. The adversary injects a set $Z3$ of $|Z3| = rC|T4|$ packets in the queue of the edge e requiring to traverse the edges e, g. The $Y1$ packets delay the $Z3$ packets in the queue e. Moreover, the packets of $Z2$ are delayed in f because edge f has unit capacity during this round. Therefore, the packets of $Z2$ in the queue of the edge f at the end of this round can be considered as a set $Z4$ of $|Z4| = |Z2| - |T4|$ packets. Thus, the number of packets in the queues of the edges f, e requiring to traverse the edge g at the end of this round is $s_{j+1} = |Z3| + |Z4|$.

In order to have instability, we must have $s_{j+1} > s_j$. Replacing s_{j+1} and s_j in the previous inequality we take $r^3(2 - (1/C)) - r^2((C - 1)/C^2) > 1$. The inequality holds for $C = 1000$ and $r = 0.8$. When $C \to \infty$, it holds that $1/C^k \to 0$ for all $k \geq 1$. Then, the inequality gives $2r^3 - 1 > 0$ which is true for $r \geq 0.794$. This argument can be repeated for an infinite and unbounded number of phases ensuring that the number of packets in the queues of the edges f, e requiring to traverse g at the end of a phase is larger than at the phase beginning.   □

Now, we consider the network $\mathcal{U}_2$ (Fig. 1) under protocol composition (FIFO, NTG, LIS).

Adversary's Strategy in Network $\mathcal{U}_2$. For the system $\langle \mathcal{U}_2, \mathcal{A}_2, (\text{FIFO}, \text{NTG}, \text{LIS}) \rangle$ the queue of the edge $e4$ uses FIFO protocol, the queue of the edge $e1$ uses NTG protocol and the queues of the rest edges use LIS protocol. We consider that each phase consists of three distinguished time rounds.

Inductive Hypothesis: At the beginning of phase j, there are s_j packets (called S packet set) that are queued in the queues of the edges $e2, e3$ requiring to traverse the edge $e1$ and the edges $e4, e1$ correspondingly.

Induction Step: At the beginning of phase $j + 1$, there will be $s_{j+1} > s_j$ packets that will be queued in the queues of the edges $e2, e3$ requiring to traverse the edge $e1$ and the edges $e4, e1$ correspondingly.
The adversary's strategy during a phase j follows:

Round 1: It lasts $|T1| = s_j/C$ time steps. During this round all the network edges have high capacity C and the adversary injects in the queue of the edge $e1$ a set X of $|X| = rC|T1|$ packets wanting to traverse the edges $e1, e2, e3$. The packets of the set S delay the packets of the set X in the queue of the edge $e1$. Therefore, X packets remain at the queue of the edge $e1$ at the end of this round.

Round 2: It lasts $|T2| = r|T1|$ time steps. During this round all the network edges have high capacity C and the adversary injects a set Y of $|Y| = rC|T2|$ packets in the queue of the edge $e2$ requiring to traverse the edges $e2, e1$ and a set Z of $|Z| = rC|T2|$ packets in the queue of the edge $e3$ requiring to traverse the edges $e3, e4$. The X packets delay the Y packets in the queue of the edge $e2$ and the Z packets in the queue of the edge $e3$. All the Y packets remain in $e2$, and all the Z packets remain in $e3$.

Round 3: It lasts $|T3| = r|T2|$ time steps. During this round the edge $e2$ has unit capacity, while all the other edges have high capacity C and the adversary injects a set $Z1$ of $|Z1| = rC|T3|$ packets in the queue of the edge $e3$ requiring to traverse the edges $e3, e4, e1$. $Z1$ packets are delayed in the queue of the $e3$.

Theorem 8. *Let $r = 0.76$. For the network $\mathcal{U}_2$ there is an adversary $\mathcal{A}_2$ of rate r that can change the link capacities of $\mathcal{U}_2$ between $\{1, C > 1000\}$ such that the system $\langle \mathcal{U}_2, \mathcal{A}_2, (\text{FIFO}, \text{NTG}, \text{LIS}) \rangle$ is unstable. When $C \to \infty$ the system $\langle \mathcal{U}_2, \mathcal{A}_2, (\text{FIFO}, \text{NTG}, \text{LIS}) \rangle$ is unstable for $r \geq 0.755$.*

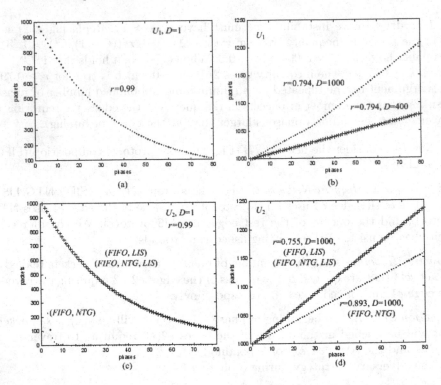

Fig. 2. Instability curves for FIFO, NTG and LIS compositions under AQMDS attacks.

We should mention that the maximum link capacity in all the above theorems is C > 1000. For values of C less than 1000 the instability injection rates are higher than the obtained ones.

6   Experimental Evaluation

For the evaluation of our theoretical results concerning the stability behavior of heterogeneous networks where FIFO compositions with other protocols are used for content-resolution on network queues under AQMDS and AQMDC attacks, we carried out an experimental study. This study uses as a test-bed the set of forbidden subgraphs for universal stability when packets are injected with paths without repeated edges [1] (Fig. 1). The experiments were conducted on a Windows box (Windows 7, Pentium III at 2.33 GHz, with 2 GB memory at 133 MHz) using C++ Builder ver. The experiments have been implemented as C++ classes by using C++ Builder. We assume that initially there are $s_0 = 1000$ packets in the system in all our experiments. Furthermore, our experiments are executed for 80 phases. We focus our interest on the evolution of the total number of packets on all the network queues in successive phases for the compositions of FIFO with any of LIS and NTG protocols under AQMDS attacks. Moreover, we are interested in the evolution of the total number of packets on all the network queues in successive phases for the specific composition (FIFO, LIS, NTG) under AQMDC attacks.

Figure 2 illustrates our experiments, considering the worst injection rate we estimated with respect to the instability, for the compositions of FIFO, with LIS and NTG protocols on forbidden subgraphs for universal stability under AQMDS attacks (x-axis coordinates correspond to time phases, while y-axis coordinates correspond to number of packets in the system). The results of our experiments agree with the theoretical results. Figure 2a and c depict the total number of packets into the queues of $\mathcal{U}_1$ and $\mathcal{U}_2$ for (FIFO, NTG), (FIFO, LIS) and (FIFO, LIS, NTG) compositions when link slowdowns are unit. Figure 2b depicts the total number of packets into the queues of $\mathcal{U}_1$ for two values of high slowdown $D > 1$ for any composition of FIFO with LIS and NTG. Figure 2d depicts the total number of packets into the queues of $\mathcal{U}_2$ for high slowdown $D = 1000$ for any composition of FIFO with LIS and NTG.

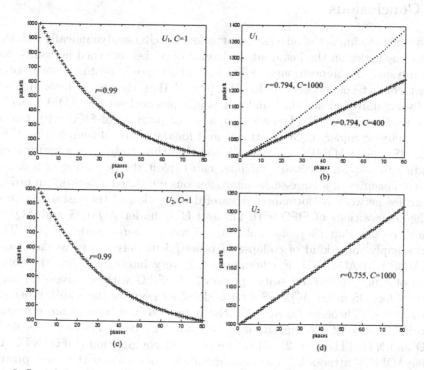

Fig. 3. Instability curves for (FIFO, NTG, LIS)composition under AQMDC attacks.

Figure 3 illustrates our experiments, considering the worst injection rate we estimated with respect to the instability, for the specific composition of (FIFO, NTG, LIS) on forbidden subgraphs for universal stability under AQMDC attacks (x-axis coordinates correspond to time phases, while y-axis coordinates correspond to number of packets in the system). The results of our experiments agree with the theoretical results. Figure 3a and c depict the total number of packets into the queues of $\mathcal{U}_1$ and $\mathcal{U}_2$ for (FIFO, LIS, NTG) composition when link capacities are unit. Figure 2b depicts the total number of packets into the queues of $\mathcal{U}_1$ for two values of high capacity $C > 1$ and the composition (FIFO, NTG, LIS). Figure 2d depicts the total number of packets into the queues of $\mathcal{U}_2$ for high capacity $C = 1000$ and the same protocol composition.

Especially, when we use unit link slowdowns (unit link capacities) the network is stable for the compositions of FIFO with LIS and NTG protocols (for the composition (FIFO, NTG, LIS)), while for high slowdown (capacity) $D > 1$ ($C > 1$) the network is unstable. Those results show that the instability properties of the set of forbidden subgraphs for universal stability in AQM model are maintained, even though we use a protocol composition for contention resolution on different network queues under AQMDS attacks (AQMDC attacks).

7   Conclusions

We studied the impact of adversarial attacks that change dynamically link slowdowns/capacities on the instability behavior of packet-switched networks when they use specific compositions of FIFO with other greedy protocols for resolving packet conflicts on network links. We proved that the set of forbidden subgraphs for universal stability under a single protocol on the AQM model [1] maintain their instability behavior for any composition of FIFO with LIS and NTG protocols under AQMDS attacks and for the protocol composition (FIFO, NTG, LIS) under AQMDC attacks. We feel that this study gives a better understanding to how an adversary/intruder can exploit the degrading of link slowdowns/capacities of a large-scale heterogeneous multimedia network in order to jeopardize network performance. A careful inspection of the instability proofs of the compositions of FIFO with LIS and NTG under AQMDS and AQMDC attacks reveals that they also hold in the more general model of [11]. These results imply some kind of collapse of powerful models [11] to weaker models (AQMDS and AQMDC). Furthermore, it is very interesting that the composition of a not universally stable protocol like FIFO with a universally stable protocol like LIS under AQMDS attacks does not improve the stability behavior of a network (Theorem 4). Actually the network could become more unstable than in the case of a composition of two not universally stable protocols like FIFO and NTG (Theorem 2). Also, the protocol composition (FIFO, NTG, LIS) under AQMDC attacks has the same instability behavior as the same protocol composition under AQMDS attacks. An open question for future work is the impact on network stability of adversarial attacks that can change dynamically network topology. Also, another question is whether there are specific networks where an unstable FIFO composition can be stable.

References

1. Alvarez, C., Blesa, M., Serna, M.: A characterization of universal stability in the adversarial queuing model. SIAM J. Comput. **34**, 41–66 (2004)
2. Alvarez, C., Blesa, M., Serna, M.: The robustness of stability under link and node failures. Theor. Comput. Sci. **412**, 6855–6878 (2011)
3. Andrews, M.: Instability of FIFO in the permanent sessions model at arbitrarily small network loads. ACM Trans. Algorithms **5**(3), 1–29 (2009)
4. Andrews, M., Awerbuch, B., Fernández, A., Kleinberg, J., Leighton, T., Liu, Z.: Universal stability results for greedy contention-resolution protocols. J. ACM **48**, 39–69 (2001)
5. Berger, D., Karsten, M., Schmitt, J.: On the relevance of adversarial queueing theory in practice. In: Proceedings of the ACM International Conference on Measurement and Modeling of Computer Systems, pp. 343–354 (2014)
6. Berger, D., Karsten, M., Schmitt, J.: Simulation of adversarial scenarios in OMNeT++: putting adversarial queueing theory from its head to feet. In: Proceedings of the 6th International ICST Conference on Simulation Tools and Techniques, pp. 291–298 (2013)
7. Bhattacharjiee, R., Goel, A., Lotker, Z.: Instability of FIFO at arbitrarily low rates in the adversarial queueing model. SIAM J. Comput. **34**(2), 318–332 (2005)
8. Blesa, M.J.: Deciding stability in packet-switched FIFO networks under the adversarial queuing model in polynomial time'. In: Fraigniaud, P. (ed.) DISC 2005. LNCS, vol. 3724, pp. 429–441. Springer, Heidelberg (2005)
9. Blesa, M., Calzada, D., Fernandez, A., Lopez, L.: Adversarial queueing model for continuous network dynamics. Theory Comput. Syst. **44**, 304–331 (2009)
10. Borodin, A., Kleinberg, J., Raghavan, P., Sudan, M., Williamson, D.: Adversarial queueing theory. J. ACM **48**, 13–38 (2001)
11. Borodin, A., Ostrovsky, R., Rabani, Y.: Stability preserving transformations: packet routing networks with edge capacities and speeds. In: Proceedings of the 12th Annual ACM-SIAM Symposium on Discrete Algorithms, pp. 601–610 (2001)
12. Chlebus, B.S., Cholvi, V., Kowalski, D.R.: Stability of adversarial routing with feedback. In: Gramoli, V., Guerraoui, R. (eds.) NETYS 2013. LNCS, vol. 7853, pp. 206–220. Springer, Heidelberg (2013)
13. Chlebus, B.S., Kowalski, D.R., Rokicki, M.A.: Adversarial queuing on the multiple access channel. ACM Trans. Algorithms **8**(1), article 5 (2012). doi:10.1145/2071379.2071384
14. Cholvi, V., Echague, J., Fernandez, A.: Stability of FIFO networks under adversarial models: state of the art, computer networks. Int. J. Comput. Telecommun. Netw. **51**(15), 4460–4474 (2007)
15. Diaz, J., Koukopoulos, D., Nikoletseas, S., Serna, M., Spirakis, P., Thilikos, D.: Stability and non-stability of the FIFO protocol. In: Proceedings of the 13th Annual ACM Symposium on Parallel Algorithms and Architectures, pp. 48–52 (2001)
16. Floyd, S., Paxson, V.: Difficulties in simulating the Internet. IEEE/ACM Trans. Netw. **9**, 392–403 (2001)
17. Koukopoulos, D.: Instability behaviour of heterogeneous multimedia networks under dynamic adversarial attacks. J. Math. Comput. Model. **57**, 2671–2684 (2013)
18. Koukopoulos, D.: The impact of FIFO compositions with other protocols on the stability of multimedia networks facing dynamic adversarial attacks. In: Proceedings of the 5th International Conference on Multimedia Information Networking and Security, pp. 575–578 (2013)

19. Koukopoulos, D.: The impact of dynamic adversarial attacks on the stability of heterogeneous multimedia networks. J. Comput. Commun. **33**, 1695–1706 (2010)
20. Koukopoulos, D.: Stability in heterogeneous multimedia networks under adversarial attacks. J. Univ. Comput. Sci. **14**(2), 444–464 (2009)
21. Koukopoulos, D.: The impact of dynamic link slowdowns on network stability. In: Proceedings of the 8th International Symposium on Parallel Architectures, Algorithms and Networks, pp. 340–345 (2005)
22. Koukopoulos, D., Mavronicolas, M., Nikoletseas, S., Spirakis, P.: The impact of network structure on the stability of greedy protocols. Theory Comput. Syst. **38**, 425–460 (2005)
23. Koukopoulos, D., Mavronicolas, M., Nikoletseas, S., Spirakis, P.: On the stability of compositions of universally stable, greedy, contention-resolution protocols. In: Malkhi, D. (ed.) DISC 2002. LNCS, vol. 2508, pp. 88–102. Springer, Heidelberg (2002)
24. Koukopoulos, D., Mavronikolas, M., Spirakis, P.: Performance and stability bounds for dynamic networks. J. Parallel Distrib. Comput. **67**, 386–399 (2007)
25. Koukopoulos, D., Mavronikolas, M., Spirakis, P.: The increase of the instability of networks due to quasi-static link capacities. J. Theor. Comput. Sci. **381**, 44–56 (2007)
26. Koukopoulos, D., Mavronicolas, M., Spirakis, P.: Instability of networks with quasi-static link capacities. In: Proceedings of the 10th International Colloquium on Structural Information and Communication Complexity, pp. 179–194 (2003)
27. Koukopoulos, D.K., Nikolopoulos, S.D.: Heterogenous networks can be unstable at arbitrarily low injection rates. In: Calamoneri, T., Finocchi, I., Italiano, G.F. (eds.) CIAC 2006. LNCS, vol. 3998, pp. 93–104. Springer, Heidelberg (2006)
28. Koukopoulos, D.K., Nikoletseas, S.E., Spirakis, P.G.: Stability issues in heterogeneous and fifo networks under the adversarial queueing model. In: Monien, B., Prasanna, V.K., Vajapeyam, S. (eds.) HiPC 2001. LNCS, vol. 2228, pp. 3–14. Springer, Heidelberg (2001)
29. Levine, D., Kessler, G.: Denial of service attacks. In: Kabay, M., Bosworth, S. (eds.) Computer Security Handbook, 4th edn. Wiley, New York (2002)
30. Lynch, N.: Distributed Algorithms. Morgan Kaufmann, San Francisco (1996)
31. Moore, D., Shannon, C., Brown, D., Voelker, G., Savage, S.: Inferring Internet denial-of-service activity. ACM Trans. Comput. Syst. **24**(2), 115–139 (2006)
32. Weinard, M.: Deciding the FIFO stability of networks in polynomial time. In: Calamoneri, T., Finocchi, I., Italiano, G.F. (eds.) CIAC 2006. LNCS, vol. 3998, pp. 81–92. Springer, Heidelberg (2006)
33. Yau, D., Lui, J., Liang, F., Yam, Y.: Defending against distributed denial-of-service attacks with max-min fair server-centric router throttles. IEEE/ACM Trans. Netw. **13**(1), 29–42 (2005)

Advances in the Parallelization
of the Simplex Method

Basilis Mamalis[(⊠)] and Grammati Pantziou

Department of Informatics, Technological Educational Institute of Athens,
Athens, Greece
{vmamalis,pantziou}@teiath.gr

Abstract. The simplex method has been successfully used in solving
linear programming problems for many years. Parallel approaches for the
simplex method have been extensively studied in the literature due to the
intensive computations required, especially for the solution of large linear
problems (LPs). In this paper, first a detailed overview is given of the
parallelization attempts concerning the standard and the revised simplex
method made to date. Next, some of the most recent and significant
relevant attempts are selected and presented in more detail along with
experimental results. The latter include some impressive results obtained
for the revised simplex method over a modern supercomputer, as well as
the recent advances in GPU-based related attempts.

Keywords: Linear programming · Simplex method · Parallel computing

1 Introduction

Linear programming (LP) is probably the most important and well studied optimization technique. The simplex method has been successfully used for solving
linear programming problems for many years [1]. Parallel approaches for the
simplex method have been extensively studied in the literature due to the intensive computations required [2]. Most research has been focused on the revised
simplex method since it takes advantage of the sparsity that is inherent in most
linear programming applications.

The revised method is advantageous for problems with a high aspect ratio;
that is, for problems with many more columns than rows. However, there have
not been seen many parallel implementations of the revised method that scale
well [2]. On the other hand, the standard method is more efficient for dense
linear problems and it can be easily converted to a parallel version with satisfactory speedup values and good scalability (e.g. [3–5,11–13]). However, lately,
some alternative very promising efforts have also been made with regard to the
parallelization of the revised method, based either on the block angular structure
(or decomposition) of the initially transformed problems or on the dual form of
the revised simplex, which is the most preferable one nowadays [6–8]. Two other
(a little earlier) valuable attempts over specific variants of the simplex method

© Springer International Publishing Switzerland 2015
C. Zaroliagis et al. (Eds.): Spirakis Festschrift, LNCS 9295, pp. 281–307, 2015.
DOI: 10.1007/978-3-319-24024-4_17

have also been presented in [14,15], and they have led to quite satisfactory results for large scale problems.

With regard to the hardware architectures used, earlier work focused mainly on more complex, and more tightly coupled, networking structures than a cluster or a network of workstations, which became a quite familiar alternative later on. Hall and McKinnon [9] and Shu [10] worked on parallel revised methods over known supercomputer environments (like Cray T3D). Thomadakis and Liu [11] worked on the standard method utilizing the MP-1 and MP-2 MasPar. Eckstein et al. [12] showed in the context of the parallel connection machine CM-2 that the iteration time for the parallel revised method tended to be significantly higher than for the parallel full tableau method even when the revised method is implemented very carefully. Stunkel [13] found a way to parallelize both the revised and standard methods so that both obtained a similar advantage in the context of the parallel Intel iPSC hypercube. Some more recent works on the standard simplex parallelization [16–18] address the significant influence of the number of columns and rows (aspect ratio) of an LP problem when a distributed-memory architecture is used, and achieve particularly high speedup values over modern (hybrid) cluster architectures, mainly following the column-based data distribution scheme [3,4,16–18].

Studying the literature one can notice that the standard (tableau-based) simplex method has been efficiently parallelized many times in the past with good speedup factors ranging from tens to up to a thousand. However, without using expensive parallel computing resources, its performance is inferior to a good sparsity-exploiting sequential implementation of the revised simplex method. On the other hand, the parallelization of the revised simplex method has not been very efficient and therefore there has been less success in terms of speedup with respect to the standard method. Indeed, since scalable speedup for general large sparse LP problems appears unachievable, the revised simplex method has been considered unsuitable for parallelization. However, since it corresponds to the computationally efficient serial technique, any improvement in performance due to exploiting parallelism in the revised simplex method is a worthwhile goal.

In the above context, throughout this paper we first try to give a detailed overview of the research attempts made till now with respect to the parallelization of the various variants of the simplex method, mainly distinguishing between the standard and the revised form. Next, we describe in more detail three of the most recent and important related attempts: (a) one presenting the efficient parallelization of the dual revised simplex method [6,7] which is considered as the most efficient and preferred variant of the simplex method nowadays, (b) one demonstrating the capability of efficiently solving large-scale stochastic LP problems with the revised simplex method, and gaining particularly high speedups (over the Clp serial solver) when implemented on a modern high-performance supercomputer [8], and (c) one presenting a notably efficient, highly scalable with almost linear speed-up implementation of the standard simplex method over a modern hybrid hardware architecture with high-speed inteconnection network and different alternatives in the software platforms used (MPI and MPI-3 Shared Memory vs. MPI and OpenMP) [16–18]. Finally, we explore separately the corresponding approaches contributed to date with the use of the CPU-GPU model trying to exploit the massive parallelism capabilities offered by the modern graphic processing units; which is one of the hottest topics in almost all the research fields of parallel computing nowadays.

Furthermore, our work can be seen as a thorough update of the survey given in [2], which is the most recent complete survey in simplex parallelization. We first summarize the most valuable works done till the end of 2010's (an interval which is covered in more details in [2]), and then we focus on the significant advances made during the last five years when the emerging technologies in hardware architectures (hybrid supercomputers, modern multicore architectures, hpc clusters, GPU computing etc.) have offered the potential for even greater achievements in response times and speedup performance. Especially, the rapid evolution of multicore technology has pushed the research in designing suitable parallelization schemes that can effectively exploit the increased computation capability of these modern hardware architectures. The first truly parallel commercial simplex solvers over multicore desktop architectures have also appeared recently (e.g. [42]), achieving significant improvements against purely sequential solutions for several kinds of LPs.

The rest of the paper is organized as follows. In Sect. 2 the necessary background with regard to the simplex method and its variants is given. In Sect. 3 the detailed overview of the research work made till now on the parallelization of the simplex method is presented. In Sects. 4, 5 and 6 the main achievements with respect to the three selected recent research attempts described in the previous paragraph, are stated respectively. In Sect. 7 the most recent approaches based on the CPU-GPU model are briefly presented, whereas Sect. 8 concludes the paper.

2 Background

In linear programming problems, the goal is to minimize (or maximize) a linear function of real variables over a region defined by linear constraints. In the standard form, it can be expressed as shown in Table 1 (full tableau representation), where A is an $m \times n$ matrix, x is an n-dimensional design variable vector, c is the price vector, b is the right-hand side vector of the constraints m-dimensional) vector of the constraints, and T denotes transposition.

Based on the full tableau representation, the basic steps of the standard simplex method can be summarized (without loss of generality) as follows:

Step 0: *Initialization*: Start with a feasible basic solution and construct the corresponding tableau.

Step 1: *Choice of the entering variable*: Find the winning column i.e., the one having the larger negative coefficient of the objective function.

Step 2: *Choice of the leaving variable*: Find the winning row by appling the min ratio test to the elements of the winning column and choose the row number with the min ratio.

Table 1. Standard simplex method with full tableau representation

Standard Full Tableau		x_1	x_2	...	x_n	x_{n+1}	...	x_{n+m}	z	
Simplex Method		$-c_1$	$-c_2$	...	$-c_n$	0	...	0	1	0
Minimize $\quad z = c^T x$	x_{n+1}	a_{11}	a_{12}	...	a_{1n}	1	...	0	0	b_1
s.t. $\qquad Ax = b$	x_{n+2}	a_{21}	a_{22}	...	a_{2n}	0	...	0	0	b_2
$\qquad\quad x \geq 0$	...	...	...	...	... ...	...	... ...	...	...
	x_{n+m}	a_{m1}	a_{m2}	...	a_{mn}	0	...	1	0	b_m

Step 3: *Pivoting:* Construct the next tableau by performing pivoting in the previous tableau rows based on the new pivot row found in step 2.

Step 4: Repeat the above steps until the best solution is found or the problem gets unbounded.

2.1   The Primal Revised Simplex Method

The revised simplex method performs the same steps as the tableau method but does not keep the tableau as an aid. Rather, whenever the algorithm requires a number from the tableau it is computed from one of several matrix equations, often involving the inverse of the basis. The data for the algorithm are the matrices A, c and b defining the original problem, the number of variables and constraints, n and m, and a record of the current basic and nonbasic variables. The basis matrix B is a square matrix composed of the columns from A corresponding to the m basic variables, whereas the columns of A corresponding to the $n - m$ nonbasic variables form the matrix N. The computational components of the primal revised simplex method are presented in Fig. 1 [2].

CHUZC: Scan $\hat{c}_N$ for a good candidate q to enter the basis.

FTRAN: Form the pivotal column $\hat{a}_q = B^{-1}a_q$, where a_q is column q of A.

CHUZR: Scan the ratios $\hat{b}_i/\hat{a}_{iq}$ for the row p to leave the basis.

$\qquad$ Update $\hat{b} = \hat{b} - \alpha\hat{a}_q$, where $\alpha = \hat{b}_p/\hat{a}_{pq}$.

BTRAN: Form $\pi_p = B^{-T}e_p$.

PRICE: Form the pivotal row $\hat{a}_p = N^T\pi_p$.

$\qquad$ Update $\hat{c}_N = \hat{c}_N - \beta\hat{a}_p$, where $\beta = \hat{c}_q/\hat{a}_{pq}$.

If {growth in representation of B} then

$\qquad$ INVERT: Form a new representation of B^{-1}.

else

$\qquad$ UPDATE: Update the representation of B^{-1} due to the basis change.

end if

Fig. 1. Operations in an iteration of the primal simplex method

At the beginning of an iteration, it is assumed that the vector of reduced costs $\hat{c}_N$ and the vector $\hat{b}$ of values of the basic variables are known, that $\hat{b}$ is feasible (nonnegative), and that a representation of B^{-1} is available. The first operation is CHUZC (choose column), which scans the (weighted) reduced costs to determine a good candidate q to enter the basis. The pivotal column $\hat{a}_q$ is formed by using the representation of B^{-1} in an operation referred to as FTRAN (forward transformation). The CHUZR (choose row) operation determines the variable to leave the basis, with p being used to denote the index of the row in which the leaving variable occurred, referred to as the pivotal row. As a result, a basis change is said to have occurred and the vector $\hat{b}$ is then updated adequately. Before the next iteration can be performed, one must update also the reduced costs (BTRAN and PRICE) and obtain a representation of the new matrix B^{-1} (UPDATE). Periodically, it is either more efficient or necessary for numerical stability to find a new representation of B^{-1} using the INVERT operation.

2.2   The Dual Revised Simplex Method

While the primal simplex has been historically more important, it is now widely accepted that the dual variant (the dual simplex method) generally has superior performance. Dual simplex is often the default algorithm in commercial solvers, and it is also used inside branch-and-bound algorithms. Given an initial partition and corresponding values for the basic and nonbasic primal and dual variables, the dual simplex method aims to find an optimal solution of by maintaining dual feasibility and seeking primal feasibility. Thus optimality is achieved when the basic variables $\hat{b}$ are non-negative. The computational components of the dual revised simplex method are illustrated in Fig. 2 [8], where the same data are assumed to be known at the beginning of an iteration. The first operation is CHUZR which scans the (weighted) basic variables to determine a good candidate to leave the basis, with p being used to denote the index of the row in which the leaving variable occurs. The pivotal row $\hat{a}_p^T$ is then formed via BTRAN and PRICE operations. The CHUZC operation determines the variable q to enter the basis. In order to update the vector $\hat{b}$, it is necessary to form the pivotal column $\hat{a}_q$ with an FTRAN operation.

3   Overview of Simplex Parallelization

The approaches contributed till now to the literature with regard to the parallelization of the simplex method can be naturally classified according to the variant of the simplex method that is considered and the extent to which sparsity is exploited. It should be noticed that parallel implementations of the simplex variants that are more efficient as a mean of solving large sparse LP problems are less successful in terms of speed-up. Conversely, the simplex variants that are generally less efficient achieve the best speed-up. A few of the parallel schemes discussed below offered good speed-up relative to efficient coeval serial solvers. However, some parallel techniques are only now seen as being inefficient in the

CHUZR: Scan $\hat{b}$ for the row p of a good candidate to leave the basis.

BTRAN: Form $\pi_p = B^{-T}e_p$.

PRICE: Form the pivotal row $\hat{a}_p^T = \pi_p^T N$.

CHUZC: Scan the ratios $\hat{c}_j/\hat{a}_{pj}$ for the row q to enter the basis.

   Update $\hat{c}_N = \hat{c}_N - \beta\hat{a}_p$, where $\beta = \hat{c}_q/\hat{a}_{pq}$.

FTRAN: Form the pivotal column $\hat{a}_q = B^{-1}a_q$, where a_q is column q of A.

   Update $\hat{b} = \hat{b} - \alpha\hat{a}_q$, where $\alpha = \hat{b}_p/\hat{a}_{pq}$.

If {growth in representation of B} then

   INVERT: Form a new representation of B^{-1}.

else

   UPDATE: Update the representation of B^{-1} due to the basis change.

end if

Fig. 2. Operations in an iteration of the dual simplex method

light of serial revised simplex techniques that either were not sufficiently known at the time or were developed subsequently. In the following two paragraphs the reader may find a brief analysis of the most representative parallelization efforts of the standard and revised simplex methods, whereas Tables 2 and 3 summarize the most significant of these efforts.

3.1   Parallelizing the Standard Simplex Method

There are many parallel implementations of the dense standard simplex method as well as of the revised simplex method with a dense explicit inverse. The simple data structures involved and the potential for linear speed-ups make them attractive implementation exercises either on shared memory machines or over distributed memory parallel environments. However, for solving general large sparse LP problems, the serial inefficiency of these implementations is such that only with a massive number of parallel processes they could conceivably compete with a good sparsity-exploiting serial implementation of the revised simplex method.

Some of the most known early works on parallelizing the standard simplex method can be found in [13,19–22]. Most of them focus on the possible data distribution and communication schemes, with implementations limited to small numbers of processes on distributed memory machines. The work of Stunkel [13] should be considered the most successful among them. He implemented both the dense standard simplex method and the revised simplex method with a dense inverse on a 16-processor Intel hypercube, achieving a speed-up of between 8 and 12 for small problem instances from the Netlib test set.

A few years later, two other valuable approaches were presented [23,24] with similar achievements. Cvetanovic et al. [23] report a speed-up of 12 when solving two small problem instances using the standard simplex method, a result that is notable for being achieved on a 16-processor shared memory machine. Luo and Reijns [24] obtained also satisfactory speedups of more than 12 on 16 transputers when using the revised simplex method with a dense inverse to solve modest Netlib test linear problems.

In the following years until 2000s, the first attempts over massively parallel computers appeared, with Eckstein et al. [12] and Thomadakis and Liu [11] contributing the most known and competent relevant works and implementations. Eckstein et al. [12] parallelized the standard simplex method and the revised simplex method with a dense inverse on the massively parallel Connection Machine CM-2 and CM-5, incorporating the steepest edge pricing strategy directly within their standard simplex implementation. As a consequence of using steepest edge weights and the expand procedure, this implementation is notable for its numerical stability, an issue that has rarely been considered in parallel implementations of the simplex method. Further details can be found in [25]. When solving a range of larger Netlib problems and very dense machine learning problems, speedups of between 1.6 and 1.8 were achieved when doubling the number of processors. They also presented results which indicated that the performance of their implementation was generally superior to MINOS (a well-known serial simplex solver), particularly for the denser problems. Thomadakis and Liu [11] also used steepest edge in their implementation of the standard simplex method on MasPar MP-1 and MP-2 machines. Solving a range of large, apparently randomly-generated problems, they achieved a speed-up of up to three orders of magnitude on the 128×128 processor MP-2.

During the next many years (till now) only a few significant new attempts and implementations were made with regard to the parallelization of the standard simplex method. Among them, a quite valuable theoretical work on parallel implementations of the standard simplex method with steepest edge, and its practical implementation on modest numbers of processors has been presented by Yarmish in [3,40]. The work in [3] has also led to high parallel efficiency and corresponding scalability for large-scale problems, whereas it has also been compared to MINOS, and it has been shown to be highly competitive even for very low density problems. Reports of small-scale parallel implementations also continue to appear. Relatively recently, Badr et al. [4] presented results for an implementation on eight processors, achieving a speed-up of five when solving small random dense LP problems.

A substantial difference between the two above attempts ([3] and [4]) was the way the simplex tableau is distributed among the processors. Either a column distribution scheme or a row distribution scheme may be applied, depending on several parameters (relative number of rows and columns, total size of the problem, target hardware environment details etc.). The most recent works following the column distribution scheme which is the most popular and widely used for practical problems, were by Yarmish et al. [3] as well as by Qin et al. [5]. On the other hand, the work of Badr et al. [4] referred above, followed the row distribution scheme and presented a well-designed and relatively efficient implementation on eight loosely coupled processors. Furthermore, a comprehensive

Table 2. Standard simplex - representative parallelization efforts

Authors	Hardware platform	Speedup
Stunkel [13] (1988)	16-processor Intel Hypercube	Between 8 and 12 for small Netlib problems
Eckstein et al. [12] (1995)	CM-2 and CM-5 with thousands of processors	Between 1.6 and 1.8 when doubling the number of processors - superior to MINOS
Thomadakis and Liu [11] (1996)	MP-1 and MP-2 (128×128 processor MP-2)	Up to 1000 on large random LPs
Yarmish et al. [3] (2009)	7 workstations - Fast Ethernet	On iteration speed: up to $\sim$ 7 for random high-aspect ratio LPs
Mamalis et al. [16–18] (2011–14)	8-nodes Myrinet-connected Intel Xeon cluster - 4 × 4 quad-core Intel with gigabit ethernet	On iteration speed: up to $\sim$ 8 for random and Netlib LPs with high-aspect ratio - 11.5 to 15.2 for large LPs of all kinds

study and comparison of both the above data distribution schemes, as well as the corresponding implementations over high-performance cluster (distributed memory or hybrid) environments achieving particularly high speedup values are given in the recent works of Mamalis et al. [16–18]. The key points and achievements of the latter are presented in more details in Sect. 6.

3.2   Parallelizing the Revised Simplex Method

Undoubtedly, the real challenge in developing a parallel simplex implementation of general practical value is to exploit parallelism when using a variant of the revised method with sparse matrix algebra techniques. Only then the resulting solver could be competitive to a good serial implementation when solving general large sparse LP problems using a realistic number of processors. Efficient serial simplex solvers are based on the revised simplex method with a factored inverse since the practical LP problems whose solution poses a computational challenge are large and sparse. For such problems, the superiority of the revised simplex method over the known serial standard simplex schemes is clear and obvious. It follows that the only scope for developing a really worthwhile parallel simplex solver is to identify how the revised simplex method with a factored inverse may be parallelized. The natural data parallelism of the PRICE operation has been exploited by most authors. Several researchers have also considered the data parallelism in other computational components, whereas others have studied the extent to which task parallelism can be exploited by overlapping operations that are then executed either in serial or, in the case of PRICE, by exploiting data parallelism.

The first worth telling research attempts were contributed by Pfefferkorn and Tomlin [26] and Helgason et al. [27]. In [26] the authors were the first to discuss how parallelism could be exploited in each computational component of the revised simplex method. On the other hand, in [27] the authors trying to contribute new ideas, beyond the classics, discussed the scope for parallelizing FTRAN and BTRAN operations based on the relatively unknown quadrant interlocking factorization technique. Further, McKinnon and Plab [28] considered how data parallelism could be exploited in FTRAN operation for both dense and sparse right-hand sides. They also investigated how the Markowitz criterion could be modified in order to increase the potential for exploiting data parallelism in subsequent FTRAN operations.

The first attempt to exploit task parallelism in the revised simplex method was reported by Ho and Sundarraj [29]. In addition to the natural data parallelism of the PRICE operation, Ho and Sundarraj identified that the INVERT operation can be overlapped with simplex iterations. The performance of Ho and Sundarrajs implementation, on an Intel iPSC/2 and Sequent Balance 8000, was quite promising, however limited in accordance with Amdahls law (since only some parts of the whole algorithm were parallelized). On a set of small Netlib and proprietary problems, they report an average saving of 33 % over the corresponding serial solution time.

The next ambitious implementation that attempted to exploit full data parallelism over the revised simplex method was that of Shu [10]. It was based on a parallel triangularization phase for the INVERT operation, a distributed sparse LU decomposition of the basis matrix for parallel FTRAN and BTRAN operations, as well as a typical parallelization of the PRICE operation. However, no significant speed-up was achieved in the corresponding experimental tests.

In the following years till now, the most known and notable corresponding atttempts were contributed by Hall and McKinnon [9,41]. Their first parallel revised simplex scheme was ASYNPLEX [9]. This corresponds to a variant of the revised simplex method in which reduced costs are computed directly. ASYN-PLEX was implemented on a Cray T3D and it was tested using four modest but representative Netlib test problems. Using between 8 and 12 processors to perform simplex iterations, the iteration speed was increased by a factor of about 5 in all cases. However, the increase in the number of iterations required to solve the problem led to a speed-up in solution time ranging from 2.4 to 4.8. Hall and McKinnons second parallel scheme was PARSMI [41]. This was developed in an attempt to address the deficiencies of ASYNPLEX. In order to make realistic comparisons with good serial solvers, PARSMI updates the reduced costs and uses Devex pricing. As the authors state, the implementation of PARSMI was a highly complex programming task, magnified by the fact that communication times are not deterministic and the order of arrival of messages determined the operation of the program. Programming difficulties, together with numerical instability meant that the implementation was never reliable. In the very limited results that were obtained on modest Netlib problems, using eight processors, the speed-up in iteration speed was between 2.2 and 2.4 (leading to a speedup in solution time between 1.7 and 1.9).

As it can be seen, all attempts to exploit parallelism in the revised simplex method have focused on the primal simplex method. The dual simplex method, which is much more efficient for many LP problems has not been addressed a lot in terms of parallelization. However, as it is explained in more detail in [2,30], there is one important distinction between the primal and dual simplex methods which has the potential to cause significant differences in parallel performance. In the primal simplex method the PRICE operation is restricted to just a subset of the non-basic variables, whereas, in the dual simplex method, especially for problems with very large column/row ratios the completely dominant cost is due to the PRICE operation. Hence its parallelization can be expected to yield a significant improvement in performance over that of the efficient serial dual simplex solvers. Bixby and Martin [30] were the first to investigate the scope for parallelism in the dual revised simplex method and chose to parallelize only those operations whose cost is related to the number of columns in the problem, that is the PRICE operation, the dual ratio test and the update of the dual variables. They implemented the dual simplex method on several architectures; however using the full Netlib set, no significant gain in performance was obtained. The latter was a normal behavior since few problems in the Netlib set have significantly more columns than rows. Focusing on this kind of problems and using up to four processors on an IBM SP2, a quite satisfactory speedup was observed, ranging from 1 to 3.

Till recently, no other valuable attempts have been made to parallelize the dual revised simplex method, thus making the one that immediately follows (Huangfu and Hall [6,7], Sect. 4) a distinguished one. Another significant parallel implementation using the revised simplex method that deserves to be presented separately (see Sect. 5) has also been recently achieved by Lubin et al. [8], demonstrating the capability of solving large scale stochastic LP problems in acceptable times within the computing environment of a supercomputer.

4   Recent Advances on the Parallelization of the Dual Revised Simplex Method

As mentioned in the previous sections, for sparse LP problems the revised (either primal or dual) simplex method is generally preferred against the simplex method

Table 3. Revised simplex - representative parallelization efforts

Authors	Hardware platform	Speedup
Ho and Sundarraj [29] (1994)	Intel iPSC/2 and Sequent Balance 8000 (primal simplex)	1.5 on average for medium sized Netlib and other LPs
Hall and McKinnon [9] (1998)	Cray T3D (8 to 12 processors) (primal simplex)	Between 2.5 and 4.8 on medium sized Netlib LPs ($\sim$ 5 on iteration speed)
Bixby and Martin [30] (2000)	Different platforms - 4 pr. on a IBM SP2 (dual simplex)	Between 1 and 3 on high-aspect ratio Netlib LPs
Huangfu and Hall [6,7] (2012–14)	8 cores of a 16xIntel Xeon E5620 (dual suboptimization)	> 2 on average for test LPs of all kinds (max of 3.5), 1.5 on average over regular dual simplex, comparable to Cplex & Clp
Lubin et al. [8] (2013)	a 320x8-node cluster with Infini-Band and a Blue Gene/P supercomputer with 40960 nodes (both primal and dual)	On iteration speed: $\sim$ 100 over Clp when using 16 nodes (128 cores) for large-scale two-stage stochastic LP problems

in its standard form since it permits the sparsity of the problem to be exploited. This is achieved using techniques for decomposing sparse matrices and solving hyper-sparse linear systems. Also important for the dual revised simplex method are advanced algorithmic variants introduced in the 1990s, particularly dual steepest-edge (DSE) pricing and the bound flipping ratio test (BFRT). These led to significant performance improvements and resulted in the dual simplex algorithm being preferred. However, for many years now, although the dual revised method is regarded as the most preferable and efficient, no practical parallel implementations appeared in this context. Towards the above direction, the authors in [6,7] introduce two novel parallel dual simplex solvers for general large scale sparse linear programming problems, over standard desktop architectures. The first approach extends a relatively unknown pivoting strategy called suboptimization and exploits parallelism across multiple iterations. The second approach exploits purely single iteration parallelism. Computational results show that the performance of the first approach is comparable with the world-leading commercial simplex solvers, and that the second approach complements the first one, in achieving speedup when it results in slowdown.

Moreover, in the past, parallel implementations generally used dedicated high performance computers to achieve the best performance. Now that every desktop computer is a multi-core machine, any speedup is desirable in terms of solution time reduction for daily use. In this direction, the authors have chosen to use relatively standard architecture to perform computational experiments with very good results. It should certainly be considered as one of the most valuable practical attempts during the last decade with respect to the general-purpose parallelization of the revised simplex method.[1]

4.1   Design and Implementation (Key Issues)

As reported in Sect. 2, the dual simplex algorithm solves an LP problem iteratively by seeking primal feasibility while maintaining dual feasibility. Considering the operations within each iteration (as given in Fig. 2), there is immediate scope for data parallelization within CHUZR, PRICE, CHUZC and most of the update operations since they require independent operations for each (nonzero) component of a vector. Additionally, the scope for task parallelism by overlapping the execution of the sub-operations within FTRAN was considered by Bixby and Martin but rejected as being disadvantageous computationally. On the other hand, Huangfu and Hall [6,7] have based their implementation on the technique of suboptimization, which is is one of the oldest variants of the revised simplex method and consists of a major-minor iteration scheme [7]. Within the primal revised simplex method, suboptimization performs minor iterations of the standard primal simplex method using small subsets of columns from the reduced

---

[1] Note also that the techniques applied in the proposed approaches, have been the basis for the integration of FICO Xpress parallel solver [42], which was the first commercial parallel simplex solver and has been regarded quite faster than the preexisting ones in various kinds of large-scale LPs.

coefficient matrix $B^{-1}A$. Suboptimization for the dual simplex method was first set out by Rosander [31]. It performs minor operations of the standard dual simplex method, applied to small subsets of rows from $B^{-1}A$. Originally, suboptimization was proposed mainly as a pivoting scheme for achieving better pivot choices and advantageous data affinity. In modern revised simplex implementations, the DSE and BFRT are together regarded as the best pivotal rules and the idea of suboptimization has been naturally forgotten. However, in terms of parallelization, suboptimization is attractive because it certainly provides more scope for parallelization.

In the design and implementation of the first proposed approach, the authors extend the suboptimization scheme of [31], incorporating (serial) algorithmic techniques and exploiting parallelism across multiple iterations. The main suboptimization steps (the exact mathematical formulation can be found in [7]) in each iteration include (a) the major optimality test, (b) the minor initialization step, (c) the minor iterations step consisting of of three basic sub-operations i.e., the minor optimality test, the minor ratio test and the minor update step, and (d) the major update step. Based on the above decomposition, the authors apply extensively data parallelism (mainly with respect to the various vector-based operations met) in almost all steps. Specifically, vector-based operations are met (and can be efficiently parallelized) on both the major optimality test and the major update step, whereas the minor initialization step offers a good opportunity for task parallelization. With regard to the composite minor iterations step, data parallelism is applied on the minor ratio test with respect to the PRICE operation and the first part of CHUZC operations, as well as on the minor update step (vector-based update operations).

In their second parallel implementation the authors introduce a relative simple approach to exploiting parallelism within a single iteration of the dual revised simplex method. The relevant approach is a significant development of the work of Bixby and Martin [30] who parallelized only the PRICE, CHUZC and update-dual operations, having rejected the task parallelism of FTRAN sub-operations as being computationally disadvantageous. The mixed parallelization scheme of this implementation can be found in more details in [7].

4.2   Experimental Results

The experimental performance of the two parallelization approaches described above has been tested using a reference set consisting of 30 problems. Most of these LP problems are taken from a comprehensive list of various representative LP problems maintained by Mittelmann [32]. The problems in this reference set reflect the wide spread of LP properties and revised simplex characteristics, including the dimension of the linear systems (number of rows and columns), the density of the coefficient matrix (average number of non-zeros per column), and the extent to which they exhibit hyper-sparsity.

The performance of both approaches has been measured using experiments performed on a workstation with 16 (Intel Xeon E5620, 2.4 GHz) cores, using 8 of the cores for the parallel calculations. With respect to the results obtained for the first approach, the main observations can be summarized as follows:

- For most of the problems included in the reference set, the speedup compared to its sequential version is more than 2 (with a geometric mean of 2.23). The best speedup obtained was equal to 3.50.
- When compared to the regular dual simplex method, the sequential version of the proposed implementation is generally less efficient (about 30 % slower). As a consequence, the overall (true) speedup is somewhat restricted, resulting in a mean speedup of about 1.5.
- It is also worth mentioning that the instances of better speedup (greater than the average) correspond largely to the sparse LP problems.

The above results are satisfactory since they refer to a general-case reference set with all kinds of problems. Furthermore, the worst performances are associated with dense LP problems, whereas the achieved performance when solving hyper-sparse LP problems is moderate but relatively stable. As it is also clearly indicated in the original paper [7], the performance of the proposed approach is comparable with the dual simplex implementation of CPLEX, a world-leading commercial dual revised simplex solver, and clearly superior to that of CLP, the world's leading open-source solver. On the other hand, the results obtained for the second approach can be summarized as follows:

- The overall performance is quite worse than that of the first approach. An average speedup of 1.13 has been achieved, with a maximum value of 2.05.
- The worst cases are associated with the hyper-sparse LP problems where, in most cases, it results in a slowdown.
- However, when applied to dense LP problems, the performance is moderate and relative stable. This is especially so for those instances where the first approach exhibits a slowdown.

In summary, the second approach is a straightforward parallelization approach which exploits purely single iteration parallelism and achieves relatively poor speedup for general LP problems. However, it is frequently complementary to the first approach in achieving speedup when the latter results in slowdown. Overall, the authors in this paper have introduced the design and development of a novel parallel dual revised simplex method implementation framework, which has been measured to provide an average speedup of 1.5 for general large scale sparse linear programming problems, over standard desktop architectures. Although this is not particularly high, the resulting performance of the first approach is comparable to the dual simplex implementation of CPLEX.

5   Parallel Distributed-Memory Simplex for Large-Scale Stochastic LP Problems

The parallel implementation of the revised simplex method for several special cases of linear programming problems may often be implemented quite more efficiently than in the general case due to the special structure of these problems [2]. Seeking towards that direction (special-purpose parallel revised simplex solvers) one of the most impressive works made recently was the one presented in [8]. In this work the authors present a parallelization of the revised simplex method for large extensive forms of two-stage stochastic linear programming (LP) problems, which can be considered one of the most interesting special cases of linear programming problems (due to their very large size as well as their significance in real life). These problems have been considered too large to solve with the simplex method; instead, decomposition approaches based on Benders decomposition or, more recently, interior point methods are generally used. However, these approaches do not provide optimal basic solutions. The present approach exploits the dual block-angular structure of these problems inside the linear algebra of the revised simplex method in a manner suitable for high-performance distributed-memory clusters or supercomputers. While this paper focuses on stochastic LPs, the work is applicable to all problems with a dual block-angular structure. The whole implementation is competitive in serial with highly efficient simplex solvers and achieves significant relative speed-ups when executed in parallel. Additionally, very large problems with hundreds of millions of variables have been successfully solved to optimality.

Moreover, as the authors claim, this is the largest-scale parallel sparsity-exploiting revised simplex implementation that has been developed to date and the first truly distributed solver. It is built on novel analysis of the linear algebra for dual block-angular LP problems when solved by using the revised simplex method and a novel parallel scheme for applying product-form updates.[2]

5.1   Design and Implementation (Key Issues)

More concretely, the proposed parallelization approach is based on the revised simplex method for linear programming (LP) problems with a special structure which is known as dual block angular or block angular with linking columns [8]. This structure commonly arises in stochastic optimization as the extensive form or deterministic equivalent of two-stage stochastic linear programs [33]. Linear programs with block-angular structure, both primal and dual, occur in a wide array of applications, and this structure can also be identified within general LPs. They are typically met in the form given below:

$$
\begin{aligned}
\text{minimize} \quad & c_0^T x_0 + c_1^T x_1 + c_2^T x_2 + \ldots + c_N^T x_N \\
\text{subject to} \quad & A x_0 && = b_0, \\
& T_1 x_0 + W_1 x_1 && = b_1, \\
& T_2 x_0 \qquad\quad + W_2 x_2 && = b_2, \\
& \quad\vdots \qquad\qquad\qquad \ddots \qquad\quad \vdots \\
& T_N x_0 \qquad\qquad\qquad + W_N x_N && = b_N, \\
& x_0 \geq 0, \ x_1 \geq 0, \ x_2 \geq 0, \ \ldots, x_N \geq 0
\end{aligned}
$$

---

[2] Note also that this paper has received recently the COAP (Computational Optimization and Applications) journal Best Paper Award for year 2013.

Borrowing the terminology from stochastic optimization, the vector x_0 is supposed to contain the first-stage variables and the vectors $x_1, \ldots, x_N$ the second-stage variables. On the other hand, the matrices $W_1, W_2, \ldots, W_N$ contain the coefficients of the second-stage constraints, and the matrices $T_1, T_2, \ldots, T_N$ those of the linking constraints.

With regard to the distribution of data across the parallel processes, the authors have adopted a carefully designed allocation scheme as follows: Given a set of P MPI processes and $N \geq P$ scenarios or second-stage blocks, on the initialization, each second-stage block is assigned to a single MPI process. All data, iterates, and computations relating to the first stage are duplicated in each process. The second-stage data (i.e., W_i, T_i, c_i, and b_i), iterates, and computations are only stored in and performed by their assigned process. If a scenario is not assigned to a process, this process stores no data pertaining to the scenario, not even the basic/nonbasic states of its variables.

Then, the authors proceed with the first (and probably the most important) step of their solution, i.e., the factorizing of the basis matrix. Accordingly, one has to form an invertible representation of the basis matrix B. This is performed in efficient sparsity-exploiting codes by forming a sparse LU factorization of the basis matrix. These factors are formed in parallel via the following steps:

– Perform partial sparse Gaussian elimination on each second-stage block.
– Collect and duplicate the necessary terms across processes.
– In each process, form and factor the first-stage block.

The first step may be performed in parallel for each second-stage block (since they have been evenly distributed to the multiple processes). In the second step the results are collected and duplicated in each parallel process by using MPI_Allgather() function, and in the third step, each process factors its local copy of the first-stage block. If then an LU factorization of the first-stage block is performed, this entire procedure could be viewed as forming an LU factorization of B through a restricted sequence of pivot choices. The remaining linear system is now trivial to solve towards the final solution. Appropriate parallelization is being applied in all the following necessary steps (solving linear systems. matrix-vector product, updating the inverse etc.) by the means of some of the well-known collective communication functions of MPI (MPI_Bcast(), MPI_Allgather(), MPI_Allreduce() etc.) [8].

5.2   Experimental Results

The proposed approach (PIPS-S) was evaluated experimentally with the use of two powerful distributed memory architectures available at Argonne National Laboratory (ANL):

– *Fusion* is a 320-node cluster with an InfiniBand QDR interconnect; each node has two 2.6 GHz Xeon processors (total 8 cores). Most nodes have 36 GB of RAM, while a small number of them offer 96 GB of RAM.

- *Intrepid* is a Blue Gene/P (BG/P) supercomputer with 40,960 nodes with a custom high-performance interconnect. Each BG/P node has a quad-core 850 MHz PowerPC processor with 2 GB of RAM.

Using suitable stochastic LP test problems, the authors present results of three different scales by varying the number of scenarios. Part of the measurements i.e. the ones for SSN and Storm problems which exhibit the best performance, are presented in Table 4. First, the authors consider instances that could be solved on a modern desktop from scratch, that is, from an all-slack starting basis. These large-scale instances (with 110 million total variables) serve both to compare the serial efficiency of PIPS-S with that of a modern simplex code and to investigate the potential for parallel speedup on problems of this size. The main observations can be summarized as follows:

- Clp is faster than PIPS-S in serial on all instances; however, the total number of iterations performed by PIPS-S is consistent with the number of iterations performed by Clp.
- Significant parallel speedups are observed in all cases; as an example PIPS-S is 5 and 8 times faster than Clp for SSN and Storm respectively when using four nodes (32 cores).
- The speedups obtained on some other instances are smaller, possibly because of the smaller number of scenarios and the larger dimensions of the first stage.

Next, some quite larger instances with 20–40 million total variables are considered. The high memory nodes of the Fusion cluster with 96 GB of RAM were required for these tests. Given the long times to solution for the smaller instances solved in the previous section, it is impractical to solve these larger instances from scratch. Instead, the authors proceed using advanced or near-optimal starting bases in two different contexts. The corresponding results can be summarized as follows:

- Clp remains faster in serial than PIPS-S on these instances, although by a smaller factor than before.
- The parallel scalability of PIPS-S is almost ideal (>90 % parallel efficiency) up to 4 nodes (32 cores) and continues to scale well up to 16 nodes (128 cores). Scaling from 16 nodes to 32 nodes is poor.
- On 16 nodes, the iteration speed of PIPS-S is about 100 times better than that of Clp for Storm and 70 times better than that of Clp for SSN.

Finally, the authors report on the solution of a very large instance with 8,192 scenarios. This instance has 463,113,276 variables and 486,899,712 constraints. An advanced starting basis was generated from 4,096 scenarios, not included in the execution time. This problem requires approximately 1 TB of RAM to solve, requiring a minimum of 512 Blue Gene/P nodes; however, results are only available for runs with 1,024 nodes or more because of execution time limits. The derived solution time was around 6 h on 1024 nodes (2048 cores), 5 h on 2048 nodes (4096 cores), and 4.5 h on 4096 nodes (8192 cores). While scaling performance is poor on these large numbers of nodes, this test demonstrates the

Table 4. Part of the experimental results of [8]

Test problem	Solver	Nodes	Cores	Time (sec.)	Iter/sec.
Solves from scratch using dual simplex					
Storm	Clp	1	1	133,047	50.4
	PIPS-S	1	1	385,825	16.5
		1	8	52,948	119.8
		4	32	15,667	405.2
SSN	Clp	1	1	12,619	93.1
	PIPS-S	1	1	58,425	17.5
		1	8	7,788	135.5
		4	32	1,931	542.1
Solves from advanced starting basis using primal simplex					
Storm	Clp	1	1	7,537	2.2
	PIPS-S	1	1	7,184	1.3
		2	16	137	47.6
		16	128	35.5	216.6
		32	256	25.2	260.4
SSN	Clp	1	1	50,737	2.0
	PIPS-S	1	1	427,648	0.8
		2	16	9,550	22.9
		16	128	1,481	143.3
		32	256	1,117	180.0

capability of PIPS-S to solve instances considered far too large to solve today with commercial solvers.

6 Revisiting the Parallelization of Standard Full Tableau Simplex Method

The fact that a parallel simplex solver based on the standard (full tableau) representation may be practical only for dense LP problems and may not easily be competitive to the fast serial revised simplex solvers of nowadays unless it uses expensive parallel computing resources, has naturally led to less corresponding efforts in the literature during the last years. However, any new intuitive corresponding study and relevant implementation would still be worthwhile as far as it achieves either particularly high speedups in absolute values (which also usually means competitive solution times to the ones of the serial solvers) or particularly high efficiency values combined with correspondingly high scalability. The latter has the potential to lead to even higher speedups and competitive solution times when executing to architectures with larger number of processors/cores.

One of the most recent and worth mentioning relevant attempts combining sufficient theoretical study and results with a relevant particularly efficient parallel implementation of the standard simplex method, was the one presented by Yarmish et al. [3]. The corresponding implementation has led to very satisfactory speedup values, whereas it has also been compared to MINOS (a well-known serial revised simplex solver), and it has been shown to be highly competitive, even for very low density problems. Moreover, together with the work of Badr et al. [4], they are the most recent works that put on the table the significant influence of the number of columns and rows of an LP problem when a distributed memory architecture is used. Being inspired by the motivation and the results of the above two research attempts, as well as by the means of the current technology (either in terms of high-speed network connections or in terms of powerful hybrid hardware architectures and corresponding hybrid software solutions), in [16–18] the authors present two very promising relevant approaches with regard to simplex parallelization in its standard (full tableau) form.

First, in [16,17] the authors present a highly scalable parallel implementation framework designed for distributed memory (message passing) environments. Two basic data distribution schemes have been implemented, a column-based one and a row-based distribution scheme, in order to measure the influence of each distribution method over LP problems with different aspect ratio and compare their performance with other works in the literature. They have experimentally evaluated their implementations over a considerably powerful parallel environment; a linux-cluster of 8 (16 threads) Xeon processors connected via a dedicated (low latency) Myrinet network interface. They have tested and compared the two implementation schemes among each other, as well as to the corresponding implementations of [3,4] referred above. Both schemes lead to particularly high speed-up and efficiency values for typical test LPs, that are considerably better in all cases than the ones achieved by the corresponding implementations of [3,4].

Next, in [18] the authors focus on the modern hybrid hardware architectures (distributed memory/cluster environments with multicore nodes) of nowadays, and they involve several different software alternatives on the parallelization of the standard simplex method with the column-based data distribution scheme. Specifically, they present relevant implementations combining pure MPI, OpenMP and MPI 3.0 Shared Memory support. They compare their approaches among each other for variable number of nodes/cores and problem size, as well as to the approach presented in [3]. The experiments have been performed over a hybrid parallel environment which consists of up to 4 quad-core processors (making a total of 16 cores) connected via Gigabit ethernet interface. All the evaluated parallelization schemes have led to particularly high speed-up and efficiency values, whereas the corresponding values for the hybrid MPI+OpenMP based scheme (which is proved to be the most efficient) are considerably better in all cases than the ones achieved in the work of [3].

6.1 Design and Implementation (Key Issues)

As mentioned above the most efficient implementations presented in [16–18] have followed the column-based distribution for spreading the initial tableau to all the processors. This is a relatively straightforward parallelization scheme within the standard simplex method which involves dividing up the columns of the simplex table among all the processors and it is theoretically regarded as the most effective one in the general case. Following this scheme all the computation parts except step 2 of the basic (sequential) algorithm (presented in Sect. 2), are fully parallelized. Additionally, this form of parallelization looks as the most natural choice since in most practical problems the number of columns is larger than the number of rows. The basic steps of the algorithm are given below:

Step 0: The simplex table is shared among the processors by columns. Also, the right-hand constraints vector is broadcasted to all processors.

Step 1: Each processor searches in its local part and chooses the locally best candidate column the one with the larger negative coefficient in the objective function part (local contribution for the global determination of the entering variable).

Step 2: The local results are gathered in parallel and the winning processor i.e., the one with the larger negative coefficient among all, is found and globally known. At the end of this step each processor will know which processor is the winner and has the global column choice.

Step 3: The processor with the winning column (entering variable) computes the leaving variable (winning row) using the minimum ratio test over all the winning columns elements.

Step 4: The same (winning) processor then broadcasts the winning column as well as the winning rows id to all processors.

Step 5: Each processor performs (in parallel) on its own part (columns) of the table all the calculations required for the global rows pivoting, based on the pivot data received during step 4.

Step 6: The above steps are repeated until the best solution is found or the problem gets unbounded.

A relevant, row-based, distribution scheme has also been implemented and studied in comparison to the one stated above (see [17] for more details). Based on the above step by step decomposition three different parallelization schemes were designed and implemented as follows:

a. Pure MPI implementation.
The well-known MPI collective communication functions MPI_Scatter, MPI_Bcast and MPI_Reduce/Allreduce (with or without MAXLOC/MINLOC operators) were appropriately used for the efficient implementation of the data communication required by steps 0, 2 and 4 of the parallel algorithm.

b. Hybrid MPI+OpenMP implementation.
Appropriately built parallel *for* constructs were used for the efficient thread-based parallelization of the loops implied by steps 1, 3 and 5. Especially with

regard to the parallelization of steps 1 (in cooperation with step 2) and 3, in order to optimize the parallel implementation of the corresponding procedures, the newly added min/max reduction operators of OpenMP API specification for C/C++ were used. Also, with regard to the parallelization of step 5, in order to achieve even distribution of computations to the working threads, collapse-based nested parallelism is used in combination with dynamic scheduling policy. Beyond the OpenMP-based parallelization inside each node, the well-known MPI collective communication functions were also used for the communication between the network connected nodes as in pure MPI implementation.

c. Hybrid MPI+MPI Shared Memory implementation.
The corresponding shared memory support functions of MPI 3.0 (mainly: MPI_Comm_split_type, MPI_Win_allocate_shared and MPI_Win_shared_query) as well as the syncronization primitives MPI_Win_fence, MPI_Win_lock/unlock and MPI_Accumulate were used for the efficient implementation of all the data communication (the initial and intermediate data sharing as well as the computation of minimum/maximum values) required by steps 0, 2, 3 and 4 of the parallel algorithm over the multiple cores of each node. The well-known MPI collective communication functions were used for the communication between the network connected nodes as in pure MPI implementation.

6.2 Experimental Results

First, in order to compare their approach to the one of Yarmish et al. [3] (which is also based on the column-based distribution scheme) the authors have run on their Myrinet-connected linux-cluster platform their basic implementation over the large size (1000x5000) linear problem presented there [3], with the same characteristics, and they have measured the execution time per iteration for 1, 2 up to 8 processors. This problem is a large-scale problem with many more columns than rows, so it is expected to have good speedup with the use of the column distribution scheme. Note also that the parallel platform used in the experiments of [3] consisted of 7 dedicated processors (the exact configuration is not mentioned) connected via Fast Ethernet network interface. The corresponding results (in terms of speedup and efficiency measures based on the execution time per iteration) for varying number of processors are presented in Table 5. Observing the results of Table 5, firstly it can easily be noticed that the execution times (in one or more processors) of the algorithm in [17] are much better than the ones of [3], which however was expected due to the fact that the test platform is quite more powerful than the platform of [3]. The most important, the achieved speedup values are also better than the ones achieved in [3]. Furthermore, observing the corresponding efficiency values in the last column someone can easily notice the high scalability (higher and smoother than in [3]) achieved. Note also that the achieved speedup remains very high (close to the maximum/speedup = 7.92, efficiency = 99.0 %) even for 8 processors.

Additionally, in other experimental measurements in the same platform (as presented in [17]), the authors compare the performance of their two different

Table 5. Comparing to the implementation of [3]

P	Yarmish et al. [3]			Mamalis et al. [17]		
#proc	Time/iter	$S_p = T_1/T_P$	$E_p = S_p/P$ (%)	Time/iter	$S_p = T_1/T_P$	$E_p = S_p/P$ (%)
1	0.61328	1.00	100.0	0.27344	1.00	100.0
2	0.31150	1.97	98.4	0.13713	1.99	99.7
3	0.21724	2.82	94.1	0.09225	2.96	98.8
4	0.15496	3.96	98.9	0.06877	3.98	99.5
5	0.13114	4.68	93.5	0.05592	4.89	97.8
6	0.10658	5.75	95.9	0.04636	5.90	98.3
7	0.09128	6.72	96.0	0.03958	6.91	98.7
8				0.03453	7.92	99.0

data distribution schemes (column-based vs. row-based) among each other (with the use of a suitable subset of NETLIB test linear problems of varying sizes), concluding to two basic remarks: (a) the column-based distribution scheme is clearly superior in most cases, however (b) there are several cases that one should choose the row-based distribution scheme instead mainly for small sized problems with almost equal number of rows and columns or greater number of rows. The high scalability of the column-based distribution scheme over sixteen processors (threads) is also demonstrated in relevant experiments for very large-scale problems. Furthermore, the authors notice that the influence of having more columns than rows in favor of the column distribution scheme is greater than the influence of having more rows than columns in favor of the row distribution scheme; which means that the communication overhead caused by the parallelization of the row distribution scheme is more significant in the general case than the one caused by the parallelization of the column distribution scheme.

Similarly, the authors in [17] have also run corresponding experiments on their hybrid hardware platform (4x4 quad-core processors connected with Gigabit Ethernet), in order to compare the performance of their two different hybrid parallelization schemes among each other (MPI+OpenMP vs. MPI+MPI 3.0 Shared Memory support), with use of another suitable subset of the NETLIB test linear problems of varying sizes. The corresponding results (speedup and efficiency values for 8 and 16 processors/cores - two quad-core processors and four quad-core processors, respectively) are presented in Table 6, and they can be summarized as follows:

- The achieved speed-up and efficiency values of the hybrid MPI+OpenMP implementation are better than the ones of the hybrid MPI+MPI 3.0 Shared Memory implementation, in all cases.
- However the achieved values for the MPI+MPI 3.0 Shared Memory implementation are also particularly high and competitive (up to 90% efficiency for medium-sized problems on eight cores).
- More concretely, for linear problems of small size the corresponding measurements are almost the same (slightly better for the MPI+OpenMP approach), whereas for problems of larger size the difference is quite clear.

Overall, one can say that the shared window allocation mechanism of MPI 3.0 offers a very good alternative (with almost equivalent results to the MPI+OpenMP approach) for shared memory parallelization when the shared data are of relatively small/medium scale, however it cannot scale up the same well (for large windows and large number of cores) due to internal protocol limitations and management costs, especially in applications where some kind of synchronization is required. Finally, in order to further validate the high efficiency and scalability of the hybrid MPI+OpenMP parallelization scheme, in more representative (closer to the real word) cases, the authors have also performed corresponding experiments for large and very large NETLIB problems. The corresponding measuremnets are shown for 2 up to 16 processors/cores in Table 7. One can easily observe the following:

- The efficiency values decrease with the increase of the number of processors. However, this decrease is quite slow, and both the speedup and efficiency values remain high ($\geq 80\%$) even for 16 cores, in all cases.
- Particularly high efficiency values (almost linear speedup) are achieved for all the high aspect ratio problems (e.g. see the values for problems FIT2P, 80BAU3B and QAP15 where the efficiency even for 16 processors/cores is over 90% - a particularly high value for realistic problems).

7   GPU-Based Simplex Parallelization Efforts

The computational power provided by the massive parallelism of modern graphics processing units (GPUs) has moved increasingly into focus over the past few years. However, in the area of simplex parallelization for several reasons (similar to the ones discussed for the conventional CPU-only parallelization) there have

Table 6. Comparing the two hybrid schemes

Linear Problems	MPI+OpenMP				MPI+MPI 3.0 SM			
	2×4 cores		4×4 cores		2×4 cores		4×4 cores	
	S_p	E_p (%)	S_p	E_p (%)	S_p	E_p (%)	S_p	E_p (%)
SC50A (50×48)	4.89	61.1	6.50	40.6	4.85	60.6	6.40	40.0
SHARE2B (96×79)	5.59	69.8	8.24	51.5	5.49	68.6	8.00	50.0
SC105 (105×103)	5.81	72.6	8.78	54.9	5.69	71.1	8.50	53.1
BRANDY (220×249)	7.00	87.5	12.17	76.1	6.60	82.5	10.63	66.5
AGG (488×163)	6.76	84.5	12.11	75.7	6.38	79.8	11.27	70.4
AGG2 (516×302)	7.00	87.5	12.89	80.5	6.58	82.3	11.99	74.9
BANDM (305×472)	7.42	92.8	13.61	85.0	6.82	85.3	12.03	75.2
SCFXM3 (990×1371)	7.60	95.0	14.38	89.9	7.16	89.5	13.05	81.5

Table 7. Speed-up & efficiency for large problems

Linear Problems	2 × 1 cores		2 × 2 cores		2 × 4 cores		4 × 4 cores	
	S_p	E_p (%)	S_p	E_p (%)	S_p	E_p (%)	S_p	E_p (%)
FIT2P (3000 × 13525)	1.977	98.9	3.94	98.5	7.80	97.5	15.24	95.3
80BAU3B (2263 × 9799)	1.969	98.5	3.91	97.8	7.72	96.5	14.92	93.3
QAP15 (6330 × 22275)	1.963	98.2	3.89	97.3	7.62	95.3	14.47	90.5
MAROS-R7 (3136 × 9408)	1.957	97.9	3.87	96.8	7.54	94.3	14.12	88.3
QAP12 (3192 × 8856)	1.953	97.7	3.86	96.5	7.50	93.8	13.97	87.3
DFL001 (6071 × 12230)	1.945	97.3	3.85	96.3	7.50	93.8	14.04	87.8
GREENBEA (2392 × 5405)	1.949	97.5	3.84	96.0	7.40	92.5	13.59	84.9
STOCFOR3 (16675 × 15695)	1.925	96.3	3.79	94.8	7.23	90.4	12.80	80.0

not been noticed as many relevant attempts as one would expect. As a consequence, no parallel GPU-based implementation of the simplex algorithm has yet offered significantly better performance relative to an efficient sequential simplex solver; at least not in all types of LPs (sparse or dense, randomly generated or benchmark etc.). Certainly, some quite significant progress (and corresponding comparative results, satisfactory speedup values etc.) has been achieved at least for dense LP problems.

The quite strict model of parallelization, the limited development tools, and the limited processing element/core speed are some of the basic disadvantages comparing to the conventional model. The relatively slow memory transfer between CPU and GPU is also a significant drawback when a fully combined processing model is to be adopted. So, although the modern GPUs offer thousands of processing cores, the revised simplex method remains difficult to be efficiently parallelized and give satisfactory/competitive results compared to the existing serial solvers, whereas a GPU-based parallel version of the standard simplex method remains to be practical only for dense problems and with multiple computing resources (i.e. multiple GPUs). Furthermore, no corresponding GPU-accelerated implementation has been reported on a supercomputer. In the above context, we present the most recent and worth telling corresponding works in the next paragraphs.

Spampinato and Elster have proposed in [34] a parallel implementation of the revised Simplex method for LP on GPU with NVIDIA CUBLAS and NVIDIA LAPACK libraries. Tests were carried out on randomly generated LP problems of at most 2000 variables and 2000 constraints. The implementation showed a maximum speedup of 2.5 on a NVIDIA GTX 280 GPU as compared with sequential implementation on CPU with Intel Core2 Quad 2.83 GHz. Bieling, Peschlow and Martini have proposed in [35] another implementation of the revised Simplex method on GPU. This implementation permits one to speed up solution with a maximum factor of 18 in single precision on a NVIDIA GeForce 9600 GT GPU card as compared with GLPK solver run on Intel Core 2 Duo 3 GHz CPU.

Lalami et al. [36] have presented a parallel implementation via CUDA of the standard Simplex algorithm on CPU-GPU systems for dense LP problems. Experiments carried out on a CPU with 3 GHz Xeon Quadro INTEL processor and a GTX 260 GPU card have shown substantial speedup of 12.5 in double precision. Double precision implementation is used in order to improve the quality of solutions. The authors have also extended their work on a multi-GPU implementation [37] and their computational results on randomly generated dense problems showed a maximum speedup of 24.5. The experiments were performed with use of two Tesla C2050 boards.

Meyer et al. [38] proposed a mono- and a multi-GPU implementation of the tableau simplex algorithm and compared their implementation with the serial Clp solver. Their implementation outperformed Clp solver on large sparse LPs. Both these papers [37,38] that extend their approach to multiple GPUs, have dealt with a complete implementation of the simplex algorithm on the GPUs including the pivoting and the selection of the entering and leaving variables in order to avoid extra communication between the CPU and the GPUs. In multi-GPU computing several decomposition schemes can be adopted. An horizontal decomposition distributes the constraints on the different GPUs. A vertical decomposition distributes the variables of the LP problem on the GPUs. Finally, one may consider also tiles. The choice of a decomposition scheme has important consequences on the resulting communication pattern and multi-GPU efficacy. A decomposition based on tiles may appear scalable; it nevertheless necessitates many communications between GPUs. In [38], the authors have adopted a vertical decomposition in order to have less communication between GPUs. An horizontal decomposition has been adopted in [37].

Finally, Ploskas and Samaras [39] propose two efficient GPU-based implementations of the revised simplex algorithm and a primal-dual exterior point simplex algorithm. Both parallel algorithms have been implemented in MATLAB using MATLABs Parallel Computing Toolbox. Computational results on randomly generated sparse and dense linear programming problems and on a set of benchmark problems (netlib, kennington, meszaros) are also presented. The results show that the primal-dual exterior point simplex implementation achieves a quite satisfactory speedup (2.3 on average) over MATLABs interior point method for the set of benchmark LPs and much greater speedups for the randomly generated LPs. However, the corresponding results (and the speedups obtained) for the revised simplex implementation, although quite good for randomly generated dense LPs, they were significantly inferior in the general case to the ones referred above for the exterior point method.

As it can be seen, although the general feeling is that the overall research work in GPU-based simplex parallelization has not yet led to significant achievements in the general case (especially for sparse problems in comparison with serial solvers), worth telling improvements have been noticed in the case of dense LP problems. Also as GPUs are rapidly evolving, we can certainly expect for such implementations a great improvement of performances in the near future.

8   Conclusion

A number of valuable recent works in the parallelization of the simplex method are presented throughout this paper. A detailed overview is also given, including the recent advances in GPU-based simplex parallelization efforts. Naturally, most of the parallelization attempts made the last years refer to the revised simplex method, however a parallel implementation based on the standard simplex method could also be practical for dense problems if powerful/expensive computing resources are used. The difficulty of implementing a parallel simplex solver that could be significantly faster than (or at least highly competitive to) the existing commercial serial solvers in all cases remains an issue. Indeed the most impressive recent work in the literature refers to the utilization of the revised simplex method for solving large-scale stochastic LP problems, achieving speed-up values more than 100 over the Clp serial simplex solver when implemented on a supercomputer. The efficient parallelization of the dual revised method exploiting the scope of parallelization offered by the technique of sub-optimization, should also be considered a significant contribution. Moreover, all the corresponding results (either the older ones or the most recent ones) definitely outline the fact that there isn't an appropriate parallel solver for all kinds of LPs. As a consequence, a valuable piece of future research should probably be the design of some kind of metasolver, that given an LP would automatically propose/select the most efficient parallel solver.

References

1. Murty, K.: Linear Programming. Wiley, New York (1983)
2. Hall, J.A.: Towards a practical parallelization of the simplex method. Comput. Manag. Sci. 7(2), 139–170 (2010)
3. Yarmish, G., Slyke, R.V.: A distributed scaleable simplex method. J. Supercomput. 49(3), 373–381 (2009)
4. Badr, E.S., Moussa, M., Paparrizos, K., Samaras, N., Sifaleras, A.: Some Computational Results on MPI Parallel Implementation of Dense Simplex Method. World Academy of Science, Engineering and Technology (WASET), vol. 23, pp. 778–781 (2008)
5. Qin, J., Nguyen, D.T.: A parallel-vector simplex algorithm on distributed-memory computers. Struct. Optim. 11(3), 260–262 (1996)
6. Hall, J., Huangfu, Q.: A high performance dual revised simplex solver. In: Wyrzykowski, R., Dongarra, J., Karczewski, K., Waśniewski, J. (eds.) PPAM 2011, Part I. LNCS, vol. 7203, pp. 143–151. Springer, Heidelberg (2012)
7. Huangfu, Q., Hall, J.A.: Parallelizing the dual revised simplex method. Technical report ERGO-14-011 (2014). http://www.maths.ed.ac.uk/hall/Publications.html
8. Lubin, M., Hall, J.A., Petra, C.G., Anitescu, M.: Parallel distributed-memory simplex for large-scale stochastic LP problems. Comput. Optim. Appl. 55(3), 571–596 (2013)
9. Hall, J.A., McKinnon, K.: ASYNPLEX an asynchronous parallel revised simplex algorithm. Ann. Oper. Res. 81, 27–49 (1998)
10. Shu, W.: Parallel implementation of a sparse simplex algorithm on MIMD distributed memory computers. J. Parallel Distrib. Comput. 31(1), 2540 (1995)

11. Thomadakis M.E., Liu, J.C.: An efficient steepest-edge simplex algorithm for SIMD computers. In: Proceedings of the International Conference on Supercomputing (ICS 96), Philadelphia, pp. 286–293 (1996)
12. Eckstein, J., Boduroglu, I., Polymenakos, L., Goldfarb, D.: Data-parallel implementations of dense simplex methods on the connection machine CM-2. ORSA J. Comput. **7**(4), 402–416 (1995)
13. Stunkel, C.B.: Linear optimization via message-based parallel processing. In: Proceedings of International Conference on Parallel Processing (ICPP), Pennsylvania, pp. 264–271 (1988)
14. Klabjan, D., Johnson, L.E., Nemhauser, L.G.: A parallel primal-dual simplex algorithm. Oper. Res. Lett. **27**(2), 47–55 (2000)
15. Maros, I., Mitra, G.: Investigating the sparse simplex method on a distributed memory multiprocessor. Parallel Comput. **26**(1), 151–170 (2000)
16. Mamalis, B., Pantziou, G., Dimitropoulos, G., Kremmydas, D.: Reexamining the parallelization schemes for standard full tableau simplex method on distributed memory environments. In: Proceedings of the 10th IASTED PDCN (Parallel and Distributed Computing and Networks) Conference, Innsbruck, Austria, pp. 115–123 (2011)
17. Mamalis, B., Pantziou, G., Dimitropoulos, G., Kremmydas, D.: Highly scalable parallelization of standard simplex method on a myrinet connected cluster platform. ACTA Intl. J. Comput. Appl. **35**(4), 152–161 (2013)
18. Mamalis, B., Perlitis, M.: Hybrid parallelization of standard full tableau simplex method with MPI and OpenMP. In: Proceedings of the 18th Panhellenic Conference in Informatics (PCI 2014), ACM ICPS, October 2–4, Athens, Greece, pp. 1–6 (2014)
19. Finkel, R.A.: Large-grain parallelism: three case studies. In: Jamieson, L.H., Gannon, D., Douglas, R.J. (eds.) The Characteristics of Parallel Algorithms, pp. 21–63. MIT Press, Cambridge (1987)
20. Boffey, T.B., Hay, R.: Implementing parallel simplex algorithms. In: CONPAR 88, p. 169176. Cambridge University Press, Cambridge (1989)
21. Babaev, D.A., Mardanov, S.S.: A parallel algorithm for solving linear programming problems. ZhVychislitelnoi Matematiki Matematicheskoi Fiziki **31**(1), 8695 (1991)
22. Agrawal, A., Blelloch, G.E., Krawitz, R.L., Phillips, C.A.: Four vectormatrix primitives. In: ACM Symposium on Parallel Algorithms and Architectures, pp. 292–302 (1989)
23. Cvetanovic, Z., Freedman, E.G., Nofsinger, C.: Efficient decomposition and performance of parallel PDE, FFT, Monte-Carlo simulations, simplex, and sparse solvers. J. Supercomput. **5**, 1938 (1991)
24. Luo, J., Reijns, G.L.: Linear programming on transputers. In: van Leeuwen, J. (ed.) Algorithms, Software, Architecture. IFIP Transactions A (Computer Science and Technology), pp. 525–534. Elsevier, Amsterdam (1992)
25. Boduroglu, I.: Scalable massively parallel simplex algorithms for block-structured linear programs. Ph.D. thesis, GSAS, Columbia University, New York (1997)
26. Pfefferkorn, C.E., Tomlin, J.A.: Design of a linear programming system for the ILLIAC IV. Technical report SOL 76–8. Systems Optimization Laboratory, Stanford University (1976)
27. Helgason, R.V., Kennington, L.J., Zaki, H.A.: A parallelisation of the simplex method. Ann. Oper. Res. **14**, 1740 (1988)
28. McKinnon, K., Plab, F.: An upper bound on parallelism in the forward transformation within the revised simplex method. Technical report, Department of Mathematics and Statistics, University of Edinburgh (1997)

29. Ho, J.K., Sundarraj, R.P.: On the efficacy of distributed simplex algorithms for linear programming. Comput. Optim. Appl. **3**(4), 349363 (1994)
30. Bixby, R.E., Martin, A.: Parallelizing the dual simplex method. INFORMS J. Comput. **12**, 4556 (2000)
31. Rosander, R.: Multiple pricing and suboptimization in dual linear programming algorithms. Math. Program. Study **4**, 108–117 (1975)
32. Mittelmann, H.: Benchmarks for optimization software (2014). http://plato.la.asu.edu/bench.html. Accessed 30 July 2014
33. Birge, J., Louveaux, F.: Introduction to Stochastic Programming. Springer Series in Operations Research and Financial Engineering, 2nd edn. Springer, New York (2011)
34. Spampinato, D.G., Elster, A.C.: Linear optimization on modern GPUs. In: Proceedings of the 23rd IEEE IPDPS09 Conference, Rome, Italy (2009)
35. Bieling, J., Peschlow, P., Martini, P.: An efficient GPU implementation of the revised simplex method. In: Proceedings of the 24th IEEE International Parallel and Distributed Processing Symposium, (IPDPS 2010), Atlanta (2010)
36. Lalami, M.E., Boyer, V., El-Baz, D.: Efficient Implementation of the simplex method on a CPU-GPU system. In: IEEE International Parallel and Distributed Processing Symposium, pp. 1994–2001 (2011)
37. Lalami, M.E., El-Baz, D., Boyer, V.: Multi GPU implementation of the simplex algorithm. In: Proceedings of the 2011 IEEE 13th International Conference on High Performance Computing and Communications (HPCC), Banff, pp. 179–186 (2011)
38. Meyer, X., Albuquerque, P., Chopard, B.: A multi-GPU implementation and performance model for the standard simplex method. In: Proceedings of the 1st International Symposium and 10th Bal-kan Conference on Operational Research, Thessaloniki, Greece, pp. 312–319 (2011)
39. Ploskas, N., Samaras, N.: Efficient GPU-based implementations of simplex type algorithms. Appl. Math. Comput. **250**, 552570 (2015)
40. Yarmish, G.: A distributed implementation of the simplex method. Ph.D. thesis, Polytechnic University, Brooklyn (2001)
41. Hall, J.A., McKinnon, K.: PARSMI: a parallel revised simplex algorithm incorporating minor iterations and Devex pricing. In: Madsen, K., Olesen, D., Waśniewski, J., Dongarra, J. (eds.) PARA 1996. LNCS, vol. 1184, pp. 67–76. Springer, Heidelberg (1996)
42. FICO Xpress Optimization Suite, A parallel simplex solver (2014). http://www.fico.com/en/products/fico-xpress-optimization-suite

An Introduction to Temporal Graphs: An Algorithmic Perspective

Othon Michail[✉]

Computer Technology Institute & Press "Diophantus" (CTI),
N. Kazantzaki Str., Patras University Campus, Rio, P.O. Box 1382,
26504 Patras, Greece
michailo@cti.gr

Abstract. A *temporal graph* is, informally speaking, a graph that changes with time. When time is discrete and only the relationships between the participating entities may change and not the entities themselves, a temporal graph may be viewed as a sequence $G_1, G_2 \ldots, G_l$ of static graphs over the same (static) set of nodes V. Though static graphs have been extensively studied, for their temporal generalization we are still far from having a concrete set of structural and algorithmic principles. Recent research shows that many graph properties and problems become radically different and usually substantially more difficult when an extra time dimension in added to them. Moreover, there is already a rich and rapidly growing set of modern systems and applications that can be naturally modeled and studied via temporal graphs. This, further motivates the need for the development of a temporal extension of graph theory. We survey here recent results on temporal graphs and temporal graph problems that have appeared in the Computer Science community.

1 Introduction

The conception and development of graph theory is probably one of the most important achievements of mathematics and combinatorics of the last few centuries. Its applications are inexhaustible and ubiquitous. Almost every scientific domain, from mathematics and computer science to chemistry and biology, is a natural source of problems of outstanding importance that can be naturally modeled and studied by graphs. The 1736 paper of Euler on the Seven Bridges of Königsberg problem is regarded as the first formal treatment of a graph-theoretic problem. Till then, graph theory has found applications in electrical networks, theoretical chemistry, social network analysis, computer networks (like the Internet) and distributed systems, to name a few, and has also revealed some of the most outstanding problems of modern mathematics like the four color theorem and the traveling salesman problem.

Supported in part by the project "Foundations of Dynamic Distributed Computing Systems" (FOCUS) which is implemented under the "ARISTEIA" Action of the Operational Programme "Education and Lifelong Learning" and is co-funded by the European Union (European Social Fund) and Greek National Resources.

© Springer International Publishing Switzerland 2015
C. Zaroliagis et al. (Eds.): Spirakis Festschrift, LNCS 9295, pp. 308–343, 2015.
DOI: 10.1007/978-3-319-24024-4_18

Graphs simply represent a set of objects and a set of pairwise relations between them. It is very common, and shows up in many applications, the pairwise relations to come with some additional information. For example, in a graph representing a set of cities and the available roads from each city to the others, the additional information of an edge (C_1, C_2) could be the average time it takes to drive from city C_1 to city C_2. In a graph representing bonding between atoms in a molecule, edges could also have an additional bond order or bond strength information. Such applications can be modeled by weighted or, more generally, by labeled graphs, in which edges (and in some cases also nodes) are assigned values from some domain, like the set of natural numbers. An example of a classical, very rich, and well-studied area of labeled graphs is the area of graph coloring [57].

Temporal graphs (also known as *dynamic, evolving* [24], or *time-varying* [16, 26] graphs) can be informally described as *graphs that change with time.* In terms of modeling, they can be thought of as a special case of labeled graphs, where labels capture some measure of time. Inversely, it is also true that any property of a graph labeled from a discrete set of labels corresponds to some temporal property if interpreted appropriately. For example, a proper edge-coloring, i.e. a coloring of the edges in which no two adjacent edges share a common color, corresponds to a temporal graph in which no two adjacent edges share a common time-label, i.e. no two adjacent edges ever appear at the same time. Still, the time notion and the rich domain of modern applications motivating its incorporation to graphs, gives rise to a brand new set of challenging, important, and practical problems that could not have been observed from the more abstract perspective of labeled graphs.

Though the formal treatment of temporal graphs is still in its infancy, there is already a huge identified set of applications and research domains that motivate it and that could benefit from the development of a concrete set of results, tools, and techniques for temporal graphs. A great variety of both modern and traditional networks such as information and communication networks, social networks, transportation networks, and several physical systems can be naturally modeled as temporal graphs. In fact, this is true for almost any network with a dynamic topology. Most modern communication networks, such as mobile ad-hoc, sensor, peer-to-peer, opportunistic, and delay-tolerant networks, are inherently dynamic. In social networks, the topology usually represents the social connections between a group of individuals and it changes as the social relationships between the individuals are updated, or as individuals leave or enter the group. In a transportation network, there is usually some fixed network of routes and a set of transportation units moving over these routes and dynamicity refers to the change of the positions of the transportation units in the network as time passes. Physical systems of interest may include several systems of interacting particles or molecules reacting in a well-mixed solution. Temporal relationships and temporal ordering of events are also present in the study of epidemics, where a group of individuals (or computing entities) come into contact with each other and we want to study the spread of an infectious disease (or a computer virus) in the population.

A very rich motivating domain is that of distributed computing systems that are inherently dynamic. The growing interest in such systems has been mainly driven by the advent of low-cost wireless communication devices and the development of efficient wireless communication protocols. Apart from the huge amount of work that has been devoted to applications, there is also a steadily growing concrete set of foundational work. A notable set of works has studied (distributed) computation in *worst-case* dynamic networks in which the topology may change arbitrarily from round to round subject to some constraints that allow for bounded end-to-end communication [5,21,41,52,53,59]. Population protocols [3] and variants [49,50,55] are collections of finite-state agents that move passively, according to the dynamicity of the environment, and interact in pairs when they come close to each other. The goal is typically for the population to compute (i.e. agree on) something useful or construct a desired network or structure in such an adversarial setting. Another interesting direction assumes that the dynamicity of the network is a result of randomness (this is also the case sometimes in population protocols). Here the interest is on determining "good" properties of the dynamic network that hold with high probability (abbreviated w.h.p. and meaning with probability at least $1 - 1/n^c$ for some constant $c \geq 1$), such as small (temporal) diameter, and on designing protocols for distributed tasks [6,17]. In all the above subjects, there is always some sort of underlying temporal graph either assumed or implied. For introductory texts on the above lines of research in dynamic distributed networks the reader is referred to [16,42,51,65].

Though static graphs[1] have been extensively studied, for their temporal generalization we are still far from having a concrete set of structural and algorithmic principles. Additionally, it is not yet clear how is the complexity of combinatorial optimization problems affected by introducing to them a notion of time. In an early but serious attempt to answer this question, Orlin [60] observed that many dynamic languages derived from **NP**-complete languages can be shown to be **PSPACE**-complete. Among the other few things that we do know, is that the max-flow min-cut theorem holds with unit capacities for time-respecting paths [9]. Additionally, Kempe *et al.* [36] proved that, in temporal graphs, the classical formulation of Menger's theorem is violated and the computation of the number of node-disjoint *s-z* paths becomes **NP**-complete. A reformulation of Menger's theorem which is valid for all temporal graphs was recently achieved in [46]. These results are discussed in Sect. 3. Recently, building on the distributed online dynamic network model of [41], Dutta *et al.* [21], among other things, presented *offline centralized algorithms* for the *k-token dissemination* problem. In *k*-token dissemination, there are k distinct pieces of information (tokens) that are initially present in some distributed processes and the problem is to disseminate all the k tokens to all the processes in the dynamic network, under the constraint that one token can go through an edge per round. These results, motivated by distributed computing systems, are presented in Sect. 4.

---

[1] In this article, we use "static" to refer to classical graphs. This is plausible as the opposite of "dynamic" that is also commonly used for temporal graphs. In any case, the terminology is still very far from being standard.

Another important problem is that of *designing* an efficient temporal graph given some requirements that the graph should meet. This problem was recently studied in [46], where the authors introduced several interesting cost minimization parameters for optimal temporal network design. One of the parameters is the *temporality* of a graph G, in which the goal is to create a temporal version of G minimizing the maximum number of labels of an edge, and the other is the *temporal cost* of G, in which the goal is to minimize the total number of labels used. Optimization of these parameters is performed subject to some *connectivity constraint*. They proved several upper and lower bounds for the temporality of some very basic graph families such as rings, directed acyclic graphs, and trees, as well as a trade-off between the temporality and the maximum label of rings. Furthermore, they gave a *generic method* for computing a lower bound of the temporality of an arbitrary graph with respect to (abbreviated w.r.t.) the constraint of preserving a time-respecting analogue of every simple path of G. Finally, they proved that computing the temporal cost w.r.t. the constraint of preserving at least one time-respecting path from u to v whenever v is reachable from u in G, is **APX**-hard. Most of these results are discussed in Sect. 5.

Other recent papers have focused on understanding the complexity and providing algorithms for temporal versions of classical graph problems. For example, the authors of [56] considered temporal analogues of *traveling salesman problems* (TSP) in temporal graphs, and in the way also introduced and studied temporal versions of other fundamental problems like MAXIMUM MATCHING, PATH PACKING, MAX-TSP, and MINIMUM CYCLE COVER. One such version of TSP is the problem of exploring the nodes of a temporal graph as soon as possible. In contrast to the positive results known for the static case strong inapproximability results can be proved for the dynamic case [23,56]. Still, there is room for positive results for interesting special cases [23]. Another such problem is the TEMPORAL TRAVELING SALESMAN PROBLEM WITH COSTS ONE AND TWO (abbreviated TTSP(1,2)), a temporal analogue of TSP(1,2), in which the temporal graph is a complete weighted graph with edge-costs from $\{1,2\}$ and the cost of an edge may vary from instance to instance [56]. The goal is to find a minimum cost temporal TSP tour. Several *polynomial-time approximation algorithms* have been proved for TTSP(1,2) [56]. The best approximation is $(1.7+\varepsilon)$ for the generic TTSP(1,2) and $(13/8+\varepsilon)$ for its interesting special case in which the lifetime of the temporal graph is restricted to n. These and related results are presented in Sect. 6.

Additionally, there are works that have considered *random temporal graphs*, in which the labels are chosen according to some probability distribution. We give a brief introduction to such models in Sect. 8. Moreover, Sect. 2 provides all necessary preliminaries and definitions and also a first discussion on temporal paths and Sect. 7 discusses a temporal graph model in which the availability times of the edges are provided by a set of linear functions.

As is always the case, not all interesting results and material could fit in a single document. We list here some of them. Holme and Saramäki [32] give an extensive overview of the literature related to temporal networks from a diverge range of scientific domains. Harary and Gupta [30] discuss applications of temporal graphs and highlight the great importance of a systematic treatment of the subject. Kostakos [39] uses temporal graphs to represent real datasets, shows how to derive various node metrics like average temporal proximity, average geodesic proximity and temporal availability, and also gives a static representation of a temporal graph (similar to the *static expansion* that we discuss in Sect. 2). Avin *et al.* [6] studied the cover time of a simple random walk on Markovian dynamic graphs and proved that, in great contrast to being always polynomial in static graphs, it is exponential in some dynamic graphs. Clementi *et al.* [17] studied the flooding time (also known as information dissemination; see a similar problem discussed in Sect. 4) in the following type of edge-markovian dynamic graphs: if an edge exists at time t then, at time $t + 1$, it disappears with probability q, and if instead the edge does not exist at time t, then it appears at time $t + 1$ with probability p. There are also several papers that have focused on temporal graphs in which every instance of the graph is drawn independently at random according to some distribution [18,31,35,63] (the last three did it in the context of dynamic gossip-based mechanisms), e.g. according to $\mathcal{G}(n,p)$. A model related to random temporal graphs, is the *random phone-call model*, in which each node, at each step, can communicate with a random neighbour [20,33]. Other authors [25,67] have assumed that an edge may be available for a whole time-interval $[t_1, t_2]$ or several such intervals, and not just for discrete moments, or that it has time-dependent travel-times [38]. Aaron *et al.* [1] studied the DYNAMIC MAP VISITATION problem, in which a team of agents must visit a collection of critical locations as quickly as possible in a dynamic environment. Kontogiannis *et al.* [37], among other things, presented oracles for providing time-dependent min-cost route plans and conducted their experimental evaluation on a data set of the city of Berlin.

2   Modeling and Basic Properties

When time is assumed to be discrete, a temporal graph (or digraph) is just a static graph (or digraph) $G = (V, E)$ with every edge $e \in E$ labeled with zero or more natural numbers. The labels of an edge may be viewed as the times at which the the edge is *available*. For example, an edge with no labels is never available while, on the other hand, an edge with labels all the even natural numbers is available every even time. Labels could correspond to seconds, days, years, or could even correspond to some artificial discrete measure of time under consideration.

There are several ways of modeling formally discrete temporal graphs. One is to consider an underlying static graph $G = (V, E)$ together with a labeling $\lambda : E \to 2^{\mathbb{N}}$ of G assigning to every edge of G a (possibly empty) set of natural numbers, called *labels*. Then the temporal graph of G with respect to λ is denoted by $\lambda(G)$. This notation is particularly useful when one wants to explicitly refer to and study properties of the labels of the temporal graph. For example, the multiset of all labels of $\lambda(G)$ can be denoted by $\lambda(E)$, their cardinality is defined as $|\lambda| = \sum_{e \in E} |\lambda(e)|$, and the maximum and minimum label assigned to the whole temporal graph as $\lambda_{max} = \max\{l \in \lambda(E)\}$ and $\lambda_{min} = \min\{l \in \lambda(E)\}$, respectively. Moreover, we define the *age* (or *lifetime*) of a temporal graph $\lambda(G)$ as $\alpha(\lambda) = \lambda_{max} - \lambda_{min} + 1$ (or simply α when clear from context). Note that in case $\lambda_{min} = 1$ then we have $\alpha(\lambda) = \lambda_{max}$.

Another, often convenient, notation of a temporal graph D is as an ordered pair of disjoint sets (V, A) such that $A \subseteq \binom{V}{2} \times \mathbb{N}$ in case of a graph and with $\binom{V}{2}$ replaced by $V^2 \setminus \{(u, u) : u \in V\}$ in case of a digraph. The set A is called the set of *time-edges*. A can also be used to refer to the structure of the temporal graph at a particular time. In particular, $A(t) = \{e : (e, t) \in A\}$ is the (possibly empty) set of all edges that appear in the temporal graph at time t. In turn, $A(t)$ can be used to define a snapshot of the temporal graph D at time t, which is usually called the *t-th instance of D*, and is the static graph $D(t) = (V, A(t))$. So, it becomes evident that a temporal graph may also be viewed as a *sequence of static graphs* $(G_1, G_2, \ldots, G_{\lambda_{max}})$.

Finally, it is typically very useful to expand in time the whole temporal graph and obtain an equivalent static graph without losing any information. The reason for doing this is mainly because static graphs are much better understood and there is a rich set of well established tools and techniques for them. So, a common approach to solve a problem concerning temporal graphs is to first express the given temporal graph as a static graph and then try to apply or adjust one of the existing tools that works on static graphs. Formally, the *static expansion* of a temporal graph $D = (V, A)$ is a DAG $H = (S, E)$ defined as follows. If $V = \{u_1, u_2, \ldots, u_n\}$ then $S = \{u_{ij} : \lambda_{min} - 1 \leq i \leq \lambda_{max}, 1 \leq j \leq n\}$ and $E = \{(u_{(i-1)j}, u_{ij'}) : \lambda_{min} \leq i \leq \lambda_{max}$ and $j = j'$ or $(u_j, u_{j'}) \in A(i)\}$. In words, for every discrete moment we create a copy of V representing the instance of the nodes at that time (called *time-nodes*). We may imagine the moments as levels or rows from top to bottom, every level containing a copy of V. Then we add outgoing edges from time-nodes of one level only to time-nodes of the level below it. In particular, we connect a time-node $u_{(i-1)j}$ to its own subsequent copy u_{ij} and to every time-node $u_{ij'}$ s.t. $(u_j, u_{j'})$ is an edge of the temporal graph at time i. Observe that the above construction includes all possible vertical edges from a node to its own subsequent instance. These edges express the fact that nodes are usually not oblivious and can preserve their on history in time (modeled like propagating information to themselves). Nevertheless, depending on the application, these edges may some times be omitted.

2.1 Journeys

As is the case in static graphs, the notion of a *path* is one of the most central notions of a temporal graph, however it has to be redefined to take time into account. A *temporal* (or *time-respecting*) *walk* W of a temporal graph $D = (V, A)$ is an alternating sequence of nodes and times $(u_1, t_1, u_2, t_2, \ldots, u_{k-1}, t_{k-1}, u_k)$ where $(u_i u_{i+1}, t_i) \in A$, for all $1 \leq i \leq k - 1$, and $t_i < t_{i+1}$, for all $1 \leq i \leq k - 2$. We call $t_{k-1} - t_1 + 1$ the *duration* (or *temporal length*) of the walk W, t_1 its *departure time* and t_{k-1} its *arrival time*. A *journey* (or *temporal/time-respecting path*) J is a temporal walk with pairwise distinct nodes. In words, a journey of D is a path of the underlying static graph of D that uses strictly increasing edge-labels. A u-v journey J is called *foremost from time* $t \in \mathbb{N}$ if it departs after time t and its arrival time is minimized. The *temporal distance* from a node u at time t to a node v is defined as the duration of a foremost u-v journey from time t. We say that a temporal graph $D = (V, A)$ has *temporal (or dynamic) diameter* d, if d is the minimum integer for which it holds that the temporal distance from every time-node $(u, t) \in V \times \{0, 1, \ldots, \alpha - d\}$ to every node $v \in V$ is at most d.

A nice property of foremost journeys is that they can be computed efficiently. In particular there is an algorithm that, given a source node $s \in V$ and a time t_{start}, computes for all $w \in V \backslash \{s\}$ a foremost s-w journey from time t_{start} [46,47]. The running time of the algorithm is $O(n\alpha^3(\lambda) + |\lambda|)$, where n here and throughout this article denotes the number of nodes of the temporal graph. It is worth mentioning that this algorithm takes as input the whole temporal graph D. Such algorithms are known as *offline* algorithms in contrast to *online* algorithms to which the temporal graph is revealed on the fly. The algorithm is essentially a temporal translation of the breadth-first search (BFS) algorithm (see e.g. [19] p. 531) with path length replaced by path arrival time. For every time t, the algorithm picks one after the other all nodes that have been already reached (initially only the source node s) and inspects all edges that are incident to that node at time t. If a time-edge (e, t) leads to a node w that has not yet been reached, then (e, t) is picked as an edge of a foremost journey from the source to w. This greedy algorithm is correct for the same reason that the BFS algorithm is correct. An immediate way to see this is by considering the static expansion of the temporal graph. The algorithm begins from the upper copy (i.e. at level 0) of the source in the static expansion and essentially executes the following slight variation of BFS: at step $i + 1$, given the set R of already reached nodes at level i, the algorithm first follows all vertical edges leaving R in order to reach in one step the $(i + 1)$-th copy of each node in R, and then inspects all diagonal edges leaving R to discover new reachabilities. The algorithm outputs as a foremost journey to a node u, the directed path of time-edges by which it first reached the column of u (vertical edges are interpreted as waiting on the corresponding node). The above algorithm computes a shortest path to each column of the static expansion. Correctness follows from the fact that shortest paths to columns are equivalent to foremost journeys to the nodes corresponding to the columns.

3   Connectivity and Menger's Theorem

Assume that we are given a static graph G and a source node s and a sink node z of G.[2] Two paths from s to z are called node-disjoint if they have only the nodes s and z in common. *Menger's theorem* [45], which is the analogue of the max-flow min-cut theorem for undirected graphs, is one of the most basic

---

[2] The sink is usually denoted by t in the literature. We use z instead as we reserve t to refer to time moments.

theorems in the theory of graph connectivity. It states that *the maximum number of node-disjoint s-z paths is equal to the minimum number of nodes that must be removed in order to separate s from z* (see also [12] p. 75).

It was first observed in [9] and then further studied in [36] that this fundamental theorem of static graphs, is violated in temporal graphs if we keep its original formulation and only require it to hold for journeys instead of paths. In fact, the violation holds even for a very special case of temporal graphs, those in which every edge has at most one label, which are known as *single-labeled temporal graphs* (as opposed to the more general *multi-labeled* temporal graphs that we have discussed so far). Even in such temporal graphs, the maximum number of node-disjoint journeys from s to z can be strictly less than the minimum number of nodes whose deletion leaves no s-z journey. For a simple example, observe in Fig. 1 that there are no two node-disjoint journeys from s to z but after deleting any one node (other than s or z) there still remains a s-z journey. To see this, notice that every journey has to visit at least two of the inner-nodes u_2, u_3, u_4. If u_2 is one of them, then a vertical obstacle is introduced which cannot be avoided by any other journey. If u_2 is not, then the only disjoint path remaining is (s, u_2, z) which is not a journey. On the other hand, any set of two inner vertices has a s-z journey going through them implying that any s-z separator must have size at least 2. As shown in [36], this construction can be generalized to a single-labeled graph with $2k - 1$ inner nodes in which: (i) every s-z journey visits at least k of these nodes, ensuring again that there are no two node-disjoint s-z journeys and (ii) there is a journey through any set of k inner nodes, ensuring that every s-z separator must have size at least k.

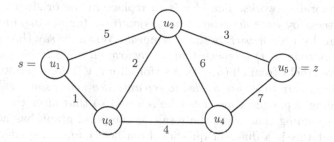

Fig. 1. A counterexample of Menger's theorem for temporal graphs (adopted from [36]). Each edge has a single time-label indicating its availability time.

On the positive side, the violation does not hold if we replace node-disjointness by edge-disjointness and node removals by edge removals. In particular, it was proved in [9] that for single-labeled temporal graphs, the maximum number of edge-disjoint journeys from s to z is equal to the minimum number of edges whose deletion leaves no s-z journey, that is, that the max-flow min-cut theorem of static graphs holds with unit capacities for journeys in single-labeled temporal graphs. The construction (which we adopt from [36]) is simply an *ad-hoc* static expansion for the special case of single-labeled temporal graphs. Let $G = (V, E)$ be the underlying graph of an undirected single-labeled temporal graph. We construct a labeled directed graph $G' = (V', E')$ as follows. for every $\{u, v\} \in E$ we add in G' two new nodes x and y and the directed edges (u, x), (v, x), (y, u), (y, v), (x, y). Then we relax all labels required so that there is sufficient "room" (w.r.t. time) to introduce (by labeling the new edges) both a (u, x, y, v) journey and a (v, x, y, u) journey. The goal is to be able to both move by a journey from u to v and from v to u in G'. An easy way to do this is the following: if t is the label of $\{u, v\}$, then we can label $(u, x), (x, y), (y, v)$ by $(t.1, t.2, t.3)$, where $t.1 < t.2 < t.3$, and similarly for $(v, x), (x, y), (y, u)$. Then we construct a static directed graph $G'' = (V'', E'')$ as follows: For every $u \in V$ let $y_1, y_2, \ldots, y_i, \ldots$ be its incoming edges and $x_1, x_2, \ldots, x_j, \ldots$ its outgoing edges. We want to preserve only the time-respecting y, u, x traversals. To this end, for each one of the (y_i, u) edges we introduce a node w_i and the edge (y_i, w_i) and for each one of the (u, x_i) edges we introduce a node v_j and the edge (v_j, x_j) and we delete node u. Finally, we introduce the edge (w_i, v_j) iff $(y_i, u), (u, x_j)$ is time-respecting. This reduction preserves edge-disjointness and sizes of edge separators and if we add a super-source and a super-sink to G'' the max-flow min-cut theorem for static directed graphs yields the aforementioned result. Another interesting thing is that reachability in G under journeys corresponds to (path) reachability in G'' so that we can use BFS on G'' to answer questions about foremost journeys in G, as we did with the static expansion in Sect. 2.1.

Fortunately, the above important negative result concerning Menger's theorem has a turnaround. In particular, it was proved in [46] that if one reformulates Menger's theorem in a way that takes time into account then a very natural temporal analogue of Menger's theorem is obtained, which is valid for all (multi-labeled) temporal networks. The idea is to replace in the original formulation node-disjointness by *node departure time disjointness* (or *out-disjointness*) and node removals by *node departure times removals*. When we say that we remove *node departure time* (u, t) we mean that we remove *all edges leaving u at time t*, i.e. we remove label t from all (u, v) edges (for all $v \in V$). So, when we ask "*how many node departure times are needed to separate two nodes s and z?*" we mean how many node departure times must be selected so that after the removal of all the corresponding time-edges the resulting temporal graph has no s-z journey (note that this is a different question from how many time-edges must be removed and, in fact, the latter question does not result in a Menger's analogue). Two journeys are called *out-disjoint* if they never leave from the same node at the same time (see Fig. 2 for an example).

Theorem 1 (Menger's Temporal Analogue [46]). *Take any temporal graph $\lambda(G)$, where $G = (V, E)$, with two distinguished nodes s and z. The maximum number of out-disjoint journeys from s to z is equal to the minimum number of node departure times needed to separate s from z.*

The idea is to take the static expansion $H = (S, A)$ of $\lambda(G)$ and, for each time-node u_{ij} with at least two outgoing edges to nodes different than u_{i+1j}, add a new node w_{ij} and the edges (u_{ij}, w_{ij}) and $(w_{ij}, u_{(i+1)j_1})$,

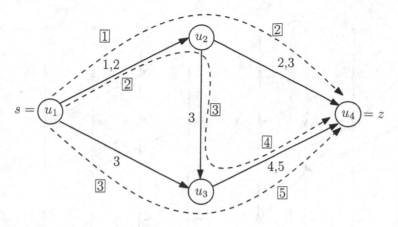

Fig. 2. An example of a temporal graph. The dashed curves highlight the directions of three out-disjoint journeys from s to z. The labels used by each of these journeys are indicated by the labels that are enclosed in boxes.

$(w_{ij}, u_{(i+1)j_2}), \ldots, (w_{ij}, u_{(i+1)j_k})$. Then define an *edge capacity function* $c : A \rightarrow \{1, \lambda_{\max}\}$ as follows: edges $(u_{ij}, u_{(i+1)j})$ take capacity $\lambda_{\max}$ and all other edges take capacity 1. The theorem follows by observing that the maximum $u_{01}\text{-}u_{\lambda_{\max}n}$ flow is equal to the minimum of the capacity of a $u_{01}\text{-}u_{\lambda_{\max}n}$ cut, the maximum number of out-disjoint journeys from s to z is equal to the maximum $u_{01}\text{-}u_{\lambda_{\max}n}$ flow, and the minimum number of node departure times needed to separate s from z is equal to the minimum of the capacity of a $u_{01}\text{-}u_{\lambda_{\max}n}$ cut. See also Fig. 3 for an illustration.

4 Dissemination and Gathering of Information

A natural application domain of temporal graphs is that of *gossiping* and in general of *information dissemination*, mainly by a distributed set of entities (e.g. a group of people or a set of distributed processes). Two early such examples were the *telephone problem* [8] and the *minimum broadcast time problem* [64]. In both, the goal is to transmit some information to every participant of the system, while minimizing some measure of communication or time. A more modern setting, but in the same spirit, comes from the very young area of distributed computing in highly dynamic networks [16,41,42,52,53,59].

There are n nodes. In this context, nodes represent distributed processes. Note, however, that most of the results that we will discuss, concern centralized algorithms (and in case of lower bounds, these immediately hold for distributed algorithms as well). The nodes communicate with other nodes in discrete rounds by interchanging messages. In every round, an adversary scheduler selects a set of edges between the nodes and every node may communicate with its current neighbors, as selected by the adversary, usually by *broadcasting* a single message to be delivered to all its neighbors. So, the dynamic topology behaves as

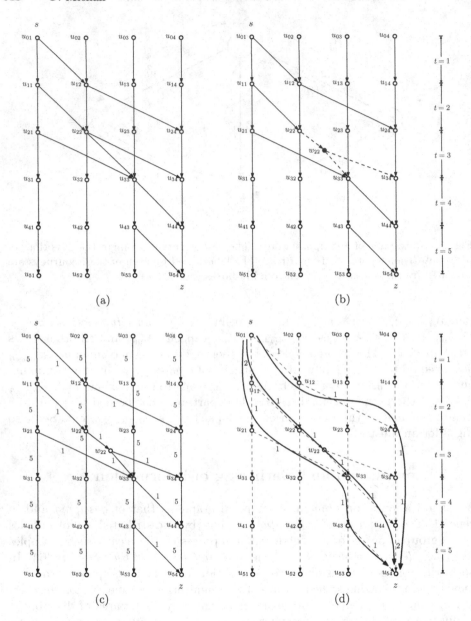

Fig. 3. (a) The static expansion of a temporal graph. Here, only two edges leave from the same node at the same time: (u_{22}, u_{33}) and (u_{22}, u_{34}). (b) Adding a new node w_{22} and three new edges. This we ensures that a node departure time can be removed by removing a single diagonal edge: removing edge (u_{22}, w_{22}) removes all possible departures from u_{22}. This ensures that separation of s and z by node-departure times is equivalent to separation by a usual static cut. (c) Adding capacities to the edges. Vertical edges take capacity $\lambda_{max} = 5$ and diagonal edges take capacity 1. (d) The maximum number of out-disjoint journeys from s to z is equal to the maximum flow from s to z and both are equal to 3.

a discrete temporal graph where the i-th instance of the graph is the topology selected by the adversary in round i. The main difference, compared to the setting of the previous sections, is that now (in all results that we will discuss in this section, apart from the last one) the topology is revealed to the algorithms in an online and totally unpredictable way. An interesting special case of temporal graphs consists of those temporal graphs that have *connected instances*. A temporal graph D is called *continuously connected* (also known as *1-interval connected*) if $D(t)$ is connected for all times $t \geq 1$ [41,59]. Such temporal graphs have some very useful properties concerning information propagation in a distributed setting, like, for example, that if all nodes broadcast in every round all information that they have heard so far, then in every round at least one more node learns something new, which implies that a piece of information can in principle be disseminated in at most $n - 1$ rounds. Naturally, the problem of information dissemination becomes much more interesting and challenging if we do not allow nodes to transmit an unlimited amount of information in every round, that is, if we restrict the size of the messages that they can transmit.

An interesting problem of token dissemination in such a setting, called the *k-token dissemination problem*, was introduced and first studied in [41]. In this problem there is a domain of *tokens* $\mathcal{T}$, each node is assigned a subset of the tokens, and a total of k distinct tokens is assigned to the nodes. The goal is for an algorithm (centralized or distributed) to organize the communication between the nodes in such a way that, under any dynamic topology (from those described above), each node eventually terminates and outputs (i.e. has learned) all k tokens. In particular, the focus here is on *token-forwarding algorithms*. Such an algorithm is quite restricted in that, in every round r and for every node u, it only picks a single token from those already known by u (or the empty token $\perp$) and this token will be delivered to all the current neighbors of u by a single broadcast transmission. Token-forwarding algorithms are simple, easy to implement, typically incur low overhead, and have been extensively studied in static networks [43,62]. We will present now a lower bound from [41] on the number of rounds for token dissemination, that holds even for centralized token forwarding algorithms. Such centralized algorithms are allowed to see and remember the whole state and history of the entire network, but they have to make their selection of tokens to be forwarded without knowing what topology will be scheduled by the adversary in the current round. So, first the algorithm selects and then the adversary reveals the topology, taking into account the algorithm's selection. For simplicity, it may be assumed that each of the k tokens is assigned initially to exactly one (distinct) node.

Theorem 2 [41]. *Any deterministic centralized algorithm for k-token dissemination in continuously connected temporal graphs requires at least $\Omega(n \log k)$ rounds to complete in the worst case.*

The idea behind the proof is to define a potential function that charges by $1/(k - i)$ the i-th token learned by each node. So, for example, the first token learned by a node comes at a cheap price of $1/k$ while the last token learned costs 1. The initial total potential is 1, because k nodes have obtained their first token each, and the final potential (i.e. when all nodes have learned all k tokens) is $n \cdot H_k = \Theta(n \log k)$. Then it suffices to present an adversarial schedule, i.e. a continuously connected temporal graph, that forces any algorithm to achieve in every round at most a bounded increase in potential. The topology of a round can be summarized as follows. First we select all edges that contribute no cost, called *free edges*. An edge $\{u, v\}$ is free if the token transmitted by u is already known by v and vice versa. The free edges partition the nodes into l components $C_1, C_2, \ldots, C_l$. We pick a representative v_i from each component C_i. It remains to construct a connected graph over the v_is. An observation is that each v_i transmits a distinct token t_i, otherwise at least two of them should have been connected by a free edge (because two nodes interchanging the same token cannot learn anything new). The idea is to further partition the representatives into a small set of nodes that know many tokens each and a large set of nodes that know few tokens each. We can call the nodes that know many tokens the *expensive* ones, because according to the above potential function a new token at a node that already knows a lot of tokens comes at a high price, and similarly we call those nodes that know few tokens the *cheap* ones. In particular, a node is expensive if it is missing at most $l/6$ tokens and cheap otherwise. Roughly, a cheap node learns a new token at the low cost of at most $6/l$, because the cost of a token is inversely proportional to the number of missing tokens before the token's arrival. First we connect the cheap nodes by an arbitrary line. As there are at most l such nodes and each one of them obtains at most two new tokens (because it has at most two neighbors on the line and each node transmits a single token), the total cost of this component is at most 12, that is, bounded as desired. It remains to connect the expensive nodes. It can be shown that there is a way to match each expensive node to a distinct cheap node (i.e. by constructing a matching between the expensive and the cheap nodes), so that no expensive node learns a new token. So, the only additional cost is that of the new tokens that cheap nodes obtain from expensive nodes. This additional cost is roughly at most 6, so the total cost have been shown to be bounded by a small constant as required. It is worth mentioning that [41], apart from the above lower bound, also proposed a simple distributed algorithm for k-token dissemination that needs $O(nk)$ rounds in the worst case to deliver all tokens.

The above lower bound can be further improved by exploiting the probabilistic method [21]. In particular it can be shown that any randomized token-forwarding algorithm (centralized or distributed) for k-token dissemination needs $\Omega(nk/\log n)$ rounds. This lower bound is within a logarithmic factor of the $O(nk)$ upper bound of [41]. As is quite commonly the case in probabilistic results, the interesting machinery used to establish the lower bound is in the analysis and not in the construction itself. Now *all* the representatives of the connected components formed by the free edges are connected arbitrarily by a line. The idea is to first prove the bound w.h.p. over an initial token distribution, in which each of the nodes receives each of the k tokens independently with probability $3/4$. It can be shown in this case that, w.h.p. over the initial assignment of tokens, in every round there are at most $O(\log n)$ new token deliveries and an overall of $\Omega(nk)$ new token deliveries must occur for the protocol to complete. Finally, it can be shown via the probabilistic method, that, in fact, any initial token distribution can be reduced to the above distribution for which the bound holds. The above lower bounding technique, based on the probabilistic method, was applied in [28] to several variations of k-token dissemination. For example, if the nodes are allowed to transmit $b \leq k$ tokens instead of only one token in every round, then it can be proved that any randomized token-forwarding algorithm requires $\Omega(n + nk/(b^2 \log n \log \log n))$ rounds.

In [21], also offline token forwarding algorithms were designed, that is, algorithms provided the whole dynamic topology in advance. One of the problems that they studied, was that of delivering all tokens to a given sink node z as fast as possible, called the *gathering problem*. We now present a lemma from [21] concerning this problem, mainly because its proof constitutes a nice application of the temporal analogue of Menger's theorem presented in Sect. 3 (the simplified proof via Menger's temporal analogue is from [46]).

Lemma 1 [21]. *Let there be $k \leq n$ tokens at given source nodes and let z be an arbitrary node. Then, if the temporal graph D is continuously connected, all the tokens can be delivered to z, using local broadcasts, in $O(n)$ rounds.*

Let $S = \{s_1, s_2, \ldots, s_h\}$ be the set of source nodes, let $N(s_i)$ be the number of tokens of source node s_i and let the age of the temporal graph be $n+k = O(n)$. It suffices to prove that there are at least k out-disjoint journeys from S to any given z, such that $N(s_i)$ of these journeys leave from each source node s_i. Then, all tokens can be forwarded in parallel, each on one of these journeys, without conflicting with each other in an outgoing transmission and, as the age is $O(n)$, they all arrive at z in $O(n)$ rounds. To show the existence of k out-disjoint journeys, we create a *supersource* node s and connect it to the source node with token i (assuming an arbitrary ordering of the tokens from 1 to k) by an edge labeled i. Then we shift the rest of the temporal graph in time, by increasing all other edge labels by k. The new temporal graph D' has asymptotically the same age as the original and all properties have been preserved. Now, it suffices to show that there are at least k out-disjoint journeys from s to z, because the k edges of s respect the $N(s_i)$'s. Due to Menger's temporal analogue, it is equivalent to show that at least k departure times must be removed to separate s from z. Indeed, any removal of fewer than k departure times must leave at least n rounds during which all departure times are available (because, due to shifting by k, the age of D' is $n+2k$). Due to the fact that the original temporal graph is connected in every round, n rounds guarantee the existence of a journey from s to z.

5 Design Problems

So far, we have mainly presented problems in which a temporal graph is provided somehow (either in an offline or an online way) and the goal is to solve a problem on that graph. Another possibility is when one wants to *design* a desired temporal graph. In most cases, such a temporal graph cannot be arbitrary, but it has to satisfy some properties prescribed by the underlying application. This design problem was introduced and studied in [46] (and its full version [47]). An abstract definition of the problem is that we are given an underlying (di)graph G and we are asked to assign labels to the edges of G so that the resulting temporal graph $\lambda(G)$ minimizes some parameter while satisfying some connectivity property. The parameters studied in [46] were the maximum number of labels of an edge, called the *temporality*, and the total number of labels, called the *temporal cost*. The connectivity properties of [46] had to do with the preservation of a subset of the paths of G in time-respecting versions. For example, we might want to preserve all reachabilities between nodes defined by G, in the sense that for every pair of nodes u, v such that there is a path from u to v in G there must be a temporal path from u to v in $\lambda(G)$. Another such property is to guarantee in $\lambda(G)$ time-respecting versions of all possible paths of G. All these can be thought of as trying to *preserve* a connectivity property of a static graph in the temporal dimension while trying to minimize some cost measure of the resulting temporal graph.

The provided graph G represents some given static specifications, for example the available roads between a set of cities or the available routes of buses in the city center. In scheduling problems it is very common to have such a static specification and to want to organize a temporal schedule on it, for example to specify the precise time at which a bus should pass from a particular bus stop while guaranteeing that every possible pair of stops are connected by a route. Furthermore, it is very common that any such solution should at the same time take into account some notion of cost. Minimizing cost parameters may be crucial as, in most real networks, making a connection available and maintaining its availability does not come for free. For example, in wireless sensor networks the cost of making edges available is directly related to the power consumption of keeping nodes awake, of broadcasting, of listening the wireless channel, and of resolving the resulting communication collisions. The same holds for transportation networks where the goal is to achieve good connectivity properties with as few transportation units as possible.

For an example, imagine that we are given a directed ring $u_1, u_2, \ldots, u_n$ and we want to assign labels to its edges so that the resulting temporal graph has a journey for every simple path of the ring and at the same time minimizes the maximum number of labels of an edge. In more technical terms, we want to determine or bound the *temporality* of the ring subject to the *all paths* property. It is worth mentioning that the temporality (and the temporal cost) is defined as the *minimum* possible achievable value that satisfies the property, as, for example, is also the case for the chromatic number of a graph, which is defined as the minimum number of colors that can properly color a graph. Looking at Fig. 4, it is immediate to observe that an increasing sequence of labels on the edges of path P_1 implies a decreasing pair of labels on edges (u_{n-1}, u_n) and (u_1, u_2). On the other hand, path P_2 uses first (u_{n-1}, u_n) and then (u_1, u_2) thus it requires an increasing pair of labels on these edges. It follows that in order to preserve both P_1 and P_2 we have to use a second label on at least one of these two edges, thus the temporality is at least 2. Next, consider the labeling that assigns to each edge (u_i, u_{i+1}) the labels $\{i, n + i\}$, where $1 \le i \le n$ and $u_{n+1} = u_1$. It is not hard to see that this labeling preserves all simple paths of the ring. Since the maximum number of labels that it assigns to an edge is 2, we conclude that the temporality is also at most 2. Taking both bounds into account, we may conclude that the temporality of preserving all simple paths of a directed ring is 2. Moreover, it holds that the temporality of graph G is lower bounded by the maximum temporality of its subgraphs, because if a labeling preserves all paths of G then it has to preserve all paths of any subgraph of G, paying every time the temporality of the subgraph. So, for example, if the input graph G contains a directed ring then the temporality of G must be at least 2 (and could be higher depending on the structure of the rest of the graph).

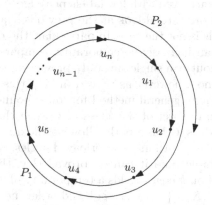

Fig. 4. Path P_2 forces a second label to appear on either (u_{n-1}, u_n) or (u_1, u_2).

Rings have very small temporality w.r.t. the all paths property, however there is a large family of graphs with even smaller. This is the family of directed acyclic graphs (DAGs). DAGs have the very convenient property that they can be topologically sorted. In fact, DAGs are the only digraphs that satisfy this property. A *topological sort* of a digraph G is a linear ordering of its nodes such that if G contains an edge (u, v) then u appears before v in the ordering. So, we can order the nodes from left to right and have all edges pointing to the right. Now, we can assign to the nodes the indices $1, 2, \ldots, n$ in ascending order from left to right and then assign to each edge the label of its tail, as shown in Fig. 5. In this way, every edge obtains exactly one label and every path of G has been converted to a journey, because every path moves from left to right thus always moves to greater node indices. As these indices are also the labels of the corresponding edges, the path has strictly increasing labels which makes it a journey. This, together with the fact that the temporality is at least 1 in all

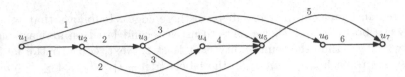

Fig. 5. A topological sort of a DAG. Edges are labeled by the indices of their tails (which are strictly increasing from left to right) and this labeling converts every possible path of the dag to a journey. For example, $(u_1, u_2, u_3, u_5, u_7)$ is a journey because its labels $(1, 2, 3, 5)$ are strictly increasing.

graphs with non-empty edge sets, shows that the temporality of any DAG w.r.t. the all paths property is 1.

In both of the above examples, all paths could be preserved by using very few labels per edge. One may immediately wonder whether converting all paths to journeys can always be achieved with few labels per edge, e.g. a constant number of labels. However, a more careful look at the previous examples may provide a first indication that this is not the case. In particular, the ring example suggests that cycles can cause an increase of temporality, compared to graphs without cycles, like DAGs. Of course, a single ring only provides a very elementary exposition of this phenomenon, however as proved in [46], this core observation can be extended to give a quite general method for lower bounding the temporality. The idea is to identify a subset of the edges of G such that, for every possible permutation of these edges, G has a path following the direction of the permutation. Such subsets of edges, with many interleaved cycles, are called *edge-kernels* (see Fig. 6 for an example) and it can be proved that the preservation of all paths of an edge-kernel on k edges yields a temporality of at least k. To see this, consider an edge-kernel $K = \{e_1, e_2, \ldots, e_k\}$ and order increasingly the labels of each edge. Now take an edge with maximum first label, move from it to an edge of maximum second label between the remaining edges, then move from this to an edge of maximum third label between the remaining edges, and so on. All these moves can be performed because K is an edge-kernel, thus there is a path no matter which permutation of the edges we choose. As in step i we are on the edge e with maximum i-th label, we cannot use the 1st, 2nd, ..., i-th labels of the next edge to continue the journey because none of these can be greater than the i-th label of e. So, we must necessarily use the $(i + 1)$-th label of the next edge, which by induction shows that in order to go through the k-th edge in this particular permutation we need to use a kth label on that edge.

Also, as stated above, the temporality of a graph w.r.t to the all paths property is always lower bounded by the temporality of any of its subgraphs. As a consequence, we can obtain a lower bound on the temporality of a graph or of a whole graph family by identifying a large edge-kernel in it. For a simple application of this method, it is possible to show that in order to preserve all paths of a complete digraph, at least $\lfloor n/2 \rfloor$ labels are required on some edge. This is done by showing that complete digraphs have an edge-kernel of size $\lfloor n/2 \rfloor$. Moreover, it is possible to construct a planar graph containing an edge-kernel

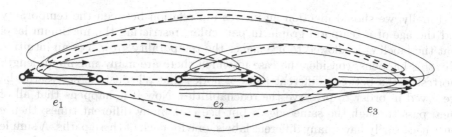

Fig. 6. The graph consists of the solid and dashed edges. The long curves highlight some of the paths that the graph defines. Edges e_1, e_2, and e_3 constitute an edge-kernel of the graph, because for every possible permutation of these edges the graph has a directed path (one of those highlighted in the figure) that traverses the edges in the order defined by the permutation. As a result, at least 3 labels must be assigned on an edge in order to preserve a temporal analogue of every possible path.

of size $\Omega(n^{1/3})$, which yields that there exist planar graphs with temporality at least $\Omega(n^{1/3})$. It is worth noting that the absence of a large edge-kernel does not necessarily imply small temporality. In fact, it is an interesting open problem whether there are other structural properties of the underlying graph that could cause a growth of the temporality.

The above show that preserving all paths in time can be very costly in several cases. On the other hand, preserving only the reachabilities can always be achieved inexpensively. In particular, it can be proved that for every strongly connected digraph G, we can preserve a journey from u to v for every u, v for which there exists a path from u to v in G, by using at most two labels per edge [46]. Recall the crucial difference: now it suffices to preserve *a single path* from all possible paths that go from u to v. The result is proved by picking any node u and considering an in-tree rooted at u. We then label the edges of each level i, counting from the leaves, with label i, so that all paths of the tree become time-respecting (this also follows from the fact that the tree is a DAG so, as we discussed previously, all of its paths can be preserved with a single label per edge). Next we consider an out-tree rooted at u and we label that tree inversely, i.e. from the root to the leaves, and beginning with the label $i + 1$. The first tree has a journey from every node to u arriving by time i and the second tree has a journey from u to every other node beginning at time $i + 1$. This shows that there is a journey from every node to every other node. Moreover, this was achieved by using at most two labels per edge because every edge of the in-tree has a single label and every edge of the out-tree has a single label and an edge is in the worst case used by both trees, in which case it is assigned two labels. Furthermore, it can be proved that the temporality w.r.t. reachabilities of any digraph G is upper bounded by the maximum temporality of its strongly connected components. But we just saw that each component needs at most two labels, thus it follows that two labels per edge are sufficient for preserving all reachabilities of *any* digraph G.

Finally, we should mention an interesting relation between the temporality and the age of a temporal graph. In particular, restricting the maximum label that the labeling is allowed to use makes the temporality grow. For an intuition why this happens, consider the case in which there are many maximum length shortest paths between different pairs of nodes that all must be necessarily be preserved in order to preserve the reachabilities. Now if it happens that all of them pass through the same edge e but use e at many different times, then e must necessarily have many different labels, one for each of these paths. A simple example to further appreciate this is given in Fig. 7. In that figure, each u_i-v_i path is a unique shortest path between u_i and v_i and has additionally length equal to the diameter (i.e. it is also a maximum one), so we must necessarily preserve all 5 u_i-v_i paths. Note now that each u_i-v_i path passes through e via its i-th edge. Each of these paths can only be preserved without violating $d(G)$ by assigning the labels $1, 2, \ldots, d(G)$, however note that then edge e must necessarily have all labels $1, 2, \ldots, d(G)$. To see this, notice simply that if any label i is missing from e then there is some maximum shortest path that goes through e at step i. As i is missing it cannot arrive sooner than time $d(G) + 1$ which violates the preservation of the diameter. Additionally, the following trade-off for the particular case of a ring can be proved [46]: If G is a directed ring and the age is $(n - 1) + k$, then the temporality of preserving all paths is $\Theta(n/k)$, when $1 \le k \le n - 1$, and $n - 1$, when $k = 0$.

6   Temporal Versions of Other Standard Graph Problems: Complexity and Solutions

Though it is not yet clear how is the complexity of combinatorial optimization problems affected by introducing to them a notion of time, still there is evidence that complexity increases significantly and that totally novel solutions have to

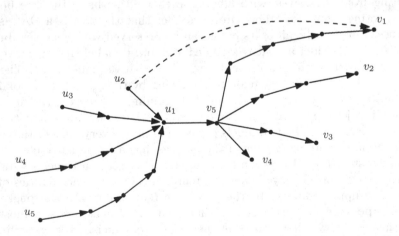

Fig. 7. In this example, restricting the maximum label to be at most equal to the diameter $d(G)$ forces the temporality to be at least $d(G)$.

be developed in several cases. In an early but serious attempt to answer the above question, Orlin [60] observed that many dynamic languages derived from **NP**-complete languages can be shown to be **PSPACE**-complete. This increase in complexity has been also reported in [10, 67]. For example, [10] studied the computation of multicast trees minimizing the overall transmission time and to this end proved that it is **NP**-complete to compute strongly connected components in temporal graphs. Important evidence to this direction comes also from the rich literature on labeled graphs, a more general model than temporal graphs, with different motivation, and usually interested in different problems than those resulting when the labels are explicitly regarded as time moments. Several papers in this direction have considered labeled versions of polynomial-time solvable problems, in which the goal is to minimize/maximize the number of labels used by a solution. For example, the first labeled problem introduced in the literature was the LABELED MINIMUM SPANNING TREE problem, which has several applications in communication network design. This problem is **NP**-hard and many complexity and approximability results have been proposed (see e.g. [14, 40]). On the other hand, the LABELED MAXIMUM SPANNING TREE problem has been shown polynomial in [14]. In [15], the authors proved that the LABELED MINIMUM PATH problem is **NP**-hard and provided some exact and approximation algorithms. In [58], it was proved that the LABELED PERFECT MATCHING problem in bipartite graphs is **APX**-complete (see also [66] for a related problem).

A primary example of this phenomenon, of significant increase in complexity when extending a combinatorial optimization problem in time, is the fundamental MAXIMUM MATCHING problem. In its static version, we are given a graph $G = (V, E)$ and we must compute a maximum cardinality set of edges such that no two of them share an endpoint. MAXIMUM MATCHING can be solved in polynomial time by the famous Edmonds' algorithm [22] (the time is $O(\sqrt{|V|} \cdot |E|)$ by the algorithm of [48]). Now consider the following temporal version of the problem, called TEMPORAL MATCHING in [56]. In this problem, we are given a temporal graph $D = (V, A)$ and we are asked to decide whether there is a maximum matching M of the underlying static graph of D that can be made temporal by selecting a single label $l \in \lambda(e)$ for every edge $e \in M$. For a single-labeled matching to be temporal it suffices to guarantee that no two of its edges have the same label. TEMPORAL MATCHING was proved in [56] to be **NP**-complete. Then the problem of computing a maximum cardinality temporal matching is immediately **NP**-hard, because if we could compute such a maximum temporal matching in polynomial time, we could then compare its cardinality to the cardinality of a maximum static matching and decide TEMPORAL MATCHING in polynomial time. **NP**-completeness of TEMPORAL MATCHING can be proved by the sequence of polynomial-time reductions: BALANCED 3SAT $\leq_P$ BALANCED UNION LABELED MATCHING $\leq_P$ TEMPORAL MATCHING. In BALANCED 3SAT, which is known to be **NP**-complete, every variable x_i appears n_i times negated and n_i times non-negated and in BALANCED UNION LABELED MATCHING we are given a bipartite graph $G = ((X, Y), E)$, labels $L = \{1, 2, ..., h\}$, and a labeling $\lambda : E \rightarrow 2^L$, every node $u_i \in X$ has precisely two neighbors $v_{ij} \in Y$, and additionally both edges of u_i have the same number of labels, and we must decide whether there is a maximum matching M of G s.t. $\bigcup_{e \in M} \lambda(e) = L$ [56].

Another interesting problem is the TEMPORAL EXPLORATION problem [56]. In this problem, we are given a temporal graph and the goal is to visit all nodes of the temporal graph by a temporal walk, that possibly revisits nodes, minimizing the arrival time. The version of this problem for static graphs is well-known as GRAPHIC TSP. Though, in the static case, the decision version of the problem, asking whether a given graph is explorable, can be solved in linear time, in the temporal case it becomes **NP**-complete. Additionally, in the static case, there is a $(3/2 - \varepsilon)$-approximation for undirected graphs [27] and a $O(\log n / \log \log n)$ for directed [4].

In contrast to these, it was proved in [56] that there exists some constant $c > 0$ such that TEMPORAL EXPLORATION cannot be approximated within cn unless **P** = **NP**, by presenting a gap introducing reduction from HAMPATH. Additionally, it was proved that even the special case in which every instance of the temporal graph is connected, cannot be approximated within $(2 - \varepsilon)$, for every constant $\varepsilon > 0$, unless **P** = **NP**. The reduction is from HAMPATH (input graph G, source s). The constructed temporal graph D consists of three strongly connected static graphs T_1, T_2, and T_3 persisting for the intervals $[1, n_1 - 1]$, $[n_1, n_2 - 1]$, and $[n_2, 2n_2 + n_1]$, respectively (it will be helpful at this point to look at Fig. 8). We can restrict attention to instances of HAMPATH of order at least $2/\varepsilon$, without affecting its **NP**-completeness. We also set $n_2 = n_1^2 + n_1$ (in fact, we can set n_2 equal to any polynomial-time computable function of n_1). If G is hamiltonian, then for the arrival time, OPT, of an optimum exploration it holds that OPT $= n_1 + n_2 - 1 = n_1^2 + 2n_1 - 1$ while if G is not hamiltonian, then OPT $\geq 2n_2 + 1 = 2(n_1^2 + n_1) + 1 > 2(n_1^2 + n_1)$, which can be shown to introduce the desired $(2 - \varepsilon)$ gap. This negative result has been recently improved by Erlebach et al. [23] to $O(n^{1-\varepsilon})$ for any $\varepsilon > 0$. In the same work, an explicit construction of continuously connected temporal graphs that require $\Theta(n^2)$ steps to be explored was also given.

On the positive side, it is not hard to show that in continuously connected temporal graphs, TEMPORAL EXPLORATION can be approximated within the temporal diameter of the temporal graph [56]. In [23], the authors additionally studied the TEMPORAL EXPLORATION problem in other interesting restricted families of temporal graphs, like temporal graphs in which the underlying graph has treewidth k (a work explicitly concerned with the treewidth of temporal graphs and its relation to the treewidth of static graphs is [44]), is a $2 \times n$ grid, a cycle, a cycle with a chord, or a bounded-degree planar graph, for which they provided upper bounds on exploration time. See also [26] for another study of the exploration problem in temporal graphs with periodic edge-availabilities, from a distributed computing perspective.

Another demanding problem that becomes even more challenging in its temporal version is the famous TRAVELING SALESMAN PROBLEM, in which a graph with non-negative costs on its edge is provided and the goal is to find a tour visiting every node exactly once (called a *TSP tour*), of minimum total cost.

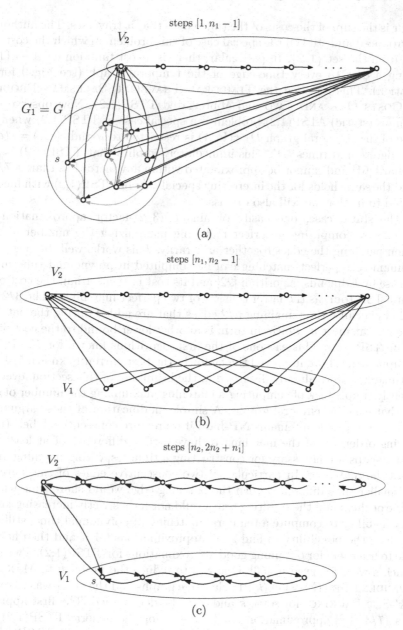

Fig. 8. The temporal graph constructed by the reduction. (a) T_1 (b) T_2 (c) T_3

In one version of the problem, introduced in [56], the digraph remains static and complete throughout its lifetime but now each edge is assigned a cost that may change from instance to instance. So, the dynamicity has now been transferred from the topology to the costs of the edges. The goal is to find (by an offline centralized algorithm) a *temporal TSP tour* of minimum total cost, where the cost of a tour is the sum of the costs of the time-edges that it traverses. The authors of [56] introduced and studied the special case of this problem in which the costs are chosen from the set $\{1, 2\}$. In particular, there is a cost function $c : A \rightarrow \{1, 2\}$ assigning a cost to every time-edge of the temporal graph (see Fig. 9 for an illustration). This is called the TEMPORAL TRAVELING SALESMAN PROBLEM WITH COSTS ONE AND TWO and abbreviated TTSP(1,2). Now observe that the famous (static) ATSP(1,2) problem is a special case of TTSP(1,2) when the lifetime of the temporal graph $D = (V, A)$ is restricted to n and $c(e, t) = c(e, t')$ for all edges e and times t, t'. This immediately implies that TTSP(1,2) is also **APX**-hard [61] and cannot be approximated within any factor less than 207/206 [34] and the same holds for the interesting special case of TTSP(1,2) with lifetime restricted to n, that we will also discuss.

In the static case, one easily obtains a $(3/2)$-factor approximation for ATSP(1,2) by computing a perfect matching maximizing the number of ones and then patching the edges together arbitrarily. This works well, because such a minimum cost perfect matching can be computed in polynomial time in the static case by Edmonds' algorithm [22] and its cost is at most half the cost of an optimum TSP tour, as the latter consists of two perfect matchings. The 3/2 factor follows because the remaining $n/2$ edges that are added during the patching process cost at most n, which, in turn, is another lower bound to the cost of the optimum TSP tour. This was one of the first algorithms known for ATSP(1,2). Other approaches have improved the factor to the best currently known 5/4 [11]. Unfortunately, as we already discussed in the beginning of this section, even the apparently simple task of computing a matching maximizing the number of ones is not that easy in temporal graphs. A simple modification of those arguments yields that the problem remains **NP**-hard if we require consecutive labels (in an increasing ordering) of the matching to have a time difference of at least two. Such time-gaps are necessary for constructing a time-respecting patching of the edges of the matching. In particular, if two consecutive edges of the matching had a smaller time difference, then the patching-edge would share time with at least one of them and the resulting tour would not have strictly increasing labels.

Our inability to compute a temporal matching in polynomial time, still does not exclude the possibility to find good approximations for it and then hope to be able to use them for obtaining good approximations for TTSP(1,2). Two main approaches were followed in [56]. One was to reduce the problem to MAXIMUM INDEPENDENT SET (MIS) in $(k+1)$-claw free graphs and the other was to reduce it to k'-SET PACKING, for some k and k' to be determined. The first approach gives a $(7/4 + \varepsilon)$-approximation $(= 1.75 + \varepsilon)$ for the generic TTSP(1,2) and a $(12/7 + \varepsilon)$-approximation $(\approx 1.71 + \varepsilon)$ for the special case of TTSP(1,2) in which the lifetime is restricted to n (the latter is obtained by approximating a temporal path packing instead of a matching). The second approach improves these to $1.7 + \varepsilon$ for the general case and to $13/8 + \varepsilon = 1.625 + \varepsilon$ when the lifetime is n. In all the above cases, $\varepsilon > 0$ is a small constant (not necessarily the same in all cases) adopted from the factors of the approximation algorithms for independent set and set packing.

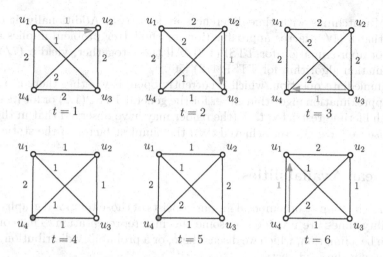

Fig. 9. An instance of TTSP(1,2) consisting of a complete temporal graph $D = (V, A)$, where $V = \{u_1, u_2, u_3, u_4\}$, and a cost function $c : A \to \{1, 2\}$ which is presented by the corresponding costs on the edges. For simplicity, D is an undirected temporal graph. Observe that the cost of an edge may change many times, e.g. the cost of u_2u_3 changes 5 times while of u_1u_4 changes only once. Here, the lifetime of the temporal graph is 6 and it is greater than $|V|$. The gray arcs and the nodes filled gray (meaning that the tour does not make a move and remains on the same node for that step) represent the TTSP tour $(u_1, 1, u_2, 2, u_3, 3, u_4, 6, u_1)$ that has cost $4 = |V|$ and therefore it is an optimum TTSP tour.

We summarize now how the first of these approximations works. Consider the static expansion $H = (S, E)$ of D and an edge $e = (u_{(i-1)j}, u_{ij'}) \in E$. There are three types of conflicts, each defining a set of edges that cannot be taken together with e in a temporal matching (with only unit time differences): (i) Edges of the same row as e, because these violate the unit time difference constraint (ii) edges of the same column as $u_{(i-1)j}$, because these share a node with e, thus violate the condition of constructing a matching, and (iii) edges of the same column as $u_{ij'}$, for the same reason as (ii). Next consider the graph of edge conflicts $G = (E, K)$, where $(e_1, e_2) \in K$ iff e_1 and e_2 satisfy some of the above constraints (observe that the node set of G is equal to the edge set of the static expansion H). Observe that temporal matchings of D are now equivalent to independent sets of G. Moreover, G is 4-claw free meaning that there is no 4-independent set in the neighborhood of any node. To see that it is 4-claw free, take any $e \in E$ and any set $\{e_1, e_2, e_3, e_4\}$ of four neighbors of e in G. There are only 3 constraints thus at least two of the neighbors, say e_i and e_j, must be connected to e by the same constraint. But then e_i and e_j must also satisfy the same constraint with each other thus they are also connected by an edge in G. Now, from [29], there is a factor of 3/5 for MIS in 4-claw free graphs, which implies a (3/5)-approximation algorithm for temporal matchings. Simple modifications of the above arguments yield a $\frac{1}{2+\varepsilon}$-approximation algorithm for temporal matchings with time-differences at least two. Additionally, it can be proved that a $(1/c)$-factor approximation for the latter problem implies a $(2 - \frac{1}{2c})$-factor approximation for TTSP(1,2). All these together, yield a $(7/4 + \varepsilon)$-approximation algorithm for TTSP$(1, 2)$ [56].

An immediate question, which is currently open, is whether there is a $(3/2)$-factor approximation algorithm either for the general TTSP(1,2) or for its special case with lifetime restricted to n (the reader may have observed that in the temporal case we have not yet achieved even the simplest factor of the static case).

7   Linear Availabilities

An interesting family of temporal graphs consists of those temporal graphs whose availability times are provided by some succinct representation. This could for example be a function, which we discuss here, or a probability distribution, which we discuss in the next section.

Such an example of a temporal graph in which a set of functions describes the availability times of the edges is the following (for other studies on periodically varying temporal graphs the reader is encouraged to consult [16, 26, 60] and references therein). The underlying graph is a complete static graph $G = (V, E)$. Each $e \in E$ has an associated linear function of the form $f_e(x) = a_e x + b_e$, where $x, a_e, b_e \in \mathbb{N}_{\geq 0}$. For example, if an edge e has $f_e(x) = 3x + 4$, then it is available at times $4, 7, 10, 13, 16, \ldots$. Clearly, the temporal graph that we obtain in this manner is $D = (V, A)$ where $A(r) = \{e \in E : f_e(x) = r$ for some $x \in \mathbb{N}\}$. If we are additionally provided with a lifetime l of the temporal graph then we just restrict $E(r)$ to $r \leq l$.

The above provides an immediate way for obtaining the rth instance for any r. For every $e \in E$, the rth instance contains edge e iff $(r - b_e)/a_e$ is integer. It is important to note that, in the above family of temporal graphs, algorithmic solutions that depend at least linearly on the lifetime l are not acceptable. The reason is that the lifetime l is provided in binary so a linear dependence on l grows exponentially in the binary representation of l. Foremost journeys in such graphs can be easily computed by a variation of the algorithm discussed in Sect. 2.1.

Now consider the following problem. We are given two edges e_1 and e_2 with corresponding functions $f_{e_1}(x) = a_1 x + b_1$ and $f_{e_2}(x) = a_2 x + b_2$ and we are asked to determine whether there is some instance having both edges, that is, to determine whether there exist x_1 and x_2 s.t. $f_{e_1}(x_1) = f_{e_2}(x_2) \Leftrightarrow a_1 x_1 + b_1 = a_2 x_2 + b_2 \Leftrightarrow a_1 x_1 = a_2 x_2 + (b_2 - b_1)$. So, in fact, we are seeking for a x_2 s.t. $a_1 \mid a_2 x_2 + (b_2 - b_1)$ (where '$\mid$' reads as "divides") and we have reduced our problem to the problem of determining whether $c \mid ax + b$ for some x. Now imagine a right oriented ring of c nodes numbered $0, 1, \ldots, c - 1$. Consider a process beginning from node b (mod c) and making clockwise jumps of length a in each round (where a round corresponds to an increment of x by 1). We have that the process falls at some point on node 0 iff $c \mid ax + b$ for some x. Viewed in this way, our problem is equivalent to checking whether $ax + b \equiv 0$

(mod c) is solvable for the unknown x. This, in turn, may easily take the form $ax \equiv b'$ (mod c) (given that $-b \equiv b'$ (mod c)) for $a > 0$ and $c > 0$ (equalities to 0 correspond to trivial cases of our original problem). Clearly, we have reduced our problem to the problem of detecting whether a modular linear equation admits a solution which is well-known to be solvable in polynomial time. In particular, a modular linear equation $ax \equiv b'$ (mod c) has a solution iff $\gcd(a, c) \mid b'$ (see e.g. [19], Corollary 31.21, p. 869). Additionally, by solving the equation we can find all solutions modulo c in $O(\log c + \gcd(a, c))$ arithmetic operations (see e.g. [19], p. 871).

Note that in the case where $b_1 = b_2 = 0$ then the answer to the problem is always "yes" as $a_1x_1 = a_2x_2$ trivially holds for $x_1 = a_2$ and $x_2 = a_1$ (provided that a_1a_2 does not exceed the lifetime of the network if a lifetime is specified). In particular, if we are asked to determine the foremost instance containing both edges then this reduces to the computation of $\mathrm{lcm}(a_1, a_2)$ (where lcm is the least common multiple) which in turn reduces to the computation of $\gcd(a_1, a_2)$ by the equation $\mathrm{lcm}(a_1, a_2) = |a_1a_2| / \gcd(a_1, a_2)$.

Now let us slightly simplify our model in order to obtain a solution to a more generic version of the above problem. We restrict the edge functions $a_ix + b_i$ so that $b_i < a_i$, e.g. $7x + 4$. Then clearly, each such function corresponds to the whole equivalence subclass of $\mathbb{N}$ modulo a_i containing b_i, that is, $[b_i]_{a_i} = \{b_i + xa_i : x \in \mathbb{N}\}$. So, for example, $7x + 4$ corresponds to $\{4, 11, 18, 25, \ldots\}$ in contrast to $7x + 11$ that was allowed before and would just give the subset $\{11, 18, 25, \ldots\}$ of the actual class. Consider now the following problem: "We are given a subset E' of the edge set E and we want to determine whether there is some instance of the temporal graph containing all edges in E'". For simplicity, number the edges in E' from 1 to k. Formally, we want to determine the existence of some time t s.t., for all $i \in \{1, 2, \ldots, k\}$, there exists x_i s.t. $t = a_ix_i + b_i$, or equivalently, $t \equiv b_i$ (mod a_i). Clearly, we have arrived at a set of simultaneous linear congruences and we can now apply the following known results.

Theorem 3 (see e.g. [7], Theorem 5.5.5, p. 106). *The system of congruences $t \equiv b_i$ (mod a_i), $1 \le i \le k$, has a solution iff $b_i \equiv b_j$ (mod $\gcd(a_i, a_j)$) for all $i \ne j$. If the solution exists, it is unique modulo $\mathrm{lcm}(a_1, a_2, \ldots, a_k)$.*

Corollary 1 (see e.g. [7], Corollary 5.5.6, p. 106). *Let $a_1, a_2, \ldots, a_k$ be integers, each ≥ 2, and define $a = a_1a_2 \cdots a_k$, and $a' = \mathrm{lcm}(a_1, a_2, \ldots, a_k)$. Given the system S of congruences $t \equiv b_i$ (mod a_i), $1 \le i \le k$, we can determine if S has a solution, using $O(\lg^2 a)$ bit operations, and if so, we can find the unique solution modulo a', using $O(\lg^2 a)$ bit operations.*

We may now return to the original formulation of our model in which $a_ix + b_i$ does not necessarily satisfy $b_i < a_i$. First keep in mind that $t_{min} = \max_{i \in E'}\{b_i\}$ is the minimum time for every edge from E' to appear at least once (in fact, at that time, the last edge of E' appears). So we cannot hope to have them all in one instance sooner than this. Now notice that $a_ix + b_i$ is equivalent to $a_ix' + (b_i \bmod a_i)$ for $x' \ge \lfloor b_i/a_i \rfloor$; for example, $7x + 15$ is equivalent to $7x' + 1$ for $x' \ge 2$. In this manner, we obtain an equivalent setting in which again $b_i < a_i$

for all i but additionally for every i we have a constraint on x of the form $x \geq q_i$. We may now ignore the constraints and apply Theorem 3 to determine whether there is a solution to the new set of congruences as there is a solution that satisfies the constraints iff there is one if we ignore the constraints (the reason being that the constraints together form a finite lower bound while there is an infinite number of solutions). If there is a solution it will be a unique solution modulo $\mathrm{lcm}(a_1, a_2, \ldots, a_k)$ corresponding to an infinite number of solutions if expanded. From these solutions we just have to keep those that are not less than t_{min} (in case we want to find the actual solutions to the system).

8   Random Temporal Graphs

Another model of temporal graphs with succinct representation, is the model of random temporal graphs. Consider the case in which each edge (of an underlying clique) just picks independently and uniformly at random *a single time-label* from $[r] = \{1, 2, \ldots, r\}$. So it gets label $t \in [r]$ with probability $p = r^{-1}$. We mainly present here a set of unpublished results concerning this model, jointly developed by the author of the present article and Paul Spirakis in 2012. We also discuss results from [2], which is a very recent paper concerned with the same issue.

We first calculate the probability that given a specific path $(u_1, u_2, \ldots, u_{k+1})$ of length k a journey appears on this path. We begin with the directed case. First, let us obtain a weak but elegant upper bound. Partition $[r]$ into $R_1 = \{1, \ldots, \lfloor r/2 \rfloor\}$ and $R_2 = \{\lfloor r/2 \rfloor + 1, \ldots, r\}$. Clearly, P(*journey*) $\leq$ P(no $R_2 R_1$ occurs) as any journey assignment cannot have two consecutive selections s.t. the first one is from R_2 and the second from R_1. So, it suffices to calculate P(no $R_2 R_1$ occurs). Notice that the assignments in which no $R_2 R_1$ occurs are of the form $(R_1)^i (R_2)^j$ for $i + j = k$, e.g. $R_1 R_1 R_2 R_2 R_2$ and there are $k + 1$ of them. In contrast, all possible assignments are 2^k corresponding to all possible ways to choose k times with repetition from $\{R_1, R_2\}$. So, P(no $R_2 R_1$ occurs) $= k/2^k$ (as all assignments are equiprobable, with probability 2^{-k}) and we conclude that P(*journey*) $\leq k/2^k$, which, interestingly, is independent of r; e.g. for $k = 6$ we get a probability of at most 0.09375 for a journey of length 6 to appear.

For any specific assignment of labels $t_1, t_2, \ldots, t_k$ of this path, where $t_i \in [r]$ ($[r] = \{1, 2, \ldots, r\}$), the probability that this specific assignment occurs is simply p^k. So, all possible assignments are equiprobable and we get

$$\mathrm{P}(journey) = \frac{\text{\# strictly increasing assignments}}{\text{\# all possible assignments}} = \frac{\binom{r}{k}}{r^k},$$

where $\binom{r}{k}$ follows from the fact that any strictly increasing assignment is just a unique selection of k labels from the r available and any such selection corresponds to a unique strictly increasing assignment. So, for example, for $k = 2$ and $r = 10$ we get a probability of $9/20$ which is a little smaller than $1/2$ as expected, due to the fact that there is an equal number of strictly increasing and strictly decreasing assignments but we also loose all remaining assignments which in this case are only the ties (that is, those for which $t_1 = t_2$).

Now it is easy to compute the expected number of journeys of length k. Let S be the set of all directed paths of length k and let Y_p be an indicator random variable which is 1 if a journey appears on a specific $p \in S$ and 0 otherwise. Let also X_k be a random variable giving the number of journeys of length k. Clearly, $E(X_k) = E(\sum_{p \in S} Y_p) = \sum_{p \in S} E(Y_p) = |S| \cdot P($a journey appears on a specific path of length $k) = n(n-1) \cdots (n-k)\binom{r}{k}r^{-k} \geq (n-k)^k \binom{r}{k}r^{-k}$. Now, if we set $n \geq r/\binom{r}{k}^{(1/k)} + k$, we get $E(X) \geq 1$. A simpler, but weaker, formula can be obtained by requiring $n \geq r + k$. In this case, we get $E(X) \geq \binom{r}{k}$. So, for example, a long journey of size $k = n/2$ that uses all available labels is expected to appear provided that $n \geq 2r$ (to see this, simply set $k = r$).

We will now try to obtain bounds on the probability that a journey of length k appears on a random temporal graph. Let us begin from a simple case, namely the one in which $k = 4$, that is, we want to calculate the probability that a journey of length 4 appears. Let the r.v. X be the number of journeys of length 4 and let X_p be an indicator for path $p \in S$, where S is the set of all paths of length 4. Denote $n(n-1) \cdots (n-k)$ by $(n)_{k+1}$ First note that $E(X) = (n)_5 \binom{r}{4}r^{-4} = \Theta(n^5)$ and clearly goes to ∞ for every r. However, we cannot yet conclude that $P(4 - journey)$ is also large. To show this we shall apply the second moment method. We will make use of Chebyshev's inequality $P(X = 0) \leq \text{Var}(X)/[E(X)]^2$ and of the following well-known theorem:

Theorem 4 [54]. *Suppose* $X = \sum_{i=1}^{n} X_i$, *where* X_i *is an indicator for event* A_i. *Then,*

$$\text{Var}(X) \leq E(X) + \sum_i P[A_i] \underbrace{\sum_{j:j \sim i} P(A_j \mid A_i)}_{\Delta_i},$$

where $i \sim j$ *denotes that* i *depends on* j. *Moreover, if* $\Delta_i \leq \Delta$ *for all* i, *then*

$$\text{Var}(X) \leq E(X)(1 + \Delta).$$

So, in our case, we need to estimate $\Delta_p = \sum_{p' \sim p} P(A_{p'} \mid A_p)$. If we show that $\Delta_p \leq \Delta$ for all $p \in S$ then we will have that $\text{Var}(X) \leq E(X)(1 + \Delta)$. If we additionally manage to show that $\Delta/E(X) = o(1)$, then $\Delta = o(E(X))$ which tells us that $\text{Var}(X) = o([E(X)]^2)$. Putting this back to Chebyshev's inequality we get that $P(X = 0) = o(1)$ as needed.

So, let us try to bound Δ_p appropriately. Clearly, p' cannot be a journey if it visits some edges of p in inverse order (than the one they have on p). Intuitively, the two paths must have the same orientation. We distinguish cases based on the number of edges shared by the two paths. First of all, note that if p' and p have precisely i edges in common then $P(A_{p'} \mid A_p) \leq \binom{r}{k-i}/r^{k-i}$ which becomes $\binom{r}{4-i}/r^{4-i}$ in our case. The reason is that the $k - i$ edges of p' that are not shared with p must at least obtain an increasing labeling. If we also had taken into account that that labeling should be consistent to the labels of the shared edges then this would decrease the probability. So we just use an upper bound which is sufficient for our purposes.

Case 1: 1 shared edge. If a single edge is shared then there are $k\binom{n-k+1}{k-1}$ $(k-1)!4 = 16 \cdot 3!\binom{n-5}{3}$ different paths p' achieving this as there are k ways to choose the shared edge, $\binom{n-k+1}{k-1}$ to choose the missing nodes (nodes of p' not shared with p), $(k-1)!$ ways to order those nodes, and, in this particular example, 4 ways to arrange the nodes w.r.t. the shared edge. In particular, we can put all nodes before the shared edge, all nodes after, 2 nodes before and 1 node after, or 1 node before and 2 nodes after. We conclude that the probability that $\sum_{|p' \cap p|=1} P(A_{p'} \mid A_p) \leq 16 \cdot 3!\binom{n-5}{3}\binom{r}{3}/r^3 = O(n^3)$.

Case 2: 2 shared edges. In this case, we can have all possible $\binom{k}{2} = \binom{4}{2}$ 2-sharings. Let us denote by e_1, e_2, e_3, e_4 the edges of p. For the sharings (e_1, e_2), (e_2, e_3), and (e_3, e_4) we get in total $3\binom{n-k-1}{k-2}(k-2)!4 = 24\binom{n-5}{2}$ paths. For (e_1, e_3), (e_2, e_4) we get $2(n-k-1) = 2(n-5)$. For (e_1, e_4) we get $(n-5)$ in case we connect the 2 edges by an intermediate node (i.e. go from the head of e_1 to some u not in p and then form u to the tail of e_4) and $2(n-5)$ in case we connect e_1 directly to e_4 and use an external node either before or after, so in total $3(n-5)$ paths. Putting these all together we get $\sum_{|p' \cap p|=2} P(A_{p'} \mid A_p) \leq$ $[24\binom{n-5}{2} + 5(n-5)]\binom{r}{2}/r^2 = O(n^2)$.

Case 3: 3 shared edges. Here there are just 2 choices for the 3 shared edges, namely (e_1, e_2, e_3) and (e_2, e_3, e_4), the reason being that if the edges are not consecutive then a fourth edge must be necessarily shared and the 2 paths would coincide. As there are $(n-k-1)$ ways to choose the missing node and 2 ways to arrange that node we get $2(n-k-1)2 = 4(n-5)$ and consequently $\sum_{|p' \cap p|=3} P(A_{p'} \mid A_p) \leq 4(n-5)\binom{r}{1}/r^1 = O(n)$.

So, we have $\Delta_p \leq \Delta = O(n^3)$ and $\Delta/E(X) = O(n^3)/\Theta(n^5) = o(1)$ which applied to Theorem 4 gives $\mathrm{Var}(X) \leq E(X)(1 + \Delta) = o([E(X)]^2)$ and this in turn applied to Chebyshev's inequality gives the desired $P(X = 0) \leq \mathrm{Var}(X)/[E(X)]^2 = o(1)$. We conclude that:

Theorem 5 [54]. *For all $r \geq 4$, almost all random temporal graphs contain a journey of length 4.*

Now let us turn back to our initial $(n)_{k+1}\binom{r}{k}r^{-k}$ formula of $E(X)$ (which holds for all k). This gives $E(X) \geq (n)_{k+1}/k^k$, which, for all $k = o(n)$ and all $r \geq k$, goes to ∞ as n grows. We will now try to generalize the ideas developed in the $k = 4$ case to show that for any not too large k almost all random temporal graphs contain a journey of length k. Take again a path p of length k and another path p' of length k that shares i edges with p. We will count rather crudely but in a sufficient way for our purposes. As again the shared edges can be uniquely oriented in the order they appear on p, there are at most $\binom{k}{i}$ ways to choose the shared edges (at most because some selections force more than i sharings to occur). Counting the tail of the first edge and the head of every edge, these i edges occupy at least $i + 1$ nodes, so at most $k + 1 - i - 1 = k - i$ nodes are missing from p' and thus there are at most $\binom{n-k-1}{k-i}$ ways to choose those nodes.

Moreover there are at most $(k - i)!$ ways to permute them on p'. Finally, we have to place those nodes relative to the i shared edges. In the worst case, the i edges define $i+1$ slots that can be occupied by the nodes in $\binom{k-i+(i+1)-1}{(i+1)-1} = \binom{k}{i}$ ways. In total, we have $N = \binom{k}{i}^2 \binom{n-k-1}{k-i} (k - i)! \binom{k}{i}$ different paths and the corresponding probability is

$$\sum_{|p' \cap p|=i} P(A_{p'} \mid A_p) \leq N \binom{r}{k-i} / r^{k-i} \leq \binom{k}{i}^2 \binom{n-k-1}{k-i}$$

$$\leq \binom{k^2}{i} \binom{n-k-1}{k-i}.$$

So we have that

$$\Delta_p = \sum_{i=1}^{k-1} \sum_{|p' \cap p|=i} P(A_{p'} \mid A_p) \leq \sum_{i=0}^{k} \binom{k^2}{i} \binom{n-k-1}{k-i}$$

$$= \binom{n+k^2-k-1}{k} \leq \binom{n+k^2}{k} = \Delta.$$

The first equality follows from the Chu-Vandermonde identity $\sum_{i=0}^{k} \binom{m}{i}\binom{z}{k-i} = \binom{m+z}{k}$ by setting $z = n - k - 1$ and $m = k^2$ as needed in our case.

Thus, we have $\Delta = \binom{n+k^2}{k}$ and for $k^2 = o(n)$ we have $\Delta \sim (n)_k/k!$. At the same time we have $E(X) = (n)_{k+1}\binom{r}{k}/r^k \sim (n)_{k+1}/k!$ (for large r), thus $\Delta/E(X) \sim (n)_k/(n)_{k+1} = o(1)$ as needed. So we have $\mathrm{Var}(X) = o([E(X)]^2)$ and we again get that $P(X = 0) \leq \mathrm{Var}(X)/[E(X)]^2 = o(1)$. Captured in a theorem:

Theorem 6 [54]. *For all $k = o(\sqrt{n})$ and all $r = \Omega(n)$, almost all random temporal graphs contain a journey of length k.*

However, there seems to be some room for improvements if one counts more carefully.

Now take any two nodes s and t in V. We want to estimate the arrival time of a foremost journey from s to t. Let X be the random variable of the arrival time of the foremost s-t journey. Let us focus on $P(X \leq 2)$. Denote by $l(u,v)$ the label chosen by edge (u,v). Given a specific node $u \in V \backslash \{s,t\}$ we have that $P(l(s,u) \neq 1$ or $l(u,t) \neq 2) = 1 - P(l(s,u) = 1$ and $l(u,t) = 2) = 1 - r^{-2}$. Thus, $P(\forall u \in V \backslash \{s,t\} : l(s,u) \neq 1$ or $l(u,t) \neq 2) = (1 - r^{-2})^{n-2}$ We have:

$$P(X \leq 2) = 1 - P(X > 2)$$

$$= 1 - P(l(s,t) \notin \{1,2\})P(\forall u \in V \backslash \{s,t\} : l(s,u) \neq 1 \text{ or } l(u,t) \neq 2)$$

$$= 1 - \frac{r-2}{r}(1 - r^{-2})^{n-2}$$

$$\geq 1 - (1 - r^{-2})^{n-2}$$

$$\geq 1 - e^{-(n-2)/r^2}, \text{ for } n \geq 2 \text{ and } r > \sqrt{n-1}.$$

So, even if $r = \Theta(\sqrt{n})$ we have that $P(X \leq 2) \to 1 - 1/e^c$ (for some constant $c \leq 1$) as n goes to infinity, so we have a constant probability of arriving by time 2 at t. Clearly, for smaller values of r (smaller w.r.t. n) we get even better chances of arriving early. For another example, let $n = 10^4$ and $r = \sqrt{n}/\log n = 25$. As $P(X \leq 2)$ is almost equal to $1 - (1 - r^{-2})^{n-2}$ we get that it is almost equal to 1 in this particular case. For even greater r, e.g. $r = \sqrt{n} = 100$, we still go very close to 1.

The following proposition gives a bound on the temporal diameter of undirected random temporal graphs, by exploiting well-known results of the Erdös-Renyi ($\mathcal{G}(n,p)$) model (cf. [13]).

Proposition 1 [54]. *Almost no temporal graph has temporal diameter less than* $[(\ln n + c + o(1))/n]r$.

To see this, observe that if $k < [(\ln n + c + o(1))/n]r$ then $p = k/r < (\ln n + c + o(1))/n$. Consider now the temporal subgraph consisting only of the first k labels $[k] = \{1, 2, \ldots, k\}$. By the connectivity threshold of the static $\mathcal{G}(n,p)$ model this subgraph is almost surely disconnected implying that almost surely the temporal diameter is greater than k.

So, for example, if $r = O(n)$ almost no temporal graph has temporal diameter $o(\log n)$. Note, however, that the above argument is not sufficient to show that almost every temporal graph has temporal diameter at least $[(\ln n + c + o(1))/n]r$. Though it shows that in almost every graph the subgraph consisting of the labels $[k]$, for $k \geq \lceil r(\ln n + c + o(1))/n \rceil$ is connected, it does not tell us whether that connectivity also implies temporal connectivity (that is, the existence of journeys).

We should also mention that [2] studied the temporal diameter of the directed random temporal graph model for the case of $r = n$, and proved that it is $\Theta(\log n)$ w.h.p. and in expectation. In fact, they showed that information dissemination is very fast w.h.p. even in this hostile network with regard to availability. Moreover, they showed that the temporal diameter of the clique is crucially affected by the clique's lifetime, α, e.g., when α is asymptotically larger than the number of vertices, n, then the temporal diameter must be $\Omega(\frac{\alpha}{n} \log n)$. They also defined the *Price of Randomness* metric in order to capture the cost to pay per link and guarantee temporal reachability of all node-pairs by local random available times w.h.p.

The idea of [2] to establish that the temporal diameter is $O(\log n)$ is as follows. Given an instance of such a random temporal clique, the authors pick any source node s and any sink node t and present an algorithm trying to construct a journey from s arriving at t at most by time $O(\log n)$. The algorithm expands two fronts, one beginning from s and moving forward (in fact, an out-tree rooted at s) and one from t moving backward (an in-tree rooted at t). Beginning from s, all neighbors that can be reached in one step in the interval $(0, c_1 \log n]$, are visited. Next the front moves on to all neighbors of the previous front that can be reached in one step in the interval $(c_1 \log n, c_1 \log n + c_2]$. The process continues in the same way, every time replacing the current front by all its neighbors that can be reached in the next c_2 steps. A similar backward process is executed from t. These processes are executed for $d = \Theta(\log n)$ steps resulting in the final front of s and the final front of t. Note that the front of t begins from the interval $(2c_1 \log n + (2d - 1)c_2, 2c_1 \log n + 2dc_2]$ and every time subtracts a c_2. Finally, the algorithm tries to find an edge from the final front of s to the final front of t with the appropriate label in order to connect the journey from s to the journey to t in a time-respecting way and obtain the desired s-t journey of duration $\Theta(\log n)$ (determined by the interval of the first front of t, and in particular by $2c_1 \log n + 2dc_2$). Via probabilistic analysis it can be proved that, with probability at least $1 - 1/n^3$, the final front of s consists of $\Theta(\sqrt{n})$ nodes and that the same holds for the front of t. Moreover, it can be proved that again with probability at least $1 - 1/n^3$ the desired edge for the final front of s to the final front of t exists, and thus we can conclude that there is a probability of at least $1 - 3/n^3$ of getting from s to t by a journey arriving at most by time $\Theta(\log n)$. Finally, it suffices to observe that the probability that there exists a pair of nodes $s, t \in V$ for which the algorithm fails is less than $n^2(3/n^3) = 3/n$, thus with probability at least $(1 - 3/n)$ the temporal diameter is $O(\log n)$, as required.

References

1. Aaron, E., Krizanc, D., Meyerson, E.: DMVP: foremost waypoint coverage of time-varying graphs. In: Kratsch, D., Todinca, I. (eds.) WG 2014. LNCS, vol. 8747, pp. 29–41. Springer, Heidelberg (2014)
2. Akrida, E.C., Gasieniec, L., Mertzios, G.B., Spirakis, P.G.: Ephemeral networks with random availability of links: Diameter and connectivity. In: Proceedings of the 26th ACM symposium on Parallelism in algorithms and architectures (SPAA), pp. 267–276. ACM (2014)
3. Angluin, D., Aspnes, J., Diamadi, Z., Fischer, M.J., Peralta, R.: Computation in networks of passively mobile finite-state sensors. Distrib. Comput. **18**, 235–253 (2006)
4. Asadpour, A., Goemans, M.X., Madry, A., Gharan, S.O., Saberi, A.: An $O(\log n/ \log \log n)$-approximation algorithm for the asymmetric traveling salesman problem. In: Proceedings of the Twenty-First Annual ACM-SIAM Symposium on Discrete Algorithms (SODA), pp. 379–389. Society for Industrial and Applied Mathematics, Philadelphia, PA, USA (2010). http://dl.acm.org/citation.cfm?id=1873601.1873633
5. Augustine, J., Pandurangan, G., Robinson, P., Upfal, E.: Towards robust and efficient computation in dynamic peer-to-peer networks. In: Proceedings of the Twenty-Third Annual ACM-SIAM Symposium on Discrete Algorithms (SODA), pp. 551–569. SIAM (2012)
6. Avin, C., Koucký, M., Lotker, Z.: How to explore a fast-changing world (cover time of a simple random walk on evolving graphs). In: Aceto, L., Damgård, I., Goldberg, L.A., Halldórsson, M.M., Ingólfsdóttir, A., Walukiewicz, I. (eds.) ICALP 2008, Part I. LNCS, vol. 5125, pp. 121–132. Springer, Heidelberg (2008)
7. Bach, E., Shallit, J.: Algorithmic Number Theory. Efficient algorithms, vol. 1. MIT press, Cambridge (1996)

8. Baker, B., Shostak, R.: Gossips and telephones. Discrete Math. **2**(3), 191–193 (1972)
9. Berman, K.A.: Vulnerability of scheduled networks and a generalization of Menger's theorem. Networks **28**(3), 125–134 (1996)
10. Bhadra, S., Ferreira, A.: Complexity of connected components in evolving graphs and the computation of multicast trees in dynamic networks. In: Pierre, S., Barbeau, M., An, H.-C. (eds.) ADHOC-NOW 2003. LNCS, vol. 2865, pp. 259–270. Springer, Heidelberg (2003)
11. Bläser, M.: A 3/4-approximation algorithm for maximum ATSP with weights zero and one. In: Jansen, K., Khanna, S., Rolim, J.D.P., Ron, D. (eds.) RANDOM 2004 and APPROX 2004. LNCS, vol. 3122, pp. 61–71. Springer, Heidelberg (2004)
12. Bollobás, B.: Modern Graph Theory. Graduate Texts in Mathematics. Springer, Heidelberg (1998). (Corrected edition, July 1, 1998)
13. Bollobás, B.: Random Graphs. Cambridge Studies in Advanced Mathematics, 2nd edn. Cambridge University Press, Cambridge (2001)
14. Broersma, H., Li, X.: Spanning trees with many or few colors in edge-colored graphs. Discuss. Math. Graph Theory **17**(2), 259–269 (1997)
15. Broersma, H., Li, X., Woeginger, G., Zhang, S.: Paths and cycles in colored graphs. Australas. J. Comb. **31**, 299–311 (2005)
16. Casteigts, A., Flocchini, P., Quattrociocchi, W., Santoro, N.: Time-varying graphs and dynamic networks. Int. J. Parallel Emerg. Distrib. Syst. **27**(5), 387–408 (2012)
17. Clementi, A.E., Macci, C., Monti, A., Pasquale, F., Silvestri, R.: Flooding time in edge-markovian dynamic graphs. In: Proceedings of the 27th ACM Symposium on Principles of Distributed Computing (PODC), pp. 213–222 (2008). http://doi.acm.org/10.1145/1400751.1400781
18. Clementi, A.E., Pasquale, F., Monti, A., Silvestri, R.: Communication in dynamic radio networks. In: Proceedings of the Twenty-Sixth Annual ACM Symposium on Principles of Distributed Computing (PODC), pp. 205–214. ACM (2007)
19. Cormen, T.H., Leiserson, C.E., Rivest, R.L., Stein, C.: Introduction to Algorithms, 2nd edn. The MIT Press and McGraw-Hill Book Company, Cambridge (2001)
20. Demers, A., Greene, D., Hauser, C., Irish, W., Larson, J., Shenker, S., Sturgis, H., Swinehart, D., Terry, D.: Epidemic algorithms for replicated database maintenance. In: Proceedings of the Sixth Annual ACM Symposium on Principles of Distributed Computing (PODC), pp. 1–12. ACM (1987)
21. Dutta, C., Pandurangan, G., Rajaraman, R., Sun, Z., Viola, E.: On the complexity of information spreading in dynamic networks. In: Proceedings of the Twenty-Fourth Annual ACM-SIAM Symposium on Discrete Algorithms (SODA), pp. 717–736. SIAM (2013)
22. Edmonds, J.: Paths, trees, and flowers. Can. J. Math. **17**(3), 449–467 (1965)
23. Erlebach, T., Hoffmann, M., Kammer, F.: On temporal graph exploration. In: Halldórsson, M.M., Iwama, K., Kobayashi, N., Speckmann, B. (eds.) ICALP 2015. LNCS, vol. 9134, pp. 444–455. Springer, Heidelberg (2015)
24. Ferreira, A.: Building a reference combinatorial model for manets. IEEE Netw. **18**(5), 24–29 (2004)
25. Fleischer, L., Tardos, É.: Efficient continuous-time dynamic network flow algorithms. Oper. Res. Lett. **23**(3), 71–80 (1998)
26. Flocchini, P., Mans, B., Santoro, N.: Exploration of periodically varying graphs. In: Dong, Y., Du, D.-Z., Ibarra, O. (eds.) ISAAC 2009. LNCS, vol. 5878, pp. 534–543. Springer, Heidelberg (2009)

27. Gharan, S.O., Saberi, A., Singh, M.: A randomized rounding approach to the traveling salesman problem. In: Proceedings of the IEEE 52nd Annual Symposium on Foundations of Computer Science (FOCS), pp. 550–559. IEEE Computer Society, Washington, DC (2011). http://dx.doi.org/10.1109/FOCS.2011.80
28. Haeupler, B., Kuhn, F.: Lower bounds on information dissemination in dynamic networks. In: Aguilera, M.K. (ed.) DISC 2012. LNCS, vol. 7611, pp. 166–180. Springer, Heidelberg (2012)
29. Halldórsson, M.M.: Approximating discrete collections via local improvements. In: Proceedings of the Sixth Annual ACM-SIAM Symposium on Discrete Algorithms, pp. 160–169. Society for Industrial and Applied Mathematics (1995)
30. Harary, F., Gupta, G.: Dynamic graph models. Math. Comput. Model. 25(7), 79–87 (1997)
31. Hedetniemi, S.M., Hedetniemi, S.T., Liestman, A.L.: A survey of gossiping and broadcasting in communication networks. Networks 18(4), 319–349 (1988)
32. Holme, P., Saramäki, J.: Temporal networks. Phys. Rep. 519(3), 97–125 (2012)
33. Karp, R., Schindelhauer, C., Shenker, S., Vocking, B.: Randomized rumor spreading. In: Proceedings of the IEEE 41st Annual Symposium on Foundations of Computer Science (FOCS), pp. 565–574. IEEE (2000)
34. Karpinski, M., Schmied, R.: On improved inapproximability results for the shortest superstring and related problems. In: Proceedings of 19th CATS, pp. 27–36 (2013)
35. Kempe, D., Kleinberg, J.: Protocols and impossibility results for gossip-based communication mechanisms. In: Proceedings of the IEEE 43rd Annual Symposium on Foundations of Computer Science (FOCS), pp. 471–480. IEEE (2002)
36. Kempe, D., Kleinberg, J., Kumar, A.: Connectivity and inference problems for temporal networks. In: Proceedings of the 32nd annual ACM symposium on Theory of computing (STOC), pp. 504–513 (2000). http://doi.acm.org/10.1145/335305.335364
37. Kontogiannis, S., Michalopoulos, G., Papastavrou, G., Paraskevopoulos, A., Wagner, D., Zaroliagis, C.: Analysis and experimental evaluation of time-dependent distance oracles. In: Proceedings of the Seventeenth Workshop on Algorithm Engineering and Experiments (ALENEX), pp. 147–158 (2015)
38. Kontogiannis, S., Zaroliagis, C.: Distance oracles for time-dependent networks. In: Esparza, J., Fraigniaud, P., Husfeldt, T., Koutsoupias, E. (eds.) ICALP 2014. LNCS, vol. 8572, pp. 713–725. Springer, Heidelberg (2014)
39. Kostakos, V.: Temporal graphs. Phys. A Stat. Mech. Appl. 388(6), 1007–1023 (2009)
40. Krumke, S.O., Wirth, H.C.: On the minimum label spanning tree problem. Inf. Process. Lett. 66(2), 81–85 (1998)
41. Kuhn, F., Lynch, N., Oshman, R.: Distributed computation in dynamic networks. In: Proceedings of the 42nd ACM symposium on Theory of Computing (STOC), pp. 513–522. ACM, New York (2010). http://doi.acm.org/10.1145/1806689.1806760
42. Kuhn, F., Oshman, R.: Dynamic networks: models and algorithms. SIGACT News 42, 82–96 (2011). http://doi.acm.org/10.1145/1959045.1959064 (Distributed Computing Column, Editor: Idit Keidar)
43. Leighton, F.T.: Introduction to Parallel Algorithms and Architectures, vol. 188. Morgan Kaufmann, San Francisco (1992)
44. Mans, B., Mathieson, L.: On the treewidth of dynamic graphs. In: Du, D.-Z., Zhang, G. (eds.) COCOON 2013. LNCS, vol. 7936, pp. 349–360. Springer, Heidelberg (2013)

45. Menger, K.: Zur allgemeinen kurventheorie. Fundamenta Mathematicae **10**(1), 96–115 (1927)
46. Mertzios, G.B., Michail, O., Chatzigiannakis, I., Spirakis, P.G.: Temporal network optimization subject to connectivity constraints. In: Fomin, F.V., Freivalds, R., Kwiatkowska, M., Peleg, D. (eds.) ICALP 2013, Part II. LNCS, vol. 7966, pp. 657–668. Springer, Heidelberg (2013)
47. Mertzios, G.B., Michail, O., Spirakis, P.G.: Temporal network optimization subject to connectivity constraints. CoRR abs/1502.04382 (2015), full version of [MMCS13]
48. Micali, S., Vazirani, V.V.: An $O(\sqrt{|V|} \cdot |E|)$ algorithm for finding maximum matching in general graphs. In: Proceedings of the IEEE 21st Annual Symposium on Foundations of Computer Science (FOCS), pp. 17–27. IEEE (1980)
49. Michail, O.: Terminating distributed construction of shapes and patterns in a fair solution of automata. In: Proceedings of the 34th ACM Symposium on Principles of Distributed Computing (PODC) (2015) (to appear)
50. Michail, O., Chatzigiannakis, I., Spirakis, P.G.: Mediated population protocols. Theor. Comput. Sci. **412**(22), 2434–2450 (2011). http://dx.doi.org/10.1016/j.tcs.2011.02.003
51. Michail, O., Chatzigiannakis, I., Spirakis, P.G.: New Models for Population Protocols. In: ynch, N.A. (ed.) Synthesis Lectures on Distributed Computing Theory. Morgan and Claypool (2011)
52. Michail, O., Chatzigiannakis, I., Spirakis, P.G.: Naming and counting in anonymous unknown dynamic networks. In: Higashino, T., Katayama, Y., Masuzawa, T., Potop-Butucaru, M., Yamashita, M. (eds.) SSS 2013. LNCS, vol. 8255, pp. 281–295. Springer, Heidelberg (2013)
53. Michail, O., Chatzigiannakis, I., Spirakis, P.G.: Causality, influence, and computation in possibly disconnected synchronous dynamic networks. J. Parallel Distrib. Comput. **74**(1), 2016–2026 (2014)
54. Michail, O., Spirakis, P.G.: Unpublished work on random temporal graphs (2012)
55. Michail, O., Spirakis, P.G.: Simple and efficient local codes for distributed stable network construction. In: Proceedings of the 33rd ACM Symposium on Principles of Distributed Computing (PODC), pp. 76–85. ACM (2014). http://doi.acm.org/10.1145/2611462.2611466
56. Michail, O., Spirakis, P.G.: Traveling salesman problems in temporal graphs. In: Csuhaj-Varjú, E., Dietzfelbinger, M., Ésik, Z. (eds.) MFCS 2014, Part II. LNCS, vol. 8635, pp. 553–564. Springer, Heidelberg (2014)
57. Molloy, M., Reed, B.: Graph Colouring and the Probabilistic Method, vol. 23. Springer, Heidelberg (2002)
58. Monnot, J.: The labeled perfect matching in bipartite graphs. Inf. Process. Lett. **96**(3), 81–88 (2005)
59. O'Dell, R., Wattenhofer, R.: Information dissemination in highly dynamic graphs. In: Proceedings of the 2005 Joint Workshop on Foundations of Mobile Computing (DIALM-POMC), pp. 104–110 (2005). http://doi.acm.org/10.1145/1080810.1080828
60. Orlin, J.B.: The complexity of dynamic languages and dynamic optimization problems. In: Proceedings of the 13th Annual ACM Symposium on Theory of Computing (STOC), pp. 218–227. ACM (1981)
61. Papadimitriou, C.H., Yannakakis, M.: The traveling salesman problem with distances one and two. Math. Oper. Res. **18**(1), 1–11 (1993)
62. Peleg, D.: Distributed computing: a locality-sensitive approach. SIAM Monographs on Discrete Mathematics and Applications, p. 5 (2000)

63. Pittel, B.: On spreading a rumor. SIAM J. Appl. Math. **47**(1), 213–223 (1987)
64. Ravi, R.: Rapid rumor ramification: approximating the minimum broadcast time. In: Proceedings of the IEEE 35th Annual Symposium on Foundations of Computer Science (FOCS), pp. 202–213. IEEE (1994)
65. Scheideler, C.: Models and techniques for communication in dynamic networks. In: Alt, H., Ferreira, A. (eds.) STACS 2002. LNCS, vol. 2285, p. 27. Springer, Heidelberg (2002)
66. Tanimoto, S.L., Itai, A., Rodeh, M.: Some matching problems for bipartite graphs. J. ACM **25**(4), 517–525 (1978)
67. Xuan, B., Ferreira, A., Jarry, A.: Computing shortest, fastest, and foremost journeys in dynamic networks. Int. J. Found. Comput. Sci. **14**(02), 267–285 (2003)

Random Surfing Without Teleportation

Athanasios N. Nikolakopoulos[1,2] and John D. Garofalakis[1,2](✉)

[1] Computer Engineering and Informatics Department, University of Patras,
Patras, Greece
{nikolako,garofala}@ceid.upatras.gr
[2] CTI and Press "Diophantus", Patras, Greece

Abstract. In the standard *Random Surfer Model*, the teleportation
matrix is necessary to ensure that the final PageRank vector is well-
defined. The introduction of this matrix, however, results in serious problems and imposes fundamental limitations to the quality of the ranking
vectors. In this work, building on the recently proposed *NCDawareRank*
framework, we exploit the decomposition of the underlying space into
blocks, and we derive easy to check necessary and sufficient conditions
for *random surfing without teleportation*.

Keywords: Link analysis · Ranking · PageRank · Teleportation · Non-
negative matrices · Decomposability

1 Introduction and Motivation

The astonishing amount of information available on the Web and the highly
variable quality of its content generate the need for an absolute measure of
importance for Web pages, that can be used to improve the performance of Web
search. Link Analysis algorithms such as the celebrated *PageRank*, try to answer
this need by using the link structure of the Web to assign authoritative weights
to the pages [16].

PageRank's approach is based on the assumption that links convey human
endorsement. For example, the existence of a link from page 3 to page 7 in
Fig. 1(a) is seen as a testimonial of the importance of page 7. Furthermore, the
amount of importance conferred to page 7 is proportional to the importance
of page 3 and inversely proportional to the number of pages 3 links to. In their
original paper, Page et al. [16] imagined of a *random surfer* who, with probability
α follows the links of a Web page, and with probability $1 - \alpha$ jumps to a different
page uniformly at random. Then, following this metaphor, the overall importance
of a page was defined to be equal to the fraction of time this random surfer spends
on it, in the long run.

Formulating PageRank's basic idea with a mathematical model, involves
viewing the Web as a directed graph with Web pages as vertices and hyper-
links as edges. Given this graph, we can construct a *row-normalized hyperlink
matrix* $\mathbf{H}$, whose element $[\mathbf{H}]_{uv}$ is one over the outdegree of u if there is a link

© Springer International Publishing Switzerland 2015
C. Zaroliagis et al. (Eds.): Spirakis Festschrift, LNCS 9295, pp. 344–357, 2015.
DOI: 10.1007/978-3-319-24024-4_19

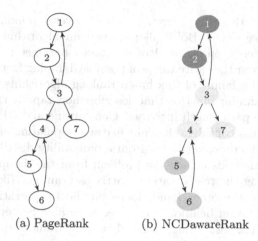

(a) PageRank   (b) NCDawareRank

Fig. 1. In the left figure we see a tiny graph as viewed by PageRank and in the right, the same graph as viewed by NCDawareRank. Same colored nodes belong to the same block and are considered related according to a given criterion.

from u to v, or zero otherwise. The matter of dangling nodes is fixed with some sort of stochasticity adjustment, thereby transforming the initial matrix $\mathbf{H}$, to a stochastic matrix.

A second adjustment is needed to certify that the final matrix is irreducible and aperiodic, so that it possesses a unique positive stationary probability distribution. That is ensured by the introduction of the *damping factor* α and a *teleportation* matrix $\mathbf{E}$, usually defined by $\mathbf{E} = \frac{1}{n}\mathbf{e}\mathbf{e}^{\mathsf{T}}$. The resulting matrix is given by:

$$\mathbf{G} = \alpha\mathbf{H} + (1 - \alpha)\mathbf{E} \tag{1}$$

PageRank vector is the unique stationary distribution of the Markov chain corresponding to matrix $\mathbf{G}$.

The choice of the damping factor has received much attention since it determines the fraction of the importance of a node that is propagated through the edges rather than scattered throughout the graph via the teleportation matrix. Obviously, picking a very small damping factor ignores the link structure of the graph and results in uninformative ranking vectors. On the other hand, setting the damping factor very close to one, causes a number of serious problems. From a computational perspective, as $\alpha \rightarrow 1$, the number of iterations till convergence to the PageRank vector grows prohibitively, and also makes the computation of the rankings numerically ill-conditioned [11,12]. Moreover, from a qualitative point of view, various studies indicate that damping factors close to 1 result into counterintuitive ranking vectors where all the PageRank gets concentrated mostly in irrelevant nodes, while the Web's core component is assigned null rank [1,4,5,13]. Finally, the very existence of the damping factor and the related teleportation matrix "opens the door" to direct manipulation of the ranking score through link spamming [6,8].

In the literature there have been proposed several ranking methods that try to address these issues. Boldi [3] proposed an algorithm that eliminates PageRank's dependency on the arbitrarily chosen parameter α by integrating the ranking vector over the entire range of possible damping factors. Baeza-Yates et al. [2] introduced a family of link based ranking algorithms parametrised by the selection of a damping function that describes how rapidly the importance of paths decays as the path length increases. Constantine and Gleich [6] proposed a ranking method that considers the influence of a population of random surfers, each choosing its own damping factor from a probability distribution.

All the above methods attack the problem from the damping factor point of view, while taking the teleportation matrix as granted. Nikolakopoulos and Garofalakis [13], on the other hand, focus on the teleportation model itself. Building on the intuition behind Nearly Decomposable Systems [7,19,20], the authors proposed *NCDawareRank*; a novel ranking framework that generalizes and refines PageRank by enriching the teleportation model in a computationally efficient way. NCDawareRank decomposes the underlying space into NCD blocks, and uses these blocks to define indirect relations between the nodes in the graph (Fig. 1(b)) which lead to the introduction of a new inter-level proximity component. A comprehensive set of experiments done by the authors using real snapshots of the Web Graph showed that the introduction of this decomposition alleviates the negative effects of uniform teleportation and produces ranking vectors that display low sensitivity to sparsity and, at the same time, exhibit resistance to direct manipulation through link spamming (see the discussion in Sects. 4.2 and 4.3 in [13] for further details). However, albeit reducing some of its negative effects, NCDawareRank model also includes the standard teleportation matrix as a purely mathematical necessity. But, is it?

The main questions we try to address in this work are the following: *Is it possible to discard the uniform teleportation altogether? And if so, under which conditions?* Thankfully, the answer is yes. In particular, we show that, the definition of the NCD blocks, can be enough to ensure the production of well defined ranking vectors without resorting to uniform teleportation. The criterion for this to be true is expressed solely in term of properties of the proposed decomposition, which makes it very easy to check and at the same time gives insight that can lead to better decompositions for the particular ranking problems under consideration.

The rest of the paper is organized as follows: After discussing NCDawareRank model (Sect. 2) we derive sufficient and necessary conditions under which the inter-level proximity matrix enables us to discard the teleportation matrix completely (Sect. 3.2). In Sect. 4, we generalize NCDawareRank model, in order to allow the definition of overlapping blocks without compromising its theoretical and computational properties. Finally, in Sect. 5 we discuss future direction and conclude this work.

2   NCDawareRank Model

Before we proceed to our main result, we present here the basic definitions behind the NCDawareRank model. Our presentation follows the one given in [13].

2.1   Notation

All vectors are represented by bold lower case letters and they are column vectors (e.g., $\boldsymbol{\pi}$). All matrices are represented by bold upper case letters (e.g., $\mathbf{P}$). The ith row and j^{th} column of matrix $\mathbf{P}$ are denoted $\mathbf{p}_i^{\mathsf{T}}$ and $\mathbf{p}_j$, respectively. The ij^{th} element of matrix $\mathbf{P}$ is denoted $[\mathbf{P}]_{ij}$. We use $\mathbf{Diag}(\omega)$ to denote the matrix having vector ω on its diagonal, and zeros elsewhere. We use calligraphic letters to denote sets (e.g., $\mathcal{U}, \mathcal{V}$). $[1, n]$ is used to denote the set of integers $\{1, 2, \ldots, n\}$. Finally, symbol $\triangleq$ is used in definition statements.

2.2   Definitions

Let $\mathcal{U}$ be a set of nodes (e.g. the universe of Web pages) and denote $n \triangleq |\mathcal{U}|$. Consider a node u in $\mathcal{U}$. We denote $\mathcal{G}_u$ to be the set of nodes that can be visited in a single step from u. Clearly, $d_u \triangleq |\mathcal{G}_u|$ is the out-degree of u, i.e. the number of outgoing edges of u.

We consider a partition of the underlying space $\mathcal{U}$ that defines a **decomposition**:

$$\mathcal{M} \triangleq \{\mathcal{D}_1, \ldots, \mathcal{D}_K\} \tag{2}$$

such that, $\mathcal{D}_k \neq \emptyset$, for all k in $[1, K]$.

Each set $\mathcal{D}_I$ is referred to as an **NCD Block**, and its elements are considered related according to a given criterion, chosen for the particular ranking problem (e.g. the partition of the set of Web Pages into websites).

We define $\mathcal{M}_u$ to be the set of *proximal* nodes of u, i.e. the union of the NCD blocks that contain u and the nodes it links to. Formally, the set $\mathcal{M}_u$ is defined by:

$$\mathcal{M}_u \triangleq \bigcup_{w \in (u \cup \mathcal{G}_u)} \mathcal{D}_{(w)} \tag{3}$$

where $\mathcal{D}_{(u)}$ is used to denote the unique block that includes node u. Finally, N_u denotes the number of different blocks in $\mathcal{M}_u$.

Hyperlink Matrix. The hyperlink matrix $\mathbf{H}$, as in the standard PageRank Model, is a row normalized version of the adjacency matrix induced by the graph, and its uv^{th} element is defined as follows:

$$[\mathbf{H}]_{uv} \triangleq \begin{cases} \frac{1}{d_u} & \text{if } v \in \mathcal{G}_u \\ 0 & \text{otherwise} \end{cases} \tag{4}$$

Matrix $\mathbf{H}$ is assumed to be a row-stochastic matrix. The matter of dangling nodes (i.e. nodes with no outgoing edges) is considered fixed through some sort of stochasticity adjustment.

Inter-Level Proximity Matrix. The Inter-Level Proximity matrix $\mathbf{M}$ is created to depict the interlevel connections between the nodes in the graph. In particular, each row of matrix $\mathbf{M}$ denotes a probability vector $\mathbf{m}_u^\mathsf{T}$, that distributes evenly its mass between the N_u blocks of $\mathcal{M}_u$, and then, uniformly to the included nodes of each block. Formally, the uv^{th} element of matrix $\mathbf{M}$, that relates the node u with node v, is defined as

$$[\mathbf{M}]_{uv} \triangleq \begin{cases} \frac{1}{N_u |\mathcal{D}_{(v)}|} & \text{if } v \in \mathcal{M}_u \\ 0 & \text{otherwise} \end{cases} \tag{5}$$

From the definition of the NCD blocks and the proximal sets, it is clear that whenever the number of blocks is smaller than the number of nodes in the graph, i.e. $K < n$, matrix $\mathbf{M}$ is necessarily low-rank; in fact, a closer look at the Definitions (3) and (5) above, suggests that matrix $\mathbf{M}$ admits a very useful factorization, which was shown in [13] to ensure the tractability of the resulting model. In particular, matrix $\mathbf{M}$ can be expressed as a product of 2 extremely sparse matrices, $\mathbf{R}$ and $\mathbf{A}$, defined below.
Matrix $\mathbf{A} \in \mathbb{R}^{K \times n}$ is defined as follows:

$$\mathbf{A} \triangleq \begin{bmatrix} \mathbf{e}_{|\mathcal{D}_1|}^\mathsf{T} & \mathbf{0} & \mathbf{0} & \cdots & \mathbf{0} \\ \mathbf{0} & \mathbf{e}_{|\mathcal{D}_2|}^\mathsf{T} & \mathbf{0} & \cdots & \mathbf{0} \\ \mathbf{0} & \mathbf{0} & \mathbf{e}_{|\mathcal{D}_3|}^\mathsf{T} & \cdots & \mathbf{0} \\ \vdots & \vdots & \vdots & \ddots & \mathbf{0} \\ \mathbf{0} & \mathbf{0} & \mathbf{0} & \cdots & \mathbf{e}_{|\mathcal{D}_K|}^\mathsf{T} \end{bmatrix} \tag{6}$$

where $\mathbf{e}_{|\mathcal{D}_k|}^\mathsf{T}$ denotes a row vector in $\mathbb{R}^{|\mathcal{D}_k|}$ whose elements are all 1. Now, using the diagonal matrix $\mathbf{\Delta}$:

$$\mathbf{\Delta} \triangleq \mathbf{Diag}\left(\begin{bmatrix} |\mathcal{D}_1| & |\mathcal{D}_2| & \cdots & |\mathcal{D}_K| \end{bmatrix} \right) \tag{7}$$

and a row normalized matrix $\mathbf{\Gamma} \in \mathbb{R}^{n \times K}$, whose rows correspond to nodes and columns to blocks and its elements are given by

$$[\mathbf{\Gamma}]_{ij} \triangleq \begin{cases} \frac{1}{N_u} & \text{if } \mathcal{D}_j \in \mathcal{M}_{u_i} \\ 0 & \text{otherwise} \end{cases} \tag{8}$$

we can define the matrix $\mathbf{R}$ as follows:

$$\mathbf{R} \triangleq \mathbf{\Gamma}\mathbf{\Delta}^{-1} \tag{9}$$

Using (6) and (9), it is straight forward to verify that:

$$\mathbf{M} = \mathbf{R}\mathbf{A} \tag{10}$$
$$\mathbf{R} \in \mathbb{R}^{n \times K} \qquad \mathbf{A} \in \mathbb{R}^{K \times n}$$

As pointed out by the authors [13], this factorization can lead to significant advantages in realistic scenarios, in terms of both storage and computability (see [13], Sect. 3.2.1).

Teleportation Matrix. Finally, NCDawareRank model also includes a teleportation matrix $\mathbf{E}$,

$$\mathbf{E} \triangleq \mathbf{e}\mathbf{v}^\mathsf{T} \tag{11}$$

where, $\mathbf{v} > \mathbf{0}$ such that $\mathbf{v}^\mathsf{T}\mathbf{e} = 1$. The introduction of this matrix, can be seen as a remedy to ensure that the underlying Markov chain, corresponding to the final matrix, is irreducible and aperiodic and thus has a unique positive stationary probability distribution [13].

The resulting matrix which we denote $\mathbf{P}$ is expressed by:

$$\mathbf{P} = \eta\mathbf{H} + \mu\mathbf{M} + (1 - \eta - \mu)\mathbf{E} \tag{12}$$

Parameter η controls the fraction of importance delivered to the outgoing edges and parameter μ controls the fraction of importance that will be propagated to the proximal nodes. In order to ensure the irreducibility and aperiodicity of the final stochastic matrix in the general case, $\eta + \mu$ must be less than 1. This leaves $1 - \eta - \mu$ of importance scattered throughout the graph through matrix $\mathbf{E}$.

Remark 1. PageRank can be seen within NCDawareRank model in two different ways:

- when there is only one block containing all the nodes – where matrix $\mathbf{M}$ collapses into the standard uniform teleportation matrix:

$$\mathbf{M} \equiv \frac{1}{n}\mathbf{e}\mathbf{e}^\mathsf{T} \Rightarrow$$

$$\mathbf{P} = \eta\mathbf{H} + (1 - \eta)\frac{1}{n}\mathbf{e}\mathbf{e}^\mathsf{T} \tag{13}$$

- when we have n singleton NCD blocks – a case where the inter-level proximity matrix coincides with the hyperlink matrix $\mathbf{H}$:

$$\mathbf{M} \equiv \mathbf{H}^\mathsf{T} \Rightarrow$$

$$\mathbf{P} = (\eta + \mu)\mathbf{H} + (1 - \eta - \mu)\frac{1}{n}\mathbf{e}\mathbf{e}^\mathsf{T} \tag{14}$$

3   Necessary and Sufficient Conditions for Random Surfing Without Teleportation

Although in the general case the teleportation matrix is required to ensure the final stochastic matrix produces a well defined ranking vector, in this Section we show that NCDawareRank model carries the possibility of discarding matrix $\mathbf{E}$ altogether. Before we proceed to the proof of our main result (Sect. 3.2) we present here the necessary preliminary definitions and theorems.

3.1 Preliminaries

Definition 1 (Irreducibility). An $n \times n$ non-negative matrix $\mathbf{P}$ is called *irreducible* if for every pair of indices $i, j \in [1, n]$, there exists a positive integer $m \equiv m(i,j)$ such that $[\mathbf{P}^m]_{ij} > 0$. The class of all non-negative irreducible matrices is denoted $\mathfrak{I}$.

Definition 2 (Period). The *period* of an index $i \in [1, n]$ is defined to be the greatest common divisor of all positive integers m such that $[\mathbf{P}^m]_{ii} > 0$.

Proposition 1 (Periodicity as a Matrix Property). *For an irreducible matrix, the period of every index is the same and is referred to as the period of the matrix.*

Definition 3 (Primitivity). An irreducible matrix with period $d = 1$, is called *primitive*. The important subclass of all primitive matrices will be denoted $\mathfrak{P}$.

Finally, we give here, without proof, the following fundamental result of the theory of non-negative matrices[1].

Theorem 1 (Perron-Frobenius Theorem for Primitive Matrices [9,17]). *Suppose $\mathbf{T}$ is an $n \times n$ non-negative primitive matrix. Then, there exists an eigenvalue r such that:*

(a) r is real and positive,
(b) with r can be associated strictly positive left and right eigenvectors,
(c) $r > |\lambda|$ for any eigenvalue $\lambda \neq r$
(d) the eigenvectors associated with r are unique to constant multiples,
(e) if $0 \leq \mathbf{B} \leq \mathbf{T}$ and β is an eigenvalue of $\mathbf{B}$, then $|\beta| \leq r$. Moreover,

$$|\beta| = r \quad \Longrightarrow \quad \mathbf{B} = \mathbf{T} \tag{15}$$

(f) r is a simple root of the characteristic equation of $\mathbf{T}$.

3.2 NCDawareRank Primitivity Criterion

Mathematically, in the standard PageRank model the introduction of the teleportation matrix can be seen as a *primitivity adjustment* of the final stochastic matrix. Indeed, the hyperlink matrix is typically reducible [12,16], so if the teleportation matrix had not existed the PageRank vector would not be well defined.

In the general case, the same holds for NCDawareRank, as well. However, for suitable decompositions of the underlying graph, matrix $\mathbf{M}$ opens the door for achieving primitivity without resorting to the uninformative teleportation matrix. Here, we show that this "suitability" of the decompositions can, in fact, be reflected on the properties of a low dimensional **Indicator Matrix** defined below:

---

[1] For thorough treatment of the theory as well as proofs to several formulations of the Perron-Frobenius theorem the interested reader can see [18].

Definition 4 (Indicator Matrix). For every decomposition $\mathcal{M}$, we define an Indicator Matrix $\mathbf{W} \in \mathbb{R}^{K \times K}$ designed to capture the inter-block relations of the underlying graph. Concretely, matrix $\mathbf{W}$ is defined as follows:

$$\mathbf{W} \triangleq \mathbf{AR}, \tag{16}$$

where $\mathbf{A}, \mathbf{R}$ are the factors of the inter-level proximity matrix $\mathbf{M}$.

Clearly, whenever $[\mathbf{W}]_{IJ}$ is positive, there exists a node $u \in \mathcal{D}_I$ such that $\mathcal{D}_J \in \mathcal{M}_u$. Intuitively, one can see that a positive element in matrix $\mathbf{W}$ implies the existence of possible inter-level "random surfing paths" between the nodes belonging to the corresponding blocks. Thus, if the indicator matrix $\mathbf{W}$ is irreducible, these paths exist between every pair of nodes in the graph, which makes the stochastic matrix $\mathbf{M}$ also irreducible.

In fact, in the following theorem we show that the irreducibility of matrix $\mathbf{W}$ is enough to certify the primitivity of the final NCDawareRank matrix, $\mathbf{P}$. Then, just choosing positive numbers η, μ that sum to one, leads to a well defined ranking vector produced by an NCDawareRank model without a teleportation component.

Theorem 2 (Primitivity Criterion). *The NCDawareRank matrix* $\mathbf{P} = \eta\mathbf{H} + \mu\mathbf{M}$, *with* η *and* μ *positive real numbers such that* $\eta + \mu = 1$, *is primitive if and only if the indicator matrix* $\mathbf{W}$ *is irreducible. Concretely,* $\mathbf{P} \in \mathfrak{P} \iff \mathbf{W} \in \mathfrak{I}$.

Proof. We will first prove that

$$\mathbf{W} \in \mathfrak{I} \implies \mathbf{P} \in \mathfrak{P} \tag{17}$$

First notice that whenever matrix $\mathbf{W}$ is irreducible then it is also primitive. In particular, it is known that when a non-negative irreducible matrix has at least one positive diagonal element, then it is also primitive. In case of matrix $\mathbf{W}$, notice that by the definition of the proximal sets and matrices $\mathbf{A}, \mathbf{R}$, we get that $[\mathbf{W}]_{ii} > 0$ for every i in $[1, K]$. Thus, the irreducibility of the indicator matrix ensures its primitivity also. Formally, we have

$$\mathbf{W} \in \mathfrak{I} \implies \mathbf{W} \in \mathfrak{P} \tag{18}$$

Now if the indicator matrix $\mathbf{W}$ is primitive the same is true for the inter-level proximity matrix $\mathbf{M}$. We prove this in the following lemma.

Lemma 1. *The primitivity of the indicator matrix* $\mathbf{W}$ *implies the primitivity of the inter-level proximity matrix* $\mathbf{M}$, *defined over the same decomposition, i.e.*

$$\mathbf{W} \in \mathfrak{P} \implies \mathbf{M} \in \mathfrak{P} \tag{19}$$

Proof. It suffices to show that there exists a number m, such that for every pair of indices i, j, $[\mathbf{M}^m]_{ij} > 0$ holds. Or equivalently there exists a positive integer m such that $\mathbf{M}^m$ is a positive matrix (see [18]).

This can be seen easily using the factorization of matrix $\mathbf{M}$ given above. In particular, since $\mathbf{W} \in \mathfrak{P}$, there exists a positive integer k such that $\mathbf{W}^k > 0$. Now, if we choose $m = k + 1$, we get:

$$
\begin{aligned}
\mathbf{M}^m &= (\mathbf{RA})^{k+1} \\
&= \underbrace{(\mathbf{RA})(\mathbf{RA}) \cdots (\mathbf{RA})}_{k+1 \text{ times}} \\
&= \mathbf{R} \underbrace{(\mathbf{AR})(\mathbf{AR}) \cdots (\mathbf{AR})}_{k \text{ times}} \mathbf{A} \\
&= \mathbf{RW}^k \mathbf{A}
\end{aligned}
\tag{20}
$$

However, matrix $\mathbf{W}^k$ is positive and since every row of matrix $\mathbf{R}$ and every column of matrix $\mathbf{A}$ are – by definition – non-zero, the final matrix, $\mathbf{M}^m$, is also positive. Thus, $\mathbf{M} \in \mathfrak{P}$, and the proof is complete.   □

Now, in order to get the primitivity of the final stochastic matrix $\mathbf{P}$, we use the following useful lemma which shows that any convex combination of stochastic matrices that contains at least one primitive matrix, is also primitive.

Lemma 2. *Let $\mathbf{A}$ be a primitive stochastic matrix and $\mathbf{B_1}, \mathbf{B_2}, \ldots, \mathbf{B_n}$ stochastic matrices, then matrix*

$$
\mathbf{C} = \alpha\mathbf{A} + \beta_1\mathbf{B_1} + \cdots + \beta_n\mathbf{B_n}
$$

where $\alpha > 0$ and $\beta_1, \ldots, \beta_n \geq 0$ such that $\alpha + \beta_1 + \cdots + \beta_n = 1$ is a primitive stochastic matrix.

Proof. Clearly matrix $\mathbf{C}$ is stochastic as a convex combination of stochastic matrices (see [10]). For the primitivity part it suffices to show that there exists a natural number, m, such that $\mathbf{C}^m > 0$. This can be seen very easily. In particular, since matrix $\mathbf{A} \in \mathfrak{P}$, there exists a number k such that every element in $\mathbf{A}^k$ is positive.

Consider the matrix $\mathbf{C}^m$:

$$
\begin{aligned}
\mathbf{C}^m &= (\alpha\mathbf{A} + \beta_1\mathbf{B_1} + \cdots + \beta_n\mathbf{B_n})^m \\
&= \alpha^m \mathbf{A}^m + (\text{sum of non-negative matrices})
\end{aligned}
\tag{21}
$$

Now letting $m = k$, we get that every element of matrix $\mathbf{C}^k$ is strictly positive, which completes the proof.   □

As we have seen, when $\mathbf{W} \in \mathfrak{I}$, matrix $\mathbf{M}$ is primitive. Furthermore, $\mathbf{M}$ and $\mathbf{H}$ are by definition stochastic. Thus, Lemma 2 applies and we get that the NCDawareRank matrix $\mathbf{P}$, is also primitive. In conclusion, we have shown that:

$$
\mathbf{W} \in \mathfrak{I} \implies \mathbf{W} \in \mathfrak{P} \implies \mathbf{M} \in \mathfrak{P} \implies \mathbf{P} \in \mathfrak{P}
\tag{22}
$$

which proves the reverse direction of the theorem.

To prove the forward direction (i.e. $\mathbf{P} \in \mathfrak{P} \implies \mathbf{W} \in \mathfrak{I}$) it suffices to show that whenever matrix $\mathbf{W}$ is reducible, matrix $\mathbf{P}$ is also reducible (and thus, not primitive [18]). First observe that when matrix $\mathbf{W}$ is reducible the same holds for matrix $\mathbf{M}$.

Lemma 3. *The reducibility of the indicator matrix* $\mathbf{W}$ *implies the reducibility of the inter-level proximity matrix* $\mathbf{M}$. *Concretely,*

$$\mathbf{W} \notin \mathfrak{I} \implies \mathbf{M} \notin \mathfrak{I} \tag{23}$$

Proof. Assume that matrix $\mathbf{W}$ is reducible. Then, there exists a permutation matrix $\mathbf{\Pi}$ such that $\mathbf{\Pi W \Pi}^\mathsf{T}$ has the form

$$\begin{bmatrix} \mathbf{X} & \mathbf{Z} \\ \mathbf{0} & \mathbf{Y} \end{bmatrix} \tag{24}$$

where $\mathbf{X}, \mathbf{Y}$ are square matrices [18]. Notice that a similar block upper diagonal form can be then achieved for matrix $\mathbf{M}$. In particular, the existence of the block zero matrix in (24), together with the definition of matrices $\mathbf{A}, \mathbf{R}$ ensures the existence of a set of blocks, that have the property none of their including nodes to have outgoing edges to the rest of the nodes in the graph[2]. Thus, organizing the rows and columns of matrix $\mathbf{M}$ such that these nodes are assigned the last indices, results in a matrix $\mathbf{M}$ that has a similarly block upper diagonal form. This makes $\mathbf{M}$ reducible too. □

Thus, we only need to show that the reducibility of matrix $\mathbf{M}$ implies the reducibility of matrix $\mathbf{P}$ also. This can arise from the fact that by definition

$$[\mathbf{M}]_{ij} = 0 \implies [\mathbf{H}]_{ij} = 0. \tag{25}$$

So, the permutation matrix that brings $\mathbf{M}$ in the form of (24), has exactly the same effect on matrix $\mathbf{H}$. Similarly the final stochastic matrix $\mathbf{P}$ has the same block upper diagonal form as a sum of matrices $\mathbf{H}$ and $\mathbf{M}$. This makes matrix $\mathbf{P}$ reducible and hence non-primitive.

Therefore, we have shown that $\mathbf{W} \notin \mathfrak{P} \implies \mathbf{P} \notin \mathfrak{I}$, which is equivalent to

$$\mathbf{P} \in \mathfrak{P} \implies \mathbf{W} \in \mathfrak{I} \tag{26}$$

Putting everything together, we see that both directions of our theorem have been established. Thus we get,

$$\mathbf{P} \in \mathfrak{P} \iff \mathbf{W} \in \mathfrak{I} \tag{27}$$

and our proof is complete. □

Now, when the stochastic matrix $\mathbf{P}$ is primitive, from the Perron-Frobenius theorem it follows that its largest eigenvalue – which is equal to 1 – is unique

---

[2] notice that if this was not the case, there would be a nonzero element in the block below the diagonal necessarily.

and it can be associated with strictly positive left and right eigenvectors. Therefore, under the conditions of Theorem 2, the ranking vector produced by the NCDawareRank model – which is defined to be the stationary distribution of the stochastic matrix $\mathbf{P}$: (a) is uniquely determined as the (normalized) left eigenvector of $\mathbf{P}$ that corresponds to the eigenvalue 1 and, (b) its support includes every node in the underlying graph. The following corollary, summarizes the result.

Corollary 1. *When the indicator matrix $\mathbf{W}$ is irreducible, the ranking vector produced by NCDawareRank with $\mathbf{P} = \eta\mathbf{H} + \mu\mathbf{M}$, where η, μ positive real numbers such that $\eta + \mu = 1$ holds, denotes a well defined distribution that assigns positive ranking to every node in the graph.*

4 Generalizing the NCDawareRank Model

4.1 The Case of Overlapping Blocks

In our discussion so far, we assumed that the block decomposition defines a partition of the underlying space. However, in many realistic ranking scenarios it would be useful to be able to allow the blocks to overlap. For example, if one wants to produce top N lists of movies for a ranking-based recommender system, using NCDawareRank, a very intuitive criterion for decomposition would be the one depicting the categorization of movies into genres [14]. Of course, such a decomposition naturally results in overlapping blocks, since a movie usually belongs to more than one genres.

Fortunately, the factorization of the inter-level proximity matrix, paves the path towards a straight forward generalization, that inherits all the useful mathematical properties and computational characteristics of the standard NCDawareRank model.

In particular, it suffices to modify the definition of decompositions as indexed families of non-empty sets

$$\hat{\mathcal{M}} \triangleq \{\hat{\mathcal{D}}_1, \ldots, \hat{\mathcal{D}}_K\} \tag{28}$$

that collectively cover the underlying space, i.e.

$$\mathcal{U} = \bigcup_{k=1}^{K} \hat{\mathcal{D}}_k \tag{29}$$

and to change slightly the definitions of the:

– Proximal Sets:

$$\hat{\mathcal{M}}_u \triangleq \bigcup_{w \in (u \cup \mathcal{G}_u), w \in \hat{\mathcal{D}}_k} \hat{\mathcal{D}}_k \tag{30}$$

- Inter-Level Proximity Matrix:

$$[\hat{\mathbf{M}}]_{uv} \triangleq \sum_{\mathcal{D}_k \in \hat{\mathcal{M}}_u, v \in \hat{\mathcal{D}}_k} \frac{1}{N_u |\hat{\mathcal{D}}_k|} \qquad (31)$$

- Factor Matrices $\mathbf{A}, \mathbf{R}$: We first define a matrix $\mathbf{X}$, whose jk^{th} element is 1, if $v_j \in \hat{\mathcal{M}}_k$ and zero otherwise. Then, if $\hat{\mathbf{R}}$, $\hat{\mathbf{A}}$ denote the row-normalized versions of $\mathbf{X}$ and $\mathbf{X}^\mathsf{T}$ respectively, matrix $\hat{\mathbf{M}}$ can be expressed as:

$$\hat{\mathbf{M}} = \hat{\mathbf{R}}\hat{\mathbf{A}}, \quad \hat{\mathbf{R}} \in \mathbb{R}^{n \times K}, \hat{\mathbf{A}} \in \mathbb{R}^{K \times n}. \qquad (32)$$

Remark 2. Notice that the Inter-Level Proximity Matrix above is a well defined stochastic matrix, for every possible decomposition. Its stochasticity can arise immediately from the row normalization of matrices $\hat{\mathbf{R}}, \hat{\mathbf{A}}$, together with the fact that matrix $\mathbf{X}$ does not have zero rows (the existence of a zero row in matrix $\mathbf{X}$ implies $\mathcal{U} \neq \bigcup_{k=1}^{K} \hat{\mathcal{D}}_k$, which contradicts the definition of $\hat{\mathcal{M}}$) neither columns (since the sets comprising $\hat{\mathcal{M}}$ are defined to be non-empty).

Remark 3. Also notice that our primitivity criterion given by Theorem 2, applies in the overlapping case too, since our proof made no assumption for mutual exclusiveness for the NCD-blocks. In fact, it is intuitively evident that overlapping blocks promote the irreducibility of the indicator matrix $\mathbf{W}$.

5 Discussion and Future Work

In this work, using an approach based on the theory of non-negative matrices, we study NCDawareRank's inter-level proximity model and we derive necessary and sufficient conditions, under which the underlying decomposition alone could result in a well defined ranking vector – eliminating the need for uniform teleportation. Our goals here were mainly theoretical. However, our first findings in applying this "no teleportation" approach in realistic problems suggest that the conditions for primitivity are not prohibitively restrictive, especially if the criterion behind the definition of the decomposition implies overlapping blocks [14,15].

A very exciting direction we are currently pursuing involves the spectral implications of the absence of the teleportation matrix. In particular, a very interesting problem would be to determine bounds of the subdominant eigenvalue of the stochastic matrix $\mathbf{P} = \eta\mathbf{H} + \mu\mathbf{M}$, when the indicator matrix $\mathbf{W}$ is irreducible. Another important direction would be to proceed to randomized definitions of blocks that satisfy the primitivity criterion and to test the effect on the quality of the ranking vector.

In conclusion, we believe that our results, suggest that the NCDawareRank model presents a promising approach towards generalizing and enriching the standard random surfer model, and also carries the potential of providing an intuitive alternative teleportation scheme to the many applications of PageRank in hierarchical or otherwise specially structured graphs.

References

1. Avrachenkov, K., Litvak, N., Pham, K.S.: Distribution of pagerank mass among principle components of the web. In: Bonato, A., Chung, F.R.K. (eds.) WAW 2007. LNCS, vol. 4863, pp. 16–28. Springer, Heidelberg (2007)
2. Baeza-Yates, R., Boldi, P., Castillo, C.: Generic damping functions for propagating importance in link-based ranking. Internet Math. **3**(4), 445–478 (2006). http://dx.doi.org/10.1080/15427951.2006.10129134
3. Boldi, P.: Totalrank: ranking without damping. In: Special Interest Tracks and Posters of the 14th International Conference on World Wide Web, WWW 2005, pp. 898–899. ACM, New York (2005). http://doi.acm.org/10.1145/1062745.1062787
4. Boldi, P., Santini, M., Vigna, S.: A deeper investigation of pagerank as a function of the damping factor. In: Frommer, A., Mahoney, M.W., Szyld, D.B. (eds.) Web Information Retrieval and Linear Algebra Algorithms, 11-16 February 2007, Dagstuhl Seminar Proceedings, vol. 07071, Internationales Begegnungs- und Forschungszentrum für Informatik (IBFI), Schloss Dagstuhl, Germany (2007). http://drops.dagstuhl.de/opus/volltexte/2007/1072
5. Boldi, P., Santini, M., Vigna, S.: Pagerank: functional dependencies. ACM Trans. Inf. Syst. **27**(4), 1–23 (2009). http://doi.acm.org/10.1145/1629096.1629097
6. Constantine, P.G., Gleich, D.F.: Random alpha pagerank. Internet Math. **6**(2), 189–236 (2009). http://dx.doi.org/10.1080/15427951.2009.10129185
7. Courtois, P.J.: On time and space decomposition of complex structures. Commun. ACM **28**(6), 590–603 (1985). http://doi.acm.org/10.1145/988672.988714
8. Eiron, N., McCurley, K.S., Tomlin, J.A.: Ranking the web frontier. In: Proceedings of the 13th International Conference on World Wide Web, WWW 2004, pp. 309–318. ACM, New York (2004). http://doi.acm.org/10.1145/988672.988714
9. Frobenius, G.: Üeber matrizen aus positiven elementen i and ii. Sitzungsber. Preuss. Akad. Wiss, Berlin (1908)
10. Horn, R.A., Johnson, C.R.: Matrix Analysis. Cambridge University Press, Cambridge (2012)
11. Kamvar, S., Haveliwala, T.: The condition number of the pagerank problem (2003)
12. Langville, A.N., Meyer, C.D.: Google's PageRank and Beyond: The Science of Search Engine Rankings. Princeton University Press, Princeton (2011)
13. Nikolakopoulos, A.N., Garofalakis, J.D.: NCDawareRank: a novel ranking method that exploits the decomposable structure of the web. In: Proceedings of the Sixth ACM International Conference on Web Search and Data Mining, WSDM 2013, pp. 143–152. ACM, New York (2013). http://doi.acm.org/10.1145/2433396.2433415
14. Nikolakopoulos, A.N., Garofalakis, J.D.: NCDREC: a decomposability inspired framework for top-n recommendation. In: 2014 IEEE/WIC/ACM International Joint Conferences on Web Intelligence (WI) and Intelligent Agent Technologies (IAT), Warsaw, Poland, 11–14 August 2014 - Volume II, pp. 183–190. IEEE (2014). http://dx.doi.org/10.1109/WI-IAT.2014.32
15. Nikolakopoulos, A.N., Kouneli, M.A., Garofalakis, J.D.: Hierarchical itemspace rank: exploiting hierarchy to alleviate sparsity in ranking-based recommendation. Neurocomputing **163**, 126–136 (2015). http://www.sciencedirect.com/science/article/pii/S0925231215002180
16. Page, L., Brin, S., Motwani, R., Winograd, T.: The pagerank citation ranking: bringing order to the web (1999)

17. Perron, O.: Zur theorie der matrices. Mathematische Annalen **64**(2), 248–263 (1907)
18. Seneta, E.: Non-negative matrices and markov chains. Springer Series in Statistics. Springer, New York (2006)
19. Simon, H.A.: The Sciences of the Artificial, vol. 136. MIT press, Cambridge (1996)
20. Simon, H.A., Ando, A.: Aggregation of variables in dynamic systems. Econometrica J. Econometric Soc. **29**, 111–138 (1961)

Of Concurrent Data Structures and Iterations

Yiannis Nikolakopoulos[1], Anders Gidenstam[2],
Marina Papatriantafilou[1]([⊠]), and Philippas Tsigas[1]

[1] Chalmers University of Technology, Gothenburg, Sweden
{ioaniko,ptrianta,tsigas}@chalmers.se
[2] University of Borås, Borås, Sweden
anders.gidenstam@hb.se

Abstract. Bulk operations on data structures are widely used both on user-level but also on programming language level. Iterations are a good example of such bulk operations. In the sequential setting iterations are easy to design on top of an algorithmic construction of a data structure and is not considered as a challenge. In a concurrent environment, such as a multicore system, the situation is completely different and the issue of extending concurrent data structure designs to support iteration operations opens new research challenges in concurrent algorithmic data structure implementations, with respect to consistency and efficiency. In this paper we take a journey through this young and evolving research topic. More precisely we describe recent advances in the area together with an overview of iteration implementations that have appeared in the research literature as well as in widely-used programming environments and we outline a range of application targets and challenging future directions.

Keywords: Iteration · Consistency · Lock-free · Concurrent data structures · In-memory computation · Range-queries

1 Introduction

Algorithms + Data Structures = Programs. Wirths book title [43] has become a famous quote and almost a synonym of what the essential components of a computer program are. It shows how data structures are a crucial part of designing and implementing efficient algorithms. An ideal data structure implementation minimizes the complexity of specific access patterns to data that an algorithm requires and integrates it to the data structure's Application Programming Interface (API) (e.g. FIFO queues, LIFO stacks, heaps).

Concurrent Data Structures

The above requirements are even more pronounced when shifting to a concurrent environment, involving multiple processing entities and units of execution. The shared memory model requires mechanisms to ensure the integrity of the

C. Zaroliagis et al. (Eds.): Spirakis Festschrift, LNCS 9295, pp. 358–369, 2015.
DOI: 10.1007/978-3-319-24024-4_20

data, which can be accessed and modified by several threads or processes. Furthermore, the access patterns to the data may be more complex and involve multiple actors with different synchronization needs e.g. getting access to data under some specific synchronization related conditions. The research community has been studying and providing algorithmic designs and implementations of shared memory data structures, including simple designs that incorporate coarse-grain locking, more complex fine-grain locking techniques, non-blocking implementations and flat combining synchronization techniques [9,15,21,24,40].

The different implementations and methodologies provide a variety of performance guarantees in several quantitative and qualitative metrics, such as throughput, scalability and fairness [8] and may comply with a variety of correctness, consistency and progress requirements, thus introducing interesting trade-offs. Balancing amongst all these requirements according to the needs of the applications that use the data structure, remains a key research and implementation issue as is also emphasized recently by Michael [32].

As with any object in a concurrent environment [17], the algorithmic design and implementation of operations provided by shared memory data structures introduces several challenges regarding the correctness requirements and the provided consistency of the operations. The standard definitions that have prevailed in the literature regarding correctness conditions of *non-blocking* implementations are *sequential consistency* [28] and *linearizability* [25]. These consistency specifications have been the main models used in the research literature for arguing about the correctness of parallel and concurrent programs in shared memory systems. In the data structure context there has been a plethora of concurrent implementations using them, cf. [9,24] and references therein.

Extended API in Concurrent Data Structures

Given the increasing interest and use-cases of concurrent data structures, implementations of them appear as part of wide spread programming frameworks [1–3] (Java, .NET, TBB), either in the language or at the library level. In such cases the API of the data structure is usually complemented with additional methods serving other parts of the programming framework like inheritance reasons, compatibility or extended functionality. As an example, Java's ConcurrentLinkedQueue, part of the java.util.concurrent package, is an implementation based on Michael and Scott's lock-free queue [33]. The API in this case, besides the initialize, enqueue and dequeue methods that a queue usually has, is extended with a variety of operations including peek, remove, size, contains, toArray, addAll and iterator. The question that naturally arises is whether the existing consistency specifications are adequate in describing the desired functionality of this extended API.

Specifically, an interesting subset of the above is *bulk operations*, i.e. "meta" operations that consist of a number of operations on the data structure, or a number of primitive operations on sub-components of the data structure. A typical example is *iteration* operations – or *enumeration* as commonly called, where the goal is to gain access to all the items stored in the underlying data structure, usually in a sequential way, without exposing the internal data structure representation. They are usually provided through the use of constructs like *iterators,* *enumerators* or *generators.*

Iterations in Sequential Programming

Iterations have been widely supported in object oriented languages in a sequential context. They were used as building blocks for other language functionalities (e.g. [4,41]), as well as for user level convenience, e.g. to create constructs that would assign values to a for-loop. Watt [41] characterizes iterators as *object-* *based* and *control-based.* The former log the state of the traversal in a separate data structure. According to this state the next steps of the iteration are decided and the new state is updated as they proceed. Algorithm 1 shows a simple iterator of single-linked list based FIFO queue. No special language support is needed in this case, but the iterator implementation gets more difficult the more complex the main data structure is. Control-based iterators rely on specific language constructs (e.g. yield and suspend) that abstract the previous mechanism and assign values to a loop variable, saving the iterator state until another value is needed.

Algorithm 1. Sequential iteration of a FIFO single-linked list based queue.

currentNode ← Head.next
while currentNode.next ≠ NULL **do**
    currentNode ← currentNode.next

Iterations in Concurrent Data Structures: Challenging Issues

Typically, none of the above constructs would take concurrency under consideration. In fact, even the iteration semantics may change when shifting to a concurrent execution. For example, protecting the state of an iteration might come in contrast with the goals of a concurrent system. In data structure implementations, the goal is to allow operations from multiple units of execution to execute concurrently, through fine-grain synchronization or lock-free/wait-free methods [24], enabling to utilize the system parallelism with anticipated benefits in throughput and latency (i.e. operations may execute on different cores simultaneously).

Moreover, such concurrent implementations introduce non-trivial *trade-offs* among the performance throughput, the consistency and ease-of-use by the programmer. Strong consistency guarantees like linearizability [25] and sequential consistency [28] are preferred by the programmer using the data structure. On the other hand, they usually come at a cost of larger algorithmic complexity in the design of the data structure. Some implementations in contemporary programming environments (cf. Sect. 4) provide weaker consistency, but with properties that either are unclear or do not match definitions in the literature.

The trade-offs above, along with the fact that iterations are bulk operations on the data structures, raise questions on the cost of iteration operations under specific consistency requirements in a concurrent implementation. How can concurrency-related behavior be characterized through consistency specifications? Do strong consistency properties have to be expensive and what are the alternatives, if any?

A problem that relates with bulk operations and iterations, is that of acquiring a *snapshot* of a shared memory register [5,14,16,27]. The similarity comes in terms of applying bulk read operations on a shared register where multiple processes write, in order to achieve a desired level of consistency for a snapshot to be returned. Consistency specifications for snapshot objects have evolved from context-specific atomicity and correctness criteria [5], to generally applicable definitions such as linearizability or relaxed guarantees like time-lapse properties [13,27].

Paper Outline

In the rest of this article we describe recent advances in problems related with iteration operations in concurrent data structures. Section 2 gives a brief description of the shared memory model. Section 3 describes the necessary consistency definitions for iteration operations, as formed by the authors of this paper in recent work [35]. Section 4 provides an overview of iteration implementations that have appeared in the research literature as well as in widely-used programming environments. Section 5 associates iteration operations with related bulk operations in current and upcoming systems; that section also outlines possible questions for future work.

2   System Model

We consider the asynchronous shared memory model commonly used in the literature, where a set of processes communicates via reading and writing in shared memory, as also used in earlier work on concurrent iterations [34,35]. The model allows to provide concurrent implementations of a container abstract data type (ADT) that represents a collection of items, including a set of *update* operations that modify the collection according to its specification.

A concurrent ADT implementation can satisfy different progress guarantees. Below we describe the standard definitions in the literature [22–24]: *Wait-freedom* ensures that any process can complete an operation in a finite number of its own steps, independently of any other process. An implementation is *bounded wait-free* if there exists a bound on the number of steps any process takes to complete an operation. In a *lock-free* object implementation it is ensured that at least one of the contending operations makes progress in a finite number of its own steps. It is common in lock-free implementations of ADTs that an operation is implemented through fail-retry loops: a retry needs to take place due to one or more *interfering* operations among the contending ones. A weaker guarantee is *obstruction freedom*: progress is only ensured for any process that eventually runs in isolation, i.e. in absence of interferences from other operations.

We define a *run* ρ (or *history*) as an execution of an arbitrary number of operations on the ADT according to the respective protocol that implements the ADT. For each update operation a of an ADT that exists in a run ρ, we call its *duration* the time interval $[s_a, f_a]$, where s_a and f_a are the starting and finishing times of a. Thus, a precedence relation $\rightarrow$ is defined over the operations, which is a strict partial order. For two operations a and b, $a \rightarrow b$ means that f_a occurs before s_b. If two operations can not be compared under $\rightarrow$, they are concurrent and we say that they overlap. In this work, we consider only runs of complete executions, where there are no pending operations. A *sequential* history ρ, is one where no operations overlap. We denote a prefix of a *sequential* history ρ ending with an operation a, as $pref_\rho(a)$. We define $state_\rho(a)$ as the postcondition of the ADT after the operation a, i.e. the items that exist in the collection after the execution of a in ρ.

A history is *linearizable* [25] if it is equivalent to a sequential history that includes the same operations and the total order of the sequential operations respects the partial order $\rightarrow$. The equivalent sequential history is also called a linearization σ. Thus, a run ρ of a linearizable ADT implementation induces a set of total orders, that extend the partial order $\rightarrow$ in a compatible way with the sequential semantics of the ADT. For each linearization σ of ρ, the respective total order is denoted as $\Rightarrow_\sigma$. As in the sequential case, for every operation a in a linearizable run ρ we respectively define $state_\sigma(a)$ as the postcondition of the ADT after operation a, in a prefix of some linearization σ of ρ that ends with a. In this notation we will drop the parameter σ when it is clear from the context.

For a given linearizable ADT implementation consider the set of all its possible states; a state S from this set is defined to be *valid with respect to a linearizable execution* ρ, if $\exists$ a linearization σ of ρ such that there exists a $pref_\sigma(a)$ and $S = state_\sigma(a)$.

The ADT includes *update* operations that can add or remove items in the collection in accordance to the specification of the ADT. We extend the ADT and linearizable implementations of them, and add *iteration* operations that will return a state of the ADT and in particular the items that are contained in it, with the following sequential specification:

Definition 1. [35] *In a sequential execution ρ, a valid iteration Itr returns the items contained in $state_\rho(a)$, where a is the latest update operation preceding Itr, i.e. $Itr : state_\rho(a)$, where $a \rightarrow Itr \wedge \nexists$ update operation a' s.t. $a \rightarrow a' \rightarrow Itr$.*

Given a run ρ, we can define the *reduced run* $\tilde{\rho}$, that does not include iteration operations.

3 Framework of Consistency Definitions for Concurrent Iterations

This section presents consistency definitions for iteration operations described in [34,35], building on the consistency-related definitions by Lamport [29] and

Herlihy and Wing [25]. In the following it is assumed that the reduced run $\tilde{\rho}$ that does not include the iteration operations is linearizable and thus for each linearization σ of $\tilde{\rho}$ the respective $\Rightarrow_\sigma$ is defined.

Definition 2. *(i)* **Safeness:** *An iteration operation $Itr \in \rho$, not overlapping with any other operation in $\tilde{\rho}$, is safe if it returns a valid state $S = state_\sigma(a)$ for some linearization σ of $\tilde{\rho}$ and some operation a, such that: $Itr \not\rightarrow a$ and $\nexists$ update operation $a' : a \Rightarrow_\sigma a' \rightarrow Itr$. If Itr is overlapping with any operations of $\tilde{\rho}$, it can return any arbitrary state of the object.*

(ii) **Regularity:** *An iteration operation $Itr \in \rho$, possibly overlapping with some $a \in \tilde{\rho}$, is regular if it returns a valid state $S = state_\sigma(a)$ for some linearization σ of $\tilde{\rho}$ and some operation a, such that: $Itr \not\rightarrow a$ and $\nexists$ update operation $a' : a \Rightarrow_\sigma a' \rightarrow Itr$, i.e. S is neither "future" nor "overwritten".*

(iii) **Monotonicity:** *For any two iteration operations Itr_1, Itr_2 that return valid states $state_\sigma(a_1)$ and $state_\sigma(a_2)$ respectively for some linearization σ of $\tilde{\rho}$, if $Itr_1 \rightarrow Itr_2$, then $a_1 \Rightarrow_\sigma a_2$ or $a_1 = a_2$.[1]*

(iv) **Linearizability:** *Itr is linearizable if it is regular and the run ρ is equivalent to some sequential history, that includes the same operations, whose total order respects the partial order of the original run ρ.*

Definition 3. Weak regularity: *Let an iteration operation $Itr \in \rho$ and the reduced linearizable run $\tilde{\rho}$. Let a be the latest update operation finished before s_{Itr}, and $pref_\sigma(a)$ the respective prefix for some linearization σ of $\tilde{\rho}$. A weakly regular Itr returns a state S such that $S = state_\tau(b)$, for some operation b in a run $\tau = pref_\sigma(a) \cup ops_{[s_{Itr},f_{Itr}]}$, that extends the $pref_\sigma(a)$ with $ops_{[s_{Itr},f_{Itr}]}$, i.e. an arbitrary number of operations that are overlapping with the execution interval $[s_{Itr}, f_{Itr}]$.*

Informally, we can see that a safe iteration implementation guarantees recent and valid returned states only in the case that it does not overlap with any modification operations. Otherwise any arbitrary state can be returned (e.g. empty). A regular iteration improves by guaranteeing a valid and "not future" state to be returned even in the present of concurrent modifications. However, there is no restriction on a regular iteration implementation on whether to actually include in the returned state the effect of one (or more) overlapping modification operations. Thus regularity can allow relaxed enough implementations for the following example to occur: let Itr_1 an instance of a regular iteration, and an overlapping modification operation a. It is interesting to note that another regular Itr_2, such that $Itr_1 \rightarrow Itr_2$ but Itr_2 still overlapping a, might return a different state – even preceding– from the one returned by Itr_1 (if for example Itr_1 includes the effect of a in its state). Monotonicity is an additional property that can clarify such behavior and the combination with regularity can guarantee

---

[1] Dwork et al. [13] in the context of composite registers used two notions of monotonicity, for scans and for updates. Notice that a regular Itr also satisfies the monotonicity of updates property, i.e. for two linearized updates, an Itr that "observes" the effects of the latter update, should also "observe" the effects of the preceding update.

linearizability for "single-scanner" iterations (cf. Theorem 1 [35]). Finally, iteration implementations in contemporary programming environments (cf. Sect. 4), motivate the need for a weaker definition between safeness and regularity. Weak regularity essentially allows to include or ignore any of the overlapping modification operations, regardless of their respective linearization order.

Correctness conditions related to the above were recently presented by Lev-ari et al. [30], where regularity is extended for single-writer data structures under read-write concurrency. The authors show similar intuition for their respective regularity definition, while they motivate the need for even weaker conditions as the ones presented above [34].

4   An Overview of Iteration Algorithms and Implementations

In the Resarch Literature of Parallel and Distributed Algorithms

Ctrie. The first design of a concurrent data structure that integrated an iteration operation was presented by Prokopec et al. [39]. They present *Ctrie*, a concurrent lock-free hash trie, that besides the usual lookup, insert and remove operations, supports a snapshot operation upon which iteration and size operations are built. *Ctrie* is designed partially as a persistent data structure [36] with immutable states, and the snapshot operation relies on the fact that modification operations will create a newer generation of the data structure content, while the snapshot retains access to the previous one. Thus, the snapshot is considered constant-time ($O(1)$), while the updating of the trie to the newer generation is delegated to the update operations, increasing their constant factor. Nevertheless, to guarantee linearizability, strong synchronization primitives are still required. The authors suggest a variation of a Double-Compare-Single-Swap (RDCSS) software primitive [20], to make sure that no concurrent updates will occur while the generation is changing.

Iterators on Sets. Iteration operations in ordered linked-list based implementations of sets were presented by Petrank and Timnat [37]. The authors build on Jayanti's single scanner snapshot algorithm on composite registers [26], which provides only scan and update operations for the individual registers. They extend it to accommodate multiple iterators as well as the necessary insert, delete and contains operations that the set semantics require. Their method includes an object that holds a list of pointers to nodes in the main data structure and a list of reports of operations that happened during the basic traversal. The commutativity properties of the set semantics are exploited, allowing the snapshot operation to linearize before the linearization points of insert operations that occurred during the traversal. The iteration operation has a complexity of $O(n + r \cdot log(r))$, where r is the size of the report list and n is the size of the main linked list traversed. However, the latter may dynamically increase by updates interfering the iteration.

Iterators in Parallel Collections. Prokopec et al. [38] present a different approach on iterators in collection data structures. They do not address issues of iterations concurrently with modification operations, but focus on the parallelization of iteration operations instead. They develop a framework for parallel programming patterns such as map-reduce or parallel looping for bulk operations, and abstract it by using *splitters.* These are abstractions for iteration operations that can be used from different threads to give access to disjoint parts of the data structure.

Iteration Consistency and the Queue Test-case. A set of consistency specifications for iteration operations (cf. Sect. 3) is proposed by the authors of the present article in [34,35]. The aforementioned work further presents an exploration of the algorithmic design space for iteration operations in shared lock-free queues and provide a set of constructions of iteration operations satisfying the consistency properties. *Weakly regular* iterations are presented based on simple traversals of the queue and by exploiting the inherent structural properties of the linked-list based queues. They are also compared with similar implementations that exist in Java's concurrency library [2]. The authors point out and study the trade-offs on achieving linearizable iteration implementations between the overhead of the bulk operation and possible support (helping) by the native operations of the data structure. *Linearizable* iterations can be achieved by typical read-validate techniques that may starve, providing only *obstruction-freedom.* Concurrent modification operations can help the iteration operation by marking nodes of the queue with appropriate timestamp information. Thus, linearizable iteration algorithms that provide *wait-free* progress guarantees can be designed, with the use of synchronization software primitives like multi-word compare and swap [20]. The reason is that due to the non-commutative nature of the queue's native operations, inconsistencies between the time of insertion and the respective timestamp have to be eliminated.

In Contemporary Programming Environments

Programming frameworks, such as Intel's Thread Building Blocks for C++ (TBB), Java and the .NET platform, include, in their standard libraries, collection data structures that support concurrent operations. These collections often support iteration over their contents while other operations may concurrently change the data structure. What kind of consistency do they offer?

Java: The standard library of the Java Platform Standard Edition 7[2] contains a number of concurrent collection or container data types that support iteration over their contents concurrently with operations that modify them. The documentation classifies the consistency of an iteration of a particular container data type as either *snapshot style*, described as capturing the state of the container at the point in time the iterator was created, or *weakly consistent*, for the ConcurrentLinkedQueue described as "returning elements reflecting the state of

---

[2] Version 1.7.0_09.

the queue at some point at or since the creation of the iterator" and similarly for other data structures. A study of the source code for the `ConcurrentLinkedQueue` reveals that the description is not entirely accurate: the result may be a mixture of the states that occur during the iteration and can include items removed early during the interval together with items added late, i.e. not reflecting the state at any particular point in time.

.NET: The .NET 4.5 Framework Class library [3] contains a number of concurrent container data structures. All of them support iteration of their contents concurrently with operations that modify them. The library documentation classifies what an iteration of a particular container type provides as either a *moment-in-time snapshot* or not a *moment-in-time snapshot*. The container types `ConcurrentBag`, `ConcurrentQueue` and `ConcurrentStack` provide *moment-in-time snapshots* while the `ConcurrentDictionary` type does not. For the latter it is stated that the contents exposed during the iteration may contain modifications made to the dictionary after the iteration started.

Intel Threading Building Blocks: It is a library for parallel programming in C++ [1] that contains a number of concurrent container data structures, some of which support iterations concurrently with other operations on the container. The support is limited to a subset of their operations; only three, namely `concurrent_unordered_map`, `concurrent_unordered_set` and `concurrent_vector` support insertion concurrently with iteration, but do not promise any particular level of consistency.

   In summary, Java's *snapshot style* and .NET's *moment-in-time snapshots* can be expected to be linearizable (or nearly so). The consistency of Java's *weakly consistent* iterators varies in detail for each implementation, and the unspecified thread-safe iterators in .NET and TBB are weakly regular.

5   Possible Applications and Research Questions

Iterations form the basis of operations that meet challenges in many of the new, demanding applications in concurrent environments. In the era of Big Data and the Internet of Things, in-memory analytics are becoming more and more important, and parallelism and concurrency are essential tools.

   Map and filter operations can in fact be built upon iterations, as also shown in Prokopec et al. [38]. Paradigms of such operations, running over large evolving data sets concurrently with other operations, may be proved valuable for real-time analytics.

   In the latest version of Java, the *stream* API is introduced. The idea is to allow parallel programming patterns such as map-reduce computations to run on streams of data that may even be unbounded. As a source of a stream, either another stream is allowed or a collection data structure, possibly concurrent. Streams from the latter are built by using bulk operations that are a generalization of iterations, called *spliterators*. For most of the concurrent collections they provide weak consistency guarantees (as in Definition 3), and they allow also parallelization (similar to the concept of [38]).

Range queries or *partial iterations* for in-memory processing is another example where iterations are useful. Essentially, range queries can be viewed as partial iterations inside a data structure. Traditionally in the database domain, data structures supporting range queries [42] were introduced to handle search queries of multiple multi-dimensional records. Examples of today's use cases are On-Line Analytical Processing systems [11,12]. These delineate algorithmic and consistency challenges for concurrent data structures. Avni et al. [6] explore designs of data structures supporting range queries, based on transactional memory support. Brown and Avni [7] present a non-blocking *k*-ary search tree that supports linearizable range queries, achieving only obstruction-freedom though. Partial iterations on concurrency- and application-aware data objects, such as e.g. sets, flat-sets and data-streaming-oriented objects [10,18,19,31], can prove very useful in this direction as well.

The questions in this domain are challenging, ranging from consistency definitions that are useful for applications, to algorithmic implementations that enable possibilities for the programmers to smoothly manage efficiency and consistency trade-offs that manifest in applications. It is expected that the consistency framework [35] will be useful for several types of such bulk operations in a wide range of concurrent objects, as it incorporates definitions across several levels of strength, that build on each-other. Besides the weakly regular constructions that already map to some state of the art implementations, *regular* iteration implementations are expected to balance consistency and performance trade-offs, and thus form a challenging direction for future work.

Acknowledgements. The research leading to these results has been partially supported by the European Union Seventh Framework Programme (FP7/2007-2013) through the EXCESS Project (www.excess-project.eu) under grant agreement 611183 and by the Swedish Research Council (Vetenskapsrådet) project "Fine-grain synchronization in parallel programming", contract nr. 2010-4801.

References

1. Intel threading building blocks documentation. http://software.intel.com/sites/products/documentation/doclib/tbb_sa/help/index.htm. Accessed on 27 November 2012
2. Java platform standard edition 7 documentation. http://docs.oracle.com/javase/7/docs/index.html. Accessed on 06 December 2012
3. .NET framework class library documentation. http://msdn.microsoft.com/en-us/library/gg145045.aspx. Accessed on 10 May 2013
4. Python v2.7.5 documentation. http://docs.python.org/2/library/itertools.html. Accessed on 10 September 2013
5. Anderson, J.H.: Multi-writer composite registers. Distrib. Comput. **7**(4), 175–195 (1994)
6. Avni, H., Shavit, N., Suissa, A.: Leaplist: lessons learned in designing TM-supported range queries. In: Proceedings of the 2013 ACM Symposium on Principles of Distributed Computing, PODC 2013, pp. 299–308. ACM, New York, NY, USA (2013)

7. Brown, T., Avni, H.: Range queries in non-blocking k-ary search trees. In: Baldoni, R., Flocchini, P., Binoy, R. (eds.) OPODIS 2012. LNCS, vol. 7702, pp. 31–45. Springer, Heidelberg (2012)

8. Cederman, D., Chatterjee, B., Nguyen, N., Nikolakopoulos, Y., Papatriantafilou, M., Tsigas, P.: A study of the behavior of synchronization methods in commonly used languages and systems. In: 2013 IEEE 27th International Symposium on Parallel & Distributed Processing (IPDPS), pp. 1309–1320, May 2013

9. Cederman, D., Gidenstam, A., Ha, P., Sundell, H., Papatriantafilou, M., Tsigas, P.: Lock-free concurrent data structures. arXiv:1302.2757 [cs], February 2013

10. Cederman, D., Gulisano, V., Nikolakopoulos, Y., Papatriantafilou, M., Tsigas, P.: Brief announcement: concurrent data structures for efficient streaming aggregation. In Proceedings of the 26th ACM Symposium on Parallelism in Algorithms and Architectures, SPAA 2014, pp. 76–78 (2014)

11. Dehne, F., Kong, Q., Rau-Chaplin, A., Zaboli, H., Zhou, R.: A distributed tree data structure for real-time OLAP on cloud architectures. In: 2013 IEEE International Conference on Big Data, pp. 499–505, October 2013

12. Dehne, F., Zaboli, H.: Parallel real-time OLAP on multi-core processors. In: Proceedings of the 2012 12th IEEE/ACM International Symposium on Cluster, Cloud and Grid Computing (ccgrid 2012), pp. 588–594 (2012)

13. Dwork, C., Herlihy, M., Plotkin, S., Waarts, O.: Time-lapse snapshots. SIAM J. Comput. **28**(5), 1848–1874 (1999)

14. Fatourou, P., Fich, F.E., Ruppert, E.: Time-space tradeoffs for implementations of snapshots. In: Proceedings of the Thirty-eighth Annual ACM Symposium on Theory of Computing, STOC 2006, pp. 169–178, ACM, New York, NY, USA (2006)

15. Fatourou, P., Kallimanis, N.D.: Revisiting the combining synchronization technique. SIGPLAN Not. **47**(8), 257–266 (2012)

16. Fich, F.E.: How hard is it to take a snapshot? In: Vojtáš, P., Bieliková, M., Charron-Bost, B., Sýkora, O. (eds.) SOFSEM 2005. LNCS, vol. 3381, pp. 28–37. Springer, Heidelberg (2005)

17. Gidenstam, A., Koldehofe, B., Papatriantafilou, M., Tsigas, P.: Scalable group communication supporting configurable levels of consistency. Concurrency Comput: Pract. Experience **25**(5), 649–671 (2013)

18. Gidenstam, A., Papatriantafilou, M., Tsigas, P.: NBmalloc: allocating memory in a lock-free manner. Algorithmica **58**(2), 304–338 (2010)

19. Gulisano, V., Nikolakopoulos, Y., Papatriantafilou, M., Tsigas, P.: ScaleJoin: a deterministic, disjoint-parallel and skew-resilient stream join enabled by concurrent data structures. Technical Report, Chalmers University of Technology (2014)

20. Harris, T.L., Fraser, K., Pratt, I.A.: A practical multi-word compare-and-swap operation. In: Malkhi, D. (ed.) DISC 2002. LNCS, vol. 2508, pp. 265–279. Springer, Heidelberg (2002)

21. Hendler, D., Incze, I., Shavit, N., Tzafrir, M.: Flat combining and the synchronization-parallelism tradeoff. In: Proceedings of the Twenty-second Annual ACM Symposium on Parallelism in Algorithms and Architectures, SPAA 2010, pp. 355–364. ACM, New York, NY, USA (2010)

22. Herlihy, M.: Wait-free synchronization. ACM Trans. Prog. Lang. Syst. **13**(1), 124–149 (1991)

23. Herlihy, M., Luchangco, V., Moir, M.: Obstruction-free synchronization: double-ended queues as an example. In: ICDCS 2003, IEEE Computer Society (2003)

24. Herlihy, M., Shavit, N.: The Art of Multiprocessor Programming. Morgan Kaufmann, Burlington (2008)

25. Herlihy, M.P., Wing, J.M.: Linearizability: a correctness condition for concurrent objects. ACM Trans. Prog. Lang. Syst. **12**(3), 463–492 (1990)
26. Jayanti, P.: An optimal multi-writer snapshot algorithm. In: Proceedings of the Thirty-seventh Annual ACM Symposium on Theory of Computing, STOC 2005, pp. 723–732. ACM, New York, NY, USA (2005)
27. Kirousis, L., Spirakis, P., Tsigas, P.: Reading many variables in one atomic operation: solutions with linear or sublinear complexity. IEEE Trans. Parallel Distrib. Syst. **5**(7), 688–696 (1994)
28. Lamport, L.: How to make a multiprocessor computer that correctly executes multiprocess programs. IEEE Transactions on Computers **C–28**(9), 690–691 (1979)
29. Lamport, L.: On interprocess communication. Distrib. Comput. **1**(2), 86–101 (1986)
30. Lev-Ari, K., Chockler, G., Keidar, I.: On correctness of data structures under reads-write concurrency. In: Kuhn, F. (ed.) DISC 2014. LNCS, vol. 8784, pp. 273–287. Springer, Heidelberg (2014)
31. Michael, M.M.: High performance dynamic lock-free hash tables and list-based sets. In: Proceedings of the Fourteenth Annual ACM Symposium on Parallel Algorithms and Architectures, SPAA 2002, ACM (2002)
32. Michael, M.M.: The balancing act of choosing nonblocking features. Commun. ACM **56**(9), 46–53 (2013)
33. Michael, M.M., Scott, M.L.: Simple, fast, and practical non-blocking and blocking concurrent queue algorithms. In: Proceedings of the Fifteenth Annual ACM Symposium on Principles of Distributed Computing, PODC 1996, pp. 267–275. ACM, New York, NY, USA (1996)
34. Nikolakopoulos, Y., Gidenstam, A., Papatriantafilou, M., Tsigas, P.: Enhancing concurrent data structures with concurrent iteration operations: consistency and algorithms. Technical report, Chalmers University of Technology (2013)
35. Nikolakopoulos, Y., Gidenstam, A., Papatriantafilou, M., Tsigas, P.: A consistency framework for iteration operations in concurrent data structures. In: 2015 IEEE 29th International Symposium on Parallel & Distributed Processing (IPDPS) (2015)
36. Okasaki, C.: Purely Functional Data Structures. Cambridge University Press, New York (1999)
37. Petrank, E., Timnat, S.: Lock-free data-structure iterators. In: Afek, Y. (ed.) DISC 2013. LNCS, vol. 8205, pp. 224–238. Springer, Heidelberg (2013)
38. Prokopec, A., Bagwell, P., Rompf, T., Odersky, M.: A generic parallel collection framework. In: Jeannot, E., Namyst, R., Roman, J. (eds.) Euro-Par 2011, Part II. LNCS, vol. 6853, pp. 136–147. Springer, Heidelberg (2011)
39. Prokopec, A., Bronson, N.G., Bagwell, P., Odersky, M.: Concurrent tries with efficient non-blocking snapshots. In: PPoPP 2012, pp. 151–160. ACM (2012)
40. Sundell, H., Tsigas, P.: NOBLE: a non-blocking inter-process communication library. In: Proceedings of the 6th Workshop on Languages, Compilers and Runtime Systems for Scalable Computers, Lecture Notes in Computer Science. Springer Verlag (2002)
41. Watt, S.M.: A technique for generic iteration and its optimization. In: Proceedings of the 2006 ACM SIGPLAN Workshop on Generic programming, WGP 2006, pp. 76–86. ACM (2006)
42. Willard, D.E.: New data structures for orthogonal range queries. SIAM J. Comput. **14**(1), 232–253 (1985)
43. Wirth, N.: Algorithms + Data Structures = Programs. Prentice Hall PTR, Upper Saddle River (1978)

On Some Combinatorial Properties
of Random Intersection Graphs

Sotiris E. Nikoletseas[1,2] and Christoforos L. Raptopoulos[2](✉)

[1] Computer Engineering and Informatics Department,
University of Patras, Patras, Greece
nikole@cti.gr
[2] Computer Technology Institute and Press "Diophantus",
Patras, Greece
raptopox@ceid.upatras.gr

Abstract. In this paper, we consider a simple, yet general family of random graph models, namely *Random Intersection Graphs (RIGs)*, which are motivated by applications in secure sensor networks, social networks and many more. In such models there is a universe $\mathcal{M}$ of *labels* and each one of n vertices selects a random subset of $\mathcal{M}$. Two vertices are connected if and only if their corresponding subsets of labels intersect. In particular, we briefly review the state of the art and we present key results from our research on the field, that highlight and take advantage of the intricacies and special structure of random intersection graphs. Finally, we present in more detail a particular result from our research, which concerns maximum cliques in the uniform random intersection graphs model (in which every vertex selects each label independently with some probability p), namely the Single Label Clique Theorem.

1 Introduction and Motivation

Random graphs, introduced by P. Erdős and A. Rényi in 1959, still attract a huge amount of research in the communities of Theoretical Computer Science, Algorithms, Graph Theory, Discrete Mathematics and Statistical Physics. This continuing interest is due to the fact that, besides their mathematical beauty, such graphs are very important, since they can model interactions and faults in networks and also serve as typical inputs for an average case analysis of algorithms. The modeling effort concerning random graphs has to show a plethora of random graph models; some of them have quite elaborate definitions and are quite general, in the sense that they can simulate many other known distributions on graphs by carefully tuning their parameters.

In this report, we consider a simple, yet general family of models, namely *Random Intersection Graphs (RIGs)*. In such models there is a universe $\mathcal{M}$ of *labels* and each one of n vertices selects a random subset of $\mathcal{M}$. Two vertices are connected if and only if their corresponding subsets of labels intersect.

Random intersection graphs have been used in various applications including secure sensor networks [4,25,27], social networks [6,26], clustering [6], and

C. Zaroliagis et al. (Eds.): Spirakis Festschrift, LNCS 9295, pp. 370–383, 2015.
DOI: 10.1007/978-3-319-24024-4_21

cryptanalysis [3]. An important application of random intersection graphs is to model the topologies of secure wireless sensor networks employing the Chan-Perrig-Song key predistribution scheme [7], which is widely recognized as an appropriate solution to secure communications between sensors. In such a key predistribution scheme for an n-size sensor network, prior to deployment, each sensor is assigned a set of distinct cryptographic keys selected at random from the same key pool containing m different keys. After deployment, two sensors establish secure communication if and only if they have some key(s) in common, and this gives rise to communication graphs that look like random intersection graphs. Furthermore, random intersection graphs are relevant to and capture quite nicely social networking. Indeed, a social network is a structure made of nodes tied by one or more specific types of interdependency, such as values, visions, financial exchange, friends, conflicts, web links etc. Other applications may include oblivious resource sharing in a distributed setting, interactions of mobile agents traversing the web, social networking etc. Even epidemiological phenomena (like spread of disease between individuals with common character-istics in a population) tend to be more accurately captured by this "proximity-sensitive" family of random graphs.

1.1 Definitions and a First Look at RIGs

Random intersection graphs were introduced by M. Karoński, E.R. Sheinerman and K.B. Singer-Cohen [12] and K.B. Singer-Cohen [23]. The formal definition of the model is given below:

Definition 1 (Uniform Random Intersection Graph - $\mathcal{G}_{n,m,p}$ [12,23]). *Consider a universe $\mathcal{M} = \{1, 2, \ldots, m\}$ of labels and a set of n vertices V. Assign independently to each vertex $v \in V$ a subset S_v of $\mathcal{M}$, choosing each element $i \in \mathcal{M}$ independently with probability p and draw an edge between two vertices $v \neq u$ if and only if $S_v \cap S_u \neq \emptyset$. The resulting graph is an instance $G_{n,m,p}$ of the uniform random intersection graphs model.*

In this model we also denote by L_i the set of vertices that have chosen label $i \in \mathcal{M}$. Given $G_{n,m,p}$, we will refer to $\{L_i, i \in \mathcal{M}\}$ as its *label representation*. It is often convenient to view the label representation as a bipartite graph with vertex set $V \cup \mathcal{M}$ and edge set $\{(v,i) : i \in S_v\} = \{(v,i) : v \in L_i\}$. We refer to this graph as the *bipartite random graph $B_{n,m,p}$ associated to $G_{n,m,p}$.* Notice that the associated bipartite graph is uniquely defined by the label representation.

It follows from the definition of the model the (unconditioned) probability that a specific edge exists is $1 - (1 - p^2)^m$. Therefore, if mp^2 goes to infinity with n, then this probability goes to 1. We can thus restrict the range of the parameters to the "interesting" range where $mp^2 = O(1)$ (i.e. the range of values for which the unconditioned probability that an edge exists does not go to 1). Furthermore, as is usual in the literature, we assume that the number of labels is some power of the number of vertices, i.e. $m = n^\alpha$, for some $\alpha > 0$.

It is worth mentioning that the edges in $G_{n,m,p}$ are not independent. In particular, there is a strictly positive dependence between the existence of two edges that share an endpoint (i.e. $\Pr(\exists\{u,v\}|\exists\{u,w\}) > \Pr(\exists\{u,v\}))$. This dependence is stronger the smaller the number of labels $\mathcal{M}$ includes, while it seems to fade away as the number of labels increases. In fact, by using a coupling technique, the authors in [9] prove the equivalence (measured in terms of total variation distance) of uniform random intersection graphs and Erdős-Rényi random graphs, when $m = n^\alpha, \alpha > 6$. This bound on the number of labels was improved in [21], by showing equivalence of sharp threshold functions among the two models for $\alpha \geq 3$. These results show that random intersection graphs are quite general and that known techniques for random graphs can be used in the analysis of uniform random intersection graphs with a large number of labels.

The similarity between uniform random intersection graphs and Erdős-Rényi random graphs vanishes as the number of labels m decreases below the number of vertices n (i.e. $m = n^\alpha$, for $\alpha \leq 1$). This dichotomy was initially pointed out in [23], through the investigation of connectivity of $G_{n,m,p}$. In particular, it was proved that the connectivity threshold for $\alpha > 1$ is $\sqrt{\frac{\ln n}{nm}}$, but it is $\frac{\ln n}{m}$ (i.e. quite larger) for $\alpha \leq 1$. Therefore, the mean number of edges just above connectivity is approximately $\frac{1}{2}n\ln n$ when $\alpha > 1$ (which is equal to the mean number of edges just above the connectivity threshold for Erdős-Rényi random graphs), but it is larger by at least a factor of $\ln n$ when $\alpha \leq 1$. Other dichotomy results of similar flavor were pointed out in the investigation of the (unconditioned) vertex degree distribution by D. Stark [24], through the analysis of a suitable generating function, and in the investigation of the distribution of the number of isolated vertices by Y. Shang [22].

In this work, we present part of our research that is related to both combinatorial and algorithmic properties of uniform random intersection graphs, but also of other, related models that are included in the family of random intersection graphs. In particular, we note that by selecting the label set of each vertex using a different distribution, we get random intersection graphs models whose statistical behavior can vary considerably from that of $G_{n,m,p}$. Two of these models are the following: (a) In the **General Random Intersection Graphs Model** $G_{n,m,\boldsymbol{p}}$ [16], where $\boldsymbol{p} = [p_1, p_2, \ldots, p_m]$, the label set S_v of a vertex v is formed by choosing independently each label i with probability p_i. (b) In the **Regular Random Intersection Graphs Model** $G_{n,m,\lambda}$ [11], where $\lambda \in \mathbb{N}$, the label set of a vertex is chosen independently, uniformly at random for the set of all subsets of $\mathcal{M}$ of cardinality λ. Finally, it is worth noting that there are other equally important generalizations of the uniform model of RIGs, perhaps most notably the random s-intersection graphs model [26], in which two vertices are connected if and only if they share at least s elements of $\mathcal{M}$ (where s is a fixed, predefined integer).

2 An Overview of Selected Combinatorial Problems

Below we provide a brief presentation of some results on RIGs obtained by our team. We also give a general description of the techniques used; some of these techniques highlight and take advantage of the intricacies and special structure of random intersection graphs, while others are adapted from the field of Erdős-Rényi random graphs.

2.1 Independent Sets

The problem of the existence and efficient construction of large independent sets in general random intersection graphs is considered in [16]. Concerning existence, exact formulae are derived for the expectation and variance of the number of independent sets of any size, by using a *vertex contraction technique*. This technique involves the characterization of the statistical behavior of an independent set of any size and highlights an *asymmetry* in the edge appearance rule of random intersection graphs. In particular, it is shown that the probability that any fixed label i is chosen by some vertex in a k-size S with no edges is exactly $\frac{kp_i}{1+(k-1)p_i}$. On the other hand, there is no closed formula for the respective probability when there is at least one edge between the k vertices (or even when the set S is complete)! The special structure of random intersection graphs is also used in the design of efficient algorithms for constructing quite large independent sets in uniform random intersection graphs. By analysis, it is proved that the approximation guarantees of algorithms using the label representation of random intersection graphs are superior to that of well known greedy algorithms for independent sets when applied to instances of $\mathcal{G}_{n,m,p}$.

2.2 Hamilton Cycles

In [20], the authors investigate the existence and efficient construction of *Hamilton cycles* in uniform random intersection graphs. In particular, for the case $m = n^\alpha, \alpha > 1$ the authors first prove a general result that allows one to apply (with the same probability of success) any algorithm that finds a Hamilton cycle with high probability in a $G_{n,M}$ random graph (i.e. a graph chosen equiprobably form the space of all graphs with M edges). The proof is done by using a simple coupling argument. A more complex coupling was given in [8], resulting in a more accurate characterization of the threshold function for Hamiltonicity in $G_{n,m,p}$ for the whole range of values of α. From an algorithmic perspective, the authors in [20] provide an expected polynomial time algorithm for the case where $m = O\left(\sqrt{\frac{n}{\ln n}}\right)$ and p is constant. For the more general case where $m = o\left(\frac{n}{\ln n}\right)$ they propose a *label exposure* greedy algorithm that succeeds in finding a Hamilton cycle in $G_{n,m,p}$ with high probability, even when the probability of label selection is just above the connectivity threshold.

2.3   Coloring

In [14], the problem of coloring the vertices of $G_{n,m,p}$ is investigated (see also [2]). For the case where the number of labels is less than the number of vertices and $mp \geq \ln^2 n$ (i.e. a factor $\ln n$ above the connectivity threshold of uniform random intersection graphs), a polynomial time algorithm is proposed for finding a *proper coloring* $G_{n,m,p}$. The algorithm is greedy-like and it is proved that it takes $O\left(\frac{n^2 mp^2}{\ln n}\right)$ time, while using $\Theta\left(\frac{nmp^2}{\ln n}\right)$ different colors. Furthermore, by using a one sided coupling to the regular random intersection graphs model $G_{n,m,\lambda}$ with $\lambda \sim mp$, and using an upper bound on its independence number from [18], it is shown that the number of colors used by the proposed algorithm is optimal up to constant factors.

To complement this result, the authors in [14] prove that when $mp < \beta \ln n$, for some small constant β, only np colors are needed in order to color $n - o(n)$ vertices of $G_{n,m,p}$ whp. This means that even for quite dense instances, using the same number of colors as those needed to properly color the clique induced by any label suffices to color almost all of the vertices of $G_{n,m,p}$. For the proof, the authors explore a combination of ideas from [10] and [13]. In particular, a martingale $\{X_t\}_{t \geq 0}$ is defined, so that X_n is equal to the maximum subset of vertices that can be properly colored using a predefined number of colors k. Then, by providing an appropriate lower bound on the probability that there is a sufficiently large subset of vertices that can be split in k independent sets of roughly the same size, and then using Azuma's Inequality for martingales, the authors provide a lower bound on $E[X_n]$ and also show that the actual value X_n is highly concentrated around its mean value.

Finally, due to the similarities that the $\mathcal{G}_{n,m,p}$ model has to the process of generating random hypergraphs, [14] includes a comparison of the problem of finding a proper coloring for $G_{n,m,p}$ to that of coloring hypergraphs so that no edge is monochromatic. In contrast to the first problem, it is proved that only two colors suffice for the second problem. Furthermore, by using the *method of conditional expectations* (see [19]) an algorithm can be derived that finds the desired coloring in polynomial time.

2.4   Expansion and Random Walks

The edge expansion and the cover time of uniform random intersection graphs is investigated in [15]. In particular, by using first moment arguments, the authors first prove that $G_{n,m,p}$ is an expander whp when the number of labels is less than the number of vertices, even when p is just above the connectivity threshold (i.e. $p = (1 + o(1))\tau_c$, where τ_c is the connectivity threshold). Second, the authors show that random walks on the vertices of random intersection graphs are whp *rapidly mixing*, i.e. the time until the random walk is sufficiently close to its steady state distribution (namely its *mixing time* [1]) is logarithmic on n. The proof is based on upper bounding the second eigenvalue of the random walk on $G_{n,m,p}$ through coupling of the original Markov Chain describing the random walk to another Markov Chain on an associated random bipartite graph whose conductance properties are appropriate. Finally, the authors prove that the *cover time* of the random walk on $G_{n,m,p}$, when $m = n^\alpha, \alpha < 1$ and p is at least 5 times the connectivity threshold is $\Theta(n \log n)$, which is optimal up to a constant. The proof is based on a general theorem of Cooper and Frieze [5]; the authors prove that the degree and spectrum requirements of the theorem hold whp in the case of uniform random intersection graphs. The authors also claim that their proof also carries over to the case of smaller values for p, but the technical difficulty for proving the degree requirements of the theorem of [5] increases.

3 Maximum Cliques

In this section, we present in more detail a particular result from our work [17] on maximum cliques in the uniform random intersection graphs model $G_{n,m,p}$, namely the *Single Label Clique Theorem* (cf. Theorem 1). Its proof includes a coupling to a graph model where edges appear independently and in which we can bound the size of the maximum clique by well known probabilistic techniques. The Single Label Clique Theorem roughly states that when the number of labels is less than the number of vertices, any large enough clique in a random instance of $G_{n,m,p}$ is formed by a single label. This statement may seem obvious when p is small, but it is hard to imagine that it still holds for *all* "interesting" values for p. Indeed, when $p = o\left(\sqrt{\frac{1}{nm}}\right)$, by slightly modifying an argument of [2], one can see that $G_{n,m,p}$ almost surely has no cycle of size $k \geq 3$ whose edges are formed by k distinct labels (alternatively, the intersection graph produced by reversing the roles of labels and vertices is a tree). On the other hand, for larger p a random instance of $G_{n,m,p}$ is far from perfect[1] and the techniques of [2] do not apply. By using the Single Label Clique Theorem, a tight bound on the clique number of $G_{n,m,p}$ is proved, in the case where $m = n^\alpha, \alpha < 1$. A lower bound in the special case where mp^2 is constant, was given in [23]. We considerably broaden this range of values to also include vanishing values for mp^2 and also provide an asymptotically tight upper bound.

We first provide some concentration results concerning the number of vertices that have chosen a particular label and the number of labels that have been chosen by a particular vertex.

Lemma 1. *Let $G_{n,m,p}$ be a random instance of the random intersection graphs model with $m = n^\alpha, 0 < \alpha < 1$ and $p = \Omega\left(\sqrt{\frac{1}{nm}}\right)$. Then the following hold:*

A. *Let L_i be the set of vertices that have chosen label $i \in \mathcal{M}$. Then*

$$\Pr(\exists i \in \mathcal{M} : ||L_i| - np| \geq 3\sqrt{np \ln n}) \leq \frac{1}{n^3} \to 0. \tag{1}$$

---

[1] A *perfect graph* is a graph in which the chromatic number of every induced subgraph equals the size of the largest clique of that subgraph. Consequently, the clique number of a perfect graph is equal to its chromatic number.

B. *Let also S_v denote the set of labels that were chosen by vertex v. Then*

$$\Pr(\exists v \in V : |S_v| > mp + 3\sqrt{mp \ln m} + \ln n) \to 0. \tag{2}$$

Proof. For the first part, fix a label $i \in \mathcal{M}$. Notice that $|L_i|$ is a binomial random variable with parameters n, p, i.e. $|L_i| \sim \mathcal{B}(n, p)$. By Chernoff bounds, for any $t \geq 0$, we have that

$$\Pr(||L_i| - np| \geq t) \leq e^{-\frac{t^2}{2\left(np+\frac{t}{3}\right)}} + e^{-\frac{t^2}{2np}}.$$

Setting $t = 3\sqrt{np \ln n}$ and noting that $t = o(np)$, we then have that $\Pr(||L_i| - np| \geq 3\sqrt{np \ln n}) \leq e^{-4\ln n}$ and the lemma follows from Boole's inequality.

For the second part, fix a vertex v. Notice that $|S_v|$ is a binomial random variable with parameters m, p, i.e. $|S_v| \sim \mathcal{B}(m, p)$. By Chernoff bounds, for any $\delta \geq 0$, we have that

$$\Pr(|S_v| > (1 + \delta)mp) < \left(\frac{e^\delta}{(1 + \delta)^{(1+\delta)}}\right)^{mp}.$$

Setting $\delta = \frac{1}{mp}(3\sqrt{mp \ln m} + \ln n)$ and using Boole's inequality we get the desired result. $\qquad\square$

Notice that the above lemma provides a lower bound on the clique number. However, a clique in $G_{n,m,p}$ can be formed by combining more than one label. Clearly, a clique Q which is not formed by a single label will need at least 3 labels, since 2 labels cannot cover all the edges needed for Q to be a clique. In the discussion below, we will provide a much larger lower bound on the number of labels needed to form a clique Q of size $|Q| \sim np$ which is not formed by a single label. The following definition will be useful.

Definition 2. *Denote by $A_{y,x}$ the event that there are two disjoint sets of vertices $V_1, V_2 \subset V$, where $|V_1| = y$ and $|V_2| = x$ such that the following hold:*

1. *All vertices in V_1 have chosen some label l_0, i.e. $l_0 \in \cap_{u \in V_1} S_u$.*
2. *None of the vertices in V_2 has chosen l_0, i.e. $l_0 \notin \cup_{v \in V_2} S_v$.*
3. *Every vertex in V_1 is connected to every vertex in V_2.*

As a warm-up, we prove the following technical lemma, which is a first indication that in a $G_{n,m,p}$ graph, whp we cannot have y too large and x too small at the same time. This lemma will also be used as a starting step in the proof of our main theorem.

Lemma 2. *Let $G_{n,m,p}$ be a random instance of the random intersection graphs model with $m = n^\alpha, 0 < \alpha < 1$ and $p = \Omega\left(\sqrt{\frac{1}{nm}}\right)$ and $mp^2 = O(1)$. Then, for any $y \geq np\left(1 - o\left(\frac{1}{\ln n}\right)\right)$, $\Pr(A_{y,1}) = o(1)$.*

Proof. Fix a particular label l_0, a subset V_1 of the vertices having chosen l_0 (i.e. $V_1 \subset L_{l_0}$) and a vertex $v \notin L_{l_0}$. The probability that v is connected to all vertices in V_1 is exactly

$$p(V_1, v) \overset{def}{=} \sum_{k=1}^{m-1} \binom{m-1}{k} p^k (1-p)^{m-k-1} (1-(1-p)^k)^y. \tag{3}$$

Indeed, $p^k(1-p)^{m-k-1}$ is the probability that v has chosen k specific labels different from l_0 and $1-(1-p)^k$ the probability that a specific vertex in V_1 has chosen at least one of those labels (so that it is connected to v).

By Boole's and Markov's inequality we then have that

$$\Pr(A_{y,1}) \leq m \binom{|L_{l_0}|}{y} (n - |L_{l_0}|) p(V_1, v) \tag{4}$$

By Lemma 1, for any vertex v, we have that $|S_v| \leq (1+o(1))mp + \ln n$ whp. Since $(1-(1-p)^k)^y$ is increasing in k and also $\binom{m-1}{k} p^k (1-p)^{m-k-1}$ is maximum around mp, we conclude that the maximum of $\binom{m-1}{k} p^k (1-p)^{m-k-1} (1-(1-p)^k)^y$ for $k \in \{1 \ldots (1+o(1))mp\}$ is attained at some index $k' = (1+o(1))mp$. Therefore,

$$\Pr(A_{y,1}) \leq m^2 n \binom{|L_{l_0}|}{y} \binom{m-1}{k'} p^{k'} (1-p)^{m-k'-1} (1-(1-p)^{k'})^y + o(1) \tag{5}$$

$$\leq m^2 n \binom{|L_{l_0}|}{y} (1-(1-p)^{k'})^y + o(1) \tag{6}$$

where the $o(1)$ term corresponds to the error term from Lemma 1. Using now the fact that (by the expansion of the natural logarithm) $(1-p)^{\frac{1}{p}} = e^{\frac{1}{p}\ln(1-p)} = e^{-\sum_{j=1}^{\infty} \frac{p^{j-1}}{j}} \geq e^{-1-\sum_{j=2}^{\infty} p^{j-1}} = e^{-1-\frac{p}{1-p}} \geq e^{-1.1}$, for any $p \to 0$, we have that

$$\Pr(A_{y,1}) \leq m^2 n \binom{|L_{l_0}|}{y} (1 - e^{-2mp^2})^y + o(1) \tag{7}$$

$$= m^2 n \binom{|L_{l_0}|}{|L_{l_0}| - y} (1 - e^{-2mp^2})^y + o(1) \tag{8}$$

$$\leq m^2 n (|L_{l_0}|)^{|L_{l_0}| - y} (1 - e^{-2mp^2})^y + o(1). \tag{9}$$

For any $y \geq |L_{l_0}| \left(1 - o\left(\frac{1}{\ln n}\right)\right)$, we then have that $\Pr(A_{y,1}) \to 0$. But by Lemma 1 we have also that $|L_{l_0}| \leq np\left(1 + o\left(\frac{1}{\ln n}\right)\right)$, which completes the proof. □

The above lemma has the following alternative interpretation, which will be useful in the sequence:

Corollary 1. *Let $G_{n,m,p}$ be a random instance of the random intersection graphs model with $m = n^\alpha, 0 < \alpha < 1$, $p = \Omega\left(\sqrt{\frac{1}{nm}}\right)$ and $mp^2 = O(1)$. Let also Q be a clique in $G_{n,m,p}$ that is not formed by a single label and also $|Q| \sim np$. If $l_0 \in \mathcal{M}$ is any label chosen by some vertex $v \in Q$, then there is a positive constant $c' < \frac{1-\alpha}{2}$, such that whp there are at least $n^{c'}$ vertices in Q that have not chosen l_0.*

Proof. Notice that, by assumption, $np = \Omega(n^{\frac{1-\alpha}{2}})$. Therefore, for any positive $c' < \frac{1-\alpha}{2}$, we have that $n^{c'} = o\left(\frac{np}{\ln^2 n}\right)$. The result then follows by Lemma 2. $\square$

We now strengthen the above analysis by using the following simple observation: For a set of vertices V_2 and $k \geq 2$, let $S_{V_2}^{(k)} \subseteq \mathcal{M}$ denote the set of labels that have been chosen by at least k of the vertices in V_2. Then the probability that every vertex of a set of vertices V_1 is connected to every vertex in V_2 is at most

$$p(V_1, V_2) \leq \left(|S_{V_2}^{(2)}|p + (1-p)^{|S_{V_2}^{(2)}|} \prod_{v \in V_2} \left(1 - (1-p)^{|S_v - S_{V_2}^{(2)}|}\right)\right)^y \tag{10}$$

$$\leq \left(|S_{V_2}^{(2)}|p + \prod_{v \in V_2} \left(1 - (1-p)^{|S_v|}\right)\right)^y \tag{11}$$

Indeed, the first of the above inequalities corresponds to the probability that each vertex in V_2 either choses one of the labels shared by at least two vertices in V_2, or it is connected to all vertices in V_2 by using labels chosen by exactly one vertex in V_2.

Lemma 3. *Let $G_{n,m,p}$ be a random instance of the random intersection graphs model with $m = n^\alpha, 0 < \alpha < 1$, $p = \Omega\left(\sqrt{\frac{1}{nm}}\right)$ and $mp^2 = O(1)$. Let also $x = \frac{1}{p^\epsilon}$, for some positive constant $\epsilon < 1$ that can be as small as possible. Then, for any $y \geq np^{1+c}$, where $0 < c < \frac{1-\alpha}{1+\alpha}$ is a constant, we have $\Pr(A_{y,x}) = o(1)$.*

Proof. Fix a set V_2 of x vertices. We first give an upper bound on the size of $S_{V_2}^{(2)}$. Towards this end, let $X = |S_{V_2}^{(2)}|$ and notice that X is binomially distributed with parameters $m, \hat{p} = 1 - (1-p)^x - xp(1-p)^{x-1}$. Since, by assumption $xp \to 0$, we have that $\hat{p} \leq \frac{x^2 p^2}{2}$. Therefore X is stochastically dominated by a binomial random variable $Y \sim \mathcal{B}\left(m, \frac{x^2 p^2}{2}\right)$.

By Chernoff bounds we then have, for any $t \geq 0$,

$$\Pr\left(X > \frac{mx^2p^2}{2} + t\right) \leq e^{-\frac{t^2}{2\left(\frac{mx^2p^2}{2} + \frac{t}{3}\right)}} \tag{12}$$

Set $t = \frac{1}{p^{2\epsilon + \epsilon'}}$, where ϵ' is a positive constant that can be as small as possible. Since $mp^2 = O(1)$, we have that $t = \omega\left(\frac{mx^2p^2}{2}\right)$. By Boole's inequality then, the probability that there is a subset V_2 of x vertices that has $|S_{V_2}^{(2)}| > \frac{mx^2p^2}{2} + \frac{x^2}{p^{\epsilon'}}$ is at most

$$n^x e^{-\frac{1}{3p^{2\epsilon + \epsilon'}}} = o(1). \tag{13}$$

Now that we have an upper bound on the size of $S_{V_2}^{(2)}$ that holds whp, notice that by the second part of Lemma 1 and the fact that $mp^2 = O(1)$, whp we have

$$\prod_{v \in V_2} \left(1 - (1-p)^{|S_v|}\right) \leq \frac{1}{2^{\Theta(x)}} = o(|S_{V_2}^{(2)}|p). \tag{14}$$

Therefore, by (11), we have that $p(V_1, V_2) \leq (2|S_{V_2}^{(2)}|p)^{|V_1|}$. By Boole's and Markov's inequality we then have that

$$\Pr(A_{y,x}) \leq m \binom{|L_{l_0}|}{y} n^x p(V_1, V_2) \tag{15}$$

$$\leq m \binom{|L_{l_0}|}{y} n^x (2|S_{V_2}^{(2)}|p)^y + o(1) \tag{16}$$

$$\leq m \binom{|L_{l_0}|}{y} n^x \left(2p^{1--2\epsilon-\epsilon'}\right)^y + o(1) \tag{17}$$

where the $o(1)$ term corresponds to the error terms from Lemma 1 and Eq. (13). Using now the first part of Lemma 1 and an upper bound for the binomial coefficient we have

$$\Pr(A_{y,x}) \leq m \left(\frac{8np}{y}\right)^y n^x \left(p^{1--2\epsilon-\epsilon'}\right)^y + o(1). \tag{18}$$

Setting $y = np^{1+c}$, for any positive constant $c < \frac{1-\alpha}{1+\alpha}$, we have ($y \geq 1$ and also) that $\Pr(A_{y,x}) = o(1)$. This completes the proof. $\qquad \square$

Lemma 3 has the following interpretation:

Corollary 2. *Let $G_{n,m,p}$ be a random instance of the random intersection graphs model with $m = n^\alpha, 0 < \alpha < 1, p = \Omega\left(\sqrt{\frac{1}{nm}}\right)$ and $mp^2 = O(1)$. Let also Q be a clique in $G_{n,m,p}$ that is not formed by a single label and also $|Q| \sim np$. Then whp, for any label $l_0 \in \mathcal{M}$, we have that $|Q \cap L_{l_0}| \leq np^{1+c}$, where $0 < c < \frac{1-\alpha}{1+\alpha}$ is a constant.*

In particular, if Q is not formed by a single label, then whp it is formed by at least $\frac{1}{p^c}$ distinct labels.

Proof. By Corollary 1, if Q is not formed by a single label, then given any label $l_0 \in \mathcal{M}$ which is chosen by some vertex $v \in Q$, there is a positive constant $c' < \frac{1-\alpha}{2}$, such that whp there are at least $n^{c'}$ vertices in Q that have not chosen l_0. Therefore, we can apply Lemma 3 using any $\epsilon < \frac{2c'}{1+\alpha}$. More specifically, for any such ϵ we have $\Pr(A_{np^{1+c}, \frac{1}{p^c}}) = o(1)$.

Additionally, this implies that whp if Q is not formed by a single label, it needs at least $\frac{np}{np^{1+c}} = \frac{1}{p^c}$ distinct labels. This is also a lower bound on the number of labels needed by a vertex v in order to connect to all vertices in Q. $\square$

Before presenting the proof of our main theorem, we prove the following useful lemma, which states that if a large clique is not formed by a single label, then it must contain a quite large clique Q' whose edges are formed by distinct labels.

Lemma 4. *Let $G_{n,m,p}$ be a random instance of the random intersection graphs model with $m = n^\alpha, 0 < \alpha < 1, p = \Omega\left(\sqrt{\frac{1}{nm}}\right)$ and $mp^2 = O(1)$. Let also Q be any clique in $G_{n,m,p}$ that is not formed by a single label and also $|Q| \sim np$. Then whp, Q contains a clique Q' whose edges are formed by distinct labels and whose size is at least $p^{-\frac{c}{2}}$, for any positive constant $c < \frac{1-\alpha}{1+\alpha}$.*

Proof. Let Q' be a subset of Q which is maximal with respect to the following property $\mathcal{P}$: "to each pair of vertices $u \neq v$ in Q' we can assign a distinct label l, such that $l \in S_u \cap S_v$".

Consider now the set of vertices $W = \{w : S_w \cap S_{Q'}^{(2)} \neq 0\}$, namely the set of vertices that share a label with at least 2 vertices in Q' (note that $Q' \subseteq W$, because every pair of vertices in Q is connected). Since Q' is maximal, the set $Q - W$ must be the empty set. Indeed, if $z \in Q - W$, then (bearing in mind that Q is a clique) z can be connected to each vertex in Q' using distinct labels, which are also different from those already used to connect pairs of vertices in Q'. Therefore, $Q' \cup \{z\}$ would also have property $\mathcal{P}$, which contradicts the maximality of Q'.

By Corollary 2 now, we have that $|W| \leq |S_{Q'}^{(2)}|np^{1+c}$, where $0 < c < \frac{1-\alpha}{1+\alpha}$ is a constant. Furthermore, by Eq. (13), we have that $|S_{Q'}^{(2)}| \leq \frac{m|Q'|^2p^2}{2} + \frac{|Q'|^2}{p^{\epsilon'}}$ whp, for any $\epsilon' > 0$ that can be as small as possible. Combining the above, and since $mp^2 = O(1)$, we have that

$$|W| \leq \frac{np^{1+c}|Q'|^2}{(1+o(1))p^{\epsilon'}}. \tag{19}$$

Consequently, the requirement $Q - W = \emptyset$ translates to

$$|Q| - \frac{np^{1+c}|Q'|^2}{(1+o(1))p^{\epsilon'}} \leq 0 \tag{20}$$

or equivalently

$$|Q'| \geq \sqrt{\frac{|Q|}{(1+o(1))np^{1+c-\epsilon'}}}. \tag{21}$$

Bearing in mind that $|Q| \sim np$ and that $\epsilon' > 0$ can be as small as possible, this completes the proof. $\qquad\square$

We now present our main theorem.

Theorem 1 (Single Label Clique Theorem). *Let $G_{n,m,p}$ be a random instance of the random intersection graphs model with $m = n^\alpha, 0 < \alpha < 1$ and $mp^2 = O(1)$. Then whp, any clique Q of size $|Q| \sim np$ in $G_{n,m,p}$ is formed by a single label. In particular, the maximum clique is formed by a single label.*

Proof. We first note that, as discussed in the beginning of Sect. 3, when $p = o\left(\sqrt{\frac{1}{nm}}\right)$, by slightly modifying an argument of [2] (in particular Lemma 5 there), we can see that $G_{n,m,p}$ almost surely has no cycle of size $k \geq 3$ whose edges are formed by k distinct labels. Therefore, the maximum clique of $G_{n,m,p}$ when $p = o\left(\sqrt{\frac{1}{nm}}\right)$, is formed by exactly one label and our theorem holds. Consequently, we will assume w.l.o.g. for the remainder of the proof that $p = \Omega\left(\sqrt{\frac{1}{nm}}\right)$.

Let Q be a clique of size $|Q| \sim np$ in $G_{n,m,p}$. By Lemma 4, if Q is not formed by a single label, then $G_{n,m,p}$ must contain a clique Q' whose edges are formed by distinct labels and whose size is at least $\beta \overset{def}{=} p^{-\frac{c}{2}}$, for any positive constant $c < \frac{1-\alpha}{1+\alpha}$. Notice also that, given the existence of any x edges, the (conditional) probability that another edge is formed using a different label from those already used by the x edges is at most $1 - (1-p^2)^{m-x} \le 1 - (1-p^2)^m$. By the union bound then, the probability that such a Q' exists in $G_{n,m,p}$ is at most

$$\Pr\{Q' \; exists \; in \; G_{n,m,p}\} \le n^\beta \left(1 - (1-p^2)^m\right)^{\binom{\beta}{2}} \tag{22}$$

$$\le n^\beta (1 - e^{-1.1mp^2})^{\binom{\beta}{2}} \tag{23}$$

$$\le e^{\beta \ln n - \binom{\beta}{2} e^{-1.1mp^2}} = e^{\beta \ln n - \Theta(\beta^2)} = o(1) \tag{24}$$

where in the second inequality we used the fact that $(1-p^2)^{\frac{1}{p^2}} \ge e^{-1.1}$, for any $p \to 0$ (for the proof of an identical fact see the proof of Lemma 2). Therefore, whp Q' does not exist in $G_{n,m,p}$, which completes the proof. $\square$

Notice that, by Theorem 1, the maximum clique in $G_{n,m,p}$ with $m = n^\alpha, 0 < \alpha < 1$ and $mp^2 = O(1)$ must be one of the sets $L_l, l \in \mathcal{M}$. Therefore, the clique number of $G_{n,m,p}$ can be bounded using the first part of Lemma 1. In particular,

Corollary 3. *Let $G_{n,m,p}$ be a random instance of the random intersection graphs model with $m = n^\alpha, 0 < \alpha < 1$, $p = \Omega\left(\sqrt{\frac{1}{nm}}\right)$ and $mp^2 = O(1)$. Then, whp the maximum clique Q of $G_{n,m,p}$ satisfies $|Q| \sim np$.*

4   Epilogue

We discussed here progress made by our team on the Random Intersection Graphs (RIGs) Model. The topic is still new and many more properties await to be discovered especially for the General (non-Uniform) version of RIGs. Such graphs (and other new graph classes) are motivated by modern technology, and thus, some combinatorial results and algorithmic properties may become useful in order to understand and exploit emerging networks nowadays.

Acknowledgment. This paper is devoted to our mentor Paul Spirakis, on the occasion of his 60th birthday. It was Paul who pointed out to us the very interesting model of Random Intersection Graphs and inspired us to work, as a team, on its exploration.

References

1. Aldous, D., Fill, J.A.: Reversible Markov Chains and Random Walks on Graphs. Unfinished monograph, recompiled (2014). Accessed on http://www.stat.berkeley.edu/~aldous/RWG/book.html

2. Behrisch, M., Taraz, A., Ueckerdt, M.: Coloring random intersection graphs and complex networks. SIAM J. Discrete Math. **23**, 288–299 (2008)
3. Blackburn, S., Stinson, D., Upadhyay, J.: On the complexity of the herding attack and some related attacks on hash functions. Des. Codes Crypt. **64**(1–2), 171–193 (2012)
4. Bloznelis, M., Jaworski, J., Rybarczyk, K.: Component evolution in a secure wireless sensor network. Networks **53**, 19–26 (2009)
5. Cooper, C., Frieze, A.: The cover time of sparse random graphs. Random Struct. Algorithms **30**, 1–16 (2007)
6. Deijfen, M., Kets, W.: Random intersection graphs with tunable degree distribution and clustering. Probab. Eng. Inform. Sci. **23**, 661–674 (2009)
7. Chan, H., Perrig, A., Song, D.: Random key predistribution schemes for sensor networks. In: Proceedings of the IEEE Symposium on Security and Privacy (2003)
8. Efthymiou, C., Spirakis, P.G.: Sharp thresholds for Hamiltonicity in random intersection graphs. Theor. Comput. Sci. **411**(40–42), 3714–3730 (2010)
9. Fill, J.A., Sheinerman, E.R., Singer-Cohen, K.B.: Random intersection graphs when $m = \omega(n)$: an equivalence theorem relating the evolution of the $G(n, m, p)$ and $G(n, p)$ models. Random Struct. Algorithms **16**(2), 156–176 (2000)
10. Frieze, A.: On the Independence Number of Random Graphs. Disc. Math. **81**, 171–175 (1990)
11. Godehardt, E., Jaworski, J.: Two models of random intersection graphs for classification. In: Opitz, O., Schwaiger, M. (eds.) Exploratory Data Analysis in Empirical Research. Studies in Classification, Data Analysis, and Knowledge Organization, pp. 67–82. Springer, Heidelberg (2002)
12. Karoński, M., Sheinerman, E.R., Singer-Cohen, K.B.: On random intersection graphs: the subgraph problem. Comb. Probab. Comput. j. **8**, 131–159 (1999)
13. Luczak, T.: The chromatic number of random graphs. Combinatorica **11**(1), 45–54 (2005)
14. Nikoletseas, S., Raptopoulos, C., Spirakis, P.G.: Colouring non-sparse random intersection graphs. In: Královič, R., Niwiński, D. (eds.) MFCS 2009. LNCS, vol. 5734, pp. 600–611. Springer, Heidelberg (2009)
15. Nikoletseas, S., Raptopoulos, C., Spirakis, P.G.: Expander properties and the cover time of random intersection graphs. Theor. Comput. Sci. **410**(50), 5261–5272 (2009)
16. Nikoletseas, S., Raptopoulos, C., Spirakis, P.G.: Large independent sets in general random intersection graphs. Theor. Comput. Sci. **406**, 215–224 (2008)
17. Nikoletseas, S., Raptopoulos, C., Spirakis, P.G.: Maximum cliques in graphs with small intersection number and random intersection graphs. In: Rovan, B., Sassone, V., Widmayer, P. (eds.) MFCS 2012. LNCS, vol. 7464, pp. 728–739. Springer, Heidelberg (2012)
18. Nikoletseas, S., Raptopoulos, C., Spirakis, P.G.: On the independence number and hamiltonicity of uniform random intersection graphs. Theor. Comput. Sci. **412**(48), 6750–6760 (2011)
19. Molloy, M., Reed, B.: Graph Colouring and the Probabilistic Method. Springer, Heidelberg (2002)
20. Raptopoulos, C., Spirakis, P.G.: Simple and efficient greedy algorithms for hamilton cycles in random intersection graphs. In: Deng, X., Du, D.-Z. (eds.) ISAAC 2005. LNCS, vol. 3827, pp. 493–504. Springer, Heidelberg (2005)
21. Rybarczyk, K.: Equivalence of a random intersection graph and $G(n, p)$. Random Struct. Algorithms **38**(1–2), 205–234 (2011)

22. Shang, Y.: On the isolated vertices and connectivity in random intersection graphs. Int. J. Comb. **2011**. Article ID 872703 (2011). doi:10.1155/2011/872703
23. Singer-Cohen, K.B.: Random Intersection Graphs. Ph.D. thesis, John Hopkins University (1995)
24. Stark, D.: The vertex degree distribution of random intersection graphs. Random Struct. Algorithms **24**(3), 249–258 (2004)
25. Yağan, O., Makowski, A.M.: Zero-one laws for connectivity in random key graphs. IEEE Trans. Inf. Theor. **58**(5), 2983–2999 (2012)
26. Zhao, J., Yağan, O., Gligor, V.: On k-connectivity and minimum vertex degree in random s-intersection graphs. Arxiv e-prints (2014). Accessed on http://arxiv.org/pdf/1409.6021v3.pdf
27. Zhao, J., Yağan, O., Gligor, V.: On the strengths of connectivity and robustness in general random intersection graphs. In: Proceedings of the IEEE Conference on Decision and Control (CDC), December 2014

Efficient Equilibrium Concepts
in Non-cooperative Network Formation

Panagiota N. Panagopoulou[✉]

Computer Technology Institute and Press "Diophantus", Patras, Greece
panagopp@cti.gr

Abstract. We review here some recently proposed models of non-coope-rative network creation games where the nodes of a network perform edge swaps in order to improve their communication costs. Our focus is on examining the structure of stable (equilibrium) networks that correspond to efficient notions of equilibria, in the sense that the nodes of the network are able to decide which links to add and which to remove in order to achieve a minimal cost, given the strategies of the other nodes. We also review results on the capability of the network nodes of converging into an equilibrium network by performing local selfish improvement steps.

1 Introduction

Large scale networks, such as the Internet, are built, maintained and used by selfish entities, all of whom aim at optimizing their own cost and quality of network usage. This suggests that such individual entities will have an incentive to form connections with others to shape the network in ways that are advantageous to themselves. A *network creation game* specifies a set of players, the link formation actions available to each player and the payoffs to each player from the networks that arise out of the link formation action profiles adopted by the players. There are many potential models of network creation games that can be considered, depending on which individuals have the decision power to form or delete a link (i.e., which subset of nodes forms the set of players, and what are their available strategies), as well as on the specification of the payoff allocation rule (i.e., what is the cost of forming or deleting a link and under which objectives do the selfish individuals evaluate the quality of a network).

The study of network creation games focuses on *strategically stable* or *equilibrium* networks, i.e., networks where there are no incentives for individual players to form or delete links and thereby alter the network. We are interested in both *static* and *dynamic* properties of equilibrium networks. Static properties include the structure (i.e., the topologies) of equilibrium networks, while, on the other

This work was partially supported by the European Social Fund and Greek national funds through the research funding program Thales on "Algorithmic Game Theory" and by the EU ERC Project "ALGAME".

© Springer International Publishing Switzerland 2015
C. Zaroliagis et al. (Eds.): Spirakis Festschrift, LNCS 9295, pp. 384–395, 2015.
DOI: 10.1007/978-3-319-24024-4_22

hand, dynamic properties of equilibrium networks specify whether (and how fast) selfish players can actually converge into a stable network and thus find a desired equilibrium.

Fabrikant et al. [4] introduced a simple network formation game, where each player is identified with a node, and each node can choose to create a link between itself and any subset of other nodes. Each link requires a fixed cost $\alpha > 0$ to be built, and each player has two competing goals: to pay for as few links as possible, and to minimize the distance to all other players in the resulting network. In particular, the objective of each player is to minimize the sum of costs of the links created by herself plus the sum of distances to all other nodes of the resulting network. In such a setting, the network is in equilibrium if no node can improve its objective cost by deleting and/or creating *any subset* of incident links.

This model of a network creation game is simple enough, while it captures the flexibility of nodes to create and delete links as well as the trade-off between the cost of creating links and the cost of reaching the other nodes of the network. However, it has a main drawback: it is NP-hard to compute a *best response* of a node. That is, a (computationally bounded) node cannot decide which links to add and which to remove in order to achieve a minimal cost, given the strategies of the other nodes. This implies that the players of the game can not even decide whether they are in equilibrium or not, which further implies that the nodes are incapable of converging into an equilibrium network by performing local selfish improvements.

In view of the above drawback, Alon et al. [2] proposed a simpler model, namely the *basic network creation game*. In this game the nodes are significantly less flexible in creating and deleting links: in particular, a node can only *swap* an existing link with another, i.e., delete an incident link and create a new incident link. Alon et al. [2] considered two different objectives for the nodes, yielding two versions of a basic network creation game: In the sum version, the cost of a node is the sum of its distances to all other nodes, while in the max version the cost of a node is the greatest distance between itself and any other node (i.e., the *eccentricity* of the node, using graph-theoretic terminology). A network is in *swap equilibrium* if no node can decrease its cost by deleting an incident link and creating a new one. With this restriction on the available strategies of each node, it is easy to see that swap equilibria (under either cost objective) can be detected in polynomial time: each node simply has to check each possible swap of a non-neighboring node with a neighboring one.

The *asymmetric basic network creation game*, introduced in [6], is similar to the basic game of [2], but here the ownership of a link plays a crucial role: only the single owner of a link is allowed to swap the link. In the *greedy buy basic network creation game*, introduced in [8], nodes have more freedom to act: a node is allowed to buy (at some cost α) or to delete or to swap one own link. It is assumed that nodes behave greedily, in the sense that they compute the best augmentation, deletion or swap by trying all possibilities and re-computing the incurred cost. This greedy behavior naturally leads to a new solution concept, the *greedy equilibrium*, in which no node can decrease her cost by buying, deleting, or swapping a link.

Even though the model of [2] and its extensions of [6,8] are more basic than the model of [4] (in the sense that better responses can be determined in polynomial time), they still rely on the fact that each vertex/player has global knowledge of the graph, which is needed to compute its cost function. In view of the above, a new swap-based network creation game was presented in [7], in which selfish costs depend on the immediate neighborhood of each vertex/player. In particular, the profit of each vertex is defined to be the sum of the degrees of its neighbors, which is also related to the number of paths of length two from that vertex. This model tends to capture selfish behavior that appears in large distributed systems of computationally bounded selfish entities. One of the interesting observations for this model is that vertices have a tendency to connect to high degree vertices.

Note that all the above notions of equilibria can be detected easily in polynomial time, in the sense that deciding whether a given state is an equilibrium can be solved in polynomial time: simply try every possible edge swap and deletion. Thus these equilibria are more natural for computationally bounded vertices.

2   Notation and Graph-Theoretic Background

Let $G = (V, E)$ be an undirected graph. For a vertex $v \in V$, we denote by $N_G(v)$ the set of neighbors of v in G. We will denote by Δ_G the maximum degree of a vertex of G, i.e., $\Delta_G = \max_{v \in V} \deg(v)$, where $\deg(v) = |N_G(v)|$. For any two vertices $v, u \in V$ we will denote by $dist_G(u, v) = dist_G(v, u)$ the length of a shortest path between u and v in G. We denote by $diam(G)$ the diameter of G, defined as

$$diam(G) = \max_{u \in V, v \in V} dist_G(u, v).$$

The *local diameter* $D_G(v)$ of a vertex v is the maximum distance between v and any other vertex: $D_G(v) = \max_{u \in V} dist_G(u, v)$. For any vertex $v \in V$ we will denote by $W_G(v)$ the sum of distances of all vertices from v in G, i.e., $W_G(v) = \sum_{u \in V} dist_G(u, v)$. If the graph is disconnected, then we define $W_G(v)$ to be infinite.

A graph is *deletion-critical* if deleting any single edge strictly increases the local diameter of both of its endpoints. A graph is *insertion-stable* if inserting any single edge does not decrease the local diameter of either endpoint.

Following the notation in [2], for any vertex $u \in V$ and any k, we will denote by $B_u(k)$ the k-vicinity of u, i.e. $B_u(k) = \{w : dist(w, u) \leq k\}$. We will omit the subscripts G in the above notation if the graph is understood from the context.

3   The Basic Network Creation Game

We will first describe more formally the model of basic network creation games proposed in [2]. We are given an undirected graph $G = (V, E)$, where each vertex corresponds to a player. A player can perform "edge swaps", i.e., replace an incident existing edge with another incident edge. More formally, let $u \in N_G(v)$ and $w \notin N_G(v)$. Then, the edge swap (u, w) of v removes the edge $\{v, u\}$ and creates the edge $\{v, w\}$. Therefore, the set of pure strategies of player $v \in V$ in graph G is $S_G(v) = \{N_G(v) \times \{V \setminus \{N_G(v) \cup \{v\}\}\}\}$. Observe that the set of pure strategies of a player depends on the current graph G and that an edge swap performed by a player modifies the graph. We denote by G_{s_v} the graph obtained from G when player v performs the edge swap $s_v \in S_G(v)$.

The *connection cost* of player $v \in V$ is the sum of distances between v and all other vertices, i.e., equals $W_G(v)$. We say that a graph is in *swap sum equilibrium* if no player (vertex) can improve her connection cost by performing an edge swap.

Definition 1. *The graph* $G = (V, E)$ *is in swap sum equilibrium if for all* $v \in V$, $W_G(v) \leq W_{G_{s_v}}(v)$ *for all* $s_v \in S_G(v)$.

We say that a graph is in *swap max equilibrium* if no vertex can improve her local diameter by performing an edge swap, and, furthermore, deleting an incident edge strictly increases the local diameter of a vertex.

Definition 2. *The graph* $G = (V, E)$ *is in swap max equilibrium if it is deletion-critical and, for all* $v \in V$, $D_G(v) \leq D_{G_{s_v}}(v)$ *for all* $s_v \in S_G(v)$.

Note that, if a graph is both insertion-stable and deletion-critical, then it is certainly in max equilibrium.

Structure of Equilibria. For the sum version, it is shown in [2] that there is essentially only one equilibrium tree. In particular, if a graph in swap sum equilibrium is a tree, then it has diameter at most 2, and thus is a star.

In contrast to the sum version, trees in swap max equilibrium can have diameter as high as 3. However, this diameter is the maximum possible. To prove this, [2] showed that, in any graph in swap max equilibrium, (i) the local diameters of any two nodes differ by at most 1 and (ii) if the equilibrium graph has a cut vertex v, then only one connected component of $G - v$ can have a vertex of distance more than 1 from v. Therefore, there are two families of max equilibrium trees: stars (of diameter 2) and "double-stars" (of diameter 3). To be in max equilibrium, the latter type must have at least two leaves attached to each star root.

For the sum version and general topologies of equilibrium graphs, an upper bound of $2^{O(\sqrt{\log n})}$ on the diameter of equilibrium graphs is proven in [2]. Furthermore, it is conjectured that the diameter of sum equilibrium graphs is polylogarithmic, and interesting evidence for this conjecture is offered. Note that the best known lower bound on the diameter is 3 (this claim appears in [2]; a correct proof is provided in [1]).

For the max version and general equilibrium graphs, a strong lower bound of $\Omega(\sqrt{n})$ on the diameter of graphs which are both insertion-stable and deletion-critical, which are graphs in swap max equilibrium, is given. In [2] it is also shown how to construct graphs that are both deletion-critical and stable under

k insertions, meaning that the graph is stable when the vertex is permitted to change any k (incident) edges. A lower bound of $\Omega(n^{1/(k+1)})$ is proven in this case, giving a smooth trade-off between diameter and computational power. In the extreme case of $k = \Theta(\log n / \log\log n)$, the lower bound becomes $\Omega(\log n)$.

For the sum version of the basic network creation model, [7] provided a new, structural property of equilibrium graphs, which roughly states that for any two vertices of degree greater than 1, the majority of the rest of the vertices are almost equidistant from them. The proof uses the probabilistic method, combined with some basic properties of equilibrium graphs. In particular, if G is a graph in swap sum equilibrium with n vertices, then the following hold:

(i) Let u, v be any two vertices of degree greater than 1. Then, there are at least two paths from u to v such that the first edge on each path is different.
(ii) If G has a vertex of degree 2, then $diam(G) \leq 9$.

For any two vertices u, v and a randomly chosen vertex $Z \in V - \{u, v\}$ of a graph $G = (V, E)$, let $D_{u,v}(Z) = |dist(u, Z) - dist(v, Z)|$. Namely, $D_{u,v}(Z)$ is the random variable of the absolute difference of the distance of Z from u, v. In [7] it is shown that, for any two vertices u, v of degree greater than 1 in a graph in swap sum equilibrium, we have that $\mathbb{E}[D_{u,v}(Z)] \leq 3$.

These structural results of graphs in swap sum equilibrium can be seen as a stronger "skewness" property like the one defined by the authors in [2] (see Sect. 5 in that paper). In fact, [7] shows how we can prove upper bounds on the diameter of equilibrium graphs in terms of the size of the largest k-vicinity, for any $k \geq 1$ and in terms of the number of edges. This partially settles positively the conjecture of [2] (that equilibria graphs have poly-logarithmic diameter), in the cases (a) of graphs that have a vertex with large k-vicinity (including graphs with sufficiently large maximum degree) and (b) of graphs which are dense enough. In particular, for an equilibrium graph $G = (V, E)$, the following hold:

1. Let $\Delta^{(k)} = \max_u |B_u(k)|$. Then $diam(G) \leq \frac{6n}{\Delta^{(k)}} + 2 + 4k$, for any $k > 0$.
2. If the maximum degree G is such that $\Delta \geq \frac{n}{\log^l n}$, for some $l > 0$, then $diam(G) = O(\log^l n)$.
3. $diam(G) \leq \frac{6n^2}{e(G) + \frac{n}{2}} + 4$.
4. If the number of edges m of G satisfies $m \geq \frac{n^2}{\log^l n}$, for some $l > 0$, then $diam(G) \leq O(\log^l n)$.

4   The Asymmetric Basic Network Creation Game

The *asymmetric swap basic network creation game*, introduced by Mihalák and Schlegel [6], is similar to the basic game originally defined in [2], but here the ownership of an edge plays a crucial role: each edge is owned by only one of its endpoints, and only the owner of an edge is allowed to swap the edge in any state of the process. However, independent of the ownership, edges are still two-way. The corresponding stable networks of this modified version are called *asymmetric* swap sum (or max) equilibria.

In particular, a graph where every edge is owned by one of its endpoints is said to be in *asymmetric swap equilibrium*, if no vertex v can delete its own edge $\{v, w\}$ and add a new edge $\{v, w'\}$ and thereby decrease the sum of distances from v to all other vertices. While the structure and the quality of equilibrium networks is still not fully understood, [6] provide further (partial) insights for this open problem. First, it is shown that every asymmetric swap equilibrium has at most one (non-trivial) 2-edge-connected component. Second, a logarithmic upper bound on the diameter of an asymmetric swap equilibrium is proven for the case that the minimum degree of the unique 2-edge-connected component is at least n^ϵ, for $\epsilon > \frac{4\log 3}{\log n}$.

As pointed out in [6], the concept of asymmetric swap equilibrium concept generalizes and unifies some other equilibrium concepts for network creation games (as the network creation game of [4] and the bounded-budget network creation game of [3]). The authors in [6] use their results to settle the conjecture of [2], concerning the diameter of sum equilibrium graphs, in the case where the minimum degree of an induced subgraph of the equilibrium graph is at least n^ϵ, for some ϵ mentioned above.

5   The Greedy Buy Basic Network Creation Game

The *greedy buy basic network creation game* was introduced and analyzed in [8]. There, greedy equilibria are introduced as a new solution concept for network creation games. This solution concept is based on the idea that players prefer greedy refinements of their current strategy (network architecture) over a strategy change which involves a radical re-design of their infrastructure. Furthermore, greedy equilibria represent solutions efficiently computed by very simple, computationally limited vertices.

In the greedy buy basic network creation game, vertices have more freedom to act as compared to the basic game of [2]. In particular, vertices check three simple ways to improve their current infrastructure: (i) greedy augmentation, which is the creation of one new own link, at some fixed cost α, (ii) greedy deletion, which is the removal of one own link, and (iii) greedy swap, which is a swap of one own link.

There are again two versions of the game, depending on the way we define the *cost* of a vertex in a network configuration: in the sum version, each vertex tries to minimize the sum of her shortest path lengths to all other vertices in the network, while in the max version, vertices try to minimize their maximum shortest path distance to any other network vertex.

Definition 3. *A graph G is in* greedy equilibrium *if no vertex in G can decrease her cost by buying, deleting or swapping one own edge.*

The Quality of Greedy Equilibria. Lenzner [8] analyzed the stability of solutions found by greedily playing vertices. For the sum version it is shown that, despite the fact that greedy strategy changes may be sub-optimal from the point of view of a vertex, greedy equilibria capture *Nash equilibria* on trees. That is, in any tree network which is in greedy equilibrium, no vertex can decrease her cost by performing *any* strategy change, i.e., create and/or delete any possible subset of edges. For general networks it is proven that any network in greedy equilibrium is in 3-*approximate* Nash equilibrium, i.e., no vertex can decrease its cost by a factor of 3 or more by performing *any* strategy change . Furthermore, a lower bound of 3/2 is provided for this approximation ratio. This shows that greedy play almost suffices to create perfectly stable networks.

For the max version, it is shown in [8] that these games have a strong non-local flavor which yields diminished stability. Even greedy equilibrium trees may be susceptible to non-greedy improving strategy changes. However, susceptible trees can be fully characterized and it is shown that their stability is very close to being perfect. Specifically, any greedy equilibrium star is shown to be in 2-approximate Nash equilibrium and that any greedy equilibrium trees having larger diameter is in 6/5-approximate Nash equilibrium. A matching lower bound for both cases is given. For non-tree networks in greedy equilibrium the picture changes drastically. For greedy equilibrium networks having a very small α, the approximation ratio is related to their diameter and a lower bound of 4 is proven. For $\alpha \geq 1$, it is shown that there are non-tree networks in greedy equilibrium, which are only in $\Omega(n)$-approximate Nash equilibrium.

6   The Local Cost Basic Network Creation Game

Even though the model of [2] is more basic than the model of [4] (in the sense that better responses can be determined in polynomial time), it still relies on the fact that each vertex/player has global knowledge of the graph, which is needed to compute its cost function. Furthermore, it is so far unknown how an equilibrium can be reached in a distributed, uncoordinated manner, starting from any initial graph configuration. In many cases though, especially for large-scale networks like the Internet, there is no coordination between nodes and only local information is at their immediate disposal. As an example, imagine a social network consisting of selfish individuals that can form relations between each other and each one measures its strength inside the population in terms of how well connected it is (so that, for example, it can receive as much information as possible from the overall network). Assuming that each individual's computational and perception capabilities are finite, each individual will only be able to assess its strength using incomplete, local information about the network (i.e., its immediate neighborhood). Investigating stable states of such systems could potentially reveal information on how groups and communities are formed inside a social network, and why certain structures appear.

In view of the above, another swap-based network creation game was presented in [7], in which selfish costs depend on the immediate neighborhood of each vertex/player. In particular, for each vertex, we define its profit to be the sum of the degrees of its neighbors, which is also related to the number of paths of length two from that vertex. This model tends to capture selfish behavior that appears in large distributed systems of computationally bounded selfish entities. One of the interesting observations for this model is that vertices have a tendency to connect to high degree vertices. This may serve as yet another interpretation of the fact that structures of large dynamic networks have many similarities with power law and preferential attachment graphs. In particular, we prove that, unlike the model of [2], this network creation game admits an exact potential, and also that any equilibrium graph contains an n-vertex star as a spanning subgraph. The existence of a potential function implies that better response dynamics always converge to an equilibrium graph within a polynomial number of steps in the number of vertices. Furthermore, we consider a case where vertices can only acquire limited knowledge concerning non-neighboring vertices and we show that we can reach equilibrium in expected polynomial time.

We now define the *local cost basic network creation game*, which is simpler than the model of [2] and also admits an exact potential. Let $G = (V, E)$ be any undirected graph with n nodes. Again, as in the model of [2], the players can be identified as the set of vertices of the graph, and any player $u \in V$ can swap one of its incident edges (which defines the set of available actions for each player). In contrast to [2] however, the payoff of a vertex depends only on the structure of its immediate neighborhood and not on the entire network. In particular, we define the *profit* of $u \in V$ in G as $\gamma_G(u) = \sum_{v \in N_G(u)} \deg_G(v)$, i.e., the profit of u is the sum of the degrees of its neighbors. (A natural generalization would be to consider nodes at distance at most k from u.)

Structure of Equilibria. A *profitable swap* is an edge swap that improves (increases) the profit of the vertex that performs it. Notice that an arbitrary sequence of profitable swaps (by nodes $v_1, v_2, \ldots$) actually transforms the initial graph through a sequence of *configuration graphs* $G_0, G_1, G_2, \ldots$. We will write $G_i \xrightarrow{v_i} G_{i+1}$ and mean that configuration G_i produces configuration G_{i+1} by a selfish swap by vertex v_i. Vertex v_i is called *deviator* in configuration G_i.

Definition 4. *A graph G is a* local cost swap equilibrium configuration *if no vertex can perform a selfish (improving) swap.*

In [7] it is shown that, if G is a local cost swap equilibrium configuration, then it contains an n-vertex star as a spanning subgraph. This follows from the fact that a vertex u does not have a profitable swap in G when $\deg_G(v) > \deg_G(w)$, for any $v \in N_G(u)$ and $w \notin N_G(u)$. This means that u connects to all vertices of maximum degree. Moreover, either all vertices are connected to all vertices of maximum degree (in which case the graph contains an n-vertex star as a spanning subgraph), or there is some vertex u not connected to at least one vertex w of maximum degree. In the latter case, u can benefit from swapping one of its edges to connect to w and thus increase the maximum degree.

7 Dynamics of Equilibria

We have seen that equilibrium networks in the models of basic network creation games we have presented have, in general, desirable properties, such as small diameter, which make them attractive for the decentralized creation of overlay networks. However, an algorithm for finding such equilibrium networks is not obvious. These games can be thought of as *sequential move games*, in order to analyze whether (uncoordinated) selfish play eventually converges to an equilibrium state: in each step, some single player (vertex) performs a myopic selfish improving move (better reply). So, in every step, some vertex myopically modifies the network infrastructure to better suit her needs. Clearly, if at some step in the process no vertex wants to modify her part of the network, then a stable network has emerged.

7.1 Symmetric, Asymmetric, and Greedy Swap Equilibria

The dynamics of the (symmetric) basic network creation game, the asymmetric swap game, and the greedy buy game, as well as the original version of network creation games defined in [4], are studied in [5].

For the basic network creation game of [2], it is shown that, if the initial network is a tree on n nodes, then the network creation process is guaranteed to converge in $O(n^3)$ steps for both the sum and the max versions. By enforcing best (instead of just better) responses on trees, this process can be sped up significantly to $O(n)$ steps. The same move policy with best responses yields a significant speed-up in the max version as well, where an upper bound of $\Theta(n \log n)$ steps is proven. Moreover, it is shown that these results carry over to the asymmetric swap basic network creation game on trees in both the sum and the max version.

These positive results for initial networks which are trees are in contrast to several strong negative results on general networks. In particular, for both the asymmetric and the symmetric cases and both the sum and the max versions on general networks, it is not guaranteed that the selfish improvement process converges if vertices repeatedly perform best possible improving moves and, even worse, *no* move policy can enforce convergence.

7.2 Local Cost Swap Equilibria

In contrast to the above described negative results, the local cost basic network creation game admits an *exact potential function*, as shown in [7]. This directly implies that, no matter what the initial network configuration is, and no matter what the move policy is, i.e., for any selfish improvement sequence, the process is guaranteed to converge to an equilibrium graph.

In particular, the function $\Phi(G) = \frac{1}{2} \sum_{v \in V(G)} \deg_G(v)^2$ is an exact potential for the game. Consider a profitable swap performed by vertex u, which swaps edge $\{u,v\} \in E(G)$ with edge $\{u,w\} \notin E(G)$ and let G' be the resulting graph. Then the following are true: (a) $\deg_{G'}(u) = \deg_G(u)$, (b) $\deg_{G'}(v) = \deg_G(v) - 1$,

(c) $\deg_{G'}(w) = \deg_G(w) + 1$ and (d) the degree of any other vertex remains unchanged. Therefore

$$\gamma_{G'}(u) - \gamma_G(u) = \sum_{z \in N_{G'}(u)} \deg_{G'}(z) - \sum_{z \in N_G(u)} \deg_G(z)$$

$$= \deg_G(w) + 1 - \deg_G(v).$$

The corresponding change in the value of the function $\Phi(\cdot)$ is then

$$\Phi(G') - \Phi(G) = \frac{1}{2}\left(\deg_{G'}(v)^2 + \deg_{G'}(w)^2\right) - \frac{1}{2}\left(\deg_G(v)^2 - \deg_G(w)^2\right)$$

$$= \deg_G(w) - \deg_G(v) + 1$$

$$= \gamma_{G'}(u) - \gamma_G(u)$$

which proves that $\Phi(\cdot)$ is an exact potential for the game.

The existence of the potential function ensures that an equilibrium graph can be found in at most $O(n^3)$ time steps (egde swaps), starting from any initial graph. However, in order for a vertex u to compute a better response (i.e., a profitable swap), it requires information about the degree from all non-adjacent vertices in the graph, i.e., all $v \in V \setminus N_G(u)$. In many cases though, especially for large-scale networks like the Internet, it is inefficient to acquire such information about all the nodes in the network. On the other hand, we can assume that any vertex u can get such information for a limited (e.g., constant) number of non-neighboring nodes by asking an oracle. In this setup the following holds:

> If any vertex u can obtain information about the degree of $c \geq 1$ randomly chosen non-neighboring vertices, then the local cost basic network creation game can converge in an equilibrium graph in a polynomial expected number of steps.

The above result was proven in [7] who defined the following procedure: Starting with the initial graph configuration $G_0 = (V_0, E_0)$, at any time $t \geq 1$, select a vertex u uniformly at random from V and then ask the oracle to reveal the degrees of c randomly chosen non-neighbors of u (we assume that u knows the degrees of its neighbors), namely $v_1, \ldots v_c \in V_{t-1} - N_{G_{t-1}}(u)$. If one of the vertices among $v_1, \ldots, v_c$ has degree equal to or larger than the degree of some neighboring vertex of u in G_t, then u performs a profitable swap. Otherwise, it does nothing. The resulting graph will be denoted by $G_t = (V_t, E_t)$.

If at any time step t, G_t is not an equilibrium graph, then there must be at least one profitable swap. In particular, there exist vertices u, v, w such that $w \in N_{G_t}(u)$, $v \notin N_{G_t}(u)$ and $\deg_{G_t}(w) \leq \deg_{G_t}(v)$. The probability that u is selected and also v is among the randomly chosen non-neighbors of u is at least $\frac{c}{n^2}$.

Consider now the stochastic process $\{X_t\}_{t \geq 0}$, where

$$X_t = \frac{1}{2} \sum_{z \in V_t} \deg_{G_t}(z)^2.$$

Notice then that, provided G_t is not an equilibrium graph, $\Pr(X_{t+1} \geq X_t + 1) \geq \frac{c}{n^2}$ and also $\Pr(X_{t+1} = X_t) = 1 - \Pr(X_{t+1} \geq X_t + 1)$. Notice also that the absorbing states of the stochastic process $\{X_t\}_{t \geq 0}$ correspond to equilibrium graphs, and we have $0 \leq X_t \leq \frac{n^3}{2}$ for any t and in particular, for any equilibrium graph G_t.

From the above, we conclude that the number of steps needed for $\{X_t\}_{t \geq 0}$ to reach an absorbing state is stochastically dominated by a geometrically distributed random variable $Geom\left(\frac{n^3}{2}, \frac{c}{n^2}\right)$. Therefore, the mean number of steps needed for absorption is at most $\frac{n^5}{2c}$. Also note that we can decide whether the procedure described above has reached an equilibrium graph with high probability. Indeed, if after at least $\Omega(n^3)$ steps no swap has occurred, then by the Markov inequality, we can correctly (positively) decide whether we have reached equilibrium with probability at least $1 - O\left(\frac{1}{n}\right)$.

8   Conclusions and Open Issues

In contrast to the well-studied general network formation games as in [4], the basic network creation games described here try to avoid (i) the dependence to the parameter α which captures the cost required to build a link and (ii) the NP-hardness to compute a *best response* of a node. The downside of this approach is that the swap equilibrium concepts are rather weak solution concepts, in the sense that nodes are less flexible to create and delete links, and much stronger structural properties are to be expected for equilibrium networks. It would be interesting to define and analyze other equilibrium concepts that allow the creation and deletion of more than one link at a time, while preserving, as much as possible, the nice properties of swap equilibria.

As already mentioned, it is conjectured in [2] that networks in sum swap equilibrium have poly-logarithmic diameter. Poly-logarithmic upper bounds on the diameter of swap sum equilibrium graphs that are either dense enough or have large k-vicinity have been proved, thus partially settling positively this conjecture for these cases. It remains open whether we can use the full power of this result to provide more general and stronger bounds on the diameter of graphs in swap sum equilibrium.

Finally, it would be interesting to extend the local costs model, so that the profit for each vertex depends on the structure of its k-vicinity, instead of its direct neighborhood only.

References

1. Alon, N., Demaine, E.D., Hajiaghayi, M., Kanellopoulos, P., Leighton, T.: Correction: basic network creation games. SIAM J. Discrete Math. **28**(3), 1638–1640 (2014)
2. Alon, N., Demaine, E.D., Hajiaghayi, M., Leighton, T.: Basic network creation games. In: Proceedings of the 22nd ACM symposium on Parallelism in Algorithms and Architectures (SPAA), pp. 106–113. ACM, New York (2010). (Also in SIAM Journal on Discrete Mathematics, vol. 27(2), pp. 656–668, 2013)

3. Ehsani, S., Fazli, M., Mehrabian, A., Sadeghian Sadeghabad, S., Safari, M., Saghafian, M., ShokatFadaee, S.: On a bounded budget network creation game. In: Proceedings of the 23rd ACM Symposium on Parallelism in Algorithms and Architectures (SPAA), pp. 207–214 (2011)
4. Fabrikant, A., Luthra, A., Maneva, E., Papadimitriou, C.H., Shenker, S.: On a network creation game. In: Proceedings of the 22nd Annual Symposium on Principles of Distributed Computing, pp. 347–351, Boston, Massachusetts (2003)
5. Kawald, B., Lenzner, P.: On dynamics in selfish network creation. In: Proceedings of the 25th Annual ACM Symposium on Parallelism in Algorithms and Architectures (SPAA 2013), pp. 83–92 (2013)
6. Mihalák, M., Schlegel, J.C.: Asymmetric swap-equilibrium: a unifying equilibrium concept for network creation games. In: Rovan, B., Sassone, V., Widmayer, P. (eds.) MFCS 2012. LNCS, vol. 7464, pp. 693–704. Springer, Heidelberg (2012)
7. Nikoletseas, S., Panagopoulou, P., Raptopoulos, C., Spirakis, P.G.: On the structure of equilibria in basic network formation. In: Gąsieniec, L., Wolter, F. (eds.) FCT 2013. LNCS, vol. 8070, pp. 259–270. Springer, Heidelberg (2013)
8. Lenzner, P.: Greedy selfish network creation. In: Goldberg, P.W. (ed.) WINE 2012. LNCS, vol. 7695, pp. 142–155. Springer, Heidelberg (2012)

Simple Parallel Algorithms for Dynamic Range Products

Christos Zaroliagis[1,2](✉)

[1] Department of Computer Engineering and Informatics,
University of Patras, 26504 Patras, Greece
[2] Computer Technology Institute and Press "Diophantus", N. Kazantzaki Str.,
Patras University Campus, 26504 Patras, Greece
zaro@ceid.upatras.gr

Abstract. We consider here the problem of answering range product queries on an n-node unrooted tree labelled with elements of a semigroup provided with an associative operator only. We present simple parallel dynamic algorithms for one of the weakest models of parallel computation (EREW PRAM). Our main result is an algorithm which answers a query in $O(\alpha(n))$ time using a single processor after $O(\log n)$-time and $O(n)$-work preprocessing, where $\alpha(n)$ is the inverse of Ackermann's function. The data structures set up during preprocessing are updated in $O(\log n)$ time and $O(n^\beta)$ work, for any (arbitrarily small) constant $0 < \beta < 1$, after a dynamic change in the label of a tree node.

1 Introduction

Developing algorithms for solving fundamental problems in parallel computing, except for being an important challenge by itself, flags the beginning of my collaboration with Paul Spirakis. Paul firmly believes that studying and solving fundamental problems, as well as possessing a solid theoretical background, is the key to the solution of virtually any problem. This belief has been the true motivation for most of my work, including the current one.

1.1 The Problem

We consider the following fundamental problem. Suppose we are given a semigroup $(S, \circ)$, i.e., a set S of elements with an associative operator $\circ$ on them, which is the only available one. Assume also that the product $x \circ y$ between any two elements $x, y \in S$ can be computed in $O(1)$ time. Let $s_1, s_2, ..., s_n$ be elements of S. We want to preprocess the sequence $s_1, s_2, ..., s_n$, such that subsequently *range queries* can be efficiently answered. A range query specifies two indices i, j, where $1 \le i \le j \le n$, and asks for the product $s_i \circ s_{i+1} \circ \cdots \circ s_{j-1} \circ s_j$. This problem is known as the *linear range product* problem.

Similarly, the *tree range product* problem is defined as follows. Let T be an n-node unrooted tree, where every node of T is labelled (or associated) with an element of S. We want to efficiently preprocess T such that, given any two nodes

© Springer International Publishing Switzerland 2015
C. Zaroliagis et al. (Eds.): Spirakis Festschrift, LNCS 9295, pp. 396–407, 2015.
DOI: 10.1007/978-3-319-24024-4_23

u, v of T, the product of the labels associated with the nodes lying on the path from u to v is computed as fast as possible. (Labels can also be associated with edges of T rather than nodes. But it is easy to see that this is a special case of the problem considered here with labels on nodes.) It is clear that the linear range product problem is a special case of the tree range product problem, where the tree is simply a path of n nodes.

In this paper, we investigate the parallel complexity of the dynamic version of the tree range product problem. In this setting, the labels of the nodes may change. After a change in a node label, we would like to update the data structures already computed during preprocessing as efficiently as possible, without recomputing everything from scratch and without sacrificing the query time.

1.2 Applications

The tree range product problem, as well as its dynamic version, has applications to all problems that can be expressed as products of labels along paths in a tree. Along with its special case (the linear range product problem), they appear to be fundamental in many theoretical applications [2] (e.g., addition in unbounded-fan-in circuits, range minima, merging two sorted sequences of elements) and also to applications of a particular practical importance. We mention below some of them.

Network Communication. Consider a network connecting various sites using a spanning tree topology. Assume also that each link of the network has a specified capacity. Each time two sites want to communicate, they have to know the maximum size of a message that can be sent. This maximum message size is equal to the minimum capacity along the tree path connecting the two sites. Moreover, the knowledge of maximum message size is even more important when a communication link between two sites is replaced by another one with a different capacity. (This may happen because of a link failure, or because at a certain time some different link is used.) This problem reduces to the dynamic range product problem on a tree, whose edges are labelled with elements of a semigroup $(S, \circ)$ and $S, \circ$ are the set of reals and the minimum operator, respectively.

Matrix-Chain Multiplication Problem. Given a chain of n matrices $A_1, A_2, ..., A_n$, where matrix A_i, $1 \leq i \leq n$, has dimension $p_{i-1} \times p_i$, we want to fully parenthesize the product $A_1 A_2 ... A_n$ such that the total number of scalar multiplications is minimized. This problem is solved by dynamic programming (see [6], Chap. 15), where the problem reduces to determining the minimum cost of a parenthesization of $A_i A_{i+1} ... A_j$, for any pair $1 \leq i < j \leq n$. If matrices A_k and A_{k+1}, $1 \leq k \leq n$, are also free to change their common dimension p_k, then clearly the dynamic matrix-chain multiplication problem reduces to the dynamic linear range product one.

Information Retrieval in Databases. Usually queries in a relational database correspond to a selection of tuples (satisfying a particular condition) from an existing relation, or from a relation generated by some relational algebra operators most of which are associative [7]. In both cases, the selection of tuples corresponds to an appropriate linear range product query made to the relation. Since values of fields in tuples change dynamically as data are updated, the same database query may result in a different selection of tuples when it is performed after such an update. Hence, an efficient solution of the dynamic linear range product problem appears to be fundamental here. Note also that the problem of generating a new relation by applying associative algebra operators on existing relations, reduces to the above mentioned matrix-chain multiplication problem, and is of particular importance in database query optimization [7,11].

1.3   Our Contribution and Related Work

In sequential computation, an efficient solution to the static tree range product problem was given independently in [1,5]. Their algorithms perform an $O(n)$ time and space preprocessing of the tree T and then any range product query is answered in $O(\alpha(n))$ time, where $\alpha(n)$ is the inverse of Ackermann's function which is a very slowly growing function with n. The algorithm presented in [1] can be also optimally parallelized on the EREW PRAM model of computation [1,8]. It performs an $O(\log n)$-time and $O(n)$-work preprocessing of T, such that afterwards a range query is answered in $O(\alpha(n))$ time using a single processor.

In this paper, we present simple and efficient parallel algorithms, on the EREW PRAM model, for the dynamic tree range product problem. Our algorithms answer a range product query in $O(\alpha(n))$ time, after an $O(\log n)$-time and $O(n)$-work preprocessing of T. The data structures set up during preprocessing can be updated, after the modification in the value of some node label, in $O(\log n)$ time and $O(n^\beta)$ work, for any constant $0 < \beta < 1$. Furthermore, we give a trade-off between query time and the work required for an update. With $O(n^\beta)$ update work, the query time is $O(\alpha(n))$; decreasing the update work towards $O(\log n)$, degrades the query time to logarithmic. It is worth mentioning here that our parallel algorithms imply a sequential dynamic algorithm for the tree range product problem with $O(n)$ time and space preprocessing, $O(\alpha(n))$ query time and $O(n^\beta)$ update time.

Our method is based on the following result: given an n-node binary tree T, partition T into $\Theta(n/m)$ node-disjoint connected components, $1 \leq m \leq n$, such that each component is of size at most m and is connected to the rest of the tree with at most 3 edges. In [4], a very simple algorithm is given that achieves such a partition in $O(\log n)$ time using $O(n)$ work on an EREW PRAM.

The main idea of our approach is the following. Based on the above tree partitioning result, we partition the tree into a small number of subtrees with disjoint node sets such that each subtree is connected with the rest of the tree with at most 3 edges. Then, we construct another tree, called the *condensed* tree, by shrinking each subtree into a tree of $O(1)$ size. The sizes of the subtrees are chosen so that the subtrees and the condensed tree have size $O(\sqrt{n})$. We then construct data structures for answering range product queries on each subtree and on the condensed tree. This enables us to answer range product queries on the initial tree. Since the node sets are disjoint, a change in a node label affects the data structure of only one subtree. Then, we update the data structures of this subtree and of the condensed tree, both of which are smaller than the original tree. Applying this idea recursively yields the trade-off between update work and query time.

We note that our approach is a generalization of a method presented in [3,4] for solving dynamic shortest path problems on digraphs of small treewidth. However, the approach in [3,4] introduces large constants and a different analysis is needed in order to reduce them substantially and thus being able to provide the (above mentioned) update vs. query trade-off.

2   Tree Partitioning

For the sake of completeness, we present in this section the tree-partitioning result in [4], which will be used for the solution of the dynamic tree range product problem.

Definition 1. *A (c, d, m)-partition of an n-node binary tree T, where $1 \leq m \leq n$ and c, d are positive integer constants, is a node-partition of T into at least n/m and at most dn/m connected components such that each component has at most m nodes and is connected to the rest of the tree through at most c edges, called the* outgoing edges *of the component.*

We give an algorithm which is a variant of the well-known parallel tree contraction algorithm (see e.g., [9]). Assign a weight of 1 to each node in the tree. By adding a leaf (with weight 0) as a child to each node that has one child, we obtain a tree in which each node is a leaf or has two children. Number the leaves of the tree from left to right using the Euler tour technique [9]. From now on assume that we have a tree with weights on the nodes adding up to n, in which each internal node has two children, and in which some of the leaves are numbered from left to right. Our algorithm for obtaining the desired partition performs a number of *rounds*. Each round (consisting of three steps) forms groups of nodes which, at the end, will give the components. The algorithm is as follows:

ALGORITHM Binary-Tree-Partition

Repeat the following steps (round) $\log n$ times.

1. In parallel, for each odd numbered leaf that is a left child, if the sum of the weights of the leaf, its parent and its sibling is at most m, then shrink the edges connecting the leaf and its sibling to their parent. Assign the parent a weight equal to the sum of the weights of the three nodes. If the sibling is a leaf, it is even numbered. Assign this number to the parent (which is now a leaf in the modified tree). If the sum of the weights exceeds m, then delete the numbers (if they exist) from the leaf and the sibling.
2. Repeat step 1 for each odd numbered leaf that is a right child.
3. After these two steps, all the numbered leaves in the tree have an even number. Divide each of these numbers by 2.

END.

In order to implement the above algorithm – as well as the subsequent ones – on an EREW PRAM, we make the following conventions for the *input-output representation*. We assume that algorithm Binary-Tree-Partition has its input tree specified as a linked structure in n contiguous memory cells. The algorithm produces its output in $O(n)$ contiguous memory cells, divided into contiguous blocks, each block containing one of the connected components in the same linked format, and one final block containing the compressed tree (i.e., the tree at the end of the shrinking process) in a linked format.

The aforementioned input-output representation can be easily accomplished using standard EREW PRAM methods [9] using $O(\log n)$ time and $O(n)$ work, which we now describe briefly. Let q be the number of nodes in the compressed tree. By assigning the preorder number to each node in the compressed tree, we can assign a unique number between 1 and q to each connected subtree. Then, by solving a prefix summation problem on q elements, where the i-th element is the number of nodes in subtree i, we can allocate contiguous memory blocks for the various subtrees. It remains to copy the subtrees into the appropriate blocks. Since each node in the compressed tree knows the memory addresses allocated for its subtree, by reversing the shrinking process we can assign a unique memory address in the appropriate block to each node in a subtree. Now it is a simple matter for each node to copy itself into this address, and duplicate its link structure.

Theorem 1. *Given any* $1 \le m \le n$, *a* $(3, 8, m)$-*partition of an n-node binary tree T can be computed in $O(\log n)$ time using $O(n)$ work on an EREW PRAM.*

Proof. It is not hard to see that after the i-th iteration, at most $l/2^i$ leaves have numbers, where l is the initial number of leaves. Thus, at the end, there are no numbered leaves. Throughout, the following invariant is maintained: if a leaf does not have a number, then the weights of the leaf, its parent and sibling add up to more than m. (Note that such a leaf will not participate in any subsequent iteration.) Call such a triple of leaf, parent and sibling an *overweight* group.

Each non-numbered leaf is contained in some overweight group, and no node can belong to more than two overweight groups. Thus, the sum of the weights of all the overweight groups is at most $2n$, hence the number of overweight groups is at most $2n/m$. Since each overweight group contains at most two non-numbered nodes, the total number of non-numbered leaves at the end is $4n/m$. Since each internal node has two children, the total number of nodes remaining in the tree is at most $8n/m$.

Each node v in the remaining tree is associated with the connected subtree induced by the nodes that were shrunk into v in the above process. These are the required groups. It is easy to see that v has a weight equal to the number of nodes in the associated subtree. Since this weight is at most m, there are at least n/m such connected subtrees. Also, as shown above, there are no more than $8n/m$ connected subtrees. It follows from the construction that each subtree is connected to the rest of the tree through at most 3 edges which are incident on at most 2 nodes of the subtree.

The complexity bounds follow by the aforementioned input-output representation of the input tree and the fact that the algorithm is a variant of the parallel
tree contraction algorithm [9]. $\qquad\square$

3 Dynamic Range Products

In this section, we shall give our algorithms and data structures for the dynamic
version of the tree range product problem. Our solution is based on the tree-
partitioning result presented in the previous section.

For a function f let $f^{(1)}(n) = f(n)$; $f^{(i)}(n) = f(f^{(i-1)}(n))$, $i > 1$. Define
$I_0(n) = \lceil \frac{n}{2} \rceil$ and $I_k(n) = \min\{j \mid I_{k-1}^{(j)}(n) \leq 1\}$, $k \geq 1$. The functions $I_k(n)$
decrease rapidly as k increases, in particular, $I_1(n) = \lceil \log n \rceil$ and $I_2(n) = \log^* n$.
Define $\alpha(n) = \min\{j \mid I_j(n) \leq 1\}$.

Recall the assumptions made for the semigroup $(S, \circ)$ in Sect. 1. As in [1], we
also assume that S has a unit element. (Otherwise, we can simply add such an
element to S.) The following has been proved in [1,8].

Theorem 2. *Let T be an n-node unrooted tree such that each node is labelled
with an element from a semigroup $(S, \circ)$. Then, the following hold on an EREW
PRAM: (i) for each $k \geq 1$, after $O(\log n)$-time and $O(nI_k(n))$-work preprocessing, the product of labels along any path in the tree can be computed in $O(k)$ time
using a single processor; and (ii) after $O(\log n)$-time and $O(n)$-work preprocessing, the product of labels along any path in the tree can be computed in $O(\alpha(n))$
time using a single processor.*

In the following, we shall denote by $\ell(u)$ the label of a node u. We define
$P[\ell(u), \ell(v)]$ to be the product of the elements associated with the nodes lying
on the path from u to v in a tree T. If u and v are the same node, then the
above product is defined to be equal to $\ell(u)$ or $\ell(v)$. For a node w of T, we shall
denote by $lc(w)$ (resp. $rc(w)$) its left (resp. right) child in T.

We shall consider first the case where the given labelled tree T is rooted and
binary. At the end of the section we shall discuss how the general case is handled.
Note that it suffices to give a data structure for answering range product queries
between any two nodes u, v of T when u is a descendant of v (called *upward
query*), or vice versa (called *downward query*). Since otherwise, let w be the
lowest common ancestor of u and v in T and w.l.o.g. assume that u (resp. v)
is a descendant of $lc(w)$ (resp. $rc(w)$). The path, in T, between u and v passes
through w. Hence, $P[\ell(u), \ell(v)] = P[\ell(u), \ell(lc(w))] \circ \ell(w) \circ P[\ell(rc(w)), \ell(v)]$, i.e.,
it reduces to the problem of computing an upward and a downward range query.
(Note that we have to consider separately upward and downward range queries,
since the operator $\circ$ may not be commutative.)

Assume we are given a $(3, 8, m)$-partition of an n-node binary tree T into
connected components T_i, $1 \leq i \leq 8n/m$. From the construction of the partition,
it is clear that each component T_i will either have one or three outgoing edges.
We use the following notation for certain nodes of the components. If T_i has only
one outgoing edge, we shall refer to the single node incident on that edge as x_i.

If T_i has three outgoing edges, we shall refer to the two nodes of T_i incident on these edges as x_i and y_i, where x_i will be the one closest to the root of T. Note that in this latter case: (a) x_i is incident on one outgoing edge and y_i on the other two outgoing edges; (b) y_i is a descendant of $lc(x_i)$ or $rc(x_i)$.

Now, we construct a binary tree T', called *the upward condensed tree* of T, as follows. Replace each T_i in T by a subtree on nodes x_i and y_i, and edge (x_i, y_i) (if y_i exists). Node x_i in T' has label $\ell'(x_i) = \ell(x_i)$. Node y_i (if exists) has label $\ell'(y_i) = P[\ell(y_i), \ell(lc(x_i))]$ or $\ell'(y_i) = P[\ell(y_i), \ell(rc(x_i))]$, depending whether y_i is a descendant of $lc(x_i)$ or $rc(x_i)$.

We can similarly construct a *downward condensed tree* T''. In T'', node x_i will again have label $\ell(x_i)$. Node y_i (if exists) will have label $P[\ell(lc(x_i)), \ell(y_i)]$ (resp. $P[\ell(rc(x_i)), \ell(y_i)]$) if it is a descendant of $lc(x_i)$ (resp. $rc(x_i)$).

The next lemma shows that the above constructions can be done optimally on an EREW PRAM.

Lemma 1. *Both condensed trees of a labelled rooted n-node binary tree can be constructed in $O(\log n)$ time using $O(n)$ work on an EREW PRAM.*

Proof. We shall show how the upward condensed tree T' is constructed. The construction of the downward condensed tree is similar. Having the $(3, 8, m)$-partition of T into q connected components and using the input-output representation described in Sect. 2, we can find in $O(1)$ time the nodes x_i and y_i for each component T_i, by assigning one processor per each node of T. Then, we allocate an array A of $2q$ contiguous memory cells for T'. Each x_i and y_i is copied into the position $2(i-1) + 1$ and $2(i-1) + 2$ of A, respectively, for $1 \le i \le q$. It remains only to establish the parent-child relationships in T'. By the construction, node y_i knows immediately its parent x_i in T'. Hence, it remains only to inform x_i for its parent in T'. But this can be done using the data structure of T. All the above take $O(1)$ time and $O(n)$ work on an EREW PRAM. The bounds now follow from Theorem 1.   □

The next lemma shows how a $(3, 8, m)$-partition of T and its upward condensed tree can be used to answer upward range product queries in T.

Lemma 2. *Assume we are given a $(3, 8, m)$-partition of an n-node labelled rooted binary tree T into connected components T_i, $1 \le i \le 8n/m$, and let T' be its upward condensed tree. If T' and all T_i's are provided with a data structure for answering upward range product queries, then: (i) We can answer correctly upward range product queries in T. (ii) If the label of a node w in T is changed, and w belongs also to component T_i, then an updating to the data structures of T' and T_i suffices to continue answering correctly upward range product queries in T.*

Proof. (i) Let u be a descendant of v in T. We want to show that $P[\ell(u), \ell(v)]$ is computed correctly using the data structures of T' and T_i's. If both u and v belong to the same component T_i, then clearly the data structure of T_i gives the correct range product. Therefore, assume that $u \in T_i$ and $v \in T_j$, $i \ne j$.

W.l.o.g. assume also that y_j, which is an ancestor of x_i, is a descendant of $lc(v)$. (The case where y_j is a descendant of $rc(v)$ is similar.)

Consider now the components T_p and T_q such that y_p is the parent of x_i and x_q is the child of y_j. From the associativity of $\circ$, we have that $P[\ell(u), \ell(v)] = P[\ell(u), \ell(x_i)] \circ P[\ell(y_p), \ell(x_q)] \circ P[\ell(y_j), \ell(v)]$. Clearly, the range products $P[\ell(u), \ell(x_i)]$ and $P[\ell(y_j), \ell(v)]$ can be obtained from the data structures of T_i and T_j respectively. In the special case where either y_p, x_q, y_j and v coincide, or y_p, x_q, x_i and u coincide, we make the convention that $P[\ell(y_p), \ell(x_q)]$, in the above product, is equal to the unit element of S.

Hence, to complete the proof, it suffices to show that $P[\ell(y_p), \ell(x_q)] = P_{T'}[\ell'(y_p), \ell'(x_q)]$, where the RHS product is taken from T' and $y_p \neq x_q$ (otherwise the proof is trivial). The proof goes by induction on the number t of nodes in the path from y_p to x_q in T'.

Consider first the basis case, $t = 0$. This means that $p = q$, and $P[\ell(y_p), \ell(x_q)] = P[\ell(y_p), \ell(x_p)] = P[\ell(y_p), \ell(lc(x_p))] \circ \ell(x_p) = \ell'(y_p) \circ \ell'(x_p) = P_{T'}[\ell'(y_p), \ell'(x_q)]$, by the construction of T' and the fact that x_p and x_q are the same nodes.

For the induction hypothesis, assume that $P[\ell(y_p), \ell(x_q)] = P_{T'}[\ell'(y_p), \ell'(x_q)]$, if the path contains at most $t - 1$ nodes.

For the induction step, let the path contain t nodes. Then $P[\ell(y_p), \ell(x_q)] = P[\ell(y_p), \ell(x_r)] \circ P[\ell(y_q), \ell(x_q)]$, where x_r is the child of y_q that belongs to component T_r. By the induction hypothesis, $P[\ell(y_p), \ell(x_r)] = P_{T'}[\ell'(y_p), \ell'(x_r)]$. By the associativity of $\circ$, $P[\ell(y_q), \ell(x_q)] = P[\ell(y_q), \ell(lc(x_q))] \circ \ell(x_q)$. But from the construction of T' we have, $P[\ell(y_q), \ell(lc(x_q))] \circ \ell(x_q) = P_{T'}[\ell'(y_q), \ell'(x_q)]$. Therefore, $P[\ell(y_p), \ell(x_q)] = P_{T'}[\ell'(y_p), \ell'(x_r)] \circ P_{T'}[\ell'(y_q), \ell'(x_q)] = P_{T'}[\ell'(y_p), \ell'(x_q)]$, as required.

(ii) We have just shown that if we have built data structures for all of T_i's and for T', we can correctly answer upward queries in T'. Therefore, it is clear that updating these data structures such that upward queries can be answered correctly in all T_i's and in T', is sufficient to answer correctly upward range queries in T. Hence, it remains to argue that we need to update only one of the components, namely the one, say T_i, which contains the node w whose label $\ell(w)$ has changed. But this follows immediately from the fact that all T_i's are node-disjoint, thus changing the label $\ell(w)$ of w in T_i does not affect any range product query in some T_j, $i \neq j$, and therefore its data structure. □

The following definition will facilitate the presentation of our results.

Definition 2. *Let $DS(T, \{P_W, P_T\}, \{U_W, U_T\}, Q)$ be a dynamic data structure for the range product problem on a tree T, where $O(P_W)$ (resp. $O(P_T)$) is the preprocessing work and space (resp. time) to be set up, $O(U_W)$ (resp. $O(U_T)$) is the work (resp. time) to update it after a modification in the value of an element associated with a tree node, and $O(Q)$ is the time to answer a product query using a single processor.*

The next lemma gives the bounds, and its proof explains the construction, of our dynamic data structures for the tree range product problem.

Lemma 3. *Let T be an n-node binary tree. Then, for each $k \geq 1$ and any integer $r \geq 0$, there exist dynamic data structures for the upward range product problem on T, with the following characteristics on an EREW PRAM:*

(i) $DS(T, \{(r+1)n - \sqrt{n}, 2\log n + 8r\}, \{c(r)n^{(1/2)^r}, 2\log n + 8r\}, 3^r\alpha(n));$
(ii) $DS(T, \{((r+1)n - \sqrt{n})I_k(n), 2\log n + 8r\}, \{c(r)n^{(1/2)^r}, 2\log n + 8r\}, 3^r k),$
where $c(0) = 1$ and $c(r) = c(r-1)[1 + 16^{(1/2)^{r-1}}]$ for $r \geq 1$.

Proof. We shall prove part (i). Part (ii) can be proved similarly. The proof proceeds by induction on r. If $r = 0$, then the update time exceeds the pre-processing and hence the static data structure of Theorem 2 suffices. In the following, we shall use the notation $D(T, n, r)$ for $DS(T, \{(r+1)n - \sqrt{n}, 2\log n + 8r\}, \{c(r)n^{(1/2)^r}, 2\log n + 8r\}, 3^r\alpha(n))$. Assume that the theorem holds for any value smaller than r. We shall show how $D(T, n, r)$ is constructed.

We first costruct a $(3, 8, \sqrt{n})$-partition of T and an upward condensed tree T'. Let $T_1, T_2, ..., T_q$, $\sqrt{n} \leq q \leq 8\sqrt{n}$, be the connected components of T, each one of size $n_i = |V(T_i)| = \sqrt{n}$ and connected with the rest of T through at most 3 edges. Also, $\sum_{i=1}^{q} n_i = n$, and T' has $n' = |V(T')| \leq 2q \leq 16\sqrt{n}$ nodes.

The data structure for $D(T, n, r)$ consists of the following: $D(T_i, n_i, r-1)$, for each $1 \leq i \leq q$, which enables us to answer upward range product queries in T_i, and $D(T', n', r-1)$ which enables us to answer upward range product queries in T'. By Lemma 2, maintaining these data structures is sufficient to answer correctly upward range product queries in T. Since in the same Lemma, we also showed how an upward query is answered having these data structures, it remains to argue here only for the resource bounds.

The time and work required for the preprocessing is equal to the time and work required for constructing: (1) the $(3, 8, \sqrt{n})$-partition of T and the upward condensed tree T', and (2) the dynamic data structures of T_i's and T' inductively. By Theorem 1 and Lemma 1, the total preprocessing work $P_W(n, r)$ is bounded by

$$P_W(n, r) \leq n + \sum_{i=1}^{q} P_W(n_i, r-1) + P_W(n', r-1).$$

By the induction hypothesis, we have

$$P_W(n, r) \leq n + \sum_{i=1}^{q}(rn_i - \sqrt{n}) + rn' - \sqrt{n} \leq (r+1)n - \sqrt{n}.$$

Similarly, the preprocessing time $P_T(n, r)$ is

$$\begin{aligned}P_T(n, r) &\leq \log n + \max\{P_T(n_i, r-1), P_T(n', r-1)\} \\ &\leq \log n + \max\{2\log n_i + 8(r-1), 2\log n' + 8(r-1)\} \\ &\leq 2\log n + 8r\end{aligned}$$

The time and work required for the update operation is the time and work to update $D(T_i, n_i, r-1)$ and $D(T', n', r-1)$. Using a similar argument as above, we can show that the time required for an update is $2\log n + 8r$. The work $U_W(n,r)$ required for an update is

$$U_W(n,r) \le U_W(n_i, r-1) + U_W(n', r-1)$$

which, by the induction hypothesis, gives:

$$U_W(n,r) \le c(r-1)n_i^{(1/2)^{r-1}} + c(r-1)(n')^{(1/2)^{r-1}}$$
$$= c(r-1)n^{(1/2)^r}[1 + 16^{(1/2)^{r-1}}]$$
$$= c(r)n^{(1/2)^r}.$$

Finally, the query time $Q(n,r)$ is bounded by

$$Q(n,r) \le 2Q(n_i, r-1) + Q(n', r-1)$$

where the first term corresponds to the time required for querying the data structures of the components in which the two nodes belong to, and the last term corresponds to the time required for querying in T'. By the induction hypothesis, this gives

$$Q(n,r) \le 2(3^{r-1}\alpha(n_i)) + (3^{r-1}\alpha(n')) \le 3^r\alpha(n).$$

Thus, we can construct $D(T,n,r)$ in the claimed bounds and hence completing the induction. □

Remark 1. Using symmetric arguments, we can prove similar Lemmata to 2 and 3 for answering downward range product queries in a labelled rooted binary tree, using the downward condensed tree T''.

We are now ready to give our main theorem.

Theorem 3. *Let T be an n-node unrooted tree such that each node is labelled with an element from a semigroup $(S, \circ)$. Then, for each $k \ge 1$ and any integer $r \ge 0$, there exist dynamic data structures for the range product problem on T, with the following characteristics on an EREW PRAM:*

(i) $DS(T, \{(r+1)n - \sqrt{n}, 2\log n + 8r\}, \{c(r)n^{(1/2)^r}, 2\log n + 8r\}, 3^r\alpha(n));$
(ii) $DS(T, \{((r+1)n - \sqrt{n})I_k(n), 2\log n + 8r\}, \{c(r)n^{(1/2)^r}, 2\log n + 8r\}, 3^r k),$
where $c(0) = 1$ and $c(r) = c(r-1)[1 + 16^{(1/2)^{r-1}}]$ for $r \ge 1$.

Proof. If T is unrooted, then we root it arbitrarily. If T is not binary, we convert it into a rooted binary tree, in the standard way, by adding dummy nodes. To these dummy nodes added, we associate the unit element of S. Note that the total number of nodes is at most $2n$. We then preprocess the tree (using e.g., the algorithm of [10]) such that lowest common ancestor queries can be answered in $O(1)$ time. All the above will cost $O(\log n)$ time and $O(n)$ work on an EREW PRAM using standard techniques (see e.g., [9]). After the above preprocessing, it follows by Lemmata 2 and 3 and Remark 1, that we can dynamically answer upward and downward range product queries in T. From the discussion in the beginning of Sect. 3, it follows that if we can answer upward and downward range product queries, then we can answer any range product query in T. The bounds follow easily by the above discussion and Lemma 3. □

An immediate consequence of Theorem 3 is a continuous trade-off between preprocessing, query, and update bounds, depending on the particular choice of r. For instance, choosing $r = -\log \beta$, where $0 < \beta < 1$ is any (arbitrarily small) constant, we get the following.

Corollary 1. *Let* $k \geq 1$ *be any constant integer and let* $0 < \beta < 1$ *be any (arbitrarily small) constant. The dynamic range product problem, on an n-node unrooted tree T, can be solved by constructing the following data structures on an EREW PRAM:*

(i) $DS(T, \{n, \log n\}, \{n^\beta, \log n\}, \alpha(n))$;
(ii) $DS(T, \{nI_k(n), \log n\}, \{n^\beta, \log n\}, k)$.

On the other hand, we may let r vary with n. For instance, choosing $r = \log \log n$, we have the following.

Corollary 2. *Let* $k \geq 1$ *be any constant integer and let* $0 < \beta < 1$ *be any arbitrarily small constant. The dynamic range product problem, on an n-node unrooted tree T, can be solved by constructing the following data structures on an EREW PRAM:*

(i) $DS(T, \{n \log \log n, \log n\}, \{\log n, \log n\}, \alpha(n) \log^{1.6} n)$;
(ii) $DS(T, \{nI_k(n) \log \log n, \log n\}, \{\log n, \log n\}, k \log^{1.6} n)$.

4   Conclusions

We have presented here simple and efficient dynamic algorithms for the tree range product problem that run on the weakest PRAM model. The dynamic tree range product problem appears to be a fundamental subproblem in many applications, as discussed in Sect. 1. We believe that our solution to this problem will help in the dynamization of graph problems which make use of tree data structures.

References

1. Alon, N., Schieber, B.: Optimal preprocessing for answering on-line product queries, Technical Report No. 71/87, Tel-Aviv University (1987)
2. Chaudhuri, S., Hagerup, T.: Prefix graphs and their applications. In: Mayr, Ernst W., Schmidt, G., Tinhofer, G. (eds.) WG 1994. LNCS, vol. 903, pp. 206–218. Springer, Heidelberg (1995)
3. Chaudhuri, S., Zaroliagis, C.: Shortest paths in digraphs of small treewidth. Part I: sequential algorithms. Algorithmica **27**(3), 212–226 (2000)
4. Chaudhuri, S., Zaroliagis, C.: Shortest paths in digraphs of small treewidth. Part II: optimal parallel algorithms. Theor. Comput. Sci. **203**(2), 205–223 (1998)
5. Chazelle, B.: Computing on a free tree via complexity-preserving mappings. Algorithmica **2**, 337–361 (1987)
6. Cormen, T., Leiserson, C., Rivest, R., Stein, C.: Introduction to Algorithms, 3rd edn. The MIT Press, Cambridge (2009)

7. Date, C.J.: An Introduction to Database Systems, Vol. I, 5th edn. Addison-Wesley, Reading (1991)
8. Hagerup, T.: Parallel preprocessing for path queries without concurrent reading. Inf. Comput. **158**, 18–28 (2000)
9. JáJá, J.: An Introduction to Parallel Algorithms. Addison-Wesley, Reading (1992)
10. Schieber, B., Vishkin, U.: On finding lowest common ancestors: simplification and parallelization. SIAM J. Comput. **17**(6), 1253–1262 (1988)
11. Ullman, J.D.: Principles of Database and Knowledge-base Systems, Vol. II. Computer Science Press, Rockville (1989)

Author Index

Printed in the United States
by Bookmasters

Printed in the United States
By Bookmasters